The Beginnings of
Western Christendom

The Beginnings of
Western Christendom

L.E. Elliott-Binns

James Clarke & Co.
Cambridge

Published by
James Clarke & Co.
P.O. Box 60
Cambridge
CB1 2NT
England

e-mail: **publishing@jamesclarke.co.uk**
website: **http://www.jamesclarke.co.uk**

ISBN 0 227 17100 4 hardback
ISBN 0 227 17099 7 paperback

British Library Cataloguing in Publication Data:
A catalogue record is available from the British Library.

First published 1948 by The Lutterworth Press
Reprinted 2002

Copyright ©1948 L.E. Elliott-Binns

CONTENTS

Definition of Terms—Cultural Boundaries—Political Boundaries—Eastern and Western Churches—Common Features—Contrasts. *Additional Note*: "The Glamour of the East".

PART I: THE SETTING

The Growth of the Empire—Its Organization—Provinces and Cities—Travel—Cultural Influences—The Romanization of the West—The Use of Latin—Education—Influence of Hellenism—The State of Roman Society—Women—Slaves—Associations.

Roman Religion—The Worship of the Emperor—Woman and Religion—Oriental Religions—The Mysteries—Mithraism—The Hermetic Writings — Philosophy — Stoicism — Neoplatonism — Roman Tolerance.

The Preparatory Work of Judaism—The Breach—Christian Jews—The Destruction of Jerusalem—Jewish Opposition—Christian Attacks—The Permanent Influence of Judaism—Jewish Christians and St. Paul.

PART II: LOCAL EXPANSION

Early Expansion—The Church in Rome—St. Peter and St. Paul in Rome—The Use of their Names—St. Peter and Rome—The Neronian Persecution—The Domitianic Persecution.

Internal Conditions—The Greek Period—Early Bishops—Victor—The Paschal Controversy—Callistus—Hippolytus—Schisms—Novatianism — Stephen — The Baptismal Controversy — Later Bishops—The Roman Primacy—The Political Causes—Rome and Corinth—The Geographical Causes—The Ecclesiastical Causes—The Petrine Claims—Rome and Alexandria—The Roman Martyrs.

General Description—The Coming of Christianity—Upper Italy—Central Italy—South Italy and Sicily.

CONTENTS

PREFACE

The first impulse to undertake the study of which this book is the outcome came to me quite suddenly in September 1933 when I was in Rome in connexion with my work on the medieval papacy. I happened to visit the catacomb of St. Sebastian and when examining the well-known *graffiti* there, was struck by the number which place the name of St. Paul before that of St. Peter. This seemed to me to be very significant, and I determined to investigate the relative importance of the two apostles in the development of the Roman supremacy, for obviously at this epoch it did not depend solely on what are called the Petrine claims. My inquiry gradually extended to the whole subject of early inscriptions and the light which they throw on the origins of the Western Church. I could not but feel that their possibilities as a means of supplementing and modifying what was known from literary sources had not been adequately realized.[1] In classical studies the results of archaeological discoveries had been utilized to the full; but this was hardly the case, at least to the same extent, with ecclesiastical studies, in which hitherto such material had chiefly been a happy hunting-ground for Roman Catholic and other scholars anxious to find traces of later practices and beliefs. But their handling of the evidence, and again I only express my own opinion, seemed to be lacking in critical judgment. It was, moreover, largely confined to the contents of the catacombs of Rome. Quite considerable discoveries, of one kind and another, had recently been made in Rome itself, and there was, in addition, the immense store of archaeological material in North Africa and Gaul made available in the excellent official publications of the French Government.

Another source of information which had not been exhausted was the apocryphal literature. To its further possibilities I was awakened by my membership for some years before his lamented death of the *seminar* conducted by Professor Burkitt. At last I found myself involved in a study of the whole matter of the origins of the Western Church. This was really ground with which I had long been familiar, for it was not for nothing that I had been the pupil of such great teachers as H. M. Gwatkin, H. B. Swete, and J. F. Bethune-Baker.

Bishop Westcott once complained that early Christian

[1] They had, of course, been used in the *Dictionary of Christian Antiquities* published in 1893.

9

inscriptions were devoid of interest (*Life of B. F. Westcott,* I, p. 289). I certainly have not found them so; for if the information which they afford is but meagre, it has about it a naturalness and intimacy which is usually lacking in the literary sources. Moreover the inscriptions, since they were contemporary, constitute something stable in the queer shifting world which formed the first three centuries of the Christian era.

The amount of material provided for study was so vast that some delimitation of area as regards both time and space was obviously necessary, so I have taken as the *terminus ad quem* the adoption of Christianity by Constantine, though I have examined much later material in the hope, not entirely unjustified, of finding matter which would throw back light on the earlier period. As to space, my inquiry was naturally limited to the West—by which I mean roughly the present division between the Roman and Orthodox obediences. It was, of course, not until the end of our period that there was a division of the Empire into East and West, whilst the ecclesiastical division came much later.

As the general outline of the story of the Beginnings of Western Christendom is readily available in textbooks on Early Church History, I have not related it in full detail, in order to give more space to what is less well known and less readily available. Much of the archaeological material, for example, is only to be found in the various journals devoted to that subject. The attention given to the political and religious backgrounds may appear to be excessive; but this is justified by their importance in the development of the Christian Church, and is, indeed, necessary in order to give a complete picture of the times in which it arose.

I have found it exceedingly difficult to obtain a clear and complete idea of the development. The mass of detail is overwhelming, and there are sad gaps in our knowledge. The simplifications of the textbooks are often deceptive, for what might at first seem clear and of a single texture proves on closer examination to be very diverse; just as a mountain seen against the light of the sun may appear to be of a uniform colour, but is not really so.[1] Much therefore must remain vague and uncertain. It would have been comparatively easy to have filled in the gaps by the use of the imagination, but I have deliberately refrained from this process; and so the narrative may be lacking in completeness and richness. But poverty, as in the economic sphere, is not always the result of sloth and indolence. It may equally well be the result of honesty. The object of my study has been to discover truth so far as it is ascertainable, not to promulgate

---

[1] cf. Ruskin, *Modern Painters*, Pt. II, sect. ii, chap. II, sect. 15.

novel theories. Too avid a quest of novelties may easily become the bane of sound scholarship.

Perhaps some into whose hands this book may come will question the usefulness, in an age like the present, of expending on such a subject the vast amount of time and labour which have been involved in its preparation. My own chief object was to clear my mind as to the origins of the medieval papacy, a subject upon which I have been working for something like a quarter of a century. There is, of course, a real danger, as Frederick Denison Maurice has pointed out, of regarding the primitive Church as a kind of pattern on the mount (cf. Exodus 25 : 40), the only true model of a Catholic Church; but it was from the primitive Church that the great structure of the Church medieval had its origin. The problem is to account for its vastly different outlook and teaching. A mere theory of development will not do so; for, as someone has said, if you begin with a hen's egg and end up with a rabbit, something more must be postulated. Obviously new elements have entered in, derived from non-Christian sources. In this matter the inscriptions with their strange fondness for pagan survivals are of immense value, as well as the whole course of early Christian art. But this pagan element, which admittedly made its way into the Church, must not be condemned out of hand; it was not without its value in broadening the Christian Gospel and its appeal. Here again I have sought merely to get at the facts, and not to pass judgment on them.

Such is my own justification for this study. But surely it can be justified on much wider grounds. We can never understand the present without an adequate knowledge of the past; and in this material age to go back to the spiritual springs of our civilization is a wholesome process. It should at least teach us the folly of confining ourselves to the world of sense and matter in trying to understand it; truly insight only comes to those whose faith allows them to reach out "beyond the flaming bulwarks of the universe" in search of a higher cause and a more perfect will. For those who have the task of guiding the life of the Church universal too much attention can never be paid to the record of the struggles of the early Christian communities, for those experiences are being lived out afresh in the younger Churches which are everywhere springing up. The failures and weaknesses of such Churches as those of North Africa and of Spain may help us to be patient with their modern counterparts in China or India, whilst their triumphs and achievements may fill us with the spirit of hope and confidence.

The comparison of the present and the past will help us to understand our own day more readily. But such a process, like

Lend–Lease, can also work in reverse, and the experiences of twentieth-century Christians may also provide new insight into the meaning of the earlier centuries. A generation has arisen in Europe which has had to learn afresh the meaning of dying for its beliefs, as well as for its country. Such a generation will have quickened sympathies with its forefathers in the faith. Nor is this reverse process confined to the sphere of religion; for as John Buchan has written, "the convulsions of our time may give an insight into the problems of the early Roman Empire which was perhaps unattainable by scholars who lived in easier days" (*Augustus*, p. 9).

It was originally intended that this volume should have been published in 1939, but the outbreak of the war made delay advisable. During the war years, in spite of other literary activities and a temporary resumption of parish work, I was able to read through once again practically the whole of the Western Fathers and the apocryphal literature, and to revise and in large measure to rewrite my thesis. A return to the neighbourhood of Cambridge has enabled me to take note of recent contributions to the subject and so to carry out further revision and supplementing.

Finally, I wish to express my gratitude to the Rev. G. H. Gordon Hewitt, the Theological Secretary of the Lutterworth Press, and to their reader, for many useful criticisms and suggestions.

L. E. ELLIOTT-BINNS

BUCKDEN
Decr. 8, 1945.

ABBREVIATIONS

Apoc. N.T.	M. R. James, *The Apocryphal New Testament*
C.I.L.	*Corpus Inscriptionum Latinarum*
Diehl	*Inscriptiones Latinae Christianae Veteres*
Euseb.	Eusebius, *Ecclesiastical History*. Other works cited by name
Gibbon	*The History of the Decline and Fall of the Roman Empire*, edited by J. B. Bury
Hippolytus	*Refutatio* (or *Philosophumena*). Other works cited by name
Iren.	Irenaeus, *Adv. Haereses*. Though I have used Harvey's edition I have adopted the divisions of Massuet which will be found in the top margin of each page. Other works cited by name
J.H.S.	*The Journal of Hellenic Studies*
J.R.S.	*The Journal of Roman Studies*
J.T.S.	*The Journal of Theological Studies*
Lightfoot	*The Apostolic Fathers*. Other works cited by name
Marucchi	*Le Catacombe romane*. References are to the posthumous edition produced by Enrico Josi
Oxford Apoc.	*Apocrypha and Pseudepigrapha of the Old Testament*, edited by R. H. Charles
P.G.	Migne, *Patrologiae cursus completus. Series Graeca*
P.L.	Migne, *Patrologiae cursus completus. Series Latina*
Styger	*Die römischen Katakomben*
Syxtus	*Notiones Archaeologicae Christianae*

PROLOGUE
THE EAST AND THE WEST

THE EAST AND THE WEST

Before entering upon our main task it will be well to glance at the influences exerted by the East upon the West, and also to take note of some of the contrasts between Eastern and Western Christianity, contrasts which are already evident in our period, a foreshadowing of even greater differences in the ages which were to follow.

In considering the question of the influences of the East upon the West, however, we have to face a preliminary difficulty. How are we to define our terms? Spatial metaphors are notoriously misleading, and even the employment of actual geographical terms is beset with obscurities. So much depends upon the standpoint of the observer. Thus when Radhakrishnan (*East and West in Religion*, p. 46) designates as Eastern that outlook on life which refuses to accept the temporal as the equivalent of the real, he has in mind an Orient which comprehends neither Orthodox Christendom nor the Semitic peoples with their stern insistence on the value of time. Europeans normally include in the term Oriental at least those who dwell at the Asiatic end of the Mediterranean. It is with this sense that it has been declared that "the religious conquest of the West by the East . . . has been a more momentous fact in the history of the world than any political conquest of the East by the West".[1]

What, it may be asked, did that conquest involve? Sir James Frazer, in a passage written more than forty years ago, would see in it the destruction, by the invasion of Oriental religious ideas, of the typically Western notion that the community is of more value than the individual. "Greek and Roman society", he affirmed, "was built on the conception of the subordination of the individual to the community, of the citizen to the state; it set the safety of the commonwealth, as the supreme aim of conduct, above the safety of the individual whether in this world or in a world to come. . . . All this was changed by the spread of Oriental religions which inculcated the communion of the soul with God and its eternal salvation as the only objects worth living for, objects in comparison with which the prosperity and even the existence of the state sank into insignificance" (*The Golden Bough*, Part IV, *Adonis, Attis, Osiris*, I, p. 300 f.). This distinction, like all attempts to compare the East and the West,

---

[1] D. G. Hogarth, *The Ancient East*, p. 14.

is too clear-cut and admits of many exceptions. To the Platonist, for example, the vision of God was the supreme good, and for many Greek thinkers salvation consisted in union with the divine. With the Jews, on the other hand, though individual prosperity might be the reward of obedience to God's commands, yet the thing that mattered most was the vindication of Israel as a whole. Furthermore there is, in practice, no necessary antithesis between the two points of view; at least as high a patriotism has been displayed by the devotees of what Frazer called "this selfish and immoral doctrine" as by the most devoted sons of Greece and Rome. The ideal which he commends is, in fact, nothing less than that of the Totalitarian State,— with all its consequences.

The interaction of the two ideals, however, has been extensive, and to trace them out in detail would be both interesting and instructive. Here it must suffice to point out that in the development of the Roman Church we have an example of the combination of the Western ideal of subordination to the community with the Oriental ideal which underlies Christianity. At the same time it would be erroneous to suppose that the idea of such subordination to "the beloved community" was absent from Christianity when it moved into the Western world. In that world during a long term of years the Church proved itself capable of holding its own against the State. Unfortunately the true balance between them could not exactly be maintained, and in this lies the tragedy of Western civilization and the source of much of our present disquiet. For though the Church came out of the conflict with unimpaired liberty, it did so only by the sacrifice of spiritual power,[1] and the loss of any immediate hope of establishing a comprehensive Christian community. In the East, on the other hand, the Church was reduced to something like a department of the State.

Thus even in things non-material the definition of East and West is a matter of standpoint, a conclusion which receives further illustration when we turn to consider cultural boundaries. An Englishman on the Acropolis may be fully conscious of the part which Greece and things Hellenic have played in the civilization in which he has been bred, as in his own life as an individual; he may be glad and proud to have his share in the ideas which animated those who built and glorified Athens; none the less he is an intrusive element, a tourist, or at best a visitor in the house of another. But let him move east to the ruins of Baalbek and his feelings will be entirely different. The architecture of the temples is broadly the same, and the civiliza-

---

[1] May I be allowed to refer for the working-out of this thought to my *Decline and Fall of the Medieval Papacy*, p. 59 f.

tion out of which they arose a development of that of Greece. But now he takes a different stand; he is here no intruder, but a member of the very Western civilization which produced those gigantic structures, with more right to be there among them than the Syrians in whose lands they have been erected.

But the cultural boundary between East and West is not that of our study, for Greek influences have always stood on the Western side, being opposed, with Latin, to those which are more definitely Oriental. It was, indeed, Hadrian, the lover of things Greek, who, at a somewhat later epoch, gave the Western twist to the Empire.

The frontier between the Eastern and Western halves of the Roman Empire would seem to fall most naturally along an imaginary line drawn from Vienna to Aquileia, for at this point it extends to hardly more than two hundred miles. In actual practice, however, it has always run further east. The division, when it came, came slowly, as would the ecclesiastical division of later centuries. The Empire, as Diocletian recognized, had become too unwieldy for administration from a single centre, and so he set up his own headquarters at Nicomedia, intending to make it, so Lactantius informs us (*De Mort. Persec.*, VII, 2), the equal of Rome. Then came Constantine's foundation of his city on the Bosporus,[1] an act which carried with it the ultimate severance of the Empire and the schism between Eastern and Western Christendom. This separation was inevitable from the simple fact that Rome would never accept a position of dependence on her own offspring; though if legend can be trusted, Rome herself had destroyed the mother city of Alba Longa, whose injuries seemed thus tardily to be avenged.

The opposition of East and West within the Empire, however, goes back to pre-Christian times and corresponds to a real difference of outlook and tradition. There had been a struggle as to which should be the dominant influence, for time and again the East had threatened to outweigh the West in the counsels of the Roman world. Even Julius seems to have considered the idea of moving the seat of government to the Troad; but the old Roman spirit rose up in protest; we can catch its echoes still in Virgil, in Horace, and in Livy.[2] It was well for Western Europe that the shifting of the capital of the Empire was postponed

---

[1] The site has always been important. Its oldest name was Lygos (Pliny, *Hist. Nat.*, IV, xi, 18); it then became Byzantium, which was still a fortified town in the days of Pausanias. The name Constantinople it would bear until our own day has seen it changed to Istamboul.

[2] cf. Horace, *Odes*, III, iii, where Rome's power is held to depend on Troy's remaining unrestored. See, further, R. S. Conway, *New Studies in a Great Inheritance*, p. 61.

until the days of Constantine, for the delay probably saved it from destruction at the hands of the barbarians, and, as Professor Conway has said, "gave it time to learn to be Christian, while Rome still stood warden of the gates of the North". Oriental influences were decisively thrown back, at least for the time, when Augustus overcame at Actium the forces of Antony and Cleopatra. But the attraction of the East still lingered.[1]

THE EASTERN AND WESTERN CHURCHES

The main divisions of Christendom as known to history are those of East and West; for the many sects and denominations of Western Europe have, directly or indirectly, broken away from the one great Mother Church of Rome. The final breach between Constantinople and Rome took place on a day in July 1054 when two legates laid on the altar of Sancta Sophia the papal bull of excommunication. Thenceforth, in spite of temporary and illusive reconciliations, schism has persisted, and the Catholic Church has been a divided Church.

In moving into the West the Church was but following the course of universal empire, whose advance, so a contemporary of Livy had noted,[2] had consistently maintained that direction, beginning in Mesopotamia and then proceeding by way of Macedonia to Rome. Christianity, it need hardly be pointed out, was by no means the first Oriental religion to seek its fortunes in the West, and when it came, it came almost without observation. Even Juvenal, as he bemoaned the flow of the Orontes into the Tiber,[3] was evidently unaware that Antioch was also the departure point of the Gospel. The modern historian sees in this transfer of Christianity to the West a striking instance of a religion finding its highest expression in an alien soil.[4] The ancient historian, however, did not trouble his head about the matter, for Juvenal was not alone in ignoring the progress of the new faith. There is something surprising about this, seeing that it was the prelude to the greatest religious change in the whole of human history; but from their own standpoint the philosophers and historians of that day can hardly be held blameworthy. After all it was one who later became a disciple of the Lord who asked "Can any good thing come out of Nazareth?" (John 1 : 46).

For the establishment and development of Western Christendom the fall of Jerusalem in A.D. 70 was of supreme importance.

[1] See the additional note "The Glamour of the East", p. 26.
[2] Pompeius Trogus in his *Universal History* which has survived only in the Epitome of Justinus.
[3] *Satires*, III, 62, *Jam pridem Syrus in Tiberim defluxit Orontes.*
[4] A. J. Toynbee, *A Study of History*, II, p. 74.

Had Jerusalem not fallen it would doubtless, from its age-long prestige, have been the shrine towards which the eyes of every Christian would have turned with reverence; the only possible seat of a theocratic government. There was also the danger, as Renan suggested in his famous *Hibbert Lectures*, that some kind of caliphate might be set up, with the family of the Messiah as hereditary rulers of Christendom. Such a course became impossible when Jerusalem was destroyed. Its vacant place was taken, not by a single new centre, but by Antioch, Ephesus, and Rome, cities which claimed to possess apostolic traditions. Each to some extent developed the original tradition in its own way; with a difference of doctrinal emphasis, a difference of organization, and even a different canon of Scripture. In the centuries which followed, one of the most urgent tasks of the Church would be to reconcile the diversities which thus arose. At the same time it had to take account of a variety of other influences pressing in from outside, for by the end of the second century Christianity had travelled far from the simple years beneath the Syrian blue; and if the triumphal dominance of the city of the seven hills was not yet even dimly visible in the West, there, and still more in the East, the tenets of the city of the violet crown had already had their effect upon the unformulated beliefs of the first Hebrew disciples of the Lord.

The East and the West, in spite of definite and increasing differences, had much in common. This was only natural, since both were parts of one Body. They had the same faith; though they might not state it in exactly the same terms, and the East would prove less accommodating than the West; for whereas the latter accepted the Nicene Creed alongside its own, the Apostles' Creed has never been used in the Greek Church; it is, perhaps, too bald and elementary for the Oriental mind, representing as it does the "popular", and not the "learned science of Christianity".[1] Though both East and West had eventually the same canon of Scripture, their progress towards fixing it was not identical. They may even have had a different Biblical text; but this is by no means so probable as Hort used to think.[2] They had, too, the same organization, though here again the development was different, and the West, in many things, waited on the East. This slower development of organization in the West may have given opportunity to the Church of Rome to exert its authority, which grew up from very informal beginnings into something rigid and exacting, so rigid in fact that it would lead in the end to schism. It was not, however, until the close of the second century that Rome itself began to be a Latin-speaking

[1] cf. Matthew Arnold, *Literature and Dogma*, p. 250.
[2] For a discussion of the so-called Western text see Part III, Chap. I.

Church and a distinctively Western type of Christianity came
definitely to take shape.

East and West had each its roll of famous martyrs, for alongside Ignatius (who·had, after all, suffered in the West and bore
a good Samnite name) and Polycarp, the West had the victims
of Nero and the martyrs of Lyons and·Vienne. In literature the
West was sadly at a disadvantage, for it was long before any
writer of the first rank began to emerge, and literature, in consequence, never played so prominent a part in the spread of
Christian ideas as in the East. In our period, apart from North
Africa, the leaders of the Western Churches were far inferior in
learning and culture; whilst even Justin and Irenaeus, the first
Western·theologians, had had their training in the East.

Such were some of the things which East and West held in
common; though even these were possessed with a difference.
When we turn to the things in which contrasts are to be found,
and these are numerous, a similar qualification is even more
necessary, for they are in general the result of a· distinctive
emphasis rather than of a fundamental cleavage. Moreover it
must constantly be borne in mind that the East itself was no
unity; how could it be with such opposing schools of thought as
those of Antioch and Alexandria, each of which had in its
different way something in common with the West. In what
follows this must constantly be recollected and such statements
as are made be regarded as generalizations which require many
exceptions.

Contrasts between East and West go back to the earliest
times; they can be discerned in the apostolic fathers, as a comparison of say I *Clement* with the epistles of Ignatius at once
makes obvious. The one is most concerned with moral and ethical considerations, and the related question of discipline; in the
other, interest in speculation and metaphysics is clearly evident.
"As we pass from Rome and Corinth to Antioch and Asia Minor,
we are conscious of entering into a new religious and moral
atmosphere" (Lightfoot, II, i, p. 1). It was no accident that
disputes in the West arose over baptism and the reception of the
lapsed, or that we find the beginnings of a penitential system in
Hermas. In the East we have, by way of contrast, the trial of
Paul of Samosata for heretical views on the Incarnation. The
same distinction persists as our period passes into the Post-
Nicene age; the typical fathers of the Eastern Church are the
two Gregories and Athanasius; their equivalents in the West are
lawyers and administrators like Ambrose, Leo, and Gregory.
The West, indeed, produced only one great theologian before
the Middle Ages, Augustine, and even for him the practical
outweighed the speculative; Christianity was valued not as a

superlative philosophy but as a scheme of redemption.

The West, as we have seen, was interested above all in discipline and morals, and as a consequence the effects of sin and the need for Atonement. Hence there is an emphasis, lacking in the East, on the redemptive work of Christ and a greater interest in the historical facts of His life. In the East, attention was mainly focused on the Incarnation and the Resurrection, and Christ was thought of as the conqueror of death rather than of sin. It was, indeed, a fundamental weakness of Eastern theology that it never acquired a fully adequate conception of the meaning of sin, regarding it more as a lack of positive goodness, or even as a necessary accompaniment of progress, than as disobedience to the divine will and an affront to the divine love.

The West, in our period, is represented most typically by the African fathers who above all others helped to shape its destinies. Tertullian, Cyprian, and Augustine had all been moulded by rhetorical studies. The two former had combined them with the rigid discipline of the law, whilst Augustine had submitted to the milder influence of philosophy. They were all, however, stern in their outlook, and very pessimistic as to human ability to achieve the good life. Like Ezekiel they were ever on the side of Jehovah against His rebellious children; not like Jeremiah, anxious to find excuses for them.[1] If they were not entirely responsible for the legalistic outlook which came to prevail, at least they strengthened its hold on the mind of the Church. It may, I think, be said that the West was naturally more closely akin to the Hebrews in its attitude towards religion than the East; for it was unspeculative, regarded life under the aspects of time and development, and predominantly legalistic in outlook. The East looked to Hellas, not Palestine, for its philosophy.

Because of its emphasis on the Resurrection, the East had a deeper note of joy in its religion, and less of that gloomy outlook which would increase with the passing of the centuries in the West. Perhaps its experiences would be less trying and depressing; or, it may be, it would seek in speculation a means of escape from the evils of life around. It was, indeed, tempted to regard life as an illusion, a trait of Oriental thought borrowed from regions still more remote.

At this epoch the Church in the East had almost a monopoly of mysticism, for in the West the seed had hardly yet been sown which would in later ages blossom in the great German mystics, and in our own Julian of Norwich and Walter Hylton. This strain of mysticism was perhaps more important than is often recognized; it forms a great part of the thought of St. Paul and is

[1] See, further, my *Jeremiah* (*Westminster Commentaries*), p. xli.

23

definitely present in contemporary Judaism.[1] But even in the Eastern Church, as in Judaism, it was not in the main stream of development or acceptance, and tended more and more to find its home in the back-waters among groups of doubtful orthodoxy, and may even have flowed into the Church from outside sources, such as the Essenes, the various Gnostic sects, and, above all, the Neoplatonists, with Plotinus as the supreme teacher.[2] Examples of mystical writings can be found in the *Odes of Solomon*, the "Hymn to Jesus" included in the *Acts of John* 94 f.,[3] and in the famous saying from Oxyrhynchus, preserved also in the *Gospel according to the Hebrews*, "Let not him that seeketh cease till he find, and when he findeth he shall marvel, and having marvelled, he shall reign, and having reigned, he shall rest."

But if Christians in the East were thus inclined to lose themselves in individualistic mysticism to the neglect of some of the wider implications of the Gospel, to depend on intuition rather than logic, immense importance was attached to correctness of belief. The title of Orthodox which designates the Eastern Church is sufficient evidence for this. But the Eastern Church, anxious it may be not to discourage further speculation, has never indulged in elaborate definitions of the faith. Even to-day its theology is much more fluid and less systematic than that of Rome, possibly because, unlike Rome, it has never been faced by the necessity for careful and exact re-statement in response to the challenge of a Reformation. The East has been the scene of many councils, it has never had a parallel to that of Trent.

There can be but little doubt that distrust of speculation hampered the Western Church in its search for truth, and some at least of its thinkers were unduly critical of human learning and philosophy. The West, as a consequence, failed to grasp the continuous nature of revelation; the faith had once for all been delivered to the saints, the Church's supreme duty was to guard the deposit. Thus its outlook, in spite of the admission of many novel dogmas, tended to become static rather than dynamic, and did not allow sufficiently for the continuous activity of God the Holy Spirit.[4] The different attitudes of East and West came out as early as the controversy with the Gnostics. In the East the Alexandrians met the challenge by demonstrating that Christianity was the true *gnosis*; the West appealed to tradition and overcame the movement not by argument but by authority.

---

[1] See Abelson, *Jewish Mysticism*, p. 21 ff.
[2] The West was, it need scarcely be said, profoundly influenced by the Neoplatonists.　　　　　　　　　　　　　　[3] *Apoc. N.T.*, p. 253.
[4] In matters of practice, Rome held a much more flexible idea of tradition: see below, pp. 113 f.

The Eastern and Western Churches in pursuing their varied lines of development were but working out their pagan heritages, for if, as Westcott has said, "the speculations of the Greek thinkers had raised problems and fashioned language which could aid Christian teachers in unfolding the doctrine of the Divine Nature, the determinations of the Roman jurists were equally powerful in preparing for the exhibition of the relations of man to God, which was the office of the Latin Church" (*The Gospel of the Resurrection*, p. 79).

In spite of a continual movement of theologians from the East to the West, that difference of atmosphere to which Lightfoot referred still persisted. It is worth noting that many of the emigrants, whether their stay was temporary or permanent, were open to Western influences; even Marcion was much more akin to the West than the East, to judge from his insistence on the literal rather than the allegorical meaning of Scripture.[1]

This flow from the East was no novelty and long before the Christian era it had been constant and considerable. Syrian traders had ever been on the move from one end of the Mediterranean to the other, and some permanent settlements had been made in Gaul and elsewhere. There were Syrian troops in North Africa, and Syrian gods were worshipped on the Roman Wall in far-away Britain. Later there would be a large Syrian Christian *diaspora*, the counterpart of the dispersion of the Jews.

After the triumph of Christianity and the expedition of the Empress Helena, the mother of Constantine, to the Holy Land, pilgrimages became a regular feature of Christian life. This was not an entirely new development, though new in the West, for in the latter half of the second century Melito of Sardis had visited the sacred sites, an example which was followed not long afterwards by Bishop Alexander (Euseb., IV, xxvi, 14; VI, xi, 2). At a later date the settlement of Jerome at Bethlehem brought East and West still closer, for he kept up a voluminous correspondence with his friends in Italy, and not a few of them made the journey to Palestine.

Intercourse between East and West continued until the progress of Islam in the eighth century made it difficult and dangerous.[2] It was only renewed on a large scale in the age of the Crusades when, in addition to the actual expeditions, there was an immense development of trade between the Italian cities and the Levant.

There was, however, one very serious barrier to any real sympathy and understanding; that was the difference of lan-

---

[1] There was, of course, much use of allegory in the West, but even St. Thomas Aquinas insisted that the literal must have control over the allegorical meaning of a verse: *De Potentia Dei*, Qu. IV, art. I, 8.

[2] cf. Pirenne, *Mahomet et Charlemagne*, p. 260.

guage,[1] and the consequent difference of theological terminology. This latter would be the source of much misunderstanding, as we shall see when we come to discuss the development of doctrine. There was something so different in the texture of the two languages and in the minds of those who used them, even if a superficial resemblance could be detected, which made it quite impossible for the Latins ever to provide adequate equivalents for the terms employed by Greek philosophers and theologians. Unfortunately very few Western theologians knew Greek. Augustine, like Cyprian, found the language repulsive and never made any great progress in it; at the same time he saw clearly the difficulty of finding suitable terms (*De Civ. Dei*, X, i) and recognized the ambiguity which must follow the confusion between "substance" and "essence" when speaking of the divine nature (*De Trin.*, VII, 10).

Additional Note: THE GLAMOUR OF THE EAST

The glamour of the East seemed never to fade from the Roman vision. The Latins might despise the Greeks and other Orientals, but they were ever anxious to establish their own connexion with the lands in which such peoples dwelt. Virgil, in attributing the foundation of Rome to the Trojan Aeneas; by no means stood alone; and even individuals sought to claim a similar derivation. Jerome tells us that some of his own contemporaries traced themselves back to Aeneas or Agamemnon (*Epist.*, CVIII), just as a noble English family might claim an ancestor who "came over with the Conqueror". The barbarians who inherited the power of Rome inherited also this tendency, and, in their turn, laid claim to an Eastern ancestry. The Franks, for example, looked to Hector and Priam, if the biographers of Charlemagne are to be trusted (the legend may even go back to Gregory of Tours, II, 9); though some preferred an eponymous founder, a Trojan named Franco (Otto of Freising, *Chron.*, I, 25). The British have claims on "Brutus the Trojan"; whilst the Danes trust in the similarity of their name to Danaus. Such legends abound in the writers of all periods of the Middle Ages. The matter is not entirely alien to our study, for it was a similar instinct which impelled many a city to seek for its Church a founder from the East, preferably of apostolic rank. There was even an attempt to connect the Jews with the same origins as the Greeks. Tacitus tells us that by some they were linked up with the Idaei who lived near Mount Ida in Crete, and that they had come to be called Iudaei "by a barbarous lengthening of the name" (*Hist.*, V, 2). It is possible that ultra-liberal Jews may have had a hand in this; such is the opinion of G. La Piana, *Harvard Theol. Rev.*, 1927, p. 382, where the reference to Tacitus is given by a slip or misprint to Bk. I.

[1] Cyprian actually disliked Greek, an early indication, according to E. W. Watson, of the severance of Eastern and Western Christianity.

PART I
THE SETTING

CHAPTER I

THE POLITICAL AND SOCIAL BACKGROUND

Any study of Western Christendom must begin with a survey, however brief, of the Empire within which it came to birth and had its development; for that development was largely conditioned by the secular world which formed its environment. The Empire, it need hardly be pointed out, embraced the East as well as the West, and included within its bounds not only Palestine, the scene of the first proclamation of the Christian Gospel, but also Asia Minor where an incipient theology had already begun to arise, even before Western Christendom in any distinctive sense had yet emerged.

THE GROWTH AND ORGANIZATION OF THE EMPIRE

When Christ was born at Bethlehem there was peace everywhere in the Empire. This peace had come to heal the wounds of a century which Horace had aptly described as "delirium", a century in which powerful military leaders had striven for dominion, and, in their insane lust for power, had been willing to sacrifice all things on the altar of their ambitions. Massacres, butchery, and proscription marked the close of the struggle, during which many of the noblest families of Rome were swept away. The revolution, for such it was, thus involved important social, as well as political, consequences.

Augustus,[1] by taming the revolutionary elements, and averting the threat from the East incarnate in Cleopatra, had brought the long conflict to an end. He was happy in his day, for men were so weary of strife and confusion that they were content to accept peace and security from any hand powerful enough to maintain them. But the price of security, then as always, was the surrender, in whole or in part, of liberty,[2] and with it other things that men value. Augustus, however, was wise enough to conceal his power by preserving the old republican forms and by claiming to be nothing more than the First Citizen (*princeps*) of Rome. In any case his power though great was by no means arbitrary since it was based on consent and delegation. But the constitution, as Syme has said, "was a screen and a sham".

---

[1] Two recent studies of Augustus may be mentioned: John Buchan, *Augustus*, 1937, and Ronald Syme, *The Roman Revolution*, 1939.
[2] Tacitus, *Ann.*, I, 2, says that this sacrifice was willingly made.

29

If personal ambition had been the motive of Augustus he became the saviour of his people. Having taken for his patron Apollo the god of perpetual youth, then but a newcomer in Rome, he based his whole policy on a revival of religion and of the old Roman virtues which had found in it their sanction and their inspiration. Alongside the restoration of traditional ideals he strove for a new way of living and new economic methods. His awareness of the need for economic reform may well have been inherited from his grandfather, the banker; for Augustus had sprung, not from the nobility, but from what we should now call the middle classes.

The period from the triumph of Augustus to the close of the second century was, as a whole, one of internal peace and growing prosperity. The death of Nero was, indeed, followed by a fresh outbreak of civic strife; but the Romans had not yet forgotten the lessons learned during the century of anarchy and the desire for quietness was still strong. In external matters the idea that limits must be set to expansion had gradually prevailed. The need for this had already been foreseen by Scipio Aemilianus some three centuries earlier when he changed the prayer beseeching the gods to make the Roman State "better and greater" into one which asked them only to preserve it.

Political stability brought in its wake commercial revival, and Rome became the great centre for the trade of the West and of the Mediterranean, which, for the only time in recorded history, was a lake surrounded by the territories of a single power. Trade was mainly in the hands of freedmen or Orientals; the latter, as we have already noted, speedily flooded the West, with consequences which were by no means limited to the sphere of commerce. But the prosperity which came to Rome was delusive, and the men of that era by their lavish spending really undermined its economic stability, and prepared the way for the grave financial difficulties which were to follow.

Internal peace and expanding trade, however, were only possible by reason of the strongly garrisoned frontiers; beyond them the forces were already gathering which would one day overwhelm the Roman world. The riches of civilization have ever been regarded as a desirable prize by the strong untutored peoples who survey them across its precarious barriers. For the moment those barriers were sufficiently powerful and sufficiently well manned to prevent serious irruptions; and further defences were constructed during the period, including Hadrian's wall in Britain. Marcus Aurelius in his day took the offensive and drove back the barbarians; had that day been prolonged their power might possibly have been broken. But this was not to be, and the close of the second century marked a definite stage in the gradual weakening of the Empire which then began to exhibit obvious signs of having passed its zenith. The age of the Antonines was, indeed, the last epoch of the ancient world which would enjoy even partial security and quiet. But even then a sense of despondency and inertia was beginning to spread, like a cloud over a summer sky, and a general belief came to prevail that the universe itself, including the physical world, was entering upon a stage of inevitable decay.[1]

Recent scholarship has considerably modified the verdict of Gibbon (I, p. 128) that Septimius Severus (193–211) was mainly responsible for the beginning of the decline of the Empire; none the less his reign certainly formed a species of watershed. Since Septimius had won his throne by the sword he regarded it as his by right of conquest and the Empire became as never before a military monarchy. One result of this was the depression of the senate. Even under Augustus, who added to its powers, it had begun to be seen that sooner or later it would become completely obsolete, and though its relations with later emperors had been friendly the impression was only deepened. From the time of Septimius its power rapidly diminished before the growing equestrian order and the provincial aristocracy whom the emperor delighted to favour. Septimius was an African by birth, but his marriage connexions were eventually to raise to the throne of the Caesars elements still more incongruous, those Syrian emperors who would help to speed the influx of Oriental ideas. Julia Domna, his wife, had a sister whose two grandsons became emperors in succession. The reign of the first, Elagabalus, has been described as "an orgy without parallel in the history of Rome".[2] He, like his much more worthy cousin, Severus Alexander, met a violent death.

In 212, Caracalla, the son and successor of Septimius, had extended the rights of Roman citizenship to all free inhabitants of the Empire.[3] This measure, though in reality a mere device to broaden the basis of taxation, by removing many inequalities and adding to the number of those directly concerned in the welfare of the State, ought to have produced new life and unity. Nevertheless decline still continued, until Decius in the middle of the third century made a desperate effort in the face of pressing dangers to revive the old Roman spirit, and incidentally brought about the first general persecution of the Christian Church. His death in battle, and the growing peril from the barbarians, led Aurelian, a generation later, to begin the con-

[1] For a Christian expression of this view see Cyprian, *Ad Demetrianum*, III.
[2] Stuart Jones, *The Roman Empire*, p. 266.
[3] The terms of the edict are uncertain: see A. H. M. Jones, "Another Interpretation of the Constitutio Antoninana", in *J.R.S.*, 1936, XXVI, Pt. II.

struction of a fresh wall to protect the city; Rome itself could no longer be regarded as exempt from possible attack. This precaution was a portent, a sign, that as Freeman has said, "the wandering of Nations had begun, that the Teutonic race had begun to play its part in the drama of human history" (*Hist. and Architect. Sketches*, p. 168). But Rome, though there might be fears for its safety, was in reality too far removed from the frontiers to be the headquarters of government of the vast territories which her sons had conquered. This fact was realized by Diocletian who became sole emperor in 285.

This remarkable man, who was of humble and probably servile birth, made it a matter of definite policy to magnify his office, and with him the process by which the Empire was turned into a despotism received its final impetus. Casting aside the obsolete traditions which had restrained his predecessors, he made access to his person increasingly difficult and gave the Imperial Court the semblance of that of an Oriental monarch. Experience had shown the ease with which an emperor might be assassinated and civil war arise. Further to discourage such attempts, Diocletian proceeded to divide up the Empire into two parts, each under an Augustus, whose burden was shared by a Caesar. Thus any claimant to the Empire would have four rulers to overcome. Diocletian took the East for his own sphere and fixed his headquarters at Nicomedia. As the Augustus of the West made Milan his capital, Rome was deprived of political importance, a step which involved a further diminution of the importance of the senate which now remained little more than an interesting relic of former times, and its chief function would be to act the part of chorus to the tragedy of the decline and fall of Rome.

In 305, Diocletian, after failing to suppress the Christian Church, abdicated and his retirement was the signal for the outbreak of a fresh series of civil wars which culminated in the victory of Constantine.

Constantine was the son of Constantius Chlorus, later the Augustus of the West, and Helena, sometimes called his concubine. She must, however, have been a lawful wife, though perhaps of a lower social status, for when Diocletian ordered Constantius to marry another she had to be divorced.[1] Constantine spent his boyhood, probably as a kind of hostage for the good behaviour of his father, at the court of Diocletian and Galerius at Nicomedia. He succeeded in escaping and joining his father not long before the death of the latter at York in July 306. The legions at once proclaimed him Augustus; an irregular

[1] Eusebius is careful to call Constantine the "lawful son" of his father (VIII, xiii, 12).

act which received an unwilling and partial recognition from Galerius, the supreme ruler. In the strife which followed, Constantine, in a series of brilliant campaigns, at last succeeded in making himself ruler of the West. In the final battle at the Milvian Bridge (or more correctly Saxa Rubra)[1] his armies consisted mainly of Germans, Celts, and Britons (Zosimus, II, 15). His triumph was followed by the issue of the so-called Edict of Milan in which, with his ally Licinius, he gave freedom of worship to the Empire. The relations between the allies, however, deteriorated and Licinius, after becoming a persecutor of the Christians, was defeated and put to death. Constantine became sole ruler in 324.

Since the appearance of the final instalment of Mommsen's *History of Rome*[2] a more adequate idea of the organization and achievements of the Empire has prevailed. For in it he showed that far from being a central despotism to which the extremities were sacrificed, the Empire exercised a civilizing influence over wide areas, bringing the barbarians within the circle of the Graeco-Roman world and laying the foundations of Europe as we know it to-day. Outbreaks of violence and destruction there may have been, but until the close of the fourth century periods of good and settled government were frequent, and even when Rome itself was the prey of conspiracy and outrage there was considerable prosperity in the provinces.

The policy of Augustus had placed Italy and things Italian very much in the foreground of the picture, but it would be a mistake to think of the Empire as in any sense a federation of provinces, each modelled on Italy. A considerable measure of political freedom was allowed to them, as well as to the subjected kingdoms, and even existing forms of government were not entirely abolished. The emperors, moreover, made a point of respecting local susceptibilities and of keeping themselves informed of local opinion. If at first there was a tendency to control or suppress national characteristics, Hadrian inaugurated the policy of enlisting them in the service of the State. It

---

[1] Different accounts of this very important battle have survived. Lactantius, who was a contemporary, places it actually at the Milvian Bridge just outside the walls of Rome (*De Mort. Persec.*, XLIV, LII); but Eusebius (*Vit. Const.*, I, 38) states that it was fought some distance away, and his account is supported by Aurelius Victor (*De Caesar.*, XL), who records that Maxentius, the opponent of Constantine, had advanced as far as Saxa Rubra, some nine miles from the city. Raphael's famous cartoon apparently placed the conflict immediately outside the walls; but the topography of artists is notoriously unreliable.

[2] Translated into English with the title *The Provinces of the Roman Empire*. Some French scholars take a very different view. cf. Camille Jullian, *De la Gaule à la France*, p. 189, and Littré, *Étude sur les Berbers et le Moyen Age*, p. xvi.

C

was under Hadrian, too, that a system of bureaucratic rule, similar to that of the Hellenistic monarchies, was established.

Under the Republic, the provinces had suffered from the lack of any settled principle of government and of continuity of policy; each was given over, and then but for a short term, to a governor who in most cases regarded it as a means of increasing his private fortune; an idea which survived, at least in popular thought, as late as the third century.[1] But the absence of corruption and exploitation did not of themselves produce efficiency, for the term of office was far too short for the peculiar problems of any area to be mastered by its nominal ruler.

Under Augustus the Empire had been divided into twenty-eight provinces of two distinct types.[2] The so-called senatorial provinces lay well inside the Empire and were governed by proconsuls; the imperial were strung along the frontiers and their governors were *propraetors*. By the reforms of Diocletian, the provinces were still further split up, civil authority was separated from military, whilst the distinction between the two types was abolished together with the privileged position of Italy.

With more equitable treatment and reasonable opportunities for developing their resources the provinces soon began to rival Italy, and by the beginning of the second century had so far progressed in material wealth and industrial efficiency as to capture markets which had hitherto been the preserve of Italian traders.

It was said above that the Roman Empire was not to be regarded as a confederation of provinces modelled on Italy; it was, in fact, much more an aggregation of cities modelled on Rome. This was especially true of the West, where towns were of recent growth and so lacked traditions of their own. Following the method of Alexander the Great and his Seleucid successors, Rome wherever she extended her rule established cities and fostered those which she found. The highest in rank was the *colonia*, a foundation of Roman citizens, often including many ex-soldiers. Next came the *municipium*, a previously existing city made to conform to Roman ways. The distinction between these two was slight and gradually disappeared. The fact that many cities were situated on the sea-coast was of great importance since it made them ready channels for the spread of ideas.

Roman cities were not limited in jurisdiction and territory to the space within the walls; each had an area around it, the

[1] See *Acts of Peter*, VIII, *Apoc. N.T.*, p. 312.
[2] See, further, W. T. Arnold, *Roman Prov. Administration*, App. I. The idea that the emperor retained the provinces which required armies to defend them requires modification: see *Camb. Anct. Hist.*, X, p. 211 f.

forerunner of the Italian *contado*, often extending to many miles over which it claimed rights. For its revenues it was dependent on various sources which were supplemented in emergencies by grants from central funds, and at all times by the patriotism of its wealthier citizens.

In the days of Rome's greatness the real power lay in the hands of the upper middle classes, and like the Whigs in England, they naturally had an eye for their own interests. The towns were therefore favoured at the expense of the countryside. From the beginning of the third century, however, the prosperity of the cities gradually declined as centralization and bureaucracy increased. The burden of administration pressed most heavily upon one class, the *curiales*, and at last became so weighty that they sank beneath it. Diocletian introduced measures intended to restore municipal life, but they only helped still further to depress it.[1] The decay of the cities also affected the peasants whose lot was closely linked with them. The increasing economic weakness was accompanied by a notable decline of enterprise and initiative, and the cities, in ceasing to be the economic *foci* of civilization, ceased also to be centres of culture and ideas.

In the heyday of their power and influence the cities were of immense service for the spread of the Gospel, for from them new ideas could radiate over the surrounding countryside, and during the whole of our period they set the norm for both life and thought. Even if the old derivation of *pagani* from "countrymen" be given up,[2] there is no doubt that Christianity was slow to advance in rural areas. The method adopted by St. Paul commended itself to his successors and it was from the city that the faith made its way into the neighbouring villages. This process seems to be known to Pliny, who speaks of the "contagion" penetrating even the villages and the countryside (*Epist.*, XCVI); whilst Tertullian states explicitly that it was in the cities that Churches were founded (*De Praes.*, XX).

If the first missionaries of the Gospel benefited from the convenience of the cities so also did they from the elaborate and comprehensive system of Roman roads. This started from the Golden milestone in the forum and penetrated every part of the Empire, crossing rivers and mountain ranges, and even, as at Brundisium and Bononia (Boulogne), leaping across the sea itself.

The construction of great highways had been originally a

---

[1] See C. E. Van Sickle, "Diocletian and the Decline of the Roman Municipalities," in *J.R.S.*, 1938, XXVIII, Pt. I, p. 8 ff.

[2] The derivation now favoured makes it represent civilians as distinct from soldiers.

matter of military necessity; those "straight dusty roads, old Rome's imperial lines, ruled for her legions" were a means of communication between the centre and the frontiers, and between one province and another. So long as Rome was strong, new roads were continually being made; roads and ports were, indeed, as vital to the Empire as veins and arteries to the human body; but after the middle of the third century, owing to shortage of labour and other factors, road-making was largely abandoned.

Travel by road was supplemented by sea and river transport. The former, of course, was only available at certain seasons; the Mediterranean, for example, was practically closed to shipping from November to March. A sea voyage could, indeed, be very dangerous, as the reader of Acts does not need to be reminded, and the small ships of the age were very much at the mercy of the elements. Even Rome's food supply might be cut off by the rise of a sudden storm.[1] There is significance in the inclusion of the shipwrecked among the regular objects of Christian charity by Tertullian (*Apol.*, XXXIX).

Except in remote districts and during civil wars, travel was reasonably safe, and this security enabled both ideas and men to pass freely from one end of the Empire to the other. For the roads not only echoed to the tramp of the legions; they were filled by swarms of traders and even of tourists. Wandering teachers also made use of them as they hurried to new scenes of activity—and not least the Christian missionary with his burning message.

CULTURAL INFLUENCES

Although Rome, from the first, had been sensitive to external influences, yet whatever she received was assimilated and made her own. In one field, however, she was not entirely successful, that of religion. None the less even here this characteristic came into play. The Oriental cults in the West, although intractable to real penetration, were different from what they had been in the lands of their origin. They were Eastern still when Rome had done her worst. Thus Rome changed all that she touched. But the process was not always deliberate, rather was it the natural outcome of the life and energy with which she was endowed. In any case the prestige of a conquering race lay behind all that was Roman, and it must not be forgotten that those whom she had subdued often acted gladly as her agents.

The means by which romanization was carried out were various. Perhaps the chief method was the establishment and development of cities, especially the foundation of colonies. Even in Macedonia there was a string of them along the Via

[1] See the description in Suetonius, *Claudius*, XVII, 2.

Egnatia. Certainly urban life was much more open to influence than the countryside, and when the imperial power grew weak the barbarism of the country began to flow back over the towns. The encouragement of agriculture also helped, for it led to the establishment of market towns which took the place of the old tribal meeting-places and so tended to break down local feeling and replace it by Roman ideas.

Even in the older towns there would be numerous officials and traders, for every conquered land quickly became the scene of the activities of the Roman merchant, and the agriculturist soon followed where conditions were suitable. Intermarriages would not be unknown and they would speed up the process of assimilation. One exceedingly fruitful means of romanization, especially in the early years of the Empire, was the camp. Camps were permanent settlements round which, through the attraction thither of traders and other dependants, a town would gradually be formed. The original nucleus would be made up of soldiers drawn from many different localities, but as the legions became permanently attached to particular stations, and soldiers on retirement settled in their neighbourhood, there would be a distinct mixture of races and cultures. The process did not, however, work only in one direction, for the legionaries tended to lose touch with a wider world, and as local recruiting became more and more the custom Roman influences grew fainter, and with the increasing entry of barbarians, many of whom came from beyond the frontier, the camp exercised influence in an opposite direction. It was, indeed, by means of the armies that the barbarians began to infiltrate into the Empire, until at last they brought about its downfall.

The establishment of schools was an obvious way of promoting romanization; the presence of Roman tutors in Britain, for example, was hailed as a triumph for Agricola, and the promise of cultural as well as military conquest. Gaul especially had a high reputation for its schools, among the most famous of which were those at Toulouse, Treves, and Marseilles.

Romanization was accompanied by the spread of the Latin language. In this connexion two things demand notice. That in the early days of the Republic the use of Latin was regarded as a privilege which was only granted by the senate; and, secondly, that it was not until the end of the Social War (90–89 B.C.) that the Latin alphabet came into general use in Italy. Before that, many districts still retained their own alphabets, based in some cases, as at Iguvium (Gubbio), on that of the Etruscans itself borrowed from the Greeks.

Latin was naturally the official language for administration and the law, as well as for the army. The ambitious soldier would

37

therefore require more than a superficial knowledge of it, and as many barbarian soldiers were exceedingly ambitious they had to give considerable attention to its study. In Syria and the East, however, Greek was recognized as an alternative language. For purposes of private intercourse the native tongues would everywhere persist; Celtic in Gaul and Britain, Punic and Berber in North Africa, with Greek and various dialects in South Italy and Sicily. The average barbarian of the upper or official classes would almost invariably be bilingual.

Latin, however, soon spread outside the boundaries of the Empire. Some knowledge of it would be retained by the barbarian soldier who returned to his homeland. Still more important was the trader; for commerce, as elsewhere, preceded culture, often in regions where no political penetration had taken place. In the East, a law school, probably started as early as the second century, which drew students from all the Orient, used Latin as the medium for instruction; and Gregory Thaumaturgus was able to acquire it even in Cappadocia (*Paneg. ad Orig.*, V, in *P.G.*, X, col. 1065).

Though many Greeks came to Rome and the West, such of them as learnt Latin did so only for practical or business purposes, for they despised Latin literature and the "barbarous" tongue in which it was written. Perhaps because of this attitude the Greeks were very poor linguists, and at the height of their cultural fame anyone who knew another tongue excited comment.[1] Although Plutarch spent some time in Rome and gave many lectures, his knowledge of Latin was defective, and he must have found a sufficiently large number of people who knew Greek to form his audiences. The history of European civilization, and of the Church in particular, might have been very different had Latin been known in the East as Greek was known in the West.

It is difficult to estimate the extent to which the process of romanization was successful; for in many cases its effects were very superficial. In particular the use of Roman names cannot be taken as evidence. When in 35 B.C. Antony enlisted Greeks and Asiatics in his army the inscriptions suggest that Latin names were conferred on them all. So too the German bodyguard of the emperors from Augustus to Galba all acquired Latin or Graeco-Latin names; Felix, Phoebus, Nereus, and Linus are especially common. The last two, it may be observed, are found among the names of early Christians. Similar names were

[1] Thucydides, VIII, 85. In the fourth century A.D. a certain Musonius attracted the attention of Constantius II because he was *facundia sermonis utriusque clarus* (Ammianus Marcellinus, XV, xiii, 1). On the other hand, a soldier in Apuleius, *Metamorph.*, IX, 39, when his Latin was not understood, spoke in Greek.

often given to slaves;[1] while freedmen, as is well known, adopted the family name of their patrons, as did foreigners who were admitted to Roman citizenship.[2] Instances of Romans taking Greek names are not unknown, but they must be unusual. There is the case of a female slave mentioned in a Delphic Oracle of 200 B.C. who is described as a Roman by race but has the name of Nicaea.

The use of Latin by soldiers, officials, and traders might often give the appearance of a romanized society; but underneath, that society was often still barbarous, and native customs and ideas, as well as native speech, would be retained. The inscriptions reveal the superficial character of the knowledge of many provincials; Latin is already breaking down into modern languages in some cases, but in general they disclose pure ignorance, with no promise of cultural development of any kind. Some races were less receptive than others, even of such superficial culture, the Scots and Irish in particular being practically impervious at this stage of their history; a noteworthy circumstance in view of the work of Ireland in the "Dark Ages" in preserving the knowledge of Greek in the West.

The world around the Mediterranean which went to make up the Empire of Rome, as it formed a single political unit, was, with a few exceptions, pervaded by a single type of culture, a culture which was destined to be one of the great moulding influences of Western civilization.

With the arms of Alexander the Great Hellenism had penetrated far into Asia. This penetration, however, had been followed by a reaction, and for a time it had seemed possible that Eastern Europe might be submerged under Oriental influences. This was prevented by the Seleucid kings who held the breach until Rome was ready to enter upon the heritage of Alexander. But Hellenism, if it repelled the onset of Oriental thought, was greatly modified in the conflict, and thereby acquired a new capacity for world penetration. In this, its latest stage, Greek culture is generally known as Hellenistic, and though it has been the fashion to belittle it when compared with the earlier Hellenic phase, from the standpoint of world history it was probably even more important, for it was to Greek culture in its Hellenistic form that Rome succumbed, and, through Rome, the nations to whom she became instructress.

Roman admiration for things Greek was coupled with a pro-

---

[1] See Miss M. L. Gordon, "The Nationality of Slaves under the Early Roman Empire," in *J.R.S.*, 1924, XIV, p. 93 ff.
[2] One well-known case was that of Archias, defended by Cicero, who took the *nomen* of Licinius from his patron Lucullus.

found contempt for those who claimed to be its living representatives. Ovid, for example, can speak of Greek eloquence and Greek cowardice in a single breath (*Fasti*, III, 102). The Greeks were everywhere despised and to call anyone a "Greekling" was to offer a bitter insult.[1] The Greeks had indeed fallen far since the heroic days, and though still possessed of great energy and aptitude, their gifts were often devoted to mean and petty objects. The loss of freedom seemed to have robbed them of all aspiration and even of self-respect. None the less they retained their pride and, as we have seen, despised the Latin speech and the Latin writings. They had an equally great contempt for those who used them. As late as the beginning of the fourth century a Greek could lump Romans and Jews together as incapable of understanding Hellenic culture owing to their barbarian nature.[2]

Long before Greece became a Roman province there had been Greek colonies in Italy and some knowledge of Greek in other parts. It is not without interest that the first mention of Rome itself speaks of it as a Hellenic city which had been captured by the Gauls.[3] With the close intercourse which followed the conquest, Greek spread very rapidly among the educated; but under the stress and strain of political strife its study was neglected (Cicero, *Pro Archia*, III), though Greek remained the language of philosophy. There was, indeed, some scorn for Romans who wrote in Greek. Horace compared them to men carrying faggots into a wood. None the less many Romans and Italians continued to adopt it as a literary medium.[4]

Under Hadrian, at the beginning of the second century, there was a kind of Greek renaissance which affected religion as well as art and letters. Later again, Greek culture found an advocate in Gallienus who thus forms a link between Hadrian and Julian. Gallienus, indeed, seems to have hoped that the advocates of Christianity might at last be driven from the field by means of the Neoplatonic philosophy. In this, too, he was a forerunner of Julian. But the decay of a living interest on a wide scale is surely to be seen in the choice by Ammianus Marcellinus, himself a Greek, of Latin as the medium for his history, especially as he was not entirely happy in his use of it.

[1] cf. Aelius Spartianus, *Vit. Hadrian.*, I, 5. The term survived into the days of Julian: see Ammianus Marcellinus, XVII, ix, 3.

[2] See Macarius Magnes, *Apocrit.*, II, 17. Some of the Romans had accepted the title of "barbarian": e.g. Plautus, *Mil. Glor.*, II, ii, 58. In 2 Macc. 2:21 Greeks or Greek-speaking Syrians are, by what must be a unique usage, called " barbarous multitudes".

[3] Heraclides Ponticus, quoted by Plutarch, *Camillus*, XXII.

[4] Among the ruling classes it was hardly considered "the thing" to profess any knowledge of Greek art, even in the days of Cicero, as can be seen from the amusing asides in *In Verrem*, II, iv, 4 f.

One outstanding service Greece was to render to East and West alike. It provided much of the terminology of Christian theology as well as the language in which the New Testament could be written. This latter was, of course, Hellenistic, a form of language which had developed outside Greece itself and under the influence of wider needs. It was, indeed, the current speech of the times, especially in the East.

THE STATE OF ROMAN SOCIETY

Opinions in regard to the moral and social condition of the Roman people in the early years of the Empire have been considerably modified in recent years owing to the realization that the authorities upon whom reliance had hitherto been placed dealt with only a restricted area in arriving at their estimates. On the one hand, these writers do not extend beyond the middle of the second century; and, on the other, they exhibit little interest in anything outside the doings of certain wealthy, but quite limited, coteries in Rome itself. Social life away from the capital was for them practically non-existent.

This obsession with things Roman, however, had exceptions, and in Pliny we have delightful glimpses of life in the purer atmosphere of a provincial town in North Italy. It was, indeed, in the provinces that the genuine Roman character, courageous and patriotic, stubborn and persistent, had generally survived. There it would linger on, even after the collapse of Rome's political greatness. The sternness and gravity of provincials had impressed Tacitus, as well as the puritan strictness of their lives (*Ann.*, II, 55; XVI, 5). This forgotten aspect of Roman society has been confirmed and illustrated by the work of archaeologists, though too much value should not be attached to memorial inscriptions, for the experience of all ages teaches us that such records are the last place where sincerity and candour are to be expected. "In lapidary inscriptions", as Dr Johnson said, "a man is not upon oath." But, when all allowances for conventional phraseology have been made, the inscriptions undoubtedly suggest that the Roman people had retained much more of its ancient character and religion than had been supposed from the literary evidence alone. These supplementary discoveries are of the highest importance for the study of Western Christendom, for they are concerned primarily not with those classes of society whose point of view and manner of life are disclosed in contemporary literature, but with the masses of simple people who remain largely unknown. It was among these, and in particular among the small shopkeepers and tradesmen, that the Gospel spread most easily.

Conditions, however, were exceedingly deplorable, even when this new evidence has been taken into account; for the capital naturally set the general tone. Unfortunately those who made up society in Rome were quite unworthy of their responsibilities, seemed indeed destitute of any awareness that such existed. They had apparently no conception of patriotism and had put behind them any attempt at a disciplined and ordered life, and even common decency. The old Roman virtues had been found too great a restraint and had been gladly abandoned. In any community, of course, it is only the few who have the means for living lives of such depravity; but the taint spreads among those who have to minister to their tastes and their follies. If luxury and vice marked the aristocracy, the populace was not behind in brutality and greed. Wealth was concentrated too much in the hands of the few, so that alongside the wastefulness of the privileged classes went a corresponding scarcity among the multitude. Hermas, writing in Rome about the beginning of the second century, speaks of those who injure their bodies because they eat too much and of those whose bodies are weakened by not having enough (*Vis.*, III, ix, 3). A century later Cyprian can also write of poverty and luxury existing side by side, and tell of the growth of large estates and the consequent eviction of the small proprietors (*Ad Donat.*, XII).

The wave of luxurious living had flowed in from Asia as the results of Roman conquests,[1] and it had come upon a people little prepared to resist it. The best stock of the nation had been almost completely eliminated, partly in warfare against external enemies of the State (the old sturdy yeoman class had practically disappeared during the long struggle with Hannibal), partly in civic strife and proscriptions at home,[2] and the ideals which had sustained Rome in the past were already in decay. Many still claimed to have noble blood in their veins; but its chief manifestation was a pride which was entirely unsupported by either character or achievement. Under Vespasian, a new nobility, created out of the middle classes, began to grow up. With their coming the crude pursuit of luxury somewhat slackened, and the hundred years of internal peace under the Flavians and Antonines may not be entirely unconnected with their rise to power.

The spread of education seems to have done little to improve the moral condition of the people. Though there was no general

[1] cf. Augustine, *De Civ. Dei*, III, xxi: *Asiatica luxuria Romam omni hosti peior inrepsit.*

[2] The same thing had occurred in Athens during the long agony of the Peloponnesian War, and Isocrates noted the disappearance of the old names from the roll of citizens and the substitution of aliens "from all sorts of places" (*De Pace*, 86–89).

system, all except the very poorest received a measure of instruction. From the time of Trajan the State made some kind of provision for the teaching of the poor, an example which was soon followed by the municipalities, and by the beginning of the third century there were schoolmasters even in the villages.[1] Private enterprise and the generosity of the rich frequently found an outlet in the provision of educational facilities. Pliny the Younger, for example, helped to found a school at Como so that the youth of the city would no longer need to go to Milan (*Epist.*, IV). That there was a fair standard of literacy seems to be established by the extensive use of coins with their inscriptions for propaganda purposes.[2] But education had largely lost its ideals. In the best period of Roman life, instruction had been begun and continued in the home under the eyes of the parent, and there had been a full recognition of the importance of moral influences and an austere environment. The basis was largely legal; Cicero learnt the Twelve Tables as a boy. But the growth of Greek influences, with their emphasis upon rhetoric, had an unfortunate effect and tended to make education superficial and purely literary.[3] The pupil was only fifteen when he went to the school of Rhetoric, the great aim of which was to produce orators and men of the world. There he learned that form was more significant than matter, or even than truth: that the chief concern of the orator was to make a good impression and to serve the interests of his party or client. It must be remembered that many of the Christian writers had been educated in this atmosphere and that they never shook it off. Their statements are as much in need of careful scrutiny as those of their pagan contemporaries.

During our period, taxation was ever on the increase and the economic strain was felt by all save the few excessively wealthy. There was also a mania for the erection of stupendous buildings which may have added to the dignity of the cities or the prestige of those who erected them but involved a heavy price in terms of social happiness for those who had to pay for them by their labour or their substance. The army, too, was becoming increasingly burdensome. The settlement of the legions in stationary camps along the frontier and the qualified recognition of the marriage of soldiers made it a much less mobile force and removed it further from the life of the civilian. This, no doubt, accounts in part for the reluctance of Romans to enlist in its

[1] See, further, Rostovtzeff, *Social and Economic Hist. of the Roman Empire*, p. 375.
[2] cf. M. P. Charlesworth, *The Virtues of a Roman Emperor*, p. 13.
[3] The demand for rhetoric was so widespread that Juvenal could ironically presume that it extended even to remote Thule (*Satires*, XV, 112).

ranks. Numbers had to be kept up by the enrolment of bar-barians.

The immense sums frittered away by the great people in vulgar ostentation had often to be raised by the sacrifice of capital, and even when capital was not actually squandered properties were neglected and land allowed to go out of cultivation. The whole method of dealing with the land, however, was unhealthy, being based on a species of plantation slavery under which the small farmer was forced out of his holding by the growth of vast estates.[1]

The small farmers and peasants, after they had been dis-possessed by the large landed proprietors, found their way only too quickly to the great towns, and to Rome in particular. Here they reinforced the swarms of unemployed and parasites already gathered there. To keep them occupied and content was essential, if inconvenient and even dangerous unrest was to be avoided; and so "bread and free amusements" became the offi-cial policy. On two days at least in every week there were "games" of one kind or another; spectacles which could hardly fail to implant or foster a lust for bloodshed and a taste for indecency in those who beheld them.[2] These games seem to have been part of Rome's heritage from Etruria, and from Italy they spread over the West. There were vast arenas in Gaul, in Spain, and in North Africa.[3] The Germans, however, seem never to have appreciated them, and by the Greeks they were at first con-demned as Roman and barbarous though later they came to patronize them. Josephus tells us that Agrippa found bloody spectacles much to the taste of his Jewish subjects and himself took genuine delight in them (*Antiq.*, XIX, ix, 5).

Originally the games had had a religious character and served to mark the changing agricultural seasons, a connexion which Augustus tried in vain to restore. They had helped to promote a sense of joyous unity with the divine powers which a less primi-tive age had completely forgotten. A similar change has taken place in connexion with our own use of the term "holiday"; which may remind us that the Church when it achieved power in the Middle Ages did not disdain to adapt such spectacles to its own purposes[4] and as a means of diverting its subjects—carni-

---

[1] The system had been begun in Sicily as early as 480 B.C. Thence it spread to South Italy after the devastation of the war with Hannibal. In the third century A.D. economic causes to which it had itself contributed brought about its collapse.

[2] These were condemned by Tertullian, *De Spectaculis*, and by Cyprian, *Ad Donat.*, VII.

[3] For their popularity in North Africa see Augustine, *Conf.*, VI, vii.

[4] For the continuation of a traditional feast under a Christian guise at Gubbio see R. S. Conway, *Ancient Italy and Modern Religion*, p. 7 ff.

vals, pageants, feastings, and festivities went to make up the Catholic holiday.

One characteristic of the Empire, as distinguished from the Republic, was the growing emancipation of women. Women with the Romans had always occupied a higher place than in the East, or even among the Greeks; there were, for example, no "women's apartments", and the wife had a much greater share in the interests and ambitions of her husband. Her ideal was, like the Claudia whose monument adorns the Appian Way, to sink into the "loveless grave" having earned her epitaph:

> Comely her speech was, graceful was her going,
> She kept house, spun her wool. 'Tis all. Farewell.

As in India in all ages, the mother had an immense influence over her sons; the mother of the Gracchi is, of course, the classic instance, though she by no means stood alone. Marriage was taken exceedingly seriously and divorce was for long unknown. The first to be recorded was granted on account of the sterility of the wife in 216 B.C. But, once introduced, divorce became a habit, and before the end of the Republic it had grown to such an extent that it was rare to find a woman who had had only one husband. Marriage alliances, which incidentally involved the divorce of a previous partner, had become a recognized means of strengthening political or personal ambitions.[1] Well might Horace declare that the decay of family life was the fountain-head of all the sorrows of Rome (*Odes*, III, vi). The same freedom persisted under the Empire, and Tertullian could scornfully declare that in his day divorce was regarded as the natural sequel of marriage (*quasi matrimonii fructus: Apol.*, VI). Another very disquieting sign, the most unmistakable symptom of a dying society,[2] was a growing unwillingness to accept the responsibilities of parenthood.

Women, in addition to being pawns on the political chess-board, soon began to take a part in the game on their own account, and behind the scenes to exercise an influence which aroused the alarm of the more conservative citizens. Juvenal is really just as shocked by the emancipated woman as by the vicious. Such an influence might be exercised for good and noble ends; more often it was inspired by motives which were entirely selfish or even evil. The figure of Cleopatra here looms large,

[1] "The ordinary educated Roman of Vergil's day would have judged it monstrous to suppose that a woman's claim on a man's affection could be weighed against his political duty, and he would point to the disasters which befell great men who had defied Roman opinion on this point" (R. S. Conway, *op. cit.*, p. 113).

[2] Polybius attributed the fall of Greece, both politically and morally, to this cause (XXXVI, 17).

for it was she who was a primary cause of the murder of Julius,[1] and, as every schoolgirl knows, of the ruin of Mark Anthony.

Among the people of the Empire, slaves formed an important class, for in number they were probably equal to the rest of the population; whilst in the propagation of the Gospel they played no inconsiderable part. Among the Romans there were two distinct classes of slaves: those who worked in gangs on plantations, and those who were employed in domestic service. The plantation system was peculiar to the West and was noted for its cruelties and horrors; but every slave was at the mercy of his master and liable to be tortured. There was, however, a growing feeling among the better type of Roman that slaves ought to be treated as human beings; in this Seneca anticipated the more humane attitude of the Antonine period. But in many cases there was real affection between master and slave, as the inscriptions testify. At first, slaves had been acquired through warfare; when this source dried up, they were imported from the East. Even under the Republic, Italian merchants were regular attenders at the great slave market on Delos.

Slavery was not necessarily a permanent condition, for the slave might acquire his freedom either as a gift from his master or he might under favourable conditions amass enough to purchase it. Freedom, however, was not coveted by every slave. He was often in a better position than the free citizen.

In course of time "freedmen", as emancipated slaves were called, came to possess immense power and influence. The beginning of the process was their introduction into the mint by Julius, and it was by way of the civil service that they often rose. The fact that trade was largely in their hands was also a considerable factor. In spite of the almost universal prejudice against them, the progress of the freedmen was probably for the good of society and the State; for it gradually built up a free industrial class and brought into the administration a body of capable and on the whole trustworthy officials. It may also be surmised that they played some part in the spread of Christianity to which they would be more likely to show sympathy than the average Roman by birth, quite apart from the fact that many of them were Orientals by origin.

One feature of Roman society, though not of its higher ranks, was the existence of innumerable clubs and associations. They possess a high significance for our study, since there can be but little doubt that they affected considerably the development of

---

[1] See Conway, *op. cit.*, p. 111 f. He refers to Cicero, *Ad Att.*, XIV, viii, 1 and xx, 2, XV, xv, 2; and to Cassius Dio, XLIII, 27.

the Christian Church and its organization. They were usually formed by people drawn from the lower ranks of society to which they provided an equivalent for the *familia* of the patrician. Our knowledge of them, for this reason, comes not from literature so much as from inscriptions. Under the Republic there seems to have been little attempt to control or regulate them, but with Julius their possibilities for evil were recognized and stringent regulations put into force; a policy which was continued under the Empire, although Augustus instructed the governors of Asia that the laws relating to assemblies were not to be rigorously applied to the Jews. There certainly was a danger in such gatherings since they might beget dangerous conspiracies.[1] The majority of these associations, like the guilds of the Middle Ages, were under some kind of religious patronage; some were definitely formed in order to promote religious objects.[2] They fulfilled many of the functions of a modern friendly or burial society, particularly in providing for the decent disposing of the remains of their members after death. They also brought a sense of fellowship and an opportunity for the exercise of powers of organization for those who had no share in governing the State.[3]

[1] cf. A statute passed in Florence in 1324 forbidding the unauthorized assembly of guilds, "since frequently under pretence of lawfulness, unlawfulness is committed . . . under any title of brotherhood for any motive or pretence of religion, or funerals, or of oblations".

[2] Perhaps in this they imitated the associations formed among the votaries of the Orphic cults: see Adam, *Relig. Teachers of Greece*, p. 93.

[3] The religious societies of the Nonconformists in England provided a similar outlet so long as their political disabilities remained: see Elliott-Binns, *Religion in the Victorian Era*, p. 419.

CHAPTER II

THE RELIGIOUS BACKGROUND

When Christianity arrived in the West it found two very definite influences at work there. On the one hand, there was the ideal of the subordination of the individual to the community, which was represented by the official religion; on the other, that represented by the various Oriental cults, by which communion with God and the search for salvation were regarded as the supreme objects of human endeavour. Although there had already been some interaction between the two they still remained distinctive and even antagonistic. From both of them the new religion was to receive deep impressions; it might indeed be said that the subsequent history of the Church records the attempt to reconcile them. One other influence of a solvent nature was also at work, the various philosophical systems which were then in vogue. On each of these three something must be said.

ROMAN RELIGION

When the religion of the Romans first comes to the notice of history it is still in a comparatively simple and undeveloped form. In each household the head of the family performed the prescribed offices in honour of the traditional deities. These in return were expected to have a special care for its interests. When compared with the worship of other peoples that of the Romans seems lacking in most of the elements which arouse ardour and devotion in the suppliant. It was formal and ceremonial, too much concerned with the family and the State, and then only with their material prosperity. None the less it proved itself capable of producing a lofty patriotism and those who entered fully into its ceremonies could scarcely fail to realize the seriousness of life or to possess a highly developed sense of responsibility. Moreover it drew the operations of the household and the field under the protection of supernatural powers and thus invested with sanctity all the common activities of its members.

The religion of the State was of a similar character. Its supreme object was to obtain and preserve the favour of the gods by the exact performance of the traditional ritual. The importance of observing the correct forms was absolute; a wrong word, a misplaced gesture, or an unlucky omen, might render the whole ceremony inoperative and void. Magic, rather than religion, lay behind this meticulous care.

But if Roman religion as established in the State and functioning in the family laid emphasis on the correct performance of ritual acts, it neglected the claims of morality. This was a fundamental weakness. Not only did it fail to provide moral guidance or stimulus, but by its influence moral standards were definitely lowered and St. Paul could attribute the failure of the pagan world to its religion (Rom. 1 : 18 ff.), a theme that Augustine developed with incisive irony.

As the life of the Romans became more complex, they encountered, of necessity, matters for which the ancient ritual made no provision. Bucolic gods could be of little avail in urban surroundings to which they were not accustomed. Livy (IV, xxx) tells us that even in the period of the kings, and a generation before the invasion of the Gauls, foreign deities were already being introduced. Additions to the objects of worship were especially liable to be made in times of disaster or military defeat. Such events seemed to demonstrate the inadequacy of the native gods and the need for supplementing them. Thus after Cannae the oracle of Delphi was consulted, a portentous act which opened the door to Greek influences. When Rome had at last overcome the menace of Carthage and embarked on its long series of conquests, cultural contacts with new peoples brought with them knowledge of other deities; and all were welcomed, even those of the vanquished. Well might the pagan in the *Octavius* of Minucius Felix, after specifying certain localities which worshipped their own gods, end up by saying that the Romans venerated them all (VI, 1).

Probably the first foreign religion to affect Rome was that of the Etruscans. Tradition attributes to them the foundation of the great temple on the Capitoline dedicated to the triad, Jupiter, Juno, and Minerva, which formed the chief object of their devotion. The Etruscans certainly had a reputation for religion, or rather for superstition,[1] and above all for the practice of divination. But their religious outlook was gloomy and rigid, and deficient in those lively and plastic elements which gave to the religion of the Greeks its joyous and stimulating tone.

In Roman religion, the gods were hardly regarded as personal, they were forces with certain offices to perform. This made it easier to amalgamate them with deities from outside whose functions were similar. In their original haunts the gods and goddesses of Greece had been vastly different from their "oppo-

---

[1] cf. Livy, V, 1: *Gens ante omnes alias eo magis dedita religionibus, quod excelleret arte colendi eas.* Arnobius, in Christian times, is more outspoken: *Genetrix et mater superstitionis Etruria* (VII).

site numbers" in Italy, none the less, as the taste for things Hellenic grew in Rome, the scope of religion was broadened and attributes characteristic of the denizens of Olympus were transferred to the native divinities. In Rome itself this hybrid mythology was current some generations before the Republic came to an end; but Rome was not Italy, and outside the capital conditions were very different. The religious practices and beliefs of rural Italy would, indeed, have a profound effect on popular Christianity in future ages.[1]

As to the exact nature of such practices and beliefs we have but scanty information; nor do we know much about the religious ideas of the common people when Christ came into the world. The gap between their conceptions, and those of the educated which have been preserved in the surviving literature, must have been considerable. Some help can be obtained from the inscriptions, but even then we are greatly at a loss. Folk-lore might also be studied by Varro, but he was not the equal of Sir James Frazer in this employ. One feature, however, is prominent, a feature which may have helped to prepare the way of the Gospel—an intense interest in life after death.[2] It may be surmised that among the educated also there was some apprehension on this score and one of the functions of philosophy was to remove it. Lucretius, like the author of *The City of Dreadful Night*, might regard as "good tidings of great joy" the message that there were no gods, and that man had but one life to endure. This attitude was but temporary and to Seneca death was the birthday of eternity, the gate of a blessed immortality, or it might be the way to absorption in the deity.

Even before the Christian era the official religion was fast losing the allegiance of the thoughtful. Philosophy had done its work, and the application of ethical standards to divinities who were little capable of enduring such an ordeal had increased the general scepticism. A similar process had taken place with the Greeks, though the gods of Olympus, never having received any formal dismissal, lingered on in obscurity, like a decayed and feeble aristocracy under a new and vigorous democratic regime. The growth of this sceptical spirit did not immediately arouse concern with the authorities since the official ceremonies were still observed even by philosophers.

In the last days of the Republic, religion was thus decaying before a variety of influences. Augustus, when he had secured his political position, made a valiant effort to revive it as a means of consolidating and safeguarding the Empire. Efforts of this kind, however, not infrequently produce not the simple faith

[1] See, further, R. S. Conway, *Ancient Italy and Modern Religion*.
[2] cf. Cicero, *Tusc.*, I, xlvi.

and ancient virtues which are the aims of their promoters, but a merely formal acquiescence, if not deliberate hypocrisy. Religion cannot be evoked by a word of command. The attempt of Augustus, which Tiberius continued, seems to have met with a better fate. It may be that as men were weary of political unrest and unsettlement so were they weary of unrest and unsettlement in the deeper matters of life, and not unwilling to accept guidance from one who had bestowed upon them peace and stability in material things. If an age of transition is often an age of scepticism, the period of adjustment which normally follows not seldom provides an atmosphere in which religion may again flourish. So it was in the second century; though not a few remained obdurate; among them Galen the physician and Lucian the satirist.[1] The revival, however, was neither deep nor lasting, and long before the triumph of Christianity its initial fervour had gone. Aurelian, indeed, endeavoured to introduce a species of monotheism based on the cult of the sun-god, but its exotic flavour hardly commended it to the Romans, and when Diocletian made a futile attempt to found a pagan Church it was based on the old gods. Monotheism remained the intellectual toy of a few philosophers.

The attitude of Christians towards the gods of the pagan varied greatly; some writers condemned them as demons, others despised them as nonentities. A like difference is to be found in the Old Testament (cf. Deut. 32 : 17 and Ps. 106 : 37, for example, with Ps. 115); whilst even St. Paul's views are by no means consistent (cf. Rom. 1 : 23 and 1 Cor. 8 : 4 f. with 1 Cor. 10 : 19 ff.). Later, the opinion that the gods were demons came to prevail, and their immense number was a matter for scorn and derision. Augustine in a clever word-play says that it was due, not to verity, but to vanity (*De Civ. Dei*, IV, xxi: *non veritas sed vanitas facit*).

One very prominent feature of Roman religion was incidentally the cause of grave hardship to the Christians—the cult of the Emperor.[2] Such an attitude towards the ruler of the State had its origin in the East where the distinction between gods and men was not so nice as in the West. In Egypt the reigning Pharaoh had for long ages been worshipped as the incarnation of the country, whilst Lysander the Spartan and Alexander had each received divine honours.

Temples had been erected to Augustus in Asia Minor, where even under the Republic Smyrna had distinguished itself by

---

[1] On this aspect of the times see M. Caster, *Lucien et la pensée relig. de son temps*, 1938.

[2] See, further, M. P. Charlesworth, "Some Observations on Ruler-cults, especially in Rome", in *Harvard Theol. Rev.*, 1935, XXVIII, p. 5 ff.

dedicating a shrine to Rome. Thus the double object of the cult, Rome and the ruling emperor, found early if divided expression. Although Augustus refused the title of *Dominus*, a point made much of by Tertullian (*Apol.*, XXXIV), he did not forbid worship being offered to him. The cult was, indeed, worthy of encouragement, for it provided a link between the various parts of the Empire and stimulated loyalty to the central government.[1] It naturally flourished most freely in the provinces where an elaborate machinery was created to foster and maintain it. Part of the propaganda consisted in the holding of annual festivals which included public games and spectacles. In the army, the cult of the emperor was encouraged by every possible device. A significant piece of evidence of its success can be found when in a dispute between a civilian and some soldiers, recorded by Apuleius (*Metamorph.*, IX, 42), the former swears by his gods, but the soldiers by the emperor.

Rome and Italy at first were content to regard the emperor as divine only after his death.[2] The soul of the dead ruler was thought to ascend from the funeral pyre into the heavens, as witnesses were produced to testify.[3] Some held that it was accompanied in its flight by Phoebus Apollo in his white-horsed chariot.[4] It was not long, however, before the living ruler, in whom the majesty of Rome was incarnate, came to be recognized as divine. On the Arch of Trajan at Beneventum the emperor, like an Egyptian or Assyrian monarch, is carved in superhuman size.[5]

To create a single cult designed to unite the Empire was a praiseworthy object, especially as it was tolerant of local worships. This aspect of emperor-worship, since it tended to co-ordinate the various faiths and accustomed the different peoples to the idea of a religion which was universal in its scope, may have prepared in some measure for the reception of Christianity. But the cult of the emperor proved incapable of this achievement and later emperors gradually came to recognize that at least in its crude form it could gain but few adherents. It may also be pointed out that from the time of Aurelian a different

[1] An instance is the well-known temple at Colchester: see Tacitus, *Ann.*, XIV, 21: *ad hoc templum divo Claudio constitutum quasi arx aeternae dominationis aspiciebatur.*

[2] Nero was much alarmed by a proposal to erect a temple to him; it seemed an omen of his death (Tacitus, *Ann.*, XV, 74).

[3] Justin I, *Apol.*, XXI. The release of an eagle from the pyre was part of the ceremonial (Cassius Dio, LVI, 42; LXXIV, 4).

[4] *Griechische Papyri zu Giessen*, I, 3.

[5] Pliny records that apostate Christians in Bithynia offered prayer and wine before Trajan's statue (*Epist.*, XCVI). The cult of the living emperor seems to have arisen through pressure from the provinces: see H. I. Bell, *Jews and Christians in Egypt*, p. 7 f.

conception of the ruler to the deity began to prevail, possibly owing to Persian influences, more and more he came to be regarded as one to whom the deity had entrusted the power of government, rather than as a god himself.

From the first, educated opinion had been critical and even scornful of the whole business, except as a political device.[1] As late as the middle of the second century Pausanias is roused to indignation by the practice. Looking back to the great ages "when the benefactors of mankind were raised to the rank of divinities", he contrasts his own age with its widespread wickedness, and regrets that "men are changed into gods no more save in the hollow rhetoric which flattery addresses to power".[2] The vulgar, no doubt, appreciated the apotheosis of its rulers, and would have been roused to fury by any attempt to deprive them of the living presence of the god.[3]

Roman religion, even at its best, was not fully capable of providing for the needs of humanity; this was especially true of women. Women, indeed, were not entirely disregarded; the institution of the Vestal Virgins was a recognition of their importance and they had a share in the family cult; but the decay of home life and the spread of Oriental religions robbed domestic worship of its unique position, and the natural demand of women for some outlet for their spiritual cravings found no adequate response in the traditional faith. It is not surprising therefore that they sought it in foreign cults; some even became proselytes of Judaism, though Judaism gave no high place to women. But it was not women alone who found the traditional religion inadequate. Those whose souls had been stimulated by the possibility of personal communion with the divine could not be content to remain passive, and leave religion to officials. Moreover the State religion was interested only in material things and had no message for those whose needs were primarily spiritual. That such formed a large proportion of the population at this epoch is not likely; when, indeed, did they? But there were many such, and they included some great names. In spite of the consolations of philosophy, Marcus Aurelius and Epictetus were desirous of a deeper knowledge of things divine. Others who had no such aid or diversion stretched out longing arms into the darkness hoping to find God. Personal salvation

[1] See two articles by K. Scott in the *Transactions of the American Phil. Soc.*: "Plutarch and the Ruler Cult" (LX, p. 117 ff.) and "The Elder and the Younger Pliny on Emperor Worship" (LXIII, p. 156 ff.).

[2] J. G. Frazer, *Pausanias and other Greek Sketches*, p. 70.

[3] When the Caliph Mansour, the founder of Baghdad, refused to allow the Persian Ramandis to worship him, a riot followed in which he nearly lost his life.

and the hope of attaining immortality were objects very near to many hearts in the first centuries of the Empire, as the multitude who turned to the mysteries and the various Oriental religions clearly manifests.

In such circumstances superstition and quackery were bound to flourish. Under the Republic, the sober Roman mind had not been greatly troubled by the rise of prophets who claimed divine inspiration, nor by the Etruscan soothsayers, the precursors of a crowd of similar adepts from the East. When once this Oriental flood had set in, the belief in astrology became widespread, and with it the acceptance of dreams as a means of revelation and guidance.[1] Magic, in all its multitudinous forms, sprang up everywhere, even in centres of culture; it was not only in Ephesus that there would have been occult books to burn (Acts 19 : 18 f.). Some, indeed, looked upon magic as stronger than the gods and capable of compelling them to do the will of its votaries; if Isis, for example, failed to carry out what was demanded of her she could be threatened with a fresh dispersal of the bones of Osiris.[2] That such arts had their perils was recognized, and the story of Lucius, who was turned into an ass by dabbling in them, was perhaps meant as a warning.[3]

From time to time the authorities would order the expulsion of those who dealt in magic arts. One of the latest attempts was an edict of Aurelian which forbade divination, together with drunkenness and gambling, in the army. Such intervention was not, of course, prompted solely by moral or even social ideals; a still stronger motive was the danger arising from the use of such means by conspirators against the emperor. But as some of the emperors themselves made frequent use of divination,[4] it is not surprising that attempts to suppress it proved abortive.

ORIENTAL RELIGIONS

The spread of Oriental cults in the West was part of that ceaseless ebb and flow between Hellenism and the civilizations of the East which had persisted for centuries; for cultural as well as political influences swing to and fro like a pendulum. With Alexander, as we have seen, the culture of Hellas had invaded the Orient; but only to arouse a counter movement

---

[1] Socrates, it will be recalled, believed in the guidance of dreams and similar phenomena: see Xenophon, *Memorab.*, IV, ii, 12; Plato, *Apol.*, XXX c; *Crito*, XLIV A; *Phaedo*, LX E.

[2] Porphyry, quoted by Augustine, *De Civ. Dei*, X, xi.

[3] Apuleius, *Metamorph.*, XI.

[4] Astrology and magic were favourite subjects of study with Septimius Severus, whilst Severus Alexander actually endowed schools for their encouragement.

which reached the very heart of the West. On its tide were borne a variety of faiths, some going back to history's dawn; others, Christianity among them, of more recent birth.

But if Christianity is to be included among these other religions its fate was to be far different from that of its rivals. Already it had something distinctive about it and in after time it would survive when they had decayed and disappeared. Before that day came, however, they would play a not inconsiderable part in its fortunes.

This factor in both the spread and development of Christianity is not always given sufficient recognition, for it was not the Jews only by their dispersion in the West who provided a soil in which the living seed of the Gospel could take root. New religions or sects habitually find their adherents among those who are already in some sense religious. Furthermore these cults had had a solvent effect on Roman religious mentality. In the old austere and rigid atmosphere of the traditional belief Christianity would have found it very difficult to flourish; but the conception of religion as something affecting the individual, which they brought in, had begun to make way among the Romans. That is one side of the picture. The other was the effect which they would have upon Christianity itself, modifying and supplementing its original teaching and practice. To this important subject we shall return in a later part of the present study.

The first foreign deity to arrive in Rome from the East was Aesculapius of Epidaurus. His worship was introduced in 293 B.C., after a consultation of the Sibylline Books, to cope with an outbreak of pestilence before which the accepted gods had proved powerless. This was not surprising, as Augustine pointed out, for Jupiter himself had spent so much of his time in rapes and adulteries that he had not been able to acquire the art of healing (*De Civ. Dei*, III, xviii). A temple to the new deity was erected on an island in the Tiber to which a sanatorium was attached, for with him had come a number of Greek physicians. At first neither he nor they received much of a welcome from the Romans.

The first genuinely Oriental deity to reach Rome, for Aesculapius had come from neighbouring Greece, was the Great Mother (Cybele). Her coming was a result of the panic which followed the disasters of the Second Punic War in 205 B.C. With the consent of Attalus, King of Pergamum, the stone which was the outward and visible sign of her presence was brought to Italy.[1]

---

[1] The cult of the Great Mother was already of profound antiquity. In various guises it underlay most, if not all, of the primitive religions of the lands bordering on the Mediterranean, as well as elsewhere. It is possible that

The cult of Cybele was well calculated to appeal to a people which was still agrarian, and in course of time it became almost completely naturalized. It was destined, often in combination with that of other divinities, to prevail until the end of paganism in the West, and who shall dare to affirm that even the collapse of paganism involved her in its ruins, for another *Mater Dolorosa* continued to claim a like devotion. The fact that as early as Minoan times she is represented as the divine Mother holding up her infant son for adoration was of great significance for the development of Christian doctrine and Christian art.[1]

Another cult which achieved much popularity was that of Isis and Osiris, or Serapis, to give him the name adopted when Ptolemy I tried to make his worship a rallying point for Greeks and Egyptians.[2] This cult probably came to the West with Egyptian traders and slaves, and though some of its features were at first regarded as revolting, by the end of the second century it was firmly established. Thenceforward, it spread with amazing rapidity, especially among women. The worship of Isis in the West, however, was very different from the same cult in Egypt, for in order to meet the prejudices of the Romans it was largely transformed. The process had indeed already begun in the land of its origin through Greek influences in Ptolemaic times;[3] one example, among many, of the working of the syncretistic process. What was left after all the modifications certainly proved abundantly attractive. "The daily ritual of Isis", Dill has said, "produced an immense effect on the Roman mind. Every day there were two solemn offices, at which white-robed, tonsured priests, with acolytes and assistants of every degree, officiated. The morning litany and sacrifice were an impressive service. The crowd of worshippers thronged the space before the chapel at the early dawn. The priest, ascending by a hidden stair, drew apart the veil of the sanctuary, and offered the holy image to their adoration. He then made the round of the altars, reciting the litany, and sprinkling the holy water 'from the secret spring'. At two o'clock in the afternoon the passers-by could hear from the temple in the Campus Martius the chant of

even in Italy she had already her worshippers, for traces of it have been found among the Etruscans. The sculptured head on the Porte all' Arco at Volterra is thought to represent her.

[1] Isis and Horus also provided models for the Virgin and Child: see E. A. W. Budge, *Legends of Our Lady Mary*, p. xli. One interesting tradition, preserved in the Syriac work, *The Cave of Treasures*, and also in the Ethiopic *Conflict of Adam and Eve*, which may be dependent upon it, states that the Virgin and Child appeared in the star of the Magi.

[2] The origin of Serapis is disputed: see Dill, *Roman Society from Nero, etc.*, p. 561 ff. The most daring suggestion is that of Tertullian who identified him with the patriarch Joseph (*Adv. Nat.*, II).

[3] See, further, Scott-Moncrieff, *Paganism and Christianity in Egypt*, chaps. I and II.

vespers. . . . There was much solemn pomp and striking scenic effect in this public ceremonial. But it is clear from Apuleius that an important part of the worship was also long silent meditation before the image of the goddess" (*op. cit.*, p. 577 f.). Thus every type of mind found something which made an appeal; those who loved spectacles, and those whose tastes were of a contemplative nature.

Other deities from Egypt besides Isis and Osiris made their way to the West. Images of the god Resheph, for example, have been found, one at Tortosa (now in the Louvre) and another somewhere in Italy, probably from Pompeii (now at Munich).

To the medley of cults Syria made her contribution, and various Baals, by the simple expedient of changing their names, became naturalized in the West. Hadad of Baalbek, under the title of Jupiter Heliopolitanus, reached Rome by way of Delos, and even penetrated to Gaul and Britain. Even better known was Jupiter Dolichenus, the Baal of Doliche, an ancient site, originally Hittite, near Carchemish.[1] In a monument at Rome he is depicted wearing the Hittite pointed cap and carrying the double axe and thunderbolt.[2]

These Syrian cults brought with them all manner of deplorable customs such as temple prostitution and human sacrifice (until Hadrian prohibited it). They reached their highest point of influence under the patronage of the Syrian emperors of the third century. Aurelian, after defeating Zenobia, raised the sun-god under the title of *Sol Invictus* to the supreme place in the Roman pantheon, erecting a temple in which the images of Bel and Helios, brought from Palmyra, were housed. In introducing his new worship, the emperor was careful to clothe it as far as possible in Roman forms. He hoped that all other cults would find a place in it.

Even from distant India, influences of a religious nature made their way. In early days communication had been rare and more Westerners went to India than Indians to the West.[3] But in 20 B.C. an embassy waited upon Augustus, to whom it was said a temple had been erected in Mysore, bringing with it the first tiger to be seen in Europe. After the Red Sea had been made available for traffic under Tiberius and Nero there was much freer intercourse. So great, indeed, was the volume of imports from India that Aelius Aristides could claim that Indians themselves had to resort to Rome if they wished to buy their own

---

[1] Now Tell Duluk. The site still retains its sacred character, being used as a Moslem shrine.

[2] See A. B. Cook, *Zeus*, I, p. 551 f.

[3] See Strabo, XV, i, 4. Virgil calls India *extremi sinus orbis* (*Georg.*, II, 123).

products.[1] But India also sent products of a different nature than the mushroom spawn so highly valued by Trimalchio.[2] Evidence of religious influence can be found in the statuette of Laksmi, the goddess of love and fecundity, discovered at Pompeii as recently as October 1938.[3] By the end of the second century A.D. Indian religious teachers were sufficiently familiar to the West that Tertullian can remind his pagan readers that Christians were neither Brahmins nor fakirs (Apol., XLII).

The extent to which Oriental religions penetrated the West can be gauged by the distribution of inscriptions. These are by no means confined to Rome and Italy, nor to great cities and towns. In North Africa the worship of Serapis is found not only among the romanized and sophisticated people of Carthage,[4] but also in country districts.[5] The cult of the Great Mother was equally widespread. In Spain there is found the worship of Jupiter Kasius, who came from the neighbourhood of Antioch; whilst in Gaul numerous Oriental deities had their votaries and the Temple Tariff of Marseilles is known to all scholars.[6] So, too, in Britain, where among others Jupiter Dolichenus was worshipped on the Roman Wall.

A careful study of the inscriptions, however, whilst it testifies to the wide area over which Oriental cults extended, also suggests that their influence may have been exaggerated, and that it was chiefly among resident aliens that they had their vogue. Certainly it is most notable in centres where such communities are known to have existed. The cults may also have flourished in a minor degree among Romans who had seen service in the East as soldiers or administrators.

The spread of Oriental cults in the West was part of a general religious awakening in the centuries immediately following the birth of Christ. It affected all classes and every clime, and arose no doubt as a kind of reaction against the scepticism and self-sufficiency which had prevailed for so long. As the various cults advanced side by side, quite inevitably they exerted influence upon each other. Syncretism and eclecticism was in the very air which men breathed, and even in the more sober world of philosophy it was at work. The exponents of one worship would not be slow to borrow features which had proved attractive in its rivals; whilst individual thinkers, despairing of truth in any single system, would combine features from each, or even hold

---

[1] See, further, H. G. Rawlinson, *Intercourse between India and the Western World to the Fall of Rome.*
[2] Petronius, *Satiricon*, XXXVIII.
[3] See *J.H.S.*, LIX, Pt. 2, p. 227.
[4] *C.I.L.*, VIII, Nos. 1002–1007, 12491–93.
[5] *op. cit.*, Nos. 14792 and 21487.
[6] See G. A. Cooke, *North Semitic Inscriptions*, No. 42.

different faiths in conjunction. All this seemed to men very natural, and very sensible, too, for as the Stoics pointed out, the sun and moon were just the same by whatever name they might be known; and so also were the gods. Religion was reaching out towards the universal.

It need not, however, always be taken for granted that similar features in contemporary religions are the result of borrowing or imitation. The possibility must not be rejected that in many of these cases, especially where the cultural conditions are alike, the same needs have fabricated the same methods of dealing with them. There must always be an allowance for the psychological factor. So again the fundamental weakness of all eclectic schools, whether in art or thought, must not be ignored; that tendency to attempt the combination of incompatibilities and to reduce their systems to a mere patchwork of ideas and customs which are not really consistent with each other. Sometimes, indeed, the new patch may destroy the whole character of the old garment. Often enough those features which are chosen for imitation are among the less admirable in the system to which they belong. In the end the eclectic cults resembled the argosies of King Solomon which had among their cargo apes and peacocks as well as gold, silver, and ivory.

One very important means by which Oriental religious ideas permeated the West were the mystery religions where they first became popular after the conquests of Alexander. The most famous were the Eleusinian which were probably based on very ancient cults. Little, however, is known about them for, in spite of the large numbers of initiates, their secret was well kept, and such accounts as are available seem to have been coloured by knowledge derived from other systems. The attachment of the rites to a particular locality may have been an innovation, for in the much older Orphic system there was no such limitation. This system, however, demanded from its adherents a more severe separation from their neighbours than other mysteries and encouraged them to form their own societies.[1]

From whatever various sources the mysteries derived and to whatever different deities they were dedicated they had much in common, both as to their aim and the means of achieving it. The final consummation of the rites was union with the divine or semi-divine being who gave to them his patronage. Beneath these rites there usually lay some kind of drama representing events in the life of the patron; but the most primitive form of mystery almost certainly had to do with the decay and revival of nature of which the god or hero was a mere symbol. This remained the central core, and round it each race grouped further

[1] See, further, Guthrie, *Orpheus and Greek Religion*.

59

details according to its own special taste and requirements. The mysteries thus had a universal element. At the same time many of them, although not in their origin the official cults of cities or states, had a strongly nationalist element, for initiation made the votary a naturalized citizen of the nation to which the cult belonged. Thus those who had been initiated into the Eleusinian mysteries could claim to be Hellenes; those initiated into the mysteries of Mithras, at least if they had attained to the rank of *Persa*, became Persians.

In theory the rites were open to all ranks of society; but the cost must have been a restriction. Lucius in Apuleius's *Metamorphoses* found the fees very heavy, and the expense of the *taurobolium* cannot have been light. However there were many grades, and it may be that admission to the lower and inferior was not too expensive. The rites were secret and guarded with great care; according to Plutarch, Alcibiades was "excommunicated" for revealing those of Ceres.[1] This element of secrecy was regarded unfavourably by philosophers. Demonax, the famous Athenian Cynic, in defending himself for not seeking initiation into the Eleusinian mysteries, said that if they were a help to men they should be proclaimed openly; a criticism which had already been put forward by Philo. Other features were also regarded unfavourably by philosophers, such as the state of ecstasy, or even frenzy, produced in the participants. On the other hand they seem to have met with modified approval from quite respectable Romans, including even Cicero. There can be but little doubt that initiation into the higher grades demanded in the devotee a high measure of self-discipline and self-control.

In what, it may be asked, lay the appeal of the mysteries and how are we to account for their popularity? One sufficient explanation is the fact that they were mysteries and conducted secret rites, for man's natural curiosity is attracted by what he is not allowed to know readily. Tertullian, rather scornfully, says that some sought admission in order to be able to wear the special dress of the initiate (*De Pallio*, IV). But the mysteries met a much deeper need than mere curiosity, for there was in the centuries in which they mainly flourished a demand, almost universal in range, for "salvation".[2] This salvation might take different forms, from the mere desire to be saved from material disasters in this life to protection from evils in the world to come. In the best teachers, however, it rose to worthy heights; Epicurus, for example, in teaching which received the approval of Seneca (*Epist.*, III, 7), declared that there could be no real salva-

---

[1] Justin infers that those of Mithras were public property (I *Apol.*, LXVI).
[2] *Niemand konnte mehr ein Gott sein, der nicht ein Heiland war*: Harnack, *Marcion*, p. 17.

tion without a previous recognition of a state of sin. Sometimes salvation was associated with a person and the title of Saviour was given to many of the gods, though not in the more philosophic systems of Posidonius and the Hermetic writings. This use of "saviour" may account for its neglect, as a term for the Lord, in orthodox Christian circles, though no such objection seems to have been felt by the Gnostics.[1]

At one time the suggestion that primitive Christianity had been deeply affected by the mysteries received some favour. There were, indeed, those who held that the simple Gospel had been corrupted into a mystery religion. It is quite true that St. Paul makes use of technical terms employed in the mystery cults, but such language had by his time come into general use. As a Jew, St. Paul could have had no dealings with the mysteries; for no Jew could be initiated and retain his privileges as a Jew. At the same time the possibility must not be ignored that his language might later be given a special significance by converts from paganism. Thus ideas which were really incompatible with Christianity might find an entry. Data for a complete judgment on these matters are lacking; but no evidence has yet been produced of any important influence being exercised by the mystery cults upon the development of the Christian faith.

On the other hand, the mysteries undoubtedly helped to prepare for the Gospel, for they stimulated men's need for spiritual satisfaction and aroused his sense of sin and failure. Like Christianity, each cult offered immortality and eternal blessedness to its initiates. It was, however, not uncommon for men to become votaries of a number of cults—just to make assurance doubly sure; and one who had been initiated might feel drawn to examine the claims and merits of the Christian "mystery".

From the apologists the various mystery religions receive little attention. Quite evidently they did not regard them as a menace to the faith, or as dangerous rivals. In the East, however, Clement of Alexandria condemned them as childish and ineffective, though he seems to have used their terminology to describe the Christian scheme of salvation (*Exhort. to the Greeks*, XII).

One Oriental religion which developed on the lines of a mystery cult has already been mentioned, but in view of its special importance more needs to be said about it.[2] Mithras was a very ancient deity; as Mitra he had been worshipped in the Amarna age (*c.* 1400 B.C.), later his cult spread among the Persians. He does not, however, appear to have been known in

---

[1] See Iren., I, i, 3. The use of the title Soter by members of the royal houses of Egypt and Syria would also be an objection.

[2] Renan regarded it as a serious rival of Christianity for the allegiance of the West: *Marc Aurèle*, p. 579. This view is criticized by A. D. Nock in *J.R.S.*, XXVII, p. 113.

the West long before the Christian era;[1] but once there he quickly won adherents, especially among soldiers and merchants, though the refusal to admit women[2] must have been an obstacle to the wider progress of Mithraism. It also benefited from imperial patronage; Antoninus Pius built a temple at Ostia and Commodus received initiation. But after the rise of Constantine to power its influence began to wane and in 378 it was prohibited. In spite of this it continued to survive for a time and there is a record of the erection of a mithreum as late as 391.[3]

Evidence for the wide diffusion of Mithraism is provided by archaeology. In every part of the West its shrines have been discovered, though not with equal density. They are comparatively rare in Western Gaul, Spain, and North Africa. In Rome the famous mithreum under the Church of San Clemente has long been an object of interest, and during the past few years there have been several further discoveries in the city, including an altar, amidst Christian remains, in the Corso Vittorio Emanuele. The most interesting discovery, however, was made in the gardens of the Barberini Palace where in August 1936 a complete mithreum, dating probably from the middle of the second century, was brought to light.[4] It contains several unusual features. Perhaps the most striking is the representation of the Sacrifice of the Bull in the form of a painting, instead of the usual carving. So far as I am aware the only other instance of this in the West is in the mithreum at S. Maria Capua Vetere.[5] Fortunately the colours can still be easily distinguished. Mithras himself is clad in a red mantle, spangled with stars, and has blue-green hose. There are ten small paintings around the central scene, five on each side, representing events in his life.

Remains have been found in many other places, including Aquileia,[6] Gaul,[7] and North Africa;[8] whilst even the tiny island of Capua had its shrine hidden away in a lovely ravine. In Britain there are no certain traces before the age of the Antonines, though a mithreum at Colchester may belong to the first

---

[1] Plutarch in his life of Pompey states that the Cilician pirates overcome by him were Mithras worshippers. Most scholars would place the entry into the West at a later date.

[2] See Porphyry, *De Abstin.*, IV, 16, for a possible membership of women; also *J.R.S.*, XIV, p. 31.

[3] *C.I.L.*, VI, No. 736.

[4] See *J.R.S.*, XXIX, Pt. I., p. 50 f.

[5] At Doura the central carving is surrounded by a number of small paintings: see Rostovtzeff, *Dura-Europus and its Art*, pp. 92, 96 f. A mithreum recently discovered at Ostia tells of the substitution of a stone statue for a painted canvas of the god.

[6] *C.I.L.*, V, Nos. 807, 809.

[7] *C.I.L.*, XII, Nos. 1535, 2706.

[8] *C.I.L.*, VIII, Nos. 2675, 6975, 8440, 9256, 18025, 18235. See, further, Gsell, *Musée de Philippeville*, p. 44 ff.

century.[1] A very interesting shrine was excavated in June 1926 at Dieburg, between Darmstadt and Aschaffenburg, in Roman-occupied Germany. It has a series of small sculptures very similar to the painted panels of the Barberini mithreum.[2]

Thus there is abundant evidence for the spread of the cult of Mithras in the West. But one people, it may be worth remarking, consistently resisted his attractions—the Greeks.[3] There was, quite evidently, something displeasing about Mithraism to the Hellenic mind and the god himself was despised as barbarous and rude. This comes out in the scene in Lucian's *Zeus Elenchomenos* where Momus is made to complain of the presence of Mithras in heaven; he "can't talk Greek, nor even understand when one drinks to him".[4]

In an age when some form of monotheism was proving attractive as a refuge from a bewildering swarm of deities, the doctrines of Mithraism had much to commend them. Another attraction lay in the high ideals which were put forth; the cult has, indeed, been described as "the purest and most elevated of all non-Biblical religions".[5] It had a number of features in common with Christianity; for Mithras, too, claimed to be a saviour and a mediator. Even in institutions there were startling likenesses. These included baptism, and a common meal in which wafers, stamped with a cross, were used.[6] Mithras was also supposed to have been born in a cave, another feature which worried the Christian fathers; for was there not a similar tradition, non-Biblical it is true, about the Lord Himself?[7] We need not suppose that these resemblances, in which other cults also shared, were the result of deliberate borrowing on either side. It is, however, possible that the figure of Mithras affected certain circles of later Judaism, for in the Merkabah mysticism, so called from the chariot in Ezek. 1, the name of Metraton, perhaps the equivalent of Mithras, is given to the charioteer.[8]

Even the *taurobolium* might seem to be a crude parody of the sacrifice on Calvary, for its cleansing blood brought forgiveness of sins and the promise of eternal life.[9] The influence of this rite can scarcely have been elevating, and even the promise

[1] See *J.R.S.*, XVIII, p. 202.
[2] See F. Behn, *Das Mithrasheiligtum zu Dieburg.*
[3] See Cumont, *Mysteries of Mithra* (E.T.), p. 33.
[4] Quoted by T. R. Glover, *The Conflict of Religions, etc.*, p. 210 f.
[5] Bigg, *Neoplatonism*, p. 56.
[6] A supposed Mithraic liturgy has survived, the only instance of such in connexion with a mystery cult: see Dietrich, *Eine Mithrasliturgie.*
[7] *Protevangelium*, XIX, 2; Justin, *Dial.*, LXX; LXXVIII.
[8] So Kohler believes (*Jew. Enc.*, VIII, p. 499b). The numerical value of the letters of Metraton is the same as that of Shaddai: see, further, Abelson, *Jewish Mysticism*, p. 67 ff.
[9] *C.I.L.*, VI, No. 510: *in aeternum renatus.*

of eternal life was not taken literally, since the rite might be repeated,[1] and twenty years was given as the term of its efficacy.[2]

Mithras was the god of light or of the dawn, but by a natural extension he came to be recognized as the sun-god as well. An inscription from Germany belonging to the mid-second century contains the phrase SOLI INVICTO MITHRAE. Mithras was not a "jealous" god, and permitted other deities to be worshipped "in his presence". In the mithreum at Saarburg, destroyed in 393, there were altars to the Celtic gods, Sucellus and Nantos-velta.[3]

Before going on to consider the question of Philosophy, a little may be said of a movement which formed a kind of bridge between it and the mystery religions, that connected with the Hermetic writings already mentioned. The movement had its origin in Egypt, probably in the second century B.C., from whence it spread to the West to become popular in the early Christian centuries. The writings were said to be the work of Hermes Trismegistos who has been identified with Thoth, the Egyptian messenger of the gods.[4] Augustine tells us that the supposed author claimed to be the grandson of the god Hermes.[5] Most of the writings, the best known of which is *Poimandres*, seem to have taken shape in the Christian era; some seem to have been composed in Latin. They are distinguished by a high moral tone, possibly derived from Jewish sources for the writings are eclectic, which at times approaches asceticism. In metaphysics they emphasize the divine sufficiency and declare that God has no need of material sacrifices which He values less than thanksgiving and praise. As in most programmes of this period redemption and immortality are promised. Amongst the various strands which go to make up the texture of the *corpus* traces of Gnosticism can be discerned, a feature which one would expect to find in eclectic documents of Egyptian origin.[6]

PHILOSOPHY

By the beginning of the Christian era philosophy had become critical rather than constructive, and its votaries gave their energies to endless discussions which, after long perambulations,

[1] *C.I.L.*, VI, Nos. 502, 504, 512: all late fourth century.
[2] *C.I.L.*, VI, No. 512: *Iterato viginti annis expletis.*
[3] See Hauck, *Kirchengesch. Deutschlands*, I, p. 15.
[4] There was a tendency to identify both Hermes and Thoth with the Logos: see P. Wendland, *Christentum und Hellenismus*, p. 7.
[5] *De Civ. Dei*, VIII, xxviii. Abailard accepted the identification (*P.L.*, CLXXVIII, col. 1009d).
[6] For texts with translations see W. Scott, *Hermetica*; and for a general treatment C. H. Dodd, *The Bible and the Greeks*, p. 99 ff.

attained no useful goal.[1] There was considerable interest in philosophical questions, though probably no great willingness to adopt the dogmas of any particular school. Philosophy had, indeed, become infected with the prevailing spirit of syncretism; it has even been suggested that, just as there was a *koine* Greek language, so was there also a *koine* Greek philosophy. In spite of the brilliance of the age men were sick at heart and turned to philosophy, not so much for a solution of the mysteries of life (that they felt was beyond them), but for guidance in the art of living. Evidence of this conception of philosophy can perhaps be seen in the temples dedicated under the Empire to abstract ideas such as Concord, Fortune, and Peace. Thus the philosopher was called upon to be a "physician of the soul".[2] The various tendencies of contemporary philosophy were conjoined in the case of Posidonius who flourished in the middle of the second century. So widespread was his influence that to it must largely be attributed that combination of Oriental religion and Greek philosophy in which the mysteries so readily thrived, and Christianity itself would not be ashamed to breathe. His own ambition aimed at a still more comprehensive target, for he desired nothing less than to unite these two elements with the Roman tradition so as to form a new universal creed.[3]

What Posidonius hoped to gain from Roman tradition it is difficult to say, for the Romans were not really interested in any kind of speculation; in Rome, as Mommsen has said, "nobody speculated except the money-changers". Philosophy was regarded as something exotic and not worthy of the attention of a Roman. Was not Agricola criticized for showing too great an interest in it? (Tacitus, *Agric.*, IV). It had no native roots and, if it was thought unworthy of the higher ranks of society, it could make no appeal to the lower and less educated who were content with the current polytheistic faiths, which might be intellectually despicable, but brought some religious consolation. Moreover a knowledge of Greek was almost essential for any comprehensive study as Greek philosophical works were seldom translated.

The principal philosophies which flourished under the Empire were Stoicism and Neoplatonism. There had been an earlier revival of Pythagoreanism, but it died out before the beginning of the third century,[4] being in part absorbed by Neoplatonism. Before going on to discuss these two philosophies and their effect

---

[1] cf. Clem., *Recog.*, I, 3. John of Salisbury noticed exactly the same thing about philosophical discussions in the twelfth century: see *Metalogicus*, II, 10.
[2] This aspect has been well brought out by Dill, *Roman Society from Nero, etc.*, p. 289 ff.
[3] See Edwyn Bevan, *Stoics and Sceptics*, chap. III.
[4] Seneca already thought of it as moribund (*Nat. Qns.*, VII, 32).

upon the growth of Christianity, something must be said of a movement which also contributed to making plain the way for the Gospel, especially among the vulgar to whom it introduced not a few novel ideas. Its votaries, known as Cynics, were characterized by a determination to reduce the necessities of life to a bare minimum. They also became notorious for their repudiation of all national or civic ties. In their methods the Cynics seem to have anticipated the friars of the Middle Ages, for they preached at the street corners and in the market-place, anywhere in fact where people assembled. They further resembled the friars in their swift fall from early purity and idealism; for like them they soon drew in quite undesirable elements. In consequence they did not escape the ridicule of Lucian and the sober condemnation of Justin Martyr;[1] whilst Dio Chrysostom speaks of them as deceiving slaves and sailors and such like in public places (*Oratio* XXXII, 10); a criticism which has a very modern ring about it. More serious were the measures taken against them by the authorities for their attacks on the emperors, for which some of them were put to death and others banished. By a recent writer they have been dismissed as "a class of itinerant moralists, who preached anarchy, inveighed against all rulers, and gloried in utter unconventionality and indecency" (*Camb. Anct. Hist.*, XI, p. 9). By the more educated some of these attributes might no doubt have been extended to cover the Christian preachers as well.

The banishment of the Cynics was not the first measure of this kind which had been taken against members of a philosophical school. As early as 173 B.C. the Epicureans were bidden to leave Italy. A certain care would henceforth be needed by all who taught publicly. But even this did not always answer, for the banishment of the Cynics, who may well have deserved it, involved the Stoics in the same fate in spite of their superior respectability. However they soon returned, and Rome quickly became the headquarters of the school. Stoicism was of Oriental origin and its founder, Zeno, had been a merchant before turning his thoughts to more intellectual pursuits; whilst Cleanthes, who succeeded him as the leader of the movement, had actually begun his career as a pugilist. The non-professional character of its first exponents may account for the interest which Stoicism exhibited towards life in general, an interest which was often absent from other schools. By the first century of the Christian era it had been so far transformed as to rank as a religion rather than a philosophy, even if the official dogmatic scheme allowed no place for a personal deity. The lack of any satisfying object for devotion, together with the severe restraints placed upon

---

[1] II *Apol.*, III. Justin's pupil Tatian seems to have been influenced by them.

the emotions, deprived Stoicism of that joyous affirmation characteristic of less sober faiths, and weakened its appeal to common men. Even its benevolence had about it something hard and unattractive, and the constant striving after invulnerability required in those who accepted its guidance, if successful, rendered them spiritually aloof and apt to be scornful of weaker mortals. Stoicism, moreover, demanded an intellectual equipment to be found only among the educated. It was, in short, better adapted to meet the needs of the aristocrat than the artisan and the slave; and this in spite of its doctrine of the equality of all men in the universal commonwealth of humanity. But if Stoicism had little to offer the populace it proved capable of drawing to itself the better type of Roman, who found in its tenets much, indeed, which he had known since childhood. And the better type of Roman was certainly drawn to Stoicism, even if its direct influence upon the lawyers who did so much to ameliorate social conditions in the second and third centuries has been exaggerated.[1] Already in the first century it had stepped, with Seneca, upon the political stage and begun to mould policy and influence the development of the Empire. A century later it would take its place upon the throne of the Caesars itself. After Marcus Aurelius, decay began, if indeed Stoicism had not already passed its prime when he became a disciple. Less rigid schools were proving more attractive and much of its teaching had been incorporated within them.

As a preparation for the Gospel, however, Stoicism must not be underrated. Before the birth of Christianity it was already at work in many quarters which would affect the coming faith; traces can be found, for example, in the *Wisdom of Solomon*, and in the *Sibylline Oracles*. The ethical terminology which it hammered out would also be of service to Christian teachers. Like the Jewish law, it set before men standards of conduct which would prove to be beyond their attaining and gave them a truer estimate of the limitations of the power of the human will and the consequent need of divine grace.

It is frequently said by witty persons that Christian Science is so called because it is neither Christian nor scientific. It might equally well be claimed that Neoplatonism was so called because it was neither new nor Platonic. Its teaching and methods were certainly very different from those of the great founder of the Academy; none the less they stood in the line of development, for Platonism had abandoned its over-critical attitude before the

[1] A. J. Carlyle, whilst recognizing that many of the ideas of the Roman lawyers were similar to those which inspired the Stoics, can find no sufficient evidence of their actually being adherents. Ulpian, indeed, seems to have depreciated philosophy (*Digest*, I, i, 1). See, further, *Hist. of Medieval Political Theory in the West*, I, p. 34.

rise of the Empire and was reaching out in various new directions. But Platonists were few in number, at least in Rome, during the first generations of imperial power (Seneca, *Nat. Qns.*, VII, 32). Neoplatonism had thus its Platonic ingredients; but there were many others, not new, but derived from previous and contemporary systems. Even Christianity seems to have been laid under contribution. It is, indeed, said that both Ammonius Saccas, who may be regarded as the founder, and Plotinus, the most famous of the advocates of the system, had been Christians. To the medley of ideas thus mingled together there was added the practice of magic arts, and a dark veil of mystery aroused the curiosity and interest of an age which was attracted by such things. It is little wonder that Neoplatonism became perhaps the most powerful of the philosophical movements of its time.

By the political leaders of paganism it was regarded as a promising means of checking the rising tide of Christianity and as giving to their outworn tenets a new cloak of intellectual respectability. For this reason it received the patronage of Gallienus; though it was with Julian, beyond the strict limits of our period, that the most deliberate and comprehensive attempt thus to use the new philosophy was made. But all chance of final victory over its rival was lost when once the elements of magic and theurgy became increasingly prominent. Neoplatonism in fact was to prove little more than "a splendid vision of incomparable cloud-land in which the sun of Greek philosophy had its setting" (Harnack).

There was no serious quarrel between Neoplatonism and Christianity. Porphyry, it is true, composed a treatise *Against the Christians* in which he condemned their theory of creation as irreligious and the doctrine of the Incarnation as an unsuccessful attempt to unite God and the world. But his polemic is not unusually bitter, save perhaps against eschatology, and there some kind of agreement might have been found within the Church. Plotinus, if in the *Enneads* he attacks the Gnostics, cannot be ranked as anti-Christian. But his system was hardly consistent with that of the Gospel. He might emphasize the value of contemplation and of communion with God; he might call men to renounce this world for the sake of a better; but his belief that the soul had power to raise itself by its own efforts and the absence of the need for a saviour from sin, these were entirely alien to the Christian scheme of salvation, as was his failure to foster love.[1]

Plotinus[2] had been born in Egypt but he came to Rome in 244, where his arrival gave a great stimulus to Neoplatonism, both

---

[1] cf. Inge, *Plotinus*, II, p. 232.
[2] For his influence in the West see Paul Henry, *Plotin et l'Occident*.

as a philosophy and as a way of life. The call to flee "to the dear fatherland of souls"[1] stirred men's hearts to their depths. Before this, in his search for knowledge, he had set out with the expedition of Gordian against the Parthians, but had fortunately made his escape from the disasters which befell it. The West, not India, was to be his goal. Here his influence became so considerable and persisted so long that a short sketch of his leading ideas will be of value. For Plotinus, matter had no real existence; nor had evil, whilst time and space were only forms of thought. The aim and consummation of man's life is union with the Absolute by means of contemplation and ecstasy. The Absolute itself was "stark unity" and beyond the reach of man's thought or conception. From it Mind, a kind of second person of the Trinity, had emanated, coming forth like light from its source. Mind is the cause of the real world of which the sensible is but a shadow. From Mind is derived Soul, the third person of the Trinity, which is diffused in all things. Much of this is pure Platonism, much probably taken over from Ammonius Saccas, whose lectures Plotinus had attended as a young man; but the various strands are woven together into a new and consistent scheme. When Plotinus died c. 270 he left behind him a large mass of writings and a numerous body of disciples. It was the most famous of these, Porphyry, who wrote the life of his master and published the *Enneads*.[2]

Porphyry himself had also come from the East, having been born in Tyre in 233. His original name was Malcho, and in adopting a Greek name he might have taken that of Basilides, the equivalent of his own, had it not already become notorious as that of a Gnostic leader. After studying under Longinus at Athens he came to Rome in 263 and attached himself to Plotinus. Later he settled in Sicily where his attack on Christianity was composed. It was a work of fifteen volumes, for like other Neoplatonic writers he was apt to be long-winded. His reputation for learning exceeded that of Plotinus, so Augustine informs us (*De Civ. Dei*, X, 10), and he certainly had a wide knowledge of the Scriptures. In him, and especially when he replies to St. Paul, Athens takes up the challenge which had been made to her philosophy by the faith which desired to supplant it. His own attack was met by Eusebius, by Methodius, and later by Apollinarius. All these works have been lost, but it is probable that the lines along which he moved have been preserved in the *Apocriticus* of Macarius Magnes, an apologetic work which adopts the

---

[1] Augustine, in *De Civ. Dei*, IX, xvii, quotes *Fugiendum est igitur ad carissimam patriam, et ibi pater, et ibi omnia* from *Ennead*, I, vi, 3.

[2] Books IV to VI had a strange fate, for on being translated into Arabic they became attached to Aristotle's *Theology* and were received as his work by medieval thinkers.

method of Origen's reply to Celsus, by taking certain arguments and then disposing of them one by one.[1]

Before finally leaving the subject of the Religious Background against which Western Christianity arose, one further matter requires to be considered: the attitude of the guardians of the official faith. The Roman authorities were exceedingly tolerant of religious beliefs so long as they did not promote a breach of the peace or threaten the unity of the State; and, of course, so long as the official religion was given due recognition by their votaries. Into the private beliefs of its subjects Rome made no inquisition as a general rule. Suspicion might, however, be aroused if a system became too powerful, and in particular if it showed signs of too compact an organization under the control of a single head; such an instrument might become dangerous.

The position of the Jews was different. Their God was a jealous God and they refused to fit Him into any political system. So a compromise had to be made. As the God of a separate nation His rights were recognized; as for the rest, the fact that His followers offered sacrifices for the welfare of the State was accepted as sufficient in normal times.[2] But times were not always normal, and there had been occasions when the Jews had been the object of attacks. The earliest of these had been in 139 B.C. when they were banished from Rome on the charge of having attempted to corrupt the morals of the people by advocating the cult of Jupiter Sabazios.[3] Later, in conjunction with those who practised Egyptian rites, they were penalized by Tiberius who ordered their vessels and vestments to be burnt. Some of them were deported to Sardinia and some were sentenced to lifelong imprisonment.[4] Under Claudius they were again ordered to leave Rome.[5]

The Jews were not the only people, apart from various philosophers and magicians, against whom measures were taken. As early as 186 B.C. the government had turned its attention to those who had been initiated into the Bacchic mysteries; many were put to death, their associations forbidden, and their books burned;[6] measures which would later be used against the

[1] Harnack thought that he was actually replying to Porphyry himself, a view which has been criticized by T. W. Crafer in *J.T.S.*, 1914, XV, pp. 360 ff. and 481 ff. Dr. Crafer has since published an edition of the *Apocriticus* in English.

[2] There was a synagogue of the Augustans in Trastevere and a Jewish association in his honour (Diehl, No. 4903).

[3] Valerius Maximus, I, iii, 3.

[4] Tacitus, *Ann.*, II, 85, and Suetonius, *Tiberius*, XXXVI.

[5] Cassius Dio, LX, 6.

[6] Livy, XXXIX, 16. The movement may have been introduced after the capture of Tarentum in 208 B.C. when many of the inhabitants were taken as slaves to Rome: see Tenny Frank, *Class. Quarterly*, XXI, p. 128 ff.

Christian Church. There are reasons for believing, however, that this action was undertaken on moral and political rather than on religious grounds. Later the Druids were suppressed. But again the primary objection to them was political rather than religious. The suppression was not complete, as it is recorded that a Druid addressed Severus Alexander in Celtic.[1] Diocletian, not long before he began the persecution of the Christians, had issued an edict ordering that the leaders of the Manichees in Africa should be burnt, and their books with them. The remaining adherents, unless of high rank (*honorati*), were to be put to death, the *honorati* being sent to work in the mines. It is probable that here too political motives may have been involved in view of the connexion between Manicheism and Persia, the enemy of Rome.

It may be permissible to express the opinion that if the Romans had possessed a powerful professional priesthood eager to maintain its rights and privileges and jealous of any potential rival, the tolerance which they exhibited would hardly have been possible.

[1] Lampridius, *Alexander Severus*, LX.

CHAPTER III

THE CHURCH AND THE SYNAGOGUE

Alexander the Great had seen in the Jews an instrument nicely adapted to the furtherance of his cherished scheme of drawing East and West together. The rise of Christianity confronted the Jews with an even greater opportunity of uniting the civilized world. Had they accepted Jesus as their Messiah and gladly shared Him with the Gentiles, the history of the Church, and of mankind, would have been immeasurably different. Even as it was, Christianity would owe an immense debt, in thought and organization alike, to the religion from which it sprang.

It was under the protecting care of Judaism that Christianity came to birth, and all through its earliest years Judaism continued to serve as a kind of breakwater against the sea of alien influences which threatened to overwhelm it. But Christianity, in order to fulfil its universal mission, had to leave its moorings and set out on its voyage into the Gentile world. Harnack, after contrasting the different part played by the Arabs in the spread of Islam (he claims that for centuries they continued to be "the main trunk of the new religion"), goes on to say that "the brief history of the Gospel within the bounds of Palestinian Judaism is a palaeontological epoch" (*Hist. of Dogma*, p. 11 f.). On both these points, however, Harnack is open to criticism; for the whole tendency of recent scholarship has been to attach much greater importance to the Palestinian period; whilst the Arabs, although they provided much of the energy and military skill which enabled the sword of Islam to achieve its conquests, made little contribution to its intellectual development. Arabic philosophy, in particular, was the work of other races.[1]

If Christianity soon outgrew its Jewish childhood, the task of propagating the Gospel had been made infinitely lighter by the preparatory work of the Jewish people. War and commerce had combined to scatter them from one end of the Roman world to the other. Josephus could claim that their law and customs had taken root in every city and tribe (*Contra Apion.*, II, 39) and quotes Strabo's testimony that the Jews dominated almost

---

[1] The only Arab philosopher of standing was Al-Khindi. Neither Avicenna (Ibn Sina) nor Averroes (Ibn Rushd) was an Arab, and Maimonides (Ibn Maymum) was a Jew. See, further, my *Decline and Fall of the Medieval Papacy*, p. 80 ff.

every place in the known world (*Antiq.*, XIV, vii, 2). This wide dispersion provided a network of centres from which the new faith might radiate. Before the breach between the Church and the Synagogue, the synagogue was the natural starting-point for the Christian missionary, for there he would not only have the opportunity of delivering his message to fellow Jews, but would, not infrequently, find among his audience men of Gentile race; for Gentiles often attended the synagogues, perhaps regarding them, from the absence of ritual and sacrifice, as philosophical rather than religious assemblies. Some of them became proselytes. Our Lord accused the Pharisees of striving to obtain such (Matt. 23 : 15), and as late as the third century Rabbi Eleazar held that it was for this that the Jews had been scattered among the nations (*Pesachim*, 87, b). The proselytizing efforts of the Jews did not pass unnoticed and Horace refers to their persuasive and compelling ways (*Satires*, I, iv, 142).

It was not only in the approach to individuals that the Jews had prepared the way; they had also made easier the approach to the Gentile world as a whole. In Alexandria, where Jews were numerous and influential, some kind of synthesis with Gentile thought had already been achieved. The Old Testament, for example, had been translated into Greek,[1] and Philo had attempted to present its teaching in a form which would appeal to non-Semites. The knowledge of the Old Testament with its monotheistic faith, its condemnation of idols, and its noble ethical teaching, was an important step towards faith in the Gospel.

The allegorical methods by which Philo had commended Jewish ideas and history to Gentile minds could easily be extended, and old forms spiritualized, until they could be quietly abandoned or transformed into Christian conceptions. This process furnishes a valuable illustration of the principle that allegorical interpretation seldom or never inaugurates new ideas; it is merely used to discover such ideas, and by so doing obtain valuable support for them, in passages which would not disclose their presence to stricter methods of interpretation. Even before the coming of Christ the allegorizing or spiritualizing of the Law had been carried so far by the Jews themselves that even Philo was moved to protest (*De Migr. Abr.*, XVI). By the use of such methods room was found for accommodation to Gentile customs and a way opened for considerable laxity of life among the Dispersion. There is much evidence for such laxity. The fact that the mother of Timothy was married to a Gentile (Acts 16 : 1) was a breach of the Law (Deut. 7 : 3); as was the marriage of Felix

---

[1] The fact that the Old Testament was not translated into Latin shows that the Jews were less numerous in the West.

and Drusilla recorded by Josephus (*Antiq.*, XX, vii, 2). So far had relaxation been carried that the moral standards and daily lives of the Jews of the Dispersion had in many cases fallen grievously below the demands of their religion. Amongst other things, the Jews had managed to acquire a most unenviable reputation for magic and sorcery.[1]

The breach between Church and Synagogue came gradually, and it seems probable that it was not complete until nearly the end of the first century.[2] But from the earliest days there must have been much in Christian teaching to cause alarm to the strictly orthodox. Even the Sermon on the Mount, with its claim to override the Law, constituted an offence. Already in the oldest of our gospels there are signs that the Christians for their part were coming to regard the Jews as enemies; the phrase *all the Jews* (Mark 7 : 3) has something hostile about it, or at least distinctive of the difference between Jews and Christians; whilst St. Luke seems determined to shift the responsibility for the murder of Jesus from the Romans to the Jews (cf. Luke 23 : 1 ff.; Acts 2 : 23; 3 : 13 f., etc.). In the last of the gospels, composed no doubt when the breach had become permanent, there is a sinister sound in the repeated mention of "the Jews".

The first Christians, like their Lord before them, frequented the temple. Did the priests who became converts (Acts 6 : 7) continue in office? Even the attacks of St. Stephen did not compromise the apostles, who were left undisturbed in Jerusalem, evidently being regarded as less revolutionary in their outlook. The Christians seem definitely to have cherished the hope that Israel would soon follow their example and acknowledge the new Messiah (Acts 3 : 19 ff.). St. Paul normally sought out the synagogue when he came to a new city and our latest knowledge of him includes his interview with the Jewish authorities in Rome (Acts 28 : 17 ff.); an interview which makes it clear that no organized opposition to the messengers of the Gospel had as yet developed. The Jewish leaders in Rome, although they had heard of the sect as being spoken against, are willing to know more about it. We must not, however, make too much of this incident; for Judaism, when Christianity began to spread, was not itself a single system, but contained within it a number of differing elements, some of which more easily tended to be drawn to the new religion; others, by a process of reaction, to become very definite opponents.[3] In the gospels it is mainly the Pharisees

[1] cf. Matt. 12: 27; Acts 19: 19; Pliny, *Hist. Nat.*, XXX, i, 11; Josephus, *Antiq.*, VIII, ii, 5 and XX, vii, 2. In the ancient world there was no distinct line between medicine and magic: cf. *Jubilees*, X, 10 ff., and Origen, *Contra Celsum*, V, 612.
[2] See J. Parkes, *The Conflict of the Church and the Synagogue*.
[3] See W. R. Arnold, "The Relation of Primitive Christianity to Jewish

who take the lead in opposing the work of Jesus;[1] in the Acts it is the Sadducees and the official priesthood who are active, no doubt because the question of the Resurrection has become prominent (cf. Acts 4 : 1 f.). In the case of St. Stephen it is the Jews of the Dispersion, who might have been expected to hold more liberal views, who initiate the persecution (Acts 6 : 9). In the early period, however, the attack is not continuous or sustained (cf. Acts 9 : 31), though some kind of persecution must have arisen almost from the first (1 Thess. 2 : 14; and cf. Matt. 10 : 17 f.); but the mission to the Gentiles was well on its way before frequent clashes occurred.

The breach was really inevitable and no possible compromise could have been reached which would have been accepted by both sides, though the inherited love of the first generation of Jewish Christians for the traditions of their fathers may have blinded them to the true state of the case. Judaism was opposed to the spirit of Jesus, and though it might contain pious and attractive elements was, in the main, according to Sanday, "a body of hard, narrow, materialized beliefs" (*Outlines of the Life of Christ*, p. 28).

The judgment of Sanday, however, probably needs considerable modification, certainly if it is to be applied to any large section of Judaism. The Jewish attitude to the Law is not easy for outsiders to grasp. The Law for many of them was no dead thing, but, by a kind of mystical conceiving, had become a "creative force expressing itself through the Holy Community to the world as a whole".[2] It might almost be regarded as an "incarnation" of the divine,[3] and in every Jewish synagogue the most impressive object was a volume of the Torah in its sacred ark with a lamp burning before it, corresponding to the altar of the Christians, and even to Jehovah sitting above the mercy-seat in the Holy of Holies of the Temple. The Law, as interpreted by the highest minds, was no mere collection of commands, but an expression of the divine mind and will. In Taoism the idea of the Way (Tao) has, in a similar manner, almost been personified. The use of the word "Law" to translate the Hebrew *Torah* is perhaps unfortunate and misleading, for it suggests something definite and not readily changed. *Torah* really means direction or instruction, and far from being a fixed code is a way of life.

Thought", in *Harvard Theol. Rev.*, 1930, XXIII, p. 161 ff. He points out that the Talmud (edited A.D. 200–500) represents "the Judaism of the opponents of Christianity as that Judaism took shape after the conflict" (*op. cit.*, p. 166).

[1] Only in John 12 : 10 do the chief priests take the lead, and there the question of the raising of Lazarus comes in.

[2] Parkes, *op. cit.*, p. 36.

[3] R. T. Herford can even say: "It is near to the truth to say that what Christ is to the Christian, Torah is to the Jew" (*Pharisaism*, p. 171).

None the less Christianity had added to the fundamentally Jewish concept of righteousness an emotional impulse. Religion was no longer the stern, even dreary, pursuit of virtue; but the glad following of a living and enabling Lord (cf. Rom. 7 : 24 f.).

The acceptance or rejection of Jesus as the Messiah must have aroused many disputes and some bitterness, but for a time the holding of such a belief would not be considered sufficient occasion for expulsion from the synagogue. Eventually, however, the issue would have to be joined at this point. So, too, the abandonment of good customs like circumcision, and the substitution of Sunday for the Sabbath, must have caused additional offence. In the West, the distinction was made still more pronounced by the adoption of Saturday as a fast day and later the careful avoidance of the Day of the Passover for the Easter celebration. In the East, the observance of Saturday as a special day continued; even to-day it is regarded as different from other days in the Greek Church; and, in the Ethiopic, as of almost equal importance with Sunday. But the really decisive act, an act which was taken at first with much reluctance by many Jewish Christians, was the admission of Gentiles as full members of the Church without requiring them to keep the Law. So long as all Christians kept the Law there was no obvious need for a breach. But, once the Gentiles came in, Christianity was seen as a rival religion and not merely as an eccentric sect. In Palestine where there would be few Gentiles the problem would not become acute. There the really decisive point was the Fall of Jerusalem in 70 and the events leading up to it. From the first the Jewish Christians took no part in the revolt (acting in this like many of the Pharisees) and in 66 they finally fled across the Jordan to Pella. In spite of the efforts of Herod Agrippa II to keep the Jews loyal to Rome in their own true interests,[1] rebellion grew, and was encouraged by a few early successes. But methods which had been successful against Antiochus Epiphanes could not hope to be effective against the mistress of the world, and Jerusalem fell at last to Titus, and her spoils went to adorn his triumph at Rome. The rebellion of the Jews in Palestine (the Dispersion had held very much aloof) brought to an end the official existence of the Jews as a separate "nation"; thenceforward they would be reckoned as part of the general population of the Empire. Individual Jews, however, still retained much influence. Bernice, the sister of Agrippa, for instance, was the mistress of Titus; and Josephus, by a well-timed submission, obtained some credit with the victors. But the Christian Jews as a class had revealed the gap between them

[1] The work of the Herods has recently been judiciously surveyed by A. H. M. Jones, *The Herods of Judaea*, 1938.

and their fellows in Palestine. After their flight it would be ever more and more difficult for followers of Jesus of Nazareth to maintain their place in the Jewish nation and in the Jewish Church.

If the Fall of Jerusalem had unfortunate political consequences for the relations of Jews and Christians in Palestine, it had also an adverse effect in the sphere of thought, and that over a much wider area. Up till then two elements in Judaism, which may be called the legalist and apocalyptic, had existed side by side. The Fall of Jerusalem discredited, for that generation at least, the dreams and forecasts of the apocalyptists, so Apocalypse was left to the Christian Jews to whom the Law was not so sacred—in the Revelation of St. John it is not even mentioned. Henceforth, legalism became the mark of Judaism. A further cause of antagonism was the growing hellenization of Christianity as Gentile influences played upon it. In Judaism the legalistic school had always set its face against such influences. Were not the Greeks pioneers of evil to all mankind? (*Sib. Orac.*, III, 553).[1] In the Dispersion, however, it had a difficult task, and as late as the middle of the third century we find a synagogue at Doura where the Old Testament prohibition of pictures is entirely disregarded. Here Hellenistic culture is seen in close contact with Jewish religion. Jewish ideas, in their turn, were also to exercise some influence in Hellenistic circles; the Hermetic writings are an example. The presence of Hebrew words and characters in magic papyri and gems can scarcely be taken as illustrations of the spread of Hebrew influence; as probably the mysterious nature of the script and sounds was sufficient to account for their use.

The method by which Jewish Christians were in the end excluded from the synagogue was quite simple. A clause against the heretics was inserted in the Blessings (the *Birkath-ha-Minim*) which no Christian could possibly repeat, and so he would cease to attend. This addition was probably made about A.D. 85 and certainly later than the Fall of Jerusalem.[2] At some time before the end of the century letters and apostles were sent out from Palestine to all synagogues informing them of the change and of the necessity of excluding Christians from the assemblies. Thus the breach was made absolute. No longer could the Jewish Christian hope to retain his nationality or preserve the link with Judaism. But if his efforts in this direction had proved vain he had still an important part to play in the fortunes

[1] "The Judaism of the Talmud killed its Greek-speaking sister, pulled down her buildings, and ploughed up their sites. What records we have are due to excavations or to occasional accidental finds" (Lietzmann, *The Beginnings of the Christian Church*, p. 95 f.).

[2] See R. T. Herford, *Christianity in Talmud and Midrash*, p. 125.

of the New Israel; though it would grow less and less as the years went by, until at length Jewish Christianity would merge in the general stream, or else flow into other channels and become definitely heretical. Before this happened, the Jewish Christian had to bear a double burden. On the one hand, he was conscious of being cut off from his nation; on the other, the failure of the Lord's return would affect him much more nearly than his Gentile fellow Christian. Once the breach was made, the flow of Jewish converts would soon dry up, and less and less would be the part which he would play in the councils of the Church which soon looked upon him with little sympathy and at times with suspicion. By the middle of the second century the observance of Jewish customs might be a ground for excommunication.[1] Even when there was no definite excommunication Jewish Christians would tend to separate into small communities of their own. In the West, the process of decay was much more speedy than in the East, where even in the time of Eusebius (III, xxv: 5) Jewish Christians were still a recognizable body. Judaism had itself always been stronger in the East, and as Christianity moved Westward the older faith had been finding new life in the Orient. Rome might be "Babylon" to the Christian; but, to the Jew, Babylon was fast becoming a New Jerusalem.

Two generations later the struggle with Rome was renewed with even greater ferocity on both sides. Once again Christian Jews, now only a small remnant, stood aside and refused to help their nation. How could they, when Bar Cochba, the leader of the revolt, himself claimed to be the Messiah? So, as Justin Martyr says, they "refused to blaspheme Christ". There had been a number of outbreaks accompanied by massacres on the part of the Jews in the years between 115 and 117. These had brought them no profit, but immense loss in men and treasure. They were but preliminaries to the final struggle. This seems to have arisen over the action of Hadrian who, when in Palestine in 130, renamed Jerusalem Aelia Capitolina after himself.[2] Rome in the end again proved victorious, but only after a protracted struggle, and she took terrible vengeance upon her defeated enemy. Aelia Capitolina was declared to be forbidden ground for all Jews—a prohibition which would affect Christians of Jewish birth. So the Church at Jerusalem became Gentile and for the time being lost its importance. It was thus in no position to maintain its claim to be the Mother Church of Christendom.

[1] See Justin Martyr, *Dial.*, XLVII.
[2] Eusebius says that the new name was given after the revolt had been crushed (IV, vi, 4). Cassius Dio, however, says it was in 130 that it occurred and formed one cause of the rebellion (LIX, 12). Spartianus, *Hadrian*, XIV, 2, says the rebellion was caused by the prohibition of circumcision.

This was a help, no doubt, to the growing importance of Rome. Later, Jerusalem would recover her prestige or some of it, and be regarded as the standard, for the East if not for the West, as we see in Firmilian's letter to Cyprian. For the Jewish nation, however, this was the end, the real termination of all hopes of national revival, a disaster greater and more conclusive than the better known fall of A.D. 70.

So far we have been concerned with the relations of the Jews to Christians of Jewish birth; their attitude towards Christianity as a whole must now receive notice.

It is often said that the Jews took a considerable part in stirring up feeling against the Church and in the instigation of persecution. It is possible, for example, that the Christians were singled out by Nero at the suggestion of the Jews acting through Poppaea, who was a Jewish proselyte. But this is only surmise. When Polycarp was martyred at Smyrna in 155, however, the writer of the account of that incident definitely accuses the Jews of habitually assisting in persecutions (*Mart. Polycarp.*, XIII, 1). The account has been rejected by some Jewish scholars on the ground that as it was the Sabbath day no Jews would have carried wood for the fire, as they are represented as doing.[1] Whether this was so or not, the part taken by the Jews in persecutions has probably been exaggerated; it was almost certainly spasmodic and unorganized.[2] None the less it formed a real element in Jewish opposition and a means of expressing the hatred felt towards the heretics who claimed to have supplanted the true Israel. It may also at times have been the means of turning attention away from themselves, for in the first days at least the missionary zeal of Christians may well have been a cause of embarrassment to the Jews from whom they were not then carefully distinguished.

Jewish opposition was naturally much greater in the East than in the West on account of the larger number of Jews who lived there. But, even in the West, Jews were numerous, especially in Rome. They were also found in considerable numbers in the Rhone Valley and in North Africa. In the West, however, they never had such freedom as elsewhere—they were not regarded as autonomous—although the jurisdiction of the High Priest, and later of the Patriarch of Palestine, would be acknowledged by all Jews, and recognized by the government. Palestine was the headquarters of anti-Christian propaganda, and Justin accuses the Jews of having sent out chosen agents to

[1] So Israel Abrahams, *Studies in Pharisaism*, II, p. 67. When Pionius was martyred at Smyrna nearly a century later, also on a Sabbath, the presence of crowds of Jews who lent a hand is reported.

[2] James the Just had been murdered in a popular uprising in the spring of 62: see Josephus, *Antiq.*, XX, ix, 1; Euseb., II, xxiii.

hinder the Christians everywhere and to denounce them and their Master (*Dial.*, CVIII and CXVII). He also affirms that they showed their hatred of the Christians by taking every opportunity of killing or injuring them (I *Apol.*, XXXI).

At the beginning of the third century the Jews were apparently active in North Africa, where they attracted the attention of Tertullian who regarded them as responsible for the persecutions which befell the Church.[1] Later still, Cyprian in his *Testimonia* also denounced them. The date and location of the mysterious Commodian have not yet been finally fixed, save that he belonged to the West and flourished not earlier than the middle of the third century. In his *Carmen Apologeticum adv. Judaeos et Gentiles* there are bitter attacks on the Jews and the renewal of the charge of helping in persecutions. As late as the Council of Elvira, c. 300, the danger of Jewish perversions and of Jewish influences in general was recognized and preventive legislation put forward. A little later, Lactantius thought the Jews of sufficient importance to contemplate writing against them (*Div. Instit.*, VII, i, 26).

From the Christian side there was also an offensive;[2] had been, indeed, from the beginning, and to it we must now turn. Its nature and extent are a subject which demands careful and unprejudiced study, for exaggeration and misunderstanding are only too easy. Dr. Parkes, for example,[3] quotes Ignatius as declaring that Judaism "is nothing but funeral monuments and tombstones of the dead". He has failed to realize that Ignatius says the same thing of Christianity—if it does not speak of Jesus Christ (*Ad Philad.*, VI, 1). There is thus no attack on the Jews as such.

The attitude of Christians towards Judaism and the Jews was by no means of a piece until well into the second century. On the one hand there was a feeling of violent repulsion, such as is found in the *Epistle of Barnabas* and the *Epistle to Diognetus*; on the other hand the *Didache*, and for our purpose still more important, *The Shepherd* of Hermas, retain a decided sympathy. This sympathy tended, indeed, towards a conception of Christianity as a new Law, rather than as a Gospel.

It was easy for Christians to taunt the Jews over the Fall of Jerusalem and to point to it as an act of divine vengeance on an apostate people. In addition there was definite propaganda to prove that the Old Testament itself had only validity as foretelling the Gospel, and that the sacrificial system was an utter

[1] See *Scorp.*, X, where he calls them *fontes persecutionum*; also *Apol.*, VII, XXI, and the treatise *Adv. Judaeos*. I do not accept the view that he is referring to the conditions of an earlier time.
[2] See, further, Canon Lukyn Williams, *Adversus Judaeos*.
[3] *The Conflict between Church and Synagogue*, p. 84.

mistake, a doctrine that would have received the approval of the pre-exilic prophets, and not least of Jeremiah. There is a striking difference between the author of Hebrews and the *Epistle of Barnabas* in their attitude in this matter which is very significant. The latter not only fails to understand the meaning of the old dispensation, but has only an inadequate idea of Christian institutions. A symptom of the growth of anti-Jewish feeling may probably be found in the preference in many Churches for *Barnabas* to Hebrews.

As to the Old Testament. Justin advanced the claim that it belonged not to those who originally received it, but to those who understood its true significance (*Dial.*, XXIX); a claim which reminds one of the German attitude to *unser* Shakespeare. That it should arouse resentment in Jewish hearts is not surprising, for the Old Testament was the dearest of their possessions, as St. Paul recognized when he placed first among the privileges of his nation the custody of the oracles of God (Rom. 3 : 2).

Even the traditions connected with the Temple at Jerusalem were transferred after a time to the Holy Sepulchre, including the claim to be the centre of the earth.[1] Anyone who has the patience to follow Justin in his argument with the Jew Trypho must feel that the truth does not lie entirely on one side; even though Justin's allegorical methods of interpretation, to us no longer convincing, were common to the disputants. Well might Trypho exclaim, after one long exposition: "The words of the whole prophecy are ambiguous, my dear man, and are no decisive proof of what you wish" (*Dial.*, LI).

One further claim by the Christian Church which aroused the scorn and indignation of the Jews was that of being the true People of God. "What are you Israel, and does God speak this of you?" Such was the very natural question which Trypho put to Justin (*Dial.*, CXXIII). There is, perhaps, something of poetic justice in this appropriation of the title and privileges by the Christian Church when one recalls that Judah itself had made the sole claim to being Israel after the Fall of Samaria and had denied the Samaritans any share in it. The conception of the Church as the true Israel, however, is one which finds much favour with modern theologians; they see in Christ, standing alone before the High Priest, the last faithful Israelite, and, as such, the founder of the new Israel.[2] But even this thought is not entirely novel, for Justin himself had anticipated it. "As

---

[1] See on the whole subject, J. Jeremias, *Golgotha.*
[2] cf. *Doctrine in the Church of England*, p. 102: "His rejection is the turning-point, decisive both for the Messiah Himself and for Israel who rejected Him. He is the sole representative at that moment of God's holy people; He bears in His own Person the whole burden of Israel's appointed destiny."

your whole race", he said to Trypho, "was called Jacob and Israel from that one Jacob who was also called Israel; so we too who obey the commands of Christ, as we are called Jacob and Israel . . . so from Christ who begat us unto God, we are called, and are, the true children of God" (*op. cit.*, CXXIV). The right to the name of the new People of God was absolutely necessary to the Church if the promises of the Old Testament were to be fulfilled in her; as Burkitt has said: "it was as essential . . . to establish her claim to be the true heir of the Covenants, as it is for the High Anglican of our day to make out a case for the apostolical succession of the English bishops" (*Early Eastern Christianity*, p. 209). But this necessity was no consolation to those who were to be summarily dispossessed of an age-long inheritance.

The Jews, however, persisted in their rejection and "so it came to pass that the Gospel of a Jewish Messiah who was God Himself incarnate was preached by Galilaeans and taken to heart by Gentiles".[1] The pressing in of the Gentiles, at first almost on sufferance, and then as their numbers grew swiftly, to a pre-dominant part in the Christian Church, increased the antipathy on both sides. The Gentile Christian was, above all, anxious to show that there was nothing Jewish about him. Professor Percy Gardner pointed out that in some early Christian sarcophagi Jesus is depicted with Jewish features (*The Growth of Christianity*, p. 49). But in the so-called Capella Graeca in the Cemetery of Priscilla at Rome, which probably belongs to the middle of the second century, He is shown as a young man, beardless and with a decidedly Roman type of face.[2] Sometimes the antipathy took on forms which later ages would frequently copy, such as attempts to molest the Jews and break up their meetings. It is said that Callistus, the future pope, was banished for creating an uproar in a synagogue.[3] Such incidents, however, were prob-ably rare under the Roman government; but attacks of a dif-ferent kind must have been increasingly common; attacks by way of controversy. The Jews, for example, are roundly accused of not even knowing God, but as serving angels, and even the moon.[4] Furthermore, various incidents of our Lord's life are so narrated as to acquire an anti-Jewish bias. In the birth narra-tives the magi, as Gentiles, are exalted at the expense of the shepherds who were Jews. In a document printed by M. R. James[5] it is even suggested that the prophecies quoted by the

---

[1] A. J. Toynbee, *A Study of History*, IV, p. 263.   [2] See Styger, p. 141.
[3] It is true that the accusation is made by his enemy Hippolytus (IX, 12); none the less it is evidence that such attacks were being made, even if untrue in this particular case.
[4] See *The Preaching of Peter* (*Apoc. N.T.*, p. 17) and cf. II. *Clem.*, II, 3, where the Jews are described as those who "seemed to have God".
[5] *Latin Infancy Gospels*, p. 94.

former are older than the Hebrew Scriptures. So, too, the emphasis laid on the washing of Pilate's hands in Matt. 27 : 24 f. is increased in the *Gospel of Peter* by the addition of the statement "of the Jews no man washed his hands" (1 : 1). The whole of this document, and there are others like it, attempts to throw the entire blame for the Crucifixion upon the Jews and to relieve Pilate of any guilt. The object may be to curry favour with the Roman authorities. Strangely enough, the Jews themselves took the same point of view.[1]

In Marcion and his followers antipathy to all things Jewish is carried to its logical conclusion. The refusal to regard Jehovah of the Old Testament as the God and Father of the Lord Jesus Christ is a natural sequel to the denial of justice to the Jews. But Marcion, who has been called, rather wittily, "an old-world Count Tolstoy",[2] cannot be taken as representative of orthodox Christian opinion. But that that feeling went at times to great extremes cannot be denied; it has even left its traces in the text of the New Testament, for our Lord's prayer in Luke 23 : 34. "Father forgive them" is left out of certain important manuscripts and versions,[3] presumably because of hatred for the Jews.[4] But not all Christian writers and advocates were narrow-minded. Justin and Trypho, perhaps because they were both philosophers, could discuss their differences quite amicably, and the former was able to affirm that the Christians, in spite of Jewish prejudices against them, did not hate in return, but prayed that repentance and mercy might be theirs.[5]

The Jews might reject their Messiah, Christian and Jew might quarrel and dispute, the Christian Church might cut itself off from the parent stem; none the less, the influence of Judaism would be permanent. How could it be otherwise when the sacred book of the new community was, and remained, a collection of Hebrew writings? If it be admitted that Christianity because it was rejected by the Jews became predominantly a Western and European religion, yet because it still clung to the Old Testament the process of westernization was stayed sufficiently long to prevent its becoming a mere mystery religion.[6] From the Old

---

[1] "The Talmud knows nothing of an execution of Jesus by the Romans, but makes it solely the act of the Jews" (R. T. Herford, *Christianity in Talmud and Midrash*, p. 86).

[2] T. M. Lindsay, *Church and Ministry*, p. 219.

[3] Amongst others who omit it are B, D, W, 579, the Sinaitic Syriac, and a and b.

[4] The Christians were not always generous in recording their triumph. On a lamp, now in the museum at Carthage, the seven-branched candlestick appears upside down.

[5] *Dial.*, CVIII. Rendel Harris has suggested that the Christian form of IV Baruch was issued in 136 as a kind of *eirenicon* to the banished Jews: *Rest of the Words of Baruch*, p. 15.

[6] "The Church accepted the Old Testament as its authoritative mythology,

Testament the Church had learned securely to grasp the doctrine of the unity of God, a doctrine which would prove essential in the coming age of controversy. A purely Gentile religion could so easily have added one more deity to its pantheon; but the Jew, both within and without the Church, was always there to compel it to face the meaning and implications of offering worship to Christ. Did it mean the abandonment of monotheism? This was perhaps the greatest service which Judaism, once the breach was made, could render to Christianity. Only less vital was its teaching of God as a living God, One who does not stand apart from the world which He has made but is prepared to intervene for the sake of righteousness. Less happy in their influence were the rather exaggerated anthropomorphic conceptions which pervaded the Old Testament, even the purer ideas of the Greeks were unable entirely to modify them; also an undue emphasis on eschatology, conceived in a very material manner. This latter found an eager welcome in the West.

These later doctrines should help to remind us that the Church, in taking over the Old Testament, and, let it not be forgotten, much other literature, from the Jewish Church, drew into the stream of its intellectual life, not only the direct influence of Palestinian thought, but also much that had come into it from Mesopotamia, Persia, and Syria. In its later stages, Judaism, as it became more self-conscious, tended to resent the intrusion of alien ideas, especially of a Hellenic nature; but this was not so in its earlier career. In the Dispersion a considerable amount of Greek influence was bound to come in through Alexandria; but even here there was a tendency, seen in Philo, to resist too great infiltration. Schweitzer has pointed out that though "he seeks to rationalize Judaism by the aid of the Platonic-Stoic philosophy . . . he gives no place to the religious and cultural ideas by which he was surrounded in Egypt" (*St. Paul and His Interpreters*, p. 176 f.).

In addition to the Old Testament, there was at least one other source of Jewish influence which was of the highest importance, that which was exercised through the cultus. Recent scholarship, even apart from what may be called the eschatological school, has reacted strongly from the views set forth by Harnack and his school a generation ago. It claims that before it came into contact with Hellenism Christianity had been decisively moulded by Palestinian Judaism in its thought, institutions, and cultus. This, it seems to me, is to go too far in the opposite direction, save in the matter of the cultus. Jewish influences

and that prevented it from ever becoming quite identical with the pagan Religion which it supplanted, monotheistic and sacramental as that Religion tended to be" (Burkitt, *Church and Gnosis*, p. 138).

here were undoubtedly much greater than had previously been supposed.[1] The rites contained in the *Apostolic Tradition of Hippolytus* are Jewish through and through, and there is scarcely a single feature for which parallels cannot be found.[2] That a strain of Jewish Christian thought, as distinct from that which welcomed Greek ideas, existed in the Church cannot, of course, be denied. It is seen in the Epistle of James with its emphasis on ethics and lack of interest in metaphysical pro- blems, phenomena which are also found in the Christian inter- polations in *The Testaments of the Twelve Patriarchs*.

The opposition to St. Paul by the Judaizers, recorded in the New Testament, continued long after his death, especially in the East. Jewish Christianity pursued a set policy of belittling him and of attributing everything to the Twelve, even the work of converting the Gentiles (e.g. *Didache*, I). In the *Apostolic Church Order* he is ignored, and though the *Didascalia* mentions his presence at the Council of Jerusalem it is only as the assist- ant of Barnabas. When, however, these documents were worked into the *Apostolic Constitutions* about the middle of the fourth century, prejudice against St. Paul had apparently been over- come and his name is introduced into the text.[3]

That there should have been this prejudice is not remarkable, for the principles for which he stood, by elevating Christianity from the position of a Jewish sect into a world-wide movement, involved the eventual disappearance of Jewish Christianity as a separate entity within the Church. Attempts to judaize still persisted for a time, but mainly in the East,[4] for I *Clement* shows no sign of their occurrence at Rome, and presumably other parts of the West were equally clear.

But if the free admission of the Gentiles, for which St. Paul fought and won, played so fundamental a part in the develop- ment of Christianity, his distinctive teaching failed to obtain any permanent recognition, though his writings were preserved and widely circulated, as was the Acts of the Apostles in which he occupies so prominent a place. Moreover his position as the Apostle of the Gentiles and a supposed founder of the Roman Church must have added to his prestige in the West. In fact his position was very high and references to him as "the Apostle" *par excellence* are common.[5] In spite of this, no real appreciation

---

[1] See C. W. Dugmore, *The Influence of the Synagogue upon the Divine Office*.
[2] See G. Dix, *The Apost. Trad. of St. Hippolytus*, p. xl ff.
[3] See the tables in C. H. Turner, *Catholic and Apost.*, p. 267–270.
[4] cf. Ignatius, *Philad.*, VI, 1; Euseb. VI, xiii, 3. The Ebionites retained a special animus against St. Paul whom they regarded as a renegade from the Law: cf. Iren., I, xxvi, 2.
[5] e.g. Augustine, *Conf.*, VIII, 12, *codicem apostoli*, and in the twelfth century, to take a much later example, Giraldus Cambrensis quotes Heb. 10:24 ff. as *illud apostoli* (Rolls Series), I, p. 250.

of his message is to be found; no school of Pauline theology came into being (the lack of any formulated system in his writings may have prevented this), and his influence on the thought of the Church was but slight. Even the synoptic gospels have no trace of it; their leading ideas are the Kingdom of God, and they make free use of the title, Son of Man, whilst St. Paul is mainly interested in Justification, Sanctification, and Reconciliation. It is true that some of his phraseology is adopted by Western writers, as for example by Clement of Rome and by Justin, but no corresponding appreciation of his doctrines seems to have accompanied it. Clement, especially, insists that we are justified by works, not words (XXX. 3, XXXII. 4), and his very quotations are often misapplied.[1] Of the Western fathers before Augustine, Irenaeus is perhaps nearest to St. Paul (though nearer still to Johannine theology). He adopts many of his ideas, but ignores the typical doctrine of Justification.[2] Perhaps there is something ironical in all this, for St. Paul in like manner had used the terminology of Greek philosophy and of the mysteries without adopting their ideas.[3]

The teaching of St. Paul thus seems to have lapsed and a different type of Christianity spread among the Gentiles for whose salvation he had laboured so abundantly. Soon they formed the chief part of the Church; and, by what seems a paradox, this prevailing type of doctrine had a legalistic tinge which probably owed but little to attempts to judaize. The Gospel, far from being the offer of free forgiveness and divine grace, tended to become but a new way of life, and justification by works displaced justification by faith. To the general neglect and misunderstanding Marcion and Augustine were exceptions; but Marcion, more Pauline than Paul himself,[4] was an extremist who was finally expelled as a heretic, and the influence of Augustine persisted in other fields, whilst his "Pauline" side, if one may so designate it, was forgotten. But the epistles were part of the canon, and sooner or later their message would be understood and come once again to light. It is a strange commentary on the blindness of the Medieval Church and its intellectual and spiritual leaders that his teaching was not rediscovered until the sixteenth century.[5]

[1] One passage may be an exception (VII, 4): "the blood of Christ . . . brought the grace of repentance to all the world".

[2] He can, for example, affirm that "godliness alone leads men to eternal life" (*Demonstration of Apost. Preaching*, I).

[3] Such is the opinion of Schweitzer, *op. cit.*, p. 238.

[4] It was Marcion and not St. Paul who first proclaimed in so many words the opposition of the Law and the Gospel: see Tertullian, *Adv. Marc.*, I, 19, 21; IV, 1.

[5] His teaching had not entirely been forgotten, and Luther himself owed a considerable debt to those who instructed him.

PART II

LOCAL EXPANSION

The Gospel, as it came to the West, was no highly articulated and definite body of teaching; it was rather an influence, a seed which was to find root in a variety of soils. In each the resulting product would not be exactly identical. For just as there were to be differences between Christianity as it developed in East and West, so would there be differences within each several nation and people. The changed climate would bring out, slowly, and at first almost imperceptibly, fresh characteristics, as the combination of the Gospel with new elements resulted in something which was at once distinctive and yet the same. St. Paul had recognized that in the case of individual Christians there must be diversities of gifts and diversities of service; in like manner the individual peoples were to make an offering of their special qualities at the feet of Christ. We are now to survey the manner in which Christianity came to the different parts of the West and the different environments which it found there. The treatment of each separate Church varies slightly in accordance with the amount and nature of the available evidence.

CHAPTER I

THE APOSTOLIC AGE

On the day of Pentecost there were dwelling in Jerusalem, Jews, devout men, out of every nation under heaven, and among them were strangers of Rome—the sole representatives of the West (Acts 2 : 6, 10). If these men really came from Rome (as is most probable) and were not merely Roman citizens as some think, then we may say that the beginnings of Western Christendom coincided with the beginnings of the Church itself. For we are surely entitled to suppose that converts were drawn from each of the several divisions mentioned. On their return to Rome, and doubtless during the voyage back, they would have been quite unable to keep to themselves the stupendous experience which they had undergone.

The Church in Palestine, however, was slow to realize that it had a message for mankind as a whole. It is true that the Gospel was to be preached to all nations; but the cities of Israel seemed to offer a wide enough field until the Lord should return (Matt. 10 : 23).[1] It was not to the original apostles, but to Saul, the persecutor so suddenly transformed into an apostle, that realization of the Church's true mission seems first to have come. Later on, in his letter to the "Ephesians", he worked out his vision, with Rome, the city from which he wrote, as the headquarters of a world-wide communion.

The story of the Church's expansion to the West is told in the later chapters of the Acts of the Apostles, and Saul, now become Paul, stands at the centre of the record. But before his conversion there had already been some expansion. Christians were to be found at Damascus (Acts 9 : 2), perhaps having come from Galilee, though some no doubt were fugitives recently escaped from Jerusalem. Ananias seems to have been of older standing (Acts 9 : 13 f.; 22 : 12); had he been, one wonders, a member of the mysterious Zadokite community which existed in that city?[2] The absence of any reference in contemporary records has probably led us to forget the possibility of quite considerable activity on the part of the earliest generation. The casual mention of Christian communities suggests that this had been

---

[1] There is no mention of such a limitation in either Mark or Luke; Loisy thinks that it is no part of the original record.

[2] See *Oxford Apoc.*, II, p. 785 ff., for a description of this community. W. K. Lowther Clarke finds resemblances to the *Didasc. Apost.* in their organization: see *Theology*, XXI, p. 331 ff.

operative. Who, for example, took the Gospel to Alexandria? It seems to have arrived there quite early (Acts 18 : 24 f.), though a long silence followed its introduction. Legend, of course, has been busy. We are told in the *Preaching of Peter* (quoted by Clement of Alexandria, *Strom.*, VI, 5) that after the Resurrection twelve years were devoted to the evangelization of the Jews before there was any thought of reaching out to the rest of mankind. *Pistis Sophia* assures us that Jesus Himself remained with the apostles during the whole of this period in order to prepare them for their wider mission.[1] When the period of preparation was ended the whole world was portioned out between them.[2]

If the older apostles occupy a prominent place in legend, and no doubt they laboured widely and strenuously, genuine history can tell us little or nothing of their activities, even in the case of St. Peter. All is concentrated on the solitary figure of St. Paul. It shows him pushing ever westward, after the vision of the mysterious Macedonian had turned his eyes to Europe. We see him sailing from Troas, past Imbros (almost lost in the towering height of Samothrace), past Thasos, the burial-place of Cassius, and so at last to Neapolis and a new continent (Acts 16 : 11 f.). Then after various returns to Palestine there comes the final voyage to Rome. The two years' sojourn there ends the narrative so far as reliable history is concerned. It was Malta,[3] however, and not Philippi, that was the true gateway to the West (using the term with the meaning that we are attaching to it, for Philippi is part of the Orthodox East) and the island is naturally full of traditions of St. Paul; the exact place of his landing, and even the house of Publius,[4] are still shown to the curious traveller; and at each site a church commemorates the supposed event.

The question has often been asked,[5] Why did Christianity move with such strength towards the West and why was the eastern extension so comparatively weak? The answer seems to

---

[1] The period was reduced to eighteen months by the Valentinians (Iren., I, iii, 2); whilst the *Ascension of Isaiah*, IX, 16, states that Christ would remain for 545 days after His resurrection. (Charles thinks that this statement is a Gnostic interpolation.)

[2] See *Acts of Thomas*, I (*Apoc. N.T.*, p. 365). In the *Acts of Philip*, 94 (*op. cit.*, p. 446), the plan is attributed to the Lord Himself.

[3] Malta is not a very suitable place for the beginning of Western expansion, for its inhabitants are mainly of Phoenician origin and speak a Semitic dialect which Strabo stated was akin to Punic (XVII, 832 ff.), though allowance must be made for subsequent Arabic influence.

[4] Legend, busy as usual, claims that St. Paul consecrated the son of Publius as the first bishop of the island.

[5] As by M. Dibelius, *Harvard Theol. Rev..*, 1927, p. 164. He finds evidence of the comparative weakness of Eastern Christianity in the lack of Aramaic literature and the use of translated Greek gospels.

be that it moved west because Rome, the capital of the Empire, lay there, and the statesmanlike mind of St. Paul early recognized its importance. His turning to the West may also have been influenced by the desire to get away from the systematic opposition of the Judaizers.

The spread of the Gospel to the West and the growth of Hellenistic influences had already robbed Jerusalem of some of its importance when the catastrophe of A.D. 70 came upon it. Strangely enough, its fall, which seems to us, as we look back, an event of major significance, passed almost unnoticed by the Church of the day. There are a few obscure references in the synoptic gospels, and that is all. Yet it involved the shifting of the headquarters of Christendom from the Mother Church in Palestine towards the West. Ephesus and the district round it seems to have become the new centre, for thither were attracted a group of apostolic figures and others who had known the Lord.

THE CHURCH IN ROME

History is almost completely silent as to the origins of the Roman Church and we are left to surmise and the sifting of the numerous legends which imagination or policy has fabricated to fill the gap. There is no evidence that it was of apostolic foundation in the narrow sense;[1] though Andronicus and Junius, "noted apostles", may have been among its original members; they had, it will be recalled, been Christians longer than St. Paul himself (Rom. 16 : 7). It was certainly not Petrine; though an appeal to Rom. 15 : 20 and St. Paul's principle not to build upon another man's foundation can hardly be taken as evidence that no other apostle had visited Rome before he wrote, or that Christianity had never been "officially or systematically preached there".[2] His delay in going to Rome, and his assurance that he was paying only a passing visit, might indeed suggest the very opposite.

St. Peter is not the sole candidate put forward by tradition as the founder of the Roman Church; there were those in the third century who regarded Barnabas as having filled that office.[3] Certainly Barnabas, whose presence in Rome is also referred to in the apocryphal *Acts of Peter*, IV,[4] seems to have played a

[1] Ambrosiaster in the fourth century denied that any apostle visited the Gentiles in Rome: see Sanday and Headlam, *Romans*, p. xxv.
[2] As is done by Sanday and Headlam, *op. cit.*, p. 409.
[3] See the *Clementine Recognitions*, I, 6 f., *Homilies*, I, 9, where he is the agent of Clement's conversion and the means of his introduction to Peter. Harnack thought that there might be some truth behind the tradition (*Theo. Lit. Zeit.*, 1876, p. 488), since it could hardly have been invented by those who held St. Peter to have been the founder.
[4] *Apoc. N.T.*, p. 307. Barnabas is there represented in a quite subordinate capacity being "sent" to Macedonia.

much bigger part in the West than the silence of the last chapters of Acts might suggest. The fact that St. Paul picked him out for special mention in 1 Cor. 9 : 6, long after their partnership had been dissolved, makes it highly probable that to the Corinthians at least he was well known.[1]

Before St. Paul's arrival in Rome the Church there can have had but little aggressive force, otherwise it would have been better known to the local Jewish community (Acts 28 : 22). At this time it may have consisted solely of a number of small, unorganized groups who perhaps had brought Christianity to the city independently of one another.[2] This might explain the absence of any mention of the "Church" in Rom. 1 : 6 f., and give additional meaning to the statement of Irenaeus (III, i, 1) that St. Peter and St. Paul not only founded the Church, but also organized it (III, iii, 2).

The earliest reference to the possible presence of Christianity is the well-known statement of Suetonius that Claudius expelled Jews from Rome in 51 owing to disputes which arose over Chrestus (*impulsore Chresto*).[3] Among them were Aquila and Priscilla (Acts 18 : 2). It is quite probable that the Messiahship of Jesus was at the root of the quarrels.

Christians in Rome, as elsewhere in the early days, would be drawn from the lowest ranks of society, and slaves and freedmen would be found among them. This assumption is supported by the names in the list in Rom. 16.[4] Their common medium would be Greek. Papias's statement that St. Peter, in addressing the Romans, had to use Mark as an interpreter (Euseb., III, xxxix, 15) hardly contradicts this, for it by no means infers that the translation was into Latin. St. Peter may not have known enough Greek to address a Roman audience, for his epistle (even if genuine) may owe much, so far as actual wording is concerned, to Sylvanus. That the Roman Church was Greek-speaking and remained so until late in the second century cannot be doubted.

Since Jews were exceedingly numerous in Rome—they not

---

[1] In the *Passion of Paul* (ed. Lipsius, pp. 108 and 109) the Latin substitutes Barnabas for Barsabas of Acts 1 : 23.

[2] For the suggestion that the Roman Church was founded from Antioch (Lietzmann, *Beginnings of the Christian Church*, p. 265 ff.) there is no evidence for or against.

[3] XXV, 4. Cassius Dio states that the decree was not strictly enforced though the synagogues were closed and Jewish associations dissolved. The spelling *Chresto* presents no difficulty, for it is found in at least one important New Testament MS. and it was not unusual for Christians to be called Chrestiani by their enemies. The spelling was also used by Christians themselves: cf. two inscriptions from the Via Latina in Marucchi, p. 659, and a Marcionite inscription at Deir-Ali of 318: see Le Bas and Waddington, *Inscr. grecques et latines*, III, p. 582 f.

[4] For its genuineness see Sanday and Headlam, *op. cit.*, pp. xciii–xcv, and Lightfoot, *Philippians*, p. 169 ff.

only lived in the region beyond the Tiber, but, as their cemeteries witness, had settlements elsewhere [1]—it is natural to suppose that among them the Gospel would first make its way. But both Jews and Gentiles were included in the earliest converts.

At about the very time that St. Paul was writing his epistle, if the usual date, the spring of 58, is accepted, an event occurred in Rome which has suggested to some scholars that the Gospel was beginning already to penetrate into higher circles. Pomponia Graecina, the wife of Aulus Plautius, was tried by a domestic court on the charge of indulging in foreign superstitions.[2] It is probable, on the whole, but by no means certain, that she was a Christian, for had she been a proselyte to Judaism, as some suppose, no such prosecution would have been likely, for Judaism was a *religio licita* (for Jews at least) and such conversions were comparatively numerous at this time,[3] and included Poppaea Sabina, the mistress, and later the wife, of Nero. Pomponia has been identified with Lucina, the founder of the cemetery which bears her name.[4] The lack of definite evidence, however, makes this a mere conjecture. It is true that fragments containing the name (e.g., Pomponius Graecinus) have been discovered in catacombs of later date, but it is by no means certain that they are Christian, or even that they belong to the sites where they were found.[5]

It has often been pointed out, and very naturally since the parallel is so obvious, that just as pagan Rome had, by tradition, two founders, so also had Christian Rome. In each case one of the supposed founders, in the course of history, came to be subordinate to the other; for Remus meant little to Republican and Imperial Rome, and the Apostle of the Gentiles, after the lapse of some centuries, gradually lost importance before the greater prestige of St. Peter. But from the first this had not been so.[6] In the catacombs their names are frequently conjoined, and in the canon of the Roman Mass, which may be as early as the close of the third century, the name of St. Paul has been included, immediately after that of St. Peter, in the list of apostles. The present custom of papal bulls bearing the heads of the two apostles is not early. Victor II (1054–57) placed the head of

---

[1] In Juvenal's day the settlement outside the Porta Capena seems to have been the most considerable and important.

[2] Tacitus., *Ann.*, XIII, 32. She was acquitted, but spent the rest of her days in "constant melancholy". G. F. Moore, *Judaism*, I, p. 350 ff., thinks that the tendency to see Judaism in accusations of "atheism" has been exaggerated.

[3] See Mommsen, *Provinces*, II, p. 166 f.

[4] De Rossi, *Roma Sottenan.*, I, p. 319; II, p. 282.

[5] Styger, p. 31 f. There is nothing to show how the name Lucina became attached to the catacomb (p. 21).

[6] C. H. Turner says, "never before the third century is the name of the one mentioned without . . . the other" (*Cath. and Apost.*, p. 219).

Peter alone on his bulls; Paul was added by Paschal II (1099–1118). There seems to have been an especial interest at the beginning of the twelfth century in the dual conjunction, for on the tomb of Pierleone (d. 1128) in the cloisters of San Paolo fuori le Mura at Rome both are invoked.[1]

There was naturally a tendency, especially in earlier times, to treat both apostles alike and to narrate of each similar stories and legends.[2] An interesting example is the preservation of the chains in which they were bound. Those of St. Peter are now well-known objects of interest in the church of San Pietro in Vincoli; legend has it that they were presented by Leo I to Eudoxia, the wife of Valentinian III, who in 442 had the church built to receive them. It is, however, doubtful whether they were known before the end of the sixth century when Gregory I mentions them (*Epist.*, V). The chains of St. Paul are referred to as being in Rome by Chrysostom in *Hom. VIII on Epist. ad Ephes.*, 2.

The conjunction of the two names, especially in the dedication of churches, is found in all parts of the West. There are a number of examples from Africa. A chapel in a cemetery at Castellum Tingitanum (Orléansville) in Algeria, according to a surviving inscription, once contained relics with a *Memoria apostolorum* (*Pet*)*ri et Pauli*. The date was about A.D. 400. A similar memorial evidently found a place in the sanctuary at Ain Ghorab which dates from about fifty years later. Mention may also be made of an inscription on a block of stone at Megroun: MEMORIA DOMNI PETRI ET PAULI.[3] In the Anglo-Saxon Church, to refer to a period still later than that which we are considering, there was widespread reverence for the two apostles and many churches have a double dedication to them, including the original dedication of St. Augustine's, Canterbury. It is also worth noting that St. Aldhelm in his poem *On Altars dedicated to the B.V.M. and the Twelve Apostles* includes St. Paul whom he places immediately after St. Peter. Finally, the first great church of Frankish Christendom which was founded by Clovis had the same twofold dedication.

The usual order puts St. Peter first, as in the canon of the Mass; but this is by no means universally observed; even in the catacombs quite a number of early inscriptions give the precedence to St. Paul. In those of St. Sebastian, for example, there

[1] In 1647 Innocent X thought it necessary to condemn the statement of Antoine Arnauld in *De la fréquente communion* that St. Peter had shared the oversight of the early Roman Church with St. Paul: see Mirbt, *Quellen zur Gesch. des Papsttums*, No. 528.

[2] Readers of the Old Testament will recall that the writer of the book of Kings followed a similar course in regard to the two prophets Elijah and Elisha.

[3] *C.I.L.*, VIII, 9714–9724, 10707–10709, and 10693.

are the well-known *graffiti*, perhaps the work of pilgrims and therefore not of "official" standing, two of which run as follows: PAVLE ED PETRE PETITE PRO VICTORE and PAVLE PETRE PETITE PRO ERATE. The same group includes two others with a slightly different wording: PAVLE PETRE IN MENTE HABETE SOZOMENVM and AT PAVLO ET PET(RO) REFRI(GERAVI).[1] To these may be added a sixth-century inscription from Aioun Berrich: HIC MEMORI(A)E SANCTORV(M) PAVLI, PETRI, DONATI, MIGGINIS, BARCIS.[2]

In the surviving literature there are not a few passages in which the greater prominence is given to St. Paul. Polycarp, for example, speaks of St. Paul and the rest of the apostles (*Ad Phil.*, IX, 1); whilst Dionysius of Alexandria records that Paul, and Peter too, are popular Christian names.[3] In the Apocryphal Literature several passages of considerable interest occur. In the *Apocalypse of Paul*, a fourth-century work which had a great vogue in the West, Noah greets him as "Paul, the best beloved of God", and Christ Himself pays him greater attention than Peter or John.[4] In Pseudo-Melito *Assumption of the Virgin* there is evidently an attempt to set St. Paul in his proper place, for when St. Peter urges him to offer up prayer he refuses because the latter stands before all the other apostles (V).[5]

The fact that in certain objects and inscriptions St. Paul's head is placed to the right whilst that of St. Peter is found on the left probably means very little. An example of this arrangement is the famous medallion found in the Catacomb of Domitilla. There is also an inscription from Neuss, near Cologne.[6] It may be noted that on the papal bulls St. Peter is placed to the left. This caused some embarrassment to medieval historians.[7]

It is a common feature in legends that the further they get from the event the more minute are the details. So in regard to St. Peter in Rome. In spite of the fact that there is no evidence that Philo ever visited the city after the embassy of A.D. 40, it has been claimed that St. Peter had an encounter with him there in the days of Claudius (Euseb., II, xvii, 1). It was not until after the lapse of two centuries that the idea that St. Peter was bishop of Rome began to be circulated;[8] an episcopate of twenty-five years is first found in Hippolytus who evidently

---

[1] See Marucchi, p. 261 f., and Styger, p. 341 ff. [2] *C.I.L.*, VIII, 18656.
[3] See Euseb., VII, xxv, 14. Both names are found among great Roman families, Paul in the Aemilian gens and Peter in the Flavian, which would give them popularity apart from the apostles.
[4] *Apoc. N.T.*, p. 553 and p. 554 f. [5] *op. cit.*, p. 212.
[6] Le Blant, *Nouveau Recueil des Inscripts.*, p. 103.
[7] Matthew Paris, *Hist. Maj.*, III, p. 416 (Rolls Series).
[8] According to Lightfoot I, ii, p. 501 f. there is no mention of St. Peter as Bishop of Rome by any writer of the first two centuries or more. The legend that he was the founder of the Church in Rome and its first bishop is, as Haller has said (*Papsttum*, p. 15), *Dichtung ohne Wahrheit*.

supposed that he immediately went to Rome after his sudden departure from Jerusalem (Acts 12 : 17). The twenty-five years are dated by Eusebius in his *Chronicle* from 42 to 67, but in the Liberian Catalogue, which is probably based on Hippolytus, the dates are given as 30 to 55.

Eusebius tells us that St. Peter came first to Rome in the days of Claudius (41–54) in order to oppose Simon Magus (II, xiv, 6). Here again we have the embellishment of a legend, for whilst Justin Martyr (I *Apol.*, XXVI and LVI) and Irenaeus (I, xxiii, 1) both mention the arrival of Simon in Rome, they apparently know nothing of his being followed there by St. Peter. Hippolytus (VI, 20) speaks of Simon's coming to Rome and withstanding the apostles, mentioning Peter by name, but from his account one would gather that St. Peter was there before Simon arrived. By the later half of the fourth century the tradition has become quite definite. According to Jerome (*De Vir. Ill.*, I, 1) St. Peter came to Rome in the second year of Claudius to oppose Simon, and remained there as bishop until the last year of Nero. He also states that St. Peter had, before this, been Bishop of Antioch and had preached to the Dispersion (with a reference to the peoples addressed in 1 Peter 1 : 1). As he had previously been to Corinth, of which tradition says he was joint founder with St. Paul,[1] and where a Cephas party existed (1 Cor. 1 : 12), there are great difficulties in fitting in an episcopate at Antioch which is said to have lasted seven years, not to mention a tour in Asia Minor, before the year 42. Fortunately these difficulties do not concern us directly; but they show the doubtful value of the whole legend.

St. Peter is connected with Antioch in various passages in Acts and also in the incident narrated in Gal. 2 : 11 ff. In this passage, as in 1 Cor. 1 : 12, 9 : 5, he is called Cephas. The apparent opposition between St. Peter and St. Paul, and above all the rebuke administered by the latter, led Christian writers, or some of them, to the conclusion that the Cephas here mentioned was not St. Peter at all, but that there was another disciple or even apostle of that name. Clement of Alexandria, who really ought to have known better, states that he was one of the Seventy (Euseb., I, xii, 2). In the *Epistola Apostolorum*, written probably in Asia Minor in the latter half of the second century, a list of the twelve apostles is given (II) in which Peter appears after John and Thomas and the list ends with Cephas.[2] So, too, in the *Apostolic Church Order* Peter follows John and Matthew, whilst Cephas comes towards the end (XXI).

When St. Peter left Jerusalem it might have been thought that as he was the apostle of the circumcision he would have

---

[1] Dionysius of Corinth in Euseb., II, xxv, 8. [2] *Apoc. N.T.*, p. 486.

travelled east where the main centres of Judaism were consolidating, and some have taken the Babylon of 1 Pet. 5 : 13 to be the Babylon, not of apocalypse which was a synonym for Rome,[1] but the actual city on the Euphrates.[2]

The absence of any reference to St. Peter in Romans and in the Captivity epistles is strong evidence that he was not in Rome during the period covered by them. Even if the Pastoral epistles are not by St. Paul, the statement in 2 Tim. 4 : 16, that no man stood by him in his trial, could hardly have been made had any tradition been current that St. Peter was then in Rome. It may be, of course, that he had already been martyred.

Such evidence as we possess leads to the conclusion that St. Peter was in Rome for but a short time before his death.[3] That this actually occurred in Rome seems highly probable in view of the early tradition to that effect.[4] The same may be said of St. Paul. The fact that their respective tombs are placed in heathen surroundings is a sign of early date, for later inventors would surely have placed them in the catacombs.

The event which first brought Christianity to the notice of the Roman world was the persecution under Nero. Different views as to the extent, causes, and effect of this outbreak have been held by different scholars, and in the absence of any fresh discoveries they are likely to persist. Each must interpret the evidence for himself in view of the general probabilities of the situation and in the light of subsequent developments.

Until Nero shed so lurid a light upon the new sect the few who had any knowledge of the Christians looked upon them no doubt as unorthodox Jews, for as Tertullian once expressed it (*Apol.*, XXI), the Church had grown up under the shadow of the Synagogue. The occasion was the great fire which destroyed half Rome in July A.D. 64. Nero at the time was at Antium, but hurried back to watch the conflagration in which, incidentally, his own palace and many works of art were lost. It is probable that the fire was the result of an accident; but suspicion gradually began to focus upon the emperor. This was both significant and tragic; for Nero had begun his reign, like Henry VIII of

[1] Rev. 16 : 19, etc. Babylon probably refers to Rome in *Sib. Orac.*, V, 143 of about this date. The *Oxford Apoc.*, II, p. 400, points out that in the *Avesta* Babylon is the seat of Azhidaka.

[2] Some recent scholars place this epistle very late, and for them the identity of "Babylon" throws no light on the question, save that it might reproduce an early tradition.

[3] There are not wanting definite statements to this effect. cf. Euseb. III, i, 2, Lactantius, *De Mort.*, I, 2, and Macarius Magnes, *Apocrit.*, III, 22, which states that "Peter, after shepherding the lambs for a few months, was crucified", though perhaps not in Rome.

[4] I have taken no notice of the various sites in Rome connected with the ministry of St. Peter which are accepted by many archaeologists. Once a tradition becomes current, sites are notoriously easy to discover.

England, under auspicious omens and had on his accession been hailed as "the hope and expectation of the world".[1] During the first five years of his rule government had been so good as to become proverbial; but in the terror of his later years the fears of men were such that death itself seemed the only safe haven.[2] "Damned to everlasting fame", no rumour was too gross for acceptation and he became a kind of symbol of tyranny at its feeblest and most cruel.

The emperor had to find a scapegoat, and the choice, possibly at the instance of the Jews, who since their chief settlement in the Transtiber region had escaped damage, may have felt that they were cast for the part, fell upon the Christians. So barbarous, however, was the treatment to which they were subjected, that the sympathies of the people began to be aroused; a regrettable weakness in the eyes of Tacitus, who thought that even if they had had no share in the fire, yet as enemies of the human race they merited punishment.[3] He tells us that the number who perished was large,[4] but makes no mention of any measures against them except for their supposed arson. The Christians may, indeed, have drawn attention to themselves by the proclamation of their belief that the world would be destroyed by fire.

The connexion of the persecution with the fire has recently been questioned in view of the possibly quite considerable interval between the two events. This interval was certainly remarkable, if we count St. Paul and St. Peter among the victims, for according to Eusebius they did not suffer until 67, which is some three years after the fire. This date may be an artificial one intended to make up the twenty-five years which St. Peter is supposed to have spent as bishop after his arrival in Rome in 42. There is what appears to be a reference to his death in the *Ascension of Isaiah* 4: 21 f., where it is "foretold" that "A lawless king, the slayer of his mother . . . will persecute the plant which the twelve apostles of the Beloved have planted. Of the twelve one will be delivered into his hands."[5] Legend has it that the victims included two Germans, Nereus and Achilles;[6] if this tradition is correct we have in them the proto-martyrs of the

---

[1] See Grenfell and Hunt, *Oxyrhynchus Papyri*, VII, 1021.

[2] Seneca, *Ad Polyb.*, IX: *nullus portus nisi mortis.*

[3] Suetonius, *Nero*, XVI, also refers to the Christians in this connexion in no favourable terms, calling them a race of men of a new and evil superstition (*maleficiae*).

[4] *Ann.*, XV, 44, Merrill, *Essays in Early Christ. Hist.*, p. 100 ff., considers that the numbers have been exaggerated.

[5] There are several references to Nero in the *Sibylline Oracles*. These are by no means confined to his supposed reappearance as *Nero redivivus* (V, 33-35, 363-377), but to the actual living man (IV, 119-122; V, 28-32, 137-152).

[6] On their legend see J. H. Crean in *J.T.S.*, XXXVI, pp. 254-265.

Teutonic race and the earliest Christians named as having suffered in Rome. There are references to the persecution in *The Acts of Paul*, where it is stated that so many Christians were slain that the strength of Rome itself was being destroyed;[1] a statement which does not suggest any real knowledge of actual events.

The uncertainties surrounding the Neronian persecution, as to its extent and the number of the victims, and also as to the actual crime supposed to have been committed by them, leave much room for speculation; but one thing it would be interesting to know—the effect it had on the composition and balance of the Church in Rome. How many of its members actually suffered and from what class were they drawn; in particular did it make any difference to the relative proportions of Jews and Gentiles? It is by no means improbable that the victims would be Gentiles for the most part, for the Jews, on occasion, gave shelter to their fellow-countrymen, even if they were Christians.

During the two closing decades of the first century Christianity appears to have made some progress among the members of the Roman aristocracy. If this is so it may have been one of the motives which prompted St. Luke to write his gospel. Its literary style would make it much more acceptable than the cruder composition of St. Mark. The Acts, which makes favourable mention of Roman officials and represents Christianity as something more than a mere Jewish sect, was equally well fitted for circulation among educated Romans. In the household of Caesar also, with its teeming multitudes of servants and others, there seems to have been considerable permeation. Before the century actually ended, however, the Church in Rome, or some section of it, had to face a further assault.

The persecution under Nero had been sufficient to attract public notice, and its spectacular nature, even if we give up, as probably we ought, the Danaids and Dircae of I *Clement*, VI, 2, was very evident. By comparison the trouble under Domitian looks like a mean exhibition of personal spite. For that emperor, not content with making a mountain out of a molehill, came to regard the mountain as possessed of all the dangerous properties of a volcano. By later writers, both pagan and Christian, Domitian was ranked as a second Nero,[2] and it is by a strange coincidence that the two earliest persecutors of the Church have both received unduly harsh treatment in the surviving literature. The reign of Domitian, like that of Nero, began well, and he was certainly a very capable administrator; but towards its

---

[1] *Apoc. N.T.*, p. 294 f.
[2] Tertullian speaks of *portio Neronis de crudelitate* (*Apol.*, V); while Juvenal, *Satires*, IV, 38, writes *calvo serviret Roma Neroni*.

close a number of prominent Romans, including some of his own kinsmen, were put to death on what appear to be quite groundless charges. Tacitus even speaks of a massacre of consulars (*Agric.*, XLV). One of his victims, Flavius Clemens, was charged with atheism and the adoption of Jewish customs, a combination which makes it more than probable that he was in reality a Christian. His wife, Domitilla, was banished to the island of Pandateria, according to Cassius Dio (LXVII, 14).[1] Another victim was Acilius Glabrio. He, too, may have been a Christian, for members of this family at a later date were buried in the catacomb of Priscilla, though, of course, this is no proof that their kinsman at the end of the first century was already a member of the Church. Domitian's interest in the worship of the Emperor may have made provincial governors more strict in their enforcement of the cult and so have made matters difficult for the Christians.

[1] It is often said that there were three ladies who bore the name of Flavia Domitilla in this period: (*a*) the wife of Titus Flavius Clemens, mentioned above; (*b*) her mother who appears in an inscription (*C.I.L.*, VI, 948); (*c*) a niece of Titus Flavius Clemens (so Euseb., III, xviii, 4) who was banished to the island of Pontia, a circumstance which was sufficiently well known for Paula, the disciple of Jerome, to pay it a visit in the fourth century (*Epist.*, CVIII). It is, however, possible, as Lightfoot has suggested (I, i, p. 49), that there has been a confusion between the wife and the niece, for the statement in the *Chronicle* of Eusebius (as preserved by Jerome, *Ad Olymp.*, 218) runs as follows: *Scribit Brutius plurimos christianorum sub Domitiano fecisse martyrium, inter quos et Flaviam Domitillam, Flavii Clementis ex sorore neptem, quia se christianam esse testata sit.* The insertion of *uxorem* after *Clementis* would eliminate the third Flavia, and *sorore* would then refer to the sister of Domitian himself. The confusion over the name of the island of exile is not without parallels, and is not enough to exclude the possibility of identification. But the suggestion is somewhat hazardous because Euseb., III, xviii, 4 calls Flavia Domitilla a daughter of the sister of Flavius Clemens, and the Armenian Version (ed. Schöne, II, p. 160) and the Syrian Epitome (ed. Schöne, p. 214) both support the reading.

CHAPTER II

THE CHURCH OF ROME

In considering the expansion of Western Christendom there is one Church, and one Church only, which in view of its central position and later importance, forms the natural starting-point. The Church of Rome was unique among Western Churches in being established in the apostolic age, and already by the beginning of the second century it was exhibiting those characteristics and virtues which made it of such outstanding significance for future ages. It was, indeed, a kind of microcosm of the West, for in it all the various types of thought and practice which affected other Churches found a home. This was doubtless a consequence of Rome's cosmopolitanism, for to it there flocked representatives of every province and city of the Empire, to influence it and in turn to be influenced by it.[1] The study of its development in our period can best be conducted by dealing first with its internal condition and then going on to its relations with other Churches, giving especial attention to the steps by which it came to exercise some kind of primacy among them.

(A) INTERNAL CONDITION

For an estimate of the state of the Roman Church at the close of the first century and in the early years of the second we are fortunate to possess two documents of considerable length, one of which is characterized by a remarkable candour; the Epistle of the Church of Rome to the Church of Corinth, generally known a I *Clement*, from the name of its writer, and *The Shepherd* of Hermas. The literary problems connected with these documents do not now concern us, they will receive attention in Part III, Chapter I; but a word must be said, in anticipation, as to their dates, a matter of obvious importance in dealing with the condition of the Roman Church. I *Clement* is almost universally assigned to the closing years of the first century, and even to the actual year A.D. 96; *The Shepherd* to a generation or so later. Some years ago, however, Edmundson in his Bampton Lectures, *The Church of Rome in the First Century*, argued strongly in favour of earlier dates. I *Clement* he would assign to A.D. 70 and *The Shepherd* to c. 90. His suggestions have not met with much

[1] See, further, G. La Piana, "Foreign Groups in Rome", in *Harvard Theol. Rev.*, 1927, pp. 183–403, a long and valuable study.

acceptance, but they are sufficiently probable to require caution in the use of the evidence of these writings which admittedly reveal a rather primitive state of affairs, especially in the matter of organization, when compared with the Churches of the East.

Both writers, whatever their exact dates, reveal in the Roman Church characteristics which would distinguish it in years to come. In the one we have an emphasis on the need for unity and good order, a recognition of the value of due subordination—the use of the title Master (δεσπότης) for God is surely not without significance. In the other, less favourable characteristics are already seen in operation, and for its writer penitence is the outstanding need. The low standard of the Church as a whole is reflected in the state of the clergy, who as a body exhibit disquieting signs of the decay of spiritual power and leadership. They are described as arrogant, self-seeking, and worldly; some are even denounced as dishonest.[1] The influx of wealthy and influential converts, of which Ignatius supplies evidence (*Rom.*, I), had had its drawbacks, and Hermas condemns certain members who hold apart from the humbler sort, of which he himself was one. Social distinctions are already erecting barriers within the fold of Christ (*Vis.*, III, ix; *Sim.*, IX, xx, xxvi).

At this epoch, and indeed until well on in the second century, there are reasons for supposing that the Church in Rome did not form a single entity. We have already seen that there were in Rome numerous groups of resident aliens. There may have been similar groups among the Christians. For instance, Christians of Jewish origin may have held apart from the rest; whilst there is good evidence for such a group of Asiatic Christians who preserved their own customs and traditions. There is also evidence for Christians among the African colony which became strong towards the end of the second century.[2] Though these immigrants were mainly of Roman blood there may have been an intermixture of Punic among them. At any rate, they were not favourably regarded by the inhabitants of Rome; and they had their own quarters in the crowded region between the Coelian and Aventine hills. Allowance must also be made for a number of congregations of semi-heretical tinge, which, later on, as the Church made more stringent its dogmatic system, would definitely be excluded as unorthodox. There were also, as we know,

[1] W. J. Wilson, *Harvard Theol. Rev.*, 1927, p. 29, has suggested that Hermas in his allusion to ecclesiastical strife (*Vis.*, III, ix) was thinking of the state of the Church in Corinth rather than that of Rome. If he was a contemporary of Clement he may have been impressed by a reading of I *Clement* to the congregation. This suggestion, though ingenious, is far-fetched and very improbable.

[2] This is suggested by the presence in the cemetery of St. Commodilla of burial customs found elsewhere only in the cemeteries of North Africa and of African names: see Marucchi, p. 126.

many heretical teachers anxious to gain influence and to "capture" the Church for their views. Thus there was real danger of disintegration and the Church might well have lapsed into a loose federation of differing schools of thought or sects. But perhaps the most interesting point to be observed is the absence of any trace of what can be described as Latin Christianity in the narrow sense from the city which was to be its most famous centre.

The reason for this lack is fairly obvious. The converts came, for the most part, from Orientals who had come to Rome, some already as Christians, the rest to be converted after their arrival. It was to such that the Gospel would make its appeal. There were very few Romans in the Church of Rome. When later on converts from noble families began to enter the Church, these, from their education, would be sufficiently familiar with the Greek language to adapt themselves to their surroundings. The presence of Latin names among the Christians is, as we have already observed, no evidence of Roman birth or even of Latin speech.

Thus until the end of the second century the Roman Church was predominantly Greek-speaking and mainly Oriental in its composition. The names of the bishops are nearly all Greek; Pius is an exception, and possibly Sixtus. Even Clement, with his Roman name, used Greek in his epistle, and Greek remained the medium of all the writers of the period who are known to us. The inscriptions on the papal tombs continue, save in the case of Cornelius, to be in Greek until nearly the end of the third century, whilst the use of Greek in the liturgy continued even longer.[1] When Latin came into use it made but slow progress, for the Roman clerics who corresponded with Cyprian had no really competent knowledge of it. There may, indeed, have been a bilingual period. This is strongly suggested by a study of the inscriptions in the catacombs, some of which hover between the two languages; it is possible to find a number which write Greek in Latin characters, and conversely, some which use Greek characters for Latin words.[2]

Of the early rulers of the Church we know very little. There are in existence various lists which profess to give their names and dates, but they cannot be relied upon, neither are they entirely consistent. Genuine traditions may indeed be preserved in them but they have been so overlaid with legendary matter

[1] See Adrian Fortesque, *The Mass*, p. 126. *Kyrie eleison*, which might readily be taken as evidence of the early use of Greek, was not actually introduced until the sixth century. The Council of Vaison in 529 looked upon its use in Rome and Milan as a novelty.

[2] See, for examples, Marucchi, pp. 421, 452, 484, and 490; Syxtus, II, p. 8 f.; Diehl, No. 4463 ff.

that any attempt to construct a reliable record seems a hopeless task.[1]

Thus no dependable traces remain of the origin of episcopacy in Rome. When Hermas wrote he quite evidently looked upon the Church as ruled by presbyters,[2] and Ignatius in addressing the Church makes no mention of any bishop. Clement does not seem to have had any definite status and was apparently a kind of secretary commissioned to write in the name of the Church. He is, in any case, a very baffling figure. In most lists he is placed third after Peter and Paul, being preceded by Linus and Anencletus[3] or Cletus. In the Clementine Romances he is said to have followed St. Peter, a position which is also assigned to him by Tertullian (*De Praes.*, XXXII). In the Liberian List he comes second, as in Augustine (*Epist.*, LIII). Many explanations have been attempted to account for the discrepancy. It was, for example, suggested by Rufinus that Linus and Cletus were suffragans of St. Peter and not full bishops. A further elaboration makes Linus an Italian from Tuscany who was thus enabled to act as bishop when St. Peter was exiled under Claudius. Epiphanius tells us that Clement, after being consecrated by St. Peter, retired in favour of Linus and Cletus, but resumed his office when they were dead (*Haer.*, XXVII, 6). A third suggestion makes them bishops of two communities, a Jewish founded by St. Peter and a Gentile founded by St. Paul. Clement, according to this theory, united the two when he became bishop. Possibly this suggestion is on the right lines, for there may well have been a number of bishops or presbyter-bishops ruling different groups in the early days of the Church in Rome. Later when a single bishop became the universal custom and when even the memory of anything different had been forgotten their names would be arranged in a succession.

Other early bishops call for little comment. Uncertainty as to their order and as to the length of their episcopates continues. The following brief notices give most of what is known of them. Sixtus is mentioned by Irenaeus (in Euseb., V, xxiv, 14) as

[1] The available evidence has been collected and discussed by Lightfoot (I, i, 201 ff.). The latest discussion will be found in Jalland, *The Church and the Papacy*, p. 83 ff. It cannot be said that it gets us any further.

[2] *Vis.*, II, iv. 3: cf. II, ii, 6 and III, ix, 7. It is interesting to notice that Epiphanius (*Haer.*, XLII, 1) says that Marcion was condemned by the Roman presbyters.

[3] Anencletus is the form found in Irenaeus and Greek writers. No Latin writer has this form before Augustine, though Optatus and others have Anacletus. The form used by the Latins is Cletus. Both names got into the Liberian List as if they represented different persons, and from that into the *Liber Pontificalis* and so into the official tradition of the Roman Church. The papal medallions in St. Paolo fuori le Mura in Rome (the early ones on the south wall escaped the fire of 1823) give the order after St. Peter, as Linus, Cletus, Clement, Anacletus. See, further, Lightfoot as referred to in the previous note.

keeping Easter after the Western reckoning, but not seeking to impose his views on others. Telesphorus suffered as a martyr and is the only early Bishop of Rome to be given the title by Irenaeus (III, iii, 3). Hyginus was bishop when Valentinus and Cerdo visited Rome (Iren., III, iii, 3).[1] With Pius, the office, if not the man, emerges into daylight. The Muratorian Fragment[2] which calls him the brother of Hermas states that he held "the see of the Church of Rome", a somewhat peculiar description. Anicetus, who may have come from Emesa in Syria, had a reign which saw much activity, including visits from Hegesippus,[3] Marcion, and Polycarp. The visit of the latter may have been connected with differences over the keeping of Easter, a controversy which came to a head in the reign of Victor. As neither could persuade the other, they wisely agreed to differ and Anicetus was content to allow the Asiatic Christians in Rome to keep their own customs, and, to show that he still retained communion with them, made a point of sending the Eucharist to them;[4] a custom which was continued by his successors. Soter received a letter from Dionysius of Corinth (Euseb., IV, xxiii, 9). Eleutherus who had been his "archdeacon", the first to be recorded,[5] is mentioned by Irenaeus and Tertullian. The latter in *De Praes.*, XXX, refers to the Church of Rome not as *ecclesia Romana*, but *Romanensis* (that is *in*, not *of*, Rome). .

If the reign of Septimius Severus may be said to have marked a turning-point in the fortunes of the Empire, the pontificate of his fellow-countryman and contemporary, Victor, was undoubtedly the beginning of a new era in the Church of Rome, and thereby in the Church as a whole.[6] From this date, moreover, our knowledge of its history becomes more exact and reliable.

We know nothing of Victor before he became bishop. According to Jerome he was an African by birth and a writer of Latin. He was, to judge from his later career, a man of great force of character, impatient of opposition, and determined in carrying out his plans. All this must have been known before his election, and no doubt something of his notions for the future of the Roman Church. The question is, Why was he chosen and why

---

[1] See p. 120, below.   [2] See p. 116, below.

[3] See p. 119 f., below.

[4] Irenaeus (quoted by Euseb., V, xxiv, 14) says that he sent the eucharist to those παροικίαι which observed the Asiatic custom. This would seem naturally to refer to dioceses in Asia Minor. But La Piana thinks that it refers to groups in Rome; a suggestion that was accepted by Streeter, *Primitive Church*, p. 225 f.

[5] Eusebius merely calls him his "deacon" (IV, xxii, 3). For a discussion of "archdeacons" see Part III, Chap. VI.

[6] In what follows I owe much to the brilliant essay of G. La Piana, "The Roman Church at the end of the Second Century", in *Harvard Theol. Rev.*, 1925, pp. 201–277.

was there at this juncture so striking a departure from the old ways? The answer must, I think, be found in a definite change of character in the Christian community. Hitherto it had been recruited mainly from Greeks and Orientals, now it was evidently attracting, in considerable numbers, native-born Romans. In addition the resident groups of aliens must themselves have been feeling the pressure of their environment and giving way to Roman tendencies. There is, also, another factor which may have been decisive in giving a Latin majority among the people, that is the presence of a large body of African Christians. We know that many Africans were arriving in Rome about this period and among them it is reasonable to suppose would be some who had been members of the African Church.

Victor found the Church in Rome split up into a number of groups whose customs were by no means uniform; there were, in addition, heretical teachers with their followers striving to gain influence if not control. With the latter he took a summary line. There could be no communion between Catholics and unorthodox, so in due course the Montanists and Theodotus the Monarchian were alike excommunicated. As to the rest, they must toe the line and submit to discipline, no kind of local anarchy was to be endured. In this task he seems to have been successful and in carrying it out greatly increased the power and prestige of the hierarchy and laid the foundations of that monarchical episcopacy which would be the characteristic of later times.

But Victor undertook another task of even greater significance. Up to this epoch the Roman Church, perhaps because of its own disunity, had made no attempt to interfere in the affairs of other Churches. Now it began, cautiously and not without reverses, the attempt to impose its own traditions upon them. Realism was to control the relations of Rome and the rest of Christendom. This came out especially in the Paschal Controversy which had arisen in the pontificate of Anicetus; but whereas Anicetus had been content to allow the continuance of different traditions Victor felt that the whole question must be raised afresh and settled once and for all.

The exact point in dispute is by no means clear and, in any case, is relatively unimportant. Some scholars think that all that was involved was the question of the date of observing the Pascha, that whilst in certain Churches of Asia this was Nisan 14th, the date of the Jewish Passover, in Rome and elsewhere it was kept on the Sunday immediately following. This would explain the term Quartodecimans applied to the recalcitrants and is perhaps the best explanation. Others think that the question was whether there should be any observance of the Paschal

Feast. They are of the opinion that it had not been observed in Rome, but that from early in the second century the custom had arisen of a yearly celebration of the Resurrection—already commemorated by the weekly observance of Sunday. This commemoration was to be preferred to that on Nisan 14th.

Victor's conduct of the controversy,[1] at least in its early stages, was wise and statesmanlike. He began by obtaining from the Churches of Gaul, Palestine, Egypt, and some in Asia Minor, the approval of the Roman tradition. He then demanded that the rest should conform with it and that the observance of Nisan 14th should be abandoned. Probably at first he made this demand on the Asiatic groups in Rome only, and in this he was only partly successful, for some of them persisted in their observance, and, withdrawing, formed a separate Church under a certain Blastus.[2] They had, it must be confessed, a real grievance, after having been allowed to continue in peace for several generations, for the policy of Anicetus had been continued by his successors. The Churches of Asia were naturally drawn into the dispute, perhaps Victor deliberately attacked them as the source of the whole trouble. But in doing so he went too far. Even those Churches which agreed with the Roman tradition were by no means ready to make its observance a matter on which the Church was to be split. Irenaeus, for example, reproves Victor for trying "to cut off whole Churches of God for observing an ancient custom handed down to them" (in Euseb., V, xxiv, 11). Other Churches were much more homogeneous than that of Rome and doubtless failed to realize how vital the matter was to Victor and his policy of unification. When Victor wished to break off relations with the Churches of Asia he was sternly rebuked by Polycrates of Ephesus. The bishops of Palestine and Egypt likewise refused to be browbeaten.[3]

If, as seems probable, Victor owed his election to the influence of his fellow-countrymen in Rome, it is natural to suppose that African traditions would be introduced into the Roman Church

---

[1] See Euseb., V, xxiii–xxv. Unfortunately his account is confused and uncertain.

[2] Euseb., V, xx, 1, does not give the reason for this schism, but it is to be found in Pseudo-Tertullian, *Adv. Omnes Haer.*, where it is stated that Blastus "wished to introduce Judaism in disguise; saying that Easter ought not to be observed save according to the law of Moses on the fourteenth of the month".

[3] I have followed the usual interpretation of this dispute, but one quite different has been suggested by N. Zernov in *The Church Quarterly Rev.*, 1933, CXVI, p. 28 ff., which is accepted by Jalland, *The Church and the Papacy*, p. 119 ff. This would limit the dispute to a group within the Roman Church and considers that there is no question of other Churches being affected save as to whether the Roman custom is apostolic or not, and no challenge to papal authority. This view is rejected by Lietzmann in *Camb. Anct. Hist.*, XII, p. 532.

and that the process of latinization would be speeded up. The Greek period was now coming to an end and room would more and more be found for the manifestation of the characteristic Roman virtues. It is to be remarked that after Zephyrinus and Callistus there was for a time an almost unbroken succession of popes bearing Latin names and, if the *Liber Pontificalis* is to be trusted, many of them were actually natives of Rome. None the less, there are still traces of Greek influence to be found. Greek characters were often used for Latin inscriptions and even those on the papal tombs up to Eutychian (d. 283) with the exception of Cornelius are in Greek.

Zephyrinus, the next bishop, was a man of humble birth and poor education and during his episcopate he was much under the influence of Callistus who eventually succeeded him. He seems to have been greatly attracted by Monarchian views and in a somewhat confused sort of way seems actually to have adopted them.[1]

With Callistus[2] we come to a man of real flesh and blood, with a practical outlook on life and the ability of a statesman such as would be characteristic of many of his successors in later ages. To rigid and puritanical souls like Tertullian and Hippolytus, his willingness to compromise with the powers of evil, if not actually to ally himself with them, was a perpetual offence. The stories told of him by the latter, although there can be little doubt of their substantial accuracy, have certainly been distorted so as to present his actions in the most unfavourable light. At this period in the life of the Church a double strife was developing, for it concerned both doctrine and practice. In both these fields Callistus was inclined to take a middle line. His policy of clemency towards sinners was adopted in order to keep them within the Church's fold when undue harshness would have driven them out and plunged them deeper into a sinful life. Penitence and a new start was their only hope. So, too, in regard to marriage. Finding that many Christian women were unable to marry men of their own faith and rank he sanctioned alliances with Christians of low birth. Such alliances were not recognized by the State and to Hippolytus seemed but concubinage. But it is quite clear that Callistus intended them to be marriages in the full Christian sense.[3] We have in his regulations an early example, which is full of significance, of the Church making its own laws and differing from the State.

Hippolytus, to whom reference has just been made, is one of

[1] See below, pp. 299.

[2] I prefer the Greek form to Calixtus, the Latin "déformation": cf. Duchesne, *Lib. Pont.*, I, p. 141.

[3] Hippolytus, IX, 12, from which our knowledge is derived, states that they were to consider such persons, even if slaves, as husbands.

the most mysterious figures in the history of the Church, a bishop for whom no see can unhesitatingly be specified. Even Jerome was quite unable to discover it.[1] Among the various suggestions that have been advanced one would make him Bishop of Portus, a suggestion, however, that is almost certainly erroneous.[2] Others see in him a bishop of the Greek congregation in Rome—on this it may be said that there is no evidence that such an office ever existed. Döllinger regarded him as the first anti-pope, a suggestion which was favourably received by Harnack and is fully accepted by Jalland (*op. cit.*, p. 130 f.). When Damasus (366–84) erected a monument to Hippolytus he called him "presbyter". This adds to the confusion; but it might be explained by his admiration for one of outstanding literary abilities, one who, moreover, may have been regarded as having been reconciled to the Roman see in later life. The irregular consecration, for such it would appear to Damasus, was quietly ignored. Hippolytus died as an exile in Sardinia (as did his rival Pontianus) in 235 or 236.[3]

Although Hippolytus, in the words of Lightfoot, "linked together the learning and traditions of the East . . . with the marvellous practical energy of the West" (I, ii, p. 435), no evidence of any actual residence in the East has survived. As the pupil of Irenaeus his knowledge of things Eastern may have been at second hand; but more than this is probable.

Anterus, the next bishop, had a very short reign; it lasted only six weeks, but it was untroubled by schism, for if Hippolytus was an anti-pope he had no immediate successor. Anterus has the distinction of being the first Roman bishop to have an inscription on his tomb.[4] At the time of his death the body of Pontianus, his predecessor, was still in Sardinia. It was brought back by Bishop Fabian, by permission of the Emperor Philip, and placed in the cemetery of Callistus. On it was placed the simple inscription, in Greek, PONTIANTOS EPISK MTR.[5]

All the Roman bishops of the first two centuries, except Clement and Alexander, were buried in the cemetery on the Vatican *juxta corpus beati Petri*, as the *Liber Pontificalis* puts it. The fate of the body of Clement is unknown;[6] but Alexander is said to have been buried on the Via Numentana some miles outside

---

[1] *De Vir. Ill.*, LXI: Hippolytus claimed to be a successor of the apostles and a "high-priest" (I. Proemium).

[2] See H. Delahaye, *Analect. Bolland.*, LI, p. 58 f.

[3] Pontianus died on September 28, 235, having ascended the papal throne on August 22, 230. These are the first authentic dates for any pope.

[4] See Marucchi, p. 193.

[5] See Marucchi, p. 193.

[6] Bones supposed to be those of Clement were deposited in the church of San Clemente in Rome during the reign of Hadrian II (867–72). They had been brought from the Crimea, whither it is said Clement had been exiled.

the city near the scene of his execution. From Zephyrinus until Miltiades (d. 314) the cemetery of Callistus was the usual burying-place. Those who found rest elsewhere were Callistus himself (d. 222) who was buried in the cemetery of Calepodio in the Via Aurelia; whilst Urban (d. 230), Marcellinus (d. 304), and Marcellus (d. 309) were deposited in that of Priscilla. It would be of interest to know why the Vatican was abandoned as the place for the burial of the bishops of Rome, and various suggestions have been made. It may be that the place had become too well known; also it is said that Elagabalus carried out certain alterations which may have interfered with it. A more probable reason seems to be that about this time the Church acquired its own burying-places and it would be natural for the bishops to be buried in them.

Returning to the succession of bishops we come across the legend, which would be repeated concerning later popes, that Fabian was chosen by the descent of a dove (Euseb., VI, xxix, 3). He was martyred on January 20, 251, and his epitaph in Greek can still be seen. The rudeness of the inscription suggests that it was done in haste, the MTR (i.e., martyr) is only slightly cut and was evidently added at a later time. The notable event of his episcopate was the division of Rome into seven regions corresponding to the seven deacons.[1] They bear no relation to the fourteen regions of civil Rome as is sometimes supposed.[2] Since the Christians were mainly concentrated in the outer districts, the allocation of the civil regions in pairs would not have been convenient.[3]

After the death of Fabian it was not found possible to elect a successor for some eighteen months and the see was administered by the Roman clergy in commission. Then the choice fell on Cornelius. Cornelius (251–253) may have been a member of the noble Roman family of that name; on the other hand, he may have been a descendant of one of the numerous slaves liberated by Sulla who would adopt the name Cornelius. The fact that his epitaph is in Latin suggests, however, that he may have had noble Roman blood. He died in exile at Centumcellae and has been accorded the title of martyr. Apart from his relations with Cyprian,[4] Cornelius is mainly remembered for his letter to Fabius of Antioch (preserved in Euseb., VI, xlvi, 11) in which he records the various stipendiaries of the Roman Church in his

[1] This division is recorded in *Lib. Pont.*, I, p. 4, and is almost certainly authentic. The Felician Catalogue text (p. 52), however, says it dates back to Clement.

[2] Mommsen in his edition of the *Liberian Catalogue*, p. 635, takes *Hic regiones divisit diaconibus* in this sense.

[3] See R. Lane Poole, *The Papal Chancery*, pp. 6 ff. and 170 ff.

[4] See below, p. 154.

day. There were forty-six presbyters, seven deacons, seven sub-deacons, forty-two acolytes, fifty-two exorcists, readers, and doorkeepers, and over fifteen hundred widows and other dependants. This catalogue gives some clue to the magnitude and wealth of the Roman Church at this period, though the huge number of widows is hard to accept unless they were drawn from a wide area.

The history of the Papacy in the Middle Ages is full of dual claims to the possession of the throne of St. Peter; incidents which, especially during the Great Schism of the fourteenth and fifteenth centuries, did not a little to undermine its power and prestige. The period with which we are concerned knows nothing of any schism on a large scale; the first real clash did not occur until 366 when Liberius was opposed by an anti-pope, Felix. All the schisms of the early Church, in the West at least, had a personal aspect [1]—the attempt by strong or assertive characters to find an expression for their gifts which was denied them within the Catholic Church. Whether Hippolytus was an anti-pope or not, he was certainly of an aggressive character and bears not a few similarities to Novatian; both were men of learning, both were rigid in their views and conduct, and both made a strong appeal to the Scriptures. The effect of Hippolytus's disagreement with the bishops of Rome, whether there was open schism or not, was but temporary and had apparently no repercussions outside the city. But his example may have encouraged the followers of Novatian, and these may well have included some who had formerly been in sympathy with Hippolytus. Novatian [2] was, indeed, so important, both in himself and as the leader of a schismatic movement, that his career demands treatment in some detail.

Novatian was a Roman by birth and a convert, having been baptized during a severe illness. Before this he seems to have been a Stoic; such is the inference from Cyprian's *alia est . . . Stoicorum ratio* (*Epist.*, LV). Later he was ordained as a presbyter and, according to the accusations of his rival Cornelius, began to desire to be a bishop (Euseb., VI, xliii, 5). Novatian was certainly outstanding as a scholar and the semi-illiterate clergy of Rome must have regarded him with mixed feelings. In addition to the writings ascribed to him, the well-known *De Trinitate* and *De Cibis Judaeis*, he was probably the author of a number of treatises once thought to have been by Cyprian.[3]

[1] The schism of Blastus in the time of Victor may have been an exception, but it was a very small and brief affair.
[2] By Eusebius and other Greek writers he is called Novatus, probably through confusion with the African of that name who took a leading part in the beginning of the schism.
[3] So Harnack, *Chronologie*, II, p. 400 ff.

In addition to being learned he was an eloquent speaker and a man of unblemished character; but like so many men of high character he seems to have been lacking in sympathy towards weaker brethren and took up a very rigorous attitude on the treatment of those who had fallen away during persecution.

The schism arose soon after the election of Cornelius in 251, and the person directly responsible seems to have been Novatus the African, who before coming to Rome had been notorious for his lax views over the reception of Christians who had lapsed during persecutions. Now he joined hands with the rigorists and persuaded Novatian to set himself up as a rival bishop to Cornelius. Novatian professed to Dionysius of Alexandria that he consented unwillingly, and Dionysius accepted his plea, but shrewdly added that if it were true it would make it all the easier for him to resign and so end the schism (Euseb., VI, xlv). The course of this, the first schism in the Roman Church, seems to have set a model for its successors even in the pleas which were advanced by the protagonists and the advice which was vainly given by onlookers. Cornelius tells us that the consecration was arranged with difficulty and only made possible by dragging in three up-country bishops, rough and very simple men, to perform it.[1] On his election, Novatian sent messengers to announce it to Carthage and to explain that he and his supporters were above all things upholders of the Gospel. The Church in North Africa refused to recognize Novatian and condemned him as a schismatic; a course which was soon afterwards followed by the Church in Rome. Thereupon some of the best of Novatian's followers, including a number of confessors, deserted him. But Novatian held on his way in spite of all. For this persistence he was severely condemned by Cyprian. Had he been the lawful Bishop of Rome his cutting himself off from the rest of the episcopate would have rendered his own office void. The end of Novatian is not fully known. He was separated for a time from his followers in Rome, perhaps during a persecution, and kept in touch with them through his writings.[2] Socrates in the fourth century states that he was martyred under Valerian (*Hist. Eccles.*, IV, 28); but as no earlier mention of this is to be found, the statement must be received with caution.[3]

[1] The letter of Cornelius to Fabius, Bishop of Antioch, has been largely preserved in Euseb., VI, xliii. Its statements, which are obviously inspired by a deep loathing and venomous rivalry, need to be taken with some reserve.

[2] There is an interesting treatment of the ideas of Novatian by A. d'Alès, *Novatien, étude sur la théol. rom. au milieu du IIIe siècle*, 1925.

[3] The tradition may be confirmed by the discovery, as recently as 1932, of an inscription in the cemetery in the Viale Regina Margherita—itself unknown

In spite of the discouraging experiences of the Novatianists in the seat of the schism, it spread rapidly over the whole Church. The reason for this may well be that a conflict between the Catholic and Puritan ideals was long overdue, and once the issue was joined at Rome it was taken up in other places. It is also possible that local disputes were tacked on to it. In spite of numerous condemnations, the schism—which found adherents as far away as Asia Minor, especially in the Phrygian mountains which had been the original home of Montanism—did not finally disappear until the end of the sixth century.

Whether the Paschal Controversy brought a rebuff to the Roman bishop or not may perhaps be disputed, but Roman claims were certainly not accepted in the dispute between Stephen, who became bishop in 254, and Cyprian of Carthage over the question of the baptism or rebaptism of heretics and schismatics.[1] The question of the latter was really the more urgent, for numbers of Novatianists, who were undoubtedly orthodox in their views, wished to return to the Church. Cyprian refused to recognize their baptism, on the ground that since there is no salvation outside the Church so there can be no valid sacraments (*Epist.*, LXIX).[2] After some hesitation the Church in North Africa gave him its support at a council held in 255. The practice in Rome was more liberal. Heretics who had received baptism in the proper form were received merely with the laying on of hands.

When the decision reached Stephen he criticized it strongly and advised the Church in North Africa to mend its ways. Cyprian thereupon held another council in 256 which reaffirmed its previous decision, though disclaiming any wish to enforce its views on other Churches. Stephen seems to have regarded this as a challenge and proceeded to excommunicate those who disagreed with him.

Stephen made a great point of the Petrine tradition, which he held to be preserved by the Roman Church, and claimed that others should submit to it. It may be remarked that already, even in the Paschal Controversy, Rome has a really different idea of what is meant by tradition than that of other Churches,

before 1926—which runs as follows:

NOVATIANO BEATISSIMO
MARTVRI GAVDENTIVS DIAC(ONVS) FEC(IT).

This may possibly refer to the schismatic; if so it suggests that martyrdom for the faith may have covered the sin of schism, since the cemetery in which he is buried apparently belonged to the Roman Church.

[1] Cyprian refused to accept the term rebaptism: *eos qui inde veniunt non rebaptizari . . . sed baptizari* (*Epist.*, LXXI).

[2] Cyprian was particularly vexed by the recognition of Marcionite baptism: *Epist.*, LXXIII–LXXV.

H

especially those of the East. The latter regarded tradition as something fixed and detailed from which it was not possible to depart even in small details. To the Roman bishops, tradition was something much more flexible and something which might be altered and adapted by rightful authority. An authority which in practice they held to belong to themselves. We have thus the beginning of the process by which the Roman Church came to identify Christian tradition with its own practice and doctrine.

In the East, heretics had generally been rebaptized, and even the orthodox, though schismatical, Montanists had had to submit to it. The practice, however, was not uniform, for Dionysius, if a Syriac fragment attributed to him is genuine, accepted even heretical baptism, if performed in the name of the Trinity.[1] This was, it may be remarked, the solution arrived at by the Council of Arles in 314 (or 316). The practice was, however, sufficiently uniform to provoke the antagonism of Stephen and so lavishly did he use the weapon of excommunication that in the end he found that he had virtually excommunicated himself. With the martyrdom of both Cyprian and Stephen, the controversy seems to have died down and been forgotten. "Forgotten too in the storms of the period were the Roman claims to primacy. But the bishops of Rome preserved them faithfully and awaited the time that would allow them to revive them once more with greater prospect of success."[2]

Stephen's successor also met a martyr's death. He was Sixtus II (257–58) and his fate has some interesting features, for he was arrested whilst preaching in the catacomb of Pretextatus on August 6, 258. The time was one of general persecution and no doubt the Christians were for this reason holding services in such a place. After being tried, it is said that he was brought back to the scene of his offence and there executed. Four days later occurred the martyrdom of one of the best known of all who suffered for their faith in the Primitive Church, St. Lawrence. Lightfoot even ventured to call him "the Stephen of the Western Church" (I, ii, p. 455). Not only is the story of Lawrence one of the most famous, it is also one of the best authenticated, although the *Acta* had disappeared before the time of Augustine. He was chief of the seven deacons of Rome and was tortured to death by being burnt over a slow fire. The story has it that by this means the prefect hoped to get from him the hiding-place of the supposed treasures of the Roman Church.

There followed Dionysius (259–68), notable for his corre-

---

[1] Feltoe, *Letters and Remains of Dionysius of Alexandria*, p. 40.
[2] Lietzmann in *Camb. Anct. Hist.*, XII, p. 541.

spondence with his namesake of Alexandria.[1] Of the other bishops who succeeded during the rest of the third century little is known. The *Liber Pontificalis* tells us that Eutychian (275–83) was a Tuscan by birth, and that Gaius whose pontificate occurred during the reign of Diocletian was, like that Emperor, a Dalmatian. The coincidence, for it cannot have been more, seemed to strike the scribe who compiled the record. The bishops for the remainder of our period had unfortunate histories. Marcellinus (d. 304) gave way under persecution and is said to have handed over copies of the Scriptures and even to have offered incense. His two immediate successors, Marcellus and Eusebius, were both banished on account of public disorders which followed their elections, a foretaste of the bloody rioting of the Roman Christians in the days of Damasus. Eusebius died in Sicily, but his body was brought back and buried in the cemetery of Callistus. Under Miltiades, who was elected in 311, the Church had internal peace and enjoyed the protection of Maxentius until Constantine came to make it finally secure.

(B) THE ROMAN PRIMACY

From the beginning of the Middle Ages until the Reformation, the primacy of the Roman Church was accepted by Western Christendom. In the East, however, the claim was either ignored or repudiated, a natural attitude in view of its much older traditions. The question which now faces us is the extent to which such a recognition was made in our period. Even before Nicaea Rome had come to occupy a position of centrality and prominence in the West, though in the East, again to emphasize the distinction, its prestige had to meet the claims of rivals, whilst the establishment, at a slightly later date, of Constantinople as the seat of the Empire raised a more serious competitor. Though our period knows nothing of any supreme bishop ruling over the whole Church of God, yet the foundations upon which later claims were to be built up can clearly be discerned, for Rome, having lost its importance as a political centre, found compensation in a new and longer lease of life as the headquarters of a great ecclesiastical system. Such a renewal of influence is not without its parallels. Perhaps the nearest comes from ancient Egypt, for when Thebes had suffered political eclipse it still retained its importance in the world of religion.

Three different elements went to make up the predominance of the Roman Church which may conveniently be named: (*a*) Political; (*b*) Geographical; and (*c*) Ecclesiastical.

[1] See p. 126 f.

(a) *The Political Causes*

Rome as the seat of the imperial government had an importance which could not fail to affect all departments of life. Even under the pagan emperors this was realized though the extent of the recognition can be exaggerated. When, for example, Aurelian decided that property in Antioch retained by Paul of Samosata after his deposition, should be returned to the Church, he specified those who were in communion with the Bishops of Italy and Rome (Euseb., VII, xxx, 19); not with the Bishop of Rome alone, nor primarily, if the order in which they are cited has any significance.[1]

In the Muratorian Fragment the wording of the reference to Bishop Pius is very significant. He is described as occupying the seat of the Church of the city of Rome *sedente cathedra [sic] urbis romae aecclesiae*, not it will be observed *cathedra Petri*. This is typical of the early Christian centuries when it was the city, not the bishop, which was all-important. Even as late as the Council of Chalcedon in 451 it is clearly stated that "the Fathers gave the primacy to the throne of the elder Rome because that was the imperial city" (Canon 28). Such an attribution was naturally not at all to the liking of the Popes, as their power and prestige increased,[2] and at an even earlier date the Law of Valentinian in 445 had placed in the forefront, not the dignity of Rome or even the authority of councils, but the merits of St. Peter which his successors were supposed to inherit.[3]

But the real debt of ecclesiastical Rome to its imperial forerunner did not end with the handing on of its prestige. The Church of Rome had behind it a thousand years of political experience, the gathered harvest of the Roman people; and, just as the rest of Italy, and eventually the whole Empire, had been drawn within the bounds of the Roman citizenship until, as a romanized Gaul of the fifth century could affirm, the world

[1] This order is often reversed by scholars who quote the decision. Duchesne, however, although a Roman Catholic, shows his usual accuracy and writes: "The emperor decided that the true bishop was the one recognized in Italy and at Rome" (*The Early Hist. of the Church*, p. 343). On p. 391, however, he is less careful and omits any mention of Italy, stating that "the Emperor Aurelian saw at once that the right [bishop] was he who was in communion with the Bishop of Rome".

[2] In the Middle Ages the extreme papalists were eager to repudiate any suggestion that the popes owed their position to the city: see my *Decline and Fall of the Medieval Papacy*, p. 10, note 30.

[3] Jalland, *The Church and the Papacy*, p. 106, considers that Rome "was honoured not because of but in spite of its imperial associations" and that the honour done to its Church was such as "no mere recognition of worldly prepotence can be sufficient to explain". This view seems to me to go against the evidence.

had become a single city,[1] so the Churches of the West would one day be absorbed within the imperial organization of Ecclesia Romana.

From the earliest days, the Church of Rome had begun to exhibit virtues which are typically Roman and a sense of responsibility for the well-being of other Churches. This sense of responsibility showed itself especially in frequent and generous efforts to relieve distress. Already to Ignatius the pre-eminence of the Roman Church lay in the domain of love (Rom., pref.). When in the middle of the third century its wealth had grown through the adhesion of numerous high-born converts (Euseb., V, xxi, 1), means were available for redeeming captives as far away as Cappadocia (Basil, Epist., LXX). Visitors to Rome were received with lavish hospitality, hospitality being a virtue which the Romans valued highly even in other Churches (1 Clem., I, 2). In the days of Soter towards the end of the second century the tradition was carefully maintained, a matter upon which Dionysius of Corinth congratulates him (Euseb., IV, xxiii, 10). It was not, however, in the provision of funds and the exercise of hospitality alone that Rome exhibited her sense of responsibility; help and advice were forthcoming for even the most distant communities (Euseb., VII, v, 2). This had come out as early as the first century in connexion with the disputes at Corinth.

The two cities of Rome and Corinth had many links, both secular and ecclesiastical; tradition even claimed that both were joint foundations of St. Peter and St. Paul (Euseb., II, xxv, 8). It was in Corinth that Aquila and Priscilla had found refuge when expelled from Rome (Acts 18 : 2) and perhaps other Jewish Christians with them. It was natural therefore that when strife arose in Corinth the Roman Church should be interested. The Corinthians may indeed have asked Rome to intervene. This is suggested by the apology at the beginning of I Clement.[2] Though the tone of the letter is urgent and serious it makes no assertion of authority. Could it have been written, one wonders, by Corinth to Rome if the circumstances had been reversed?[3] Certainly there is nothing to suggest subordination, and the final appeal is to the Scriptures.[4] The value attached to the com-

---

[1] Rutilius Namatianus, De Reditu Suo, I, 66: Urbem fecisti quod prius orbis erat. His love for Rome did not extend to the new religion which then had its headquarters there, though probably his opposition had been exaggerated: see Pichon, Les Derniers Écrivains profanes, p. 266.

[2] Zahn, Int. to N.T., I, p. 269, thinks that Fortunatus mentioned in LXIX may have been a messenger from Corinth.

[3] Lietzmann, however, comments, "one gets the impression that the Romans would have been greatly surprised had Corinth . . . dispatched such a letter of admonition to Rome" (Camb. Anct. Hist., XII, p. 530).

[4] So R. van Cauwelaert in Rev. d'hist. ecclés., 1935, p. 267 ff.

munication by the Church in Corinth can be judged from the fact that even as late as the time of Dionysius (c. 166) it was habitually read in the public services.

The letter to Corinth also exhibits other virtues characteristic of the Roman mind, such as a sense of order and proportion, a recognition of the need for stable organization, and in general what may be called a legal outlook. One other supreme mark of the Roman genius the Church would also share; the power of adaptation.[1] The problems which faced it were not materially different from those which occupied the thoughts of other Churches; but whereas they were content, for the time at least, to tolerate a wide diversity, Rome, from the days of Victor onwards, was anxious to discover solutions in practical matters, and to press them upon other Churches.[2] Uniformity and rigidity were even then at work to stiffen the power of Rome. This desire, however, was no mere craving for power and authority, it sprang largely from that more kindly virtue already referred to, a sense of responsibility. This was surely a symptom of greatness and of an imperial outlook. The Roman Church, here again treading in the steps of its pagan predecessor, from the first tended to see all things from the point of view of the society.

(b) *The Geographical Causes*

Since the earth is a globe, any single locality may be regarded, quite legitimately, as its centre. To the Greek, Delphi had been such a centre, the navel of the earth; to the devout Jew it had been Jerusalem.[3] The Roman had been content to define only the centre of his city, and the remains which marked *umbilicus urbis Romae* may still be seen. At the beginning of the Christian era, and in the centuries to come, no rival, however, could have been found to challenge its right to be the virtual centre of the civilized world, and that not only in the political sphere.[4] In the world of commerce its importance was great, not because it produced anything, but because on that very account it had to import everything to meet its needs. Rome was also a great religious centre, and many Oriental cults, after considerable

---

[1] cf. *Camb. Anct. Hist.*, X, p. 160: "The genius of Rome had shown itself in the method by which, when change was called for, she set up new organs of State beside the old and left them to find their *modus vivendi*, often turning to new uses those which had outlived their original purpose".

[2] Contrast the view of Firmilian in his letter to Cyprian (*Epist.*, LXXV): *Multa pro locorum et hominum diversitate varientur.* The attitude, it may be pointed out, of those who framed the Articles of the Church of England.

[3] cf. Ezek. 38 : 12: *Jubilees*, VIII, 19; I *Enoch*, XXVI, 1; *Sib. Orac.*, V, 250.

[4] Of modern countries France alone has created a "myth of centrality". In the Department of Cher, a Roman milestone at Buère is held to be the *centre géographique de la France*: see E. R. Curtis, *The Civilization of France*, p. 45.

groups of Orientals had come to live in Rome, moved thither their headquarters. It was also to Rome that Lucius had to go to receive his final initiation into the mysteries of Isis (Apuleius *Metamorph.*, XI, 26). G. La Piana ends his exhaustive survey of this matter by saying that "In the first three centuries of the empire Rome had become the great religious centre of the world, where all religions and cults of importance established their headquarters and under official protection carried on their work of propaganda".[1] This was true also of philosophy, for in the first century B.C. Rome had become the centre of Stoicism. Later, Galen (129–c. 200) left his native Pergamum and came to Rome and so added medicine to its attractions.

Because Rome was thus the centre of the civilized world, the focal point of all the busy activities of mankind, men· were drawn towards it from every quarter. Among them were many Christian leaders and thinkers. Justin paid two visits, though he seems to have held a little aloof from the Church in Rome.[2] He lectured in the house of a certain Martin near the Baths of Timothy on a site now probably occupied by the Church of Santa Pudenziana. It was at Rome that Justin met his death, along with six companions, under the prefect Rusticus whose term of office covered the years 162 to 167.[3] His fears of denunciation by Crescens, a Cynic philosopher (II *Apol.*, III), were fulfilled, as his pupil Tatian informs us, whilst expressing fears on his own behalf (*Ad Graec.*, XIX). But Tatian returned in safety to his native Mesopotamia.

Polycarp visited Rome in 155,[4] perhaps in company with Irenaeus who was there about the same time. The latter tells us (III, iii, 4) that Polycarp brought back many of the followers of Valentinus and Marcion to the faith by his exposition of apostolic doctrine. About this time also Rome received a very interesting visitor in Hegesippus who compiled or was given a list of early bishops which has become famous. Hegesippus is said to have composed five volumes of Memoirs (Euseb., IV, viii, 1 f.); but his scope was too limited, being almost entirely doctrinal and practical, to justify the title of the father of Ecclesiastical History which is sometimes applied to him.[5] An even more interesting, if not so important, visitor about this

---

[1] *Harvard Theol. Rev.*, pp. 282–320. I find myself again quite unable to agree with Dr. Jalland, who is inclined to belittle this factor (*op. cit.*, p. 106).

[2] So K. Lake, *Landmarks of Early Christianity*, p. 127.

[3] *Acta Mart. Just.*, II. The Paschal Chronicle is more definite and states that he suffered *c.* 165. Eusebius erroneously places the event in the reign of Marcus Aurelius (IV, xvi).

[4] C. H. Turner in *Studia Biblica*, II, pp. 105–155 dates the martyrdom on February 22, 156.

[5] See Lawlor, *Eusebiana*, p. 1 f.

time was Avercius Marcellus, better known as Abercius,[1] Bishop of Hieropolis in Phrygia.[2] In an epitaph, prepared during his lifetime, he describes his various travels including a visit to "royal Rome" and the "golden-robed and golden slippered queen".[3]

Clement of Alexandria, although he spent some time in South Italy, seems not to have visited Rome; but Origen fulfilled his desire to see the ancient Church of the Romans and paid a short visit while Zephyrinus was bishop (Euseb., VI, xiv, 10). His disciple Pierius, who suffered in the Diocletianic persecution, later went to Rome. He was the author of many works, all of which have perished, and may have been head of the Catechetical School at Alexandria.

The Diocletianic persecution furnished Rome with several Eastern martyrs, including the Phrygian Pancras, a boy of fourteen who was put to death on the Via Aurelia. His name and fame spread to England, where a number of churches are dedicated to him. There were also two noble Persians, Abdon and Sennen, who were on a visit to the tombs of the apostles.[4] Pictures of them in native dress can be seen in the cemetery of Pontianus.[5]

Rome was thus a natural meeting-place for Christians, as for others. In it could be found representatives of the most distant Churches, as well as groups from every part of the Empire. The opportunity thus presented for influencing the whole Church was recognized by every leader of a new movement and numbers of heretics and protagonists of conflicting sects sought it out in hopes that their wares would find a mart in the metropolis of the Empire. The visits of Marcion and the various Gnostic and Monarchian leaders are too well known to demand more than a bare mention. Others included Cerdo, an Asiatic who arrived in the first half of the second century (Iren., III, iv, 3); Epigonus, a disciple of Noetus, by some identified with Praxeas,[6] who arrived about 200; and Alcibiades of Apamea, who came a little

---

[1] The name seems to be Celtic or Italian rather than Phrygian. See, further, Lightfoot, II, i, p. 477 ff.; W. M. Ramsay, *Cities and Bishoprics of Phrygia*, p. 679 ff.; and W. M. Calder, in *J.R.S.*, 1939, XXIX, Pt. I, p. 1 ff. The epitaph itself is now in the Lateran Museum (Marucchi, p. 671).

[2] Not to be confused with Hierapolis in the Maeander valley.

[3] This is based on the reading of Lightfoot and Ramsay. Calder decides for $\beta\alpha\sigma\iota\lambda\epsilon\iota\alpha\nu$ against ΒΑΣ[Ι]ΛΗ; "to Rome to look on sovereignty".

[4] It is of interest to note that in 1332 the men of Bordeaux, then under English rule, petitioned Parliament for approval of the ordinances of a confraternity "*al honour de Dieu et de seynte eglise et des martirs Seint Abdon e Sennen*": see *Chancery Parliament Roll*, No. 3, §8.

[5] See Marucchi, p. 80 f. Christianity spread early to Persia. There had been Parthians, Medes, and Elamites at Pentecost (Acts 2 : 9). Other Persians are mentioned in the *Passio S. Valentini* (Marucchi, p. 588).

[6] De Rossi, *Bull. Arch. Crist.*, 1866, p. 69. Epigonus is mentioned by Hippolytus: IX, 7.

later from the valley of the Orontes to be met and denounced by Hippolytus (IX, 8). There were among the visitors a number of women. Marcion, indeed, is said to have sent a female disciple before him, whilst Apelles came under the influence of a Gnostic virgin named Philumene who claimed to receive revelations. Marcellina, a Carpocratian, led many astray.

Not all the reported visits to Rome can, of course, be accepted as representative of real happenings. Many are undoubtedly spurious, whilst in regard to others doubts are bound to arise. That St. Peter was in Rome for a timè and was there martyred seems probable, though many legends concerning his sojourn are later inventions. But the supposed visit of St. John must definitely be rejected. The tradition that he was plunged into a cauldron of boiling oil outside the Latin Gate was, indeed, known to Tertullian[1] and other Latin writers, but strangely enough it receives no mention in the East. The visit of St. Barnabas also has little evidence in its favour.

One legend has aroused especial interest in the West, that of Thecla.[2] Some Greek MSS. of her *Acta* record that when she was ninety years of age, being attacked on Mount Calamon in Asia Minor by some young men, in response to her prayers the rock opened, and so she disappeared from this life. Her grave, however, is shown near Seleucia, where it has become a shrine.[3] Another series of traditions claims that her body travelled underground to Rome where it is now supposed to rest near that of St. Paul.[4] In the Roman Breviary in the order *Commendationis*, after a number of Old Testament examples have been cited, there is mention of the deliverance of St. Peter and St. Paul from prison, and of Thecla from three terrible martyrdoms. In later histories her name by some obscure process was transformed into Tigris or Tigeria.[5]

(c) *The Ecclesiastical Causes*

Haller in *Das Papsttum*, p. 455, expresses the opinion that for Eusebius the most important see in the Church was that of

---

[1] *De Praes.*, XXXVI. The supposed event is commemorated by the Festival of St. John ante Port. Lat. (May 6). According to a rival tradition the incident took place in Ephesus. Turner, *Studies in Early Church Hist.*, p. 198, is inclined to accept the story.

[2] She is mentioned by Tertullian, Ambrose, Sulpicius Severus, Augustine, and Jerome, among others. A cemetery in Rome bears her name (see Marucchi, p. 128) and in the Capitoline Museum a fragment of a fourth-century sarcophagus shows a ship with the name Thecla in large letters on its side. There is a reproduction in Marucchi, p. 627.

[3] See Delahaye, *Origines du culte des martyrs*, p. 161 f.

[4] *Apoc. N.T.*, p. 281. The story of the underground journey is not actually narrated in the Greek; it is inferred from her disappearance into the rock and subsequent emergence in Rome.

[5] R. Lane Poole, *Studies in Chron. and Hist.*, p. 130.

Alexandria, and that he regarded the lists of bishops of Rome as of no more interest than those of that see, or of Jerusalem, or Antioch. "The father of Church History", he concludes, "knew nothing of any Roman primacy." With this conclusion I agree fully, though I cannot help feeling that Haller has underestimated the interest which Eusebius took in the bishops of Rome. In spite of his neglect of the West he frequently takes the Roman episcopates as periods in his history.[1] But since the object of his labours was to preserve a record of those who had presided over the most prominent local dioceses (I, i, 1), the comparatively small space which he devotes to Rome shows clearly that he was not aware that it possessed any unique standing. But if Eusebius knew of no Roman primacy and preferred, it may be, the see of Alexandria to that of Rome, in the West, Rome had no possible rival. From the ecclesiastical standpoint it was the only see which had any serious claim to apostolic foundation. At first, as we have seen, all the emphasis was on the joint foundation by St. Peter and St. Paul; later, when the Petrine claims began to be formulated, the stress was shifted to St. Peter alone.

It is no uncommon thing in the history of institutions to find that legends have been invented or manipulated in order to account for existing facts. So it was with the Roman see. Its admitted primacy in the West was gradually exalted, so that eventually, though not in our period, it claimed sovereign power over the other Churches. At the same time the connexion with St. Peter, and St. Peter's own relations to the other apostles, were suitably adjusted so as to give a historical basis for the claim. The legend thus followed the fact; the fact was not built up on the legend.

Though there is no trace in the New Testament of any claim by St. Peter to exercise authority over the rest of the apostles, it would be idle to deny that he possessed some kind of primacy among them. This is evident in all the gospels, not only in the charge narrated in John 21 : 15-17, but in the story of St. Peter's confession as recorded in Mark 8 : 29, and in the command to stablish his brethren (Luke 22 : 32).[2] So, in the early chapters of Acts, St. Peter is everywhere prominent. On the other hand, the sons of Zebedee certainly knew of no primacy such as would preclude their own sitting one on either side of the Master in His kingdom (Mark 10 : 35 ff.); a narrative, it may be

[1] See Lawlor and Oulton's edition of Eusebius, *Ecclesiastical History*, II, p. 13. As early as the last quarter of the second century the Roman Church was reckoning dates by the episcopates—so Harnack states: *Constitution and Law of the Church*, p. 122.

[2] This was first taken as implying any kind of supremacy by Ambrose, *In Ps. XLIII, enarr.* 40 (*P.L.*, XIV, 1163).

pointed out, which would hardly have been handed down in a community which regarded St. Peter as occupying a unique position among the Twelve. So far I have said nothing of the text upon which the most extravagant claims have been based: "Thou art Peter, and upon this rock I will build my church" (Matt. 16 : 18). This promise was taken by Tertullian to refer to St. Peter himself (*De Praes.*, XXII) but to him personally, a point which he brings out very clearly in *De Pudic.*, XXI, written it is true in his Montanist days. In both East and West, however, this was not the only interpretation; the "rock" upon which the Church was to be founded was not the man, but the faith which he exhibited, a view held by both Augustine and Chrysostom, to name two representative theologians. Here it may be remarked that such a personal qualification could obviously not be transmitted. Now, with what might seem to be proud effrontery did one not know the long process of development behind it, the text appears in letters six feet high round the dome of St. Peter's in Rome.

Before going on further to consider how far any promise made to St. Peter was intended to be handed on to any possible successors it will be well to notice that in some parts of the early Church the ruler of the whole Christian community (by a kind of process of caliphitism) was not St. Peter but St. James. This is the view of the Clementines (late documents coming, it must be confessed, from no very orthodox source). From them we hear that Clement, after his consecration by St. Peter as his successor at Rome, is bidden to report his appointment to St. James at Jerusalem, since the latter is the "bishop of bishops", and ruler of "the Churches everywhere".[1]

Returning to the question of the ability of St. Peter to hand on any authority over the Church which he may have possessed, we recall Tertullian's insistence that any promise to him was purely personal. Cyprian goes further than this; for, while recognizing that the Church is founded upon St. Peter, he seems not to be aware that the bishops of Rome were concerned in the matter (*Epist.*, LXX). Even if for purpose of argument we allow St. Peter's ability to transmit his authority, any trustworthy evidence that he was ever Bishop of Rome is entirely lacking; in fact it is not until after the second century that there is any mention of his having filled that office.

---

[1] *Letter of Clem. to Jas.* in *Clem. Hom.* In the *Clem. Recog.* also St. Peter is given a position of inferiority to St. James. The latter was appointed by the Lord (I, 43) and he orders St. Peter to go to Caesarea (I, 72). He and his successors have the power to license teachers (IV, 35). Epiphanius, *Haer.*, LXXVIII, 7, speaks of St. James as having been entrusted by the Lord with "His throne on earth as first bishop" of Jerusalem. Significance may have been attached to the order of names in Gal. 2 : 9, "James, Cephas, and John".

The first Bishop of Rome to claim special powers as the successor of St. Peter was Callistus, though actual appeals to the Lord's commission are unknown before Damasus in the fourth century. If such authority had been admitted by the Church as a whole, the course of its history would have been very different from what it was, since the decision of the Bishop of Rome would have been decisive in all matters. There would, for example, have been no Arian dispute, for the question would immediately have been solved by an *ex cathedra* ruling of the supreme pontiff.

One passage is often invoked as evidence of the recognition of the sovereignty of the Roman Church in the latter part of the second century, the well-known reference by Irenaeus to Rome as the guardian of the apostolic tradition, which whilst shared with other Churches, belonged especially to her on account of her pre-eminent position *propter potentiorem principalitatem* (III, iii, 2). The Greek original of this passage has been lost and even the meaning of the key-word *principalitatem* is disputed. Archbishop Benson claimed that according to Roman usage it involved no idea of rule (*Cyprian*, pp. 537–540). Irenaeus's appeal to Rome as preserving apostolic tradition has an instructive parallel in Tertullian, *De Praes.*, XXXVI, where a like appeal is made not to Rome only but to other Churches. Convenience of situation is here the governing motive, so that those in Achaia are recommended to look to Corinth, those in Macedonia to Philippi or Thessalonica, and those in Asia to Ephesus. Rome is the natural centre for those in Italy. Here there is recognition of Rome, but not as possessing anything unique for the whole Church, but only for the West where Rome was the only apostolic see.

We have already seen that, until the pontificate of Victor, the Roman Church, because of its own lack of unity, was in no position to make any attempt to impose its traditions upon others, and that early attempts to do so were by no means successful. Other similar disputes will be noticed in subsequent chapters.[1] Here it is sufficient to point out that the fact of Rome's being thus involved in disputes with other Churches shows that no recognition on their part of any kind of sovereign authority vested in Rome had even been thought of. In the matter of the lapsed, for instance, it is Cyprian who takes the lead; Rome and the rest of Christendom follow.[2] Firmilian is plainly unaware of any right of the Roman bishop to guide the

[1] Stephen and Cyprian had other disputes. That concerning the Spanish bishops will be found treated in Part II, Chap. V; that concerning the see of Arles in Part II, Chap. VI.

[2] This is admitted by the great Roman Catholic historian, Tillemont, *Mémoires*, IV, *S. Cyprien*, § 23.

Catholic Church. In his letter of sympathy to Cyprian,[1] after Stephen's attack, he likens the action of the Bishop of Rome to that of Judas; a daring comparison. For Firmilian, the right to set the standard belongs not to Rome, but to Jerusalem.

Cyprian, in addition to engaging in disputes with the bishops of Rome on a number of occasions, put forth a reasoned theory of the Unity of the Church and its basis, in the treatise *De Unitate*. This may have been provoked by the Novatianist schism or by the attempt to appoint a rival Bishop of Carthage in Felicissimus. His ideas on the subject are clear and consistent. The Church, in order that its complete unity might be demonstrated, was founded upon a single individual, St. Peter (Matt. 16 : 18); but any privileges which he might have been given were afterwards shared by the other apostles (John 20 : 21-23). Unity therefore is based upon the episcopate as a body. Each bishop in consequence has a responsibility not only to his own Church but to the Church as a whole. The Bishop of Rome is to be honoured and respected as a kind of senior, but he has no superior status, much less any kind of jurisdiction over the rest, any more than St. Peter had over the other apostles. Never by word or act does Cyprian recognize such authority over himself or any other bishop. The same attitude, it may be remarked, was maintained by Augustine more than a century later; he, too, would admit the primacy of Rome, but not anything approaching supremacy.

In view of Cyprian's consistent attitude it is strange to find in some MSS. of *De Unitate* IV passages in which the peculiar authority of St. Peter and the Roman see is admitted. By the great majority of scholars, including the Roman Catholic, Hugo Koch,[2] these passages are rejected as interpolations. Others attribute *both* versions to Cyprian, but find difficulty in deciding which is the original form![3]

If, however, Cyprian offered a firm resistance to exaggerated claims on the part of Rome, he more than any other was ulti-

---

[1] A Latin version of the original Greek is preserved as *Epist.* LXXV, in Cyprian's Letters. Its genuineness has been questioned: see the discussion in Benson, *Cyprian*, p. 377 ff.

[2] Hugo Koch, *Cyprien und die röm. Primat* (*Texte und Unters*, III, Pt. V, 1). In a more recent work, *Cathedra Petri* (*Zeit; für N.T. Wiss.*, Supp. XI, 1930), he shows that Cyprian's phrase *matrix et radix catholicae ecclesiae* is never used for the Roman Church in early Christian writings.

[3] See two articles by Dom Chapman in *Rev. Bénéd.*, 1902 and 1903, and his notice of Koch's book, 1910, p. 447 ff. Also M. Bévenot, *S. Cyprian's De Unit., Chap. IV, in the Light of the Manuscripts*. The conclusions of the latter are accepted by Jalland, *The Church and the Papacy*, p. 161 ff., who takes the longer recension as the original and intended to support Cornelius against Novatian. Later, Cyprian realized that it might be used against his theory of the episcopate and in consequence he eliminated the reference to the primacy. It may be pointed out that Fr. Bévenot's survey of the MSS. was far from complete.

mately responsible for their growth in the West, for it was he who made "the Petrine primacy in relation to the Roman Church an integral element of a theory of the episcopate".[1]

Most of Rome's relations were inevitably with the neighbouring Churches of the West. With one Church in the East, however, that of Alexandria, she seems to have had specially close relations. In the early attempts to spread the Gospel Alexandria played a surprisingly small part. The first Christian to be mentioned as living there is, so far as I know, a young man who wished to anticipate Origen by becoming a eunuch (Justin, I *Apol.*, XXIX). We have no information as to when the Gospel arrived in Egypt,[2] where the presence of large numbers of Jews, and those of a liberal type, might have been thought to provide the very soil in which Christianity would most readily take root; there were, moreover, Jews from Egypt present at Pentecost (Acts 2 : 10), whilst Apollos was an Alexandrian (Acts 18 : 24 f.), and according to an addition in the Western text had been instructed "in the word of the Lord in his own country". Although there is no official mention of the Church in Egypt until well on in the second century, Hadrian in 130 refers to the presence of Christian bishops.[3] Possibly the explanation is that the first Egyptian Christians were Gnostics and in consequence the record of their activities has been deliberately suppressed.

That there was a close link between the two Churches is definitely recognized by Julius I in 340.[4] Lietzmann considers that the Gospel, in its orthodox form, reached Alexandria from Rome and that a memory of this event is enshrined in the tradition that Mark was the first Bishop of Alexandria.[5] The theory gains support from the similarity of the canons of Scripture of the two Churches, as well as from the presence of a number of readings in the Sahidic version found also in Codex D and the Old Latin. The constant intercourse between the cities, as for example in connexion with the corn supply, would provide ample opportunities for Christian teachers to go from one to the other.

In view of all this, it was quite natural that when Dionysius of Alexandria was suspected of heretical views his critics should appeal to Rome. Though there is no evidence that any jurisdiction was admitted, the mere fact that the appeal was made

---

[1] C. H. Turner, *Catholic and Apostolic*, p. 228.

[2] Alexandria is not necessarily typical of Egyptian Christianity as a whole for it was primarily a Greek city, and is often referred to as "Alexandria ad Aegyptum".

[3] Vopsius, *Vita Saturn.*, VIII. The genuineness of the Letter to Servianus in which this occurs has been questioned.

[4] So Athanasius, *Apol. contra Arian.*, XXXV.

[5] *The Founding of the Church Universal*, pp. 85 and 363.

must have added greatly to the prestige of the Roman Church.

One of the chief causes of Rome's importance in later Christian opinion was that it had been hallowed by the blood of the martyrs, and above all that it contained the actual bodies of St. Peter and St. Paul. This, Chrysostom regarded as Rome's greatest distinction, with special emphasis, it may be noted, on St. Paul (*Hom. 32 in Rom.*). Innumerable pilgrims journeyed to see the tombs of the great apostles and the last resting-places of those who had made a like heroic sacrifice. For their use special Itineraries were prepared, just as for the modern tourist, and some of these have survived. It was with the thought of the sacred dead who lay within its walls that the medieval pilgrim caught his first glimpse of the eternal city.

> O Roma nobilis, orbis et domina
> Cunctarum urbium excellentissima,
> Roseo martyrium sanguine rubea,
> Albis et virginum lilliis candida;
> Salutem dicimus tibi per omnia,
> Te benedicimus—salve per saecula.[1]

As elsewhere, so at Rome, martyrdom had been rated very high from the earliest times, as we can see from the reference in Hermas *Vis.*, III, i, 9. In spite of this, the earliest Roman Festival Calendar, the *Depositio Martyrum*, gives the names of no Roman martyrs, except St. Peter and St. Paul, before the third century. Yet the record of Rome is very impressive, for it begins with the first victims, those who perished under Nero, and stretches right down through our period by a continuous succession. Well might Ignatius call Rome the instructress of others in the art of dying for the faith.[2] Included in the roll are several bishops: Alexander, Telesphorus, Pontianus, Fabian, Cornelius, Stephen, and Sixtus II. Many, too, came to Rome from elsewhere to die; such were Ignatius himself, and Justin Martyr. This cause, even within the period with which we are concerned, must already have been a potent means of adding to the prestige of the great Western see.

---

[1] *Oxford Book of Medieval Verse*, p. 39.
[2] *Rom.*, III, 1: This is obviously the meaning of the passage, though Streeter, *Primitive Church*, p. 158, takes it of instruction in general and consequently finds it difficult to explain.

CHAPTER III

ITALY

To think of Italy, with Rome apart, is difficult; so many details are involved, and the natural centre round which they might be grouped is no longer available. None the less, for our purpose, Italy must be envisaged as a separate entity, and the development of the Christian Church outside Rome must be studied. This can best be done under three heads—the Churches in the North, in the Central regions, and in the South, including Sicily.

Before, however, we go on to a detailed consideration of the ecclesiastical expansion something must be said of Italy in general. Although it formed a geographical unity there was within that unity a wide diversity. This can be seen by a comparison between the North, with its ancient cities and flowing streams,[1] and Calabria with its sheep-runs and the townships of Magna Graecia. Italy as a whole in the early days of the Empire was very prosperous, agriculture flourished and trade was expanding. There was security of person and property and an eager development of municipal life. Italy also at this period prided herself on her unique position of political privilege; and was above all else determined not to be treated merely as a province of Rome. But gradually, for reasons of expediency and to further efficient government, her privileges were taken away. Under Hadrian, and later under Marcus Aurelius, various measures were introduced which had the effect of increasing central control; it was, however, not until the close of the second century that the position of Italy began seriously to be threatened, when Septimius Severus became emperor. He had no desire to bolster up what he regarded as obsolete privileges and in things military treated Italy like the rest of the Empire. By granting the *Jus Italicum* to cities outside the peninsula he raised them to a position of equality. Thus a double process was at work; on the one hand, the privileges of Italy were being ignored; on the other, those that were retained had to be shared with others. The extension of the franchise by Caracalla had the same effect. By the reforms of Diocletian, Italy was divided into

---

[1] cf. The well-known lines of Virgil, *Georgics*, II, 155 ff.:
> . . . *tot egregias urbes operumque laborem*
> *Tot congesta manu praeruptis oppida saxis*
> *Fluminaque antiquos subterlabentia muros.*

two vicariates, one based on Milan, the other on Rome, and definitely placed on a level with the rest of the Empire though for the moment the actual title of province was not applied to it.

In addition to its native races Italy had within its borders numbers of immigrant peoples. In the South there were numerous colonies of Greeks; while in Sicily the mixture of races was notorious, for the island had received Carthaginian as well as Greek settlers upon its soil. In the North there were many Celts. The territory beyond the Apennines, known as Cisalpine Gaul, did not become part of Italy proper until 42 B.C., though its inhabitants had enjoyed the citizenship for a few years before that date. The incorporation of this region into Italy seems eventually to have had a deadening effect upon local initiative.[1] In South Italy, as in Rome itself, there were many Jews, so we learn from inscriptions and other sources; but they do not seem to have been numerous in the rest of Italy. This may help to explain the presence, during our period, of many more Churches in the South than in the Centre or the North; for Christianity would best flourish where the Jews had prepared the way.

THE COMING OF CHRISTIANITY

Apart from the notices in the Acts of the Apostles, the first direct trace of Christianity in Italy in general is to be found in the salutation which "they of Italy" desired to make at the end of Hebrews (13:24). This phrase may refer to a group of Italian Christians away from their native land who send greetings to it; or it may mean a group of Christians living in Italy at the time of writing. The answer will depend on the place where the epistle was composed. In any case, these Christians were probably connected with Rome rather than the rest of Italy. Apart from a vague reference to Churches in "the central regions of the world", which may mean Italy, in Irenaeus (I, x, 2), the next notice is concerned with the consecration of Novatian. This, according to Cornelius, could only be performed when he had enticed three bishops from "a small and very insignificant part of Italy" (Euseb., VI, xliii, 8). At a council subsequently held in Rome to deal with the case of Novatian there were present sixty bishops, a list of whom, with their sees, was compiled by Cornelius, together with others who supported him (Euseb., VI, xliii, 21 f.). Unfortunately, this list has not come down to us. This was in 251, and presupposes a large number of Christian centres, though we must not be led astray into thinking that a bishop

[1] For a study of this interesting and important region see G. E. F. Chilver, *Cisalpine Gaul: Social and Economic History from 49 B.C. to the Death of Trajan.*

meant a "diocese" in anything resembling the modern sense. The jurisdiction of the bishop was much more like that of the parish priest of later times.[1] Then we have the recognition, by the Emperor Aurelian, of the bishops of Italy and Rome;[2] and, finally, the record of the presence of numerous Italian bishops at the Councils of Rome and of Arles.

Our information is thus rather scanty. It can be supplemented by later lists of council-attending bishops, by notices in inscriptions, and by the not very reliable *Acta* of the martyrs. Legends, it need scarcely be said, form a perfect labyrinth; but they add to our knowledge little that can be relied upon. I have, in what follows, made occasional use of them, not so much for the value of their references, but as illustrating the kind of background against which Italian Christianity grew up.[3] Apart from these unreliable sources, the evidence that we can assemble enables us to construct little more than a bare catalogue of names and places.

(a) *Upper Italy*

Christianity seems to have entered Upper Italy with considerable difficulty, and, even when an entry had been made, progress was very gradual. No doubt the Gospel was carried by travellers along the great roads from Rome and the South; but the first teachers may well have come from the Balkans, especially on the east coast where the great harbours of Ravenna and Aquileia gaze across the Adriatic. One reason for the slow advance of Christianity in this region, apart from the absence of Jews in any number, was doubtless the conservative nature of the population. In Upper Italy there had survived much of the old Roman character with its austere and frugal outlook. The people were absorbed in rural pursuits and simple pleasures and would be much less likely to feel the need of a new religion. They were, in this, very different from the cosmopolitan and disillusioned society of Rome and the South. There was really a threefold strain in the population, for considerable Etruscan settlements are known to have been made before the Gaulish invasion (Polybius, II, 17), and even under the Empire Mantua retained its Etruscan character, though probably this was a feature not shared by its neighbours.[4] The Gaulish or Celtic

---

[1] On the growth of Italian dioceses, see F. Lanzoni, "Le origini delle diocesi antiche d'Italia", in *Studi e Testi*, XXXV, p. 261 ff.

[2] Euseb., VII, xxx, 19. Haller thinks that as late as the Council of Sardica (343) Upper Italy was not included in ecclesiastical Italy and that the jurisdiction of Rome did not extend so far: see *Das Papsttum*, p. 79.

[3] Gregory the Great collected the stories of the saints up to his own day in *De Vita et Miraculis Patrum Ital.* The collection was known to Bede. As a historical source its value is negligible.

[4] Virgil says of it, *Tusco de sanguine vires* (*Aeneid*, X, 203); whilst Pliny the Elder calls it *Tuscorum trans Padum sola reliquia* (*Hist. Nat.*, III, 19).

element in Cisalpine Gaul went further south than is sometimes realized, for Sinigaglia represents Sena Gallica. No doubt many Celtic traditions survived beneath the romanized crust. A further element was added after A.D. 174, when masses of the defeated Marcomanni were transported to North Italy, where an outbreak of plague had reduced the population. The danger of bringing in large numbers of barbarians was soon demonstrated, for there was a rising in Ravenna and the seizure for a time by the Marcomanni of the city itself (Cassius Dio, LXXII, 11).

Aquileia, in the north-eastern corner, was an important commercial centre, the emporium of a trade which reached northwards to the Danube and eastwards to Byzantium. From it Christianity, when once established, would naturally spread throughout the surrounding region. It cherishes a tradition, valueless from the historian's point of view, that Mark was its bishop before going to Alexandria.[1] A more substantial testimony to the presence of Christianity in the city is the record of its bishop's attendance at the Council of Arles. The present cathedral is supposed to occupy the site of an earlier structure built by Bishop Theodorus at the beginning of the fourth century.[2] Aquileia, which in the days of Ausonius was the ninth largest city in the Empire, is now an insignificant and poverty-stricken township, its position having been usurped by Venice to which it supplied citizens. It seems to have enjoyed some kind of religious eminence, for in the fourth or fifth century a certain African named Restutus made a pilgrimage *ut istam urbem videret*. There he died and was buried.[3]

Moving west from Aquileia we come to Verona, the city which to Ruskin "represented the faith and beauty of Italy" (*Praeterita*, II, § 140). But that was Italy of the Middle Ages. What is notable about its history, or supposed history, in earlier times is the restraint which forbore to claim an apostolic founder. It was content with a certain Euprepius said to have been one of the seventy disciples of Luke 10 : 1.[4] During the Diocletianic persecution two martyrs, Fermus and Rusticus, are said to have perished. We reach more solid ground with St. Lucillus, claimed as the sixth bishop, who attended the Council of Sardica in 343. The early Christians are supposed to have worshipped in the Grotto of St. Nazarus, a small chapel cut in the rock. The neighbouring Brescia (Brixia) sent its fifth bishop to Sardica.

[1] See Galliciolli, *Delle Memorie Venete*, II, p. 332. The *Liber Pontificale* says that Pius, Bishop of Rome, was *natione Italus . . . de civitate Aquileia*.
[2] The church was rebuilt in the eleventh century, but mosaics from the original basilica were discovered in 1910.
[3] *C.I.L.*, V, No. 1703.
[4] Ughelli, *Ital. Sacr.*, V, p. 677.

Legend tells of a predecessor, Flavius Latinus by name, in the first century.[1]

Turning south we come to Padua (Patavium). Its ambitions seem to have been of a secular nature, for it was apparently satisfied with its claim to have been founded by Antenor, the brother of Priam of Troy. What is actually a medieval sarcophagus is still shown as his tomb. Christian legends of ancient growth are lacking and the first bishop to be named is Euparius (d. 293). His successor, Felix, was not without distinction, if the custom of having separate Christian burial-grounds was, as is alleged, his invention. Felix died in 313 and was followed by Paulus, a Roman by birth.

Further to the south and east, Ravenna lies near the coast amidst its pines. Before the sea retreated, Ravenna was a busy seaport and one of the most important Roman naval bases. During the winter months when the fleet was laid up the marines were housed in the Castra Ravennatium in the Trastevere region of Rome. This continual intercourse between Rome and Ravenna cannot be neglected as a factor in the spread of Christianity. As one of the most ancient cities of Italy, and later the ecclesiastical rival of Rome, Ravenna is naturally well supplied with legends, and has the distinction of being mentioned in the *Sibylline Oracles*, V, 204 f. Its ecclesiastical legends, however, were not sufficient to satisfy the curiosity of the medieval chronicler Agnello, who, in a most ingenuous and illuminating passage, has informed us that in compiling the lives of the early bishops he filled up any gaps from his imagination, assisted by the prayers of his brethren.[2] The first bishop is said to have been Apollinarius who had been sent there by St. Peter himself. He is said to have left Antioch in 44, and was skilled in both Greek and Latin literature.[3] Four of his disciples followed him, one of whom, Eleuchadius, was bishop in 100.[4] It is said that before his conversion Eleuchadius had been a philosopher. Leaving such legends aside we find that a bishop, who is claimed to be the twelfth to occupy the see, attended the Council of Sardica. Of lesser folk, in the ecclesiastical world, Fosca, a maiden of noble birth, is said to have been put to death, together with her nurse Marca, in the Decian persecution. The twelfth-century church of Santa Fosca at Torcello, once in ruins but recently restored, claims to enshrine her remains.

Bologna, in spite of its great age and continuous importance,

---

[1] Ughelli, *Ital. Sacr.*, V, p. 728. There seems to have been a Bishop of Brixen (Bressanone) of this name in the third century (Syxtus, II, p. 183). They may have been confused.

[2] See Muratori, *Rerum Ital. Scriptores*, II, Pt. II, p. 62.

[3] His life is included in *Vita Sancti Exuperantii* of Agnello.

[4] There is a sermon upon him by Peter Damien (*P.L.*, CXLIV, col. 534).

seems to have few early legends, and Christianity was slow to
make an entry there. During the Diocletian persecution a certain
Agricola and his slave Vitalis were crucified. Their bodies were
deposited in a Jewish burying-ground and only discovered in
393 with supernatural aid. The relics were taken to Florence.[1]
The patron saint, Petronius, to whom the largest church is dedicated, died in 430. It has, however, been claimed that the old
cathedral of Santi Pietro e Paolo went back to the previous
century.

Pavia (Ticinum) holds that Felix, the ninth of her bishops,
was martyred as early as 255 after filling the see for only two
years.[2] In spite of these details there is much doubt as to whether
he even existed. A church at Ticinum about 326 is, however,
mentioned by Sulpicius Severus (*Vita S. Martini*, II), and an
ancient sarcophagus, said to contain the remains of the first
bishop, Syrus, who lived in the second century, still exists.[3] The
combination of the two names Felix and Syrus is also found in
the episcopal lists of Genoa. A Felix succeeded St. Valentine,
famous for his combination of learning and holiness of life, in
307. He in turn was followed by Syrus who had been his pupil.
To the north-west of Genoa we find that Asti (Asta) honoured
as its first bishop Evasius, who was martyred in 265; whilst at
Como (Comum), further to the north and east, there appears to
have been a church before the close of the third century as well
as a number of martyrs. It is surprising that we know so little
about Como; it was perhaps not ambitious to make ecclesiastical
history, having its secular fame as the birthplace of the two
Plinys, and later as the refuge of Julian,[4] and its lovely lake
"with its scent of myrtles and everlasting spring" which Paul
the Deacon far away in the court of Charlemagne could never
forget.[5]

Last of all, in Upper Italy, we come to the great see of Milan
(Mediolanum). In later times it claimed to have been founded
by St. Barnabas,[6] but there is no early evidence in favour of the
legend. Milan had a fine record of martyrs, among whom two
brothers, Gervasius and Protasius, are said to have suffered in

---

[1] See Paulinus, *Vita Ambrosii*, XIV; Ambrose, *Exhort. ad Virgin.*; and
Paulinus of Nola, *Carm.*, XXIV.
[2] Ughelli, *Ital. Sacr.*, I, p. 1078.
[3] See De Rossi, *Bull. Arch. Crist.*, 1876, p. 95 ff.
[4] Ammianus Marcellinus, XV, ii, 8.
[5] *Carm.*, IV (*Poet. Lat. Carolini Aevi*, i).
[6] The earliest mention is in the *Datiana Hist. Eccles. Mediolanensis* (ed.
Biraghi), so called from Datio, Archbishop of Milan in the middle of the sixth
century. The episcopate of Barnabas naturally became part of the stock of
every chronicler. In the *Opusc. de situ Mediolani* (*Rerum Ital. Scriptores*, I,
Pt. II), for example, a whole section is devoted to *De adventu Barnabae Apostoli*
(p. 205).

the days of Nero. Their chief importance lies in the dedication to them in 387 by Ambrose of the Basilica which later was to bear his own name. Another martyr was Faustinus who suffered in 182, having been baptized, together with his father Philip, by Caius who is reckoned as the third bishop. Still another victim was Nabor, put to death in 304.[1] So far, legends of a not very reliable character have been our guide in dealing with the affairs of Milan. Our first really authentic information is concerned with Bishop Merocles (304–15), who attended the Councils of Rome and of Arles. We know nothing more about him, and even the correct spelling of his name is uncertain. When Milan became the headquarters of the government in the West the city acquired new importance and became a serious rival to Rome. Under Ambrose its prestige would be raised yet higher. But the retirement of Honorius to the safety of Ravenna removed any real threat to Roman supremacy. In the Middle Ages, however, the rivalry of the fourth century would flare up once again.

(b) *Central Italy* [2]

Beginning from the north-east we find that Faenza (Faventia) was represented at the Council of Rome by Constantius, the first of its bishops, from whom the cathedral takes its name.[3] Rimini (Ariminum) near by was also represented at Rome, but claimed to have had a bishop as early as 260. Later it was to be the scene of the notorious council (359) after which Christendom was amazed to find itself Arian. Further down the east coast Pesaro (Pisaurum) lays claim to a bishop named Florentius in the middle of the third century. He is said to have built a church there.[4]

Moving across the mountains into Tuscany we come to Florence. Here tradition has it that Christianity was introduced in the days of Nero, and that St. Miniato was martyred under Decius. The evidence in support of each of these claims is, however, but meagre and of little value. The importance of Florence lay in the future. The same applies to Siena some thirty miles to the south. It may be the Siena which sent a bishop to the Council of Rome, but its claim could be disputed by both Cesena and Segni. The small church of St. Quirino is said to occupy the site of the Temple of Quirinus, an interesting example of the persistence of sacred sites and sacred names.

In Umbria the queenly city of Perugia (Perusia) has, as might

---

[1] Mentioned by Ambrose, *Epist.*, XXII.
[2] Some scholars think that up to the close of the second century at least the Churches of Central Italy were directly dependent on Rome: see F. Lanzoni, *Le origini delle diocesi antiche d'Italia*, p. 595 ff.
[3] Optatus of Milevis, *P.L.*, XI, col. 931.
[4] Ughelli, *op. cit.*, II, p. 948.

have been expected, many romantic legends concerning its origin. Justinus had attributed its foundations to the Achaeans (*De Hist. Philipp.*, XX, 1), but in the Middle Ages exiles from Troy were considered more appropriate. The origin of the Church in the city aroused similar fanciful stories; it was traced back to apostolic times and Ercolanus, a disciple of St. Peter, is named as its founder.[1] But history has preserved no record of the coming of Christianity to Perugia. The so-called apostle of Umbria, St. Felicianus, had his see in the third century at Foligno (Folginum), where he is said to have had three predecessors. It was at Foligno that Heraclius, Justus, and Mauros are supposed to have suffered during the Decian persecution. In the persecution of Diocletian, the neighbouring city of Spoleto (Spoletium) lost its bishop, Sabinus, and two deacons. Ferento (Ferentum) also had a martyr, Eutychius by name, who suffered in 269. He is mentioned by Gregory the Great (*Dialog.*, III, 38).

Turning now to the west coast, we find that Civita Vecchia (Centum cellae), whose harbour was planned by Trajan, sent Bishop Epictetus to the Council of Arles. It was in 253 the scene of the exile and death of Cornelius, Bishop of Rome. Moving further down the coast we come to the famous twin harbours of Portus and Ostia. Portus[2] had been founded by Claudius when Ostia became choked up, but it soon shared the same fate. Trajan refounded it in 103 and made a canal which now forms the main stream of the Tiber. The harbour itself has become a shallow lake, and that constructed by Claudius has completely dried up. Ecclesiastically, Portus is notable as the suggested see of Hippolytus. It sent a bishop to the Council of Arles,[3] but apparently not to that of Rome. Some authorities consider that Christianity made an early appearance at Portus. This is quite a probable supposition, though there is no actual evidence to support it. The city claimed a number of martyrs.[4]

At Ostia, important excavations have recently been carried out. It seems to have begun with a small stronghold in the fourth century, though Virgil may have intended it for the scene of the first settlement of Aeneas at the mouth of the Tiber. Later it became very important as the massive ruins still testify. Its harbour, known as the *Emporium*, became choked up by the

[1] See Ciatti, *Memorie annali et istoriche di Perugia*, Pt. I, Bk. I, p. 423. The successor of Ercolanus is said to have been martyred under Marcus Aurelius —see Pellini, *Dell' Historia di Perugia*, I, p. 95—which leaves an awkward gap of over a century between them.
[2] The wide extent and importance of Portus can be inferred, not only from literary notices, but also from the results of excavation: see De Rossi, *Bull. Arch. Crist.*, 1866, pp. 37 f., 63, 99, 193.
[3] The description which follows his signature is a little unusual: *Gregorius episcopus de loco qui est in Portu Romae.*
[4] See Marucchi, p. 654.

Tiber at the beginning of the Christian era. Claudius dug a new channel and made many other improvements in the port and city, whilst Trajan added still further to the amenities of the place. For the Romans, under the Empire, it was a popular summer resort and bathing place; the Brighton, so to speak, of Rome. Ostia, as an important port, was a ready means of entry for all kinds of foreign influences. It was here in 205 B.C. that Scipio had welcomed the Black Stone in which was embodied the Magna Mater of Pessinus. It was at Ostia, too, that the worship of Isis was first introduced, and to the end it remained the centre of that worship in Italy. There was, which may account for the ease with which strange faiths came to Ostia, a large resident population of Orientals, including not a few Syrians. We have little information concerning Christianity and its coming, though an apostolic founder has been claimed. Minucius Felix, it will be remembered, made it the scene of his delightful dialogue *Octavius*, at the close of the second century; but this is no evidence of the presence of Christianity as the speakers are there on a visit from Rome. Under Claudius II (268–70) a number of martyrs are said to have been put to death, including St. Ciriacus, the bishop, and St. Aurea, who became the patron saint of the city. Ostia, as every reader of the *Confessions of St. Augustine* will recall, was the scene of the touching farewell and death of Monnica. At the Council of Rome in 313 Ostia was represented by its bishop, Silvester. As the ground is not suited to the construction of catacombs the remains are few, but there are some Christian cemeteries. One remarkable feature is the frequent use of *hic dormit* on the tombstones.[1]

South of Rome there lies Antium (Anzio),[2] the Volscian capital in which Coriolanus sought refuge. It also provided a retreat to Callistus, and from it he returned to Rome to undertake the charge of the cemetery which bears his name on the Appian Way. Harnack has apparently misunderstood the statement of Hippolytus, IX, 12, and so places the cemetery at Antium, and takes this location as evidence for a Church there.[3] Antium was the birthplace of two of the emperors of our period, Caligula and Nero. Leaving the coast and turning east we come, at a distance of some fifteen miles, to Tres Tabernae, known from its mention, together with Appii Forum, in connexion with St. Paul (Acts 28 : 15). It sent a bishop, Felix by name, to the Council of Rome. Going north-west from this town towards Rome we come to the Alban Mountains and here we find the famous site of Aricia.

---

[1] It is perhaps worth mentioning that Ostia retained its importance as a port until Pope Pius V in 1612 reopened the right arm of the Tiber at Portus.

[2] Since I first wrote this paragraph Anzio has acquired a new and splendid significance.

[3] *Mission und Ausbreitung*, p. 811 (E.T., II, p. 391).

This place, which lies to the south of present-day Ariccia, was once the central shrine of the Latin League and had a grove sacred to Diana into which no horse was ever allowed to enter (Virgil, *Aeneid*, VII, 761 ff.). Her priest was the *rex nemorensis*, a runaway slave who acquired his office by slaying his predecessor (Strabo, V, 239). Its only early connexion with Christianity is the statement in *Acts of Peter*, XXXII (*Apoc. N.T.*, p. 332) that Simon Magus took refuge there for a time. The story is, of course, unworthy of credence, but the choice of the locality suggests that Christians were living there. In the same passage Terracina is also mentioned as the scene of Simon's end. It sent a bishop to Rome in 313. Unlike Aricia there are a number of legends, apart from Simon Magus, connecting the town with Christianity, for Nereus and Achilles, disciples of St. Peter, are said to have been martyred there,[1] as well as Julian and Caesarius.[2] Terracina, which stands on a conspicuous limestone rock, was the Anxur of the Volscians.[3]

Fifteen miles north-east of Ariccia lies Palestrina (Praeneste), famous in the Middle Ages as the chief stronghold of the Colonna family. It claimed to be one of the oldest cities of Italy. Sulla, after besieging and destroying it, had it rebuilt to become a favourite summer resort of the Roman aristocracy. In Christian times it laid claim to a martyr, St. Agapitus, who is said to have met his death in the reign of Aurelian.[4] Its bishop, Secundus, attended the Council of Rome.

(c) *South Italy and Sicily*

South Italy is, as it has always been, a very different land from Italy further north. In the south, good harbours towards the east are to be found and these attracted immigrants who brought with them the brilliant culture of Hellas and gave as a perpetual inheritance characteristics which are not to be found among the inhabitants of the more purely Latin heart of the land.

The first mention of Christians in South Italy is in Acts 28 : 13 f., when St. Paul, on his way to Rome, landed at Puteoli, now Pozzuoli, and found certain brethren there. Since he was desired to tarry with them, we may safely conclude that they were residents and had not, like the brethren at Appii Forum (Acts 28 : 15), merely come for the purpose of meeting him.

---

[1] Their *Acta* belong to the fifth or sixth century but seem to contain a few reliable details. Their bodies were eventually taken to Rome.

[2] Mentioned by Bede, *Martyr.* (ed. Smith), p. 439.

[3] Horace, after passing through Ariccia and Appii Forum, speaks of *impositum saxis late candentibus Anxur* (*Sat.*, I, v, 26).

[4] The *Acta* are late but may well contain authentic matter: see Marucchi, *Notizie storiche sul mart. S. Agapite*, Rome, 1874.

Columns from the Temple to Augustus, which must have gazed down on St. Paul as he landed, have been incorporated in the cathedral of San Proculo which crowns the height above the city. Puteoli was the natural landing place for anyone coming from the East. Titus, after the fall of Jerusalem, sailed from Alexandria, and after touching at Rhegium, landed there (Suetonius, *Titus*, V). According to the Antiochene *Acts of the Martyrdom of Ignatius*, which were accepted as genuine by Ussher and other older authorities,[1] the saint was bitterly disappointed when bad weather forced the ship in which he was travelling to go on to Portus. He had wished to follow in the footsteps of St. Paul. Puteoli was the port at which the famous Alexandrian grain fleet used to arrive; its coming has been vividly described by Seneca (*Epist.*, LXXVII). In spite of its distance from Rome it was the port for that city and, indeed, the chief port of Italy until the improvements carried out at Ostia and the construction of the harbour at Portus began to rob it of its importance.

The commerce of Puteoli had been greatly increased under the Republic when the slave trade which Italian merchants had carried on at Delos was moved further west. Puteoli, indeed, came to be known as Little Delos. Its importance as a link with the East led to many settlements of Orientals near the port, and Syrians became so numerous that a special tax was imposed for permission to carry on a native cult.[2] There were also many Jews. Thus all the elements which would make for the favourable reception of the Gospel were present. In spite of this, however, we hear little of any Church life there. In the *Acts of Peter*, VI (*Apoc. N.T.*, p. 309), a certain Ariston is mentioned, and an alarming apostasy among the Christians owing to the activities of a Jew named Simon. Such statements have little value save in suggesting that Christians, in some numbers, were actually to be found in Puteoli, otherwise the stories would not carry conviction. Januarius, the famous Bishop of Beneventum whose miraculous blood brought such ecclesiastical profit to Naples, of which he is the patron saint, actually met his death at Puteoli during the Diocletian persecution and his body was not taken to Naples until 432.

Naples, of which Pozzuoli is now a suburb, may well have had Christians in quite early days as it possessed a numerous Jewish community. It claimed as its first bishop St. Aspren who, having been cured of a disease by St. Peter, was afterwards baptized and later consecrated by him. But the real patron saint of Naples is Virgil, who spent most of his latter days there and was

---

[1] Lightfoot, however, rejects them (II, i, p. 382 ff.).
[2] See Mommsen, *Provinces*, II, p. 138 f.

there buried. An anonymous Latin poet quoted by T. R. Glover, *Virgil*, p. 332 f., has described an imaginary visit to his tomb paid by St. Paul: [1]

> Virgil's tomb the saint stood viewing,
> And his aged cheek bedewing,
>   Fell the sympathetic tear;
> "Ah! had I but found thee living,
> What new music wert thou giving,
>   Best of poets and most dear."

Naples, it need hardly be said, was an important centre for the radiation of Greek culture and learning. One interesting feature of the city is the presence of five catacombs, four to the north and a fifth under Sant' Efremo. They contain wide and lofty corridors and chapels, but the date of the latter is uncertain. A first-century bishop, Epitimitus, has been claimed for Naples, as well as several predecessors. [2]

Among the numerous and varied remains of Pompeii, if there is nothing which can be claimed as Christian without qualification, certain inscriptions strongly suggest that the Gospel had reached the city before its destruction. There is, for example, a mutilated inscription which reads HRISTIAN. [3] The words "Sodom and Gomorra", found written on the walls of a house, must also have come from a Christian or possibly a Jewish hand. [4] The Jews had settlements at Pompeii and one of their synagogues, "Synagoga Libertinorum", recalls Acts 6 : 9. [5]

Some sixteen miles to the north-east of Naples lies Nola, which had the strange double distinction of witnessing the death of Augustus in A.D. 14 and the birth of Giordano Bruno in 1548. In the middle of the third century it was the scene of the labours of St. Felix of Nola. He was ordained *c.* 250 by Maximus the bishop, and suffered in the Decian and Valerian persecutions. His fame depends upon the eulogies of St. Paulinus, perhaps the greatest saint of the fifth century, who surrendered great possessions to serve humbly at his shrine. [6] Some forty miles further on

---

[1] The original can be found in Comparetti, *Vergil in the Middle Ages*, p. 78:

> *Ad Maronis mausoleum*
> *Ductus fudit super eum*
> *Piae rorem lacrimae;*
> *Quem te, inquit, reddidissem,*
> *Si te vivum invenissem,*
> *Poetarum maxime.*

[2] See Ughelli, *Ital. Sacr.*, VI, p. 26.   [3] *C.I.L.*, IV, No. 679.
[4] *C.I.L.*, IV, No. 4976. See Nestle, *Zeitschrift für N.T. Wissenschaft*, V, p. 167 f.
[5] See Lanciani, *Pagan and Christian Rome*, p. 310.
[6] *Carm.*, XII. (*P.L.*, LXI, col. 463):

> *Et foribus servire tuis, tua limina mane*
> *Munditiis curare sines; et nocte vicissim*
> *Excubiis servare piis: et munere in isto*
> *Claudere promeritam defesso corpore vitam.*

in the same direction is the city of Beneventum, famous alike in classical and medieval times. Christianity penetrated to it during our period, for, apart from St. Januarius, there is record of its having sent a bishop to the Council of Rome. A certain Erasmus, who is described as Bishop of Campania, was martyred under Diocletian. From him was taken one of the most famous names in history, Erasmus of Rotterdam. In Apulia there was a Church at Arpi, a city founded according to Virgil, *Aeneid.*, XI, 243, by Diomedes, for its bishop attended the Council of Arles.

It is very surprising that we have so few traces of the progress of the Gospel in the extreme south of Italy, for, since it was Greek-speaking, no more likely region for missionary activity could have been found apart from Rome itself. Clement of Alexandria, it will be recalled, lived here for a time and found Christian teachers (*Strom.*, I, i, 11); whilst among the very few bishops from the West who were present at the Council of Nicaea was Marcus, Bishop of Calabria. The incidental mention, in Acts 28 : 13, of a possible visit of St. Paul to Reggio (Rhegium) has been sufficient to form the basis of the usual legends. It is claimed that he spent some time there, and that on one occasion he silenced the grasshoppers who interfered with his preaching.[1]

By the time that Christianity began to arrive in the West, Sicily had been displaced as the granary of Rome by Egypt and Africa. Much of the land had therefore become pasture and was farmed by landlords who lived at Rome and on the mainland. An attempt by Augustus to revive agriculture by settling colonies of small farmers had not met with much success. The population of the island was made up of the most diverse elements, it was a very mosaic of civilizations; but the landowners were a Roman aristocracy who did not take much interest in the country itself apart from its productivity. Latin was the official language, but it seems to have been little spoken by the common people, although in use among the clergy until the end of the sixth century. St. Paul spent three days in Syracuse on his way to Rome (Acts 28 : 12), but there is no trace of Christianity in Sicily until Cyprian records that during the Decian persecution the Roman clergy wrote to the island (*Epist.*, XIII: cf. XXX, 5). An earlier piece of evidence may perhaps be found in an inscription to one Callistus, a native of Sicily, in the Great Cemetery in the Via Nomentana in Rome.[2] As Greek letters are used, it is presumably pre-Nicene. But Callistus may have been converted after his arrival in Rome.

. Syracuse seems to have been the most important centre of

---

[1] It is curious that Pausanias should mention the fact that the grasshoppers there are supposed to be silent.

[2] In Marucchi, p. 410.

Christianity in our period, and its bishop, Chrestus, was the first to subscribe his name at the Council of Arles. A letter addressed to him by Constantine has been preserved by Eusebius (X, v, 21 ff.). There are in Syracuse a number of catacombs known as the grottoes of St. John which are of early date; they may, indeed, originally have been used in pre-Christian times. Some think that they are evidence for Christianity in Sicily in the second century.

Pantaenus, the head of the Catechetical School at Alexandria, who gave up Stoicism to become a Christian, seems to have been a native of Sicily, for Clement, who may have met him there, calls him a "right Sicilian bee" (*Strom.*, I, i, 14). It is also possible that Porphyry's attacks on Christianity, composed in Sicily, may have been provoked by its local manifestations.

Sicily seems to have had its due quota of martyrs. At Leontius a virgin named Euthalia is said to have been put to death by her own brother in 257 for professing the faith. Possibly earlier is the martyrdom of St. Agatha at Catania. Her cult has been a most flourishing one, and even at the present day it is believed that to carry her veil in procession is the most certain way of averting eruptions of Mount Etna. St. Agatha was not the only saint who was powerful against Mount Etna, for Taormina holds that its own patron, San Pancrazio, has always saved it, even though streams of lava have often come very near. At Catania there also suffered a deacon named Euplius during the Diocletian persecution. The same outbreak witnessed the martyrdom of St. Lucia at Syracuse.

There are not many legends about Christianity in Sicily though the *Acts of Peter and Paul*, VII (ed. Lipsius, p. 182) claim that when St. Paul was at Reggio he crossed over to Messina and appointed Bacchylus as bishop of that city. To end on a more authentic note it may be recorded that a bishop named Capito, from a see in Sicily which is not mentioned, was present at Nicaea.

CHAPTER IV

NORTH AFRICA[1]

The Church in North Africa is perhaps the most romantic of all the early Christian Churches. We admire its vigorous growth, the constancy of its martyrs, whilst even the bitterness of its sectarian struggles is but the reverse of a high virtue, the defect of its qualities. Above all, the African Church was adorned by a succession of great names—Tertullian, Cyprian, and Augustine. Perhaps our interest is quickened, especially for the third century, by the possession of unusually full information in the form of those intimate letters of Cyprian which throw so vivid a light on its proceedings. Unfortunately after his death that light is withdrawn and a curtain seems to descend on the stage of North Africa; to rise again with the development of the Donatist Schism at the beginning of the following century. But while the curtain is drawn back and the lights are full on we have a stage crowded with living and moving figures. And the background, for those who have an eye for such matters, is a thing of beauty and historic interest. The very name of Carthage is a poem in itself; and the architectural remains—one need think only of Timgad, "the African Pompeii", with its noble ruins and the mountains stretched along the near horizon—testify to a vanished past of high achievements.

Geographically, North Africa forms a distinct area. Later on the Arabs, recognizing this, would call it Djezirat el-Maghreb, the isle of the West. The sea cuts it off from the north and the west alike, whilst the desert separates it from the south, as well as from Cyrene and distant Alexandria to the east. It is true that a road ran through Cyrene to Egypt, but the terrors and discomforts of the Western desert were such as to make it little used. It would require the age of mechanical transport to overcome them.[2] The real affinities of North Africa were with the lands across the Mediterranean rather than with the rest of the continent; in the fourth century the province of Tingitania was

---

[1] On the Church in North Africa, see, amongst other works: Leclercq, *L'Afrique chrétienne*, 1904, and Ernesto Buonaiuti, *Il cristianesimo nell' Africa Romana*, 1928. On the literature: the monumental work of P. Monceaux, *Hist. littéraire de l'Afrique chrét.* (Vols. I to VII, 1901–23). On Christian remains: J. Mesnage, *L'Afrique chrétienne*, 1912.

[2] The North African campaigns of 1940–43 will have made all this very familiar to English readers.

actually regarded as part of Spain for purposes of administration. Until Diocletian made further divisions it consisted of three provinces: Africa Proper, Numidia (a land of forts and camps), and Mauretania. These corresponded only roughly to the modern divisions, for Africa Proper included Tripoli and Tunisia; Numidia had part of Algeria; while Mauretania claimed the rest of Algeria and part of Morocco. Constitutionally and economically it was almost a century behind the other regions of the West.

Before the dawn of our period, Carthage, once the rival and then the victim of Rome, had risen from its ashes and again looked out across the distance which Cato found so menacing—with a favouring wind a ship could reach Carthage on the second day from Ostia. After being refounded as Colonia Julia by Julius Caesar it had been populated with colonists from Italy—veteran soldiers, hard-working agriculturists, and the necessary allowance of slaves. By the third century, which was a time of vigorous activity among all the cities of Roman Africa, it had become second only to Rome in wealth and population among the cities of the West, and even a rival of Alexandria in the East; a position which it still occupied in the late fourth century, though in the East its dispute for the place of second city of the Empire was with Constantinople, and not Alexandria, which had dropped back a little in the race.[1] From Carthage, which has now disappeared as completely as the North African Church itself, colonists pushed on to other growing cities, each modelled on Rome. Hadrian made a magnificent road nearly two hundred miles in length to link up Carthage and Theveste (Tebessa) and keep the rich cities of the Mount Aures region in touch with the centre of government. Dr. Jalland has expressed the opinion that Carthage was "more authentically Roman, because less exposed to the allurements of a decadent Hellenism and the insidious propaganda of an aggressive Orientalism than the imperial city itself" (*The Church and the Papacy*, p. 123). With this opinion I cannot fully agree, even for the late second century of which he is speaking, for if the Romans in Africa escaped these influences they succumbed to others even more deadly. The luxury and effeminacy which had exercised such an enervating effect upon earlier races of settlers found in them ready victims and after a time their condition was very much that of the descendants of the Crusaders in Syria and Palestine. In the

[1] Ausonius in his *Ordo Urbium Nobilium* writes, after giving the first place of all to Rome:

> Constantinopoli adsurgit Carthago priori,
> Non toto cessura gradum quia tertia dici
> Fastidit, non ausa locum sperare secundum
> Qui fuit ambarum.

second century itself the Romans of North Africa were despised by their fellow-countrymen in Italy. Even the famous author Fronto never felt really happy in Rome, although he was honoured and held to be the most elegant writer of his time. When all the flattery had been lavished upon him, he was still a "colonial".

The basis of the economic life of North Africa was agriculture, with the breeding of horses and mules as a profitable side line. From the beginning of the Roman occupation the cultivation of wheat had been intensified until it became the outstanding harvest. Thus it had continued for some centuries, but later other products had received more attention. In part this was due to the bringing of fresh land into cultivation which was not so well suited to the production of grain; in part to the appearance of new needs, especially in the matter of oil, among the Romans in Italy. So the vine and the olive were encouraged, as well as the fig tree and more humble members of the vegetable kingdom. The African native has ever been averse to industrial activity, and so manufactures were of but small account in the economic life of the people and there was little to export apart from grain and oil. In fact much had actually to be imported in the way of pottery, metal-work, and even building materials, though there were quarries which produced stone for local needs.

The people of North Africa, in spite of the infiltration of other races, were in the main from a single stock, that commonly known as Berber (the Greek "barbarian"). Other names, such as Libyan, Numidian, Moor, or Gaetulian, "corresponded to no intrinsic difference of race, but only of geographical position" (*Camb. Anct. Hist.*, XI, p. 481). The Berbers were a non-Semitic race and have persisted down to the present day as the predominant people of the land. In Numidia, for example, the natives to-day speak Berber and Arabic, as their forefathers spoke Berber and Punic under the Romans.[1] In the course of the centuries they have changed but little.

The intruding races were three: the Phoenicians, the Romans, and the Jews. The Phoenicians had been in North Africa for several centuries before the Christian era. But their migration from Syria was not nearly so ancient as the reader of the *Aeneid* is led to imagine. Actually it took place, not at the time of the Fall of Troy, as Virgil, wishing to ante-date the fatal connexion of Rome and Carthage, would have us believe, but some four centuries later. When Christianity first came in the Phoenicians had been almost completely romanized and still remained, as they had always been, an aristocratic class comparatively small

[1] cf. Boissier, *L'Afrique romaine*, p. 350.

in numbers. They were first and foremost traders, and during their period of rule had taken but little interest in the people and country away from the coast. They had, however, been the introducers of the vine, olive, and date-palm amongst other things. The Phoenicians had, of course, no complete monopoly of trade, for Greeks and Syrians also had their share and brought fresh influences and ideas to the country. The Romans had come in gradually, in the wake of the conquering legions. (Reference has already been made to the presence of colonies of veterans.) These formed the largest non-Berber element and contained other elements, Gallic, Spanish, German, and even Asiatic, as well as Italian. Many of them sought wives among the native population, and their posterity soon mingled with it. This process was helped by the recruitment of the army, from the second century onward, from the peoples on the spot, though there were in addition purely native forces, the so-called *limitanei* and *foederati*. The Romans naturally made their first settlements on the coast and then gradually spread into the fertile districts. Later still they pushed towards the south, bringing fresh lands into cultivation and robbing the "desert" to increase the "sown". In course of time they reproduced on the soil of Africa those great estates which had marked the economy of the land of their origin. Last of all came the Jews, cousins as it were of the Phoenicians. They were quite numerous, especially in the coast towns[1] where they were grouped in settlements with their own synagogues and cemeteries. They seem to have exercised, as elsewhere, some religious influence, and to have made converts among the native population, for the fourteenth-century Arabic writer, Ibn Khaldun, observed that in his day many Berber tribes in Tripoli and Morocco were Jews by religion. As it is most unlikely that they had adopted Judaism after the Moslem conquest, the conclusion that their conversion dates back to Roman times can hardly be avoided.[2]

As there were four chief races in North Africa, so also were there four languages in use. But these do not actually coincide with the races, for Hebrew demands no consideration, and Greek was brought in by the Romans as well as their own Latin. We have already noticed the use of Berber, usually in conjunction with Punic, and its survival to the present day. It was Punic, however, which was the popular speech among the natives, being employed even by the upper classes, although the Romans never gave it official status or themselves made use of

[1] See, further, Noeldechen, *Tertullians Gegen die Juden* (*Texte und Unters.*, XII, Pt. II, pp. 3–14), and Monceaux, "Les colon. juives dans l'Afrique romaine", in *Rev. Études juives* for 1902.

[2] Some historians, however, think that Ibn Khaldun mistook for Judaism some kind of debased Christianity which had survived to his day.

it:[1] Apuleius, a little beyond the middle of the second century A.D., reproached an African youth for speaking Punic; he had almost forgotten Greek, and Latin he knew not at all (*Apol.*, XCVIII). Greek, it should be noticed, remained for long the language of those who wished to be thought cultivated, and in the flourishing schools of Carthage it received as much attention as Latin, though it would seem that by the time of Augustine Greek studies had rather fallen into the background (*Conf.*, I, xiii f.). The early Christian martyr Perpetua spoke both Greek and Latin.[2]

Latin was the official language and was probably understood and employed on occasion by all better-class Africans, who would also know Greek or Punic in addition, as the case might be. But as in all parts of the Empire, the Latin spoken in everyday life, especially among the vulgar, was very different from the literary language. Even so Africa was especially noted for its dialect, which did not pass without criticism in Rome;[3] probably because, like the English spoken in New England, it contained a number of archaisms, as well as vulgar expressions. There was also an African "accent" which differed from the standard "Italian" current in Rome, even Augustine could be recognized as of African origin by his pronunciation, that *stridor punicus* to which Jerome refers (*De Ordine*, II, xlv). The numerous inscriptions are full of errors in grammar and idiom, though it would be a mistake to take them as evidence of defects in African Latin; in most cases they are doubtless due to the ignorance of the mason or his patrons.

Africa gave a number of literary men to the Latin world, the best known of whom is Apuleius. Apuleius was born at Madaura, "a very splendid colony", he calls it (*Apol.*, XXIV), about A.D. 125. Later he settled at Carthage, and like several of the Christian writers, for whose views he would have had but scant sympathy, he was a lawyer and rhetorician. He used Latin in both speaking and writing, but it was not his mother-tongue. He claims that he learnt it in Rome by his own efforts and without any instruction (*Metamorph.*, I, 1). Hence, no doubt, the

---

[1] Punic was evidently used in municipal affairs for a time: see Mommsen, *Provinces*, II, p. 326 f. In its native Syria, Punic, it may be worth noticing, had long been superseded by the kindred Aramaic; in Africa it was to disappear with the coming of Arabic.

[2] *Passio Perpet.*, XIII: *Coepit Perpetua Graece cum eis loqui.*

[3] Apuleius, *Metamorph.*, I, 1. Whether the so-called African was a dialect or not has been much disputed. In the second and third centuries Latin literature was almost entirely in the hands of Africans and so there is little with which to compare it. Miss M. D. Brock, *Studies in Fronto and His Age*, pp. 161–261, after a very careful examination comes to the conclusion that there was no African dialect; that which is called such was but the Latin of a certain epoch.

obscurities of his style. His best-known work, the *Metamorphoses* or *The Golden Ass*, as it is often called in English, was derived largely from *The Ass* of Lucius, the authorship of which has been attributed, almost certainly erroneously, to Lucian. But *The Ass* has been greatly enlarged and supplemented by the addition of many stories which Apuleius probably borrowed from the Milesian Tales which had been translated by Sisenna in the first century B.C. Apuleius is constantly referred to by Augustine as "Platonicus Apuleius" (e.g. *De Civ. Dei*, VIII). One significant fact in regard to African literature has often been noted; it never produced a single poet whose verse, or name, has been considered worthy of preservation. African genius sought other heights than those of Parnassus. With the emergence of Tertullian, to be followed by other Christian writers, the pre-dominance of Africa in Latin Literature is carried a stage further.

The subject of African religion calls for little comment and, in fact, not much is known about it. Already two outside streams of influence had come in to affect the native ideas of the super-natural, the Phoenician and the Roman. Both would naturally bear more strongly and more immediately upon the urban popu-lations and only gradually reach the countryside and the nomad peoples. The Berbers themselves appear to have had but rudi-mentary conceptions of things divine, it has even been sug-gested that they had no idea of God at all. Each village or settlement, however, probably had some kind of tutelary deity, and in the towns the native gods were soon identified with those of the Romans when the latter came in as conquerors.[1] Among the civil population there was a flourishing cult of the Great Mother, whilst at Lambaesis and other garrison towns traces of Syrian and Egyptian worship have been found as well as the cult of Mithras.

THE COMING OF CHRISTIANITY

Just as the exact date of the Phoenician occupation of the ports and markets of North Africa is unknown, so also Christi-anity when it came, came unobserved. In view of the close connexion of Carthage with Rome and the presence in North Africa of many colonists from Italy as well as of large estates belonging to Roman families,[2] it may reasonably be supposed

[1] In Dougga (Thugga), for example, south-west of Carthage, many temples, although dedicated to Punic deities, bear Roman names.

[2] cf. J. Mesnage, *L'Évangélisation de l'Afrique, part que certaines familles rom-africaines y ont prise.*

that it arrived from across the Mediterranean. Both Tertullian and Cyprian, it may be noted, regarded Rome as the source from which African Christianity drew its origin.[1] Be this as it may, it is clear that it was among Romano-Africans that the Gospel spread most rapidly.[2]

The natural way for Christianity to reach North Africa would be through Carthage, and Carthage by reason of its commerce was in close touch with Rome. But not with Rome only, for in spite of the dangers of the sea route along the North African coast,[3] there was regular intercourse with Alexandria and Antioch. From these eastern sources Christian influences may well have come in as well as from Italy, though we are not in a position to say in what particular order they were exerted or to assess their relative importance. The possibility that converts from Cyrene (Acts 2 : 10) had a hand in carrying the Gospel to their western neighbours, even if communication between them was difficult, cannot be entirely excluded. Christian missionaries were accustomed to overcome the most serious obstacles. Eastern influence may perhaps be found in the wide popularity of the cult of St. Stephen.[4] There are also a number of legends which connect the foundation of the Church in North Africa with Syria and Palestine;[5] among them are accounts of two visits paid by St. Peter during which he appointed Crescentius to be the first Bishop of Carthage. This tradition was accepted as genuine by Salvian of Marseilles in the middle of the fifth century, and, what is less surprising, by the bishops of Numidia in that which followed. Direct evidence of definite connexions with the East during our period can be found in the relations of Tertullian with the Montanists and in the correspondence of Cyprian with Firmilian of Caesarea in Cappadocia. Neither of these, it may be remarked, throws any light on origins.

There is, however, one other rather interesting link, that of architecture. In view of the connexion with Rome it is surprising to find that, in spite of much that is common, there are striking differences between Rome and African ideas of church-building. The most notable of them is the absence in Africa of transepts

---

[1] Gregory the Great claimed that the African bishops derived their succession from Rome (*Epist.*, VIII).

[2] See J. Mesnage, *L'Évangélisation de l'Afrique.*

[3] At one time part of the Alexandrian and Syrian fleet was stationed at Caesarea (Chercell) to protect the coast against pirates.

[4] See Toulotte, *Nuovo Bull. Arch. Crist.*, 1902, VIII, p. 211 ff. Relics of St. Stephen were claimed to exist at Rusicade (Philippeville) (see Augustine, *Epist.*, CCXII) as well as at Carthage, Kairouan, and Tichilla (Testour in Tunisia).

[5] See Leclercq, *L'Afrique chrét.*, p. 34, note 2. Augustine also seems to recognize some close link with Jerusalem (*Enarrat. in Ps. xliv : 23 and Ps. xlix : 3*) as well as with the East in general (*Epist.*, LII, 2).

and *atria*, both of which are regular features of Roman churches. Gsell, after a detailed survey, concluded that the architectural affinities of North Africa are with Egypt and Syria rather than with Italy and Rome (*Les Monuments antiques de l'Algérie*, II, p. 150).[1]

The Church in North Africa, like its sister across the Mediterranean, went through a stage of some duration in which it was Greek-speaking. Such is the conclusion to be drawn from the use of that language by Tertullian in some of his early writings and also from the *Passio S. Perpetuae* if, as seems probable, it was originally written in Greek.[2] But this stage came earlier to an end than in Rome, for the Roman Church first shows signs of latinization under the African Victor, its bishop in the last decade of the second century.

The first recorded event in the life of the North African Church was a martyrdom. This was in July 180 when, under the proconsul P. Vigellius Saturninus, who is mentioned as a persecutor by Tertullian (*Ad Scap.*, III), twelve Christians, seven men and five women, were put to death at Carthage. They came from Scillium and so are known as the Scillitan martyrs. Several of them bear Punic names. An account of their sufferings and fortitude, written in simple non-literary language, has been preserved.[3] It describes the proconsul as making every effort to avoid carrying matters to extremes. He argued patiently with the Christians and finding this of no avail gave orders that the men alone were to be put to death. Then after a delay he reluctantly enforced the same penalty on the women who still remained obstinate. The victims gave thanks to God that He had judged them worthy to suffer and then quietly went to the place of execution.[4] They were, so far as we know, the first sheaves of the great harvest of African martyrs.[5] The title of archi-martyr has, however, been claimed for Namphano, one of a small band who met their end at Madaura, some think in the same year. There are, however, reasons for placing the event in the middle of the fourth century and for thinking that the

---

[1] Monceaux, *Hist. litt. de l'Afrique chrét.*, I, p. 7, considers that certain features in the African liturgy support an Eastern connexion. He concludes that Christianity was first introduced from the East and then propagated in the hinterland through the Roman Church.

[2] Rendel Harris and Gifford, who recovered the Greek MS. of the *Acta*, consider that it is the original, but Armitage Robinson (*Texts and Studies*, I, No. 2) dissents. Harnack thinks that it may have appeared in a bilingual form (*Altchrist. Lit.*, p. 819).

[3] Printed as an appendix to Armitage Robinson's *Passio Perpetuae*.

[4] A basilica built over their tomb is mentioned by Victor Vitensis, *De Persec. Vandalorum*, I, iii, 9. It was perhaps at Coudiat Tsalli on the way to Utica.

[5] cf. Augustine, *Epist.*, LXXVIII: *Africa sanctorum martyrum corporibus plena est.*

victims were members of the Circumcellion sect of the Donatists.[1]

After the Scillitan outbreak there came a lull of some years,
though sporadic cases seem to have occurred between 198 and
212, and even the cemeteries were attacked. Amongst the
victims were Celerina and her two sons (Cyprian, *Epist.*,
XXXIV); whilst Aemilius and Castus, after an apostasy, suffered in May 203 (Cyprian, *De Lapsis*, XIII). It was in this
latter year, almost certainly, that Perpetua and her companions,
the most famous of all African martyrs, also suffered. An
interesting fact about this group is that they were Montanist in
sympathy, if not in actual allegiance, though this is quite likely,
especially as Montanism did not involve unorthodox views.

Perpetua herself was a young married woman and at the time
of her martyrdom had an infant son. Among her companions
were two slaves, one of whom, Felicitas, enjoyed with her considerable fame in the Western Church. They all came from
Thuburbo Minus (Tebourba), not far from Carthage, and had
been converted by a priest named Saturus. It was not until
after their arrest that they were actually baptized. Saturus himself suffered with them after having been vouchsafed a number
of visions. One pathetically human touch has been preserved in
connexion with him. He prayed that however he was to suffer it
might not be by being hugged to death by a bear. The sufferings
endured by these simple Christian folk were truly horrible and
they have been recorded in some detail—Perpetua, for instance,
was tossed to death by a cow—but they are for this reason all
the more impressive and witness to their amazing constancy.[2]
When Christianity became a legal religion their bodies were
placed in the Basilica Majorum at Carthage, though it was not
until 1907 that the inscription on their tomb was discovered.[3]

The rule of C. Julius Asper and his successor passed without
incident, and then came two years of persecution under Scapula
Tertullus (211–13) against whom Tertullian uttered his sinister
warnings. Tertullian also wrote at this time his *De Corona
militis*, which was inspired by the fate of a Christian soldier at

---

[1] Four of them—Namphano, Lucitas, Mygdon, and Samae—bear Punic
names. Namphano and Miggo(in) are common names in North Africa, but
Lucitas seems to be unique. The title *archimartyr* was given to the first of
them by a pagan writer, Maximus of Madaura, and has been preserved by
Augustine, *Epist.*, XVI. It may be the equivalent of *protomartyr* (cf. Lightfoot,
II, i, p. 463) or it may mean martyr-in-chief. The latter meaning is favoured
by J. H. Baxter in *J.T.S.*, XXVI, p. 21 ff.

[2] For an English rendering see A. J. Mason, *Historic Martyrs*, or E. C. E.
Owen, *Some Authentic Acts of the Early Martyrs*.

[3] It was discovered by Père A. L. Delattre of the Musée Lavigerie at Carthage
and has been reproduced by Mr. Owen as a frontispiece to the work mentioned
in the previous note.

Lambaesis.[1] During this crisis many of the bishops deserted their flocks; so Tertullian on the eve of his departure from the Church into Montanism has informed us (*De Fuga*, XI).

Tertullian played so important a part in the fortunes of the Church in North Africa that some details of his career must be given. He stands out as one of the most significant figures in the whole history of the Western Church and in the development of the Latin speech; for he set that Church moving along certain lines of thought and development and gave to it the rudiments of an ecclesiastical vocabulary. In him the characteristics of the African Church and of the Phoenician people, of whom he was so proud (cf. *De Pallio*, II), are combined. A combination which was to lend vital force to his personality.

The exact date of Tertullian's birth is not known, but it must have been soon after the middle of the second century. His father, a soldier in the service of the Proconsul of Africa, gave him a good education, which included a sound knowledge of Greek. Although Tertullian was never an exact scholar,[2] he had wide knowledge, and in the practice of the bar he found a congenial exercise for his very considerable talents. His instinct for rhetoric, which the whole course of his education and manner of life had tended to foster, was never overcome even when he became a Christian; it is especially noticeable in *De Pallio*. His conversion did not take place until he was nearly forty, and was followed, although he was a married man, by ordination to the priesthood.[3] The outstanding literary gifts which were his, together with his training as a lawyer, made him an ardent and useful advocate of his new faith; but unfortunately his fiery nature could not endure restraint or compromise, and after being what E. K. Rand has called the "self-constituted prosecuting attorney against all heretics", he himself stepped over the dividing-line and became a Montanist. He had then been a Christian less than ten years, and as he was to live a further twenty or more, two-thirds of his Christian life were spent outside the Church. Tertullian's real importance lies in his literary work—he was no statesman or organizer—and this side of his activities can be more conveniently studied in connexion, not with the development of the Church in North Africa, but with that of Christian thought in the West as a whole (see Part III, Chap. V). His influence was no doubt prejudiced by the lapse into Montanism, as is expressly stated by Hilary (*In Matt.* 5 : 1), but the recognition of him by Cyprian and the use of his writings by

---

[1] Lambaesis was the headquarters of the Third Legion at this time. The Roman camp there is one of the best preserved which has survived.

[2] So F. G. Kenyon, *Text. Criticism of the New Test.*, p. 254.

[3] Jerome is our sole authority for his having taken orders: see *De Vir. Ill.*, LIII.

the latter did much to counteract this. The ideas of the older man, softened and modified by Cyprian, gained currency in both West and East. By the time of Jerome, his works were so well known that he apologizes for mentioning them by name (*De Vir. Ill.*, LIII).[1]

We turn now to one whose activities furnish a complete contrast to those of Tertullian, to one who was the greatest statesman and organizer of the Western Church in the pre-Nicene age, a forerunner of great Latin bishops like Ambrose and Gregory the Great, and an example of "a creative personality . . . breaking his way out of the social framework in which his creative powers had been baulked and . . . setting himself in a new framework in which those powers were offered an outlet".[2]

Cyprian was born early in the third century, probably at Carthage, the city in which most of his busy life, both before and after his conversion, was spent. Although no record of his family has been preserved he was evidently a man of high social position and of considerable wealth, and his accession to the Church in North Africa must have been regarded as a notable triumph. Following the adhesion of Tertullian, it witnessed to the progress which Christianity was making in cultivated and influential circles. Like Tertullian he was a barrister, and like Tertullian he did not become a Christian until in mature years. From what fierce spiritual and intellectual struggles he emerged when accepting Christianity we cannot tell, for when he comes before us the inner turbulence has been quelled; but one who could call Tertullian his master can scarcely have escaped his own inner conflicts. Perhaps a recognition of his failure to live the highest life, or perhaps the failure of his times in which he himself was involved, may have driven him to seek new power and possibilities in the Gospel message and in the ordinances of the Church.

A presbyter named Caecilian was the means of his conversion and in gratitude he thereafter called himself Thascius Caecilius Cyprianus. This event occurred in 246, and only two years later on the death of the Bishop of Carthage he was forced, much against his own wishes, and mainly by pressure from the laity, to succeed to the office. A small body of the clergy, under the leadership of Novatus, disgusted by his promotion, were thrown into opposition; the root of much subsequent disquiet. The approval of the neighbouring bishops—by custom they should have made the original choice—regularized the position of the new bishop and Cyprian duly set out on his stormy career.[3]

[1] A sect of Tertullianists survived in North Africa until the days of Augustine: see *Haers.*, LXXX.
[2] Toynbee, *A Study of Hist.*, IV, p. 55, but with no reference to Cyprian.
[3] For the importance of Cyprian as a writer and as a theologian see pp. 262, 290 below.

The years which had preceded the election of Cyprian had been a time of peace and rapid expansion and the Church seemed firmly settled in the land, and even settled on its lees. Tertullian in the whole of his writings mentions less than half a dozen Christian congregations; but there must have been many more, for as early as 198 a synod at Carthage under Agrippinus was attended by seventy bishops, as many as were present at the synod of Lambaesis c. 240. After the persecution under Decius, nothing like such large numbers came to the numerous synods held by Cyprian; the average was about fifty, though at a synod in the autumn of 256 ninety bishops attended. These figures imply that considerable progress had been made, though at this stage of the Church's organization a bishop represented only a single city. The spread of the episcopate had doubtless been furthered by the elaborate municipal organization which went back to Phoenician times and furnished an obvious model. Under Cyprian's powerful leadership there was a large influx into the Church; but the subsequent relapse when persecution came reveals the shallowness of many of the converts.

It was in 249 that the African Church received its first severe testing, and Cyprian, with rare wisdom and restraint, retired before the storm. He saw that he could be of more service to the Church by continuing to direct its fortunes from a safe hiding-place than by a spectacular martyrdom. From his refuge, which was known to his intimates, and visited by some of them, he kept in close touch with all that was happening, bringing encouragement to those in prison by his letters and messages, and helping them from his considerable private resources. Meanwhile the clergy remained at their posts.

The persecution was the cause of many apostasies of one type or another, and when its main force had spent itself a grave problem was raised as to the treatment of those who wished to return. Cyprian took a reasonably severe line, though not sufficiently severe for some ardent spirits. The Church could not simply refuse to have any further responsibility for the lapsed; but they must be moved to remorse and penitence. The question of their complete restoration might be left to the end of the persecution and in the meantime it was possible for some to witness to the genuineness of their penitence by making a good confession. In cases of dangerous illness communion might be allowed on the intervention of a confessor. Such briefly was Cyprian's position. But if it was not sufficiently severe for some, it was too drastic for others, and soon the confessors began to issue *libelli pacis* granting restoration to the lapsed. The practice in the end became a positive scandal, for careful inquiries were not always made as to the penitence of those who received the letters; some confessors, indeed, seem to have issued what were virtually "blank cheques". Furthermore they gave orders that Cyprian and the other bishops were to recognize their action. This was too much for the Bishop of Carthage; it seemed a presumption on the value of confessorship which was quite unjustified, and likely to undermine completely the discipline of the Church. He consulted the Roman clergy as to the action which they were taking in similar circumstances and then took a strong line himself.

Differences over the lapsed gave an opportunity to the group of presbyters who had always resented Cyprian's appointment to add to his difficulties. But he refused to be shaken and insisted on treating each case on its own merits. Passion ran high and Cyprian was accused of belittling the confessors who had endured persecution when he himself was in hiding. Matters were made worse when his opponents succeeded in gaining control of the finances of the Church in Carthage. His sentence of excommunication against them seems to have had little effect.

It was at this stage of the dispute that Cyprian wrote his treatise *De Lapsis* in order to set out his exact position. Not all the lapsed were equally guilty. The worst were those who had offered sacrifice in order to safeguard their possessions before any compulsion had been applied to them. Less blameworthy were those who had broken down under torture. The former must not hope to be received back into communion, though God in His mercy might forgive them. The latter might be received after penitence. Those who had purchased *libelli* without having actually done sacrifice must also submit to penance. The letters issued by the confessors he virtually ignored.

Cyprian's position and his action against the rebellious presbyters was approved by a synod of bishops which met probably in May 251. A year later the rebels tried to upset this decision, and failing to do so chose a bishop, one Fortunatus, for themselves. He claimed to have the support of twenty-five bishops and very astutely sent messengers to Cornelius, the newly-elected Bishop of Rome, assuring him that Cyprian was losing ground and that he himself was the true bishop. For a moment Cornelius seems to have been impressed by this measure and Cyprian wrote a stern letter to him (*Epist.*, LIX) explaining the exact situation. This was effective. In the meantime the position in North Africa had been further complicated by the appearance of a Novatianist bishop, Maximus, who gathered around him those extremists who would not hear of the reception of any of the lapsed. Thus there were three parties in the Church of Carthage.

Cyprian's position was improved by concessions which he

made in May 253 when persecution seemed again about to break out. In order to strengthen the Church in view of the crisis it was agreed to receive back all those who had submitted to discipline. A safe move, for it was no time for waverers to place themselves again in jeopardy, and sincere Christians ought not to be deprived of the means of grace when facing the new peril.

After a delay the storm broke at last, and it found a Church much better prepared to meet it than in the days of Decius. This time Cyprian felt that his witness must be full and complete, that a purified Church would be strong enough to stand without his guidance, and so after a period of exile he met a noble death on September 14, 259. There were numerous other victims, including St. James and St. Marian.[1]

It has been suggested that one reason for the severity of the persecutions in North Africa at this time was the disturbed condition of the country. There had been widespread plagues in 252—Cyprian incidentally had taken measures both for the care of the living and the burial of the dead—and many raids by Berber tribes. This made the government anxious to suppress any kind of suspected movement. The Christians may even have been thought of as in league with the Berbers. In any case, since they took no share in the ceremonies intended to placate the offended gods, they became objects of dislike.

After the death of Cyprian the Church in North Africa enters on a period of obscurity; we do not even know with certainty the name of his successor, though it was probably Lucian.[2] Then at the end of the third century persecution again broke out, sporadically and mainly in the army, the prelude to the final testing under Diocletian. It happened, however, that North Africa in this escaped comparatively lightly, for the proconsul, Anulinus, was seemingly not an advocate of stern measures.[3] Some churches were seized, but not destroyed;[4] though even when the persecution was over they were not immediately restored, for a synod of bishops at Cirta (Constantine) in March 305 had to meet in a private house because no church was available.[5] Under Maxentius there was some renewal of oppression, but on political rather than religious grounds,[6] and with the victory of Constantine in 312 North Africa passed under his rule and the Church had no more need to fear the secular arm. But unfortunately this did not mean that the secular arm no longer had to interfere, for the Christian emperors were compelled to

---

[1] Referred to by Augustine, *Sermons*, CCLXXXIV. An account of their sufferings is printed in E. C. E. Owen, *Some Authentic Acts*, p. 105 ff.
[2] See *Passio Montani, Lucii et aliorum*, XXIII.
[3] So Augustine states in *Brev. Coll.*, III, 25.
[4] Gsell, *Les Monuments antiques*, II, p. 116.
[5] Optatus of Milevis, I, xiv.   [6] *idem*, I, xvii f.

copy the methods of their pagan predecessors and to use force to suppress religious opinions. This was due to the rise of what is known as the Donatist Schism.

The Donatist Schism really lies outside our period, but as its actual beginnings come within it and as it throws light on the mentality of African Christians, some brief notice must be taken of it. The schism arose in the following way. Mensurius, Bishop of Carthage, ably supported by his deacon Caecilian, took strong measures to discourage a fanatical desire for martyrdom which manifested itself during the Diocletianic persecution. For this, and his supposed leniency towards lapsed Christians, he and Caecilian incurred considerable unpopularity. Mensurius died in 311 and Caecilian was chosen to succeed him. But the bishops of Numidia had not been consulted over the appointment and they at once held a synod which declared his consecration invalid, not ostensibly on the ground that they had not been consulted, but because Felix of Aptunga, who had performed it, was believed to have been guilty of handing over sacred writings during the persecution. This accusation was almost certainly false, but it served their turn. In place of Caecilian they proceeded to appoint a certain Majorinus who seems to have been a mere figure-head, for the moving spirit was Donatus, Bishop of Casae Nigrae, from whom the sect probably took its name;[1] unless the honour, if such it can be called, belongs to Donatus the Great who soon afterwards succeeded Majorinus as Donatist Bishop of Carthage.

The African Church, even more than the remainder of Western Christendom, had little interest in speculation, hence its resistance to Gnosticism and its aloof attitude to the various schools of thought, Logos theologians, Marcionites, and Monarchians, who disputed between them. Tertullian might give forth his thunders, but the Church took no active measures. But if this aloofness saved it from heresy, it took a delight in schism. So now the dispute which had begun in a single see quickly spread over a great part of North Africa, especially in the country districts of Numidia, and rival bishops were soon to be found in many cities.

The Donatists, however, were not content with their progress, or were, perhaps, emboldened by it to take further measures. So they denounced Caecilian to Anulianus, the proconsul, and requested that the matter should be reported to Constantine. In order that their case might obtain a fair hearing they asked that a judge should be sent over from Gaul. The matter was finally transferred to Rome where a council was held in the Lateran on October 3 of the same year under Miltiades the bishop. Each side sent ten bishops to support its case. The in-

[1] So Augustine, *Haer.*, LXIX.

quiry resulted in a complete acquittal for Caecilian. But still the Donatists were not content and a more important council was held at Arles in August 314 (or 316), but with the same verdict. A direct appeal to the emperor for his personal investigation led to another rebuff for the Donatists at Milan in November 316.

In spite of all attempts to check them by the peaceful means of argument or the more doubtful method of persecution[1] the Donatists continued to flourish. They seem to have made an especial appeal to the native inhabitants, offering them something which corresponded to their special temper of mind, a temper of mind which had found expression in the writings of Tertullian and possibly the sect of Tertullianists fostered the speedy growth of the Schism. The Africans may also have seen in the movement an opportunity of protesting against Italian rule, or at least of taking a line of their own. The reason which may also account for the rapid spread, during the eighteenth century, of Methodism in Wales and Cornwall, districts which had hitherto been free from Dissent. Donatism had thus a social and political significance, and it is possible that had the Church in North Africa found means to reconcile the sectaries its whole history would have been very different. The schism never spread beyond Africa, but in Africa the struggle which it aroused was fierce and bitter, and the tide of martyrdom again flowed wide and deep; with the tragic difference that now Christians were slaughtering their fellows. After the work of Augustine, a truly doughty opponent, the movement gradually decayed.

The final efforts of the Empire to crush the Church had no permanent effect and Christianity made such rapid progress that the whole population, apart from the Berbers, seemed on the way to accepting it in one form or another, for the rescript of Constantine to Miltiades, if taken literally, almost presupposes that all the inhabitants were either Catholic or Donatist (Euseb., X, v, 18). A most imposing list of bishops and sees can certainly be compiled.[2] As elsewhere the Gospel had first spread among the lower ranks of society and the bishops, with a few striking exceptions such as Cyprian, probably came from the same humble order of society.[3] Later it reached the better-educated middle classes, but failed to penetrate among the native in-

---

[1] After 321 Constantine stopped persecution, but it was revived by Constans.
[2] Our knowledge of many of them is due to the large number of councils held by Cyprian and the survival of the recorded names. At the Council on Rebaptism held in September 256 no less than eighty-seven bishops were present from Proconsular Africa, Numidia, and Mauretania. Lists will be found in Benson, *Cyprian*, 575 ff., with notes; in Harnack, *Mission and Expansion*, II, pp. 242 ff.; and in great detail in J. Mesnage, *L'Afrique chrétienne*, under the names of the sees.
[3] J. Toutain, *Les Cités romaines de la Tunisie*, quoted by Leclercq, *op. cit.*, I, p. 43.

THE BEGINNINGS OF WESTERN CHRISTENDOM

habitants. This largely accounts for the rapid decline and subsequent disappearance of Christianity in North Africa. When the Roman power was driven out, those of Roman descent returned to the continent of Europe, to Italy and Spain for the most part; so Ibn Khaldun has recorded (III, pp. 191, 193). Many, however, had become mingled in the native population and many were too poor to arrange for evacuation. These last were mostly enslaved. The decline of Christianity was not, however, so sudden or so complete as is generally supposed. At the time of the Arab conquest Christian Berbers are said to have retreated to the mountains and the depths of the Sahara.[1] The Church certainly existed under Arab domination and Carthage long remained the seat of the primate.[2] It was not indeed until 1583 that the Turks finally abolished the practice of the Christian religion and the last vestiges were swept away.[3]

It has just been stated that one of the main reasons for the decline of the North African Church was its failure to enlist to any extent those who had not already been affected by Roman culture. Among the Berbers, for example, the Gospel spread very slowly. They were out of touch with the towns and therefore not so likely to come under its influence as more urban peoples. At the same time there may have been a much deeper penetration than is usually supposed, for a mausoleum at Blad-Guiton, which is undoubtedly Christian, preserves features of great antiquity and seems to have been erected by native princes who still retained some of the customs of their ancestors. It is, however, scarcely older than the fifth century and may possibly have been the work of a wealthy Roman with antiquarian tastes.[4] Another similar mausoleum has been found at Djedar. It is difficult to arrive at any satisfactory conclusion on this matter owing to our ignorance of rural, as distinguished from urban North Africa, as the former is not so fruitful a field for archaeological research. However, such researches have recently been carried out and reveal unexpected evidence of the spread of Christianity. The actual remains, however, are later than our period.[5]

Among the Phoenician inhabitants of North Africa the Gospel seems at first to have made but slow progress, for neither Tertullian nor Cyprian makes any mention of Punic Christians.

[1] See E. W. Bovill, *Caravans of Old Sahara*, p. 115 f.
[2] An interesting piece of evidence of the survival of Christianity is a medal bearing the figure of the Virgin and beneath it the words, in Arabic, "Mary protect thy servant". It is dated 711 A.H. (i.e. 1312) and was found at Tazmalt in Algeria.
[3] On the later history see L. R. Holme, *Christian Churches in North Africa*, p. 211 ff.
[4] See Gsell, *op. cit.*, II, p. 412 ff.
[5] See A. Berthier, *Les Vestiges du christianisme antiq. dans la Numide centrale*, 1943.

By the time of Augustine, however, they were apparently numerous.[1] Of the hundred and fifty or so bishops mentioned in the days of Cyprian hardly one has a Punic name. But this does not mean that there were no Punic bishops, for the latinization of names was very common. There were, as we have seen, Punic names among the martyrs, and symbols derived from Punic sources, such as the doves of Tanit and a horse-shoe shaped cake, have been found on objects in use among Christians. But the most striking evidence of the weakness of Punic Christianity is the complete absence of any reference to a version of the Scriptures in that language.

One inevitable result of the advance of Christianity after its adoption by the emperors was the decay of rival religions. As early as the beginning of the fourth century the temples are described as deserted. But paganism was never eradicated, and even in the days of Augustine North Africa was looked upon as a stronghold of heathenism (*Epist.*, CCXXXII). One notable centre of pagan survival was Madaura, once a colony of veterans. The Christian basilica there was of only moderate dimensions, some ninety by sixty feet,[2] which suggests that the Church was but weak. Even in Carthage the cult of the goddess Juno-Caelestis continued to attract some of the leading men; among them were those who tried to combine it with membership of the Christian Church (Salvian, *De Gubern. Dei*, VIII, 2 f.). As elsewhere, epitaphs containing heathen phrases have been discovered, such as one at Madaura itself which reads *Dis manibus sacrum Juli Meggenti in pace fidelis*,[3] though taken alone they are no evidence of any mixture of religions. At Cuicul (Djemila) a Christian who acted as *flamen sacerdotalis* is known.[4]

North Africa is full of archaeological remains, many still of surpassing beauty and magnificence. Outstanding among them is Timgad already referred to above. The Christian remains, in spite of the overthrow of the Church, are also considerable. Most of them, it is true, are in a poor state of preservation; some have been built over, and not a few churches were turned into mosques. There are also numerous inscriptions,[5] but these are often undated and as a whole of no great value for our period.

[1] He regards a knowledge of Punic as necessary for the clergy in some districts: see *Epist.*, CVIII and CCIX; *Sermons*, CLXVII.
[2] Gsell, *op. cit.*, II, p. 227.
[3] Mesnage, *op. cit.*, p. 339.
[4] De Rossi, *Bull. Arch. Crist.*, 1878, p. 31; 1880, p. 167.
[5] These include two dated 225 and 226 from Sitifis (Sétif), *C.I.L.*, VIII, 8501 a and b; another of 227 probably from Auzia (Aumale), *C.I.L.*, VIII, 9162. At Tipasa there is an epitaph of 238, as well as other early inscriptions: *C.I.L.*, VIII, 9289, 20892–20894. An inscription of 302 comes from Altava (Hadjar-Roum), *C.I.L.*, 9862.

Quite a large proportion refer to the cult of the martyrs which made a strong appeal to Catholic and Donatist alike. Of the architectural remains little has survived which can with certainty be dated before Constantine. But many earlier buildings undoubtedly existed. Their sites, as in Gaul and Italy, are often on the outskirts of the cities, a sign that they go back to a time anterior to the triumph of the Church.[1] The earliest Christian building in Algiers is the church at Orléansville (Castellum Tingitanum) erected in 324.[2] Nothing now remains but the foundations which show that it measured eighty by fifty-two feet. There were also a primitive sanctuary at Tipasa and a church at Cuicul (Djemila), as well as the Basilica Novarum at Carthage.

In addition to buildings there are records of Christian cemeteries, the *areae* to which Tertullian refers (*Ad Scap.*, III). An inscription from Caesarea (Chercell) mentions an *area ad sepulcra* given by Servianus, a senator (*C.I.L.*, VIII, 9585). This was the normal method of Christian burial, but in addition the African Church made use of catacombs.[3] Some of these have been discovered, and doubtless there are others which a happy chance may yet reveal. The most important already known are at Susa (Hadrumetum) with 7,300 burials and 137 inscriptions, at Arch-Zara near Sallakta (Sullechtum),[4] at Djebel Djabba near Khenchela (Mascula),[5] and at Addoufen (Varturliani).[6] Augustine says that in his day some Christians went below ground to worship God (*Sermons*, XLV), a custom which may have been borrowed from paganism, or may recall times when, as in Rome, it was unsafe to worship in public. In this connexion mention may be made of the hypogeum at R'ar Brid which may possibly have been of Christian construction since its Arabic name means "the grotto of faith".[7]

During its brief but significant career, the Church in North Africa probably had a greater influence on the future development of Western Christendom than Rome itself. It was, indeed, in North Africa that Latin Christianity had its cradle. This influence can be grouped round three great names; for it was Tertullian who first provided it with a vocabulary and did much to popularize an ascetic Puritanism; it was Cyprian who moulded its organization; and from Augustine it received its most abiding theological impress. Augustine, it need hardly be said, lies out-

[1] See, further, Gsell, *op. cit.*, II, p. 115 ff.
[2] This date is sometimes given as 252 owing to a failure to realize that it is that of the Mauretanian era.
[3] On these, see Leynaud, *Les catacombes africaines*.
[4] De la Blanchère, *Bull. du Comité*, 1895, p. 371 ff.
[5] Vars, *Rec. de Constantine*, 1898, p. 362 ff.
[6] Gsell, *op. cit.*, II, p. 184.   [7] No. 107 in Gsell.

side our period, for it was not until night was about to descend
upon this short-lived Church that it produced the greatest and
perhaps most typical of its sons. Earlier Tertullian with his
combination of solid Roman thought and Punic fire, might have
stood as the typical North African Christian; but Augustine has
the final claim, for in Africa alone could he have emerged. "A
mind", as Mommsen has said, "intoxicated first by the whirl of
a dissolute life, and then by the fiery enthusiasm of faith, such
as utters itself in the *Confessions* . . . has no parallel elsewhere in
antiquity" (*Provinces*, II, p. 345).

But were these great men in any way typical of North African
Christianity as a whole? I am inclined to doubt it, and cannot
help feeling that the presence of such outstanding figures has
tended to give an exaggerated idea of what it actually accom-
plished, for, after all, the Church in North Africa was not so very
effective, and it would be as great a mistake to judge its condition from them as to take the prophets of the Old Testament as
samples of the contemporary religion of Israel and Judah.

But if we are to allow to the Church in North Africa a lower
measure of attainment than is usually admitted, and this seems
to me to be inevitable from a close study of its condition, we
must not ignore the immense difficulties with which it had to
cope in its efforts to influence that strange congeries of peoples
who found their dwelling along the southern margin of the Mediterranean. The very mixture of races and languages was itself
no small obstacle, we see it at work in the Donatist Schism which
so weakened the Church. There was also something rigid and
unreceptive about the mind of the Africans as a whole. If literary
circles in Rome regarded even a great writer like Fronto as a
"colonial" they had probably some justification, for the African
outlook, if not exactly "colonial", was certainly provincial, and
this was something to be reckoned with in things ecclesiastical.
Had the Church in North Africa been left to itself it would
probably have been lost in "the paradoxical ecclesiology of the
Donatists" and, forgoing its universal character and aspirations,
have been reduced to "a fanatical congregation of beggars".[1]
In addition, account must be taken of the vast differences in
social development of the various sections of the community, for
the luxury and corruption of the cities was in strong contrast
with the crudity and barbarism of the desert tribes, and both
with the state of ignorance and depression which was characteristic of the cultivators of the soil. The consequence was, as we
have already seen, that the Gospel message made but a limited
appeal and seems not to have penetrated far beyond the Graeco-
Roman elements of the population. But even with them its

[1] G. La Piana, *Harvard Theol. Rev.*, 1925, p. 277.

effects seem to have been only superficial, for the Church carried on a losing battle against the licence and luxury of its environment and the perpetual attraction of pagan ideas and practices. Tertullian had already denounced the growing laxity, especially among the women, in *De Cultu Feminarum*, and Cyprian again took up the theme in *De Habitu Virginum*, whilst in *De Lapsis* he disclosed the depths to which nominal Christians were capable of sinking.

As we know nothing of the first Christians of North Africa we can have no means of judging with what enthusiasm they received the pioneer missionaries; but everything suggests, when at length we gain authentic tidings of the Church there, that its religion had already become conventional, that it had reached that stage which is so urgent a problem in the Mission field to-day—what is sometimes called second- and third-century Christianity. Persecution, from time to time, pruned away the weaker elements and so purified the Church, but its effects were only transient. The early martyrs were undoubtedly genuine and sincere in their faith, and exhibit a simplicity and steadfastness of conduct which have never been excelled; but the attitude of the "confessors" of the days of Cyprian and the morbid zest for suffering which seems to have passed in a kind of wave of hysteria over many during the Diocletian persecution give no high notion of their spiritual condition. What seems to have been the most prominent weakness of the Church and the root of its ultimate failure to survive—and here again a parallel can be found in the Native Churches of to-day—was its inability to produce strong and spiritual leadership. Tertullian already knew of bishops who abandoned their flocks in time of danger, and the picture which Cyprian gives of some of the episcopate of his day is sufficiently gloomy. Many of them were engaged in secular pursuits which they quite evidently regarded as of more importance than the care of their dioceses. What could be done under wise and stimulating guidance can be seen from the career of Cyprian, but there was alas only one Cyprian during our period. It will, however, be but just to end by thinking of the Church in North Africa as it was in the later days of his episcopate. Its high reputation can be judged from the letter of the Roman presbyters printed as *Epist.* XXXVI among Cyprian's correspondence. Three points stand out as especially noteworthy: its faith, its institutions, and its generosity. Its generosity was, indeed, remarkable, and in proportion to its more limited resources Carthage was in this respect no mean rival of Rome itself.[1]

[1] Cyprian himself sent money to redeem Christian captives in Numidia, and much hospitality was shown to strangers and help given to other Churches (*Epist.*, LXXI–LXXIX).

CHAPTER V

SPAIN

When Christianity was first preached in the West, Spain had been under Roman rule for a longer period than any other province. But even before the coming of the Romans the peninsula had, for many centuries, been open to a wide variety of influences; and a succession of different cultures had contributed to make Spain what she was at the time of the conquest. The chief task of the Romans would be to complete and systematize this age-long process, and at the same time to broaden her horizons and bring political coherence. There was, indeed, already some measure of stable political and social life, but the fact that Spain had been populated by successive waves of immigrants, coming in both by sea and by land, made real unity difficult. Even the efforts of the Romans to that end were not entirely successful. Spain continued to be a collection of separate and jealous entities. Within her borders there were over five hundred cities, most of which were independent of their neighbours, and anxious to remain so.[1]

Communication was comparatively easy, as the Romans had established an elaborate road system, the work of Augustus, Tiberius, and Claudius. Three main trunk roads entered the country from Gaul, and went respectively to Gades (Cadiz), to the Lusitanian coast by way of Saragossa, and through Pampeluna to Brigantium (Corunna). With the outside world there was also much intercourse, mainly commercial in character, and especially with the neighbouring lands of Gaul, Italy, and Africa. Many Africans, indeed, were resident in Spain, and, as we have seen, in the fourth century Tingitana was actually grouped with the Spanish provinces for purposes of administration. In some of its geographical features Spain is closely akin to Africa, for it is not until the Pyrenees are reached that damp mossy woods, the real distinguishing mark between the North and the South, are to be found.

From an economic standpoint Spain was valuable to the Romans chiefly on account of its rich mines which they regarded as the proudest fruit of their conquest, if we take their boasts to Judas Maccabeus as an index (1 Macc. 8 : 3). The ancient world

[1] C. H. V. Sutherland, *The Romans in Spain, 217 B.C.–117 A.D.*, 1939, is the latest work on the subject.

looked upon them as the most productive of all mines.[1] Wheat and oil were also found in the peninsula, and there were manufactures of ironwork and of textiles. The littoral was very fertile, whilst the high central region produced a hardy and warlike population, toughened by wind and sun, a ready source of fighting men.

The smooth and regular progress of the country was interrupted in A.D. 256 by a sudden invasion of Frankish tribes, who after remaining some dozen years crossed over into Africa where any further trace of them was lost (Aurelius Victor, *De Caesar.*, XXXIII, 3). Many cities were sacked, including Tarragona, some of which never recovered, for their ruins could still be seen in the fifth century (Orosius, VII, xxii, 8). By the time of the raid Christians were sufficiently numerous to suffer with the rest of the nation.

It was in Spain that the work of romanizing the West was really begun, and Gades (Cadiz) was the first native city outside Italy to adopt Roman law and the use of the Latin tongue. The process of romanization, as well as the development of municipal life, was encouraged by Vespasian's grant of Latin rights to all Spain, and it was not long before the whole country, or the greater part of it, had submitted to the new influence. The success and speed with which this was achieved was all the more remarkable as the number of actual immigrants of Latin speech and Roman ways was never considerable. They sufficed, however, to direct the native population into the new manner of living. The process was not, of course, uniform, and different parts of the land and different classes were differently affected by it. The towns naturally were in advance of the countryside, and the upper classes came under Roman influences and submitted to them much more readily than the mass of the population. The Spanish upper classes were indeed noted for their high level of culture and education.

Though the process of romanization advanced with such speed it did not go entirely without opposition. Some of this was deliberate, and some due to circumstances. Among the latter may be noticed the fact that the native Iberian language did not belong to the Indo-Germanic group and those who used it found some difficulty in acquiring the Latin speech. The same was true of the Punic-speaking group which inhabited the coast opposite to Africa. More definite opposition came from religion, but even here it was not entirely deliberate or sustained, and if the native cults remained practically unaltered, the deities were given Roman names. This did not, however, interfere with the

[1] So Diodorus Siculus V, xxv, 1. For other references see Pliny, *Hist. Nat.*, XXXIII, iv, 21, 23.

general process which, in spite of these small obstacles, made a deep impression upon the Spanish people, and was sufficiently strong to survive the barbarian and Moslem conquests and to furnish a basis for a genuine Spanish culture in later ages.

Soon after the rise of the Christian era Spain began to make a noteworthy contribution to Latin literature, and if she failed to produce a poet or thinker of quite the first rank, the two Senecas, Lucan, Martial,[1] and Quintilian form a group of which any nation might be proud. Later there would arise a Christian poet in the person of Prudentius. But Spain, like North Africa and Gaul, was criticized for her peculiarities in the use and pronunciation of Latin. Even as early as the days of Cicero the poets of Cordova had acquired an unenviable notoriety (*Pro Archia*, XXVI). Provincialisms were even supposed to occur in the dispatches of Hadrian (Spartianus, *Vit. Had.*, III). But Spain's contribution to the Roman world was not restricted to literature; she was the mother of hardy and forceful sons. Prominent among them were two emperors, Trajan and Hadrian; whilst if Spain had no part in the upbringing of Marcus Aurelius, he came ultimately of Andalusian stock.

Since Spain had been invaded by peoples of several races whose comings were separated by distinct intervals of time, her population was very diverse and varied. The Romans recognized three main divisions; the Iberians in the east, north, and south of the peninsula, the Celts in the north-west, and the Celtiberians in the centre. Celtic names are to be found in parts which were not ranked as definitely occupied by this race; a sign, probably, that they had been driven out of them by later invaders. The Iberians[2] were, it need hardly be pointed out, the predominant stock, and ancient writers often speak of the whole peninsula as Iberia. They had in quite remote times built their own walled towns whose masonry still provides the lower courses of some modern cities. The Celts came in about the sixth century B.C. In addition to the principal races already mentioned, there were others who helped to enrich the gorgeous fabric of Spanish civilization. The Phœnicians had traded with Spain from almost prehistoric times, but if archaeology is a safe guide they affected its life but little. They were content to establish what a later age would have called "factories" or trading posts, and apart from Gades, possibly the oldest city in Europe, no settlement of theirs has been discovered. Their trade was, after a time, threatened by the arrival of Greek merchants, who, in striking contrast,

[1] Martial had a great fondness for his native land, and above all for "rugged Bilbilis", the city of his birth. To it he was content to return at the end of his days.

[2] There are Iberians mentioned in *Sib. Orac.*, V, 116. But as they appear between Persia and Babylon they were obviously not natives of Spain.

made a real contribution to the life of the country; the native Iberian art, for example, shows distinct traces of Hellenic influence, and the earliest coinage was definitely copied from Greek models. The invasion of the Carthaginians in the fourth century B.C. does not seem to have done much to reinforce the meagre Phoenician influence, and was in any case transitory as they were driven out by the Romans at the end of the following century. Somewhat unexpectedly, traces of one race are not found, at least in earlier times—the Jews.[1] St. Paul, if ever he visited Spain, would have had no synagogues to act as starting-points of his propaganda. By the beginning of the fourth century, however, in view of the canons of the Council of Elvira directed against them, the Jews must have been both numerous and influential.

Under the Empire, Spain was divided into three provinces—a number afterwards increased by subdivision—Tarraconensis, which included the north, north-west, the centre, and the east coast as far as New Carthage; Lusitania in the west; and Baetica in the south. There was a tendency to speak of two Spains, divided by the Ebro into North and South, but this does not seem to have been very common.[2]

THE COMING OF CHRISTIANITY [3]

As in the case of most other regions, history can give us no definite information as to the manner in which Christianity came first to the peninsula; but numerous legends have arisen which attempt to supply the deficiency. They are, like most legends, full of minute details. One of them tells how St. Peter sent seven bishops from Rome with a complete scheme for the occupation of the country. Their names are given as Torquatus, Secundus, Indalecius, Ctesiphon, Caecilius, Hesychius, and Euphrasius;[4] and they founded respectively the sees of Acci (Guadix), Abula (Abla), Urci, Vergium (Berja), Illiberis (Granada), Carcesa (Cazoria), and Illiturgi (Andujar). It should be remarked that nearly all these places are in Baetica and have this much of historic probability behind them, that this province, being the most completely romanized, was the most likely to receive the Christian faith.

[1] cf. Renan, *St. Paul*, p. 194, and W. L. Knox, *St. Paul and the Church at Jerusalem*, p. 330.

[2] See Pliny, *Hist. Nat.*, IV, 22. The Greek text of Iren., I, x, 2 speaks of Spain in the plural, but as the Latin has *in Hiberis* (Iberians) it may be a misreading.

[3] On the history of Christianity in Spain see H. Leclercq, *L'Éspagne chrétienne*, 1906, and Gams, *Kirchengeschichte von Spanien*, 1862–64. The latter is uncritical but contains much information.

[4] They are celebrated together in the Mozarabic Liturgy on May 15 in a hymn whose piety is more respectable than its metre.

The Spanish Church had an amazing power of invention. Not content with affirming that the three wise men came from Iberia, it also averred that Cornelius the centurion was a naturalized Spaniard. But the outstanding achievement was the claim that it had a special connexion with St. James. That a late and utterly unsubstantiated legend should have been received so widely is an extraordinary testimony to the credulity of mankind. But Britain is in no position to criticize other nations in such matters in view of the even later tradition invented by the monks of Glastonbury in the twelfth century that Joseph of Arimathaea once visited that place. Strangely enough, the first recorded notice of the legend of St. James occurs in an English writer, in a poem attributed to Aldhelm of Malmesbury at the end of the seventh century (*P.L.*, LXXXIX, col. 293). Had the legend been known earlier it would assuredly have received some notice. Prudentius, for example, who is ever anxious to glorify his native land and its saints,[1] would surely have mentioned it, whilst neither St. Isidore (d. 636) nor St. Julian of Toledo (d. 690) has any apparent acquaintance with it. The legend was carried a stage further by the discovery of a tomb purporting to be that of the apostle at a site near Amala in Galicia. It became known as Santiago of Compostella and to it the see was transferred from Iria Flavia. An attempt to justify the tradition by a supposed transfer of the relics of St. James from Palestine is first found in Notker Balbulus (d. 912).

There is, however, one legend which, even if it is not genuine, has a respectable flavour lacking in those previously mentioned, that which looks upon St. Paul as the founder of the Spanish Church. It is based, it need hardly be said, on the apostle's expressed intention of visiting Spain (Rom. 15 : 24), supported by the statement in I *Clement*, V, 7 that he "reached the terminus of the West". This description would suit Spain admirably, for, not long before, Horace had called it *Hesperia ultima* (*Od.*, I, xxxvi, 4); and Lucan, himself a Spaniard, speaks of *extremique orbis Iberi* (*Pharsalia*, VII, 511), and in another passage *extremaque mundi* (*Pharsalia*, III, 453). The Muratorian Fragment, which probably reflects the opinion current in Rome at the end of the second century, also mentions the story.[2] In addition there is the somewhat dubious testimony of the so-called Vercelli Acts, belonging to the third century or even earlier, which describe the starting out and sojourn of the

---

[1] His famous *Peristephanon* devotes more than half its bulk to four Roman martyrs—Lawrence, Romanus, Hippolytus, and Agnes. The rest, save for a short poem on the passion of St. Peter and St. Paul, commemorates martyrs of the Spanish Church.

[2] *Profectionem Pauli ab urbe ad Spaniam proficiscentis* (ll. 30 f.).

apostle (I–III and VI).[1] As is natural, the story grew, and later writers profess to have much more detailed knowledge than those who came before. By the fourth century Jerome is able to tell us that St. Paul travelled by sea;[2] which may well have been the case if the voyage were actually made, for the usual route was from Ostia and took four days (Pliny, *Hist. Nat.*, XIX, 1). To reach the actual "terminus of the West", Gades,[3] would require a further three days.

The suggestion has been put forward by some scholars that by the "limit of the West" St. Paul meant Rome itself. It is true that in the *Psalms of Solomon*, viii, 16 Rome is called "the uttermost part of the earth"; but it is difficult to imagine that such a phrase would be used by Clement, writing actually in Rome, and knowing the large stretch which lay beyond it.[4]

At first sight it seems unlikely that St. Paul would have chosen to spend valuable time and labour on a visit to Spain, which was mainly Latin-speaking and where, as we have seen, there were few if any synagogues from which he could have worked. But we have his own statement that he contemplated such a step. What he had in view, it may be surmised, was a series of visits to the seaports where a certain number of Greek-speaking people would doubtless be found. Whether his plan ever came to anything is uncertain, and even in the Middle Ages its fulfilment was not universally accepted. Abailard, for example, denies it (*Sic et Non*, Prolog.). One statement, however, seems definitely to rule out the foundation of the Spanish Church by St. Paul. That is the declaration by Pope Innocent I in 416 that no Church had been founded in Italy, Gaul, Spain, Africa, Sicily, or the islands, except by bishops commissioned by St. Peter or his successors (*Epist.*, CCCXI). This declaration with its sweeping claims can hardly be taken seriously; but it suggests that unless St. Paul carried the commission of St. Peter, which is most unlikely, no tradition was accepted in Rome of his having been the founder of the Church in Spain.

Whether St. Paul visited Spain or not the Spanish Church certainly took a great interest in him, as can be seen from surviving inscriptions. One from Guadix near Granada (it belongs to the middle of the seventh century) claims that Pauline relics are preserved there;[5] a claim which is also made by a monastery

---

[1] *Apoc. N.T.*, pp. 304–306, 309.
[2] *In cap. XI, Isaiae: Hispaniam alienigenarum portatus est navibus.*
[3] Silius Italicus, *Punica*, XVII, 637: "*terrarum finis Gades.*"
[4] It has been suggested that Clement's phrase may mean "the goal in the West". Possibly he was using vague language, perhaps based on Mal. 1 : 11, where the Gentiles "from the rising of the sun even unto the going down thereof" are spoken of as worshippers of Jehovah.
[5] See Hübner, *La arqueologia de España*, No. 175.

at Obena, near Oviedo.[1] Sometimes his name is coupled with that of St. Peter, as in an inscription from a church in the same neighbourhood,[2] and in one of the sixth century found on a deserted site near Loja, west of Granada.[3] In a late inscription of about A.D. 1000 he is named alongside St. Peter as an apostle.[4] The name Paul seems to have been given to many Spaniards, though this is not necessarily of much significance. It is found on a gravestone (A.D. 544) at Evova in Portugal,[5] whilst relics of PAVLI CONF. are preserved at La Morera not far from Zafra in south-west Spain.[6] A marble dedication tablet, dated A.D. 577, at Illiberis is inscribed A S̄C̄O PAVLO ACCITANO PONTF̄C̄.[7]

Christian inscriptions are not numerous in Spain; but many must have been destroyed during the Moslem occupation, whilst some doubtless suffered from the Visigoths. Early inscriptions are in fact almost unknown. Those that survive generally bear a date, usually according to the era of Spain, which was thirty-nine years in advance of the Christian era, a usage sometimes found in African inscriptions and those of Narbonne.

The earliest notices of the Church in Spain which can be accepted as authentic are rhetorical and vague. Irenaeus mentions Churches in Iberia (I, x, 2), while Tertullian refers to all parts of Spain as having accepted Christ (Adv. Jud., VII). The latter statement does something to justify the assertion of Bury that "Christianity made such rapid strides, and the Spaniards adapted it so skilfully to their pagan habits, that before the time of Constantine Spain had become, throughout its length and breadth, a Christian land" (Life of St. Patrick, p. 4). This estimate is certainly an exaggeration; but it brings out one grave defect of the Spanish Church, to which reference will be made below, its readiness to make terms with paganism. There was little, at this time, of the martyr spirit, or even of strong and definite faith, among some at least of its leaders. The first detailed notice, indeed, records the apostasy, during the Decian persecution, of Basilides, Bishop of Leon, and Martial, Bishop of Merida. The latter, it is reported, had even buried his children with pagan ceremonial. The neighbouring bishops took action, degrading them from their office and appointing, and perhaps consecrating, successors. But the offenders were not willing to be so easily disposed of. Basilides seems to have submitted at

---

[1] op. cit., No. 263; cf. Nos. 379 (Barcelona), 390 (Saragossa), and 471.
[2] No. 146. It runs as follows: OFFERET FLAINVS ABBA IN ONORE APOSTOR DI SCOR PETRI PA[VLI].
[3] No. 374: CONSECRATIO DOMINORVM PETRI ET PAVLI.
[4] No. 466: SCS PAVLVS APOSTOLVS SCS PETRVS APOSTOLVS. In No. 255, a wooden box from Oviedo, he appears with Christ and His apostles.
[5] No. 11: DEPOSITIO PAVLI FAMVLVS [sic] DEI.
[6] No. 57.   [7] No. 115.

first and done penance, but later he made his way to Rome, where by some means or other he gained the ear of Stephen, the newly-elected bishop of that see. He proved sympathetic and probably restored him or expressed his intention of doing so. The Spanish Churches thereupon appealed to Carthage, and Cyprian held a council in 254 which reversed the decision of Stephen; Cyprian being careful to suggest that the Bishop of Rome had been deceived or was ignorant of the true state of affairs (*Epist.*, LXVII). The whole affair is rather vague but quite obviously the age of appeals to Rome is not yet, and the African bishops conceive that they have the right to reverse an erroneous decision made by its bishop. Unfortunately, Stephen did not agree and resented their action. He refused to see a deputation of bishops from North Africa, and even discouraged the Christians in Rome from showing them hospitality. Cyprian himself he denounced as "a false Christ, a false apostle, a treacherous doer" (*Epist.*, LXXV).

There was, however, a brighter side to the picture, and in the persecutions under Valerian in 258, Fructuosus, Bishop of Tarragona, and two deacons, Eulogius and Augurius, met a worthy end.[1] Tarragona was the headquarters in Spain of emperor-worship and severity was natural. The bishop seems to have been beloved not only by his flock, which would be natural, but even by the heathen.[2]

One distinction the Spanish Church can claim: that of having held the first ecclesiastical council of which the findings are still extant. This was the Council of Elvira (Illiberis, probably Granada) held at the beginning of the fourth century, before, it would seem, the outbreak of the Diocletian persecution, since there is an air of peaceful security about the proceedings which persecution would have made impossible. It was attended by nineteen bishops and a number of priests. The most famous of the bishops was Hosius of Corduba (Cordova), the home of the Senecas. He was then not yet fifty years of age and had been bishop but a short time. After suffering under Maximian he came into favour with Constantine whose chief ecclesiastical adviser he seems to have been. He presided at the Council of Nicaea, for the calling of which he was probably responsible. When a very old man he was compelled to sign the Arianizing Creed of Sirmium in 357. He died soon after at an incredible age.

---

[1] The *Acta* are evidently used by Prudentius, VI, and Augustine, *Sermons*, CCLXXIII, and are accepted as genuine by Harnack. They can be read in Owen, *Acts of the Early Martyrs*, p. 100 ff. All three are mentioned in inscriptions (Hübner, Nos. 57 and 85), but as these are not earlier than the sixth century, they merely bear witness to the preservation of the tradition.

[2] *Acta S. Fructuosi*, III: *Talem amorem habebat non tantum a fratribus, sed etiam ab ethnicis.*

The senior bishop at Elvira was the Bishop of Acci (Guadix) and he presided. The great bulk of the bishops came from the south and east; but Galicia was represented by the Bishop of Legio (Leon), Tarraconensis by the Bishop of Caesaraugusta (Saragossa)—Tarragona itself sent no representative—Lusitania by three bishops.

The canons passed by the council were eighty-one in number and it must be confessed that they reveal a very disquieting picture of the state of the Spanish Church at this epoch. There is, as Harnack has said, "a combination of coarse worldliness and fanatical severity such as has been characteristic of the Spanish Church in every age". Compromise with paganism, cruelty, and immorality seem to have been rife, and the attempts to check them show, by their extreme severity,[1] the extent to which the evil had penetrated. Perhaps the most disquieting revelation is that the clergy were as bad as their flocks.

We find that Christians are found who accept office as *flamens* (canons 1–4, 55). As the duty of the *flamen* was to preside over the annual games it was hardly consistent with the profession of Christianity, though doubtless by this time the religious side had become merely conventional and the office was valued as an honour. Some parents were willing to give their daughters in marriage to pagan priests (canon 17); others, it is shameful even to relate, gave them in prostitution (canon 12). The low state of Christian morals is also revealed by the provision of punishment for those who commit "a second adultery" (canon 7), as well as for those of the clergy who condone adultery in their wives (canon 64). A sidelight on the brutality of the age is thrown by canon 5 which inflicts perpetual excommunication on mistresses who beat their slaves to death. Other canons which are interesting are canon 36, which forbids pictures in churches, and canon 60, which refuses the title of martyr to those who bring their fate upon themselves by attacking pagan images, and so forth. In view of the unworthy state of the Christian body in Spain, it is not surprising to learn that attendance at divine service was much neglected (canons 21, 45, 46). Part of the worldliness of the Church may have been due to the presence in it of wealthy members (canons 40, 41).

Such was the state of the Spanish Church on the eve of the outbreak of the last great persecution; and in view of them it rose to face the test amazingly well. The best side of the Spaniard, a characteristic, however, which is closely akin to fanaticism, is his ability to bear punishment and torture. The persecution seems to have been carried out under the direction of a very vigorous magistrate, Datianus by name, whose exact office is

[1] Gibbon, II, p. 52 ff., contrasts the treatment of *lapsi* in Gaul and Spain.

not clear. He may have been a kind of commissioner appointed for the special purpose, as he exercised his powers without any regard to provincial boundaries.

Many of the cities of Spain had at this crisis their martyrs, but Saragossa seems to have achieved the primacy, such is the opinion of Prudentius who was probably one of her citizens.[1] Prudentius has preserved the names of many of these witnesses to the truth of their religion; most of them are otherwise unknown, but one famous case stands out—that of St. Vincent. He was a deacon of Saragossa and was arrested with Valerius the bishop. In the story of his death, legend and history are strangely mingled but the *Acta* are certainly early and contain authentic matter.[2] Another interesting case was that of Eulalia, a child of twelve and a member of a noble family at Merida. She was so much impressed by the constancy of the martyrs that she longed to imitate them. Her parents removed her to the country, but she managed to elude their vigilance and returning to the city presented herself before the tribunal of the magistrate. Her subsequent behaviour suggests the fanatic rather than the Christian, for she scattered the corn offered to the idol and struck Datianus himself. After horrible tortures she was burnt.[3] Persecution in Spain was very fierce, but it did not last long, being probably ended by the succession of Constantius in 305.

Already in the period before Nicaea certain characteristics of the Spanish Church of later days had begun to stand out and crystallize. There was, for example, a certain secular outlook which revealed itself in the willingness to compromise with paganism. This was, perhaps, ultimately a legacy from Roman ideas of a state religion with a ritualistic expression, but no great interest in ethics or metaphysics. The pride and arrogance, characteristic of the race, would also appear in the Church. Still far in the future the builders of the cathedral at Seville would resolve that it should be so vast that posterity should think them mad. The experiences of the Spaniards as the western outpost of Christendom against Islam, in which much of the country was overrun, no doubt did much to reinforce that fanatical devotion which sought martyrdom, but which also showed itself in ferocious cruelty. Spain, too, was a land in which heresy was apt to spring up; though the instances of it are a little later than

---

[1] See *Peristephanon*, IV, 57 f.:

    Sola in occursum numerosiores
    Martyrum turbas Domino parasti.

[2] The *Passio S. Vincentii Levitae* belongs to the late fourth century. It was read publicly in the Church of Africa—so Augustine, who himself quotes from it, informs us: *Sermons*, CCLXXV. Prudentius devotes Hymn V to this saint.

[3] See Prudentius, *op cit.*, III. It is worth while recalling that she is referred to by Bede, *Hist. Eccles.*, IV, 20.

our period. In the fourth century Montanism, after apparently disappearing in the West, suddenly reared its head again in Barcelona. It was in Spain also that Priscillianism came to light; with Agape, a Spanish lady and the disciple of Marcus of Memphis, to form a link with the Gnosticism of the East.[1] The first heretics to suffer death at the hands of Christians were part of the crop of this sowing. The chief home of the Inquisition was already foreshadowed.

[1] See Sulpicius Severus, *Chron.*, II, 46; Jerome, *Epist.*, LXXV.

CHAPTER VI

GAUL AND GERMANY

Gaul and Roman Germany really formed a unity and are best considered together, for the same life pulsated at Treves as in Lyons, in Mainz as in Vienne. Things might have been very different if the defeat of Varus and his legions in A.D. 9 had not prevented the establishment of a separate province of Germany, stretching from the Rhine to the Elbe. The Romans, to conceal their mortification, still retained, at least in name, the lost Germany, but it lay almost entirely on the left bank of the Rhine. The two provinces of Upper and Lower Germanica were in reality marches, to use a later name, and important mainly from a military point of view as protecting Gaul from invasion. There was a strong Gallic element in them, for Gauls had even crossed to the right bank of the Rhine when the inhabitants had fled or been expelled. The boundaries between Gaul and Germany were always very fluid; Belgica, for example, contained parts of what is now Germany, including Treves. This vagueness persisted well into modern times, for Erasmus at the beginning of the sixteenth century could speak of that part of Holland in which he had been born as belonging to Gaul rather than to Germany.[1]

With Free, or as we should now say unoccupied, Germany there was considerable intercourse, mainly by way of trade. Some of this went up the Rhine valley and along the north coast, some even along the Danube and as far as South Russia. Trade between Italy and Germany, extending as far as Scandinavia, had begun to flourish in the early days of the Empire, and, notwithstanding the opinion of Tacitus, Germany was open to Roman influence. Roman money circulated widely beyond the frontiers,[2] and even Roman methods of house-building. As late as the fourth century, Julian's soldiers who penetrated east of the Rhine found and burned houses constructed in the Roman style.[3]

The trader, although probably the most important link be-

---

[1] See *Eras. Epist.* (ed. P. S. Allen), IV, p. 354: *Si cosmographorum picturis credimus, magis vergat ad Galliam quam ad Germaniam.* In the twelfth century Otto Bishop of Freising speaks of Cologne as being in Belgic Gaul (*Chronicle*, VII, 12).

[2] See *J.R.S.*, XXVI, 1936, p. 195 ff.

[3] See Ammianus Marcellinus, XVII, i, 7: *ritu Romano constructa.* Their conduct was different from that of the troops who found a palace at Ctesiphon built in Roman style and spared it for this reason: *op. cit.*, XXIV, v, 1.

tween the two territories, did not stand alone. Many Germans crossed into the Empire as agricultural labourers, many as captives. When slaves acquired their freedom, as many did, they might return to their native land, as might also the mercenary soldier when his time of service was completed.[1] Probably the barbarian peoples knew more of Rome than Rome knew of them. The capture of slaves was by no means all on one side, for there were many raids into the Empire by the barbarians, especially in later times, and those seized were sometimes numerous. The family of Wulfilas, the Apostle of the Goths, had originally been abducted from Cappadocia by Gothic bands.

(A) GAUL

From the point of view of the Roman government, Gaul was important as a link with Germany and as the gateway to Britain. More, perhaps, than any other province it helped to widen the horizon of the Roman people, and conversely to extend the civilization to which they had given birth. The destruction of various great fortified centres, Alesia, Gergovia, and Bibracte, among others, prevented the rise of strong reaction against romanizing tendencies, whilst the towns which took their place provided new centres of Roman influence.

Gaul was divided into four provinces, one of which was far older than the rest and stood in a distinct category. This was Narbonensis in the south, which corresponded with the later Provence and even then, as in the Middle Ages, had a civilization of a somewhat exotic character. It had long been subjected to Roman influences and in Pliny's eyes could hardly be distinguished from Italy itself (*Hist. Nat.*, III, 31). Its numerous cities filled up the land and each had but a small district depending upon it. Narbonensis was a senatorial province, the other three were imperial, and had been added to the Roman State by the conquests of Julius Caesar. Among them cities were comparatively few, and in consequence the territory depending upon them was much greater than in the south. The population of the three imperial provinces was not uniform. Aquitania in the south-west was mainly Iberian, with Celtic lands between the Garonne and the Loire; Lugdunensis in the west and centre was Celtic; whilst Belgica in the north had a mixture of Celts and Germans. To the latter was added the country stretching along the left bank of the Rhine from the Lake of Geneva to the Moselle, a region almost purely Celtic. Under Tiberius, Rheims

[1] The employment of mercenaries was very common. Both Gauls and Germans were to be found in the bodyguards of Herod the Great: see Josephus, *Bell. Jud.*, I, xv, 6; xviii, 3; xxxiii, 9.

was the largest town in Belgica and the seat of the government, but it was later displaced by Treves, which became for a time the capital of the West and an important depot for the equipment of the imperial armies.[1]

Gaul was a land of much prosperity; it was, indeed, taken by Josephus as a synonym for wealth (*Bell. Jud.*, II, xvi, 4), and among its inhabitants were many rich merchants and nobles dwelling in magnificent country houses. As in Italy there were large estates, though not on quite so considerable a scale. The names of some of them still survive as those of French villages; a contrast to Britain where the older names have completely disappeared, owing no doubt to the breach in the methods of agriculture which followed the Saxon conquest. Agriculture was, indeed, the foundation of Gallic prosperity, for Gaul was rich in grain and all manner of green stuff; the cult of the vine, however, dated back only to Roman times. Once it had had great mineral wealth, and though the writers of the *Sibylline Oracles* still thought of it as rich in gold (V, 200), in the Christian era this had diminished. It had busy manufactures and workshops, especially in pottery and glass making, carried on mainly as family affairs. In early times Italy had sent its merchants and craftsmen into Gaul and as far as Germany, and even in the days of Cicero trade seems mainly to have been in Italian hands (*Pro Fonteio*, V); but the Gauls were apt pupils and soon rivalled their masters, even competing with them in their home markets.

The road system was good, and still more useful were the facilities provided by the great rivers. The valley of the Rhone as a means of communication between the Mediterranean world and the North must have been used as early as the bronze age, and it was quickly colonized by the Greeks. At the beginning of our period the communities of the Rhone valley still had Greek-speaking elements and kept up contact with the cities of Ionia from which they had come.[2] Marseilles had been colonized from Phocaea in the sixth century B.C. Further up the river lay Arles, partly on the east bank and partly on an island in the stream —hence the *duplex Arelate* of Ausonius. It too was an important centre of trade and gradually displaced Marseilles.

The centre of government was Lyons (Lugdunum),[3] which

---

[1] cf. Ausonius, *Ordo Urbium Nobilium*, VI, 4: *Imperii vires quod alit, quod vestit et armat.*

[2] This was true of the Christians of Lyons and Vienne at the end of the second century. Three inscriptions set up by people *natione Graeca* and one by a lady *natione Asiana* are mentioned by Vasile Pârvan, *Die Nationalität der Kaufleute im römischen Kaiserreiche*, pp. 90 and 107.

[3] The name Lugdunum was derived from Lug, a solar deity, who may also have provided the Lugones of Spain with their appellation. There was another city of this name, Lugdunum Batavorum, near Leyden. On Lyons and Vienne see H. Bazin, *Vienne et Lyon gallo-romain.*

was held with a garrison of only 1,200 men, who sufficed to keep the whole of Gaul in check, so Josephus tells us (*Bell. Jud.*, II, xvi, 4). The city had been founded by Plancus in 43 B.C. for Italians driven out of Vienne, but its inhabitants included men of divers races; it was, indeed, a cosmopolitan city, full of Greeks, Syrians, and other Orientals. Owing to its excellent communications, it was connected through the valley of the Dorea Baltea by a military road with Italy and also with the camps guarding the Rhine, it was well fitted to be a centre not only for government and trade, but for romanizing influences.[1] It suffered through the desperate battle fought there in A.D. 197 between Septimius Severus and Clodius Albinus in which many Romano-Gauls were killed; but it was not until Treves became prominent in the fourth century that its importance began seriously to decline. Not far away from Lyons was Vienne, with which it was in perpetual feud (cf. Tacitus, *Hist.*, I, 65). Vienne had been the chief settlement of the Alpine tribe of the Allobroges and was Latin rather than Roman; but it had a temple to Augustus and Livia, and Gaius granted it the Roman franchise. Vienne was apparently notorious for the low tone of its morals, for it received, by an obvious pun, the name of Via Gehennae.[2]

Since Marseilles and the Rhone valley had been colonized by Greeks it was natural that their culture should have spread in the surrounding country. Marseilles itself took a prominent part in the promotion of Greek studies, being called a school for barbarians by Strabo;[3] so great, indeed, was its reputation that many Italians preferred it to Athens. Its siege and capture during the Civil War reduced its political importance without affecting its reputation as a centre of culture. The presence, however, of numerous Roman soldiers and Italian traders soon began to have effect, and by the second century A.D. Marseilles was transformed into a Latin city and Greek was displaced.[4] In the rest of Gaul there seems not to have been any wide diffusion of Greek culture, though Greek characters are used in inscriptions;[5] the total number of inscriptions is, however, very small, a dozen at most, of which three come from Treves.[6] On the

---

[1] From A.D. 12 a yearly Diet for the whole of Gaul was held there. This did much to unify Gaul and to spread Roman influence.

[2] See *The Death of Pilate, Apoc. N.T.*, p. 158, which may not be earlier than medieval times.

[3] IV, 5: cf. also Cicero, *Pro Flacco*, XXVI, and Tacitus, *Ann.*, IV, 44. The latter mentions its happy combination of frugality and refinement (*Agric.*, IV).

[4] Favorinus, who lived early in the second century, although born in Gaul, wrote in Greek, a circumstance which he reckoned among the remarkable things of his life.

[5] Camille Jullian, *De la Gaule à la France*, p. 149 ff. On the decay of Greek in Gaul see F. E. Brightman in *J.T.S.*, 1900, I, p. 451 ff.

[6] See Le Blant, *Manuel d'épigraphie, etc.*, p. 44.

other hand, there is evidence that Greek influence persisted in some quarters after its main force had abated. Ausonius, for example, in the fourth century, preferred it as a means of expression, although, as a boy, he had found difficulty in acquiring it. Later in the same century, Paulinus of Pella knew Greek better than Latin (*Eucharisticos*, LXXV). Greek is also used, alongside Latin, in a system of popular psalmody at Arles which probably dates from the beginning of the sixth century.[1]

By the early years of the first century, so Mommsen claims, all the country on both banks of the Rhone had been thoroughly romanized in language and manners (*Provinces* I, p. 87). This statement may be a slight exaggeration, but it cannot be denied that the influence of Rome and things Latin spread with extraordinary rapidity among the Gauls. Perhaps the fact that there is some affinity between the Celtic and Italian dialects may have helped in the process. Cultural influence was naturally most active in the towns and among the upper classes, and there was a great fondness among them for rhetoric, even before Gaius established contests for orators at Lyons.

Although the Christians at Lyons and Vienne who were martyred in 178 were mainly Greek-speaking, yet Eusebius's account (V) bears witness to the prevalence of Latin. Sanctus, when questioned, for example, replied in Latin, as did Attalus; and when the latter was taken round the amphitheatre he was preceded by a placard in Latin. The use of Latin was, of course, natural in an official proclamation, but no doubt it would be understood by the spectators. Latin culture was still flourishing at Lyons in the days of Ausonius, when Bordeaux also had a great reputation, being the chief school of rhetoric in the West. Treves, too, was on the way to becoming an academic centre when the German invaders swept it away. In the fifth century Arles was known for its legal studies. There is no doubt that in the closing age of the Empire in the West Gaul was the strongest centre of culture. The process of romanization had certainly gone sufficiently deep to enable the Gallo-Romans to romanize the Germans who occupied their land and eventually to displace the laws and judicial institutions of the invaders by their own.[2] Tacitus, with his admiration for the noble savage, regretted that romanization and subjection had had the effect of making the Gauls slothful and cowardly and even effeminate (*Agric.*, XI, *Germ.*, XXVIII). Be this as it may, the Gauls succeeded in assimilating Latin civilization as no other people have ever done, a fact of considerable importance for the future history

---

[1] It is mentioned by Cyprian of Toulon in his *Life of Caesarius of Arles*, I, 19 (*Script. Rerum Merovig.*, III, p. 463).
[2] cf. Kiener, *Verfassungsgesch. der Provence*, p. 85 ff.

of Europe. They themselves were to become the typical Latin people.

The process of romanization, however, was by no means complete, nor did it proceed without opposition. In spite of an outward acceptance of things Roman, the Celt remained a Celt at heart, and never entirely surrendered himself to the world-wide culture to which he was exposed.[1] To the end, membership in a universal empire meant little to him in comparison with his own local and individual interests. A strong national feeling always persisted, which comes out in the writings of a fifth century writer like Sidonius, as well as in the attempt by his contemporaries to set up, with Gothic and Burgundian aid, a Gallic emperor in the person of Marcellinus. So, too, the persistence of the Celtic language was such that it continued to be recognized by Roman Law as late as the third century (*Digest*, XXXII, i, 11). It was not, indeed, until the fourth century that the Latin language and Latin literature became fully naturalized in Gaul. In other matters reaction was easier. When the barbarians, for instance, came in, the people of Alesia—and no doubt others with them—reverted to their old ways of life and even to the pre-Roman manner of architecture.

Another stream of influences which flowed into Gaul must not be forgotten, that of the numerous Oriental peoples who were for purpose of convenience classed as Syrians.[2] They were to be found not only in Narbonensis,[3] but also in the more recently acquired provinces. Even as far as Treves there is evidence of Oriental penetration, for an inscription has been discovered there in Greek to a certain AZIZOS AGRIPPA recording that he was of Oriental origin. Even more definite is the case of an Oriental named Abraham, who died at Clermont; of him it is recorded that he had been born near the Euphrates.[4] Intercourse with the East persisted for a considerable time; was, indeed, only brought to an end when Saracen pirates made the Mediterranean unsafe for commerce. Phoenician wines were still being imported into Gaul in Merovingian times, and Gregory of Tours at the end of the sixth century records that the Syrian tongue was still in use.[5] The influence of Oriental ideas, especially Syrian, was most pervasive and extended to art, and in particular, for some reason, to memorials of the dead. Among the latter a good

[1] cf. Hubert, *Les Celtes*, I, p. 18.
[2] Bréhier, "Les Colonies des Orientaux", in *Byzant. Zeitschrift*, 1903, XII, says that: "For more than eight hundred years Syrians, Armenians, Egyptians, Persians and Greeks, all soon included under the designation of Syrians, established themselves in the main cities of the Empire". Later on, Syrians in the West would be absorbed by the Jews: so F. Rozen surmises in *Juden und Phönizier*.   [3] See Lentheric, *La Grèce et l'Orient en Provence*.
[4] See Le Blant, *Inscr. chrét. de la Gaule*, No. 557.
[5] *Hist. Franc.*, VIII, 1: cf. Salvian, *De Gubern. Dei*, IV, 69.

example is the sarcophagus of Boethius, Bishop of Carpentras.

It is probable, in the nature of things, that the early Greek settlers in Gaul exercised some influence on the religion of the native peoples. Ammianus Marcellinus, writing in the fourth century, tells us that the Druids had borrowed ideas from Pythagoras (XV, ix, 8); and Justinus speaks of Gaulish kings wishing to enter Marseilles in order to share in the worship there prevalent: *ut deos eorum adorare liceret* (XLIII, v, 5). No doubt Herodotus was not the only Greek who loved to discuss religion with the priests of barbarian cults, and there may be something in these stories. But if Greek or other early influences affected the religion of the Gauls it remained a thing of predominantly native growth, and it is with the Druids that it is chiefly associated. Although their worship had been suppressed by the Romans before the coming of Christianity, it doubtless continued to be effective and would persist into Christian times, modifying the character of its supplanter.[1] For one thing, the Druids were greatly interested in the future life; ethics, with them, were based on the supposition of immortality, and in their ritual they were careful to remind the worshipper that this earthly life was not all.[2] They had, moreover, an organized cult of heroes which would be a ready preparation for the cult of saints. In their worship, no use was made of temples; the sacred places were on hill tops or near springs, or in clearings in the forests; it was only when Celtic deities were equated with Roman that temples came to be built. The chief function of the Druids seems to have been divination and the instruction of the young; some scholars have found in them a species of priest-king.[3] The origins of Druidism can no longer be traced, they may extend into pre-Celtic days;[4] certainly the cult extended widely among Celts in all lands and, whilst bringing some kind of unity among the Gallic tribes, linked Gaul as a whole to a larger world.[5] It may be worth noting that in the Iberian parts of Gaul a different series of deities was honoured. When the Romans came in there was an inevitable tendency for the religion of the victors to affect that of their subjects; Celtic gods received Latin names and to them the attributes of similar Roman deities were soon transferred. Even the mystery cults were introduced and penetrated as far as the Rhineland.[6] The excavation of the temple area at Altbachtal near Treves has recently thrown a good deal of light on the local

[1] cf. Sulpicius Severus, *Vita Martini*.   [2] Hubert, *Les Celtes*, II, p. 280.
[3] So, e.g., Camille Jullian; but Hubert, *op. cit.*, II, p. 277, rejects the idea.
[4] Camille Jullian, *De la Gaule, etc.*, p. 94.
[5] *Le sacerdoce des druides est une institution panceltique, ciment de la société celtique*: Hubert, *op. cit.*, II, p. 273.
[6] See H. Lehner, "Mysterien-Kulte im röm. Rheinlande", in *Bonner Jahrbuch*, 1924, pp. 36–91.

religious conditions in the first four centuries of the Christian era.[1]

THE COMING OF CHRISTIANITY [2]

Of the origins of Christianity in Gaul we have no sure knowledge. A historian of the standing of the late Herbert Fisher may allow himself to refer, without qualification, to the "humble Syrian traders who first brought the Christian message to Marseilles" (*Hist. of Europe*, I, p. 512); but lesser scholars must speak with more caution. It may be that his surmise is correct; but it is equally probable that, just as Southern Gaul was indebted to Asia Minor for its first colonists, so also was it indebted to Asia Minor for its first knowledge of the Gospel; the Christian missionary following, at a long interval, in the steps of the Greek trader. Early Gallic Christianity, as we know it from Eusebius's account of the martyrs of Lyons and Vienne and from the pages of Irenaeus,[3] is certainly Greek and linked closely with Asia Minor. Of the martyrs named by Eusebius, Attalus came from Pergamum, Alexander from Phrygia, and Ponticus was a slave from Pontus. The reference to "those through whom our affairs had been established" (V, i, 13) suggests that Christianity was not of long standing in the Rhone valley; a suggestion which is supported by Sulpicius Severus (*Chron.*, II, 32), who, writing in the latter half of the fourth century, tells us that the Gospel was slow to cross the Alps into Gaul and that it had only recently been established there when the persecution broke out.

Legends there are in plenty which officiously take upon them to supplement the silence of history, or the bare statements of early writers. Some of these arose as late as the Middle Ages, such as the tradition that the family of Bethany, including Lazarus, came to Gaul.[4] They are, of course, of no value to the historian of early times. Others, even if they do not record actual events, give a clue to the course which they pursued. This applies to the claim made by both Vienne and Mainz that Crescens, sent to Galatia [5] by St. Paul (2 Tim. 4 : 10), founded its Church. Other Churches are equally definite in discovering founders from among the apostolic circle. Avignon, for example, claims as its

[1] See S. Loeschcke, *Die Erforschung des Tempelbezirks im Altbachtale zu Trier.*
[2] On Christianity in Gaul, see T. Scott Holmes, *The Christian Church in Gaul*, and Duchesne, *Fastes épiscopaux de l'ancienne Gaule.*
[3] Irenaeus definitely mentions an Asiatic deacon in Gaul (I, xiii, 5).
[4] For this legend see Scott Holmes, *op. cit.*, p. 19 ff.
[5] Eusebius, III, iv, 8, took Galatia as meaning Gaul, as did later writers, a view supported by its proximity to Dalmatia. In the *Monumentum Ancyranum* Gaul comes between Spain and Dalmatia: see Zahn, *Int. N.T.*, II, p. 25 f. Two important MSS. actually read Gaul. A similar confusion is found in the *Acts of Paul* (ed. Lipsius, p. 105) where the Greek text has Gaul, but the Latin the curious reading "Galilee", which no doubt represents an original "Galatia".

first bishop the Rufus who is mentioned by St. Paul in Rom.
16 : 13, and avers that he was sent from Rome by the apostle
himself. Arles, even more ambitious, has fixed on Trophimus of
Ephesus (2 Tim. 4 : 20); and to heighten its glory states that he
was consecrated by St. Peter in Rome and then installed in his
see by St. Paul.[1] It is a little strange that no see in Gaul lays
claim to apostolic foundation. Possibly Arles had at one time
advanced such a claim, for on the diptychs of one of the churches
in that city Trophimus is named as the *second* bishop. This
restraint is all the more remarkable in view of the great interest
which Gaul seems to have taken in St. Peter and the claims put
forth on his behalf. The giving of the keys, for example, is a
subject which appears as frequently among Gallic monuments
as in Rome itself.[2]

The best known and most widespread tradition in connexion
with early Gallic Christianity—it appears not only in Gaul and
Germany, but in Spain and Italy, and even in the East—is that
concerning St. Denys, identified with Dionysius the Areopagite
(Acts 17 : 34).[3] He is said to have arrived in Rome in the days of
Clement by whom he was sent on to Gaul.[4] This legend has a
genuine basis, for a certain Denys came to Paris in the middle
of the third century, being one of the seven bishops mentioned
by Gregory of Tours (*Hist. Franc.*, I, 28). He was not, however,
identified with the Areopagite before the ninth century.[5] Two
centuries later Abailard, noticing that Dionysius is regarded as
Bishop of Corinth by Bede in his commentary on Acts, stirred
up much excitement in the Convent of St. Denys by rejecting
the accepted tradition (*Hist. Calam.*, X, col. 154). Less ambitious legends tell of Clarus who, after preaching in Aquitania
in the first century, was martyred at Lectours in Gascony; of
Benignus, later the patron saint of Dijon, who with two companions was sent to Gaul by Polycarp of Smyrna;[6] and of
Marcellus, who with Valerian escaped from the persecution at
Lyons with angelic aid, only to meet his death at Chalons-sur-
Saône. The first mention of Christianity in Britanny is the
martyrdom of two brothers at Nantes, *c.* 288. Their names are

[1] The tradition is known to Pope Zosimus in the fifth century who speaks of
Trophimus as the fountain from which the rills of faith spread to all Gaul
(*Epist.*, I). Gregory the Great also accepted Arles as the channel through which
Christianity came to Gaul (*Epist.*, V).
[2] See Le Blant, *Les Sarcoph. chrét. de la Gaule*, p. xiii.
[3] More appropriately he was claimed by Athens as her first bishop.
[4] The statement of Sulpicius Severus that no martyrs suffered in Gaul before
the days of Marcus Aurelius would rule him out (*Chron.*, II. 46).
[5] By Abbot Hilduin in *Areopagitica*, *P.L.*, CVI, cols. 23–50.
[6] The mention of Polycarp is interesting in view of his close connexion with
Irenaeus, though the statement of Gregory of Tours (*op. cit.*, I, 29), that the
latter was sent to Gaul by Polycarp, has no evidence to support it.

given as Donatianus and Rogatianus. Of Clarus, claimed as first bishop of Nantes, nothing is known.

The North also had its traditions. The subterranean church under St. Gervais at Rouen, said by some to go back to the fourth century, once contained the tombs of Avitianus and Mellonus,[1] pioneer missionaries in that neighbourhood. Amiens attributed its faith to Firminius who preached there for forty days in 101 and, being denounced by heathen priests, was beheaded by the governor. His body was buried by a Roman senator in his garden where subsequently a small oratory was built. The site is now occupied by the great cathedral.

Another more comprehensive legend states that Irenaeus sent missionaries (as he may well have done) to various parts of Gaul. Felix, Fortunatus, and Achilles went to Valentia, to be martyred in 202; Ferroleus and Ferrutio to Vesontio (Besançon). A later mission, already referred to, consisted of seven bishops, who founded sees at Tours, Arles, Narbonne, Toulouse, Paris, Clermont, and Limoges.[2] These legends, and others like them,[3] deeply overlaid as they are by later traditions, are not without historical substructure, and give some clue to the course of the Gospel in Gaul.

From whatever quarter Christianity first came to Gaul there can be little doubt that it came from over the sea—in spite of Sulpicius Severus and his mention of the Alps. Marseilles, or Arles, would be a likely starting-point for the missionaries of the Gospel, and from there the message would be carried up the Rhone valley. Such Christian remains as have survived go to confirm this supposition, for, except at Autun, all the early monuments come from places near the Mediterranean seaboard or from the Rhone valley. The latter possesses by far the largest number of inscriptions.[4] Christianity, having taken root in the south-west, was long in spreading to the other parts of Gaul and it was not until the second half of the fourth century that there was any rapid advance, and not until well into the fifth before paganism was finally overthrown.

The first clear evidence of the existence of the Christian Church in Gaul is contained in the noble and tragic story of the martyrs of Lyons and Vienne[5] to which reference has already

[1] He is said to have been a native of Britain who had been converted at Rome: Ussher, *Antiq.*, p. 75.
[2] Gregory of Tours, *op. cit.*, I, 28. His statement that Tours had no church before Constans (X, 31) seems to contradict this.
[3] See, for some of them, Scott Holmes, *op. cit.*, p. 60 ff.; Duchesne, *Fastes*, I, p. 45 ff.
[4] Le Blant, *Manuel de l'épigraphie*, p. 41. The remains are later than our period and four only are probably as early as the fourth century. The earliest with a definite date comes from 334 (pp. 14 and 27).
[5] A full account will be found in Scott Holmes, *op. cit.*, p. 34 ff.

been made more than once. Eusebius has preserved the letter sent by the survivors to the Churches of Asia and Phrygia recording the "mighty rage of the heathen against the saints and all that the blessed martyrs endured" (V, i). It tells of the sufferings of Pothinus, the aged Bishop of Lyons, of Maturus and Sanctus, and of Attalus, a man of rank. Above all, it preserves the heroic fortitude of Blandina, the slave-girl, and her brother [1] Ponticus, still a boy. Such was their courage and patience that even the spectators, hardened to bloodshed and cruelty, could not withhold their admiration.

Pothinus, the bishop, is said to have been ninety years old when he met his death in 177. He had come from Asia Minor and as one born in the first century must have had precious recollections of the famous circle there. His successor was a man notable in the history of the early Church—Irenaeus. The name itself is probably the Greek form of one originally Semitic and all the examples of its occurrence recorded in the *Dictionary of Christian Biography* come from the East. I have, however, found one instance of its use in the West in an inscription in the Great Cemetery on the Via Nomentana in Rome which is of some antiquity. It runs as follows:

C. PISONIVS . ET . ANNIA . ZOSII E . PARENTES IRENEO .
FILIO . DVLCISSIMO.[2]

Irenaeus, like his predecessor, had come from Asia Minor, having been born at Smyrna in the first half of the second century. Harnack gives the date as about 140, but this is surely much too late, for Eusebius tells us that while still a young man he had seen Florinus in the company of Polycarp (V, xx, 5). As Polycarp survived until 155 or 156 this statement would not be inconsistent with Harnack's date, if he saw him at the end of his life; but it is quite ruled out by his referring to the reign of Domitian as "almost in our generation" (V, xxx, 3). Irenaeus is said to have been lecturing in Rome at the time of Polycarp's death and may well have accompanied him thither on the visit paid by the latter shortly before that event. When Irenaeus first went to Gaul we do not know. He was the bearer of a letter from the Christians awaiting martyrdom in 177 to Eleutherus, Bishop of Rome, commending to his favour the Montanists of Asia Minor (Euseb., V, iv, 1). This was evidently before the death of Pothinus and his own appointment to succeed him. The last

---

[1] Unless "sister" in Euseb., V, i, 54 refers to a spiritual and not a natural relationship, as it well may do.

[2] See Marucchi, p. 401. A few other instances appear in Diehl, III, p. 88. The name was also used by the Jews, for two examples are known, one on a tomb in the Randarnini cemetery in the Via Appia (Diehl, No. 4908A), the other in that in the Via Nomentana (Diehl, No. 497A).

we hear of Irenaeus is in connexion with disputes over the date of Easter about 195 when he made a protest on behalf of the custom of Asia Minor (*op. cit.*, V, xxiv, 11 ff.). His end is unknown. Of the literary labours which made him so famous, more will be said in a subsequent chapter; here it will suffice to say that his chief work *Adversus Haereses* was probably written about 185.

The next important event in Gallic Christianity is connected with the case of Marcian, the Novatianistic Bishop of Arles in the middle of the third century. Faustinus, Bishop of Lyons, had written to Stephen of Rome complaining of the activities of this schismatic; but getting no satisfaction he appealed to Cyprian. The latter wrote a strong letter to the Bishop of Rome urging him to inform the bishops of Gaul that he considered Marcian as excommunicated and his see as vacant (*Epist.*, LXVII).

Arles again became prominent in the eyes of the Church when in August 314 [1] or 316 it became the scene of the first council which was more than a mere meeting of local bishops. Its main business was to inquire into the Donatist Schism. Among other matters then decided was that of the baptism of heretics. The following decision was made: "As the Africans are in the habit of re-baptizing according to their law, we decree that a heretic coming to the Church shall be questioned as to his creed. If they are satisfied that he was baptized in the Father, and the Son, and the Holy Ghost, only the hand is to be laid upon him that he may receive the Holy Ghost. If, however, he does not confess this Trinity, then let him be baptized" (canon 8).

Meanwhile persecution had been continuing sporadically and the toll of martyrs had been steadily rising. Numerous legends, in addition to those already referred to, have been preserved. One concerns Symphorian, who may have escaped from the persecution at Lyons. It is certainly an early story, even if not contemporary. He suffered at Autun. Others were Florentius, Bishop of Vienne, who perished in 253; Fabius Victor, a soldier, who met his death at Marseilles c. 290; and Ferreolus, a military tribune, who tried to protect Christians at Vienne just before the outbreak of persecution under Diocletian, and was himself put to death in consequence. Maximian, who was then ruling Gaul, was very zealous, especially against soldiers. Of those who suffered, in addition to Ferreolus, was his friend Julian martyred at Brivas (Brioude on the Allier).[2] As Constantius was the ruler of Gaul when the last persecution actually broke out it escaped

---

[1] This is the generally accepted date, but Seeck has suggested that the real date was 316: see *Zeitschrift für Kirchengesch.*, X, p. 509.

[2] He became a popular saint and is mentioned by Sidonius, *Epist.*, VII, and *Carm.*, XXIV, whilst Gregory of Tours devotes considerable space to him (*De Glor. Mart.*, II).

lightly, as his obedience to the imperial edicts was merely formal. In the south Datianus, notorious for his activities in Spain, was responsible for the death of St. Faith at Aginnum (Agen in Aquitania). For some reason she aroused special interest in England where the crypt of Old St. Paul's was dedicated to her, as well as at least seventeen other churches.

But if the Christians of Gaul escaped comparatively lightly they endured much from barbarian inroads; churches were destroyed and abandoned; even their sites became overgrown and cattle grazed in the sanctuaries. The sacraments could no longer be administered to the faithful. But the Church in Gaul soon recovered and in the latter part of the fourth century Gaul was noted for its missionary activity and sent over St. Ninian to Whithorn in Galloway. A church was built there in 397 "after the manner of the Romans" by masons sent from Tours and dedicated to St. Martin. Under the name of Magnum Monasterium it became known far and wide as a great centre of education, both sacred and secular.[1] From it Christianity spread into what is now Cumberland and Westmoreland, and even into Northern Ireland.

Paganism, in the meantime had been slowly dying out, and in general wherever its remnants are found, there, alongside them, are Christian remains. But Nîmes is a striking exception, for Christian remains are there practically unknown. For some reason or other the people of the place were persistently opposed to the Gospel,[2] and even after the triumph of Christianity St. Baudilius was martyred there.[3]

The ecclesiastical development of Gaul is by no means clear. The cantonal basis of Gallic life may have made organization difficult, but by the time that the Gospel entered, towns had been sufficiently established to have made this no great obstacle. Duchesne, while recognizing the supremacy of Arles in Narbonne, thinks that the Bishop of Lyons was supreme over all Celtic Gaul, including Germany, until the middle of the third century.[4] It is surely not without significance that though Vienne was in the province of Narbonensis the Christians there joined with those of Lyons in the letter to Asia in 177. But at this period the number of Christians must have been very small and the organization correspondingly primitive.[5]

Lists of bishops have been compiled based on the records of the Councils of Rome and Arles and from other less reliable sources. They make clear that in Narbonensis there were sees

[1] See Skene, *Celtic Scotland*, II, chap. II.
[2] Tillemont, *Hist. Eccles.*, IV., p. 725.
[3] Le Blant, *Inscript. chrét. de la Gaule*, p. lxviii.   [4] *Fastes*, I, p. 38 ff.
[5] Gregory of Tours, *op. cit.*, I, 29, states that Pothinus was the first bishop of Gaul.

already at Vienne, Arles (whose bishop Marinus was at Rome),
Marseilles where Christian inscriptions have been discovered,
Vasio (Vaison), Portus Nicaenus (Nizza), Arausio (Orange), Apt,
and Tolosa (Toulouse). In Lugdunensis there were Lyons itself,[1]
Autun (whose bishop Reticius was at Rome), Duja (Diê) which
had the distinction of being the only city in Gaul to send a
bishop to Nicaea, Lutetia (Paris), and Agedincum (Sens). From
Aquitania four bishops went to Arles; they were those of
Burdigala (Bordeaux), Eauze, Minate (Mendê), and Avaricum
(Bourges). From Belgica came bishops from Treves and Duro-
cortorum (Rheims). In several other cities the presence of
Christians can be surmised and these may have had their
bishops; among them may be mentioned Geneva and Augustoritum (Limoges). The first bishop of Augustoritum, St. Martial,
has been identified by local patriotism with the boy who provided the five loaves and few small fishes for the feeding of the
Five Thousand (John 6 : 9)! Eventually every city which in
pagan times had a *flamen* probably had its own bishop.[2]

Christianity in Gaul during its early period hardly developed
any of the characteristics which marked it in later times. This
was probably because it continued to retain something derived
from its Eastern origin. Greek, as in Rome, was for long its usual
language, and Irenaeus, the greatest figure which adorned it
before the Nicene age, was still in some ways an Oriental. The
first definitely Latin figure to arise is Hilary of Poitiers. The persistence of Eastern elements can be traced in the inscriptions.
There are, for example, six at Vienne which include expressions
characteristic of the prayers of the Eastern rather than the
Western Church: IN SPE RESVRRECTIONIS MISERICORDIAE
CHRISTI.[3] This influence received further reinforcement later on
with the arrival, from the East, of monasticism.[4] The reluctance
of the Church in Gaul to sever its connexion with Asia Minor can
also be seen in its continued interest in Montanism. The success
of the heretic Marcus, a disciple of Valentinian, among the
Christians of the Rhone valley may have been due to his adopting the Montanist device of employing prophetesses in his work
(Iren., I, xiii, 3).

Thus the Eastern element remained strong in Gaul; but alongside it there soon grew up a native, Celtic element. Irenaeus tells
us that he had to preach in Celtic and, indeed, to use it more
than any other language (I, Pref. 3).

[1] See Hirschfeld in *Sitzungsber. d. K. Preuss. Akad. d. Wiss.*, 1895, p. 381 ff.
Bishop Voccius was at Arles, and Gregory of Tours mentions a bishop named
Helius who occupied the see "in pagan times" (*Gloria Confess.*, LXI).
[2] Such is the suggestion of E. Desjardins, *Géog. hist. et administ. de la Gaule
rom.*, III, p. 524. [3] Le Blant, *Manuel d'épigraph. etc.*, p. 93 f.
[4] Harnack, *Mission and Expansion*, II, p. 399.

One characteristic Gallican feature has sometimes been claimed as going back to the earliest days of the Church in Gaul, and even to Irenaeus himself, that is the special Rite of Lyons. But here, as so often, tradition has been found to be misleading. The rite is no older than the close of the eighth century.[1] None the less, the liturgical uses of Gaul and of Rome were different at the beginning of the seventh century, as Bede informs us (*Hist. Eccles.*, I, xxvii); a difference which probably goes back to quite early times.

(B) GERMANY

The failure of the Romans to penetrate the dark forests of Germany and to subject their denizens to her influence is one of the tragic facts of history, for it has led to a deep fissure in European society, a fissure which is ultimately responsible for most of the conflicts which have delayed its ordered development. Liberal Germans, such as Thomas Mann,[2] realize how much the nation has lost by never having been exposed to the full influence of that genuine European civilization which is based on Graeco-Roman culture. In consequence it has no true conception of the beauty and dignity of man, and of the things which made life worth living in the Roman West. The German feels himself close to the primitive world and at bottom has an immense belief in its scale of values, and, more readily than other Europeans, is prone to revert to pagan conceptions and ideals. When he does so he reacts strongly against those alien influences which have been superimposed upon him, including Christianity itself, and seeks to rid himself of them. In consequence the Germans have proved a more intractable element in European society than the Jews whom they so bitterly despise.

In Celtic lands there was worked out through the interpenetration of the different peoples a species of mixed culture in which each provided certain elements. This failed to happen in the case of the Germans, though on the left bank of the Rhine, where they were mingled with Celtic elements and came under Roman influences, something of the kind took place and apparently went deep, for Mommsen considered that Germans of this type adhered more firmly to Roman rule than the Celts, and that it was not they who opened the doors to their fellow-countrymen across the Rhine (*Provinces*, I, p. 25). Such Germans, it need hardly be said, are not regarded by modern Teutons as at all the genuine article, and are sharply to be distinguished from the "Wotan-Germans" who have never sub-

---

[1] Dom Buenner, O.S.B., *L'Ancienne Liturgie romaine : le rite lyonnais*, 1934.
[2] cf. *Betrachtung eines Unpolitischen*, published in 1918.

mitted to the corruptions of an alien culture. Thus, when at
length the barriers fell and the barbarian tribes poured into the
Empire, the Empire became barbarized and even Germanized.
But had the German people been overcome by the arms of Rome
they would have given themselves up to Christianity as readily
it may be as Gauls and Britons. To many of them it came at last,
backed by force of arms in the days of Charlemagne and later
of the Teutonic Knights. For this reason, among others, it failed
to penetrate the hard core of the German soul, which remained
impervious to all outside influences, and looked back to its own
past by a kind of ancestor-worship which, as Collingwood (*The
New Leviathan*, p. 271) has pointed out, is not far removed from
autocrat worship, and so of that "worship of the herd" which
accounts for so much in the behaviour of the German people,
otherwise so inexplicable.

For our purposes Germany is taken to include not only the
two provinces of Upper and Lower Germany but those parts of
Belgica which in recent times have formed part of the German
Empire. Even so, the great bulk of that empire lies outside our
survey; Christianity in the early centuries may have penetrated
beyond the frontiers so carefully guarded by the Roman legions,
but if so we have no certain records of its progress. The Church
in Germany was of late origin and growth, especially when compared with that in North Africa, in Italy, or even in Southern
Gaul. There were highly developed congregations in Carthage
and in Lyons before ever we hear of the presence of any
Christians in Treves or Mainz. Hauck began his monumental
Kirchengeschichte Deutschlands by remarking that there is no
really German Christianity until the baptism of Clovis in 496.
Before that there were only fragments. Here and there small
groups of Christians might appear no one knows whence or how;
just as in the evening sky stars emerge one by one.

Christian remains are naturally few. A number of objects bearing Christian signs have been found scattered up and down
various parts, but they are only few and of uncertain date and
furnish little reliable evidence of the spread of Christianity in
our period. There is, for example, a bronze seal from Wiesbaden
with a monogram of Christ,[1] a fragmentary inscription at
Bingen,[2] a couple of rings from Kreuznach,[3] and a few others.
When the large cemetery at Andernach was excavated no
Christian remains were found.[4]

The earliest references to Christianity in Germany are naturally vague and general. Tertullian in a highly rhetorical passage
can speak of it as having reached even the Germans (*Adv. Jud.*

---

[1] Kraus, *Die christ. Inschrift. der Rheinlande*, No. 54.   [2] *op. cit.*, No. 60.
[3] *op. cit.*, No. 64.   [4] *Bonner Jahrbuch*, 1886, p. 148 ff.

VII); and, a little earlier, Irenaeus is able to refer to the orthodoxy of the faith of the Churches in Germany, as though these
were well organized and already of some duration.[1] Origen likewise speaks of Britain and Germany as having had the Gospel
preached to them (*On Matt.* 24 : 9). On the other hand it must
be noted that Eusebius omits Germany from his list of provinces
(*Vita Const.*, III, 19), as does Athanasius (*Contra Arian.*, I);
though the latter makes mention of Britain. Moreover Bede's
statement that Severus became Bishop of the Treveri early in
the fifth century and preached the word to the people west of
the Rhine (*Hist. Eccles.*, I, xxi) suggests that up to that time
Christianity had failed to make any deep impression. Probably
the earliest assemblies of Christians on German soil consisted
mainly of people drawn from other races, Celts and the mixed
inhabitants of romanized towns. Soldiers, traders, and slaves
from the Rhone valley may have been among their number.
Just as to-day in some distant lands where Christians are few,
a handful of British and others will combine for worship with
perhaps the encouragement of an occasional visit from a missionary to keep them together. Such small congregations could play
no part in the life of the Church and little in that of the surrounding heathen.

In the absence of early and authentic information about the
earliest times, the legend-makers have inevitably been busy to
fill the gap. But their efforts bring little satisfaction to the
historian and the value of the numerous legends is very slight.[2]
Their chief value, as elsewhere, is the light which they throw on
the mentality of later centuries. We begin with Treves, which
in secular matters was extremely ambitious; did it not claim to
be the oldest city in Europe and to have been founded by Tre-
bates, the son of Ninus? It professes to contain the tomb of St.
Matthias, but for its first bishops is content to set out the names
of Eucharius, Valerius, and Maternus, all envoys of St. Peter.[3]
As Bishop Cyril, in the middle of the fifth century, dedicated an
oratory to the first two of these,[4] they must go back to a com-

---

[1] I, x, 2. The Latin version speaks of Germany in the singular; but the
original Greek, as preserved by Epiphanius, has the plural, and Harvey thinks
that this signifies both free and occupied Germany (I, p. 92). It may be pointed
out that Caesar always speaks of Germany in the singular, but later writers,
such as Pliny and Tacitus, use the plural. But this might well be a reference
to the two divisions of Roman Germany as in *Agric.*, XXVIII; the singular is
used of Germany beyond the Rhine.

[2] I have ignored the so-called Council of Cologne, said to have been held in
346, with its list of attendant bishops. It is obviously pure invention. See, for
a discussion, Duchesne, *Fastes épiscopaux de l'ancienne Gaule* (ed. 2), I, p.
361; and, for a more recent treatment, W. Neuss, *Die Anfänge des Christentums
im Rheinlande.*

[3] Garenfeld, *Die Trierer Bischöfe*, p. 72 f.

[4] Kraus, No. 77.

paratively early date. Maternus is also claimed by Cologne and
Tongern; and there are reasons for believing that the first Bishop
of Cologne actually bore this name, though, far from being a
disciple of St. Peter, he lived in the fourth century. Mainz has
chosen for its founder that Crescens who was sent to Galatia by
St. Paul (2 Tim. 4 : 10); whilst Metz lays claim to Clement, who
was sent by St. Peter.

The above legends are obviously unauthentic and not even
impressive. There are, however, others which, though they may
not be entirely genuine, witness to probabilities; for they make
much of the part played by the army. The legions in both Upper
and Lower Germany, so far as is known, were not changed much
during the first few centuries of the Christian era, so that there
would be no opportunity for soldiers, who had served in the
East, to bring Christianity with them. However, the legend of
the Thundering Legion suggests a link with the East, for the
legion concerned (XII) had been recruited in Melitene in Cappadocia, where there may well have been a considerable number of
Christians towards the end of the second century. The story
narrates the plight of a Roman army which had run short of
water and was relieved by rain sent in response to the prayers
of this Legion. The actual narrative contains many inconsistencies;[1] there are, for example, reasons for doubting whether
Legio XII was present on the occasion; but the incident has
evidently some historical foundation, for it is mentioned by
Cassius Dio who attributes the sudden relieving shower to the
arts of an Egyptian magician (LXXI, 8, 10).[2] The usual date is
c. 174, but it has recently been suggested that the actual year
was 171.[3] A similar legend tells of the so-called Theban Legion,[4]
or a cohort belonging to it, being put to death under Maximian
in 286 for refusing to attack fellow-Christians against whom they
had been marched.[5] The incident, which is very obscure, may
rest on some actual event, but this is by no means probable. It
is usually located at Agaunum near Martigny, and the name of
their leader is given as St. Maurice. But rival claimants exist in
Xanten[6] (with St. Victor as the principal martyr), Cologne, .

[1] For a full discussion, see Lightfoot, II, i, p. 469 ff.
[2] Tertullian, *Apol.*, V, refers to an account of the incident said to have
been compiled by Marcus Aurelius himself; whilst an appendix to Justin, II
Apol., contains what purports to be a letter written by him to the senate,
probably a quite early forgery.
[3] See A. von Domaszewski, "Die Chron. des Bell. Germ. et Sarmat.", in
Neue Heidelberg. Jahrbücher, V, p. 120 f.
[4] There was a church dedicated to the Theban Legion at Canterbury in
the eleventh century: see Goscelin of Cant., *Hist. Trans. S. Aug.*, II, i (*P.L.*,
CLV, col. 30).
[5] See Scott Holmes, *The Christian Church in Gaul*, p. 85 f.
[6] Xanten as the scene of the boyhood of Siegfried is also connected with a
very different series of legends.

Treves, and Bonn. However, St. Maurice commands by far the greatest measure of support and the bones of the legionaries are said to lie buried in his abbey.[1]

Cologne, however, has, or had, a church of St. Gereon, dedicated to the leader of the band and his three hundred and eighteen men; and not far away is a church dedicated to St. Ursula, said to occupy the site of one of the fourth century. This brings us to a very interesting legend which may have behind it a genuine tradition. In its popular form, so well known through the paintings of Carpaccio, it tells of the massacre of Ursula and her eleven thousand virgin companions by the Huns. She is said to have been a British princess and to have suffered in 451. But the dates 238 and c. 283 have also been claimed and it is possible that she may have been a genuine martyr and that the number of her companions has been greatly exaggerated. However, as the legend is not mentioned by St. Jerome or even by Gregory of Tours, this seems unlikely.[2]

Leaving legends aside and coming to a consideration of genuine evidence, we turn again to Treves as the natural starting-point. Christians may have been found there as early as the second century, but the number can never have been large, for up to 336, when it was burnt down, one small church had sufficed to accommodate them;[3] whilst the larger building which took its place remained the only Christian edifice in the city as late as 385.[4] Even after the recognition of Christianity by Constantine, and in spite of the frequent presence of Christian emperors, the Gospel seems to have made but little appeal to the natives; as the services would be conducted in Latin the religion would be regarded as Roman and so patriotism would tell against it. To become a Christian would be to cease to be a German. The capture of Treves in 464 by the Ripuarian Franks, who were heathen, no doubt caused the destruction of many Christian remains, but enough have survived to make it clear that the Church consisted entirely of Roman and romanized converts, for there is a complete absence of purely Celtic or Teutonic names from the inscriptions,[5] though Greeks and Orientals are found.[6] The first bishops, as already noticed, were Eucharius and

---

[1] In 1070, Anno, Archbishop of Cologne, obtained permission to remove some of these bones to his cathedral: In order to avoid trouble he did this by night: *Vita Annonis, M.G.H., Script.*, XI, p. 480.

[2] See, further, W. Levison, "Das Werden der Ursula-Legende", in *Bonner Jahrbuch,* 1927, p. 1.

[3] Athanasius, *Apol. ad Const.*, XV.

[4] No other seems to be known to Sulpicius Severus, *Vita Mart.*, XVI, 18.

[5] Kraus, *Die christ. Inschrift. der Rheinlande*, I, includes a hundred and eighty-two (Nos. 74–255). A certain Hariulfus appears in No. 102, but it is not certain that he was a Christian.

[6] Kraus, Nos. 80, 160, 163, and 164.

Valerius, and Treves was represented at the Council of Arles. Maternus, the third bishop, bears the same name as bishops of Cologne and Tongen, and it is possible that he is the same person and exercised jurisdiction over the whole district.[1] Metz (Divodurum) claims as its first bishop St. Caelestius, who died in 320, whilst Victor may have been the bishop of that name at Sardica.[2]

Cologne (Colonia Agrippina) was late in receiving the Gospel and it is doubtful whether any kind of organized Christianity existed there before the fourth century.[3] However, Bishop Maternus was present at the Council of Rome in 313 and at Arles in 316, when Eusebius tells us he was specially consulted by Constantine about the Donatist Schism (*Hist. Eccles.*, X, v, 18). Compared with those at Treves the number of Christian inscriptions, seventeen, is but meagre.[4] In the middle of the fourth century Ammianus Marcellinus speaks of the Christians as worshipping in a tiny conventicle (*conventiculum ritus Christiani*), XV, v, 31, though his remark does not exclude the existence of other churches in the city. Tongern, near by, seems at the beginning of the fourth century to have been attached to Cologne. There was a bishop here in 344 named Servatius.[5]

Mainz (Moguntia) lags even behind Cologne, for it had no bishop at Arles and its name does not occur in connexion with the Arian controversies. By the middle of the fourth century it apparently possessed a large church, for Ammianus Marcellinus speaks of the greater part of the inhabitants being gathered there when the city was attacked by barbarians.[6] No certain Christian inscriptions have been found at Mainz,[7] and the first bishop whose name is known is Sidonius, as late as the first half of the sixth century.[8] Augsburg (Augusta Vindelicorum) is content to mention a visit from Narcissus, a bishop of Oriental birth who converted St. Afra and then went on to meet his death in Spain.

For the spread of Christianity beyond the frontiers of the Roman Empire, we have, as has been said, no evidence for our period. There is no doubt that there was constant intercourse across the frontier; we know, for example, that when Catualda conquered Maroboduus he found, in what is now Bohemia, merchants from the Roman province (Tacitus, *Ann.*, II, 62). Such traders might include Christians. From a later time we

---

[1] So Duchesne, *Fastes*, I, p. 15.
[2] So Hauck suggests: *Kirchengesch. Deutschlands*, I, p. 32.
[3] So Kleinen, *Einführung des Christent. in Köln*, p. 10. Hauck, however, is critical of this view: see *op. cit.*, I, p. 7.
[4] Kraus, Nos. 283–299.
[5] Athanasius, *Contra Arian.*, L.
[6] XXVII, x: Jerome speaks of many having been butchered (*trucidata*) in the church (*Epist.*, CXXIII, 16).
[7] Possibly Kraus, No. 33 is an exception.
[8] Fortunatus, *Carm.*, II, 11 f.; IX, 9.

have, indeed, an instance of the Gospel being introduced by such, for Ambrose corresponded with Fritigal, a Marcomanni queen who had been converted by an Italian trader (*Vita Ambrosii*, XXXVI).

The majority of the Germans in the North finally accepted Christianity, as we have seen, not as the result of persuasion but of force. Such mass conversions sometimes have happy results in the long run if the second generation becomes amenable to Christian education; but in the case of Germany, even of those parts which accepted the faith through the labours of such outstandingly skilled missionaries as Boniface and his fellows, evil was to follow the delayed conversion; for, by that time, the "mythology" of Christianity had largely become static, and thus a very different fate befell the ancestral gods of the Teutons from that of the deities of the Mediterranean peoples. In the case of these latter their objects of worship remained much the same, though the names were altered and the old gods and goddesses, from the Great Mother downwards, were still revered as saints. But in Germany it was far otherwise. There the ancestral gods were destined for destruction, and objects associated with their worship were obliterated and the whole mythology despised and condemned.[1] Had Germany been converted earlier and her deities received within the Christian pantheon what a difference might have been made. The Nazis at least would have been deprived of one great argument.

[1] They did indeed give their names to the days of the week, a small concession; and objects such as the maypole have survived in popular use.

CHAPTER VII

THE BRITISH ISLES

Although Britain was little known to the Roman world before the expedition of Julius Caesar it had for long been in close touch with the continent of Europe and, above all, with neighbouring Gaul. In fact, it may be said, perhaps with a touch of exaggeration, that the further back one goes in history the closer the connexion is seen to be; until a time is reached at last when Britain is actually part of the mainland and the white cliffs of Dover are one with the sandbanks of Calais. None the less, its real significance only begins with the invasion and brief occupation in 55 B.C. and the following year.

After its temporary appearance within the sphere of their influence, Britain for nearly a century was left unmolested by the Romans, though relations between it and the Continent continued to be close and friendly. The tribute imposed by Caesar was, one imagines, seldom or never paid; whilst the hegemony of the Trinovantes which he had imposed was not uniformly accepted, as is shown by the visits of affronted rulers to Rome itself. But these were not matters to stir the Empire into renewed military activity against the offending islanders. But the idea of permanently occupying this remote region, a legacy from Caesar, continued to be cherished, and poets could compose odes to celebrate its coming acquisition. But the time was not yet ripe, even when Augustus had brought peace at length to the troubled world. Augustus might, indeed, play with the thought of taking up the unfinished task of his great kinsman, but other, more pressing, duties prevented his embarking actually upon it. From a military point of view, the necessary expedition would bring little of either profit or glory. The Gauls would, of course, be deprived of a handy place of refuge, and agitators and rebels of a convenient base; but this was hardly sufficient compensation. Moreover, to occupy the island would mean an increase in the standing army, and any additional revenues which might accrue from the conquest would scarcely offset the necessary expenditure. The memory of Caesar's uncompleted conquest, however, weighed upon the minds of imperial statesmen, until at length, under Claudius, the work was taken in hand. It had, perhaps, become urgent, and there was, moreover, an ostensible excuse for intervention.

It was the Trinovantes themselves, Caesar's chosen instru-

ments of government, who provided the occasion. Under Cunobelinus, a name better known in the form Cymbeline, which
Shakespeare used, they had thrown off the last perfunctory
acknowledgment of Roman suzerainty and proceeded to subject
the neighbouring tribes. A family quarrel then broke out and
one of the sons of Cunobelinus fled to Rome and appealed to
Gaius for his protection. Here was a clear call to intervene, and
in A.D. 43 a strong expeditionary force under the command of
Aulus Plautius was sent to Britain. It met with only slight
resistance and soon the Roman army was halted along the banks
of the Thames awaiting the arrival of Claudius, who was now
emperor, to put the final touches to the conquest. In its course
one brave antagonist had to be overcome, Caractacus, the son
of Cunobelinus who was now dead. Camulodunum, the capital
of the Trinovantes, was captured and transformed into a Roman
colony by the settlement there of a body of veteran soldiers.

Thus the initial conquest had been a comparatively easy task.
Later, outbreaks would come, provoked as a rule by unwise
methods on the part of the conquerors, of which the most serious
was that under Boudicca or Boadicea, to give her the popular
name. During this rising the Roman forces were in danger of
annihilation and Roman rule itself was nearly swept away.
This and other storms were, however, successfully weathered
and Britain settled down at last as a Roman province.

The coming of the Romans meant that Britain, like every
other conquered territory, would be romanized. But the process
of romanization,[1] for good or for evil, had already been at work
for a considerable time, as can be seen from the results of excavations at Colchester and other sites. Much of it was a consequence of commercial relations with the Continent, for Britain
was largely engaged in what would now be called "luxury trades"
—the export of slaves, skins, hounds, precious metals, as well
as the more useful grain and cattle. On the site of London itself
there had been a settlement of traders for more than a generation before the Christian era: humble forerunners of those who
should in later years dwell in that

> monstrous ant-hill on the plane
> Of a too-busy world.

The native rulers, or some of them, had been in favour of closer
relations with Rome, and Strabo considered that they had, even
before a single Roman landed on their shores, made the whole
island almost a Roman territory (IV, 200). This estimate is no
doubt a gross exaggeration, though it is probable that in the

---

[1] On the different views as to the extent to which Britain was romanized,
see Gougaud, *Christianity in Celtic Lands*, p. 5 f.

south and especially in the south-east of Britain there had been a perceptible spread of Roman ideas.

But Britain had a quite ancient and considerable culture of its own, and the people were far from being the naked savages imagined by our ancestors. It is, indeed, held by some scholars that in art at least the coming of Roman influences was a real set-back. "Before the Roman conquest," wrote Professor Collingwood, "the Britons were a race of gifted and brilliant artists: the conquest, forcing them into the mould of Roman life with its vulgar efficiency and lack of taste, destroyed that gift and reduced their arts to the level of mere manufactures" (*Roman Britain*, p. 247). Conquering peoples are often apt to despise the arts and customs of the vanquished, and probably there is no people which is not able to "surprise the world with native merchandise". Even the African who was once regarded as little more than a savage is now known to possess quite an admirable social system and a definite culture. For evidence of the high artistic achievements of the Britons, the bronze mirror found at Gloucester may be adduced. With the Romans, Gallo-Roman Samian pottery came flooding in, though remains of Italian pottery of an even earlier date have been discovered at Silchester. It is pleasing to know that the native ware, after a time, recovered itself and began gradually to supplant that of the invader. The chief centre of manufacture was Durobrivae (Castor in Northamptonshire) where pottery remarkable for the vigour and life of its decoration was produced.[1]

In the wake of the legions came a whole crowd of "hangers-on", merchants and traders and others drawn by the prospect of exploiting the newly acquired territories and their inhabitants. The process of romanization, which depended largely on the contacts made by people of this class, as well as by officials, naturally first affected the dwellers in cities. It had but indifferent success and diminished with the decay of the towns in the third century. A later stage came with the development of the "villa" system, the establishment of large country estates, the forerunners of the medieval manor, which included masses of dependants. The second stage was carried on principally by those who had been born in Britain and were sometimes of native race, with here and there a wealthy merchant from across the channel. The earlier, urban, stage had affected rich and poor alike; the second or rural stage seems to have left the peasants almost untouched, Roman ways of life being regarded as the privilege of the wealthy. The spread of Roman influence among the native rulers was mainly the work of Agricola, who encouraged romanization both by his personal influence and by

[1] See Foord, *The Last Age of Roman Britain*, p. 64 f.

grants of public money towards the erection of buildings. It was numbered among his triumphs that Roman tutors were finding employment in Britain.[1] Tacitus is scornful of the effects, which ruined many ambitious native rulers. "Step by step," he says, "they were led to things which dispose to vice. . . . All this in their ignorance they called civilization, when it was but part of their servitude" (*Agric.*, XXI).

Except in the case of the ruling classes and those whose occupations brought them into close contact with Roman officials and such like, romanization hardly penetrated below the surface of the people's life. There might be some adoption of Roman ways of living and of Roman fashions; but the bulk of the population remained immune from their influence. The Briton, like the Gaul, was very proud of his native culture and manner of life, and tenacious to maintain them in spite of all efforts to change him. As one moved north and west such influences would almost completely disappear.

Scotland and Ireland, to use modern names, although of races akin to the Gauls and Britons, spoke different dialects and had had little intercourse with the Romans. They had probably reached a much lower level of civilization; the Caledonians in particular seem to have advanced very little beyond the stage of savages. There was some intercourse, however, for traders seem to have frequented the coastal districts of Scotland bringing domestic wares, wines, and raw metal. There was also some flow of trade across the northern border, and quantities of Roman coins have been found in North Britain. Ireland remained almost untouched; but had Agricola been granted the additional legion which was all, so he declared, that was necessary to enable him to occupy the island, the story of Western civilization might have been very different, at least so far as the British Isles are concerned.

What has been said of romanization in general may also be said of one of its most striking manifestations, the use of the Latin tongue. The process by which it spread was doubtless only slow, but it seems to have covered a sufficiently wide extent; some have even affirmed that archaeology affords "ample evidence that . . . Latin was spoken, not only in the towns, but also in the rural country-houses and farms".[2] It is remarkable, too, that whilst no Celtic inscriptions have, so far as I know, ever been discovered, vulgar *graffiti* in Latin are not uncommon.[3] No

---

[1] Plutarch tells us that he met at Delphi a Greek teacher of languages on his way from Britain to his home in Tarsus. A vivid illustration of the variety of races included within the Empire and of the extent of the communication between them.

[2] Zachrisson, *Romans, Kelts, and Saxons in Ancient Britain*, p. 25.

[3] Haverfield, *Romanization of Roman Britain* (Ed. 4), p. 209.

literature of the Roman period, however, seems to have been preserved. With the withdrawal of the Romans and some consequent severance of intercourse with the Continent, the use of Latin would naturally grow less and less, save among scholars and writers. The Latin of St. Patrick is barbarous, but that of Gildas is excellent of its kind and he refers to it as "our own tongue". It was perhaps no misfortune that the Anglo-Saxon invasion had the effect of almost completely wiping out the use of Latin, for when it came again to Britain with the Christian missionaries it came as a literary language and in a purer form than if it had survived, as on the Continent, as a living tongue.

In a paper read before the British Association in 1935 Mr. R. Jackson challenged the prevailing notion that Latin was widely used in Roman times, limiting it to officials, military and civil, and to the native upper classes when on their best behaviour. He suggested that the *graffiti* found at Silchester may well have come from artisans using Celtic as their spoken tongue, but writing a rude kind of Latin. He cited as a parallel the Erse-speaking people of Kerry who always use English when signing their names or writing a letter.

Before leaving the subject of Latin in Britain, it may be worth while to recall the amusing story told in the thirteenth century by Giraldus Cambrensis in his *Gemma*, of a priest who explained that the festival of St. John before the Latin Gate (*ante portam Latinam*) was intended to commemorate the introduction of Latin into Britain by that apostle. The story, if not deliberately invented by the witty Anglo-Norman, throws more light, it must be confessed, on the ignorance of contemporary clerics than on the use of Latin in this island.

Economically, the country was reasonably prosperous. Foreign traders may have done much in the way of exploitation, but the natives were not without benefits. There were, for example, the great roads carried along the tops of the hills, not probably as was once thought so as to avoid valleys and forests which might conceal foemen, but so as to do away with the necessity for crossing rivers, with the cost of bridges and the danger of floods. The countryside was cared for and agriculture stimulated. In the fens, there was a wonderful system of drainage, subsequently allowed to decay and only discovered with the aid of air-photography. The great achievement of the Romans, however, was the creation of towns. These seem to have been designed on military rather than civil lines, possibly because military architects alone were available. They were adorned by large and ambitious buildings which must have involved heavy taxation, and were protected by fortified walls or, in the case of the smaller towns, by earthworks. During the decay of civic life in the third century which affected all parts of the Empire, Britain did not escape.[1] At the end of the century an attempted revival appears not to have been a success. Part of it was the restoration of Verulam by Constantius, who also rebuilt the fortress of York. The growing importance of the countryside can be traced in the foundation of small market towns; but the larger continued to decay and many of them were simply left to squatters.[2]

Romanization was even extended to include religion, and Celtic and Roman deities lived side by side in perfect amity, terms which favoured some interchange of influence and attributes. This can be judged from an inscription set up in 237 by a certain M. Aurelius Lunaris and dedicated to the goddess Tutela Boudiga, i.e., to the Great Mother and the Celtic Victory.[3] It is remarkable that most of the Romano-Celtic temples are of late date and show the strength of paganism, even in the fourth century, when it was about to be proscribed. There are in Britain traces also of Oriental cults, and strange gods from Syrian climes were worshipped on the bleak northern wall. There is, for example, an altar to Jupiter Heliopolitanus from Baalbek at Carvoran, near Greenhead, and not far away is another to the goddess Atargatis, placed there by a band of archers from Hamath stationed on the wall in the time of Hadrian. In the same neighbourhood, at Cilurnum (Chesters) a mutilated monument of Jupiter Dolichenus, whose home was less than two hundred miles north of Baalbek, has also been discovered. These remains were the work of the mixed races who were present on the wall for military reasons. Their variety can be gathered even more clearly and in greater detail from the numerous tombstones which have been preserved. These include memorials, not only to Syrians, but also to Greeks, Pannonians, Thracians, and indeed to men from practically every province of the Empire. One interesting case, which must have had many parallels, shows how one such immigrant settled down in his new country and became part of its people. Near Newcastle-on-Tyne there is a tombstone of a certain Barates, a Syrian from Palmyra, who married a British wife and made his home there. Sometimes, so records reveal, there would be transfers of military forces on a large scale. In A.D. 119, for example, after the Ninth Legion (Hispana) had been annihilated, the Sixth (Victrix) was brought over from Gaul, with auxiliary troops, to take its place. The

---

[1] Rostovtzeff has argued that Britain escaped the wave of depression and bankruptcy which affected the rest of the Empire at this time. He bases his objection mainly on the evidence of the villas. Recent excavations at Verulam seem to tell against him. See *Camb. Anct. Hist.*, XII, p. 282.
[2] Much of the above account is based on Collingwood, *Roman Britain.*
[3] See *J.R.S.*, 1921, XI, p. 100 ff.

soldiers and their dependants would thus be added to the permanent population. Similarly, towards the end of the third century, Probus transferred to Britain large numbers of Burgundians and Vandals captured during his campaigns in Germany. Thus it will readily be seen that the people among whom Christianity was to attempt to appeal in this island were by no means all of the same race or even on the same level of civilization; a fact which is often forgotten.

THE COMING OF CHRISTIANITY

Legends concerning the advent of Christianity to Britain are numerous and highly imaginative. It has been claimed, for example, that St. Paul, accompanied by a disciple of Welsh birth named Aristobulus, once paid it a visit. The legend may have originated in the mind of some patriotic writer who considered that Britain had an even clearer claim to the title of "terminus of the West" than Spain.[1] Other legends tell how Bran the Blessed, the father of Caractacus, brought the Gospel from Rome itself. Others again trace the introduction to Pudens and Claudia, mentioned in 2 Tim. 4 : 21. They would identify Pudens with Aulus Pudens, the friend of Martial, who married a British maiden.[2] One legend stands apart from the rest in having some kind of historic, even if mistaken, basis. Bede, who is the first to mention the story, tells how Lucius, King of the Britons, wrote to Eleutherus, Bishop of Rome, in 171, asking to be made a Christian (*Hist. Eccles.*, I, iv). There actually was such an appeal at that time from a King Lucius, but he was Lucius Abgar, King of Edessa. It has been suggested that the confusion between the two monarchs may have arisen owing to the fact that the citadel of Lucius was called Birtha (Britium). One other legend demands notice on account of its wide popularity, although it is of very late origin, that of Joseph of Arimathaea. It is said that he and twelve companions set out from Jerusalem bringing with them the Holy Grail, and finally settled at Avalon, the future Glastonbury. This beautiful and poetic legend is, as a matter of sober fact, quite unknown before the end of the twelfth century. Actually the first mention is in 1191 and there can be but little doubt that, together with another legend calculated to appeal to a rather different public—that King Arthur was buried there—it was the invention of the monks of Glastonbury after the disastrous fire of 1184.[3]

[1] See Ussher, *Brit. Eccles. Antiq.*, I, and Haddon and Stubbs, *Councils*, I, p. 22 f.

[2] For a discussion of this theory, which has, of course, no historical value, see Lightfoot, I, i, p. 76 ff.

[3] See J. Armitage Robinson, *Two Glastonbury Legends*, p. 50.

The first reference to Christianity in Britain is contained in the well-known passage of Tertullian (*Adv. Jud.*, VII) in which he makes very ambitious claims for the extent of the spread of the Gospel. There are also references by Origen (*6th Hom. on Luke, 4th Hom. on Ezek.*, and *Comm. on Matt., XXXIX*) as well as Eusebius (*Demonst. Evangel.*, III, 5). When and how it first reached Britain is quite unknown. One surmise, and it is nothing more, is that soldiers in some of the legions introduced it. This is a possibility which cannot be ignored, but it seems more probable that, to quote the words of Wakeman: "it came in the wake of the rich civilians of Gaul who built their villas at Silchester or Verulam, bathed in the medicinal waters at Bath, or ate the best oysters the world produced at Colchester or Canterbury" (*Hist. of the Church of England*, p. 1). It spread, no doubt, at first among the townspeople, who had already been subject to Roman influences, though mainly among the poorer sections. In any event, there is little trace of its effective presence before the later part of the fourth century, and even then paganism was still active, for a temple was built to the Celtic god Nodens at Lydney as late as 365.

Bede tells us that there was no persecution in Britain before Diocletian (*Hist. Eccles.*, I, iv) and that even then the land escaped comparatively lightly owing to the clement disposition of Constantius. There are stories of a few martyrs, among them the famous St. Alban who was put to death on a hillside outside the city.[1] Miracles were still being performed in Bede's day (*op. cit.*, I, vii), which suggests that there had been a continuous cult. A Welsh tradition says that he suffered at Caerleon where St. Julius and St. Aaron are also said to have given up their lives; and, with less of historical probability, St. Socrates and St. Stephen at Monmouth. In spite of Bede, and Gildas upon whom he depended, it is by no means certain that these outbreaks took place under Diocletian. Constantius is said to have avoided any bloodshed (Lactantius, *De Mort. Persec.*, XV, 7) and the Donatists of Africa believed that he took no part in the persecution (Optatus, I, 22); moreover, the Anglo-Saxon Chronicle definitely states that St. Alban suffered in 283 (A) or 286 (EF). Gildas himself is slightly vague about the matter (*Chron.*, X, *ut conicimus*). British bishops attended the Council of Arles. Their names are given as Eborius, Restitutus, and Adelfius. Eborius is described as *episcopus de civitate Eboracensi*, Restitutus as Bishop of London, and Adelfius of *Colonia Londinensium* (?*Lindensium* or *Legionensium*, which may be Caerleon).[2]

[1] Gildas, *Chron.*, X, states that a multitude of other Christians also suffered at this time, in various localities.

[2] Mansi, *Concilia*, II, p. 476. See also S. N. Miller in *Eng. Hist. Rev.*, XLII, p. 79 f.

Christianity only penetrated the northern part of the island at the end of the fourth century; that is, beyond the limits of our period. It began with the arrival of Ninian, the Romano-Briton who had been educated at Rome. On his way home he had visited St. Martin at Tours, and inspired by this he built a monastery at Whithorn in Galloway which he dedicated to that saint. It became a great centre of missionary activity.

The organization of the Church in Britain was doubtless similar to that of Gaul, and by the end of the fourth century, it may be supposed, every walled city (there were scarcely more than fifteen of them) possessed a church and a bishop.[1] Up till then it had been poor and struggling, with little power of influencing the upper classes. The near neighbourhood of Gaul would be a source of strength and reinforcement so long as communication could be maintained.

Christian remains in Britain are almost entirely lacking.[2] In view of the secular history of the island this is hardly surprising, for remains in general from the fourth century are scanty, especially those concerning the poorest classes from whom Christianity would draw. Forts and camps have also largely disappeared, and such inscriptions as have been discovered are mainly the work of soldiers, among whom the Gospel made little progress. After the end of the third century they are chiefly milestones and tombs. Many sites which the Romans and the Britons of their day had occupied became deserted; the fact that the Anglo-Saxons, when they came, lived in settlements rather than in scattered hamlets meant that many sites would be abandoned. This was sometimes all to the good, for though such sites might become, in later days, stone quarries for new buildings, many of them were lost until discovered by the archaeologist; among them are such important sites as Verulam, Silchester, Wroxeter, and Caister near Norwich.

Pagan remains in addition to inscriptions, such as those already referred to in connexion with the spread of Oriental religions, included quite a number of temples. These were small structures intended for the use of the officiating priest and of any worshipper who "assisted" at the ceremony; there was no kind of provision for a congregation. One interesting inscription from the early fourth century records that one Septimus by

---

[1] The manner of the attestation of the British bishops at Arles, if sufficient reliance can be placed upon it, seems to prove that the organization was on a diocesan basis, not as under the Celtic system where the abbot was supreme, and the bishops, unless themselves abbots, whilst discharging their special functions such as ordination, had no jurisdiction.

[2] When Richard of Cirencester was compiling his *Speculum Hist. de Gestis Regum Angliae* at the end of the fourteenth century one of his superiors asked scornfully: "Where are the vestiges of those cities and names which you commemorate? There are none" (I, vii).

name restored a statue of Jupiter at Corinium (Cirencester). The most numerous remains are connected with the cult of Mithras; so numerous are they in fact that they suggest that during the Roman occupation Mithraism had a greater following than the Church. It is worth mentioning that no Anglo-Saxon temples have survived, though the evidence of place-names bears witness to the existence of many local sanctuaries. No doubt they were deliberately destroyed when the population adopted Christianity, and the site occupied by a Christian church.

As many Christian churches must have been built by British Christians, some reason for the lack of remains is required. One possible cause is the use of unsubstantial materials in their construction. Celtic churches were generally simple oratories of wood or stone and might not possess even a separate chancel.[1] Bede tells us, for what it is worth, that the Britons were not accustomed to build their churches in stone (*Hist. Eccles.*, III, iv). There seems, indeed, to have been a general reluctance to make use of stone during this period, for even the amphitheatres were constructed of wooden seats with earth banks, never of solid masonry. Another cause would be deliberate destruction on the part of the heathen invaders, and also, for the possibility must not be neglected, by the Roman Church when England became Christian once again.

The theory that the Britons were entirely dispossessed and exterminated in those districts which the Anglo-Saxons conquered is no longer held, at least in its crudest form. Quite probably in many parts the Britons continued to exist in subjection to their conquerors and were no doubt allowed to carry on their worship. All the same, there must have been a vast amount of destruction. One striking piece of evidence for the ruthlessness of the invaders is the total disappearance of most of the place-names which appear in records relating to the Roman period. They cannot even be traced in an English guise. But still more destruction of British Christian remains must have taken place after the coming of the Italian mission under Augustine. Bede tells us that when he arrived in Kent he found the queen was using a British church, St. Martin's, Canterbury,[2] and that later, King Ethelbert gave him permission to repair other British churches (*Hist. Eccles.*, XXVI and XXXIII). Professor Hamilton Thompson has pointed out that Augustine and his companions departed, in a remarkable way, from the usual Roman custom by making their chancels at the east end; and that at St. Pancras there is a western porch, the origin of which

---

[1] See Hamilton Thompson, *Ground Plan of the English Parish Church*, p. 25.
[2] See, on this, C. R. Peers, "The Earliest Christian Churches in England," *Antiquity*, III, p. 67.

is probably the non-Roman *narthex* (*op. cit.*, p. 24). This departure from traditional arrangement may have been due to the adoption of a building or foundation belonging originally to British Christians. One student of the period has gone so far as to declare that "it was the settled policy of the Roman Church to exterminate all traces of Celtic Christianity once they had got the upper hand—so much so that there is not one old dedication to St. Aidan in all the north of England".[1] Bede's History is full of stories showing how much the Romans despised the Celts, and the Celts hated the Romans. Even before this, Gildas, a romanized Briton, represents Celtic Christianity as corrupt and lacking in zeal. This feeling persisted for centuries. St. Aldhelm, who died in 709, tells us that in his day British priests in the country beyond the Severn would not worship with Saxons; and Theodore's *Penitential* regards all British and Irish bishops as being in a state of excommunication and refuses to recognize their acts (II, ix, 1 and 3). Even when malicious destruction was not present, the tendency to make use of older material would always be there. An example can be found in the small church of Escomb, near Bishop Auckland, which was constructed almost entirely of masonry taken from a Roman building; whilst at Brixworth, near Northampton, tradition (possibly mistakenly)[2] says that the church was a transformed Roman basilica.

The oldest Christian site in Britain is probably Glastonbury. The little church of wattle in Avalon was perhaps built as early as the second century. It survived because when the Saxons conquered that part of England they were already Christians. Early in the seventh century St. Paulinus covered it over with wood and lead; but unfortunately it was burnt with the rest of the abbey buildings in 1184. Thus though it no longer exists we have clear proof of its having survived the Saxon invasion. Of remains actually existing to the present day the most famous is the small basilican church at Silchester. It contains some interesting features including a *narthex* extending across the entire east end, a characteristic of eastern architecture. It is, in this, akin to the basilicas in North Africa, although it retains the apse at the west end, which is a Roman characteristic.[3] Another building which was probably a Christian church was discovered at Caerwent (Venta Silurum) in excavations carried on in 1923–1925 by Mr. V. E. Nash-Williams. It forms part of a block of buildings, including shops and baths, near the forum and has some peculiar arrangements. The *narthex*, measuring 70 ft. from north to south, was only 12½ ft. in depth; from it there extended

[1] J. L. G. Meissner, *The Celtic Church in England*, p. 3.
[2] So Hamilton Thompson, *op. cit.*, p. 21.
[3] See Hamilton Thompson, *op. cit.*, p. 14, for a fuller description.

a small nave which measured 25 ft. by 10 ft., ending in an apse at the east end.[1]

IRELAND

Although Ireland was never part of the Roman Empire it was not entirely cut off from all dealings with it. There is, indeed, some evidence of regular intercourse with both Gaul and Spain, and Tacitus could claim that its harbours and approaches were familiar because of commerce (*Agric.*, XXIV). Further evidence can be found in the presence of Roman coins, a hoard belonging to the second century was discovered at Bray Head, whilst others from the time of the Republic have been found. In fact, they are quite common on the east coast.[2] There was also a close religious link with Gaul. It has, indeed, been suggested that the Druids of Gaul went to Ireland in order to be trained, rather than to Britain.[3] Curiously enough, there seems to be no evidence of Druidism in southern Britain, apart from the notice in Caesar: *De Bell. Gall.*, VI, 13. It existed, of course, in Anglesey, the ancient Mona.[4]

Christianity does not seem to have made any effective entry into Ireland until the fifth century; such, at least, is the opinion of those who have given special attention to the subject. Legends here do not pretend to add much to our knowledge, though it has been claimed that an Irishman named Altus who was serving in the Roman army was present at the Crucifixion and returned home to proclaim the Gospel to his fellow-countrymen. Although the real beginnings are associated with the visits of Palladius and St. Patrick in 431 and 432, there can be little doubt that Christianity was already in existence in some parts of the island at an earlier date.[5] It has even been suggested that this was of a Pelagian type and that they came, like St. Germanus in Britain in 429, to stamp out heresy rather than to convert a heathen people.[6]

It was a common practice for Irish kings to make raids on Britain; and Cormac MacArt, the founder of Tara, is said to have carried out a particularly successful one in the middle of the third century. Among the booty brought back would be slaves, and some of them, even at that date, might be Christians. The presence of such is, however, more likely at a later period, and it is thought that the Gospel may have been brought in this way

---

[1] See *Archaelogia*, 1930, p. 229 ff., and *Arch. Camb.*, 1931, p. 210 ff.
[2] See *Proceedings of Royal Irish Academy*, II, p. 184 ff.; VI, pp. 441 ff., 525; XXX, p. 176.
[3] By Professor Rhys, *Studies in Early Irish History*, p. 35.
[4] Tacitus, *Ann.*, XIV, 29.
[5] Bury, *Life of St. Patrick*, pp. 89 f., 129, 349 ff.
[6] Sheldon, *The Transition from Roman Britain to Christian England*, p. 42.

to Munster after a large-scale raid in 368. A little later, parts of Northern Ireland were evangelized from the monastery which St. Ninian had established at Whithorn in Galloway.

When Christianity finally made an effective entry into the island it seems to have made rapid progress, mainly by a rather easy compromise with paganism and by the adoption of many magical practices.[1] As the Irish had never been subject to the Roman Empire, they had no natural reverence for Rome or for its bishop, and adopted their own form of organization. The legend that St. Teilo, St. David, and St. Padarn made a pilgrimage to Jerusalem in order to receive episcopal consecration from the Patriarch there,[2] even if it is not good history, testifies to the desire to avoid any recognition of the papal supremacy.

Before leaving the subject of Christianity in Ireland, which seems scarcely to have existed in our period, mention must be made of a theory advanced by the Dean of Elphin (Dr. Ardill) which would actually date its coming as early as the end of the second century.[3] He finds the difficulties of trying to place St. Patrick in the fifth century quite insuperable—Professor Zimmern tried to avoid them by identifying Patrick and Palladius—and falls back on this earlier date as the best way out. Moreover, he brings evidence to show that the circumstances of his career fit in well with the second century. The theory met with some amount of approval from the late Professor Burkitt, who, however, suggested that the middle of the third century might be an even more suitable period.[4]

[1] Sheldon, *op. cit.*, p. 95 f.
[2] *ibid.*, p. 124.
[3] In his volume *St. Patrick, A.D.* 180.
[4] In a review in *J.T.S.*, 1932, XXXIII, p. 404 ff. Prof. Souter also seems to think the theory is a possible one: *J.T.S.*, XXXVI, p. 334; as did Prof. J. P. Whitney in conversation with the present writer.

PART III
BELIEF AND ORGANIZATION

CHAPTER I

LITERATURE: (a) CANONICAL

For the purposes of our study it is necessary to survey not only such literature as was produced in the West, but also that which circulated there. The canonical writings, it is probable, came exclusively from the East or were produced by Eastern Christians, a fact of considerable importance, for the writers, even under the burden of inspiration, still retained their characteristic love of symbolism and hyperbole. When the Scriptures appeared in the more literally minded West, this was often not realized. The same is true of other writings from the apostolic and sub-apostolic age which failed to get into the canon, and with them also we shall deal in this chapter.

THE CANON OF SCRIPTURE

The determining of a canon of New Testament scriptures, which should be accepted alongside that of the Old, was not the act of any official body, but the result of a consensus of public opinion. As in the case of the typically Western Creed (that known as the Apostles'), no oecumenical council gave a decision in the matter; this was the work of the Church as a whole, not, we may believe, without the guidance of the divine Spirit. The books of the New Testament were the product of a living and worshipping community, written, indeed, by individuals, but by individuals as members of that community. They too were not without divine guidance and inspiration. A council could only approve books which were already received as inspired by the people, and the chief function of the authorities during the period of transition was negative—the exclusion of writings held to be undesirable. In the West the main criterion was apostolic authorship.

At one time it was held that until the beginning of the fourth century only small collections of writings could be circulated together, owing to the fact that a papyrus roll was of such limited size. It has, however, recently been discovered that papyrus codices came into use at a much earlier date.[1] Christian codices, if the dating of the Chester Beatty Papyrus and of the

---

[1] See C. H. Roberts in *J.T.S.*, XL, p. 256. He suggests that Caesar may have used a papyrus codex for dispatches to the senate: *J.R.S.*, XXIII, p. 139 ff.

fragment of the Unknown Gospel (Egerton Papyrus, No. 2) is correct, were in use in the second century. The use of vellum,[1] from the fourth century onward, must, however, have made it much easier to bind together large collections of documents, and the whole of the New Testament could then be included within the covers of a single volume. It is not until the seventh century, however, that we get Latin Pandects which contained the whole Bible.

So long as the belief in inspiration and the spirit of prophecy was alive in the Church, there was no attempt to fix the limits of the canon; individual writings would be either accepted or rejected, but the canon itself would not be closed. After a time various pronouncements were made, but it was Athanasius in his Festal Letter of 367 who first authorized our present collection. His decision met with the approval of the West; but the Syriac-speaking Christians of the East, with others, retained a canon of their own. The first official statement of the Western Church was the decretal of Damasus in 382.

The canon, then, was of slow growth. For the earliest generation of Christians the Old Testament was the only recognized collection of Scripture, and, it need hardly be said, was retained by the Church alongside the New when the latter came into being. This was not so with the Marcionites; in fact it was Marcion's rejection of the Old Testament which may have suggested to him the formation of a new collection of sacred books. This consisted of the Gospel of Luke, revised and expurgated, and the *Apostolicon*, that is, the Pauline epistles,[2] omitting the Pastorals. Even before Marcion, signs had not been lacking that some of the New Testament writings were already rising to the same level of authority with the Old. This can be seen by comparing the usage of Clement of Rome with that of Polycarp in the manner of making quotations. Each of them, it may be noted, records sayings which they attribute to the Lord in a form which is not found in any canonical gospel. This suggests that other gospels[3] were in circulation or a definite oral tradition. It has been surmised, not without probability, that in Egypt at least gospels which the later instinct of the Church felt compelled to reject were preferred to those which became canonical,[4] though the recent discovery of a papyrus fragment of John

[1] It is not without interest to note that in the Papal Chancery papyrus was retained until the time of Benedict VIII (1020–22), although instances are known of parchment being used before that date: see Bresslau, "Papyrus und Pergament in der päpst. Kanzlei", in *Mittheilungen*, 1888, IX, p. 1 ff.

[2] Marcion included an Epistle to the Laodiceans, almost certainly our Ephesians, which is not otherwise represented.

[3] Such as the *Unknown Gospel* edited by Bell and Skeat in 1934.

[4] P. D. Scott-Moncrieff, *Paganism and Christianity in Egypt*, p. 55.

belonging to the middle of the second century shows that the gospel was known in Egypt.[1] Clement of Alexandria tells us that in his day the *Gospel according to the Hebrews* and that *According to the Egyptians* were still in general use.

From the first, no doubt the sayings of the Lord were regarded as possessing complete authority and inspiration; then the facts of His life as they came to be collected in the gospels would be added. The writings of the various apostles also would have a place apart from other literature, especially in such Churches as had received epistles of their own.[2] These would be read in the public services and copies exchanged for those of epistles to other Churches. Thus they would take their place alongside the Law and the Prophets and come to be regarded as Scripture.[3] In the West, the first suggestion of a canon is to be found in the *Acts of the Scillitan Martyrs* (180), for when the judge asked them what they had in a certain box, they replied, "The books [i.e., the gospels] and the epistles of Paul the Righteous".

It was probably the challenge of heresy which made the formation of a canon really urgent, for if there was to be an appeal to Scripture it is obviously necessary to know what is included in the term. The nucleus was quickly settled, a matter of great importance,[4] consisting of the gospels, the Acts, and the writings of St. Paul. About the rest there was some uncertainty and many claimants for inclusion.

Of such claimants none in the form of gospels was taken very seriously, except perhaps at Alexandria; and the four canonical gospels quickly assumed a unique position, although others were in circulation and also perhaps separate sayings of the Lord. Our four gospels were probably preferred to their rivals owing to some connexion with the more important Churches, as well as by claims to distinguished authorship. Matthew, which incorporates much of Mark, seems to be connected with Antioch; the fourth gospel, whoever wrote it, with Ephesus; the writings of St. Luke, even though we cannot connect them with any particular locality, carry the weight of a companion of St. Paul. The case of Mark is of especial interest, for, after most of its contents had been incorporated into Matthew and Luke, it might well have fallen out of use; Burkitt, in fact, thought that this actually occurred (*Two Lectures on the Gospels*, p. 33 f.). What finally saved it? Presumably its link with Rome. That such a link

[1] C. H. Roberts, *An Unknown Fragment of the Fourth Gospel.*
[2] cf. Tertullian, *De Praes.*, XXXVI.
[3] See Iren., I, iii, 6.
[4] cf. Streeter, *The Four Gospels*, p. 499: "It was the acceptance by the leading Churches at an early date of an authoritative Life of Christ, interpreted in the light of the great Epistles of Paul, that made it possible for some kind of unity in the direction of doctrinal development to be preserved".

existed is almost certain;[1] though it is unlikely that it was originally written in Latin, as some scholars suppose,[2] and as is definitely stated by a colophon at the end of the Peshitta version of the gospel, by many Greek MSS., as well as by Ephraim in his commentary on the *Diatessaron*. If such a Latin original ever existed it may be represented by Cod. Bobbiensis (k); but since the Church in Rome was Greek-speaking until a late period it seems unlikely that a gospel in Latin would be produced there.

The West was very cautious in admitting new names to its canon, especially when compared with Alexandria. This attitude can be illustrated by the contents of MSS. usually associated with Alexandria. Cod. Sinaiticus includes *Barnabas* and *The Shepherd* in the New Testament; Cod. Alexandrinus, both I and II *Clement*. The Roman Church, on the other hand, hesitated long over the fourth gospel; whilst Hebrews, although used in I *Clement*, was only received at last owing to its supposed Pauline authorship.

The books which were accepted at Rome towards the end of the second century are known from the so-called Muratorian Fragment, a Latin document, behind which there almost certainly lies a Greek original—it has even been said that this original was in iambics—containing a list of canonical writings. It includes the gospels,[3] Acts, and the Pauline epistles, which by this time had come to be received in all Christendom. Of books that were still in dispute, it has 2 and 3 John, Jude, and the Apocalypse; but not Hebrews, James, or either of the epistles of Peter, unless I Peter has been omitted by mistake as it finds a place in the Old Latin version of about this date. Hebrews, however, was included in the Old Latin soon afterwards, Westcott thinks before the time of Tertullian (*Canon of the N.T.*, p. 263).

Among the first Christians, the term Gospel meant the Christian message. Later it came to be limited to written records of the life and teaching of the Lord. Harnack finds the transition stage in the epistles of Ignatius *Ad Philad.* and *Ad Smyrn.*[4]

It is by no means clear how long the four gospels which are now alone regarded as canonical had occupied their unique position. Irenaeus, writing about 185, looks upon the number as

[1] See B. W. Bacon, *Is Mark a Roman Gospel?* (Harvard Theol. Studies, No. VII).

[2] P. L. Couchoud in *Rev. de l'hist. des rel.*, 1926, pp. 161–192; and Burkitt's discussion in *J.T.S.*, 1927–28, p. 375 ff.

[3] The beginning is lost but it starts with the third gospel (Luke) and goes on to John, so that the gospels presumably followed their present order. This was not fixed in the West until the Vulgate. A common order, found in Codex Bezae (D), the Gothic version, and several Old Latin MSS., changes the places of Mark and John. It is expressly stated to be the order in the Monarchian prologue to John.

[4] See his interesting study of the use of Gospel appended to *The Constitution and Law of the Church*, p. 315 ff.

almost part of the natural order, like the four quarters of the earth, or the four winds. This suggests that they had long been accepted as works apart; they may, indeed, have been so accepted by Hermas,[1] but the evidence of Justin, who comes between them, makes this unlikely. He is quite indefinite in the matter.

Justin, however, marks a distinct step from Papias who preferred spoken reminiscences to the written word. But by his time the living voice was no longer there; written traditions had perforce to be accepted. In his own writings, Justin refers from time to time to what he calls the *Memoirs* [2] of the Apostles, and in several places actually uses the word gospel.[3] He fails to give a name to any of these documents or even to mention their number; but since the facts which he cites are found in the canonical gospels it is natural, at first sight, to conclude that he refers to them, possibly excepting St. John with which there are no certain parallels. But other possibilities must not be ignored. He may, for example, have been using sources now lost which lie behind them, or some gospel harmony, or one or more lost gospels.[4] It has even been suggested that the *Gospel of Peter* was his source of information.[5] In favour of this may be adduced the statement in I *Apol.*, XXXV, found also in *Gospel of Peter*, III, that Christ was placed on the judgment seat. Justin certainly preserves several traditions which otherwise have only survived in non-canonical gospels, such as the light on Jordan (*Dial.*, LXXXVIII), also recorded in the *Gospel of the Ebionites* and in other places. These traditions are included among matters stated to come from the apostolic memoirs. His possible use of a harmony may have been suggested by the circumstance that his disciple, Tatian, did actually construct such a work. But this, it must be remembered, was based on the canonical gospels alone. The *Diatessaron* was composed in Syriac and was for a time preferred to the four gospels themselves in Syriac-speaking Churches. Burkitt once made the interesting suggestion that before leaving Rome Tatian made an earlier harmony in Latin

---

[1] C. Taylor thinks that Irenaeus, who accepted *The Shepherd* as scripture (IV, xx, 2), borrowed the idea from Hermas: see *Hermas and the Four Gospels*, p. 12 ff.

[2] τὰ ἀπομνημονεύματα, a word found also in Euseb., V, viii, 8: cf. III, xxxix, 15; VI, xxv, 13. A third-century papyrus cited by Moulton and Milligan, *Gk. Test. Voc.*, p. 67, uses it in the sense of a concise statement referring to a person and intended for oral delivery.

[3] There are two references in I *Apol.*, and ten in the *Dial.* The word gospel is used I *Apol.*, LXVI, and *Dial.*, C. For Justin's use of the gospels see Sanday, *The Gospels in the Second Century*, pp. 91 ff., 113 ff.

[4] cf. E. R. Buckley in *J.T.S.*, 1935, XXXVI, p. 174 ff.

[5] See Credner, *N.T. Kanon*, p. 22. He connected the *Gospel of Peter*, the *Gospel of the Hebrews*, and Tatian's *Diatessaron*. Harnack is inclined to favour the theory: *Texte und Unters.*, IX, Pt. III, p. 37 ff.

for the use of Latin-speaking Christians, who at that date had, so far as we know, no gospel in their own language.[1] His theory, however, has not met with much favour, and the subsequent discovery of a small fragment in Greek at Doura opens the possibility that both the Latin and Syriac forms depended on a Greek original.[2]

The Acts of the Apostles is so closely linked to the third gospel that nothing further need here be said about it, and we can pass on to the epistles of St. Paul. These, as we have seen, found early acceptance. It is, however, worth noticing that in addition to the canonical epistles there were a number which were apocryphal. The Muratorian Fragment mentions Epistles to the Laodiceans and Alexandrians respectively, but condemns them as Marcionite forgeries. They are no longer extant, unless the quite innocuous *Epistle to the Laodiceans* printed by Lightfoot in his Colossians is the document in question.[3] Zahn placed it in the second century, but it is probably much later. In any case it is made up of a string of Pauline phrases. The so-called *Third Epistle to the Corinthians* is preserved in the *Acts of Paul*.[4] It was apparently received as genuine by some Western Christians and translated into Latin in the third century, possibly from a Syriac version. Before leaving the Pauline epistles it is worth noticing that their order is by no means established. In the Muratorian Fragment, 1 Corinthians heads the list, and this arrangement may have been that current in Rome in the first century.[5] Both Tertullian and Cyprian place Romans last, and differ in the order of the other epistles. The third-century Chester Beatty Papyrus, No. 46, has the present order but inserts Hebrews after Romans.

Turning to the rest of the canonical epistles, we notice at the outset the strange fortunes of Hebrews. At the end of the first century, in view of the use made of it by Clement, and possibly by Hermas, it was in high favour at Rome. Later, although Justin may have known it, it fell into disuse, being absent from the Muratorian Fragment and from the earliest strata of the Latin version. This neglect may have arisen from doubts as to its authorship. Tertullian's suggestion that it was by Barnabas (*De Pud.*, XX) probably helped to restore its credit, and by his time it probably formed part of the Latin version. But Cyprian's failure to cite it in support of his view of the value of the priest-

[1] See *J.T.S.*, 1924, XXV, p. 129. On the subject of the two forms of the *Diatessaron*, see 1935, XXXVI, p. 256 ff.

[2] See C. H. Kraeling, "A Greek Fragment of Tatian's Diatessaron", in *Studies and Documents from Doura*, 1935, III.

[3] An English translation will be found in *Apoc. N.T.*, p. 479.

[4] *Apoc. N.T.*, p. 289 f.

[5] See I *Clem.*, XLVII, 2, with Lowther Clarke's note.

hood shows that it was not much esteemed in the West, an estimate which is confirmed by a similar abstention on the part of Novatian when denying the possibility of a second repentance. In the East it had a better reception, for Clement of Alexandria and Origen both accepted it as Pauline, even if not actually written by the apostle himself. But doubts lingered in the minds of many, largely due to the refusal of the Church of Rome to admit that it was by St. Paul (Euseb., III, iii, 5).

A similar course was taken in regard to James, which was first accepted as a "religious classic" and then omitted from the canon. Streeter thinks that in each instance the real author was known in the West (*Primitive Church*, p. 191 f.). It was probably used by Clement of Rome, and many parallels can be found in Hermas; but it is missing from the Muratorian Fragment and the Old Latin version. Neither Tertullian nor Cyprian makes use of it.

The Muratorian Fragment as we now have it makes no mention of 1 Peter; the omission, however, may be due to the faulty state of the text. But as it is omitted from the Syriac canon it is possible that it had not been accepted by the Roman Church at the time, for, if it had been known as "Scripture" in Rome, Tatian would doubtless have taken it with him when he returned to the East, *c.* 172. Beyond two quotations in doubtful works of Tertullian it was hardly used in the West.

The other epistles, except 1 John, were probably ignored rather than rejected. There was no occasion for their use. Tertullian, however, quotes Jude as apostolic (*De Cult. Fem.*, III), and, together with 2 and 3 John, it appears in the Muratorian Fragment and in the Old Latin. Later tradition held that 2 and 3 John were by the Elder and not the Apostle.[1] 2 Peter, which has apparently some kind of relationship with Jude and the *Apoc. of Peter*, is evidently a late work, perhaps coming from the middle of the second century.

Until recent times it was generally held that 1 John was the work of the Evangelist, but this opinion has now its critics.[2] In the East, it may have been known very early to Polycarp and Ignatius; and possibly also in the West, for there are suggestive parallels to be found in I *Clem.*, XLIX, 5 and L, 3 (cf. 1 John 4 : 18), and perhaps in Hermas, *Mand.*, III, i (cf. 1 John 2 : 27). Its wide acceptance before the end of the second century is shown by its inclusion in the Muratorian Fragment and its use by Irenaeus (III, xvi, 5 and 8) and Tertullian (*De Pud.*, XIX).

[1] Jerome, *De Vir. Ill.*, XVIII. The Decretal of Damasus in 382 says: *Johannis apostoli epistula una, alterius Johannis presbyteri epistulae duae.*
[2] Holtzmann, however, rejected the authorship of the Evangelist for all three epistles. C. H. Dodd regards the First Epistle as being the work of a disciple of the Evangelist who was steeped in his ideas and style.

For the Apocalypse there is early and positive testimony. Many parallels are to be found in Hermas, and it was evidently known to the writers of the Epistle of the Churches of Lyons and Vienne (Euseb., V, i, 10, 22); whilst it is definitely ascribed to John by Justin Martyr (*Dial.*, LXXXI) and Tertullian. Both the Muratorian Fragment and the Old Latin include it. The differences of style which are so apparent in the Greek would not be obvious to those who may have read it in a Latin version only; and so it was natural that doubts on the subject should first arise in the East, where Dionysius of Alexandria subjected it to acute criticism (Euseb., VII, xxv).

THE LATIN VERSIONS

The history of the various Latin versions is very obscure in its beginnings, but their importance for a study of Western Christendom can hardly be exaggerated, affecting as they did not only the language, but even the thought of the West. Latin versions tended to be very literal, and their style was such as to discourage educated readers.[1] Arnobius, indeed, tells us that the heathen openly scoffed at the possibility of those responsible for such productions being trustworthy guides in philosophical or religious matters.[2] But the Old Latin survived for a time, even when the more polished Vulgate was on the way to universal acceptance. Some of its defects may have been due, not to uneducated translators, but to the fact that their proper language was Greek.

Apart from the Vulgate, which arose after our period, three Latin versions are known: the African, the European, and the Italian. As to the latter, the *Itala* of Augustine, Burkitt thinks that it was only another name for the Vulgate itself, and not a separate version.[3] The relations between the other two are complicated, but the majority of scholars look upon the African as the older and think that it spread to Italy, Gaul, and Spain to form the European.[4] Others think that the two versions are entirely independent. Streeter made the ingenious suggestion that the African version represents a text that circulated in

---

[1] They made use of the vulgar speech, the so-called *sermo plebeius*, not the classical *sermo urbanus*.

[2] Boissier, *Le Fin du paganisme*, I, p. 351, speaks of the translators torturing the ancient language without pity and of the shock which their efforts must have caused to those accustomed to classical Latin.

[3] *The Old Latin and the Itala (Texts and Studies*, IV, No. 3), p. 54 ff. See also De Bruyne, *Rev. Bénéd.*, 1913, XXX, p. 294 ff.

[4] Kenyon, *Text. Crit.*, p. 198 f., Sanday and Turner, *Novum Test. S. Iren.*, p. xvii f., consider that the Old Latin version used in Italy had been affected by the African.

Rome before the entry, through Justin, Tatian, and Irenaeus, of what he calls Ephesian influences.[1]

The African Latin is found at its best in two fifth-century codices, Bobbiensis (k)[2] and Palatinus (e), which agree with the quotations in Cyprian. Together they represent the text current in North Africa in the middle of the third century and are thus the earliest known version.[3] The text and version used by Tertullian, in so far as it differed from those of the African version, would, of course, be earlier. But the question is beset by difficulties as he apparently makes use of two distinct types.[4] As Tertullian was familiar with both Greek and Latin he may well have made his own renderings.

Of the African Latin as a whole it may be said that it shows an independent character and has a somewhat unusual vocabulary.[5] Some of its renderings are very striking when compared with those of the Vulgate, for example the opening words of the fourth gospel are given as *In principio fuit sermo*[6] instead of *In principio erat verbum*; again "the light of the world" (John 8 : 12) is rendered *lumen saeculi* which later versions gave as *lux mundi*. But the interest and importance of the African version are not confined to vocabulary. It seems, in addition, to witness to a Greek text different from that which formed the basis of the European. The best representatives of this version are two codices, Vercellensis (a) and Veronensis (b). Both contain only the gospels. The former probably belongs to the fourth century, the latter to the sixth.

Before leaving the subject of the Latin versions, mention may be made of certain so-called Monarchian prologues to the Latin gospels which are printed in Wordsworth and White's edition of the Vulgate. They are probably of later date than our period, being usually attributed to Priscillian and the year 380, but some authorities would bring them down much earlier. A Greek original for the Lucan prologue survives and probably all the prologues were originally written in that language. The suggestion has been made that they formed an introduction to a

---

[1] Harnack believed that a Marcionite version of such Scriptures as were accepted was made in Rome in the latter part of the second century (*Marcion*, p. 47 ff.).

[2] This MS. was damaged by fire but fortunately C. H. Turner had previously made a careful collation: see *J.T.S.*, 1904, V, p. 88 f.

[3] See, further, von Soden, *Das latein. N.T. in Afrika zur Zeit. Cyp.* (*Texte und Unters.*, XXIII).

[4] P. Capelle, *Le Texte du psautier latin en Afrique chrét.*, I, p. 105 f.

[5] Much useful information will be found in Sanday's detailed study of (k) in *Old Latin Bib. Texts*, II. Burkitt gives several lists of characteristics: *op. cit.*, p. 12 ff.

[6] This rendering was adopted quite independently by Erasmus and aroused much criticism. The Reformer Theodore Beza also used *sermo* and not *verbum* in his version.

canonical collection of the gospels set up in opposition to the canon of Marcion.[1]

THE WESTERN TEXT

From the Old Latin version it is an easy transition to the so-called Western Text of the New Testament of which it provides one of the principal examples. The title "Western" was given by Hort, although he had to admit that it also circulated in the East in the Ante-Nicene period. Since his days fresh discoveries have been made which emphasize this aspect. His theory as to its origin has therefore been by no means universally accepted by scholars. Kenyon, who hardly looks upon the Western Text as a unity, suggests that it may have been brought to Gaul by Irenaeus from Asia Minor;[2] whilst von Soden, who gives it the symbol "I", regarded it as having originated in Jerusalem.

In addition to the Old Latin, the Western text is found in a number of Greek MSS., the chief of which is the famous Codex Bezae (D), written in Greek and Latin; it is also found in the Curetonian Syriac, the Sinaitic Syriac versions, and in a number of Fathers. Of these Justin Martyr, Tatian, and Hippolytus wrote in Greek; as did Marcion, who also supports this type of text; whilst Tertullian, Cyprian, and Novatian wrote in Latin. The case of Irenaeus presents more difficulty as the Greek original is lost, save for fragments, and the Latin version is of uncertain date. Nor can we be certain that the translator preserved the Greek text of quotations used by Irenaeus; he may have been influenced by Latin versions current in his day.[3] Allowance must also be made for subsequent corruption of the text in transmission in order to make it conform to the Vulgate. Considerable Western elements have also been found in Clement of Alexandria[4] and in the writings of Origen after he moved to Caesarea in 231.

Amongst the fresh material which needs to be taken into account since Hort's day are two Greek uncials: the Freer Gospels (W), a MS. of the fourth or fifth century which originated in Egypt,[5] and the Koridethi MS., so-called from a monastery on the Black Sea to which at one time it belonged; as well

---

[1] De Bruyne, *Rev. Bénéd.*, 1928, XL, p. 193 ff. P. Corssen in *Texte und Unters.*, XV, Pt. I, dates them in the third century. See, further, Harnack, *Die ältest. Evangelien-Prologe und die Bildung des N.T.*

[2] *Text. Crit.*, p. 339. It is possible that Justin may have introduced the text if it came from the East.

[3] Dom Chapman thinks not: see *Rev. Bénéd.*, 1924, XXXVI, p. 34 ff.

[4] See P. M. Barnard, *The Biblical Text of Clem. of Alex.* (*Texts and Studies*, V, No. 5). Clement might have acquired a "Western" text when in South Italy.

[5] In Mark 1–5 : 30 the text is strangely mixed, having affinities with the African Old Latin as found in (e).

as the Ferrar Group of cursives which are thought to have circulated in Palestine,[1] and the Sinaitic text of the Old Syriac. In view of the wide circulation of the "Western" text, can it still be claimed that the geographical title is anything more than a convenient label? Streeter would separate it into three distinct groups, a true Western group circulating in Africa and Italy, and two Eastern, based respectively on Antioch and Caesarea (*The Four Gospels*, p. 64 ff.). He considers that the text represented by the Koridethi MS. and its allies, which he identifies as that found at Caesarea by Origin (*op. cit.*, p. 100 ff.), as of sufficient importance to rank beside the Alexandrian, Western, and Byzantine texts; that is, in Hort's terminology, the Neutral, Western, and Syrian (*op. cit.*, p. 84). It has been suggested by Burkitt that the text current at Antioch in the second century is represented by the Old Syriac.[2] Though not identical with that of the *Diatessaron*, this version may have been influenced by it.

That a definite text existed in the West would not be denied by any scholar. It may be located at Rome in the middle of the second century, and the evidence for its use is contained in the quotations of Marcion, Justin, and Tatian. Can its influence be traced in the similar texts which Hort grouped with it under the title Western, or are these, as Streeter and others think, distinct texts? It seems to me that the possibility of this influence is not to be ignored. The prevalence of a "Western" type of text in Syriac-speaking circles may be the result of the influence of Tatian,[3] whilst Alexandria, in view of the constant intercourse between that city and Rome, may well have received it from Rome.[4] It is rather more difficult to account for "Western" readings in Palestine, especially if the Ferrar Group is Palestinian, though this is by no means certain.[5]

One characteristic of the Western text, even in the narrower sense, is the presence of a number of fragments not generally found in other texts.[6] Some of the best known are the man working on the Sabbath in D only (at Luke 22 : 53); the light at the Baptism (Matt. 3 : 15), and the light at the Resurrection (Mark 16 : 3) occurring in Cod. Vercellensis and Cod. Bobbiensis respectively, though not in D. The incident of the light at the Baptism was widely known in various forms. It is referred to by Justin

---

[1] See Kirsopp Lake, *Codex 1 of the Gospels and its Allies* (*Texts and Studies*, VII, No. 3).

[2] *Evangelion Da-Mepharreshe*, II, p. 254.

[3] This suggestion had already been made by Burkitt, *Early Eastern Christianity*, p. 75.

[4] Streeter, *op. cit.*, p. 57, allows for the possibility of Western readings having been taken from Rome to Alexandria.

[5] Rendel Harris, *On the Origin of the Ferrar Group* and *Further Researches into the History of the Ferrar Group*.

[6] See the lists in Burkitt, *Old Latin and the Itala*, p. 47 ff.

(*Dial.*, LXXXVIII) who calls it "fire", and by Tatian, since it finds a place in the *Diatessaron*. The *Gospel according to the Ebionites* (quoted by Epiphanius, XXX, 13) mentions a "light", but the *Preaching of Paul* (quoted by Pseudo-Cyprian, *De Rebapt.*) refers to fire on the water.[1]

It may be worth adding two further supposed sayings of the Lord known in the West which do not actually occur in any MS. of the New Testament. They have been preserved by Tertullian. "No man who is not tempted shall obtain the Kingdom of Heaven" (*De Bapt.*, XX)[2] and "Thou hast seen thy brother: thou hast seen thy God" (*De Orat.*, XXVI).[3]

THE APOSTOLIC FATHERS

With the Gospel message a new power had come into the world: vivid, creative, even, if one may be allowed the term, explosive, which found an outlet in diverse directions and in various manners. Christianity, although deriving much from things ancient and old-established, set out on its way with an intense life of its own. But the initial impulse could not be maintained. To an age of diversity and experiment there succeeded one of consolidation and unification. This change is reflected in the literature of the period.

The writings of the Apostolic Fathers cover a period of some fifty years round the turn of the first and second centuries. Thus they are contemporary with writings which now form part of the canon. Some of them were for a time candidates for admission, though unsuccessful in the end. None the less, as Gwatkin used to point out, the distinction between canonical and uncanonical writers, "so studiously ignored by some of the literary critics, is not a fiction of some church authority, but a fact which no serious reader can fail to notice" (*Early Church Hist.*, I, p. 99). The Apostolic Fathers though aware that they stood on a lower plane than their predecessors, having neither the authority nor ability of Peter and Paul,[4] were yet insistent that they also spoke with divine inspiration.[5]

As a body they exhibit no great literary merit or high intellectual quality, the writer of the *Epistle to Diognetus* being here an exception; they are, for the most part, practical men striving to deal with the needs of their day, to cultivate the Christian way of living and to bring others into the Christian society,

---

[1] *Apoc N.T.*, p. 298.
[2] cf. *Didascalia*, II, 8: "The Scripture saith, A man that is not tempted is not approved".
[3] Also in Clement of Alexandria, *Strom.*, I, xix, 94 and II, xv, 70.
[4] cf. Ignatius, *Rom.*, IV, 3; *Eph.*, III, i; *Trall.*, III, 3; Polycarp, *Phil.*, II.
[5] cf. I *Clem*, LIX, 1; LXIII, 2; Ignatius, *Phil.*, VII, 1.

rather than to add to the Church's treasury of learning. No better summary of their attainments can be found than that of Lightfoot when he said: "There is a breadth of moral sympathy, an earnest sense of personal responsibility, a fervour of Christian devotion, which are the noblest testimony to the influence of the Gospel on characters obviously very diverse, and will always command for their writings a respect wholly disproportionate to their literary merits" (I, i, p. 7).

They had no ambition to work out a system of theology, or even to explore the implications of the doctrines handed down to them. Judged by the standards of later orthodoxy they were not always very cautious in their statements. But though they might fail to perceive all the richness of their inheritance they preserved it unsullied for the generations to come. And that was the supreme need of the moment. Renan might complain that Polycarp was ultra-conservative (*L'Église chrét.*, p. 433), but as Lightfoot commented "His was an age when conservatism alone could save the Church".[1] Before advance could be renewed there was need for consolidation and assimilation of what had already been received in face of the influx of new and possibly dangerous influences.

The following works, all written in Greek, are included under the term of Apostolic Fathers: I and II *Clement*; seven epistles of Ignatius; Polycarp to the Philippians; the *Didache*; the *Epistle of Barnabas*; *The Shepherd* of Hermas; the *Martyrdom of Polycarp*; and the *Epistle to Diognetus*. Several of these have been included in MSS. of the New Testament; I and II *Clem.* in Cod. Alexandrinus (fifth century); *Barnabas*[2] and Hermas in Cod. Sin. (fourth century); and Cod. Claromont (sixth century).

For the West, those mainly important are I *Clem.* and *The Shepherd* of Hermas (incidentally they are greater in bulk than all the rest put together), since they were written in Rome, and the epistle which Ignatius wrote to that city. The others, even if they have no specific connexion with the West, are valuable as showing the conditions of Christian life and thought during the period. About the date of the *Didache* much has been written, especially in view of its relation with *Barnabas* with which it has "The Two Ways" in common.[3] The *Epistle to Diognetus* is probably later than the others (unless the *Didache* is to be assigned

---

[1] II, i, p. 427. Well might Ignatius appeal to Polycarp to stand firm as an anvil when it is smitten (III, 1).

[2] Though Barnabas was accepted as Scripture by Clement of Alexandria and Origen, Eusebius includes it among "spurious" works (III, xxv, 4). A tenth-century Latin version is known.

[3] Muilenburg, *The Lit. Relations of the Epist. of Barnabas and the Teaching of the Twelve Apost.*, accepts the dependence of the *Didache*. The most recent survey is that by the late Professor Creed in *J.T.S.*, XXXIX, 1938, p. 370 ff.

to the third century); the last two chapters belong to a separate work and have been attributed to Hippolytus. It never aroused much interest in the West.

Of works which were actually written in the West, the first in order of time was the letter written by the Church of Rome to that of Corinth known as I *Clement*. Clement, the scribe who wrote in the name of the Church (Euseb., III, xvi), was at one time identified with the companion of St. Paul mentioned in Phil. 4 : 3. But the suggestion seems not to have been made before Origen in his *Homily on John*, 6 : 36 and is improbable on chronological grounds. Hermas mentions a Clement who was a kind of foreign secretary to the Church of Rome (*Vis.*, II, iv, 3) who may have been the author if *The Shepherd* is dated early. The epistle was read in the Church at Corinth and elsewhere (Euseb., IV, xxiii, 11) and acknowledged by all (III, xxxviii, 1). It was apparently very popular in Egypt for it was included among canonical scriptures in Cod. Alexandrinus and was also translated into Coptic; two MSS. have survived, one of the fourth, the other of the seventh century.[1] The existence of a large Clementine literature in the East also shows the interest which was taken in Clement in that part of the Church.[2] In view of this and his frequent mention of the epistle, it is strange that Eusebius does not include it in his catalogue of canonical and sub-canonical writings (III, xxv). In the West the book was never popular. It was translated into Latin, according to Harnack and Lake, in the second century, but Zahn places it between the fourth and seventh;[3] but it is never quoted by any Latin Father who did not also know Greek.[4] From the age of Constantine until the Reformation I *Clement* seems to have been unknown in the West.

The date of the epistle is assigned by almost universal consent to the last decade of the first century.[5] Merrill's recent suggestion that it was not composed until 140[6] can hardly be taken very seriously, especially if the epistle was known to Polycarp. There is, however, something to be said in favour of an earlier date. The chief reasons for the generally accepted date, *c.* A.D. 96, are

---

[1] Both were discovered in the present century and were therefore unknown to Lightfoot. The Coptic is unique in omitting Clement's name from the title, which it gives as: "The Epistle of the Roman Church to the Corinthian Church."

[2] It is difficult to account for the popularity of the book in the East, as the writer seems to be ignorant of Eastern customs; such, at least, is the inference to be drawn from the substitution of "an upper room" for "house-top" in the story of Rahab (XII, 3).

[3] C. H. Turner, *Studies in Early Church Hist.*, p. 255, takes a middle line and places it in the second or third century.

[4] So Lightfoot states: I, i, p. 146.

[5] See Lowther Clarke, *The First Epistle of Clement*, p. 11 f.

[6] *Early Christian Hist.*, p. 217 ff. This date is rejected by Streeter, *Four Gospels*, pp. 4, 527 f.

the identification of the evil experiences which the Church of Rome had recently endured with the persecution of Domitian, and the idea that the epistle was written by Clement when Bishop of Rome. Neither of these reasons has any real weight, for the persecution under Domitian was not a general outbreak or such as would be likely to affect the life of the Church as a whole, and there are no signs that the epistle was written by a single official. It is true that until the recent discovery of the Coptic version all known authorities for the text mentioned Clement in the title, but there is nothing in the body of the epistle to justify such an ascription. It is, as the Coptic calls it, an epistle from the Church of Rome to that of Corinth, and may well have been written by Clement in his early days before he had attained any high dignity. The description of the sufferings of the Christians fits what we know of the outbreak under Nero very exactly, and they seem to be so vivid as to suggest that they were very recent. In Chapter XLI the temple at Jerusalem seems still to be standing. A date about A.D. 70 seems to me to be much more probable, and I am inclined to agree with Edmundson in seeing in the repeated calamities which have prevented the Romans writing to Corinth (I, 1) disasters which had befallen, not merely the Church, but the entire city.[1] If the epistle is dated as early as this the primitive organization, with the absence of any "bishop", would be accounted for. The chief objection lies in the difficulty of dating some of the canonical writings which are used by Clement, especially the Epistle to the Hebrews.[2]

The work known as II *Clement* has a very obscure history. Its date and origin are both matters of dispute, and it seems probable that it was not even an epistle at all though called such by Eusebius (III, xxxviii, 4). In this it had a predecessor, for the so-called first epistle of St. John was quite probably a sermon. Harnack thinks that it was the letter sent to Corinth by Soter, Bishop of Rome, casually mentioned by Eusebius (IV, xxiii, 11), but that he made use of an old homily.[3] The connexion with Rome is not accepted by many scholars,[4] as most prefer Alexandria. Lightfoot thought that it was composed in Corinth between 125 and 150. Probably a date about the middle of the second century, with Egypt as its location, is as near the truth as we can arrive. It is included in Cod. Alexandrinus and there

---

[1] "In the whole course of its long and chequered history the city of Rome has never experienced so many 'sudden and successive troubles and calamities' as befell it in the course of the year A.D. 69." (*The Church of Rome*, p. 192).
[2] Lake, in his edition of *The Apost. Fathers* in the Loeb Library, allows a wide range of choice,—from 75 to 110.
[3] *Chronologie*, I, p. 440 ff.
[4] Lietzmann, *Beginnings of the Christian Church*, p. 267, is an exception.

is a Syriac version, but no Coptic has ever been discovered nor any Latin. It is never quoted by Clement of Alexandria and the West ignored it altogether.

Thus, in the West, both the so-called epistles of Clement fell out of use and perhaps out of knowledge. Their place was taken strangely enough by two other epistles[1] supposed to have been addressed by Clement to James (to the earlier an epistle of Peter to James was added). This earlier epistle was apparently composed about 200 and now, with many additions, forms the first part of the Pseudo-Isidorian Decretals. In its original form it was probably prefixed to the *Periodoi of Peter*. This document is mentioned by Epiphanius (*Haer.*, XXX, 15) as the work of the Ebionites, though in this he was almost certainly mistaken. Earlier still it may have been known to Origen and perhaps underlies the reference in Eusebius III, xxxviii, 5. It is generally thought to have been the source from which the two best-known Clementine writings, the *Homilies* and the *Recognitions*, took their origin.[2] These two writings, although definitely related, have their differences, mainly of emphasis. The former is chiefly interested in doctrine; the latter in edification. They profess to relate the adventures of Clement and his relations with St. Peter. In their present form they hardly go back before the fourth century and were not well known in the West until Rufinus at the end of that century translated the *Epistle to James* and a little later the *Recognitions*.[3] Hort considered that the latter has much of the Roman spirit and may have been composed in Rome (*Clementines*, p. 90), an opinion which has been approved by both Harnack and Waitz. But in view of its obviously Syrian background it is better with Lightfoot (I, i, pp. 55 f., 64, etc.) to derive it from the East.

The author of *The Shepherd*, like Clement, has been identified with a companion of St. Paul, the Hermas of Rom. 16 : 14, but the probabilities in his case are even more slight. Hermas gives a good deal of information about himself, but it must be received with some reserve.[4] The vivid and exact descriptions of Arcadia[5] have led some scholars to suppose that that was his

[1] In the Syriac-speaking Church, by another odd coincidence, the two epistles of Clement would be those *On Virginity* which were unknown in the West.

[2] The latest study is Waitz, "Die pseudoklem. Hom. und Rekog.", in *Texte und Unters.*, X, Pt. III.

[3] The *Recognitions*, as a whole, are now known only in this Latin version; the *Homilies*, in the original Greek. In both cases Syriac versions were made, of which parts are extant.

[4] It was usual to regard the work as one of pure fiction until the appearance in 1868 of Zahn, *Der Hirt des Hermas*. Since then the personal references have been accepted as substantially genuine.

[5] See J. Rendel Harris, "Hermas in Arcadia", in the *Journal of Bib. Lit.*, 1887, p. 69 ff.

original home; there is, however, small justification for this opinion. He probably knew very little about his origins, for it seems likely that as a child he was exposed and then found by someone who later sold him to a slave dealer (a common process in his days). At any rate, he was in due time purchased by a lady in Rome for whom he worked as an agricultural labourer; later he gained his freedom and set up in business. He claimed to be a prophet, and may thus be regarded as an earlier Piers Plowman, though sadly lacking in the literary gifts of William Langland. Hermas was notable for an intense curiosity; he himself admits that he was shameless in trying to find out things. In spite of his many misfortunes he always remained optimistic both for himself and for those who fell into sin. This would make an appeal to the many who were in like case.[1]

The date of *The Shepherd* is uncertain. According to the Muratorian Fragment it was written whilst Pius, the brother of Hermas, was Bishop of Rome; that is, in the middle of the second century. But this seems unlikely. Hermas was probably a Greek; Pius (the Latin name is itself no evidence) is said by the Felician abridgment of the *Liber Pontificalis* to have been an Italian. Confusion may have arisen from the fact that Pius had a brother Pastor by name, and in at least one Latin version the book is called *Liber Pastoris*. In any case a date in the middle of the second century is hardly consistent with the citation of the work as Scripture by Irenaeus. No doubt he was influenced by the belief that the author had been a companion of St. Paul, but if it had been composed only a short time before his own arrival in Rome it is unlikely that he would not have known of the fact. A much earlier date seems to be called for, as its contents suggest a very primitive organization. There is no apparent distinction between bishops and presbyters (*Vis.*, II, ii, 6; iv, 2 f.; III, i, 8; v, 1; ix, 7) and the persecutions (*Vis.*, III, ii, 1) might almost be those of Nero. I am myself inclined to place it in the first century and to regard the reference to Clement (*Vis.*, II, iv, 3) as genuinely meant to apply to the writer of I *Clem.* The fact that Hermas shows no knowledge of its contents need occasion no difficulty, as the two works are so different and proceed from quite different circles in the Church: the one from what may be called the official classes, the other from the rank and file.[2] It is even possible that *The Shepherd* is the earlier work.

[1] See, further, W. J. Wilson, "The Career of the Prophet Hermas", in *Harvard Theol. Rev.*, 1927, XX, p. 21 ff. Reitzenstein very ingeniously connects Hermas with Hermes Trismegistos; in Greek the two names have the same genitive, whilst ὁ ποιμάνδρης and ὁ ποιμήν might easily be confused.

[2] Students of medieval history may care to be reminded of the very different account of the Fourth Crusade given by Villehardouin who represents the great people, and that of Robert de Clary, the simple knight in his less-known *La Prise de Constantinople*.

The reason for giving it a late date may have been a wish to discredit its claims to sub-apostolic authorship in view of the rise of Montanism which its prophetic outlook might seem to favour. It is a common device to emphasize the recent origin of "heresy".[1]

At the same time it is possible that the book at first circulated in two parts, *Vis.*, I–IV, and the rest. The Visions seem designed for oral use and perhaps the idea of writing them down came later. From *Vis.*, V the book takes on a more literary character, though there is sufficient similarity in style and outlook to discount theories of a different authorship. The probability that two works have been combined is supported by the recent discovery of the Michigan papyrus which begins at *Vis.* V, the point at which the Shepherd first makes his appearance. A further possible argument in favour of this theory is that nearly all citations in Christian writers are taken from the later part.[2]

The work is of an apocalyptic nature and has many of the characteristics of similar productions which enjoyed a wide circulation among the vulgar. This must have made it popular with the common folk. The chief interest of the book, which is divided into five visions, twelve mandates, and ten similitudes, is the problem of post-baptismal sin. Actually its real value lies in the glimpse which it gives of what the Roman Church was like at a period before it had felt the influence of outside traditions, and also as revealing the mentality of at least one, probably not untypical member of the community.

The Shepherd was accepted as inspired by Irenaeus, Clement of Alexandria, and Origen, but was scornfully rejected by Tertullian.[3] At one time it had some popularity in the West, but soon fell into disfavour, probably owing to the statement in the Muratorian Fragment and the condemnation of Tertullian; but it continued to be much read in Egypt, where papyrus fragments are continually being discovered.[4] Although never, so far as we know, translated into Syriac, it circulated among the Manichees, possibly as Burkitt suggests (*Religion of the Manichees*, p. 96), because of the resemblance between Hermas and

[1] Streeter, *The Primitive Church*, pp. 203–213, suggests a date about 100. Harnack would spread the composition over a considerable period, though retaining the single authorship.

[2] See Harnack, *Altchrist. Lit.*, p. 51 ff. Irenaeus, however, quotes *Vis.*, IV, xx, 2 and *Mand.*, I, i, and Clement Alex. knew both parts.

[3] He called it *illo apocrypho pastore moechorum* (*De Pud.*, XX), and mentions that it had been rejected by a number of Church councils. One of its offences was the encouragement of the objectionable practice of sitting during prayers (*De Orat.*, XII).

[4] A list will be found in Kirsopp Lake's edition in *Apost. Fathers* (Loeb Classics), II, p. 4 f. I have noted the following more recent discoveries: Oxyrh., No. 1783 (from *Mand.*, IX); Mich., Pap. No. 917 (*Sim.*, II, ix, to IX, v, 1); and Mich., Pap. No. 44, a fragment only, probably of the late second century.

Hermes Trismegistos already referred to, for Hermes was held in high honour among the followers of Mani.[1]

The Epistle of Ignatius to the *Romans* was apparently well known in the West, and it became, in Lightfoot's words "a sort of martyr's manual". Its influence can be seen in the Epistle of the Churches of Vienne and Lyons, and in the *Passion of Perpetua and Felicitas*. The only Western Father, however, who definitely quotes the work is Irenaeus (V, xxviii, 4). As a pupil of Polycarp he would naturally be interested in Ignatius, and his knowledge of the writing might have been gained in Asia Minor before his migration to the West. There are parallels in Tertullian but no definite quotations. No early Latin version of his epistles has survived; of what is now regarded as the genuine corpus of seven epistles,[2] there is none earlier than the thirteenth century. The longer recension, which includes interpolations in the genuine epistles, was the form which was used in the West during the Middle Ages.

Ignatius was never a popular saint in the West, and even had some difficulty in retaining his place in the calendar. The name, however, found favour, for some reason unknown, with the Spaniards; and, as Lightfoot has said, "in the sixteenth century it acquired unwonted prominence in the founder of the most powerful order in Christendom" (II, ii, p. 427). The prevalence of the name, however, is no certain index to the popularity of the saint, for "Ignatius" was of Latin or Samnite origin and known apart from the Bishop of Antioch.

Lucian,[3] who flourished soon after the middle of the second century, may have had Ignatius in mind when describing Peregrinus in *De Morte Perigrini*, though this is evidence for the East and not the West.

Polycarp, in spite of his visit to Rome, does not appear to have aroused much interest in the West, and his epistle was hardly known. There is, it is true, a Latin version, but it is very late and probably owes its existence to the epistle having been included in the Ignatian corpus. On the other hand the *Martyrdom of Polycarp*, a contemporary letter written by the Smyrneans, seems to have been known, for the martyr Germanicus who is mentioned in III, 1 is included in Western calendars on January 19. Rather curiously, he is absent from those of the Greek Church.

[1] See Ephraim's *Refutation of Mani* (ed. C. W. Mitchell), II, p. xcviii, and Augustine, *Contra Faustum*, XIII.
[2] The matter seems decisively to have been settled by Lightfoot, though E. T. Merrill, *Early Christ. Hist.*, p. 13, expresses "grave doubts".
[3] Lucian was probably the inventor of the "comic" dialogue, a literary form previously used only by serious writers. It became a potent weapon in the hands of Erasmus.

CHAPTER II

LITERATURE: (b) APOCRYPHAL

The gap which Gwatkin found to exist between the canonical writings and those of the Apostolic Fathers had a counterpart, even more distinct, in that between the latter and the numerous apocryphal writings which characterized the period immediately following. In this literature, although genuine traditions not otherwise preserved may be included, the narratives as a whole are obviously the product of minds whose critical faculty has been entirely subordinated to the desire to edify or to astound. The tendency thus manifested grew with time until historical and even doctrinal truth became a matter of little moment. At last, especially as heresy began to exploit this field, there was little care for anything except the sensational and the miraculous. Thus the demands of the imagination, which, when all is said and done, requires sustenance as well as the reason, were met; for the one finds it in facts, the other in fancies. None the less, this type of literature undoubtedly exerted a very harmful influence on ordinary Christians, and in addition furnished the heathen with some justification for the charge that Christians, like Jews, took an unhealthy interest in the practice of magic.

The Christians, however, were not the inventors or sole exponents of this tendency. The second and third centuries of our era saw the rise and wide diffusion of many similar romances —stories such as the *Leucippe and Clitophon* of Achilles Tatius, the *Daphnis and Chloë* of Longus, the *Satiricon* of Petronius, and most popular of all the *Metamorphoses* or *Golden Ass* of Apuleius. The last termed his work a Milesian tale—*sermone isto Milesio* (I, i); which reminds us that behind many of these stories lay a much older tradition, the so-called *Milesian Tales* compiled by a certain Aristides in Greek and translated into Latin by Sisenna shortly before the Christian era. The term, indeed, became a popular equivalent for anything romantic, and therefore presumably, untrue. Tertullian, for example, applies it to the speculations of the Valentinians (*De Anima*, VII). Other similar productions took the form of travel tales. One and all reveal the kind of thing which appealed to contemporary taste—in which the average Christian no doubt shared. It was avid of the marvellous and the crude, and ready to gulp down the most absurd narratives so long as they ministered to this depraved appetite. The Christian apocryphal writings must be regarded as both rivals of and substitutes for these popular productions; intended, on the one hand, to supplant them in the reading of converts, and at the same time to provide for the need which they revealed. The subjects were, indeed, very different, save perhaps in the Clementine Romances; but the influence of secular literature may perhaps be traced. Merrill has made the interesting suggestion that some of the writings, and, in particular the correspondence, have been influenced by the schools of rhetoric in which the pupils "were taught to compose on themes or situations from past history".[1] This may have been so, but contemporary travel narratives probably furnished the most attractive models; the *Acts of Thomas*, for example, seem to be indebted to such writings, especially to Philostratus's *Life of Apollonius of Tyana*. At the same time the canonical Acts of the Apostles was ever at hand for imitation, although there is either a surprising ignorance of its contents or else a culpable readiness to manipulate them.

Although this large mass of Christian literature appeared under names that were demonstrably false, and have rightly been classed for this reason as Pseudepigrapha, it is not necessary to suppose that there was in all cases (there certainly was in some) any desire to deceive. They were not forgeries in the modern sense, since forgeries attempt to imitate the style, manner, and message of the supposed original. A forgery, for this reason, is bound to be a lifeless thing from the mere fact that it is an imitation. These writings, though often crude and childish, are living and possess a definite point of view. In fact they preserve for us samples of the strange unbidden guests who were clamouring for admission within the Christian scheme of things. The Christians were, it would seem, exceedingly gullible, for Lucian claimed that his hero Peregrinus had written works which were accepted by them as genuine.

These writings had an extraordinary popularity, being, as Harnack has put it, "the favourite reading of Christians from Ireland to the mountains of Abyssinia, and from Persia to Spain". Nearly all of them were produced in the East and were part of that tremendous outburst of literary and dogmatic activity in Christian circles which marked the second century. But if they were produced in the East their influence was very widespread in the West, and not only widespread, but persistent. The extent to which incidents recorded only in these apocryphal writings have entered into the mind of the West can be seen from the

[1] *Early Christ. Hist.*, p. 8. The same phenomenon is found in the Middle Ages, and some of the compositions, for example, of Peter of Blois, are to be suspected for this very reason.

Chronicles,[1] as well as from the Liturgies, and, most obvious of all, from art. So, too, the various visions and apocalypses of medieval literature, not excepting Dante's *Commedia*, owe a large debt to the same source.

The student of the beginnings of Western Christendom, as of Christendom in general, cannot afford to neglect these documents. Their importance, indeed, can scarcely be exaggerated. This importance, however, lies not in the facts which they purport to narrate—these are often enough the fruit of over-zealous imaginations—but in the clues they furnish to the mind of early Christians in the humbler ranges of society; and of such, it must be remembered, until well into the second century, the Church largely consisted. Thus these writings light up the dim corners of Christian life, exposing the ideas and beliefs which circulated among less instructed believers, and revealing a background which, with all its crudity and pathos, may easily be forgotten or ignored.

Much space in these writings is naturally devoted to supplying details of the earthly life of Jesus and His chief disciples. In strong contrast to the canonical Scriptures, they show great interest in the Blessed Virgin;[2] the Gnostics, indeed, had a *Gospel of Mary*, a fragment of which has survived. Much of the new matter is childish and unedifying; much unorthodox when judged by later standards; whilst magic, as an unfailing means of converting the heathen and of moving the sinner to repentance, is very prominent. Many of the stories of feats of magic, though well fitted to impress the vulgar, must have created an atmosphere quite unworthy of the Gospel and its teaching, blinding men to the true proportion of things and giving them an unhealthy taste for the marvellous and the bizarre. Two examples may be adduced. In the *Gospel of Thomas*, IV,[3] the boy Jesus is said to have struck dead one who by chance hit Him with a stone; an act which cannot be described as otherwise than vindictive. Then in the *Acts of Peter*, XIII,[4] the apostle, in order to prove the truth of his message, caused a dead fish to swim in a bowl of water. Stories such as these are not such as to commend themselves to a genuine Christian piety. Another feature which is prominent is an intense curiosity as to the future life and the state of the departed. This desire was common at the time and would be especially natural for men who had to face danger and persecution.

The writings, however, are not without their better side and

---

[1] An example may be cited in Otto of Freising, *Chron.*, III, 14.
[2] The New Testament makes no mention of her, after Acts 1 : 14, and the first generation seems to have had but little interest in her.
[3] *Apoc.*, *N.T.*, p. 55.　　　　　　　　　　　　　　　　[4] *op. cit.*, p. 316.

exhibit an unbounded faith and trust in the Master, and a praiseworthy readiness to go to all lengths in His service. In spite of much that is open to criticism, they testify to the unrivalled interest taken by orthodox and heretic alike in the earthly life of Jesus. This gives a complete denial to those who would have it that Christianity was speedily severed from its roots in history to become a mere syncretism. Some Gnostic sects did indeed attempt to make it such; the wide circulation of the apocryphal literature, for some of which they were responsible, gives a clue to the cause of their failure. The common people could make little of mere abstractions; they were anxious for solid facts, or what were presented to them as such.

The Apocryphal Literature[1] can most conveniently be surveyed under four headings: (A) Gospels; (B) Acts; (C) Epistles; (D) Apocalypses.

(A) GOSPELS

A number of fragmentary gospels have survived, the best known and most considerable of them is the *Gospel according to the Hebrews*. This was originally written in Aramaic or Hebrew and was regarded by some as the original of the canonical Matthew. Eusebius included it among the antilegomena (III, xxv, 5), adding that it found favour with Jewish Christians. It does not seem to have been used in the West, although it is probably referred to as the Gospel of Matthew by Irenaeus (I, xxvi, 2; III, xi, 7). The author of the pseudo-Cyprianic *De Rebapt.*, XVII, quotes the *Preaching of Paul* to the effect that the fire which appeared on the Jordan at the baptism of Jesus was not recorded in any gospel; this shows that he had no knowledge of the *Gospel according to the Hebrews* which contains the incident. Clement of Alexandria appears to look upon it as Scripture (*Strom.*, I, ix, 45; V, xiv, 96). Some scholars, H. G. Evelyn White among them, think that the celebrated *Sayings of Jesus* discovered in two papyri at Oxyrhynchus in 1897 and 1903 formed part of *Hebrews*. There is no evidence that these sayings were current in the West.

Akin to the *Gospel according to the Hebrews* and possibly identical with it is the *Gospel of the Ebionites*, six fragments of which have been preserved in Epiphanius, *Haer.*, XXX. They

---

[1] A useful introduction to the apocryphal literature can be found in A. F. Findlay, *Byways in Early Christian Literature*; whilst most of the works in an English translation are included in M. R. James, *The Apocryphal New Testament*. Those who read German can consult Harnack, *Altchrist. Lit.* The texts are available in *Neutest. Apok.*, edited by Hennecke and others. For the acts, there is Lipsius, *Acta Apost. Apocrypha*, with useful critical apparatus. Many of the originals appear in a convenient form in the *Kleine Texte* series.

probably come from the first half of the second century. Of the *Gospel according to the Egyptians* a few fragments are known from the writings of Clement of Alexandria and it is referred to by Hippolytus, V, 7.

Next in order are the so-called Infancy Gospels of which much more has survived. The numerous traditions concerning the events which preceded the birth of our Lord of which Medieval Art and Literature are so full have been derived from them. The direct source is the *Pseudo-Gospel of Matthew*, a Latin compilation which may go back to the end of the eighth century. It was used by Hroswitha, the famous abbess of Gandersheim, in the tenth. Behind it lie two apocryphal works, the *Book of James* or the *Protevangelium*, and the *Gospel of Thomas*.

The *Book of James* was written originally in Greek and in the second century; a Latin version appeared soon afterwards.[1] It is full of traditions concerning a period upon which the canonical gospels are wisely reticent. These have to do with the relations of Joachim and Anna, the parents of the Blessed Virgin, and her own early life. By them a simple village damsel is transformed into the daughter of wealthy parents surrounded by attendant maidens; she becomes, in fact, almost a princess in a fairy tale. The author is obviously quite unacquainted with both the geography of Palestine and the customs of the Jewish people. The *Gospel of Thomas* is given by M. R. James in three forms, two Greek and one Latin. The Greek MSS. are all late and the work may have originally appeared in Syriac. It is mentioned by Hippolytus, V, 7. The contents are mainly concerned with the boyhood of the Lord and are of an unedifying nature for the most part.

The next class of gospels are those which supplement the scriptural accounts of the Passion. The first and most important of them is the *Gospel of Peter*, a very early document. In a recent study, P. S. Gardner Smith brings it down to the end of the first century.[2] M. R. James, however, does not consider it much earlier than the middle of the second. Some scholars see a reference to it in Justin's statement in *Dial.* CVI, that Jesus changed the name of one of his apostles to Peter, as it is written in *his* memoirs; taking the pronoun to refer, not to Jesus, but to Peter. If this is so we have evidence for its circulation in Rome in the middle of the second century. But the reference is doubtful, for even if the pronoun refers to Peter it might be a way of citing the canonical Mark. Later, the writing disappeared without leaving, as Stanton once put it, "a ripple upon the surface

---

[1] Published in James, *Latin Infancy Gospels*. This volume appeared after the issue of *Apoc. N.T.*, which it supplements.
[2] See *J.T.S.*, 1926, XXVII, pp. 255 ff. and 401 ff.

of the waters".[1] Probably it was never very widely known,[2] and traditions contained in it did not have much influence. An example of the neglect of its contents has been found in the persistence of the name Longinus for the centurion who stood by the cross, and the ignoring of the name Petronicus given in *Gospel of Peter*, VIII. But those who cite this circumstance have failed to observe that Petronicus is the centurion in charge of the guard set over the tomb, who may well have been a different person from the officer who was present at the Crucifixion.

The author seems to have been familiar with all four canonical gospels, even including John.[3] That of Mark he apparently knew in a form which contained the lost ending.[4] Traces of the use of *Peter* may be found in several passages in the Latin translation of Origen's *Commentary on Matthew*.[5] In outlook the writer is strongly anti-Jewish and has a markedly docetic tendency. At the early period from which the gospel comes, this need not, however, be taken as a sign of definite unorthodoxy.[6]

Another work of a similar scope is the *Gospel of Nicodemus*, or the *Acts of Pilate*. This is much later in date and can hardly have been written before the fourth century, possibly as a reply to the *Acts of Pilate* put out by Maximin Daza in 311 for the confusion of the Christians. The concluding part, which purports to describe the Descent into Hell, is even later. In a Latin version it had great popularity in the West and became a favourite subject for Miracle plays. Its object is to provide irrefutable evidence for the truth of the Resurrection. The Holy Grail *motif* of the Arthurian legends of the twelfth century may possibly have been derived from it. No more than a bare mention of the *Assumption of the Virgin* is called for. It was written originally in Coptic, but had a Latin version which claimed, quite falsely, to have been composed by Melito of Sardis.

(B) ACTS

Of the various and numerous apocryphal acts there are five which stand out from the rest in a class by themselves. These are the acts respectively of John, Paul, Peter, Andrew, and Thomas. All of them can be dated in the second and third centuries. By the Manichees of North Africa they were collected into a *corpus* and used in preference to the canonical Acts of the Apostles.

---

[1] *J.T.S.*, 1901, II, p. 18.
[2] It is mentioned by Origen, *On Matt.* X, 17; and by Eusebius, III, iii, 2, and VI, xii, 2.
[3] So C. H. Turner thinks: see *J.T.S.*, 1913, XIV, p. 168.
[4] So Burkitt, following Harnack. See *Two Lectures on the Gospels*, p. 33; also Streeter, *The Four Gospels*, p. 353 f.
[5] J. O. F. Murray, *The Expositor*, XCIII, p. 55 ff.
[6] So L. Vaganay, *L'Évangile de Pierre*, p. 118 ff.

This set of five works is sometimes referred to under the title of the Leucian Acts. The title, however, is late, having been first used by Photius, Patriarch of Constantinople, in the ninth century. He says that their author was Leucius Charinus, of whom nothing is known. It is, however, not without significance that the author of the comparatively late Part II of the *Acts of Pilate* gives to the supposed narrators the names of Leucius and Karinus; but what connexion there is between these two persons and the one mentioned by Photius it is impossible to say.

A certain Leucius is considered to have been the writer of the *Acts of John*, and possibly also of the *Acts of Andrew*. But the five works (unless *John* and *Andrew* are from the same pen) seem to have had different authors and have by no means the same outlook, especially in doctrine. The *Acts of Paul*, in particular, stand apart; at one time they were almost regarded as canonical in some quarters. Asia Minor is the most likely place of origin for the whole series, but some scholars think that the *Acts of Peter* were written in Rome.[1] This is hardly likely, as, although there is frequent mention of sites in Rome, the way in which they are referred to suggests the effort of an active imagination to realize places known by name only.

The theory held by Lipsius that our present Acts represent orthodox editions of more primitive works which had a strong Gnostic bias has not met with any favour. They probably all came more or less in their present form from orthodox or semi-orthodox circles, as the term was understood in the second and third centuries. They have certain common features, such as the love of marvels, the dislike of marriage, the denial of the resurrection of the "flesh", and other similar docetic tendencies.

The so-called *Acts of Linus* appear to be a Latin paraphrase,[2] probably of the fourth century, of the *Acts of Paul* and of *Peter*, with a small amount of additional matter. The chief interest of the compiler was in the martyrdoms of the two apostles.

The earliest of the works was probably the *Acts of John* and it may have served as a model for some of the others. Leucius, its supposed author, has been claimed as an actual companion of the apostle whose adventures he relates.[3] If the work may be dated in the early part of the second century, as is done by James,[4] there is no bar on chronological grounds. Certain

[1] Findlay, *Byways in Early Christian Literature*, p. 208. This is denied by Lietzmann, *Beginnings of the Church Universal*, p. 102, and also by M. R. James.
[2] The paraphrase may have been written in Greek, the language of the Acts themselves, and then been translated.
[3] See Epiphanius, *Haer.*, LI, 6.   [4] *Apoc. N.T.*, p. xx.

Gnostic terms appear and there are traces of docetic influence; but neither has much significance in this period. No complete text has survived, but there is enough to show that the author possessed distinct literary gifts and a deep religious nature. "Some of the mystical passages may be ranked with the best products of second-century religion."[1] The work identifies John of Ephesus with the apostle, the first clear instance of this equivalence.

The *Acts of Paul* belong, in their present form, to the latter half of the second century, but contain earlier matter. The text is defective, but much has been recovered in a papyrus acquired by the Hamburg Library in 1927.[2] Tertullian tells us that these acts were composed by a certain priest in honour of St. Paul, and that on the discovery of the forgery the author was degraded from his orders (*De Bapt.*, XVII). In Alexandria, however, they appear to have been accepted as genuine, and almost as canonical;[3] whilst, in Rome, according to Hippolytus, *Comm. on Daniel*, III, xxix, 4, they were highly valued. One part, devoted to the *Acts of Paul and Thecla*, circulated as a separate work and had an immense popularity, being translated into many languages from the original Greek.[4] Thecla may well have been a real person; and her cult became widespread, as we have already noted, in both East and West. Queen Tryphena, who appears prominently in the narrative, was actually the great-niece of the Emperor Claudius.

The *Acts of Peter* belong to the late second century. They show the influence of the *Acts of John* and are especially fond of miraculous stories. Although written in Greek, a good part of the original is now preserved in a Latin version of the seventh century, the so-called Vercelli Acts. There is a possible reference to the acts in Hippolytus, VI, 15. Events and places in the West fill a large part of the narrative but, as already stated, they do not suggest first-hand knowledge on the part of the author.

The *Acts of Andrew* may be by Leucius, but seem better to belong to a later date, the third century. In doctrine they skirt the boundary line of orthodoxy but without any distinct crossing of it into heresy. The book had a certain vogue in the West, and Gregory of Tours made an abstract of it in Latin to which he contributed a prologue.[5]

The *Acts of Thomas* also belong to the third century and are

---

[1] Kirsopp Lake in Hastings, *Dict. of Ancient Church*, I, p. 36.
[2] Edited by Carl Schmidt and W. Schubart, 1936.
[3] Origen, *De Princ.*, I, ii, 3 and *On John*, XX, 12.
[4] For the Latin version, see von Gebhardt, *Die lateinische Uebersetzung der Acta Pauli et Theclae* (*Texte und Unters.*, VII, Pt. II).
[5] Printed in his works in *Monumenta Germ. Hist.*, II, p. 821 ff.

even less observant of the boundary between orthodoxy and heresy than those of Andrew. They reflect the use of a vivid imagination, and the accounts of the travels of Thomas in India are worthy to be compared with the narratives of Marco Polo. It is possible that the acts were originally written in Syriac,[1] though Greek is, on the whole, more likely. The author has incorporated the famous "Hymn of the Soul" and other similar matter which probably had an independent circulation. These acts are not of any great service as throwing light on Christianity in the West; but the survival of Latin versions, even if they have been "much adulterated",[2] shows that they were read; whilst the traditional figure in art of Thomas carrying a spear is probably derived from them.

(C) EPISTLES

Among the apocryphal literature which has survived are a number of letters. But this type of forgery, if the name is not too harsh, was not attractive, since it involved more difficulty for the composer; although the gullibility of the public was such that no consistency of style was required. The following are worthy of mention, among many others.

The *Letters of Christ and Abgarus* have been preserved by Eusebius (I, xiii), who claims to have copied them from the Syriac originals in the archives at Edessa and translated them literally.[3] One letter only from each of the supposed correspondents makes up the collection. More important for our study is the *Correspondence of Paul and Seneca*, though not so important as might be imagined, as the forgery was not carried out before the fourth century. It had an immense vogue in the West right down to the Reformation, and its genuineness was widely held in uncritical days.[4] Seneca was exalted almost to the rank of an apostle in consequence.[5] The first actual notice of the collection occurs in Jerome, *De Vir. Ill.*, XII. It consists of fourteen letters, eight by Seneca and six by Paul. They are quite

---

[1] So Burkitt in *J.T.S.*, I, 1900, p. 280 ff.   [2] James, *op. cit.*, p. 364.

[3] A lintel discovered at Ephesus in 1900 has an inscription of both letters in an early fourth-century Greek translation: see Burkitt, *Early Eastern Christianity*, p. 15.

[4] In view of this it is strange that the genuine works of Seneca were difficult to procure. Roger Bacon tried in vain to obtain copies of them: *Opus Tertium*, XV (Rolls Series, p. 56), though the Abbey of St. Albans possessed a copy in 1290 made by Abbot Robert. See *Gesta Abbatum Mon. S. Albani*, I, p. 483 (Rolls Series).

[5] One school of German critics gave great importance to Seneca as a factor in the rise of Christianity. Bruno Bauer, for example, thinks that it had its origin among slaves in Rome who had been influenced by him; whilst Steeck and Van Manen consider that the canonical Pauline epistles were a product of the second century and influenced by Seneca and Philo.

unskilful productions and it is exceedingly difficult to understand their popularity and even their acceptance in any shape or form.[1]

The *Epistle of the Apostles* is a strange document. Some critics think that it belongs to the latter half of the second century and comes from orthodox circles in Asia Minor, or even more definitely from Ephesus.[2] It appears to have had little influence and but small popularity as it receives no mention in any ancient writer. The Greek original has been lost, but a complete Ethiopic and an incomplete Coptic version have survived. A Latin version was made in the fifth century of which only a fragment remains. Streeter claims that the quotations, which use all four canonical gospels, demonstrate the existence of a type of text similar to that of the Western in its narrower sense. He thinks that it may actually have been imported to Rome from Ephesus: *The Four Gospels*, p. 70 f.

(D) APOCALYPSES

A number of apocalypses bearing the names of apostles have been preserved. The most important of them is the *Apocalypse of Peter* which made a bid for inclusion in the canon, appearing as Scripture in Cod. Claromontanus, a sixth-century MS., together with the *Epistle of Barnabas*, *The Shepherd* of Hermas, and the *Acts of Paul*. It was probably composed in the second century, and was perhaps originally part of the *Gospel of Peter*, as fragments of the two writings have been discovered together. The Muratorian Fragment mentions it, a testimony to the high regard in which it was held in Rome. In Palestine it was customary to read it in some churches on Good Friday. It seems to have enjoyed a very wide circulation, though this was doubtless limited to the unlearned. The writer of II *Clement* evidently knew it, whilst Commodian made use of it in framing his picture of the end of the world.[3] Heathen writers, such as Celsus and the Neoplatonist in Macarius Magnes (*Apocriticus*, IV, 6), seem to have regarded it as a Christian scripture. This commendation or use by heathen may have damaged its reputation in the eyes of the learned. Some of its ideas seem to have been borrowed from the Egyptian Book of the Dead.[4]

Other similar works are the *Apocalypse of Paul*, which dates from the fourth century but contains earlier matter (it was popular in the West and a complete Latin version has survived); and the *Apocalypse of Thomas*, which may have been written in Latin in the fifth century and also includes earlier elements.

[1] See, further, Lightfoot, *Philippians*, p. 329 ff.
[2] See C. Schmidt in *Texte und Unters.*, XLIII, 1919.
[3] See *J.T.S.*, XVI, p. 405 f.   [4] A. Boulanger, *Orphée*, p. 127 ff.

OLD TESTAMENT APOCRYPHAL WORKS

In addition to these works there are a considerable number which, although appearing under the guise of names from the Old Testament, are definitely Christian or have been worked over by Christian writers. There are also a number of interpolations in a Christian direction in some of the well-known Old Testament Pseudepigrapha themselves. These all require to be taken into account and also the extent to which the Pseudepigrapha themselves were in circulation in the West. Their circulation among non-Jews may have been very much wider than is generally supposed. Israel Abrahams (*Judaism*, p. 38) has even ventured to claim that Horace had read some of them in view of the opening lines of *Ars Poetica*, which seems based on apocalyptical visions:

> *Humano capiti cervicem pictor equinam*
> *Iungere si velit, et varias induere plumas*
> *Undique collatis membris, ut turpiter atrum*
> *Desinat in piscem mulier formosa superne,*
> *Spectatum admissi risum teneatis, amici?*

To seek out quotations and so to find evidence for the use of such works in the West would be an immense and, for our purposes, an unprofitable task; so I have contented myself with regarding the existence of a Latin version as sufficient testimony for their use. In addition, it has to be remembered that, during the first two centuries of our era at least, they would have found a considerable number of readers in a Greek form. The Old Testament itself was thus circulated, and included in the Septuagint version was what we call the Apocrypha. In addition, many well-known Jewish Apocalypses were current, and to judge by quotations were regarded as of equal value with the Old Testament itself by Christian writers. But for the emergence of the New Testament there might well have arisen a Christian Old Testament different from that of the Jews.[1] The Western Church was not so much impressed by the *dictum* of Jerome[2] as were the framers of the Sixth Article of the Church of England, and was inclined to use them not only for examples of life and instruction in manners, but also for the establishment of dogma.

The circulation of the Septuagint is of interest to the student of Western Christendom because upon it the Old Latin versions

---

[1] cf. Harnack, *History of Dogma* (E.T.), I, p. 115.
[2] *Prologus in Libros Salom*: *haec duo volumina* (i.e., Ecclesiasticus and Wisdom) *legat ad aedificationem plebis, non ad auctoritatem ecclesiasticorum dogmatum confirmandam.*

were based. When Jerome compiled the Vulgate he made a fresh translation from the Hebrew for all the canonical books except the Psalms.[1] For the Apocrypha, except Judith and Tobit, for which he made translations from the Chaldee (that is Biblical Aramaic), the Old Latin version was retained.

In addition to the works which have been included in the Apocrypha there exists a large mass of literature to which the general name of Pseudepigrapha has been given. The influence which some of them exerted, and, above all, Enoch,[2] was immense. Enoch, no doubt, owed its position to the fact that it had been quoted by Jude (13–15) (so Tertullian, *De Cult. Fem.*, I). The extent of their circulation can be judged from the very numerous quotations and references to be found in Western writers and by the existence of Latin versions.

The *Book of Enoch* is a composite work in which many authors have taken a hand. The original was written partly in Hebrew, partly in Aramaic, and dates from 200 B.C. onwards. The full text is now preserved in Ethiopic only. A Greek version exists for part of it, but evidence for the existence of a Latin version can be found only in a quotation in Pseudo-Cyprian, *Ad Novatianum*, and in a small fragment covering 18 verses.[3] Enoch was a favourite book with the Western Fathers, and indeed, with Christian writers of the first three centuries in general. After that, it began to be regarded with some suspicion, possibly because it had been excluded by the Jews from their canon. The Western Fathers who made use of it include Justin, II *Apol.*, V; Tatian, *Ad Graec.*, VII and XX; Irenaeus, in at least three passages in *Adv. Haer.*; Minucius Felix, *Octavius*, XXVI; and many times in Tertullian. The latter, who accepts the authorship of Enoch as a literal fact, naïvely wonders how the work managed to survive the Flood, concluding that Noah must have taken special precautions in the matter. There are also references in the *Passio Perpetuae*, in Cyprian, *De Hab. Virg.*, XIV, and in numerous passages in Lactantius. A work which also bears the name of the same author, *The Secrets of Enoch*, now exists in Slavonic only. It was used by Irenaeus, amongst others.

The *Assumption of Moses* is alluded to in Jude 9 and comes from a Jewish source which had some sympathy with the Christian point of view. It was written in Hebrew during the first century A.D. and a Greek version was quickly produced.

---

[1] Jerome later translated the Psalter, but the Vulgate is based on the Septuagint.
[2] Charles, *Book of Enoch*, p. xcv ff., considers that its influence was greater than that of the other apocryphal and pseudepigraphical books combined.
[3] Edited by M. R. James in *Texts and Studies*, II, No. 3, pp. 146–150.

From this a Latin version followed, though at some distance in time; it may be as late as the fifth century.[1]

Another important work is IV *Ezra*.[2] This also was probably written in Hebrew originally, but both the Hebrew and the Greek version[3] have perished. It was from the Greek that a number of other versions were made. Several of these have survived. The most important is the Latin;[4] the others are the Syriac, Ethiopic, Armenian, and two different Arabic versions. The Latin is included in the Vulgate as an appendix. In the English Apocrypha the book has the title II *Esdras*. The work contains sixteen chapters, of which the first two and the last two are found in the Latin version alone. Its main part was probably composed by a Jew shortly before the close of the first century, A.D., but the additional matter appears to be Christian. The book is referred to by Giraldus Cambrensis at the end of the twelfth century as by "Ezra the prophet".[5]

Closely akin to IV *Ezra* (by some it is held to be by the same author) is the *Apocalypse of Baruch*, to be distinguished from the *Book of Baruch* which forms part of the Apocrypha. The original was doubtless composed in Hebrew, from which a Greek version was made, which in turn was translated into Syriac. No Latin version is known before Ceriani translated it in 1866, but Cyprian contains a fragment of a Latin *Apocalypse of Baruch* which is probably based on this work. The point of view of the book is Pharisaic, but several hands seem to have been at work in writing or compiling it. Although earlier matter may have been incorporated, it must mainly be dated after the Fall of Jerusalem in A.D. 70. Another *Apocalypse of Baruch*, known as the Greek, was discovered some years ago and edited by M. R. James in *Texts and Studies*, V, No. 1. Its connexion with the Syriac Apocalypse seems only to be remote. Other works purporting to come from Baruch include the *Rest of the Words of Baruch*, a Christian work surviving in Greek, Ethiopic, and Armenian.

The *Book of Jubilees* was written originally in Hebrew. A few fragments of a Greek version have survived, and of the Latin which was made from it, about a quarter.[6] Rönsch, with something of the confidence of a Sherlock Holmes, says that the latter was made by a Palestinian Jew living in Egypt about the middle

[1] A large fragment was discovered by Ceriani in a sixth-century palimpsest at Milan.
[2] See, further, G. H. Box, *The Ezra Apocalypse*.
[3] For references to this version see *Apost. Constit.*, VIII, 7, and perhaps II, 14; Hippolytus, *Frag. contra Plat.*; and perhaps *Epist. of Barn.*, V. This last is questioned by Box, *op. cit.*, p. 44.
[4] Edited by Bensley and James in *Texts and Studies*, III, No. 2.
[5] *De Rebus a se Gestis*, III, 2 (Rolls Series), I, p. 91.
[6] It was published by Ceriani in *Monumenta sacra et profana*, 1861.

of the fifth century.[1] It was probably known to Hippolytus,[2] and to the author of the *Clementine Recognitions*.[3]

The *Book of Adam and Eve* was a Jewish romance of which the original form has perished. Various parts, however, survive in other writings such as the Greek *Assumption of Moses* as well as in an Arabic and Ethiopic work which has been considerably christianized. The *Testament of Adam*, of which fragments in Greek, Syriac, and Arabic are known,[4] also belongs to the same cycle. For the West, the most important is the Latin *Vita Adae et Evae* of which many MSS. have been preserved, a testimony to its popularity in the Middle Ages.

The *Martyrdom of Isaiah* has disappeared in the Greek, save for a fragment recently discovered; but two incomplete Latin versions are known. The original may have been written by a Jew about A.D. 40. In the West it is quoted by Justin, *Dial.*, CXX; Tertullian, *De Patientia*, XIV; *Scorp.*, VIII; and, later, by both Ambrose and Jerome. It is from this source that the tradition of Isaiah's being sawn asunder is probably derived (cf. Heb. 11 : 37). To this work two Christian writings of perhaps the end of the first century, the *Vision of Isaiah*[5] and the *Testament of Hezekiah*, were attached by a Christian editor who also interpolated additional matter into the original. The whole now forms the *Ascension of Isaiah*, a complete text of which is found only in Ethiopic. From the third century onwards the composite work had a wide circulation among the unorthodox.[6]

The *Book of Eldad and Medad* was known to the Roman Church, being quoted by Hermas, *Vis.*, II, iii, 4; Lightfoot has also suggested that the "scriptural" quotation in I *Clem.*, XXII (and also in II *Clem.*, XI) was taken from it (I, ii, p. 80 f.). The book may be a Christian forgery to sustain the courage of converts in the face of persecution.

One book or rather collection which was much used by the Christians was the *Sibylline Oracles*,[7] though it goes back into pre-Christian days. In 75 B.C. the Roman senate ordered a collection of the sayings then extant to be made. The Hellenistic Jews were adepts at inventing fresh sayings for propaganda pur-

---

1 *Das Buch der Jubiläen . . . latein. Fragmente*, p. 459 ff.
2 See Charles, *The Book of Jubilees*, p. lxxx.
3 See Rönsch, *op. cit.*, pp. 322–325.
4 Edited by M. R. James in *Texts and Studies*, II, No. 3.
5 This work is docetic in outlook. The birth of Jesus was not accompanied by any natural pangs (XI, 7–11; cf. *Odes of Solomon*, XIX). It is fond of the title *Dilectus* for the Messiah; cf. Eph. 1 : 6, I *Clem.*, LIX, Ignatius, *Smyrn.*, Int., *Epist. Barn.*, III, 6, IV, 8, and *Acts of Paul and Thecla*, I.
6 Jerome connects it and the *Apoc. of Elias* with the followers of Basilides and locates them both in Spain: *In Is. lxiv. 4* and *Prol. Gen.*
7 The use made of the Sibyllines by Christians led Celsus to call them Sibyllists. Origen, *Contra Cels.*, V, 61.

poses, and later the Christians adopted the same methods. The original collection at its greatest extent consisted of fourteen books, but only twelve have survived. Hermas made use of the Sibyl (*Vis.*, II, iv), but no actual references are found in *The Shepherd*. Justin says that it was a capital offence to read the *Sibyl* or the *Prophecy of Hystaspes* (I *Apol.*, XLIV).[1] He again refers to the same two works as foretelling the final conflagration (I *Apol.*, XX). There are references in I *Clem.*, VII and XXXV, whilst Tertullian refers to the Sibyl in *Ad Nation.*, II. Lactantius, who seems to look upon the oracles as heathen, though at times inspired, makes abundant use of them. In the Middle Ages the *Sibylline Oracles* were in much request. Geoffrey of Monmouth, *Hist. Brit.*, IX, xvii, claims that they foretold that three natives of Britain would be emperors of Rome: Belinus, Constantine, and Arthur. Whilst the reference in the *Dies Irae* is very familiar:

> *Dies irae, dies illa*
> *Solvet saeclum in favilla,*
> *Teste David cum Sibylla.*

A number of Jewish Pseudepigraphal works have been the object of Christian interpolations, mainly in order to provide "prophecies" of events. There are many in the *Testaments of the Twelve Patriarchs*,[2] a work of which no surviving Latin version exists, but its use in the West can be affirmed from references in Hermas, Irenaeus (*Fragt.*, XVII), and Tertullian (*Adv. Marc.*, I; *Scorp.*, XIII). Such interpolations and additions have already been referred to in the case of the *Sibylline Oracles* and other works, and there have been references to deliberate Christian forgeries in the *Prophecy of Hystaspes* and the *Vision of Isaiah*. Many similar works undoubtedly existed but no record of them now remains beyond the bare names, for Christian writers, for their own purposes, were very ready to assume the mantle of Old Testament patriarchs and saints. There are apocalypses[3] attributed to Elijah, to Zephaniah, and to Daniel; another to Sedrach, and probably to Ezekiel. Then there are testaments such as that of Job, and three of Abraham, Isaac, and Jacob.[4] The last are referred to in the *Apostolic Constitutions* and may be Jewish works with a Christian veneer.

One work seems to stand by itself and demand a separate

---

[1] This lost work was probably a Christian "forgery". Its supposed author was the father of Darius. It is referred to by Clement of Alexandria, *Strom.*, VI, 5 (quoting the *Preaching of Peter*), and by Lactantius.

[2] See R. H. Charles, *The Greek Versions of the Testaments of the Twelve Patriarchs* and *The Testaments of the Twelve Patriarchs*. The question of the Christian interpolations is discussed on p. xlviii ff. of the former, and p. lxi. ff. of the latter work.

[3] Some of them have been edited by Steindorff, *Texte und Unters.*, II, Pt. III.

[4] See M. R. James in *Texts and Studies*, II, No. 2.

treatment, that is the collection of hymns known as the *Odes of Solomon* discovered in 1909 by Rendel Harris. They were written in Syriac and known already, before the actual recovery of the text, by name. Lactantius evidently regarded them as a collection, for he says "Solomon in the nineteenth Ode says thus". Five of the odes had been preserved in full, being quoted in the *Pistis Sophia*. By the end of the third century they were evidently regarded as Scripture and were perhaps in use in public worship,[1] which suggests that they had been in existence some time. There has been much dispute as to the date of their composition as well as to the original language and location. The latest date is probably 180 but Harris himself thinks that they were the work of a Jewish Christian writing at the end of the first century, and that Greek was the original language. Harnack suggests that the original author was a Jew and that Christian interpolations were introduced later. The full number of the Odes is forty-two, but one of them has not been recovered.[2]

When Rendel Harris discovered his MS. he found that there was attached to it a Syriac version of the *Psalms of Solomon*.[3] This work, probably written originally in Hebrew, had long been known to scholars in a Greek version.[4] It includes eighteen psalms which emanated from a Pharisaic circle, probably about the middle of the first century B.C. The psalms had a considerable circulation among Christians in primitive times, but soon lost their popularity. As no traces of a Latin version have been discovered they can have had but little influence in the West. They became known again in 1626 when a printed edition appeared.

[1] J. H. Bernard suggests a possible reference in *Testamentum Domini*, which in a rubric orders the singing of hymns by Moses, Solomon, and other prophets.
[2] There is an edition by J. H. Bernard in *Texts and Studies*, VIII, No. 3, and by Rendel Harris, the third edition of which (1916–1920) in two volumes was produced jointly with A. Mingana.
[3] See *The Odes and Psalms of Solomon published from the Syriac Version*. The two works appear together in two lists of scriptural books, the *Synopsis Sacrae Scripturae* (sixth century) and the *Stichometry of Nicephorus* (ninth century).
[4] Edited by Ryle and James, *The Psalms of the Pharisees*.

CHAPTER III

LITERATURE: (c) PATRISTIC

We come now to a survey, which limitations of space compel to be somewhat brief, of the remaining Ante-Nicene literature; the literature, that is, which, with the exception of the Church Orders, never made any claim to having been produced by apostles or apostolic men, and was never considered for inclusion in the canon.

Before embarking upon the task, however, it will be well to make a few observations on early Christian literature in general with which a modern reader is apt to be impatient. He finds the writers profuse and even dull, and in places almost puerile. But any one who studies these writings with sympathy cannot escape feeling that the authors are endeavouring to mediate valuable experiences, and if he makes up his mind to follow a hard and oft-times obscure path, he will at length arrive at a special and privileged standpoint from which to view the development of Christian life and thought.

Although our interest is fixed on the West, the survey which we shall make cannot be confined strictly to that portion of the Ante-Nicene Church, for works produced in the East undoubtedly in this era played their part in the development of Western ideas. This applies, above all, to the writings of the Alexandrian school. In any case the earliest writings in the West itself were in Greek, for it was not until the close of the second century that any clear traces of Christian Latin literature can be discerned.

The amount of the literature that we have to consider is not very vast and no doubt much has disappeared. The question thus arises as to how far what survives can be taken as representative of the mind of the Church as a whole. No doubt many works of a heretical tinge have deliberately been suppressed or allowed to perish, but probably what remains of the literature as a whole gives a balanced view of the main line of development in our period. Certain authors have, of course, been fortunate in this matter; more survives of Tertullian, for example, than of Cicero, but we shall not on this account give them undue weight.

But if the amount of literature is not very vast it has striking variety, especially after the middle of the second century and the end of the so-called age of the apologists. This last may roughly be dated from 120 to 170 and it has earned its name through the survival, when much else has perished, of works of an apologetic nature. The value of these works is unfortunately rather limited, for in writings in defence of Christianity against the attacks of pagans, and even of Jews, not a great deal is said about the faith and practices of the Church—though here Justin Martyr is an exception. The early Christians up to the time of the triumph of the Gospel were exceedingly reticent in such matters, and in strong contrast to modern ideas the Scriptures themselves were often withheld from heathen notice.

After about 170, Christian literature made a great advance, especially in the West, with the emergence of Latin writings, with a parallel in the East in those of the school of Alexandria. In place of short compositions of no particular literary merit we have elaborate treatises and a definite advance in craftsmanship. This change was due to the gradual penetration by Christianity of the higher levels of intellectual and social life. Clement and Origen were worthy to take their place in any literary or philosophical circle, and, in the West Minucius Felix, Tertullian, and Cyprian were writers of outstanding merit. The same age saw also the production of numerous letters and essays, of chronicles, and even of romances, such as those considered in the previous chapter. All alike were intended to meet the new needs which had arisen with the growth of the Christian community, needs which were at once practical and intellectual. Before going on to the more regular line of development represented by the apologists and theologians, two classes of writing may conveniently be considered—the acts of the Martyrs,[1] and the Church Orders.

There are scholars who consider that behind the various descriptions of the sufferings and trials of the martyrs we have definite official records of the Roman courts. But this is hardly likely to have been the case, although reminiscences of legal language may undoubtedly be found in them and the use of technical terms, due perhaps to those who had actually been present at their trials. The genuineness of most of the acts of the martyrs has been questioned, and rightly so, for many original accounts may have perished in the Diocletianic persecution when there was a considerable destruction of Christian records. That it was the custom to collect accounts of various martyrs we know from Eusebius (IV, xv, 46–48). The best known and most authentic accounts of definite incidents which we possess are concerned with the Scillitan martyrs,[2] Perpetua and her companions,[3] the sufferings of the martyrs of Vienne and

[1] See E. C. E. Owen, *Some Authentic Acts of the Early Martyrs.*
[2] Edited by Armitage Robinson in *Texts and Studies*, I, No. 2, pp. 112–117.
[3] Both the Latin and the Greek forms are edited in the volume mentioned in the previous note.

Lyons (in Euseb., V, i-xi), and the Proconsular Acts of Cyprian,[1] all of which have already received notice in their appropriate places in Part II.

Although the Church Orders, with the possible exception of the so-called *Egyptian Church Order* which will be discussed later, are all the products of the East, it is necessary to take some notice of them, as they are known to have circulated in the West; the Verona Manuscript is evidence of this,[2] though it is probable that they exerted no great influence during our period. The most comprehensive of them, *The Apostolic Constitutions*, after being almost forgotten in the West, came to play a considerable part in post-Reformation controversy. Although *The Apostolic Constitutions* belongs to the latter part of the fourth century, it is based upon much earlier material and therefore forms a good starting-point for an inquiry into the whole subject;[3] though the editor made some additions of his own and also modified the material which he used. The work is divided into eight books. Behind the first six lies the *Didascalia Apostolorum*,[4] which comes from North Syria and, apart from later additions, may belong to the middle of the second century. It exists in a Syriac version and fragments in the Verona MS. Behind Book VII is the *Didache* and other matter; whilst Book VIII is based on what used to be known as the *Egyptian Church Order*, but is now generally referred to as the *Church Order* or *Apostolic Tradition* of Hippolytus.[5] In spite of their diverse origins, the various sections are traditionally said to have been the work of the apostles assembled at the Council of Jerusalem (Acts 15).

The question of the authorship of the *Egyptian Church Order*, which survives in Coptic, Ethiopic, and Arabic versions, together with fragments in the Verona MS., and the various documents allied to it,[6] is of great importance for our study, for if any of them can be traced ultimately to Hippolytus we have evidence for conditions in the West which otherwise would be lacking, so far as Church Orders are concerned. The suggestion that Hippolytus was responsible for the *Egyptian Church Order* was first made by Baron Eduard von der Goltz in 1906, but it

---

[1] Benson considered that these *acta* were older than the *Vita Cypriani* of Pontius who had been his deacon.

[2] This palimpsest has been edited by E. Hauler, *Didasc. Apost. Fragmenta Veron. Latina.* It includes fragments of the chief orders.

[3] The standard edition is F. X. Funk, *Didascalia et Const. Apost.*, published in two volumes in 1905.

[4] See, in addition to Funk, R. H. Connolly, *Didascalia Apostolorum*, 1929.

[5] The latest edition, of which Vol. I was published in 1937, is by G. H. Dix.

[6] These consist of *Canones Hippolyti*, existing in an Arabic document published by Achelis in 1891 (*Texte und Unters.*, VI, Pt. IV); the *Epitome*, a summary of Book VIII of *Apost. Const.*, often referred to as the *Constitutions of Hippolytus*; and *The Testament of our Lord*, which is contained in the *Syrian Octateuch*.

attracted little attention until a few years later when Edward Schwartz quite independently arrived at the same conclusion. The authorship is now generally accepted, though it has been challenged by R. Lorentz in *De Egyptische Kerkenordening en Hippolytus van Rome*,[1] and, in this country, by J. Vernon Bartlet in his Birkbeck Lectures on *Church-Life and Church-Order*. The question is too technical for discussion here, but in view of the arguments of Bartlet I feel that anything in the so-called Hippolytean Church Orders must be used with caution when considering conditions in the West.

Another collection which so far as its first two books are concerned is connected with the same Order is *The Syrian Octateuch*. An edition with a Greek translation was published by Lagarde as long ago as 1856,[2] but it failed to arouse any notice, and in any case gave not the full text but only generous extracts. Books I and II were published in Syriac by Rahmani in 1899.[3] Five years later came Horner, *The Statutes of the Apostles or Canones Eccles.*, and finally in 1913 F. Nau, *La Version syriaque de l'octateuque de Clément*. The last title is due to the tradition that the work was issued by Clement of Rome for the apostles.

An earlier work was *The Apostolic Church Order*[4] which appears to come from a Church, perhaps in Egypt, which was still in what may be called the missionary stage. Its various sections, like those of the *Apost. Const.*, are attributed to the different apostles. The first fourteen sections deal with ethics (cf. the early part of the *Didache*) and the latter sixteen with organization.

In view of the picture of ordinary church life which these Orders present, it will be useful to give some idea of the contents of that associated with Hippolytus. It is divided into three parts which deal respectively with the Clergy, the Laity, and Church Observances. The part dealing with the clergy begins naturally with the choice and consecration of bishops; this is followed by a description of the eucharist which the newly consecrated bishop celebrates. Then come forms for blessing oil, cheese and olives. The remaining sections deal shortly with the ordination of presbyters and deacons and the position of confessors, widows, readers, virgins, and subdeacons. The part concerned with the laity deals with those who are attracted to the faith, with a

---

[1] H. Elfers, *Die Kirchenordnung Hippolyts von Rom*, 1938, claims to have refuted Lorentz.

[2] *Reliquiae Juris eccles. antiquissimae.*

[3] *Test. Domini nostri Jesu Christi*. There is an English translation by Cooper and Maclean.

[4] The Greek text is appended to Harnack, "Die Lehre der zwölf Apost." in *Texte und Unters.*, II, Pt. V. See also F. X. Funk, *Doctrina Duodecim Apost.*, and the Syriac version, with variants from the Coptic, by J. P. Arendzen in *J.T.S.*, 1901, III, p. 59 ff. Latin fragments are contained in the Verona MS.

special notice of the position of slaves. There follows a long catalogue of crafts and professions which are to be avoided by Christians. It then returns to the preparation of catechumens and provides a prayer for their use. There is then a description of Baptism and Confirmation. The third part dealing with Church Observances is comprehensive and slightly discursive. It has sections on the Stationary Mass, Agapes in private houses, the importance of giving thanks over a meal and of remembering the sick to whom food should be sent. One interesting section is concerned with the bringing in of lamps for suppers at which the congregation assembles together. Then there is a command that first-fruits are to be brought to the bishop to be blessed by him. Fasting before the Paschal Feast is then noticed and there are several sections on the times for prayer. Especial care is ordered for the reverent treatment of the consecrated elements when they are taken home instead of being consumed at the Eucharist. There is a section on the Public Cemetery and another on the use of the sign of the cross in temptation. This outline gives us something of the background of the everyday life of Christians in the early centuries, a subject which receives detailed treatment in Part III, Chap. VII.

THE APOLOGISTS

In the face of persecution and misrepresentation, the Christian Church was compelled to explain itself and its teaching, and in so doing it entered for the first time into the common world of literature. The writings of the apologists "thus possess a significance out of all proportion to their intellectual ability or to the intrinsic literary merits of their works" (*Camb. Anct. Hist.*, XII, p. 460). Apart from the numerous productions of Tertullian, two only of the works, which appeared before the third century was well on its way, exhibit outstanding literary aptitude, and both of them are comparatively short. They are the anonymous *Epistle to Diognetus*, written in Greek and mentioned in Chapter I above; and the *Octavius* of Minucius Felix, in Latin. By some critics the latter is said to have been more interested in literary art than in the Christian religion.

The apologists had to meet attacks on two different planes, the practical and the intellectual. They had, that is, to defend their way of life from calumnies and to justify it to the governing authorities; they had also to expound their special beliefs to the pagan world and its thinkers. There was nothing exactly novel in this double procedure, for Philo and Josephus had undertaken the same task in defence of Judaism, and doubtless the way of approach of their Jewish predecessors was of assistance to the Christian writers. In the New Testament itself the two writings of St. Luke had possibly the same object. Some of the apologies are addressed to individuals, the emperors and others, some to the senate, some apparently to the general public. It may be remarked that those intended for rulers may never have reached the persons to whom they are addressed; possibly they were not even expected to do so, but were a kind of academic exercise calculated to enhance the intellectual and social prestige of Christianity. The apologists are not above stooping to the use of rhetoric, as when Tertullian claims that only bad emperors like Nero and Domitian had been persecutors (*Apol.*, V), or makes exaggerated claims of the influence and extent of the Christian Church. Others were more cautious: Tatian bitterly condemned the use of rhetoric in any shape or form, it was only good to serve injustice and slander (*Ad Graecos*, I); whilst Cyprian deprecated its use in the cause of Christ, it was better to let the facts speak for themselves (*Ad Donatum*, X).

In attempting to persuade pagan philosophers and men of culture of the truth of the Gospel, the apologists were undertaking a hard task and it is doubtful if their writings, at least before the rise of the Alexandrians, had much effect. It is true that Justin Martyr, a typical inquirer as his story tells us, after failing to find satisfaction in any philosophical system, was drawn at last to Christianity by the testimony of a believer (*Dial.*, II–VIII). But what had really aroused his interest and sympathy was the constancy of Christians (I *Apol.*, VIII; II *Apol.*, XII). It must be confessed that the methods adopted by the apologists were scarcely likely to appeal to cultivated thinkers who were not already disposed to give them a sympathetic hearing. Origen might recognize the futility of appealing to allegory when arguing with the heathen; but others, both before and after him, were not so circumspect. As one studies their writings, although one may agree with the positions they strive to maintain, the arguments adduced strike one as being quite unconvincing to an outsider who did not accept their premises. But probably such works were intended primarily for "home consumption", to convince the simple believer that a good case could be made out for Christianity and to repel the onslaughts of the pagans. This would explain, perhaps, the large amount of space devoted to the exposure and belittling of the gods of the heathen.

One remarkable feature of the writings of the apologists, however, tells against this supposed use of their works: the strange absence of appeals to the Scriptures. This can be seen, for example, by comparing Tertullian's *Apology* with his other works. They followed in this the principle laid down by their

Master (Matt. 7 : 6) of not casting pearls before swine. The method was evidently widely accepted, for Lactantius (*Div. Instit.*, V, 4) could condemn Cyprian because he quoted Scripture in a work intended for pagans. Tertullian, although he would even disallow any appeal to the Scriptures when arguing with heretics (*De Praes.*, XIX), was quite willing that they should not be kept back from pagans who cared to read them (*Apol.*, XXXI). Some of the opponents of the Gospel seem, indeed, to have had an intimate knowledge of their subject, such as Celsus and Porphyry, the latter may indeed have been a renegade. In any case the New Testament, so far as it then existed, would have carried little weight with the heathen, though the Old, on account of its antiquity, might have commanded more respect.

The line of attack which such opponents took up can be surmised with some accuracy from the replies which they called forth. The criticisms of Celsus, for example, are known from the detailed refutation of them made some sixty years later by Origen. The same is true of the arguments of the pagan philosopher in the *Apocriticus* of Macarius Magnes. The latter, who represents the point of view of Neoplatonism, was a very dangerous, if much more sympathetic antagonist; for whereas earlier attacks had belittled the Founder of Christianity and poured scorn on the attempts of His illiterate followers to solve problems which had baffled the learned of all ages, this writer professes to hold Jesus in high regard; but he condemns the Christians for having completely misunderstood His teaching. The arguments advanced by the heathen in the *Octavius* have been thought by some to be those of Fronto, the tutor of Marcus Aurelius.[1]

The first apologies of which we have record are said by Eusebius to have been presented or dedicated to Hadrian in 126 by Quadratus and Aristides respectively (IV, iii, 1–3, *Chron.*, p. 281). There is, however, some doubt about the date, though Hadrian, with his tolerant outlook and insatiable curiosity, might seem to have been likely to take favourable notice of a Christian approach. In 1889, however, Rendel Harris discovered a Syriac version of the *Apology of Aristides*[2] which, as Armitage Robinson pointed out, was identical with a speech in *The Life of Barlaam and Josaphat*. As this was written in Greek, it gave presumably the original text, and was addressed, not to Hadrian, but to his successor Antoninus Pius. A Greek fragment has also been discovered in a papyrus.[3]

[1] Especially by Schanz. Fronto was certainly very different from Caecilius for he was a rhetorician with an aversion for philosophy and an adherent of the old religion, while Caecilius was a sceptic.
[2] *Texts and Studies*, I, No. 1, with an appendix by Armitage Robinson.
[3] Now in the British Museum. Text in *J.T.S.*, 1923, XXV, p. 73 ff.

The first apologist to have close connexions with the West was, however, Justin Martyr,[1] who, as we have seen, lived and died in Rome after coming from Palestine. Flavia Neapolis, where his family had been settled for two generations, was the ancient Sychem and the modern Nablous. It was a Roman colony named after the emperor Flavius Vespasian, and possibly Justin may have had Roman or Italian blood in his veins. Many of his works have been lost (cf. Euseb., IV, xviii), but we possess three that are of first-rate importance as revealing the life of the Church in the middle of the second century as well as the attitude of liberal minded Judaism to its Christian supplanter. These works are the two *Apologies*[2] which bear his name and the *Dialogue with Trypho*;[3] the last is much the largest in bulk. In addition a number of works claiming to be by Justin are known; but their claim cannot be upheld. The most important of them is the *Oratio ad Graecos*, which, however, is probably very much later and may even belong to the third century. The suggestion that it is the work of a Greek convert to Hellenistic Judaism,[4] though most ingenious, cannot readily be accepted.

Justin was a truly devoted follower of his Master and his works are of outstanding importance; but he was by no means a clear thinker, and, in spite of his varied contacts with the leading philosophies of the day, and though he raises such fundamental questions as the relation of faith and reason, of natural and revealed religion, was hardly abreast of the culture of the times.[5] His pupil Tatian, after receiving a good classical education, definitely repudiated that culture.[6] Tatian has been called an Assyrian Tertullian, and certainly there are distinct points of resemblance, for, like Tertullian, he professed to despise Greek learning; and, like Tertullian, he passed at length outside the boundaries of orthodox Christianity.

Tatian was born about 110 in Assyria, and later came to Rome, where he adopted Christianity, through reading the Old Testament,[7] and it may also be surmised through the influence of Justin Martyr. After the death of the latter he became a

---

[1] In the Middle Ages Justin was apt to be confused with his namesake, Junianus Justinus, the Roman historian, who was probably a contemporary.
[2] For the dates, see Lawlor and Oulton, *Euseb.*, II, p. 140.
[3] Trypho may well have been a real person. The name is not uncommon, nor was it specially Jewish. The feminine form, Tryphena, is found in Rom. 16 : 12.
[4] See E. R. Goodenough, *Harvard Theol. Rev.*, XVIII, 1925, p. 187 ff. He claims that the work belongs to the early part of the first century and that St. Paul made use of it in Galatians.
[5] See E. R. Goodenough, *Theology of Justin Martyr*, p. 292 f.
[6] *Ad Graecos*, I: "We have renounced your wisdom, though I was once a great proficient in it".   [7] *op. cit.*, XXIX.

heretic, puffed up, so Irenaeus thought, by being himself a teacher (I, xxviii, 1). This was in 173, and soon afterwards he returned to his native regions, arriving back in Mesopotamia about the time of the founding of the Church in Edessa. This led Burkitt to make the exceedingly interesting suggestion that he is actually Addai, the traditional founder of that Church.[1] To most people Tatian is best known, not as an apologist, but as the compiler of the famous *Diatessaron*, the first known harmony of the gospels.[2]

Far more important than Justin or Tatian was Irenaeus. The work by which he is best known is the treatise *Against Heresies* written in Greek about 185. This has been described as "A literary expression of the Catholic system, so complete and successful that the whole history of the Church from Irenaeus to the Reformation, and even later, may be viewed as a natural development of it" (*Camb. Anct. Hist.*, XII, p. 450). In compiling his great work, Irenaeus made use of sources, some of them oral,[3] and it has even been suggested that he incorporated wholesale the lost treatise of Theophilus of Antioch against Marcion mentioned by Eusebius (IV, xxiv).[4] The original Greek has been lost,[5] but as later writers, and Hippolytus in particular, made use of it, numerous extracts have been preserved. There is also a Latin version which may have been made during the lifetime of Irenaeus, since it appears to have been known to Tertullian.[6] The translator has not done his work particularly well and a comparison with the surviving Greek passages shows that he did not always grasp the meaning of the original. The version itself nearly passed out of use, for no copies of it were to be found in either Rome or Lyons at the end of the sixth century.[7] This suggests that the influence of Irenaeus, which was never of much consequence in the East, was also declining in the West. In this connexion it is worth noting that the author of the *Apocriticus* of Macarius Magnes, who probably wrote in the later part of the fourth century in Asia Minor, valued Irenaeus, not for his writings, but for his practical abilities: placing him with Fabian of Rome and Cyprian of Carthage

---

[1] See *J.T.S.*, XXV, 1924, p. 130.

[2] Harnack finds many points of agreement with Marcion, whose activities may have suggested the idea of a harmony: see *Marcion*, p. 236*.

[3] cf. IV, xxvii, 1, *audivi a quodam presbytero*, and *passim*.

[4] This is the theory of Loofs, *Texte und Unters.*, XLVI, Pt. II. It has not met with much favour. For detailed criticisms see F. R. Montgomery Hitchcock in *J.T.S.*, 1937, XXXVIII, pp. 130–139, 255–260.

[5] A fragment written *c.* 200 was discovered at Oxyrhynchus: see *Papyri Oxyrhyn.*, III, No. 405.

[6] This is doubtful: see *J.T.S.*, 1922, XXIII, p. 51. A. Souter, *Nov. Test. S. Iren.* (*Old Latin Bib. Texts*, No. VII), dates it *c.* 400. B. Kraft, *Die Evangelienzitate des heil. Iren.*, p. 47, suggests *c.* 300. [7] Souter, *op. cit.*, p. lxvii.

as outstanding benefactors of humanity (III, xxiv). In addition to the treatise *Against Heresies*, a number of extracts from smaller works, chiefly letters, have been preserved; the most important of them is the *Letter to Florinus* from which Eusebius quotes a long passage (V, xx). He also makes mention of the *Demonstration of Apostolic Preaching* or *Epideixis*. This work had been lost until an Armenian version was discovered in 1904.[1] It was evidently composed after the bigger work, and forms a kind of Christian *vade-mecum* for laymen.

The literary methods of Irenaeus are not such as will appeal to a modern reader. He is much too diffuse and discursive. Proofs and examples are piled one upon another until the mind is weary of them, especially as it is often difficult to find any relevance in them. He is full of long digressions, and his dialectical ingenuity may have impressed his contemporaries but has now lost its force. None the less, his writings played their part, and that no small one, in the defence and propagation of the Christian message.

The next writer to be considered is Hippolytus who is stated by Photius (*Bibliotheca*, p. 121) to have been the pupil of Irenaeus. This is possible, but is more probably based on conjecture, in view of the generous use which Hippolytus made of the writings of the earlier writer. Hippolytus was notable for the immense amount of literature which he produced; it was apparently his activity in this direction which suggested to Ambrose, the patron of Origen, that the latter should employ himself in a similar way.[2] Our knowledge of the full extent of his labours has a strange and unusual source. In 1551 there was discovered in Rome a mutilated statue which scholars have agreed to be that of Hippolytus, and on the sides and back of the chair in which the figure is seated there is a long list of theological works, some of which were known already to be his work. It is also a remarkable fact, in a life and career which are beset with unusual circumstances, that the writings now held to be by him have in a number of instances been previously attributed to others.[3] The *Refutation of all the Heresies*, for example, was included in the works of Origen and known as the *Philosophumena*. The discovery in 1842 at Mount Athos of a manuscript of the treatise proved that it was actually the work of Hippolytus. So too the last two chapters (XI and XII) of the *Epistle to Diognetus*, which had long been suspected of being by another hand were

---

[1] See *Texte und Unters.*, XXXI, Pt. I. There is an English edition by Armitage Robinson.

[2] Euseb., VI, xxii and xxiii with Lawlor's note.

[3] His treatise περὶ τοῦ πάσχα has recently been discovered in a collection of *spuria* of Chrysostom.

claimed for Hippolytus.[1] Then there is the vexed question of the *Church Order* to which reference has already been made. Genuine writings by Hippolytus seem certainly to have been included in the source which lies behind the various documents which go to make up the tradition.[2] Lightfoot was fond of attributing writings to Hippolytus, and not content with giving him the Muratorian Fragment (I, ii, p. 411 f.), went on to identify him with the presbyter Gaius mentioned in Euseb., II, xxv, 6 f., etc.), though of this he later became uncertain. Gaius may have been the author of the *Little Labyrinth* (Euseb., V, xxviii), but he prefers Hippolytus (*op. cit.*, p. 379).[3] Hippolytus he regarded as "by far the most learned man and the most prolific writer whom the Church of Rome produced before Jerome" (*op. cit.*, p. 427). That he was a prolific writer none would deny, but the question of his learning is not by any means so clear. It is with very great hesitation that I venture to differ from the judgment of so great a critic as Lightfoot, but the learning displayed by Hippolytus seems to me to partake too much of the "parade" variety, and to be very similar to that of some who in the Middle Ages gained a reputation by the lavish use of epitomes, the so-called "Florilegia" which were common in their day and not unknown in earlier times. In the first days of Christianity there existed a large literature of elementary introductions and summaries of philosophical works which were widely used.[4] His accounts of the various philosophies would seem to have been based on such sources and exhibit no mastery of their principles, besides being guilty of numerous contradictions.[5] The impression left on my own mind by a careful study of the *Refutation* is that it is the product of a well-meaning but not too careful writer. His defects are due not to lack of good faith but to confused thinking and a failure fully to understand or master his material. Hippolytus might even be accused of being an intellectual "snob" anxious to impress his readers. Incidentally, he was the last of the writers of the Roman Church to make use of Greek.

One great service, however, it seems that Hippolytus did render. He saved exegesis from becoming a Gnostic monopoly.[6] In his manner of interpretation he stood between the schools of

---

[1] Originally by Bunsen and questioned by many scholars. It is accepted by R. H. Connolly, *J.T.S.*, 1936, XXXVII, p. 2 ff.

[2] See Bartlet, *Church-Life and Church-Order*, p. 105 ff., and an article by Bishop Frere in *J.T.S.*, 1915, XVI, pp. 323–371. For unknown reasons Hippolytus, like Clement of Rome, was held in high esteem in the East and there was a tendency to attribute documents to him or to use his name.

[3] Harnack, *Chron.*, II, p. 224 f., accepts this.

[4] cf. Nock, *Conversion*, p. 179.

[5] See on this point F. Legge, *Hippolytus, Philosophumena*, I, p. 9.

[6] Pantaenus, it must not be forgotten, had also written a Commentary on the Bible which was known to Jerome, *De Vir. Ill.*, XXXVI.

Antioch and Alexandria (as they afterwards developed) by striving to combine allegorical and historical methods of interpretation. In the West, it was long before he found any worthy successor; in the East, he was the forerunner of Origen.

With Hippolytus we leave the Greek writers of the West and turn to Latin literature. As versions of I *Clement* and of *The Shepherd* of Hermas had appeared before the end of the second century, not to mention the existence of a Roman Creed in Latin, there was evidently a Latin-speaking community growing up in the West. When Tertullian wrote *De Spect.*, XXIX, that is, just before the close of the second century, he could claim that the Christians had a considerable literature of their own, and a literature which was based on the truth and not on fables. He may be referring to the Scriptures,[1] or his words may have a wider application,[2] but if there was any considerable secular Christian literature in Latin it has completely disappeared. Tertullian wrote in the very midst of what may be regarded as the period of transition, which stretched from the middle of the second to the middle of the third centuries, during which the Church in the West was gradually transformed from a Greek-speaking to an entirely Latin-speaking body. In this work of transformation Africa took the lead, with Rome close behind.[3] Africa was the natural leader because there the number of Christians who were of Roman origin and Latin speech was probably far greater than in so cosmopolitan a city as Rome. The letter written to Cyprian by the Roman clergy reveals the low standard of Latin scholarship in the Roman Church. It is not only defective in style, but also ignorant in places of grammar.[4]

Jerome (*De Vir. Ill.*, LIII) tells us that the first Latin authors were Bishop Victor and Apollonius, the senator and martyr who made a speech before the senate. But the real pioneer was Tertullian or possibly Minucius Felix. In Rome itself Novatian holds the claim to first place unless the works, falsely attributed to Cyprian, *De Aleatoribus*[5] and *De Montibus Sina et Sion*, are of Roman authorship.

Heine once observed that Latin "was a lapidary speech fit for the stone-hard Roman people . . . Christianity with a true Christian patience tormented itself with the attempt to spiritualize this tongue".[6] The attempt was remarkably successful as the

---

[1] This is the opinion of P. Monceaux, *Hist. litt. de l'Afrique chrét.*, I, p. 50.
[2] cf. Leclercq, *L'Afrique chrét.*, I, p. 90.
[3] cf. Augustine, *duae urbes literarum Latinarum artifices Roma atque Carthago.*
[4] It appears as VIII in the collection of Cyprian's *Epistles.*
[5] Harnack thinks that this was written by Victor and that it is the first Latin Christian document which we possess.
[6] Quoted by Allen, *The Continuity of Christian Thought*, p. 249.

writings of Prudentius and of some medieval verse-makers testify; but in the period around the turn of the second and third centuries the task had only begun. It was the creative genius of Tertullian which was there at hand to undertake it and see it well on the way to future perfection. Classical literature and the rude attempts of the African version to present the Scriptures, these were the raw materials out of which he carved the new medium of theological Latin; later, Cyprian would do his part, and to these two the Church owes a profound debt. "The lamp which all runners in the sacred race have received is that which Tertullian lit and Cyprian trimmed."[1] It was the combination of qualities and environment which gave them their peculiar importance and effectiveness; native qualities already conditioned, for good or evil, by that environment. They lived at a great crucial moment in the history of the Christian religion, the moment when it was endeavouring to naturalize itself in the West. Behind it lay the Semitic and the Hellenistic phases; now was to come, supplementing and modifying them, the Latin phase of Christianity.

Such a process, of necessity, involved the coining of new terms to represent ideas which up till then had appeared in a Greek dress. The attempt to coin these terms was but moderately successful; completely successful it could never have been, for the translation from one language to another always involves limitation and the introduction of new shades of meaning which were not present in the original. The practical Romans were not well qualified for discovering equivalents for terms which represented the abstract ideas of the Greeks.

Some of the new terms employed by the Latins had unfortunate connotations: e.g., to use *substantia* for οὐσία was to invite disaster, on account of the materialistic suggestions which it contained; it was really much nearer in meaning to ὑπόστασις. For this latter word *persona* was used, another word with unfortunate antecedents since it had already a legal flavour. Such imperfect and misleading renderings of important theological terms were bound to lead to confused thinking and to eventual misunderstanding with the Eastern Church.

Tertullian has been described as "the first instance of a Christian author who rose even on formal grounds far above his contemporaries, and proved himself a master of his own language".[2] His immense output, from both the orthodox and the Montanist periods of his activity, forms a literary whole of outstanding value, even apart from its style. That style is the product of an unusual combination of qualities in an unusual

---

[1] Benson, *op. cit.*, p. 531.
[2] Lietzmann, *The Founding of the Church Universal*, p. 290.

person. Tertullian had that greatness of passion and emotional intensity which is one of the essentials of a great writer; by comparison Cyprian, if we leave aside some of the epistles, seems cold and colourless. But this natural fervour was ever at war with that strict legal training which had moulded so decisively his outlook and methods. To this tension may be attributed the obscurity which at times overclouds his writings, an obscurity which rendered them unpopular.[1] The Greek writings which he composed have all disappeared,[2] but Latin was his natural means of expression and to it he gave a new meaning and a new sphere. In this he had had at least one predecessor, though in a very different context, for his fellow-countryman Apuleius had already shown what could be done by a free and original treatment of the Latin tongue.

Tertullian's great achievement was to coin a new theological terminology for the Latin Church. This does not mean, of course, that all the terms found in his writings were actually his own invention. Many of them were perhaps already being used in Latin versions of the Scriptures, but he gave them authority and a wider operation. It has already been pointed out that some of the equivalents selected would later have unfortunate consequences: for these he was not entirely responsible; they were inherent in any attempt to find for Greek ideas and Greek terms their corresponding Latin equivalents. Some of the words used were borrowed from Roman religion itself; words such as *pius, religio, sacer, sacramentum,* and *sanctus.*[3] Some were coined by simply transliterating the Greek; such were *ecclesia,*[4] and *parochia,* as well as various designations for clerical orders, *episcopus, presbyter, diaconus.* Some words seem to have been derived from military usage, a sign perhaps of the extent to which Christianity was spreading in the army; the fact that Tertullian's own father was a centurion had possibly some effect in providing this military element in ecclesiastical vocabulary. At the same time it is possible that Tertullian was not to the extent that is often supposed the inventor of new terms. They may well have been gradually brought into use. For instance, in *De Orat.,* XIX and elsewhere, he uses *statio* for a set fast, its first

---

[1] So Lactantius says, *Div. Instit.,* V, 1. But when he couples with it the charge of lack of polish, *minus comptus et multum obscurus,* we are puzzled to know what he means.

[2] For references to them, see *De Cor. Mil.,* VI; *De Bapt.,* XV; and *De Virg. Vel.,* I. Eusebius, who took comparatively little interest in the West, save when the Roman Church was concerned, thought that Tertullian himself was a Roman (II, ii, 4; xxv, 4).

[3] See Warde Fowler, *Relig. Experience of the Rom. People,* p. 459 ff.

[4] This adoption was already current in secular speech: see Deissmann, *Light from the Ancient East,* p. 112 ff., who refers to a bilingual inscription at Ephesus (*c.* A.D. 103).

appearance in a Latin writing. But strangely enough this very term had been used by Hermas, *Sim.*, V, i, 16, in a Greek form, nearly a century before. It may well be that in the case of other words examples of earlier usage have been lost.

Tertullian's writings are very numerous, both those which belong to the time when he was an orthodox churchman and those from his later Montanist period. They divide naturally into three groups: (*a*) Apologetic; (*b*) Dogmatic; and (*c*) Practical. In his apologetic writings, which come mostly from his earlier days, Christianity takes the offensive against paganism, for he is not content merely to explain the Christian point of view, but goes out of his way to attack the absurdities of the popular religion. The most famous of his writings in this class are the *Apology* and *Ad Nationes*. The dogmatic works are mainly anti-heretical and anti-Jewish. His point of view becomes narrower as he singles out individual antagonists. This can be seen by comparing the earlier *De Praes. Haeret.* with *Adv. Valent.*, *Adv. Marc.*, and *Adv. Prax.* The treatise *Adv. Judaeos*[1] is almost certainly genuine so far as Chapters I–VIII are concerned; the later chapters are parallel to *Adv. Marc.* and a rather clumsy addition. His treatise *De Anima* is important as the first attempt at a Christian psychology; but, probably in reaction from the super-spirituality of the Gnostics, it seems to go too far in the opposite direction and defends the corporeality of the soul. The same tendency can be found in *De Carne Christi* and *De Resurrectione Carnis*. The remaining works of a practical character are marked by a strong asceticism which increased as he drew nearer and nearer to Montanism.

Between Tertullian's *Apology* and the *Octavius* of Minucius Felix some measure of dependence seems undoubtedly to exist. The question as to which is the borrower has often been debated, and no final decision has yet been reached on the point. In modern times, the first to suggest the prior date of the *Octavius* was Ebart, in 1870. Lactantius, in commenting upon the work of previous apologists, had already placed Minucius before Tertullian (*Div. Instit.*, V, i), but the consensus of opinion had been in favour of the priority of the latter. The *Octavius* evidently comes from a period when there is no persecution and when Christianity has spread among the educated classes; when, indeed, Christians could take the offensive without fear. This would suit the end of the second century and the first half of the third; somewhere within this period the work obviously belongs, but to fix it within narrower limits is hardly possible. The mention of a certain Marcus Caecilius Natalis, a native and official

---

[1] It is in this treatise, in the earlier chapters, that the use of Theodotion's version of Daniel is found: see, further, Burkitt, *The Old Latin, etc.*, p. 30 n.

of Cirta, in several inscriptions dated 210–217,[1] does not get us much further, for we cannot be certain that he is the Caecilius of the dialogue. The question must remain an open one; those who consider that Tertullian is the more likely borrower will place the *Apology* later, and those who hold a different idea will make Minucius the debtor.[2]

Minucius Felix was probably an African like Tertullian, and, like Tertullian, he went to Rome to become a successful advocate. He seems to have taken up his permanent residence there. The scene of the *Octavius* is Ostia. The author, his friend Octavius, and Caecilius, a heathen, begin a discussion on Christianity. Caecilius speaks first, and condemns Christians for their unsatisfactory manner of life, for their disloyalty, for their secret and shameful ceremonies, and because their God left His Son to die on the cross. In the end, however, he allows himself to be convinced by Octavius. The dialogue is a charming piece of work of high literary merit; its atmosphere of easy and cultivated toleration recalls vividly the *New Republic* of W. H. Mallock. It is full of reminiscences of Latin authors which reveal a mind steeped in the best culture of the times. Cicero seems to have provided the model for the work as a whole, and his spirit permeates it. Numerous borrowings can also be discovered, especially from *De Natura Deorum*. It is to be remarked that the name of Christ nowhere appears in the dialogue, a phenomenon which has led some critics to question the writer's complete sincerity and knowledge of Christianity.

As a piece of literature, the *Octavius* is highly pleasing, though possibly it rather "smells of the lamp" and gives the impression of being much more of a literary exercise than a spontaneous composition. There is no passion about it, and the author seldom ventures far from his classical models. Even the Christian parts have been suspected of being borrowings from Tertullian. But the work, taken at its lowest, is an important witness to the spread of Christianity among the educated. But what a reduced Christianity! It is clearly held as a philosophy, not as a religion, and the authority of Cicero and Seneca is at least as great as that of the Scriptures. The background is that of a debating society or a school of rhetoric in which the real beliefs and passions of men were not involved.[3]

[1] *C.I.L.*, VIII, 6996, 7094–7098.
[2] In favour of the earliness of Minucius among recent scholars are H. J. Baylis, *Minucius Felix and his Place among the Early Fathers of the Latin Church*; and P. de Labriolle, *La Réaction païenne*, p. 93. Against it is A. Amatucci, *Africa Romana*, p. 191. J. Martin, *Minucii Felicis Octavius* (1930), places the *Octavius* later than *Quod Idola* of Cyprian.
[3] The preservation of the *Octavius* may be due to a fortunate accident. In a Paris MS. of the ninth century it is added as an eighth (!) book to Arnobius, *Adv. Nationes.*

Cyprian, although he valued Tertullian and regarded him as his master, and although he obviously made large use of his writings, nowhere definitely quotes him by name. This is the more surprising as some of his writings are little more than a restatement of the thoughts and ideas of the earlier author. It is interesting, in this connexion, to compare Cyprian's *De Habitu Virginum* with Tertullian's *De Cultu Femin.* Cyprian's literary labours began immediately after his conversion when he put forth a pamphlet, based on the *Apology* of Tertullian and the *Octavius* of Minucius Felix, with the title *Quod idola dii non sunt.* It was followed by *Ad Donatum.* Later on there came *Testimonia ad Quirinum,* a collection of proofs taken from the Scriptures for use against the Jews, and *De Cath. Ecclesiae Unitate.* Other treatises also came from his pen, but his supreme contribution was the priceless series of letters which he wrote; [1] a collection which is unique in the early Church, for those of Ignatius, which might offer a parallel, are rather discourses than letters, and give but little information about the circumstances of the writer or of those to whom he wrote. The letters of Cyprian, however, constitute a source of outstanding importance for the condition of the Church in North Africa and, indeed, of Western Christianity in general for the middle of the third century.[2]

In any survey of Latin writers Novatian cannot be missed out for he was perhaps the first Christian author who wrote in Latin only. His extant works are not numerous, there are two letters written to Cyprian in the name of the Roman clergy (*Epist.* XXX and XXXVI), the treatise *De Trinitate,* the only book of its kind produced by the Roman Church before the fourth century, and *De Cibis Judaeis.* Harnack would also assign to him four works mistakenly ascribed to Cyprian: *De Spectaculis, De bono Pudicitiae, Adv. Judaeos,* and *De Laude Martyrii.*

A writer who seems to have depended for his matter on the works of Cyprian, with which his own are often edited, was Commodian, the first of Christian poets in order of time. He was certainly not the first, by any other method of calculation; for he was no Keble and his doctrine is better than his poetry, which is written in barbarous hexameters, similar, it is said, to some found in African inscriptions. But even his doctrine was not impeccable, for it contains traces of Patripassianism and of Chiliasm and his works were put on the Index by the *Decretum Gelasianum.* He probably belonged to the latter part of the third century and to North Africa. His longer poem *Instructiones* was

---

[1] On Cyprian's letters, see C. H. Turner, *Studies in Early Church History,* p. 97 ff.
[2] See, further, E. W. Watson, "The Style and Language of St. Cyprian", in *Studia Biblica,* IV, pp. 189–317.

in two books; the shorter *Carmen Apologeticum* was discovered by Cardinal Pitra in 1852.

Julius Africanus belongs to the East rather than the West, for he wrote in Greek and spent most of his life in Palestine. He came to Rome in 222 or thereabouts on an embassy to the Emperor Elagabalus and remained there in order to design a handsome library in the Pantheon for Severus Alexander.[1] He was the author of a celebrated work on world history which formed the basis of Eusebius's *Chronicle*, whilst his chronological calculations inspired Hippolytus to undertake similar enterprises and so to popularize such matters in the West.

Before we leave the Latin writers, two other names must receive attention, Arnobius and Lactantius. They were both laymen, both apologists, and both had been pagans. Their works are probably based on earlier material and their theology is neither profound nor exact.

Arnobius was born at Sicca, the Colonia Julia Veneria of the Romans and the El Kef of the Arabs, which stands on the highway between Cirta and Carthage not far from Madaura. His life overlapped that of Cyprian, since he was born before 250. The best-known of his works is a polemical treatise in seven books, *Adv. Nationes*,[2] composed about 300. Its strength lies in its exposure of the follies and shortcomings of paganism rather than in any positive exposition of the Christian faith. This may be accounted for by the fact that until his sixtieth year Arnobius had been a violent opponent of Christianity. He is said to have been converted by a dream. But whatever may have been the cause of his sudden change, and the matter is somewhat obscure, it did nothing to modify the violence of his methods, although it may have altered the object against which they were directed. Amidst his denunciations of the absurdities and immoralities of the popular deities he makes one good point, however: national gods cannot be true gods, for true gods must extend their power impartially to all peoples (*Adv. Nat.*, IV).

Lactantius, who was a pupil of Arnobius, was born probably in North Africa about the middle of the third century. Like his master, he did not adopt Christianity until well advanced in years. Arnobius is not likely to have had any hand in the matter, for his conversion took place at Nicomedia where he held a professorship. This he lost during the Diocletian persecution of 303; but on the accession of Constantine he came into favour and was appointed tutor to Crispus, the latter's young son. He spent his last years at Treves where he died in extreme old age.

Lactantius was a great admirer of Cicero and had caught

[1] See *Papyri Oxyrhyn.*, III, No. 512 f.
[2] See F. Gabarrou, *Arnobe, son Œuvre* and *Le Latin d'Arnobe*.

something of the beauty of his style. The writing with which his name is usually associated, however, the *De Mortibus Persecutorum*, is of a very different style and the attribution has not gone unchallenged.[1] The Ciceronian style is more evident in his other considerable work, the *Institutiones Divinae*. The latter was written about 320 and dedicated to Constantine. If the *De Mortibus* is by Lactantius it shows that he was no very reliable authority, as he is far too apt to allow his prejudices against the persecutors to overstimulate his imagination. The delight of the author in describing the misfortunes which overtook them and their relations is certainly morbid and unchristian. Many other smaller works are catalogued by Jerome, but two only are still extant, *De Opificio Dei* and *De Ira Dei*.

From about the beginning of the Christian era, Alexandria had gradually been taking the place of Athens as the leader of culture. It was more accessible and more settled, and the Museum with its body of teachers and students was a centre from which intellectual influences radiated over a wide area. Whilst Athens gradually sank into a kind of city of tourists, living on the glories of the past, Alexandria developed a busy life of its own and had its face set towards the future. Even before the rise of Christianity it had been the meeting-point of three exceedingly important tendencies: Egyptian symbolism, Jewish Monotheism, and Greek science and philosophy. In the Christian School these tendencies continued to play their several parts and thus gave to it an intellectual strength and experience which hitherto had been painfully lacking on the Christian side in its struggle with pagan thought and philosophy. It was at Alexandria first that the initiative passed to the exponents of the Christian faith.

In view of its importance in the history of liberal Judaism it is strange that Alexandria made so tardy an appearance in the development of the Christian faith; but once it had emerged its contribution was noble and effective. The centre from which, during our period, that contribution was chiefly to be made was the so-called Catechetical School. The first head of whom we have knowledge was Pantaenus, whose numerous writings have all perished. Under his pupil Clement it became famous, and with Origen it took the foremost place in Christian thinking.

Clement was probably born of pagan parents; but curiosity led him to seek for a more profound knowledge of ultimate things than Hellenic culture, or even the mysteries, could provide. In his search after truth he travelled widely and, like Plato, spent some time in southern Italy. The achievements of Clement

---

[1] See Appendix I to Bury's edition of Gibbon. Lawlor, *Eusebiana*, p. 237 ff., is in favour of the authorship of Lactantius.

have perhaps never received an adequate recognition. To most people his chief significance is as the predecessor of Origen. This is due probably to the unsystematic nature of his writings and the vagueness of his teaching. He had undoubtedly great learning and his interests covered an exceedingly wide field. But his critical faculty was not equal to the strain placed upon it by such vast accumulations. Though prepared to welcome truth from whatever quarter it might come he was not a really deep thinker, owing mainly to his habit of going off at a tangent and failing to see the due proportion of things. But for him Christianity was the final philosophy and Christ was the Truth.

Origen may have been of Coptic descent and his name has been interpreted as "the child of Hor",[1] but his mother was apparently a Jewess.[2] Born about 186, he succeeded Clement as head of the Catechetical School at the age of eighteen; and though he had attended the lectures of his predecessor—Eusebius is surely conclusive on this point (VI, vi; cf. xiv, 9)—he never, so far as I know, alludes to him or acknowledges any indebtedness. In 212, accompanied by his friend and patron, Ambrosius, he paid a visit to Rome (Euseb., VI, xiv, 10) where according to Jerome (De Vir. Ill., LXI) he heard Hippolytus. Into the rather chequered career of Origen in the East we cannot enter; it will suffice to recall the quarrels with the ecclesiastical authorities at Alexandria which compelled him to spend the later part of his long life at Caesarea in Syria.

Origen was one of the greatest and most original thinkers ever given to the Christian Church and with his supreme power of thought he had a hospitable mind, avid of ideas, and a most retentive memory. The weight of his learning never became overwhelming for he had the ability to arrange his ideas in a systematic form. In this he excelled Clement, as also in the extent of his knowledge. Holding, with Clement, that Christianity is the final philosophy, he endeavoured to show that it covered the whole of life and thought. His chief work, De Principiis, exists only in Latin, and a comparison with such Greek fragments as have happened to survive shows that the translation by Rufinus is by no means reliable.[3] As an apologist, he undertook to answer the notorious attack on Christianity by Celsus, written about the time of his own birth. Of this work Hort has said that it is "at once the best and most comprehensive defence of the Christian faith which has come down to us from the days of the Fathers" (Ante-Nicene Fathers, p. 131).

[1] See Bigg, The Christian Platonists of Alexandria, p. 152.
[2] So Jerome says, Epist. XXXIX.
[3] An English edition of the De Principiis has recently appeared by G. W. Butterworth. He prints translations of the Greek fragments alongside that of the Latin.

In addition to his work on doctrine and apologetics, Origen was a pioneer in the art of textual criticism and in the exegesis of the Bible. His exegesis, however, was marred by a too great use of allegory; for in this matter he failed to rise above his early training and the methods of his times.

The ideas of Origen had considerable influence in the West, as can be seen from the number of his works which were translated into Latin, and by the extent to which his thought, and even his language, has permeated the writings of the three great Latin teachers of the fourth century—Hilary of Poitiers, Ambrose, and Jerome. It was, however, as an exegete that he found most favour with them, for his doctrinal works were regarded with some suspicion; and when Rufinus translated *De Principiis* he ventured to make numerous modifications in the original in the interests of what he considered orthodox dogma,[1] whilst Jerome has confessed that his study of Origen had misled him (*Epist.*, CXXIV). Origen was fearless in his pursuit of truth, and at times came very near to the verge of heresy. His followers, with less caution and less balance than their master, at times pressed his ideas beyond the limits of what was allowable and so brought his whole teaching into disrepute.

[1] He admits in his preface that the translation was made in response to a widespread demand.

CHAPTER IV

THE CONFLICT OF THOUGHT

The history of the intellectual development of any epoch is a history of contending forces; though the conflict is not on the intellectual plane alone. Developments take place under the leading of novel religious experiences and the pressure of newly realized spiritual needs. The ebb and flow of the contest is to be gauged by individuals, none of whom reflects exactly the thought of his age; in fact the greater he is as a thinker the less will he reflect it. In the case of the Christian Church in our period there were not many thinkers of genius, though we have to take note of the sudden emergence of writers who seem to concentrate what has gone before and to express it concisely in some new formula. It is a ready temptation to regard such writers as mere thinkers or fabricators of systems, and to forget that they were living men faced by the greatest of all problems, the meaning of life and the relation of God and man. In their efforts to solve these problems they may have made mistakes in the course of their thinking; experiments which, so to speak, went wrong, and have been condemned by the more mature experience of later ages. But such experiments are necessary if progress is to be made, for new truths, and fresh aspects of truths already known, are wont to be discerned by those who leave the beaten highway and boldly take their own separate course. It is surely not without significance that two of the thinkers who stand out in the pre-Nicene Church, the one in the East and the other in the West, Origen and Tertullian, have not unblemished reputations. But even heretics and schismatics have their part to play by exploring the limits of the faith and revealing the necessity for defining its boundaries.

The immense development which took place in fundamental doctrines is not always fully realized even by professed students of the subject, and I cannot do better than quote the words of a profound scholar who was also a Churchman of unquestioned orthodoxy, to emphasize this. The late C. H. Turner once affirmed that "it would be puerile to deny . . . that development has taken place between the Christology of the first chapters of Acts and the Christology of the Council of Nicaea. . . . If the Creed of Nicaea—the confession that Jesus Christ is co-eternal and consubstantial with the Father—had been put before any ordinary Greek-speaking Christian of the primitive community of Jerusalem, he would certainly have found it quite unintelligible" (*Catholic and Apostolic*, pp. 100 and 117).

In a small volume which I published some years ago entitled *The Church in the Ancient World*, I had a chapter on "The Struggle with Heresy and Schism". Such a title reflects the standpoint of a later age when the struggle was over, and one side had been definitely declared to be the victor, and so orthodox. But from the point of view of those who were engaged in the actual contest it is apt to be misleading, for it suggests that even from the earliest years there was an elaborate and clearly defined standard of Christian belief against which those whom we call heretics deliberately rebelled. Such was not the case, at least until well into the second century and even beyond it. The so-called heretics claimed that they held the orthodox position and complained when Catholics stood aloof from them (cf. Iren., III, xv, 2). The statement of Dr. Pusey that "The Catholic Christian regarded his faith as a matter of external Divine Revelation; the heretic held what he held as a philosophy"[1] is only partially true and does not take full account of the extraordinary diversity in both life and thought in the Church of the first two centuries. Its variety was at least as great as that of Christendom to-day. In the New Testament itself, very divergent views are already at work and a steady development of doctrine can be traced, with the fourth gospel as a final term. No doubt the presence of different sects, Pharisees, Sadducees, and Essenes, among the Jews accustomed primitive Christians to differences of outlook within the People of God. They were the separate embodiments of those conflicting tendencies which coexist everywhere in religious societies.

In speaking of the conflict of thought, however, I have no wish to suggest that the result of the clash of opinions was fortuitous, or the decisions erroneous; I wish merely to avoid injustice to thinkers who felt sincerely, if mistakenly, that their view of Christianity was the true one. All heresies contain some measure of truth, even if only because, as Feuerbach has affirmed, they come to birth at the call of some human need, and the real views of a defeated party are apt to be misrepresented by the victors. But Dr. Pusey is right in so far as the Church held that it had received a divine revelation of which it was the guardian. This can be seen from the high value which is attached in the New Testament itself to faith, not only in the sense of personal trust, but also as implying intellectual assent to certain propositions. Passages to this effect are found not only in the fourth gospel and the Pastoral epistles, but even in the synoptic gospels and those epistles of St. Paul whose genuineness is

[1] *Justin Martyr*, Library of the Fathers, p. xiii.

beyond question, as well as in the Acts. The Apostolic Fathers, in their turn, testify to the existence of a common faith; and after the middle of the second century Hegesippus identifies it with what was preached by the Law, the Prophets, and the Lord (Euseb., IV, xxii, 3); whilst it is significant that the Churches of Vienne and Lyons, when writing to Asia and Phrygia, speak not only of their common hope, but also of their common faith (Euseb., V, i, 3).

It is necessary, therefore, to recognize alongside a great variety of opinions a deep underlying unity. We must beware of what Professor Dodd has called "a piecemeal treatment of early Christian thought": Christianity, he says, "however it arose, is a distinct phenomenon in the spiritual life of mankind. It is not to be confused with anything else, however close its resemblances may be, in certain respects, to other spiritual movements, and however real its affinities with them. Nor is it a mere collection of various religious ideas, but an organic unity" (*The Present Task in N.T. Studies*, pp. 32 and 35).

The founder of Christianity left behind Him no instructions on the intellectual life; neither commending it, nor, as other religious reformers (e.g., St. Francis) have done, condemning it. Nor did He enunciate any theological system; whilst even in ethics there is nothing entirely new in what He taught. It is true that we possess no complete account of His teaching as a whole, but only fragments, preserved by the pious memory of the first disciples. If we find this matter for regret it is because we have mistaken the function and mission of Jesus. He was not primarily a teacher, but a revealer: what He said, and even what He did, was not the supremely important thing, but what He was. As Burkitt has finely said: "It is not as a Philosopher, but as a Prometheus, that we worship Christ—the Man who came down from Heaven to give men the Divine Fire" (in *Camb. Biblical Essays*, p. 198).

This being so, dogma, although only of a rudimentary kind, was a necessity so soon as records began to be made, and there is no period in the life of the Church, of which we have knowledge, when dogma is not found. There may have been a "pre-theological age", but if so we know nothing about it, and if ever there was a "simple Gospel" entirely free from the complications of "theological sophistication" it has been lost. The synoptic gospels in their present form may be later in date than the epistles of St. Paul; but it can hardly be denied that they represent a more primitive and less developed type of Christianity; but even they have theological presuppositions. Between the stage which they represent and Christianity as we find it in the middle of the second century there is a wide gap, both in thought and organization, and the one does not seem to be an obvious outcome of the other. Fuller knowledge would, no doubt, enable us to fill this gap, for breaks in the history of doctrine are seldom or never abrupt; they only seem so from our defective information.

In spite, however, of the gap between the synoptic gospels and the Christianity of the mid-second century, by that time those gospels, with John and the epistles of St. Paul, had taken their place alongside the Old Testament, and come to be recognized as a standard by which the belief of the Church was to be tested and regulated. Thus, as Sanday has said, "Christian theology . . . already bears the stamp that marks it throughout succeeding centuries, viz., that it is not free speculation, but reflexion based on *data* given by the Bible" (*Outlines of the Life of Christ*, p. 223). Even the Gnostics held this position (Iren., III, xi, 7), though with a difference. But the acceptance of the principle did not make matters too simple. For one thing there was, as we saw in Part III, Chap. I, much divergence of opinion as to what constituted Scripture, and the use of allegorical methods of interpretation allowed a wide difference in the results which might follow an appeal to it. A further difficulty was due to the lack of any accepted text; that, I imagine, underlies the accusation of corrupting the Scriptures,[1] though we cannot rule out deliberate attempts to interpolate, nor the invention of documents purporting to be apostolic.[2]

Already in the New Testament there are signs that ideas of a dangerous character are at work in the Church. In the next generation warnings against them are found in Ignatius and Hermas. Such views generally arise from the vagaries of individual thinkers who have no conscious intention of departing from orthodoxy. This constitutes their gravest threat, for the nearer heresy is to received beliefs, the more insidious will be its attractions, and the greater the need to expose and denounce it. Heresy and orthodoxy have the same origins, their divergence is only perceived as they develop. In the Early Church heretical developments were the fruit of attempts to find room within the borders of orthodox Christianity for elements drawn from the previous mental and philosophical background of new converts, both Jewish and pagan. Every form of teaching, since it arises in a particular environment, must savour of the soil, and its vital elements need to be disengaged from their temporary setting. So, too, as it takes root in fresh environments it draws to

[1] One is reminded of the naïve observation of the editors of the Douai Bible (1609–10) that the Vulgate was better than the original Hebrew as being free from Jewish corruptions.

[2] Such as those noticed in Part III, Chap. II: cf. also the observations of Dionysius of Corinth in Euseb., IV, xxiii.

itself other elements from the air above it. Dissent is never merely perverse since it arises from a desire to take up some aspect of truth which the Church of the day is neglecting. In its emphasis on such neglected truth it may pass over into heresy or schism, whilst the Church in its turn may become more rigid in its refusal to allow an adequate place for it. A principle which, in our period, is perhaps illustrated in the rise of Montanism. Before, however, the Christian tradition had been defined and stabilized, attempts to supplement it had their dangers; but it is well to observe that heresies usually diverged in opposite directions, thus giving testimony to the central truth which lay between them.

The first Christians were Jews by birth and upbringing, and although the Gospel was to be subjected to Hellenistic and pagan influences, about whose extent scholars may argue, one fact is certain; it never lost entirely its contact with the Judaism out of which it had emerged. But Jewish Christianity, like orthodox Jewry, was not interested in metaphysics, and if the Church had remained predominantly Jewish there would have been little need for any but elementary doctrinal statements. The coming in of the Gentiles, however, changed all that. The first influx may have been of the uneducated; but once those who had had a philosophical training were enrolled their needs would have to be met. They themselves, indeed, would be compelled by sheer intellectual honesty to apply methods and training acquired in their old life to the contents of the religion which they had come to adopt. The process has already begun in the New Testament with the fourth gospel and its surprisingly complete fusion of Hebrew and Hellenic elements, "the boldest 'restatement' of Christianity in terms of contemporary thought ever attempted in the history of the Church".[1] Ephesus, the probable scene of this restatement, was the only great city which could with certainty claim an apostolic founder, and it lies on the fringe of Asia Minor, whence European philosophy had its origin in the past. Was it only coincidence that it became once more the seed-plot of the West?

The development of the Church, both ecclesiastically and intellectually, gave less and less place to the Jewish Christian, and he tended gradually to disappear from it. After the second century, Hebrew thought, although it still exercised through the Old Testament, a controlling influence, made no fresh contribution to Christianity. The struggle between Hebraism and Hellenism which had begun on other fields, long before Jesus Christ appeared on earth, had ended in the victory of the latter. It was not a victory of the West over the East, for Hellenism itself,

[1] Streeter, *The Four Gospels*, p. 468.

although the spirit of Greece had breathed upon it, had much that was Oriental in its component elements. Thus defeated, the Jew began to pass outside the Church into heresy, as did, indeed, the victorious Hellene on his side.

The Judaizers of the New Testament appear to have exerted but little influence in the following generation, though Justin tells of successors (*Dial.*, XLVII f.); some of whom, however, were content with keeping the Law themselves and not insisting that Gentiles should be subject to it. The principal Jewish heresy was that of the Ebionites, a term first used by Irenaeus (I, xxvi, 2), and probably derived from the Hebrew word for "poor". Eusebius, who says that it was applied to them"from the first", explains it as given on account of the "poor and low opinions about Christ" which they held (III, xxvii, 1). Whether this derivation is correct or not, what is certain is that these and kindred heresies tended to deny the Incarnation and to regard Jesus as a mere man and born of men. Such are mentioned by Justin (*op. cit.*, XLVIII). Those critics who look upon St. Paul as the real founder of "developed" Christianity consider that they represent its original form. Some Ebionites, however, whilst rejecting any kind of eternal Sonship, accepted the supernatural birth. The earliest Ebionites were found in the East, some lived in communities beyond Jordan and may have been recruited from among those who abandoned Jerusalem in A.D. 66. Irenaeus noted as one of their characteristics that they adored Jerusalem as if it had been the house of God (I, xxvi, 2). In the West, they were represented by the Elchasites, so-called from the *Book of Helxai* which was said to have fallen from heaven with strange secret doctrines. As the movement did not appear in Rome until the beginning of the third century, when it was introduced by Alcibiades of Apamea (Hippolytus, IX, 13–17), its connexion with the earlier movement is not very clear. There were Ebionites in the fourth century, for Epiphanius devotes much attention to them (*Haer.*, XXX), though the connexion with the Clementine Romances which he propounds is probably a mistake.[1]

If many Jewish heresies regarded Jesus as a mere man, the last of a series of prophets who had been the bearers of the divine revelation, others were pronouncedly docetic in tone and presented Him in such a way as to destroy His true humanity and to reduce the experiences which He underwent to mere illusions. In modern times it is the divinity of Jesus which arouses difficulty; we must not forget that in the first days of the Church the humanity was much more of a stumbling-block. Those who held docetic views were naturally put to great shifts

[1] cf. E. Schwartz, *Zeit. für die N.T. Wissenschaft*, XXXI, p. 151 ff.

to explain the various narratives in the gospels; incidentally some of them preferred Mark to the rest (Iren., III, xi, 7). Many of these attempted explanations are truly amazing. An example may be quoted from the source, possibly part of the *Gospel of Peter*, which lies behind one of the Latin Infancy Gospels.[1] It purports to give an account of the birth of Jesus—but what is born is nothing human, but a light. This by a process of consolidation gradually takes on the form of a child.

Before proceeding to consider the various Gnostic heresies, mention may be made of Cerinthus, the Egyptian heretic, who forms a kind of link between them and the Ebionites; for Irenaeus comments on the similarity of their views (I, xxvi, 2), and the *Epistle of the Apostles*, I,[2] couples him with Simon as a false apostle. So far as is known, Cerinthus had no influence in the West, though the actual name (a strange one)[3] is to be found in a pagan inscription now in the Lateran Museum.[4] Like Marcion, he made a distinction between the supreme deity and the creator and some of his views are akin to those of the Monarchians.

The most active and significant movement of thought in our period was carried on by that congeries of sects which bear the title of Gnostic. Its effect upon the development of Christian ideas and institutions was so considerable that a detailed survey is demanded, even though, in the West, its direct influence was not so great as in the East. Many of the leading exponents of Gnosticism did indeed make their way to Rome and other centres in the West, but their ideas were too speculative to find there any permanent home, except among those Christians, and they formed a decreasing number in proportion to the rest, who had themselves come from the East.

Whether Gnosticism is rightly regarded as a Christian heresy, or merely as a species of Oriental philosophy which attached itself to Christianity among other systems of thought, has been much disputed. Irenaeus held that the Gnostic teachers borrowed their views, with but a change of name, from pagan thinkers (II, xiv, 1 ff.); whilst Hippolytus scornfully likened them to cobblers patching together the blunders of the ancients (V, 6). He looked upon the Gnostic systems as combinations of heathenism and philosophy—the Valentinians, for example, got their ideas from Pythagoras and Plato—which had no right to the name of Christian (VI, 21).[5] The Gnostics themselves, however, insisted that they were Christians; and not only so, but

---

[1] See M. R. James, *Latin Infancy Gospels*, p. 66 ff.   [2] *Apoc. N.T.*, p. 485.
[3] Names ending in *-inthos* seem to go back to Minoan times: cf. *labyrinthos*.
[4] In Marucchi, p. 414.
[5] Justin tells us that the title Christian, like that of philosopher, was applied rather loosely (I *Apol.*, XXVI).

that they were Christians of a superior order to whom had been committed a "secret tradition" by the apostles themselves.[1] To this claim there was an obvious reply. The apostles would surely have entrusted any secret teaching to those whom they themselves had appointed over the Churches (Iren., III, iii, 1). None the less the fact remains that the Gnostics claimed the title of Christian, and recent scholarship tends to accept their claim. Burkitt,[2] for instance, pointed out that in all Gnostic systems the central figure was Jesus the Saviour, though salvation might consist only in "knowledge",[3] and very diverse ideas about Him might be held. In other words the rise of Gnosticism was a sign "not that the Christian had lapsed into the pagan, but rather that the victory of Christianity over paganism had begun".[4]

Orthodox opinion looked upon Simon Magus as the originator of Gnosticism, a convenient and useful attribution which was calculated to discredit the movement in the eyes of all who had read, or who would read Acts 8 : 9 ff. It is quite probable that a teacher of this name flourished in Samaria and drew to himself a following; but it is difficult to suppose that he was the Simon mentioned in Acts.[5] Samaria was notorious as a centre of religious syncretism and would provide a suitable environment for the growth of views such as those generally described as Gnostic. Irenaeus states that Cerdo came to Rome having received his doctrines from the followers of Simon (I, xxvii, 1), but other traditions, of a far from satisfactory character, make Simon himself go to Rome. He plays a big part in the *Clementines* and in some of the apocryphal acts. In the former he is called Simon the Magician,[6] and is said to have come from a village of the Gettones.[7] A sect of Simonians was still in existence in the latter part of the second century (Iren. I, xxiii, 4), and persisted even longer (Euseb., II, xiii, 6).

The task undertaken by the Gnostics was, in their view, identical with that of the Schoolmen of the thirteenth century, being

---

[1] The Naassenes claimed that James, the brother of the Lord, had handed it on to Mariamne (Hippolytus, V, 7). Basilides affirmed that his tradition came from the Lord Himself through Matthias (VII, 20).

[2] In his valuable and sympathetic study, *Church and Gnosis*, pp. viii f., 87 f.

[3] The story of the Fall in Genesis makes knowledge equivalent to sin, as Hegel has pointed out (*Phil. of Hist.*, p. 333).

[4] Preuschen, quoted by Edwyn Bevan in *Hibt. Journ.*, October 1912, p. 152.

[5] Justin, I *Apol.*, XXVI, does not definitely identify Simon with Simon Magus.

[6] As also by Irenaeus (I, xxiii, 1). Rendel Harris in *The Expositor*, 1902, V, p. 190 ff., identified him with the Simon, a native of Cyprus (cf. Acts 13 : 8), employed by Felix, Governor of Judaea (see Josephus, *Antiq.*, XX, vii, 2).

[7] The statement in *Sib. Orac.*, III, 63, that evil would come from the stock of Sebaste (Samaria) has been applied to Simon; but R. H. Charles, *Ascension of Isaiah*, p. lxviii, thinks that Sebaste has no geographical connexion in this passage and that the reference is to Nero Redivivus.

nothing less than the restatement of Christian truth in the literary and scientific terms of the day. The spread of the Gospel in a Graeco-Roman civilization certainly demanded such a restatement, for the ideas of God and the world contained in the Old Testament were not well adapted to such an environment. Above all, the eschatological teaching which formed so large a part of the original Gospel was unacceptable. There were, however, some Gnostics who found nothing limiting in Jewish and Semitic ideas.[1]

A positive exposition of the Gnostic scheme can only be attempted in brief outline, for the subject is obscure and not of general interest. The Gnostics faced two major problems, the existence of evil, and the reconciliation of the finite and the infinite. The fact of evil was accounted for by dualism, that is, the belief that two opposing deities, one good, the other evil, control the destinies of the world. Both physical and moral evil, between which they made little distinction, have their root in matter. From this various consequences must follow. For example, the world itself cannot have been created by the good God, since it is material; nor could Jesus have taken actual flesh and blood. Man himself has within him a divine spark, but, since it is contained in a material body, his life is one perpetual struggle. The gap between the finite and the infinite they met by presupposing a number of emanations from the deity, a doctrine that was not without its parallels in later Judaism in which the angels were so regarded.[2]

Mankind was divided into three classes. The spiritual, in whom the divine element was supreme and whose salvation was assured (these were the Gnostics); the psychical,[3] in whom it was mixed with material elements, their future was uncertain and depended upon the victory of one element or the other (these were the ordinary Christians); and the material, in whom the divine element was subordinated.

One reason why Gnosticism never had the same attraction for the West as for Orientals has already been mentioned; it was too speculative and theoretical. Its doctrines, indeed, have the appearance of having originated with thinkers whose imagination was greater than their intelligence; for speculation may easily become over-subtle, and the thinker more anxious to display the sharpness of his weapons and his own skill in wielding them, than to arrive at the truth. Truth, indeed, may be counted as a poor prize when compared with novelty. Another example

[1] Hegesippus stated that Palestinian Gnosticism derived from Jewish sources (Euseb., IV, xxii, 5).
[2] See Abelson, *Jewish Mysticism*, p. 54.
[3] Tertullian in his Montanist days called the Catholics "psychic" (*De Monog.*, I).

of the lack of relevance to practical life can be found in the Gnostic idea of salvation which consists in knowledge.[1] It was, as Gwatkin has said, "much more at home in cosmogonies than in a world of sinners" (*Early Church Hist.*, II, p. 21). Another weakness revealed by Gnosticism when compared with Catholic Christianity—perhaps not entirely unconnected with its over-intellectualized outlook—was a quite inadequate conception of the Church and of the obligations attending membership in the Body of Christ.

But if the Gnostics had an imperfect idea of the Church, some of them at least attached a high value to rites and ceremonies. This may seem inconsistent with the theory that all matter was evil, but was no doubt based on practical considerations. It is an established fact that ritual makes a strong appeal to certain types of mind, and if the Gnostic sects hoped to compete success-fully with the Church and with the mystery religions, some kind of ceremonial was essential. Gnostics of a stricter type, how-ever, rejected such outward aids and attractions, insisting that worship must be of a purely spiritual nature.

In their attitude to the body, the different sects, and even the different individuals who composed them, exhibited a like incon-sistency. Accepting the theory that matter was evil, some treated it with harshness and severity in order to bring it into subjection or, it may be, to demonstrate their contempt for all that con-cerned it; others, denying that the material could affect the spiritual, plunged into all kinds of excesses. Thus from the same root grew up asceticism and gross immorality. The evidence of the writings recently discovered in Egypt shows, however, that many Gnostics lived lives of strict morality; though the presence of some who behaved very differently is admitted, even in Gnostic sources.[2] Hippolytus readily believes that for the initiates there were secret orgies (I. proem). There were some, too, who added the practice of magic to immoral habits of life; such was Marcus, who led many astray in the days of Irenaeus (I, xiii, 1 ff.). That the Gnostics should deny the resurrection of the flesh was natural, in view of their attitude towards matter, and this denial may account for the general unwillingness which they are supposed to have shown to seal their witness by martyrdom.

The Gnostics attached great importance to the influence of the written word, and Irenaeus speaks of "the indescribable number of apocryphal and spurious books forged by them"

---

[1] The idea that knowledge and salvation are identical is Pythagorean. Even the orthodox Gnostic exalted knowledge above faith. Clement of Alexandria, for instance, held that the first step in the Christian life was from paganism to faith, the next from faith to knowledge (*Strom.*, VII, 10).

[2] See, for example, *Pistis Sophia*, 387.

(I, xx, 1). Much of their immense output has perished, but in recent years some of it has been recovered in Egypt, mostly the product of obscure sects. Many of the surviving apocryphal gospels and acts have a Gnostic tendency, though the mere presence of Gnostic ideas or phraseology is in early days no proof of heresy.[1] Like the Essenes[2] they made much of the possession of secret books which contained the keys to perfect knowledge.[3]

If a great deal of Gnostic literature was worthy of the strictures of Irenaeus, such as the *Gospel of Judas* which he tells us the Cainites had produced (I, xxxi, 1), some of it attained a high level of usefulness. In the work of exegesis Gnostic scholars may have given a lead to their more orthodox brethren. Basilides, for instance, compiled twenty-four books on the gospels,[4] whilst Valentinus produced many homilies.[5] The Muratorian Fragment, in rejecting the writings of Valentinus, Basilides, and their fellows, mentions that they had composed a long[6] book of Psalms.

Irenaeus has observed the readiness with which heretical teachers break away from the central body in order to start their own societies, and attributes the tendency to their being blind to the truth and therefore apt to wander off in all directions (I, xxviii, 1; V, xx, 1). The "dissidence of dissent" is already at work, and was certainly a feature of Gnosticism.

Gnosticism had its origin in the East and flourished especially in Syria and Alexandria. It was in the latter city that the most famous leaders arose, such as Basilides, Carpocrates, and, above all, Valentinus, who later came to Rome. His system is well known owing to the attention which it received from Irenaeus.[7] This system, in addition to being the best known, was probably also the most orthodox and the least given to curious speculations. But the number of sects was almost endless, and they differed among themselves to such an unbelievable extent that any attempt to delineate their varieties would be an unprofitable enterprise. Irenaeus, who does not miss the opportunity of jibing at their patent inconsistencies and contrasting their variations with the unity of the Catholic faith, states that they took pride in novel doctrines which they invented daily; novel

---

[1] Ignatius is full of Gnostic terms: e.g. *Eph.* init.: πλήρωμα, I, 1: φύσει and the very striking phrase in *Magn.*, viii, 2: λόγος ἀπὸ σιγῆς προελθών (cf. *Wisdom*, xviii, 14).   [2] See Josephus, *De Bell. Jud.*, II, viii, 12.

[3] Origen, *De Princip.*, IV, ii, 3 (Greek fragt.).

[4] Clement of Alexandria, *Strom.*, IV, 12.

[5] Tertullian, *De Carne Christi*, XVII, XX.

[6] That is, if we accept Zahn's proposed emendation for line 83, where *marcioni* is taken to be a mistranslation of μακρόν.

[7] See, further, R. P. Casey, "The Eastern and Italian Schools of Valentinians", in *Harvard Theol. Rev.*, 1930, XXIII, p. 291 ff.

doctrines were, indeed, a sign of "perfection". The same teachers would hold different ideas at different times, and so they never came to well-grounded knowledge (I, x, 2; xviii, 1; xxi, 5; III, xxiv, 2).

In spite, however, of the inconsistency of its various advocates and the multiplicity of its sects, Gnosticism undoubtedly exercised a remarkable influence and made a very wide appeal. In the early second century, when it began first to flourish, men were in a state of deep perplexity owing to the delay of the Lord's coming and to the anomalies in the world around them. They were thus a ready field in which the seeds of novel teaching could take root. One cause for its attraction was the spirit of assurance displayed by its various exponents. The Gnostic leaders spoke with much personal authority and highly extolled their several notions; in which, no doubt, many of them sincerely believed. Such fanaticism is always attractive to the weak and curious.[1] There was also the claim to a secret tradition derived from the Lord Himself. This could not fail to be very impressive. Gnostic writings, in significant contrast with the canonical gospels and the Acts, are full of discourses said to have been uttered by the Lord after His resurrection. There was, however, another side. The movement was not all magic and curious speculation, and some of its writings exhibit deep spiritual insight. This is true above all of the *Hymn of the Soul* of which A. A. Bevan has written: "Gnosticism is here displayed to us not as it appeared to its enemies, not as a tissue of fantastic speculations, but as it was in reality, at least in some of its adherents, a new religion" (*Texts and Studies*, V, No. 3, p. 7).

Gnosticism grew up and developed in the East, but it was not long before traces of it became only too evident in the West; the Gnostic leaders in point of fact made special efforts to spread their doctrines in the capital of the Empire by personal visits. In the middle of the second century this migration had hardly begun, if Justin is a reliable authority, but before the century was ended Rome itself and the congregations on the Rhone had been deeply affected. Into North Africa, however, it seems never to have penetrated; the soil was too arid, although later it was to prove not unfriendly to the Neoplatonists.

In the time of Hyginus, Bishop of Rome *c.* 138–144, Cerdo came from Syria (Iren., I, xxvii, 1); he was later to influence Marcion. In the same episcopate another Gnostic leader of more profound significance also came to the Eternal City; this was

---

[1] The extent to which such things as British Israelitism and astrology prevail at the present day makes it impossible for us to be unduly scornful of the superstitious weaknesses of the early centuries. For the same spirit is exhibited in both alike.

Valentinus (Iren., III, iv, 3) of whom mention has already been made. He remained on in Rome for many years and acquired such influence that Tertullian could state, probably with exaggeration, that Gnosticism was at this time stronger there than in any other place. The same authority informs us that Valentinus retained his membership of the Church for a considerable time but was eventually excommunicated after a number of lapses and reconciliations (*De Praes.*, XXX). Among his followers were Ptolemy whose *Letter to Flora* has been preserved by Epiphanius (*Haer.*, XXXIII, 3–7), and Heracleon who wrote a *Commentary on St. John.* Marcus, to whom reference has been made, was also a Valentinian, though quite unworthy of his master. Valentinus seems to have left Rome in the days of Anicetus, in whose episcopate a certain female teacher of Gnosticism, Marcellina by name, took up her residence there and led many astray (Iren., I, xxv, 6).

But the Gnostics did not have it all their own way. The unswerving testimony of Polycarp during his visit to Rome to the identity of the faith of the Church with that handed down by the apostles induced many to abandon their Gnostic views (Iren., III, iii, 4). None the less one of his own disciples, Florinus, the friend of Irenaeus, fell under such influences, and received an epistle from the latter (*c.* 190) imploring him to give up his heretical beliefs (Euseb., V, xx, 1 ff.). But Gnosticism in Rome and in the West generally had but a fitful existence; it may have flamed up for a time, but it soon burnt itself out in the absence of fresh fuel. That it persisted for a time, however, we have evidence in a Gnostic burial-place in Rome, dating from the beginning of the third century.[1]

The most potent danger of Gnosticism to the Church, however, lay in its secret and pervasive methods. Those who held Gnostic views considered that they had every right to remain in the Church, and, indeed, that they were perfectly orthodox, though adding certain esoteric views to their orthodoxy. Even Valentinus, as we have seen, was long a member of the Roman Church. No doubt they formed cells within the larger congregations and drew to themselves such souls as seemed especially likely to accept their teaching. Those who had been brought up as pagans, and even in the later part of the second century they probably formed the bulk of the average congregation, would find much that was familiar in their doctrines, and this would make them all the more attractive. The different systems seem not to have been at all well known to those writers who undertook to reply to them; Irenaeus, for example, claims that he was

[1] It is a vault in the Viale Manzoni: see G. Bendelli in *Monumenti Antichi*, 1922, XXVIII.

a more effective apologist for the Catholic faith than those who had gone before him, not through any special merit of his own, but merely because he possessed more accurate information as to Gnostic ideas (IV, Pref., 2); so, too, Hippolytus claims to be the first to have full knowledge of the teaching of the Peratae (V, 12).

It was the fashion at one time to regard Marcion as a Gnostic. This was a mistake, for though he came under Gnostic influences, especially as exerted by the Syrian Cerdo,[1] his outlook and teaching were quite distinct. For one thing he was little affected by Hellenic ideas. Burkitt has called him "a great and original religious genius, the most remarkable Christian of the second century". He goes on to say that "The essential fact about Marcion is that he was a Christian Dissenter. Other heretics were heretics because they were only half-Christian, but Marcion's religion was essentially Christian and Biblical" (*The Rel. of the Manichees*, p. 80).

This extraordinary man was the son of the Bishop of Sinope, and as Sinope had been colonized by Italians in the time of Julius Caesar, was perhaps of Italian descent. In the early part of the second century, when Marcion was growing to manhood, there was much religious activity in Pontus, the famous "prophet" Alexander of Abonuteichos was a neighbour and contemporary, and he may well have caught the general infection. We are told that he was compelled to separate himself from the Catholic Church, c. 137.[2] Soon afterwards he is found at Rome where he signalized his coming by a gift of £2,000 to the Church, a gift which was returned when his questionable position became manifest.

The teaching of Marcion was really an attempt at simplification in the face of the prevailing syncretism; he was a disciple of St. Paul striving to restore what he held to be his master's doctrine. Neander has well called him the first Protestant, and in some sense he anticipated the work of Luther, and even nearer to his own times, that of Augustine. Although he has many affinities with the fourth gospel (Harnack, *op. cit.*, p. 236 ff.), Marcion considered that the disciples of Jesus had failed to understand Him. The work of Jesus was to redeem us, not from demons, death, sin, or guilt, but from the world and its Creator and Lord, the God of the Old Testament, and to make us children of the true God whom He came to reveal. He found support for his distinction in the reference to "the god of this world" (2 Cor. 4 : 4). Moreover the refusal to call down fire from heaven showed that Jesus was no Son of Jehovah (Luke 9 : 54 f.). The

[1] See Harnack, *Marcion: das Evangelium vom fremden Gott*, p. 32* ff.
[2] The Chronicle of Edessa says in 449 of the Seleucid era: see Hallier, *Texte und Unters.*, IX, Pt. I, p. 89.

latter was manifestly not the true God, otherwise He would not have made men so weak and helpless, or have exhibited such favouritism in His dealings.[1] The attempt to combine a belief in Jesus with a rejection of the Old Testament was, of course, impossible to maintain, and is evidence of Marcion's lack of depth as a teacher. He was, however, conscious as few men were in that age of the limitations of knowledge,[2] and may have recognized the inconsistency without striving to remove it. Another defect of his system, when compared with that of the Church, was the absence of any interest in sacramental theology,[3] though in practice baptism was highly regarded and preparations of an ascetic nature demanded (Tertullian, *Adv. Marc.*, I, 29 and IV, 11).

Strangely enough, Marcion, although he rejected Jehovah as the supreme God, believed in the historical accuracy of the Old Testament,[4] and it is probable that he was the first to conceive the idea of putting alongside it another collection of writings. As he held that the gospels and epistles used by the Church had been falsified, his New Testament was of a restricted character, for he accepted Luke only of the gospels,[5] and ten of the Pauline epistles; all of these he drastically revised in order to remove what he regarded as interpolations.[6]

The followers of Marcion, like the Gnostics, split up into a number of sects, the principal of which was led by Apelles.[7] Apelles was the greatest and best known of the Marcionites, and in many ways the most consistent, although he differed from his master by rejecting the idea of two gods and the infallibility of the Old Testament, which he ascribed to one of the fallen angels. Like Marcion, Apelles came to Rome. One strange aspect of his career was his submission to the influence of a certain Philumene, "a maiden possessed of the devil" according to Rhodo, to expound whose teaching he composed a volume entitled *Phaneroseis*. Other Marcionite leaders whose names have been preserved (Euseb., V, xiii, 3 f.) had but little significance for the West, except Lucanus or Lucianus who flourished at Rome and founded a sect which bore his name. For knowledge of his teaching, which seems to have departed from orthodoxy much more widely than that of Marcion and Apelles, we are indebted mainly to Tertullian.

[1] Harnack has collected a list of the "offences" of the God of the Old Testament: *op. cit.*, p. 141 ff.
[2] Harnack, *Mission und Ausbreitung*, p. 256 (E.T., I, p. 299).
[3] *op. cit.*, p. 250 (E.T., I, p. 289). [4] Harnack, *Marcion*, p. 67.
[5] It is not known why he chose this gospel. Harvey, *Irenaeus*, I, p. 216, says that he believed that it was written by the Lord Himself.
[6] The contents of Marcion's Gospel and Apostolicon are outlined in Harnack, *op. cit.*, pp. 39*–236*. [7] On Apelles, see Harnack, *op. cit.*, pp. 323–339.

In addition to various denunciations of Marcion and his disciples by well-known writers such as Irenaeus, Hippolytus, and Tertullian, whose works have survived, there was also an earlier attack by Justin.[1] Writers, too, of less established orthodoxy made it their business to oppose the Marcionites; among them were Bardaisan[2] who wrote in Syriac (Euseb., IV, xxx, 1), and Rhodo, an Asiatic who came to Rome and was a disciple of Tatian (Euseb., V, xiii, 1 ff.).

Marcion was a skilful organizer and his Church spread with extraordinary rapidity, in spite of the refusal of his followers to marry and beget children, and by the middle of the second century it had become a serious rival of the Church in almost every province of the Empire. Justin says that it was found among all races of mankind (I *Apol.*, XXVI), and by the end of the century it had, according to Tertullian (*Adv. Marc.*, V), filled the whole world. In the West its chief centres were Rome, Lyons, and Carthage. Constantine tried to suppress it (Euseb., *Vit. Const.*, III, 64), but it still continued, and as late as the fifth century was receiving attention from Catholic antagonists.[3] But by this time its race was nearly run, even in the East, and the Marcionites were gradually becoming, as Burkitt has said, "an unlicensed and vanishing society" (*Church and Gnosis*, p. 112). But they had played a great part in Eastern Christianity and not least in the contribution which they made to the "new theology" of Mani.

Although Manichaeism did not become active in the West until well on into the third century it will be convenient to deal with it here; more especially as Marcion supplied some of its very heterogeneous elements. The founder, Mani, was born in 215 and spent his boyhood in South Babylonia. At the age of twenty-four he set out to convert the world to a new religion which was to supersede and include all others. Much of its contents was drawn from Zoroaster, some from Buddhism, a little from Hellenism, and a great deal from various types of Christianity.[4] Mani looked back to Jesus as his divine forerunner, opening his letters with the phrase "Mani, apostle of Jesus Christ". He himself claimed to be the Paraclete of the fourth gospel. Mani exalted asceticism and regarded the material world as the province of the devil, held that good and evil were co-eternal, and condemned marriage. Here can be traced the

[1] Mentioned in Euseb., IV, xi, 8 f. and quoted by Irenaeus. For others see Euseb., IV, xxiv and xxv.
[2] He was in turn attacked by a Marcionite, Prepons by name: see Hippolytus, VII, 31.　　　　　　　　　　　　　　[3] Harnack, *Marcion*, p. 307 ff.
[4] Burkitt in his *Rel. of the Manichees* considers that the kernel of the system was definitely Christian. Euseb., VII, xxxi, 1, it may be noted, regarded it as a heresy. The newly found documents in Central Asia confirm this.

influence of Persian dualism and ideas which became popular during the Middle Ages in various Western heresies. Mani paid a visit to India where he founded a Church, but later returned to Persia which soon became the headquarters of an organization having adherents in all parts of the world. In 273, however, he met his death, by crucifixion, mainly it is said, through the jealousy of the Persian religious authorities.

Mani left behind him numerous writings, none of which has survived in full, so we are dependent on notices of other writers and the recent discovery of a few fragments.[1] His system, which was considerably modified by his followers, appealed to the multitude by its strict morality, whilst a severely rational outlook attracted the educated. This rational outlook, however, did not preclude an interest in elaborate speculations—such speculations are, indeed, frequently an unexpected fruit of the rational spirit—and a number of Gnostic writings were given a high place in the literature of the movement. The various apocryphal acts, which circulated under the names of different apostles, were formed into a kind of corpus and probably displaced the canonical Acts of the Apostles.

Manichaeism spread rapidly in all directions from its original home, and reached China in one direction and North Africa in the other. By the close of the third century it was a rival of Christianity and Neoplatonism for the religious allegiance of the Empire.[2] In North Africa, to which it is supposed to have been carried by Adamantus, one of the twelve apostles of Mani, it soon aroused the alarm of the imperial authorities and an edict was sent by Diocletian ordering its suppression. In spite of this and later attempts to check its progress, Manichaeism continued to flourish in North Africa, especially among the native population, though not among them alone, for Augustine, it will be remembered, was a Manichee for nine years of his life. It also persisted in the remainder of the West, taking various guises in different parts. The Priscillianist heresy which sprang up in Spain and southern Gaul in the fourth century may have been influenced by it, whilst its most famous manifestation occurred in much the same region with the rise of the Albigenses. But if it survived in the West it was in Asia that its main field of development undoubtedly lay. Here it lasted for a thousand years and was only finally submerged beneath the ever-widening flood of Islam.

[1] On the latest literature see C. R. C. Allbury in *J.T.S.*, 1938, XXXIX, p. 337 ff.
[2] So Harnack, *Dogmengesch.*, I, p. 766 f.

THE GROWTH OF DOGMA

The challenge of the heretics was met by an appeal to history. If the Gnostics claimed to possess a secret tradition, the Catholics replied by citing the open tradition in each several Church, guaranteed by the succession of its bishops from the apostles. Emphasis was also laid on St. Paul's teaching that the Church was to be one in faith; whilst intercourse between the different Churches helped to ward off attempts at innovation in any one of them. The heretical novelties were often concerned with abstract points of speculation and endeavoured to explain and elucidate matters which lay beyond human ken. Simple Christians, especially in the West, were not greatly interested in such activities. Ultimately, heresies were to be overcome and the authentic tradition of the Church to be preserved rather by the common sense and loyalty of such, than by the skilled arguments of the learned. None the less it was a weakness in the pre-Nicene Church in the West that, largely owing to the absence of an educated laity, there was a gap between the ordinary Christian and the theologian. In the East the laity soon joined in the exciting pastime of theological controversy; but in the West there was no such development and the rights of the common folk were safeguarded mainly by the bishops of Rome whose outlook was unspeculative and practical.[1] A study of later developments suggests that while the Greek Church met heresy by argument and so built up a Christian philosophy, the Roman Church imposed silence by an appeal to a rigid dogmatic standard held to have come down from the apostles. This double tendency was already at work before the age of the councils.

Thus the growth of dogma, especially in the West, was due to practical needs; the necessity for exposing and excluding false and dangerous teaching and the ambition to preserve for future generations the faith handed down from the past. This, however, involved an added emphasis on authority, and was not without its own dangers, for it might result in a conception of the faith as something static, and sacrifice truth on the altar of unity. Unity is bought at too high a price if truth is in any way suppressed, and creeds, instead of representing the glad pro-

[1] cf. J. Lebreton, "La foi populaire et la théologie savante", in *Rev. d'Hist. ecclés.*, 1924.

fession of those who believe, are transformed into instruments for searching out the heretical.

The most certain thing that may be affirmed of all dogma is that it is inadequate; an attempt to express, in human words and forms, eternal truths which ever elude them. None the less, dogma is a necessity for any religious organization after its initial stages; there must be a definite pattern of fundamental beliefs. For dogma not only crystallizes experience, it may also promote it, and the intellectual as well as the emotional needs of mankind demand satisfaction.

Christianity, however, did not resist heresy and overcome the paganism with which often enough it was allied merely by appealing to tradition. It overcame them by absorbing into itself the best elements of its rivals and by claiming them for its own. "Whatever things have been rightly said among men belong to us Christians", so Justin affirmed (II *Apol.*, XIII). But it must not be supposed that the Gospel was simply a nucleus round which every variety of current religious ideas might gather, or that the Church submitted too readily to outside influences. Had it done so it would scarcely have differed from its contemporaries. If it borrowed freely it consistently stamped its borrowings with something of itself, and so preserved its own peculiar identity. The real miracle of Christianity is not that it survived amid the welter of competing religions, but that it made so few concessions to them. It was an age of tolerance and had Christianity been less rigid it might well have been submerged. None the less the influx of pagan ideas was considerable, and was largely the result of the noiseless pressure of the inarticulate masses. That is why medieval religion contained so considerable an element of pagan ideas, survivals of folk-religion which the Church had "scotched", but by no means destroyed. Under a thin disguise they still maintained their existence.

Such accommodation to pagan ideas may have been justified on the ground that it was better to have a superstitious Christian than a superstitious heathen, and with the hope that in due course unworthy ideas would be purged from the convert. Unhappily such a hope proved an illusion, for there were few who attained to sufficient spiritual insight to know what to reject. But the thought and culture upon which the intellectual life of the age had been nourished was not entirely a snare; it had its better side, and after all it was possible that God had not left the heathen world entirely without witness of Himself.

Accretions on the faith came in mainly from the Graeco-Roman world and were Hellenic in character. But there were other sources of influence; the apocryphal literature, for example, contains large masses of mythological and romantic material of a very different nature. These, too, found a home in some sections of the Church, even if the learned despised them. For it must be remembered that it was not only the ideas of the learned, but the superstitions of the vulgar which made their way into Catholic faith and practice. The notions and customs to which men had been accustomed since childhood were not easily surrendered when they became Christians. The tragic thing about such retentions is that often enough it is the less desirable elements which tend to persist in the new environment. Such at least is the experience of missionaries in the present day.[1]

So began a process which Harnack has described in its more advanced stages. "Saints and intercessors, who were thus semigods, poured into the Church. Local cults and holy places were instituted. The different provinces of life were distributed afresh among guardian spirits. The old gods returned; only their masks were new. Annual festivals were noisily celebrated. Amulets and charms, relics and bones of the saints were all objects of desire" (*Mission und Ausbreitung*, p. 328, E.T., I, p. 395).

The People of God under the Old Covenant had had their own struggle with heathenism, and because their hold on the fundamental truths was less firm, and the body of religious experience which they possessed more meagre, they were compelled to take up a less receptive attitude. It might have been well for the Christian Church if it had been as strict. But the example of the Old Testament, paradoxically enough, seems to have excused a spirit of complacency. Did it not teach the legitimacy of learning from those outside; for Moses, although he was taught by Jehovah Himself, had not disdained the counsel of Jethro. This spirit became even more prevalent as the ceremonial part of the Jewish Law began to be suspected of a heathen origin. This was the opinion of Chrysostom,[2] who though he belongs to the East and to a period later than that of our study, may well have had those who anticipated him in the West.

In the days before Constantine there was much difference of opinion among Christian teachers as to the proper attitude to be taken up towards the philosophy and learning which was part of the world in which they had grown up. In the East, and at Alexandria in particular, learning was highly valued by the

[1] cf. Westermann, *Africa and Christianity*, p. 23: "School teaching will seldom succeed in destroying religious and magical beliefs altogether, but it will push them into the lower regions of the mind, and gradually their best features, reverence for the ancestors and gods and the moral sanctions growing out of them, will disappear, while the darker sides, fear of spirits, spells and witches remain and enter into an unholy alliance with scientific and religious ideas learnt at school".

[2] "The sacrifices and the cleansings and the new moons and the ark and the temple itself had their origin from heathen grossness" (*Hom. in Matt.* 6 : 3).

cultivated. Clement looked upon philosophy as a schoolmaster to bring men to Christ (*Strom.*, I, v, 28); but he complained that the average Christian was as frightened of it as of a hobgoblin. In the West there was not the same admiration for philosophical studies, though Irenaeus had a high opinion of Plato (III, xxv, 5); and Minucius Felix, not unexpectedly, regards Christianity as the equivalent of true wisdom (*Octav.* I). But to Tertullian philosophy was the mother of heresy, and he could ask with bitter scorn: "What has Athens to do with Jerusalem, the academy with the Church?" (*De Praes.*, VII). From the middle of the third century, however, in order to facilitate the evangelization of the educated heathen, dangerous concessions were made; "a grave intellectual blot . . . worse perhaps in the West than in the East".[1]

In the post-Nicene period the Church, after much hesitation, took over what was best in the literary tradition of the Empire, a momentous decision, for the Church thus became the chief means of its survival. But the hesitation was real and significant. We find it epitomized in Jerome, who was both a considerable scholar and a devout Christian. The manner in which now one side of his nature, now another, swayed his mind is well illustrated from his writings. He records a dream in which he was condemned as a mere Ciceronian (*Epist.*, XXII), and in a letter to Pope Damasus he denounces pagan literature as only fit for demons (*Epist.*, XXI). But, in another mood, he upholds the value of learning and justifies it by St. Paul's use of Aratus and Menander (*Epist.*, LXX) and even ventures to assert that Christian girls should be familiar with both Greek and Latin writers from their earliest youth (*Epist.*, CVII).

One of the attractions of Christianity, however, to thinking men was that, as its system developed, it showed itself capable of providing answers to many of the great ultimate questions which contemporary philosophers were apt to avoid or leave unsolved, either from despair or from a too ready contentment with solutions handed down from the past. Thus the labour of Christian thinkers and scholars gradually placed the Gospel in a wider setting and achieved for it a more universal significance.

After the second century and the contest with Gnosticism the development of thought took on new aspects and new standards began to be set up. By this time there was an especial value placed upon all that could claim to be apostolic. So the apostolic writings, the apostolic orders, and the Apostles' Creed came to hold a unique place. This is doubtless one reason for the appearance at this epoch of the many romances which profess to give details of their lives.

[1] Bigg, *The Church's Task in the Roman Empire*, p. 83.

Christianity is a historic religion with its basis firmly established on a considerable body of historic facts. These, it must not be forgotten, were accepted long before attempts were made to build up dogmas upon them. The Atonement, to take a doctrine which during our period had not yet become the subject of controversy, might be differently explained; no one questioned that Christ was a Saviour. But dogma was necessary in spite of the danger of too great a striving to enforce orthodoxy. This may eventually flare up into persecution.

The definition of Christian doctrine may be said to begin with the third century, though before that thinkers were feeling their way towards formulations. The chief interest at this stage was in the relations of the persons of the Trinity—that of the two natures in Christ belongs to the post-Nicene age, though incidentally it affected the earlier controversies, and, it is worth recalling that, until Abailard gave it a wider application, *theologia* to the Latins meant Christology.

It may be said that until late in the second century Christian thinking had all been done in the East, mainly in Asia Minor, the first home of Greek philosophy. But just as the centre of Greek philosophy had shifted to Athens, so too the rise of the schools of Antioch and Alexandria would once again rob Ionia of its predominance. It was at this period that there also emerged the first typical western theologians in North Africa. It is true that before Tertullian and Cyprian we have, in the West, the names of Justin and Irenaeus, as well as Hippolytus. But all three wrote in Greek, and Justin and Irenaeus came from Asia Minor; whilst Hippolytus can hardly be claimed as having introduced anything specifically Western into Christian thought. That would come with the use of the Latin language.

It was in North Africa that Latin Christianity was first evolved as an intellectual force, and that through the genius of one man, Tertullian.[1] Tertullian was by temperament typical of African Christianity, which has been described as "harsh and hard like the soil and climate". Towards classical learning on its philosophical side he adopted, as we have already seen, an attitude of scornful isolation; but to the part of his early education which formed the staple fabric in that of so many Romans, the law, his attitude was very different; it seemed to enter into the very texture of his mentality, and so great was the legal knowledge exhibited by him that it has led to the suggestion that he was in fact the famous jurist of that name.[2]

Tertullian, with this legal trend, was naturally not so much a

[1] See, further, A. d'Alès, *La Théologie de Tertullien.*
[2] Alexander Beck, "Römisches Recht bei Tert. und Cyprian", in *Schriften der Königsberger Gelehrtengesellschaft*, VII, 2.

pioneer as an organizer of thought; even his bending of the Latin speech to serve the uses of theology may not have been entirely novel; whilst the "legalizing" of the Gospel had been begun long before. In his theological ideas he certainly owed much to those who had preceded him, above all to Irenaeus. It might, indeed, be asserted that he took the thought of the latter and pressed it into a legal mould. It has been suggested by Harnack that Tertullian stands to Irenaeus as Calvin did to Luther. The parallel is an apt one, for Calvin approached theology from the standpoint of law; it was not for nothing that he too had had a legal training.[1] It was an easy matter for one who had an intimate knowledge of the Roman penal system and the Roman view of debts to find phraseology in which to state the problems of theology, and in so stating them to give them a twist which definitely modified them. "Tertullian did serious injury to the Church of his own age and of later ages by beginning the process of casting the language of theology in the moulds supplied by the law courts. In the Bible, legal images take their place among a variety of other images; but that is quite another thing from the supremacy which legal conceptions of spiritual things acquired through the reckless use of legal phraseology."[2] It was no doubt because of this obsession with the Roman penal system that in one point at least Tertullian anticipated, if he did not actually originate, a typical Western development: the emphasis which he placed on the importance of the death of Christ. Western theology has always valued the Atonement more highly than Eastern; with the Greek thinkers, the Incarnation is primary.[3]

Tertullian's use of legal phraseology might cramp the Gospel and be misunderstood in the East; but in some respects it seemed to make the doctrine of the Trinity more comprehensible, for *substantia* was used of property [4] and so might be shared by

[1] John Buchan (*Montrose*, p. 48) has pointed out how Calvin's use of legal phraseology set the fashion and was imitated by the Covenanting preachers who constantly speak of "surety", "cautioner", "bond", and "writs". Even Donne adopts a similar usage: see *Sermons*, I and XXXIV.

[2] Hort, *The Ante-Nicene Fathers*, p. 105 f. The following comment of a great medieval scholar is of interest in this connexion: "The civil law of Rome had entered into the composition of the law of the Christian Church at every stage of its formation. Its subtle and unrecognized influence upon forms, institutions, and organizations of the Christian Church—nay, in the West, even upon the very content of the theology—dates from the earliest days of Gentile Christianity. Every growth of systematic theology—at least in the Latin half of Christendom—deepened its influence" (Hastings Rashdall, *Medieval Universities*, ed. Powicke and Emden, I, p. 132).

[3] For Tertullian's application of "legalism" to penance see below, p. 344.

[4] It is a temptation to exaggerate the legalism of Tertullian, as Harnack perhaps does. His "conceptions and expressions . . . were by no means entirely controlled by legal usage, and the philosophical sense of the terms must also be borne in mind" (Bethune-Baker, *Early Hist. of Christian Doctrine*, p. 138, note 2).

T

several *personae*. His influence in the East was, in fact, considerable, it might almost be said decisive, for Bishop Alexander was led to see the dangers of Arianism because his predecessor Dionysius had been a student of the Western Father. In such matters Tertullian was quite orthodox, and if he has been accused of subordinating the Son, it was only in the sense that the Son had His origin in the Father. As Bethune-Baker has said: "Certain crudities of thought may perhaps be detected, but as having developed and created a series of most important doctrinal formulae which became part of the general doctrinal system of the Catholic Church, his importance cannot be over-estimated" (*Early Hist. of Christian Doctrine*, p. 144).

As a thinker, Tertullian is lacking at times in critical power; he is too ready to accept any kind of story which will help his case: as, for example, the forged letter of Marcus Aurelius in reference to the Thundering Legion, and in his representation of the attitude of the emperors in general (*Apol.*, V). A more serious defect was his narrow outlook. For him the rule of faith contained all knowledge, other things were of little consequence. If his mind had moved in a wider orbit it may well be that Montanism would have had no attraction for him.

The next great African Father made no contribution of his own to the development of abstract Christian thought. Cyprian, like Tertullian, had been a lawyer and the effects of his legal training can be seen in his keenness for precedents and perhaps in his lack of reflective power. He did much to propagate the ideas of Tertullian, especially his ethical teaching and the doctrine of merit. Cyprian's range of interests was strangely like that of some of the Church Orders, such as the *Didascalia*; it did not extend beyond ethics and organization, and if the West had produced a Church Order of its own, one would have thought that Cyprian, not Hippolytus, would have been its author. He was, however, above all, a great statesman and administrator of the type of Ambrose and Leo, and his interest in doctrinal matters was practical rather than theoretical. Such questions only became urgent when they were likely to lead to controversies and schism.

After the death of Cyprian, controversies and schisms did indeed break over the African Church; but the most important of them, the Donatist, led right on to the greatest of all African and Western theologians, Augustine. In him Latin Christian thought would find its highest expression and exercise its widest and most enduring influence.

Montanism, the strange sect which drew away Tertullian in his later days, arose in Asia Minor soon after the middle of the second century, and the first reference to it in the West is found in the appeal sent by the martyrs of Lyons and Vienne, by the hands of Irenaeus, to Eleutherus, Bishop of Rome in 177.[1]

The movement is named after Montanus and was a species of revivalism, accompanied by outbursts of prophesying and the gift of tongues. Two women, Priscilla and Maximilla, were associated with Montanus in the leadership of the movement whose headquarters were at Perpuza in Phrygia which was looked upon as the New Jerusalem. Montanism was probably in part a protest against over-organization and over-intellectualism, in part a spontaneous outbreak such as over-organization would attempt to check unduly. The whole history of the Church is full of such outbursts and of the conflict of the religions of authority with the religions of the Spirit.

It is probably better to regard Montanism as a schismatic rather than a heretical movement, for though one section was accused of holding Patripassian views,[2] the main body seems to have been quite orthodox. In the West, where it began to gather influence during the episcopate of Zephyrinus (197–217), it was apparently much more sober than in its original haunts. There was an absence of wild ecstasies, and apparently there were no female prophets. Tertullian, no doubt, had a powerful influence over its development, and, indeed, may have brought to it more than he gained. At any rate it received a favourable reception in Rome, where perhaps the circulation of the writings of Hermas, with their similar outlook, had prepared the way. Before this, Irenaeus had condemned the movement because it denied the gift of prophecy to the Church and rejected the teaching of the fourth gospel.[3] Tertullian claimed that a bishop of Rome whom he does not specify (it was probably Eleutherus)[4] had expressed his approval of Montanism in a letter which was afterwards withdrawn (*Adv. Prax.*, I). The first Montanist teacher to appear in the West was probably Proclus. His views were orthodox and though he came from Asia he may have had a Western origin.[5] He was well received until the arrival of Praxeas, the Modalist leader, who gained the confidence of the

---

[1] Euseb., V, iii, 4; iv. 1 f. See, further, P. de Labriolle, *La Crise montaniste*, p. 213 ff.

[2] Pseudo-Tertullian, *Haer.*, XXI. Hippolytus says that some Montanists had adopted the views of Noetus (VIII, 19).

[3] III, xi, 9. Irenaeus does not specifically mention the Montanists by name but the reference is clear. In view of this it is difficult to account for the theory of Neander that he had been influenced by the movement, unless he had reacted strongly from it. Rendel Harris also thinks that he had been subject to Montanist influences in his early days (*Study of Codex Bezae* in *Texts and Studies*, II, No. 1, p. 194). He thinks that Rome, Carthage, and Lyons all "montanized" in the second century (*op. cit.*, p. 153).

[4] For a discussion of his identity see G. La Piana in *Harvard Theol. Rev.*, 1925, p. 245 f. He thinks that Victor was the bishop.

[5] So Lawlor, *Euseb.*, II, p. 76.

bishop and opened his eyes to its dangers. Tertullian with great scorn exclaims that he thus did two successful jobs for the devil; he expelled prophecy and introduced heresy; he drove out the Paraclete and crucified the Father.[1] Proclus, who remained on in Rome, was later to find an opponent in Gaius, a Roman presbyter. The controversy between them is of much interest, since against the claim of Proclus that Philip and his daughters had prophesied at Hierapolis where their tombs still existed (Euseb., III, xxxi, 1), Gaius retorted by pointing to the trophies of St. Peter and St. Paul in Rome (Euseb., II, xxv, 6 f.).

Though the Jews were not really interested in metaphysical problems, sooner or later Jewish Christians had to think out the relations of Jesus and the Father; but it was the influx of converts accustomed to Greek ways of thought that made the question really urgent. The Church might reject the speculations of the Gnostics, but simple rejection was not enough; the doctrine of the Incarnation must be formulated. In this emergency Christian thinkers were attracted by a term which seemed ready at hand to meet their needs, that of the Logos, or Word of God.

Hellenic thought had consistently regarded the deity as so exalted that only negative propositions could be postulated concerning Him, an attitude which the Schoolmen of the Middle Ages, as followers of Aristotle, would likewise adopt. In the Logos, first used by Heracleitus [2] (c. 500 B.C.), they found a link between the incomprehensible divine nature and mankind. The conception of the Logos as the divine "reason" was, of course, a commonplace of Stoicism, in which system it virtually usurped the place of the deity Himself. It had also been adopted by Philo, the Jewish Alexandrian philosopher, who regarded it as a principle going forth from God and sharing His nature, but distinct and subordinate. Some scholars hold that it was through Philo that the idea penetrated into Christian thought,[3] though Palestinian or Jewish sources are now thought to be much more probable.[4] In the Old Testament there is mention of the Word as a means of God's activity. This is especially clear in Ps.

---

[1] *Adv. Prax.*, I. The extremities to which Tertullian could go may also be seen in his condemnation of episcopacy as unspiritual; no really spiritual Church could be ruled and directed by bishops (*De Pudic.*, XXI).

[2] Heracleitus claimed to be the mouthpiece of the Word, which he probably identified with "fire" and so with the deity: see J. Adam, *Relig. Teachers of Greece*, p. 216 ff. Heracleitus, together with Socrates and others, was recognized by Justin as a Christian before Christ (I *Apol.*, XLVI).

[3] So Bigg, *Christian Platonists of Alexandria*, p. 15.

[4] cf. J. Abelson, *Immanence of God in Rabbinical Lit.*, p. 146 ff. In IV *Ezra*, VI, 38, and *Apoc. of Abraham* the "word" has a quasi-personal significance. The *memra* of the Targums, however, is now generally regarded as merely a periphrasis of the divine name.

33 : 6, which is several times referred to by Irenaeus (e.g., I, xxii, 1; III, viii, 3; *Demons.*, V). The recent tendency is to derive the use of the Logos primarily from this source.

Philo certainly had no thought of identifying the Logos and the Messiah—he was not interested in the Messiah—and his ideas, though never consistently worked out, were too philosophical to have had much attraction for the first generations of Christians. The conception of the Logos in the fourth gospel [1] is quite unphilosophical; it is not the "reason" of the Stoics and of Philo, but the agent of revelation. Furthermore, St. John regards the Logos as no intermediate being but the Son Himself, and so as God in the fullest sense; and, what is more important, he identifies Him with a historic person, Jesus of Nazareth.

Before the rise of the Gnostic controversy the term Logos was not much used by Christian writers, and then in the sense of reason, and in a vague and unsystematic way, though Ignatius declared that Jesus was both Logos and Son (*Magn.*, VIII, 2). The growth of a Logos theology in the West, and with it a more favourable attitude towards the fourth gospel, was, so far as evidence is available, the work of Justin; though if John was the source of his teaching, he makes curiously little direct use of it.[2] For Justin, the Logos is always personal; and though he allows no division in the godhead, the Logos is distinct from the Father (*Dial.*, LXI and CXXVIII). He recognizes the soteriological activities of the Logos who reveals the Father and interprets Him to mankind, but He is of lower rank, though before all things and begotten. It was the Logos who became man in Jesus (I *Apol.*, XII f.; II *Apol.*, VI). Justin's pupil, Tatian, declared that the Logos springs forth from the Father, but without taking from His "Logos-power", just as one torch is lighted from another without diminishing its flame (*Ad Graec.*, V).

A further stage is reached with the writings of Irenaeus. But before going on to consider his theories something must be said of his general importance, for Irenaeus, in spite of some obvious defects, is one of the outstanding figures in the history of Christian doctrine. No theologian since the days of the apostles had so clearly discerned the purpose of God for His world.[3] But his attitude was inclined to be too static, the faith was to be held in its entirety, without "adding thereto or diminishing therefrom" (*Demons.*, II). He was, also, uncritical with a curious

---

[1] On the use of the term in the fourth gospel, see W. F. Howard, *Christianity according to St. John*, p. 34 ff., and R. G. Bury, *The Fourth-Gospel and the Logos Doctrine*.

[2] cf. Burkitt, *Church and Gnosis*, p. 93.

[3] cf. Armitage Robinson, *St. Iren. The Demonstration of Apost. Preaching*, p. vii.

fondness for peculiar traditions; such as the idea that our Lord's ministry lasted more than ten years, and that He was about fifty when He was crucified.[1] This uncritical tendency, however, adds to his value as a witness to the past, though a habit of depending on his memory and making no written records, may weaken confidence in his testimony.

Thus Irenaeus is important, not because he was a brilliant or original thinker, or of exceptional intellectual powers,[2] but on account of his cautious and conservative outlook, his ambition to "keep the middle way of truth", as Bartlet has well expressed it (*Church Life and Church Order*, p. 52). In addition he exhibited an admirable perseverence in the pursuit of knowledge and was at great pains to acquire full and exact information concerning any question with which he had to deal. Thus he grounds his claim to a more exhaustive acquaintance with the various heretical systems than previous apologists on the greater labour he had given to their study (IV Praef., 2). As a young man he had heard Polycarp (Euseb., V, xx, 5 f.), and he continually refers to an unnamed but venerable teacher, who may have been Polycarp, or perhaps more probably Pothinus, his predecessor in the see of Lyons. It is characteristic of his modest, yet confident, spirit that though he claims extensive knowledge he gladly attributes it to those who had taught him.

When all allowances have been made for credulity and a conservatism which was at times excessive, the contribution which Irenaeus made to the development of Christian thought on wise lines can hardly be overestimated. At a time when it was rising above the first somewhat naïve period to a higher level upon which a process of standardization could be conducted, the presence of a teacher whose sane and cautious outlook was combined with an extensive knowledge of the past was of immense value. Innovations were clamouring for admission into the Christian scheme; but not all of them were serviceable, and the test upon which Irenaeus insisted, conformity to what he believed to be the apostolic tradition, was certainly demanded.[3] At the same time he himself seems quite unaware that much in that tradition was of only recent growth. This can be seen in his

---

[1] II, xxii, 5 f.; *Demons.*, LXXIV. cf. also the theory of Eve's adolescence (III, xxii, 4; *Demons.*, XXXIII). It is not likely that Irenaeus originated these theories, but I have not been able to trace them in earlier writers in the form in which he presents them.

[2] His superiority over his predecessors can best be described as moral rather than intellectual. In his treatment of heretics, for example, he is not merely anxious to refute them, but to restore them to the true faith, having a better love for them than they have for themselves (III, xxv, 7).

[3] Such a test had been applied by the Jews who carefully preserved the succession of witnesses from Moses up to the Men of the Great Synagogue, ending with Johanan ben Zakkai: see *Pirke Aboth*, I and II.

statements about the early history of the Church in Rome (e.g., III, iii, 2 f.), as well as in his more detailed accounts of the composition of the canonical gospels (III, i, 1) when compared say with those of Papias (Euseb., III, xxxix, 13 ff.).

Although he came from the East and wrote in Greek, Irenaeus had sympathy with the Latin and Western outlook. This comes out in his definitely practical conception of religion, in his interest in the daily life of the believer, and in his emphasis on the sacraments as a means of grace. In speculation he followed the line of development laid down by Justin, though everywhere carrying it on further;[1] but in his thought on the Incarnation the Logos is not so prominent as is the historical significance of the Incarnate Son. Any attempt to separate the persons of the Trinity he regarded with distrust, insisting that the Logos is co-eternal with the Father (II, xxx, 9) and one with Him (IV, xxviii, 2). At times there are signs of confused thought, for in *Demons.*, II, it is the Logos who said "I am that I am", but in III, vi, 2, the Father. The Logos was the agent in creation (III, xi, 2) and it was He who became flesh (III, xi, 3). Irenaeus is also at pains to distinguish the Logos from Wisdom who is the Holy Spirit (IV, xx, 3).

Hippolytus[2] derived much from Irenaeus and was at the same time in agreement with Justin, for, like him, he subordinated the Logos. He recognized the possibility of divisions within the divine nature, but held that the Logos only became Son at the Incarnation (*Contra Noet.*, IV, XI). Whilst Justin had called the Logos a "second god" (*Dial.*, LVI), Hippolytus is more cautious and more vague, referring to Him as "another" (*op. cit.*, XI). He carries on from earlier thinkers what is to us the strange notion that the Holy Spirit who came upon the Blessed Virgin (Luke 1 : 35) was the Logos, who thus brought about His own incarnation. Justin had put forward the same idea (I *Apol.*, XXXII), but Irenaeus is vague and probably represents a transitional stage to later theories, for whereas in *Demons.*, LXXI, he states that "Christ's body was made by His Spirit", in V, i, 3 he is less definite.[3]

The Logos theology, even in its most orthodox form, was beset by two dangers. On the one hand He may be regarded as a mere attribute of God; on the other, if undue emphasis is laid upon His derivation, He may appear to be a kind of demi-god, such as the Gnostics loved to postulate in their various systems. The task of meeting these difficulties was first undertaken, not in the

---

[1] On the debt of Irenaeus to Justin see Armitage Robinson, *op. cit.*, pp. 6–23.

[2] See, further, A. d'Alès, *La Théologie de St. Hippolyte.*

[3] On this obscure subject see H. J. Carpenter, "The Birth from Holy Spirit and the Virgin in the Old Roman Creed", in *J.T.S.*, 1939, XL, p. 31 ff.

West, but by the rising school of Alexandria. In order to clarify the process of development it will be necessary to turn aside for a brief consideration of their ideas.

Clement recognized the activities of the Logos in creation and His incarnation (*Strom.*, V, iii, 16) and is careful to insist on His distinct personality (V, i, 1); but he goes beyond the Western Fathers by a firmer grasp of the unity of the Logos and the Father, whilst avoiding any excessive subordination. Origen, by his theory of the eternal generation of the Son, tried to meet all the difficulties; but he placed the Son in a definitely subordinate position, and the Holy Spirit below the Son.[1] He insisted, however, that both of them partake of the divine nature, and neither may be regarded as a mere attribute.

Returning to the West and to a time slightly anterior, we find the *locus classicus* in Tertullian, *Apol.*, XXI. The main points that he makes are that God possessed the Logos from all eternity; that the Logos came forth to create the universe, and that thenceforth He was called the Son of God; that He partakes of the one divine substance from which He is derived, and, as begotten, is distinct from the Father in manner of subsistence (*modulo*) as in rank (*gradu*). Thus the Logos was not from the beginning a person, though He may have been so in essence, a position which is worked out in *Adv. Prax.*, V, in which treatise he also recognizes the subordination of the Logos (IX and XIV). Tertullian, though he had his share in spreading the Logos doctrine in the West, was aware of its defects, and he did even more to popularize the thought of the divine sonship.

Although the Logos theology had the support of the ablest of the early Western thinkers and was useful in commending the doctrine of the Incarnation to educated pagans, it was by no means accepted by all Christian teachers, and never really took deep root. It was, for one thing, too intellectual, the object of its advocates seemed to be to establish a coterie of *illuminati* rather than a fellowship of saints. The Logos was the last term of an evolutionary development in revelation; what the ordinary Christian wanted was a Saviour from sin and death. Moreover it tended to obscure the historic Jesus. It is not therefore surprising to find that after the middle of the third century it drops definitely into the background and that the bishops assembled at Nicaea deliberately rejected the use of the term. For this omission there were many sound reasons. It was too closely akin to Gnostic speculations, and possibly the fact that it was used in Egyptian theosophical literature, as, for instance, in the

---

[1] *Ascens. of Isaiah*, IX, says that both the Son and the Holy Spirit worship and glorify God; whilst even Irenaeus explains that the Son is called servant because subject to the Father (*Demonst.*, LI).

Poimandres of Hermes Trismegistos, laid it open to suspicion.

In both Irenaeus and Tertullian the thought of the Son is becoming more prominent than that of the Logos, and it was along this line that advance towards a doctrine of the Incarnation was to move. It was a relationship which all could comprehend, though not without its own special dangers, for the recognition of the Logos had helped to preserve the thought of the immanence of God; but the Son tended to share the transcendence of the Father.

There was, however, another line of interpretation which in its different types was of great importance for the development of Christian doctrine, this was Monarchianism. About this heresy there is much that is uncertain, and even its advocates have around them an element of mystery.[1] As in the case of other unsuccessful movements we have to depend on opponents for knowledge of its tenets; an obviously unreliable source, for it is notoriously difficult not to misrepresent the point of view of an adversary, even when the will deliberately to do so is absent. Monarchianism probably originated in Asia Minor, where Christian thought was most active in the second century, and for a time it may have become the prevailing form of Christology. On its appearance in Rome it seems to have received some kind of official recognition. There are, indeed, scholars who claim that Monarchianism represents the original Christology of the Roman Church before it had been diverted, through the teaching of Justin and his successors, and the introduction of African influence with the coming of Victor.[2] They trace a line of succession through Hermas and Artemon. Such a theory, however, is open to serious criticism, for Hermas was no theologian, and even if statements which have a Monarchian flavour can be found in his writings—which is very doubtful—they are the result of ignorance.[3]

Monarchianism[4] arose from a desire, perfectly unobjectionable in itself, to preserve the unity of the godhead, and to emphasize the sole rule of God. But in the attempt to preserve the unity it was led to a denial of the distinction between the persons within it; and in emphasizing the rule of God it suggested the possibility, to those outside, that there were inferior gods; for no one can be called a monarch who has no subjects, as was urged by the

[1] Tertullian seems to know only Praxeas. De Rossi made the bold suggestion that he should be identified with Epigonus (*Bull. Arch. Crist.*, 1866, p. 69 f.). Epiphanius (*Haer.*, LVII), since he states that Noetus came from Ephesus, may have confused him with Praxeas.

[2] See Kirsopp Lake in *Harvard Theol. Rev.*, 1924, XVII, p. 177; and Harnack, *Dogmengesch.*, I, p. 160.

[3] See, further, R. L. Ottley, *Doct. of the Incarnation*, I, p. 158 f.

[4] The first suggestion of the name is contained in the title of a treatise of Irenaeus (Euseb., V, xx, 1).

heathen advocate in the *Apocriticus* of Macarius Magnes (IV, 20).[1]

The Monarchians may be divided into two distinct groups according to the attitude which they took towards the relation of Jesus to the Father. One group denied the divinity of Jesus, regarding Him as a mere man upon whom the divine power descended at His baptism; the other identified Him so completely with the Father as to earn the title of Patripassians.

The first type of Monarchians are called Dynamic or Adoptionist. This latter title is used by Harnack and accepted by Tixeront, but it is better to reserve it, as Bethune-Baker does,[2] for a mode of thought of a later date to which it has usually been confined. Such views were brought to the West by Theodotus, the leather-seller, who came to Rome from Byzantium towards the end of the second century. He was a man of wealth and culture who is said to have apostasized during a persecution. His defence, not very satisfactory even from his own standpoint, was that he had denied not God but a man. Theodotus accepted the miraculous conception of Jesus, although regarding Him as only a man before His baptism. The idea that the heavenly Christ descended upon the man Jesus receives support from the Western reading of Luke 3 : 22: "Thou art my son, this day have I begotten thee"; and it might well be argued that anyone coming to the fourth gospel without knowing the Church's tradition or the synoptic gospels would receive the impression that the Holy Spirit suddenly descended upon a man who thus became the Son of God.[3] Some of the followers of Theodotus postponed the full acquisition of divinity until after the Resurrection.[4]

Theodotus was excommunicated by Victor, Bishop of Rome, in 195; none the less, he succeeded in gaining disciples. They were mainly "intellectuals" and resembled a literary circle rather than a Church. Among them was a namesake, called by way of distinction, the banker. He was notorious as the upholder of a cult of Melchizedek. Another follower of Theodotus was a certain Artemon, about whom little is known save that he was active in Rome in the early part of the third century, and claimed that his views had the support of both Scripture and tradition. He was opposed by the author of *The Little Labyrinth* (possibly

---

[1] With this opinion may be compared that of Xenophanes, as preserved by Theophrastus, that "there is no hegemony among the gods; for it is unholy to suppose that any of them is subject to a master": see Adam, *Relig. Teachers of Greece*, p. 204. Tertullian argued that a ruler could share his powers (*Adv. Prax.*, III). [2] *Early Hist. of Christ. Doct.*, p. 97 n.

[3] A Christian interpolation into the text of *The Testaments of the Twelve Patriarchs* (Test. Judah, xxiv, 1 ff.) suggests the same point of view.

[4] There were Gnostics, if the strange story preserved in *Pistis Sophia* is good evidence, who held that the union of the Heavenly Christ and the human Jesus took place during His boyhood.

Hippolytus) who affirmed that Jesus had always been regarded as divine. Dynamic Monarchianism did not persist in the West with much vigour after the time of Artemon; there are in fact few traces of it; none the less it had sufficient influence to come to the notice of Augustine before his conversion and be accepted by him (*Confessions*, VII, xix). In the East, similar views were held by Paul of Samosata, Bishop of Antioch, who looked upon Jesus as a man in whom the Logos had taken up His abode in such a way that Jesus progressed towards divinity. For these views he was condemned in 268 and deprived of his bishopric.

The other type of Monarchianism was much more influential, perhaps because it approached much nearer to orthodoxy; for there can be no question that the divinity of Jesus had always been firmly held, even if its implications had not been worked out. The confession which Hippolytus puts on the lips of Zephyrinus, Bishop of Rome, "I know only one God, Christ Jesus, and no other in addition to Him, He was born and suffered",[1] would doubtless have been echoed by the vast majority of Christians who, like the bishop himself, were unversed in theological niceties.[2]

Teaching of this nature, which sought to preserve the unity of the godhead by denying any permanent distinctions within it, was brought to Rome by Praxeas about the time that Theodotus was airing his different doctrines. Praxeas, who has already been noticed in connexion with Montanism, is a mysterious figure and only comes into the full light when he goes to North Africa and arouses the hostile attention of Tertullian. As he is apparently unknown to Hippolytus, his efforts in Rome can have had but little effect. The name Patripassianism, which became attached to this type of Monarchianism, may well have been devised by Tertullian who was good at inventing nicknames. It was applied to them because, since it identified the Father and the Son, the former must also have suffered. The followers of Praxeas refused to accept this inference and explained that the Father suffered *with*, but not *in*, the Son.

The most noteworthy of the Monarchians of this type was Noetus, who, according to Hippolytus, came to Rome after having been condemned by the presbyters of his native Smyrna (*Contra Noet.*, I), for his unorthodox views. He held that the

---

[1] See Hippolytus, IX, 11. There is a curious parallel to the confession of Zephyrinus in a Coptic fragment of the *Acts of Paul* in which the father of a boy who has been raised from the dead by the apostle exclaims: "I believe . . . that there is no other God than Jesus Christ, the son of the blessed". See *Apoc. N.T.*, p. 271.

[2] Hippolytus says that Zephyrinus was ignorant and uncultivated, as well as unskilled in theological definitions (IX, 11). He also claims that he was inconsistent, as on one occasion he denied that it was the Father who died.

Father was born, had suffered and died, but he strove to avoid the objections of his opponents by distinguishing between God in His essence and God as He allows Himself to become visible and passible. His teaching was continued in Rome by Epigonus and Cleomenes (Hippolytus, IX, 7).

The most famous name among Monarchians was Sabellius, probably a Libyan by origin. He arrived in Rome in the early part of the third century, and so rather later than the Monarchian teachers just mentioned. He taught that God had revealed Himself under three different forms; as the Father in creation, as the Son in redemption, and as the Holy Spirit in sanctification. Thus the distinction of persons, according to his view, may be said to arise from the religious experience of man, rather than from anything inherent in the godhead itself. Sabellius differed from Noetus chiefly by his clearer recognition of the Holy Spirit; but he allowed no really fuller distinctions within the godhead. A council at Rome in 258 condemned his views, but they continued to flourish, especially in the East, and played their part in many controversies. The treatise *De Trinitate* of Novatian shows that in Rome they had no great following after the middle of the third century.

It was in connexion with Sabellianism that the important correspondence between Dionysius of Alexandria and his namesake of Rome had its origin. The bishop of Alexandria in combating the heresy allowed himself to use expressions which, when taken from their context, savoured of an opposite form of heresy. His opponents reported the matter to Rome, making five distinct accusations, of which the most serious were that he had separated the Father and the Son, had denied the eternity of the Son, and had made Him a creature. These views were condemned by a synod in Rome in 260 and the bishop followed up the decision by sending two letters, one to the Church at Alexandria, and the other to the bishop. The latter replied by way of explanation, and his explanations were accepted. Thus the controversy ended in a much more satisfactory manner than is customary in such affairs.

The correspondence was important as illustrating the relations between Rome and another Church—an aspect which has already received attention. It was also important from the doctrinal point of view, for it brought into prominence the unity of the divine essence as it subsisted in the three persons. Thus it forms a convenient transition to a consideration of the doctrine of the Trinity.

The actual term triad or Trinity was first used in connexion with Christian doctrine by Theophilus in *Ad Autol.*, II, 15, and in the West by Tertullian (*trinitas*) in *De Pudic.*, XXI. The idea of three persons in the godhead had, of course, been long recognized in view of certain statements in the New Testament; the interpolation in I John 5 : 7, however, which was such a standby of the Latin fathers, had not yet been made. The material which goes to make up the doctrine is found mainly in John among the gospels, though the only definite statement, oddly enough, is Matt. 28 : 19. Elsewhere, 2 Cor. 13 : 14 is almost a formulation of later belief. Three persons are taken for granted in I *Clem.*, XX and LVIII, but not much interest was displayed as to the relations between them before the rise of the Monarchian controversy, and then it was concerned with the Father and the Son. Several passages in Irenaeus suggest that he accepted two persons only as belonging properly to the godhead. In *Demons.*, XLVII, he writes: "The Father is God and the Son is God, as that which is begotten of God" (cf. III, xviii, 3). Irenaeus finds it difficult to distinguish between the Son and the Spirit, the two hands of God (V, xxviii, 3) and usually couples the Word and the Wisdom (IV, xx, 1 ff.; *Demons.*, V). In Justin, it should be noted, Wisdom is the second person of the godhead (*Dial.*, LXII and CXXVI). Later, Tertullian defends himself against charges not of Tritheism, but of Ditheism.

In the earliest days, baptism seems to have been in the name of the Lord Jesus alone, or in that of the Trinity. Oblations were blessed in the name of the Maker of all, through His Son, Jesus Christ, and through the Holy Spirit (Justin, I *Apol.*, LXVII). From the inscriptions, we gain little evidence as to the extent to which any formal doctrine was recognized, and what there is is mainly of a negative character. As a rule, they mention only the Father and the Son; for references to three persons are extremely rare in both East and West.[1] One imperfect inscription in the cemetery of Domitilla can, however, be cited. It probably belongs to the third century:

[IV]CVNDIANV[S QVI CREDIDIT IN]
CRISTVM IESV[M VIVIT IN]
[PATR]E ET FILIO ET IS[PIRITV SANCTO] [2]

In our Lord's teaching as reported in the synoptic gospels there is little mention of the Holy Spirit; it seems to belong to the second, more sophisticated, stage of Christian development of which the fourth gospel is the representative. But the Acts of the Apostles and St. Paul's epistles show what a large part the Holy Spirit played in the life of the primitive Christians. The manifestations of His presence and influence, however, were, as Celsus pointed out, not dissimilar from those experienced by the heathen. It has, in fact, been suggested that the third person

[1] Syxtus, II, i, p. 81.   [2] Marucchi, p. 170.

of the Trinity may have come ultimately from Zoroastrianism in which the premier of the *Amesha Spentas* (immortal holy ones), *Vohu Manah* (good mind), performs similar functions and has an almost identical name.[1]

During the first Christian centuries not much was written about the Holy Spirit. There was a belief in His person, but it was seldom put into words; and His relation to the other persons of the Trinity, and even to the believer, seems to have aroused little attention.[2] This may have been on account of the thought of our Lord as the Logos; whilst the Montanist emphasis on the Spirit and the identification of His manifestations with ecstatic outbursts may have made men suspicious and anxious to avoid using His name. The Gnostics also had their ideas on the matter.

This does not mean that references to the Holy Spirit and His work are entirely lacking. In the West, Clement refers to the outpouring of the Spirit (II) and to His speaking through the Old Testament (XVI). He also recognizes His personality and divinity (LVIII). Other references, however, in entering into more detail, reveal some crudity of conception and uncertainty of usage. The term in Hermas, for instance, seems to connote the spirit dwelling in man (*Mand.*, IV, v, 2). If it is oppressed it can call upon God to allow it to depart (X, ii, 5). Those who defile the flesh defile the Holy Spirit also (*Sim.*, V, vii, 2). On the other hand, the Spirit is called the Son of God (*Sim.*, IX, i, 1); but the maidens round the Tower are also called holy spirits, and "powers of the Son of God" (*Sim.*, IX, xiii, 2).

Justin says that Christians worship and reverence the Father, the Son, "the host of other good angels who follow and imitate Him", and the Spirit of Prophecy (I *Apol.*, VI). Later in the same treatise he says that the Spirit of Prophecy is worshipped in the third place (XIII). This aspect of His work, represented later by the phrase in the creed, "Who spake by the prophets", is prominent in writers of the second century.

With Irenaeus, as we might expect, a more constructive level is gained, though he begins by clearing away some mistaken ideas, such as the Valentinian, and the conception of the Holy Spirit as a mere emanation (II, xix, 9). He refers to Him, with the Son, as the hand of God (IV, xx, 1) and as the image of the Father, and His Wisdom (IV, vii, 4). The mission of the Holy Spirit is mainly to teach, thus continuing His earlier activity as shown in the inspiration of prophets and apostles (III, xxi, 4).

---

[1] See E. Meyer, *Ursprung und Anfänge des Christentums*, II, p. 441. In criticism of this view I would point out that the term Holy Spirit (*Spenta Mainyu*) is itself found in Zoroastrianism; it is used of Ahura Mazda: see Dhalla, *Zoroastrian Theology*, p. 24.

[2] It is a rare thing to find any reference to the Holy Spirit in ante-Nicene inscriptions: Syxtus II, i, p. 74 ff.

Irenaeus is insistent on the thought of the Church as the sphere of the Spirit's operations and on His working through the sacraments (III, xxiv, 1). Hippolytus tends to attribute to the Logos activities usually associated with the Holy Spirit, and seems to place Him in a category different from that of the Father and the Son, though he recognizes His distinction from them (*Contra Noetum*).

In North Africa, Tertullian raises the question of the divine procession and uses a term for the Holy Spirit similar to that employed by Justin, speaking of Him as the third from the Father (*Adv. Prax.*, VIII). He also makes mention of His work in the Church and through the sacraments. The thought of the Holy Spirit working in the Church is also prominent in Cyprian, but apart from this he makes little mention of Him. This tendency to restrict the operations of the Spirit to what may be called ecclesiastical channels was unfortunate, especially as it coincided with the substitution of the idea of the Son for that of the Logos in reference to the second person of the Trinity. Thus the thought of the immanence of God was liable to be obscured.

THE GROWTH OF CREEDS

Whilst speculation was going on among the learned, the need for definite teaching of a simple nature for those entering the Church had been met by the provision of credal statements which would serve as an outline for instruction. Much uncertainty, however, enshrouds the early history of the creeds, probably because for long it was considered unsafe to commit them to writing. It seems probable, on the whole, that it was in connexion with the instruction and baptism of converts that they first arose.[1] They were, however, not designed for instruction alone, but also to provide a confession of faith.[2] At a slightly later date, when heretical ideas were current, they would also be used as tests for the exclusion of doubtful or erroneous opinions.[3] It should, however, not be forgotten that there were tests of belief even in New Testament times (cf. 1 Cor. 12 : 3; 1 John 2 : 22; 4 : 2 f., 15; 2 John 7), as well as in the next generation (Ignatius, *Trall.*, IX). The initial intention, no doubt, was to obtain the consent of all to what was an embodiment of the

[1] A. C. M'Giffert thinks that the old Roman Symbol was meant to counteract erroneous teaching (*The Apostles' Creed*, p. 12).
[2] Baptismal creeds are, as a rule, in the singular: "I believe"; those issued by councils, in the plural. It is sometimes stated that "We" is a characteristic of Eastern, and "I" of Western, creeds; but this is almost certainly an error: see *Early Hist. of the Church and Ministry*, p. 335, note 2.
[3] cf. The statement of Herbert Loewe in *Judaism and Christianity*, I, p. 155, that in Judaism a creed is an educational convenience, not a dogmatic test.

common faith; the acceptance of Jesus as Lord being the chief requisite for membership. On other matters much latitude of opinion was apparently allowed. But gradually the need for elaboration became evident. In later times, when creeds were recited in public worship, liturgical requirements helped in the process of development, but this lies well outside our period.[1]

In the New Testament a number of credal forms of an elementary nature are to be found. These may have been in the form of hymns, so as to make them easy to remember.[2] The foundation belief is, as stated above, the acknowledgment of Jesus as Lord (Rom. 10 : 9; 1 Cor. 12 : 3), probably coupled with the statement that God raised Him from the dead (Rom. 10 : 9; cf. Acts 17 : 18). Fuller details are added in passages like 1 Cor. 15 : 3 f.; Phil. 2 : 5 ff.; and 2 Tim. 2 : 8. They are all concerned with the second person of the Trinity; but there are also two passages which foreshadow the threefold creed of later times (Matt. 28 : 19 and 2 Cor. 13 : 14). Some scholars have suggested that these different interests correspond to two distinct types of creed in use in primitive times, and that the greater detail found under the second article is due to the incorporation of the one into the other.[3]

Credal passages, though not grouped together as such, can also be discovered in the works of Christian writers of our period. Although only incidental they are sufficiently numerous, especially in the West, to throw considerable light on what was believed and taught. From the writings of Justin, for example, a really elaborate creed can be constructed.[4] Tertullian records that candidates for baptism had to make a rather fuller response than a bare confession of belief in the Trinity (De Cor. Mil., III). His own creed evidently included a clause concerning the Church (De Bapt., VI). From two of Cyprian's letters (LXIX, LXX) we can construct his own Baptismal Creed. It is in the form of questions:

> Dost thou believe in God the Father,
> and in Christ the Son,
> and in the Holy Spirit?

[1] Percy Dearmer says that creeds were not used liturgically before the fifth century and then only locally. Rome did not add the creed to the liturgy before the eleventh century for, when the Emperor Henry II was crowned at Rome in 1014, he commented on its absence and requested that it might be added according to German usage: see *The Church in the Twentieth Century*, p. 143.

[2] It is possible that in the original Aramaic the Lord's Prayer was in rhyme. Such devices were common before the invention of printing. In the fourteenth century, for example, John Myrc, a canon of Lilleshall, produced a well-known manual for parish priests full of ministerial technicalities in rhyme.

[3] Hausleiter thinks they were combined in Rome early in the third century; see Kirsopp Lake, "The Apostles' Creed", in *Harvard Theol. Rev.*, 1924, XVII, p. 173 ff.

[4] As has been done by T. H. Bindley, *Oecumenical Docts. of the Faith*, p. 60.

> Dost thou believe in the remission of sins
> and eternal life through the Holy Church?

The clause concerning eternal life is interesting as it was not added to the Apostles' Creed until much later.

The earliest creed to which an approximate date can be given comes from Asia Minor and belongs to about the middle of the second century. Its contents, as preserved in the *Epistle of the Apostles*, run as follows:

> In the Father, the Lord Almighty,
> And in Jesus Christ our redeemer,
> In the Holy Ghost the comforter,
> In the Holy Church,
> And in the remission of sins.[1]

In the West the creed attributed to the apostles seems to represent, with some slight differences, that current in the Roman Church, perhaps as early as the later half of the second century.[2] The West was much more interested in the historical facts of our Lord's life than in their interpretation; the clause "under Pontius Pilate", though derived from the New Testament (1 Tim. 6 : 13), is typical of its point of view. This lack of interest in questions of interpretation doubtless enabled the West to arrive at a statement of belief which suited it long before the East, and that without the approval of a council. It was, moreover, retained with very slight alteration. One feature of the Roman Creed is the omission of any reference to our Lord's baptism. It has been suggested by Harnack that this was due to the difficulty, felt in many parts of the early Church, that Jesus should have undergone a rite which was intended for the remission of sins.[3] It is to be noted that no Western creed includes any reference to the sacraments.[4]

Though the Apostles' Creed is very early, it did not reach its final form before the middle of the eighth century. Some of the typical clauses, such as "He descended into Hell" and "The Communion of Saints", although current in the East, are among the later additions. One clause in the creed, as known to the pre-Nicene age in the West, was "to judge both the quick and the dead". This is of much interest as the only clause which gives a

---

[1] *op. cit.*, V (*Apoc. N.T.*, p. 487). A much more elaborate statement is contained in III of the same work (*Apoc. N.T.*, p. 486).

[2] The theory of F. J. Badcock (*Hist. of the Creeds*, chap. I) that the Apostles' Creed is a typical fourth-century document, and therefore much later, has not met with much acceptance.

[3] How early this feeling arose can be seen by a comparison of Mark 1 : 9 with Matt. 3 : 13 ff. Ignatius explained that our Lord submitted to baptism in order to "purify" water for Christians (*Eph.*, XVIII, 2). Another passage which attempts to deal with the difficulty is the extract from the *Gospel according to the Hebrews* preserved in Jerome, *Dial. adv. Pelag.*, III, 2.

[4] The Eastern creeds refer to baptism.

reason. The thought of judgment to come was a practical thing and in all ages loomed large in the mind of Western Christendom. But the belief in "the life everlasting" was, as we have seen, a late addition. The belief in the resurrection of the flesh (*carnis*) in its crude form is rejected by modern ideas, but for the ancients held no difficulty, even though it seems to contradict St. Paul's idea of the "spiritual body" (1 Cor. 15 : 44). In the *Epistle of the Apostles*, XXI (*Apoc. N.T.*, p. 493) Jesus is represented as telling the disciples that He had come in the flesh that they might rise in their flesh, and the *Apoc. of Paul*, XIV (*Apoc. N.T.*, p. 531) says plainly that the body on the day of Resurrection will be the same body.

Matters such as the Last Judgment and the Resurrection lead on to a consideration of those many questions which are usually grouped under the term eschatology. In the New Testament eschatology bulks large,[1] and its exact significance and the extent to which it formed part of the original Gospel message have been fiercely debated. To enter into this subject is not within the scope of the present study; it will suffice to notice that ideas of this nature were current in the earliest Christian literature.

In considering the various eschatological notions which have arisen, it is necessary that two distinct ideas should be kept separate—in thought at least—the fate of the individual, and the accomplishment of the divine purposes. In the New Testament it is the latter idea which is prominent; in the mystery religions the former. The shifting of emphasis among Christians to the thought of the individual may well have been due to outside influences, or it may have arisen naturally. It is certainly the prevailing concern when men to-day allow their minds to dwell on a future life and the end of the ages. Any attempt, however, to picture the other world under the forms of space and time must, with our limited knowledge, be of the nature of analogue and poetry; and all descriptions of the life beyond the grave are either crude continuations of this life, or highly symbolical and imaginative. At times, indeed, they are apt to be, as Israel Abrahams has remarked, "monstrously inartistic" (*Judaism*, p. 23).

Among the Jews there had been a very deep and widespread interest in eschatology, as the survival of a huge mass of apocalyptical literature sufficiently testifies. But this form of thought fell out of favour towards the end of the first century A.D., though the Fall of Jerusalem seems to have inspired at least two

---

[1] Even in the fourth gospel the eschatological element is much greater than is often realized: see W. F. Howard, *Christianity according to St. John*, p. 109 ff.

works of this nature, IV *Ezra* and the *Apòc. of Baruch.* Josephus, however, is very anxious that the Romans should not think that eccentric notions of this kind were at all typical of his nation. Among Christians, however, they continued to flourish, and many writings, including the canonical Revelation and the *Ascension of Isaiah*, were produced by them.

One idea which was eagerly taken up by some Christians was that of the Millennium, the rule of Christ upon this earth which would last for a thousand years. This notion was closely connected with belief in the resurrection of the flesh, for if men were to take their place in such a scheme they would obviously require bodies. This theory was held by many, including the author of *Barnabas*, and Papias; and, in the West, by such influential teachers as Justin, Irenaeus, Hippolytus,[1] and Tertullian. In the East, men were more critical of such high-flown notions;[2] Eusebius makes fun of poor Papias in this connexion (III, xxxix, 12 f.), whilst the Revelation itself is often omitted from Eastern lists of Scripture. "Hellenic culture revolted against what seemed the crude and violent imagery, the unrestrained Orientalism, of the prophecy attributed to St. John."[3] In the West, on the contrary, the book aroused considerable interest, as can be seen from the numerous commentaries which were written upon it.

In the latter half of the second century, men's thoughts, and not least in the West, turned strongly to the idea that the end of the world was approaching. Wars were constant and there had been widespread and alarming outbreaks of plague. As a consequence, there was much excitement among the common folk, and even Tertullian expected the end to arrive speedily (*De Resr. Carnis*, XXIV); the power which was delaying it was the Roman Empire (*Apol.*, XXXII; cf. 2 Thes. 2 : 6 f.). Cyprian, a little later, had the same conviction (*Epist.*, LVIII). Views as to the speedy end must have been profoundly modified by Constantine's adoption of Christianity—the idea of a catastrophic introduction of Christ's kingdom would no longer seem desirable.[4] But as late as the fourth century a great and wealthy noble like Paulinus of Nola could give up his rank and become a hermit in order to prepare himself better for the second coming.[5]

---

[1] See especially the fragments on *Daniel* and *The Apocalypse.*
[2] For Origen, the "second coming" represented merely the passage from the temporal to the eternal. He put aside the thought of the visible return and earthly rule of Christ.
[3] C. H. Turner, *Studies in Early Church Hist.*, p. 193.
[4] Even in Tertullian's time, not all were anxious for the end, since they prayed for its postponement (*Apol.*, XXXII, XXXIX).
[5] Paulinus, *Carm.*, X, 304.

The question of the future world and the fortunes of the soul after death had long been a matter for speculation among the Romans; though here as elsewhere they had been mainly content to borrow the ideas of other races. But one thing stood out: the passionate desire of the individual that his existence should not be forgotten when he was dead. He "had a horror . . . of the day when no kindly eye would read his name and style upon the slab, when no hand for evermore would bring the annual offering of wine and flowers".[1] To provide for this service he would make lavish endowments, and so anticipate the wealthy of the Middle Ages with their chantries which, whatever other effect they had, did at least commemorate the names of the benefactors.

One of the most famous descriptions of the other world in Latin literature is, of course, contained in Book VI of the *Aeneid*. Virgil probably derived many of his conceptions, through the Greek poets, from Orphism. The Orphic rites, among other offices, prepared men and women for the under-world, and those who had been initiated acquired valuable privileges and immunities. They were, however, not entirely magical in their working, for a life of purity on earth was necessary for the attainment of immortality. Another nearer source of influence would be found in the Etruscans, who had an almost morbid interest in the after life, and especially in its punishments and torments, as anyone must realize who has seen reproductions of Etruscan tombs and their paintings.

Ideas from all these very diverse sources were part of the common inheritance of the Roman world and passed over into the Christian Church in one form or another. Even literature was deeply affected by them, and the various visions of Heaven and Hell which are so common in medieval writings, with Dante's *Commedia* as the supreme example, owe not a little to pagan traditions.

One of such traditions was the doctrine of purgatory which is found in the Orphic teaching and emerges in Christian circles as early as the beginning of the third century. Clement of Alexandria speaks of the salutary nature of the sufferings, leading to the conversion of the soul, to be endured there (*Strom.*, VI, 6). At about the same time, Tertullian in the West was teaching that after death the souls of the martyrs alone went straight into the presence of their Lord (cf. 2 Cor. 5 : 8), those of ordinary Christians descend into the Lower World (*De Resr. Carnis*, XLIII). He, too, refers to the purifying punishments which are the lot of men until the day of the Lord (*De Anima*, LV–LVIII).

The idea that the time in purgatory could be avoided, or curtailed, by the payment of fees to a professional priesthood,

[1] Dill, *Roman Society from Nero, etc.*, p. 258.

or in reward for services rendered to the deity or his representatives, is very old; it is found, for example, among the Egyptians,[1] and was common in Italy, through the Etruscans, long before the Christian era. The time would come when it would be carried "by the priests of the Roman form of Christianity as part of their professional and financial apparatus all over this long-suffering world".[2]

For the majority of Christians, death was the door to a new and better life, or a return of the soul to its real home; hence arose the practice, not found among the heathen, of placing the date of death on their memorials,[3] and even the simple expression, REDIIT. An example may be quoted from the inscription on the tomb of a married couple at Brioude: TRANSIERVNT AD VERAM REMEANS E CORPORE VITAM. [4] It had evidently been adapted from an earlier inscription of a single person, and the substitution of *transiervnt* for *transiit* has spoilt the hexameter. Another memorial reveals the intense desire for the coming of the Lord:

HIC PATER EST ATOLVS NATO NATAQUE SEPVLTVS
EXPECTANTQVE DIEM NVNC DOMINI PROPERAM.[5]

[1] See E. A. W. Budge, *The Book of the Dead*, III, p. 10.
[2] R. S. Conway, *Ancient Italy and Modern Religion*, p. 65.
[3] For the custom in Gaul see Le Blant, *L'Épig. chrét. en Gaule*, p. 7 f.
[4] Le Blant, *Inscript. chrét. de la Gaule*, No. 380.   [5] *op. cit.*, No. 334.

CHAPTER VI

THE CHURCH AND THE MINISTRY

When we look back and try to envisage the life of the early Christian community we are apt, having in mind the manner in which the Church to-day is introduced into a mission field, to think of a definite organization gradually spreading from place to place with the preaching of the Gospel upon which it depended. Such a picture is by no means in conformity with the facts so far as we know them. Christianity seems to have spread in divers ways, but apparently without any elaborate or highly developed organization.

The information which we possess about the Church and Ministry in the first days is by no means as adequate as we could desire. For this, two reasons may be responsible. In the first place the writers of the New Testament and those who immediately followed them would not be concerned to describe in minute detail matters which would be familiar to their contemporaries; and secondly, they were not greatly interested in such matters. Christ would soon return and then would come the end.[1] Meanwhile, all that was necessary was to provide means by which the fellowship of the Body could find expression, such as opportunities for the simple worship which grew up to supplement that of the Temple, and to maintain the care of the poor and indigent. At first, it may be, the hope was cherished that the Jewish people as a whole would recognize their Messiah, especially when a great company of the priests believed (Acts 6 : 7); in that case there would be no need to set up a rival organization.

The foundation of any definite society by Jesus Himself is often denied. He was not, it is urged, interested in institutions but in individuals. In reply it may be pointed out that the choice of the Twelve, a very significant number,[2] and the establishment of an apostolate, did in fact provide an institution of a very definite and momentous character, and a nucleus round which an organized society could develop. The stewards set over the household (Matt. 24 : 45; Luke 12 : 42; cf. 1 Cor. 4 : 1 f.) point

---

[1] The belief in an earthly kingdom, with the apostles ruling over the twelve tribes of Israel, may, however, have involved the idea of others to help them in their task.

[2] cf. Quick, *Doctrines of the Creed*, p. 327: "The choice of twelve means that the new Israel . . . is making a fresh start from the twelve apostles, as the old Israel started its history from the twelve sons of Jacob".

in the same direction, as well as the allegory of the Good Shepherd and His fold (John 10). St. Paul quite evidently looked upon Christ as the founder of the Church for which He had, indeed, given His life (Eph. 5 : 25). To the early Christians, however, with their strong conviction that the risen and ascended Lord was with them and inspiring them, the exact method by which the Church was founded would have been of little consequence. It was He who was responsible.

A superficial reading of the New Testament might suggest that Christendom then consisted of a number of small independent communities, such as those to whom St. Paul wrote his various letters. But the term *ecclesia* which is used to describe the Christian Body means primarily the whole fellowship of believers, and not those of a particular district. Moreover there was an underlying conviction, common to them all, that the Christian Church was the new People of God, united, not as the Jewish Church had been by racial unity, but none the less bound together into a single Body; the Body of Christ in St. Paul's own phrase. I think a parallel may be found in the history of Islam: for those who accept belief in Allah and recognize the authority of Muhammed become members of a new community (*ummah*) which takes the place of the traditional community founded on kinship. As with the primitive Christian community, not descent but "faith" is the bond. So, too, in regard to the Ministry. If there is no trace of anything at all resembling the monarchical episcopate of later times, there is at least the recognition of the delegation of authority by the apostles.[1]

THE CHURCH

The various Christian societies, if they lacked any rigid organization, had a definite unity, a common faith, and already common traditions and ways of doing things (1 Cor. 11 : 16). They regarded themselves as parts of a single whole, of that new People of God which had taken the place left void by the apostacy of the Jews. Many may have been isolated from the main body, and some may even have preferred to remain so; such perhaps was the community which produced the *Didache*. The Church, in claiming to be the successor of the Jewish people (and the choice of the term *ecclesia*, with all its associations, is strong evidence of this), must at the same time have realized that it was claiming to be the inheritor of the world-wide empire which

[1] In his brilliant essay contributed to *Episcopacy Ancient and Modern*, Lowther Clarke suggests that at first the ministry was quite undifferentiated, the apostles simply making use of assistants as Moses had done (Num. 11 : 16 ff.). There was, in other words, function, but not office.

Daniel had foretold and John had elaborated in the Apocalypse. The Church, then, is no mere organization such as the pagan fraternities; no mere association for the improvement of morals; but a society filled with the life of God and conscious of the continuous guidance of His Spirit. Ideas about organization might differ in different parts, but all alike recognized its value and significance. This was of great importance in view of the craving for salvation which was widespread in the Empire at this epoch. For it tended to emphasize the needs of the individual and obscure the idea of the Church as the People of God (especially for those who had not early come under the influence of the Old Testament) with a mission as a community. Even the phrase *extra ecclesiam nulla salus*, though it emphasizes the predominant importance of the community, does so by bringing out its significance as the ark of salvation for the individual.

Ideas of the Church current in East and West did not differ greatly during our period, though there was already a difference of emphasis. The West naturally placed a high value on any kind of association; it was part of the Roman *gravitas* for a man to look upon the society to which he belonged as no chance affair but "the ordered outcome of the experience of his fathers and an inheritance which he must keep ordered to hand on to his descendants".[1] Thus the Gentile had had his training as well as the Jew. As time went on more and more value was attached to the idea of the visible Church, until at last the very name of Christian could be refused to those who were outside its bounds.[2] Cyprian, rigid as ever, even denies that heretics have any Church at all, a sentiment with which his correspondent, Firmilian of Caesarea, was in full agreement (*Epist.*, LXXV).

The Church was a single body, and all lesser communities, whatever their size, are members of the one primitive society which has come down from the apostles (Tertullian, *De Praes.*, XX). The Church, indeed, might be regarded as part of the original creation and older than sun and moon (II *Clem.*, XIV, 1 ff.); and for its sake all things were made (Hermas, *Vis.*, II, iv, 1). The Church is our Mother just as God is our Father, says Tertullian (*De Orat.*, II). Irenaeus looks upon it as the seed of Abraham through Jesus Christ (IV, viii, 1). Some of these claims, and the figures employed to enforce or illustrate them, may strike us as eccentric. They are at least evidence of the high conception which Christian teachers cherished. In a less figurative vein it could be claimed that the Church was the unique sphere of the operations of the Holy Spirit (Iren., III, xxiv, 1)

[1] R. W. Moore, *The Roman Commonwealth*, p. 27.
[2] Cyprian, *Epist.*, LV: *Christianus non est qui in Christi ecclesia non est.*

and that through it alone remission of sins and eternal life were possible.[1]

In different lands and among different peoples organization took different forms, even the officials do not seem to have been identical. Communities which were originally Jewish would naturally adopt forms which differed from those originally Gentile. The political and social organization of the Jewish communities themselves had not been entirely uniform. In Alexandria they were under the rule of a single official, the ethnarch; but this was not the case in Rome where the community had a species of president, but power was in the hands of the several groups which composed it. These probably were not sufficiently homogeneous to make complete subordination advisable. The organization of the Jews, however, seems to have provided a model for the Christians;[2] how far this went may be inferred from descriptions in Philo (*De Vita Contemp.*, LXVII, LXXV, etc.) which mention a president who expounds the Scriptures, elders (presbyters) who occupy the highest places at the common meal, and young men who serve at the tables.

Among the Gentiles the influence of associations could hardly be avoided. One difference, however, there must have been; the officials of the Christian Church were not merely elected by each several group, there was some kind of higher authorization (Acts 6 : 3, 6). Even in Acts 14 : 23 and Titus 1 : 5 no idea of choice by the congregation is implied in the Greek. In I *Clem.*, XLII, 1–4 (cf. XLIV, 2 f.), which may be taken as representing the view current in Rome towards the end of the first century, it is stated that the apostles received the Gospel from Jesus Christ and appointed of their first-fruits as bishops and deacons. To these, subject to the approval of the whole community, belongs the right to fill vacancies. The principle of authorization is here exemplified, for the apostles or those selected by them, appoint or ratify the local officials.[3]

THE MINISTRY

In the New Testament no exclusive form of government is specified or even inferred. The very names of the ruling officials are not uniform, for there are bishops and deacons in some Churches, but apparently not in others. At Antioch, important as the starting-point of expansion to the West, the leaders seem

---

[1] Cyprian, *Epist.*, LXIX. He quotes the form of creed current in North Africa: *Remissionem peccatorum . . . et vitam aeternam per sanctam ecclesiam.*
[2] See, further, G. F. Moore, *Judaism*, I, p. 308 ff., and Oesterly and Box, *Religion and Worship of the Synagogue.*
[3] Tertullian would allow the title "apostolic" to Churches which were the offspring of those founded by apostles (*De Praes.*, XX).

to be prophets and teachers, who themselves commission "apostles" (Acts 13 : 1 ff.).[1] Harnack, as is well known, had a theory that there was a primitive ministry of "gifts", consisting of apostles, prophets, and teachers. This ministry was mobile and belonged to the Church as a whole. To it a local ministry of "office", with bishops, priests, and deacons, at length succeeded, as the Church passed from the missionary stage. In the Pauline epistles there are certainly traces of two ministries, local and mobile, existing side by side. Harnack's theory, however, is probably too rigid, and he presses it unduly; but the problem which it raises has been recognized by C. H. Turner,[2] and the theory itself is still maintained by Harnack's successor at Berlin, Hans Lietzmann (*Beginnings of the Christ. Church*, p. 187 ff.).

According to Mark 3 : 14 (Luke 6 : 13, but not Matt. 10 : 2) the title "apostle" was actually given by the Lord.[3] This may underlie the distinction made by St. Paul between the Twelve and apostles in general (1 Cor. 15 : 5 and 7 and the reference in 2 Cor. 8 : 23 to a kind of secondary apostleship, that of the Church). Perhaps it was such a limited apostleship that he was repudiating in Gal. 1 : 1. It is interesting to observe that, though the Twelve were careful to maintain their original number by the election of Matthias in the place of Judas (Acts 1 : 15 f.), so far as we know, further vacancies were left unfilled.[4] There was no attempt to continue the Twelve as a kind of college of cardinals to rule the Church. In the second generation the title of the Twelve was gradually abandoned as a description of the earliest disciples in favour of the Apostles. The latter was a Greek word and could also be used of St. Paul and others. In the Jewish Church the term was used to describe the collectors sent out by the Jewish Patriarch some time after the Fall of Jerusalem.

Harnack's higher ministry was a mobile ministry moving about from place to place. Its powers may have come gradually to be concentrated in the presiding member of the presbytery in each Church, whether with Hort we regard him as holding merely temporary rank or, like the later bishop, permanently elevated above his brother presbyters. A link between the visiting apostle and the resident bishop can perhaps be found in Timothy and Titus who were apparently resident for a limited

---

[1] Hort thinks that there must also have been elders, *Christ. Eccles.*, p. 90.
[2] *Studies in Early Church Hist.*, p. 13 f. For a criticism of Harnack see Armitage Robinson in *Early Hist. of the Church and Ministry*, p. 66 ff.
[3] The title is applied to the Lord in Heb. 3 : 1, and Justin, I *Apol.*, XII; cf. the constant use in the fourth gospel "He that sent me" though with a different Greek word.
[4] Hort thinks James may have taken the place of his namesake (*op. cit.*, p. 77).

period. It is possible, also, that Hippolytus was some kind of bishop with a roving commission. Early in the second century Ignatius could lay it down that the threefold ministry of bishop, priest, and deacon was necessary in every Church (*Trall.*, III, I). But recollection of an older state of affairs seems to have lingered; Hermas apparently tries to combine both types of ministry by speaking of apostles, bishops, teachers, and deacons (*Vis.*, III, v, I).[1]

It is very doubtful whether any definite order of prophets ever existed in the ancient Church. Ignatius at the beginning of the second century claimed to possess prophetic powers (*Trall.*, V; *Philad.*, VII), but for him as for Polycarp (*Phil.*, VI, 3), "the prophets" were those of the Old Testament.[2] So in I *Clem.* no reference is made to any other prophets, which is perhaps surprising in a letter to Corinth. Tertullian, in his pre-Montanist days, when mentioning various orders who might fall from the faith, does not include prophets, and may therefore not have known them as an order.[3] It seems best to regard prophecy as a gift which might be exercised by anyone. There were, indeed, wandering prophets who went from place to place much in the manner of the American revivalists of more recent days, but perhaps they were exceptional. A little consideration makes it evident how unsuited prophecy is as the basis of an order, depending as it does on visions and other spasmodic means of guidance.

Those who had the gift, whether an order or not, and whether local or mobile, evidently presented a serious problem in the early days of the Church, before organization had been developed and in the absence of formulated doctrines. The numerous warnings against "false prophets" show this clearly.[4] Even in the second century Hermas tells us that there were prophets who engaged in fortune-telling, but that the true prophet sought no reward and was further distinguished from the false by his humility and gentleness (*Mand.*, XI). Though Hermas himself claimed to be a prophet, his position in the Roman Church was

[1] At an even earlier date, this time in the East, Polycarp is described as an apostolic and prophetic teacher, and also as bishop of the holy Church (*Mart. Polycarp*, XVI, 2).

[2] See *Magn.*, VIII, 2; *Philad.*, V, 2; IX, 1 f. Kirsopp Lake is surely mistaken in claiming that *Philad.*, V, 2 refers to Christian prophets.

[3] *De Praes.*, III. But as he likewise passes over presbyters the inference is not very certain. There may be a reference to the prophets as an order in a papyrus recently discovered in Egypt where ἡ προφητικὴ τάξις is mentioned: see Grenfell and Hunt, *Oxyrhyn. Pap.*, I., p. 8 f. But the term may have no technical significance, as Eusebius refers to Montanism as the "lying organization (τάξεως) called the New Prophecy" (V, xix, 2).

[4] cf. Matt. 7 : 15 ff., 24 : 11 f.; *Didache*, XI f. In the Akhmim fragment of the *Gospel* or *Apoc. of Peter* it is again recorded that the Lord foretold the coming of "false prophets" (*Apoc. N.T.*, p. 507).

evidently very subordinate. Certainly there is nothing in his writings to suggest that any order existed either then or earlier.

A generation later Justin tells us that prophetic gifts were common (*Dial.*, LXXXII); whilst they were known to Irenaeus (V, vi, 1). An anonymous writer against Montanism, quoted by Eusebius (V, xvii, 4), affirms that according to the Apostle (i.e., St. Paul) the prophetic gift ought to continue in the whole Church until the Lord's return.

We come now to Harnack's third order, that of the teacher. Here again it is not easy to find traces of anything definite. The nearest approach is Acts 13 : 1 f. where prophets and teachers are mentioned as being in charge of the Church at Antioch. Doubtless, teaching was part of the Church's activities from the very earliest days, and those who had the necessary gifts would take their share in it. But not everyone had such qualifications, for the writer of the *Epistle of Barnabas* disclaims their possession (I, 8; IV, 9: cf. Ignatius *Eph.*, III, 1)—the real Barnabas, the companion of St. Paul, however, seems to have been a teacher (Acts 13 : 1). The office was certainly recognized as apostolic,[1] though the use of the title itself had been forbidden by the Lord (Matt. 23 : 8). In spite of this prohibition it was probably that by which He Himself was originally known (John 13 : 13),[2] just as His followers were called "disciples", a term common in the gospels, found in Acts, but unknown in the epistles where "saints" or "believers" is the usual designation of Christians. This change of nomenclature is quite a natural one, for it witnesses to the different relationship between the Lord and His followers when He was no longer with them in the flesh.[3] The title "disciple" did not, however, disappear at once, it is used in several passages by Ignatius (e.g., *Eph.*, I, 2; III, 1; *Magn.*, IX, 1 f.; *Trall.*, V, 2).

The function of the teacher is never clearly defined, but no doubt whilst he might be an evangelist the term would chiefly be applied to those who instructed candidates for baptism and others who were already Christians. St. Paul taught daily in a hired lecture-room at Ephesus (Acts 19 : 9); where a school was set up by Justin, as also at Rome, a practice which was carried on by Tatian. Such halls would correspond to the "preaching

---

[1] So Iren., IV, xxvi, 2, 4 f., where *magistratum* must mean "teaching office" and not "government" as Harnack, *Dogma*, II, p. 84, seems to think. It is the equivalent of διδασκαλία: see Mason in *Early Hist. of the Church and Ministry*, p. 46, n. 3.

[2] But always with the idea that He is *magister vitae* rather than *scholae*. The use of the term in the *Apost. Church Order* has no value, being an obvious fiction in conformity with the claim that the apostles themselves issued the injunctions.

[3] In the *Fragment of an Unknown Gospel* (*Egerton Pap.*, No. 2, 33) the Lord is addressed as Διδάσκαλε Ἰη[σοῦ].

halls" of pagan professors or to the similar institutions of the modern missionary.

In North Africa certain presbyters seem to have been set apart for the work of teaching, which suggests that it was no necessary activity of the presbyter. But teachers were not invariably members of the clergy, for *Apost. Trad.*, XIX, 1, speaks of both ecclesiastics and laymen engaging in the work, and adds that either may lay hands upon and pray for the catechumens whom they instruct.

For Harnack the work of the teacher had immense importance,[1] and he cites Jas. 3 : 1 as evidence of the attractiveness of the office. This importance was retained when both apostles and prophets had disappeared. But if ever there was a separate order, and the evidence makes it hardly probable, it must eventually have been merged in that of the reader.

If a threefold ministry of apostles, prophets, and teachers ever existed, by the middle of the second century it had completely disappeared. Even earlier, as we have seen, Ignatius could claim that bishops, priests, and deacons were essential to the life of the Church. To Irenaeus and Tertullian this latter ministry is as much a part of the nature of things as the fourfold gospel. They seem hardly aware of a time when it was not everywhere established. Above all, they recognize the supreme importance of the episcopate.

The theory that the terms "bishop" and "presbyter" originally represented the same office (just as under the old dispensation priests and levites were originally one) which was made popular by Lightfoot, probably goes too far. It seems, on the face of it, that such different terms would scarcely have been used with an identical meaning. In Acts 20 : 17 and 28 the two seem definitely to be identified, but, as Lowther Clarke has pointed out, "In view of the LXX colouring we may suppose that *episcopi* is here used of function rather than office" (in *Episcopacy Ancient and Modern*, p. 17). The truth of the matter seems to be that whilst every bishop was a presbyter, not every presbyter was a bishop.[2] The equation of the two offices seems, however, to have persisted in Alexandria until the third century, as it is apparently recognized by Clement;[3] and Jerome records that up to his time the presbyters of Alexandria ordained one of their number to be bishop (*Epist.*, CXLVI). The idea of a threefold order is, however, frequently found in early writings. In addition to the well-known passage from Ignatius already quoted, it appears in

---

[1] *Mission und Ausbreitung*, p. 365 ff. (E.T., I, p. 444 ff.).
[2] This seems to be the case in I *Clem.*, whilst Irenaeus often speaks of the bishop as presbyter (e.g., III, ii, 2; IV, xxvi, 2 ff.), never, I believe, *vice versa*.
[3] See Tollinton, *Clem. of Alex.*, II, p. 111 ff.

Hippolytus (IX, 12) and in Cyprian (*Epist.*, LXXX), to name but a few instances. It is, of course, definitely recognized by the Council of Nicaea (canon 3). In the East, at any rate, certain distinctions between the two offices were maintained. The so-called *Canons of Hippolytus* preserved in an Arabic version, point out that the bishop differs from the presbyter by having his own seat and by the power of ordaining.[1] Moreover, a confessor who has suffered torture may be accepted as a presbyter without ordination, but not as a bishop.[2] In the Middle Ages the Papacy pursued a policy of limiting the power of the episcopate, and perhaps as a consequence the distinction between bishop and priest was declared to be one of grade and not of order.[3]

The bishop's right to ordain is so important that something more must be said about it. Ordination seems to go back to primitive times in the Christian Church, for the laying on of hands in 1 Tim. 5 : 22 can hardly have any other meaning. In the second century it was even held that the Lord had so ordained the apostles (*Acts of Peter*, X).[4] Lowther Clarke (*op. cit.*, p. 42 f.) thinks that it may have been a Palestinian custom which was not at once taken over by Gentile Christians. Be this as it may, the custom of ordination, and that by the bishop, soon became the accepted means of conveying holy orders. In the West, the presbyter assisted by "touching" the candidate for the priesthood when the bishop actually ordained him.[5] It was not, however, required for minor orders, as a rule, though there is some difference of procedure in the case of certain offices. In *Apost. Const.*, VIII, 19 ff., both the reader and the subdeacon receive the laying-on of hands, but this is forbidden in *Test. Domini*, I, 40 ff. Cases in which presbyters alone are supposed to have conferred holy orders are of doubtful value. The well-known instance of the supposed custom of the Alexandrian presbytery cited above is open to several objections. C. H. Turner has suggested that it was invented by the Arians to discredit Athanasius.[6]

The process by which the bishop came to be distinguished from his fellow presbyters and at last to occupy a position of authority over them and the Church can no longer be traced.

---

[1] *Die Canones Hipp.*, IV, 32 (ed. by Achelis in *Texte und Unters.*, VI, iv, p. 61): *Episcopus in omnibus rebus aequiparetur presbytero excepto nomine cathedrae et ordinatione, quia potestas ordinandi ipsi non tribuitur.*

[2] *op. cit.*, VI, 43–45 (p. 67 f.), *Apost. Trad.*, X, 1.

[3] Canon law only recognizes the bishops as having a higher degree within the order of the priesthood (Gratian, I, lx, 4). The Roman Church confirmed this at Trent: see *Catechism of the Council of Trent*, Pt. II, chap. VII, qu. xxv.

[4] *Apoc. N.T.*, p. 314.

[5] *Apost. Trad.*, VIII, 1. Dix states that this custom was unknown in the East (*op. cit.*, p. 16).

[6] In *Camb. Med. Hist.*, I, p. 160 f., and, for a discussion of the whole matter, see F. E. Brightman in *Early Hist. of the Church and Ministry*, p. 401 ff.

Doubtless it took place gradually and almost unperceived—for the bishop remained a presbyter and performed the same functions, though he began to draw to himself greater powers. Various lines of development have been suggested. In a college of presbyters it would be necessary to have a chairman or president.[1] This need not always have been the same person, though perhaps the senior presbyter may have held the office; but the possibility of the various members presiding in rotation must not be excluded. In this case, the very term "bishop" may have represented at first merely a temporary office which any presbyter might hold, rather than a permanent order. The same applies to the administration of the eucharist. Then, again, each Christian community in its relations with other communities and with the world outside would need a representative; the presiding elder would be the obvious person to take over such a responsibility and there would be an advantage if the same person acted each time. Again, the growth of heretical views made it advisable, if not essential, that there should be an official with full authority to expound the traditional doctrines. At some period or other the power of ordaining was confined to the bishop, as we have already seen in the quotation from the *Canons of Hippolytus*, IV, 32. This concentration of power, however, is more likely to have followed the emergence of a monarchical episcopate than to have been a means by which it developed.

Another line of explanation would regard the bishops as having been selected by the apostles as definite heads of each Church. In this case the office would have been a permanent one and there would have been a distinction between the bishop and the presbyter from the first. But this idea seems to find no justification in the earliest literature, for, as we have seen, the office hardly became universal until well on in the second century.

In considering the question of what is called the Apostolic Succession it is necessary to distinguish carefully between the facts and theories which may have been built upon them. In the New Testament the fact is stated (e.g., Acts 14 : 23; Titus 1 : 5); but the writers "show no consciousness of any idea that Apostolic appointment . . . is essential to a valid ministry or that it has been specially determined by revelation of God's will".[2] So again in I *Clem.*, XLII, XLIV, we have the fact stated, but the only theory advanced is the necessity for a regular performance of divine worship. In Irenaeus the thought of the transmission of authority is certainly present (cf. III, iii, 2; IV, xxxiii, 8), but it is not confined to the episcopate (III, ii, 2 speaks of *succes-*

[1] In the synagogue a permanent Head was chosen from the elders: see G. F. Moore, *Judaism*, I, p. 289.   [2] Hamilton, *The People of God*, II, p. 122.

siones presbyterorum), and the succession is valued as a guarantee of the truth of the tradition which the bishops upheld, the object being the "establishing the purity of the Church's faith rather than its continuity as an institution".[1] So, too, Tertullian insists on the bishops being able to trace themselves to an apostolic source (*De Praes.*, XXXII). Headlam, indeed, claims that in the early Church there is no thought of the transmission of grace, the whole emphasis is upon obedience to the apostolic ordinances and a due succession.[2] The succession is not from consecrator to consecrated but from predecessor to successor.[3] Alike to Irenaeus, to Hegesippus, and to Tertullian bishops have their place in the apostolic succession only in connexion with the Churches over which they preside.[4]

The Christian Church, like the Jewish, was careful that continuity should be maintained, but on different grounds and by different methods. For just as the new People of God were to be drawn from all the races of mankind, so the new order of ministry was to be perpetuated, not in a single tribe or family, but by an ecclesiastical tradition.

The manner in which a bishop was chosen is not quite clear. The *Apost. Trad.*, II, 1 (cf. *Apost. Const.*, VIII, i, 2) lays it down that he is to be selected by all the people. This does not seem to have been the invariable rule in the West, he might be chosen by neighbouring bishops in the presence of the people. Certainly the people had their rights in the matter, for Cyprian reminds them that if they have an unworthy bishop it is their own fault for not having objected to his appointment (*Epist.*, LXVII). One thing, however, is clear: that, however chosen, a bishop had to be consecrated by those who were already bishops.

The exaltation of one presbyter above the rest so that, either at once or by a gradual development, he became permanently a ruler of the Church and its representative to those outside, was undoubtedly an advantage and filled a definite gap in the organization of the Church as a whole. The various challenges by which it was confronted could only be met with any hope of success by a united body acting under a recognized leader. Once his authority was recognized, however, fresh powers would inevitably accrue to him. Hermas had already emphasized the part taken by bishops in providing hospitality (*Sim.*, IX, xxvii, 2),

[1] N. P. Williams in *Northern Catholicism*, p. 199.
[2] *The Doctrine of the Church and Reunion*, p. 131. But 2 Tim. 1 : 6 seems to imply a special grace transmitted by the laying-on of hands by St. Paul.
[3] C. H. Turner, *Catholic and Apostolic*, p. 280 f., expresses his agreement with Dr. Headlam on this point. Elsewhere he has himself quoted the view of Augustine that "the apostolic succession of the church of Rome is, as with St. Irenaeus, from holder to holder not from consecrator to consecrated" (in *Early Hist. of the Church and Ministry*, p. 193).
[4] C. H. Turner in *Early Hist., etc.*, p. 129.

a very important function in times when there was much moving about from place to place. In this connexion the bishop would be the appropriate official to grant letters of identification to Christians wishing to proceed to some other Church. Within the community the bishop would be the natural arbitrator if disputes arose. Under Roman civil law disputants were allowed to refer their case to an arbitrator and his decision was recognized as binding. Christians naturally chose the bishop; the custom was, indeed, so usual that Constantine later made it de jure.

In the struggle with heresy it was to the bishops, as representing apostolic tradition, that recourse would be made for a testimony as to the genuine belief of the Church, and later still the bishops meeting in synod would decide what that faith actually was. Considerable sums of money would also pass through the hands of the bishop as the ruler of the congregation and it was for him to arrange for the distribution of alms. The position of the bishop as the representative of the Church on what may be called the business side was recognized by Gallienus when he restored the places of worship which had been seized during the persecution. It was the bishop, too, who corresponded with other Churches, or rather with the bishops who represented them. The development of systematic penance also brought fresh power to the bishop, for in course of time the right to receive penitents became vested in him, with power to appoint subordinates to act in his stead.

All the evidence which is available points to the East as the part where the Episcopate first arose, and some scholars would connect it with the presence of St. John in Asia Minor.[1] The Church there was stronger and more homogeneous than in the West, and more able to absorb elements which came in from outside. In Rome, the only place in the West of which we have any knowledge before the later half of the second century, there seem to have been a number of separate groups within the Church; possibly Rome's task was to reduce these groups to unity as a stage towards the unification of the whole Western Church under its leadership. There is no trace of episcopal rule before the second century, however, and even in Philippi presbyters and deacons seem to bear rule.[2] The bishops of Rome seem first to have begun to extend their powers under Anicetus (155–167) who was a Syrian and to have made even greater headway under the African Victor (189–199). Streeter had an interesting theory that the Eastern idea of the episcopate was brought to

---

[1] Tertullian traces the succession of bishops in Asia Minor to St. John (Adv. Marc., IV).
[2] cf. Polycarp, Phil., V, 3; VI, 1.

Rome by Ignatius (*The Primitive Church*, p. 227 ff.); but, though the theory is attractive, we have no means of either proving or disproving it.

The function of the presbyter was twofold, to govern and to teach. So Lightfoot concluded from the mention of pastors and teachers in Eph. 4 : 11, which he takes to apply to a single set of officials (*Philipp.*, p. 194). In the pastoral epistles there is certainly much stress laid on the ability to teach as a qualification for the bishop, who here may perhaps be supposed to include the presbyter (1 Tim. 3 : 2; Tit. 1 : 9). In North Africa teaching seems to have been a prominent part of the duty of presbyters, for *Passio Perpetuae*, XIII, speaks of *presbyterum doctorem*[1] and the same phrase is used in Cyprian, *Epist.*, XXIX. But it was mainly in administrative and judicial work[2] that they were normally engaged. It was to the presbyters that Barnabas and Saul handed over the funds sent to Jerusalem (Acts 11 : 30). Dr. Jalland, indeed, concludes that "the presbyter of the second and third centuries was far more of a Christian 'magistrate' than a 'priest' ", and that the bishop alone was the proper priest; and that, when absent, "his liturgical function would be supplied, not by a presbyter, but a deacon" (*The Church and the Papacy*, p. 143 f.). But to deny liturgical functions to the presbyter is surely to go too far, for Tertullian repeatedly calls them *sacerdotes*, and if Benson denied that Cyprian did so (*Cyprian*, p. 33, n. 3) his statement was not quite accurate, though the only instances are in *Epist.*, XL (cf. *Epist.*, LXI, *cum episcopo sacerdotali honore conjuncti*). As the Church grew it would be necessary to develop a kind of "parochial system";[3] for the whole body of Christians in a single city would no longer be able conveniently to meet together for common worship. Presbyters it may be supposed were given the charge of definite churches and became responsible for their worship.

The term diaconate was used at first of any kind of service, and had no definite connotation. Thus, St. Paul could call himself a deacon (Eph. 3 : 7) and speak of his ministry as a diaconate (Rom. 11 : 13). Contrary to popular opinion, the "seven" appointed to assist the apostles in Acts 6 are not given the title in the New Testament. The work of the later deacons was not, however, limited to "serving tables" as Ignatius reminded them (*Trall.*, II, 3); other tasks were theirs, especially as helpers of the

[1] The Greek text, however, has no equivalent for *doctorem*.
[2] In the Jewish Church the elders acted as judges.
[3] The term parish (*parochia*) has a long and varied history into which we cannot here enter. With the Jews it could mean a community in a foreign land (*Ps. of Sol.*, XVII, 19); with the Christians it is often the equivalent of diocese, even in the Middle Ages. See, further, Harnack, *Const. and Law of the Church*, p. 47.

bishop,[1] though apparently not of any high spiritual significance.[2] After a time they came to work under the presbyters,
though still retaining their intimate relation to the bishop,[3]
whilst some of their more mechanical duties were transferred to
the lesser orders. Because the deacons were few in number (the
traditional seven was retained in Rome) and because they were
in close attendance upon the bishop, they had considerable influence, and rivalry with the priesthood was not uncommon.
What are now considered the rights of the priesthood were sometimes undertaken by them, such as the offering of the eucharist,
a practice which was sufficiently common to require condemnation at the Council of Arles (canon 15).

It seems to have been the custom for one deacon to have an
especially close relation with the bishop (cf. Euseb., IV, xxii, 3),
and he may have taken a leading place in the order. But to speak
of him as an archdeacon, as is often done by modern scholars, is
an anachronism; for, with the exception of one isolated instance,
the title was not used before Jerome.[4]

In the West, although *ordo* itself is Latin, most of the titles
used are Greek: episcopus, presbyter, and deacon being all retained. *Sacerdos*, although it was available and used by Tertullian
and Cyprian, failed to maintain its place, perhaps because it was
a common name for heathen priests. In the Old Latin version of
Acts, it is the usual equivalent of ἀρχιερεύς (e.g., 4 : 1; 5 : 27;
7 : 1; 9 : 14, 21; 23 : 4, 14). It was, in general, limited to the
bishop, though Cyprian, as we have seen, in a few passages
applies it to a presbyter. An interesting illustration of the usage
can be found in a church dedication at Castellum Tingitanum
(Orléansville) where the name of the founder, who was a bishop,
is given as *Marinus sacerdos*.

There was, it would seem, no hard and fast rule as to the application of ecclesiastical terms borrowed from other religions by
the Church. Levite is used by Cyprian of presbyters (*Epist.*, I);
but it is also used of deacons, as of the father of Pope Damasus,
and in the account of the martyrdom of St. Vincent of Saragossa
written at the end of the fourth century under the title of *Passio
S. Vincentii Levitae*.

---

[1] See *Apost. Trad.*, IX, and Cyprian, *Epist.*, III. Their dependence upon
the bishop, to whom they formed a kind of personal staff, was brought out at
the Council of Nicaea (canon 18).

[2] cf. C. H. Turner, *Cath. and Apost.*, p. 330 f. He concludes:" At best [the
deacon] will have been . . . a sacristan or server".

[3] Ignatius regards the deacon as subject to the bishop and the presbytery
(*Magn.*, II).

[4] The exception is Optatus of Milevis, I, xvi (*P.L.*, XI, col. 915), who applies
it to Caecilian of Carthage. Lipsius, *Chron. der röm. Bischöfe*, p. 120, says that
no such office is found in the Roman Church before the end of the fourth
century.

Presbyter and its Greek original had also a wide usage;[1] like the Saxon "elder" it could be used of local or village officials. There is a strange reference in a papyrus of A.D. 159–160[2] to the priests of the Socnopaeus temple as being divided into tribes each of which is under an "elder-priest".[3] Episcopus was also common in Hellenistic Greek and was used of officials in pre-Christian days.[4]

In the East the reader was an important official ranking with prophets (*Didasc.*, II, 20) and drawing as large a share of the clerical allowance as presbyters and deacons (*Didasc.*, II, 28). In Rome also, in the middle of the second century, if the reference in II *Clem.*, XIX, 1, is to an official, as seems probable, he was held in high regard. There is an inscription in the church of St. Agnes, Rome, which may belong to the second century in commemoration of FAVOR, LECTOR.[5] In North Africa, Tertullian groups readers with the three highest orders (*De Praes.*, XLI). There are also many references to readers by Cyprian who regards them as only just outside the ranks of the clergy (*Epist.*, XXIX: *clero proximo*). Later they seem to have become less important, for in the list of Roman ecclesiastics given by Cornelius (in Euseb., VI, xliii, 11) they are simply lumped together with doorkeepers and exorcists at the end.[6] However, in the *Apoc. of Paul*, XXXIV–XXXVI (*Apoc. N.T.*, p. 543 f.), a fourth-century work which had some popularity in the West, they are the only minor order mentioned in a vision of evil clerics.

The work of the reader included more than mere reading aloud, it required in addition powers of simple exposition,[7] as an ancient prayer for use at the admission of a reader preserved in *Apost. Const.*, VIII, 22, testifies. There may be traces of the activities of the reader in the New Testament (e.g., Mark 13 : 14; Matt. 24 : 15; Rev. 1 : 3; cf. 1 Tim. 4 : 13). His functions, however, seem to have differed. In North Africa, he read both the gospel and the lessons (Cyprian, *Epist.*, XXXVIII, XXXIX); in Rome, the epistle, but not the gospel. In the *Apost. Trad.*, XII, the reader is appointed by the bishop handing him "the book". This is more fully, though by no means consistently, specified in other church orders; the *Egyptian Church Order*, V f., calls it the book of the Apostle (i.e., St. Paul), whilst the *Canons of Hippolytus* call it the gospel.

[1] See H. Hauschildt, *Zeit. für N.T. Wiss.*, 1903, IV, p. 235 ff.
[2] G. Milligan, *Selections from Greek Pap.*, No. 33.
[3] "Clearly a title not of age but of dignity" say Moulton and Milligan, *Vocab. of the Greek Testament*, p. xvii.
[4] See Deissmann, *Bib. Studies*, p. 230 f.   [5] Marucchi, p. 386.
[6] Marucchi, p. 658, prints an inscription to a certain Proficius who was both LECT. ET EXORC.
[7] In later Greek ἀναγινώσκειν is used with the sense of read and make comments: cf. Epictetus, *Diss.*, III, xxiii, 20.

Just as the original "seven" were·appointed to relieve the apostles from the serving of tables, so the various minor orders seem to have sprung up in order to relieve the deacons themselves of their less important duties. For our period they are almost confined to the West, except the reader who has already received attention, and are not found in the East before the fourth century. In the West, they seem to have been well developed by the middle of the third century, and we have good evidence for their existence in the Letter of Cornelius and the various writings of Cyprian.

The most important of the minor orders was the sub-deacon. In the Middle Ages the office would still further be magnified and come to rank as a major order being part of the diaconate. The number, like that of the deacons, was apparently at first seven, if Rome is any criterion for other Churches. Acolytes are first found in the middle of the third century in the West (in the East, hardly before the sixth). In the list of Cornelius they appear after the sub-deacons. The list then goes on to mention exorcists, readers, and door-keepers, without separate enumeration. The exorcist, however, seems to have played a great part in the Early Church, or perhaps it would be more correct to say the practice of exorcism, for it may be that no separate order existed at first, since the gift was possessed by many Christians (cf. Justin II *Apol.*, VIII). The extent to which it was used is startling to a modern mind; catechumens, for example, were exorcized daily during their long term of preparation and finally by the bishop himself before being baptized (*Apost. Trad.*, XX, 3, 8). In the New Testament, exorcism is one of the principal works of the disciples (Mark 1 : 39; 3 : 15), but it seems to be intended for cases of obvious possession. The office as it came to be developed took over much of the work of the healer of earlier days and might be combined with that of reader. Two inscriptions in a cemetery in the Via Latina can here be cited, that of Proficius already noticed, and another which runs as follows: FAVSTVS EXORC[ISTA] IN P[ACE].[1] Several other early inscriptions have also survived; one from the beginning of the fourth century in the cemetery of Trasone in the Via Salaria commemorates MACEDONIVS EXORCISTA DE KATHOLIKA [ECCLESI]A.[2]

The desire for pre-eminence has, unfortunately, been ever a mark of Christian leaders. It was not Diotrephes alone in the primitive Church who desired to have the pre-eminence (3 John 9),. for the synoptists (Mark 10 : 42 f.; Luke 22 : 24; Matt. 20 : 25 f.) as well as the fourth gospel (John 13 : 13 ff.), contain warnings uttered by the Lord to His disciples against this very fault. The strife at Corinth with which I *Clement* deals is an

---

[1] Marucchi, p. 658. [2] *op. cit.*, p. 447.

example of the need for such warnings and at Rome itself similar conditions were found (Hermas, *Mand.*, XI, 12; *Sim.*, VIII, vii, 4).

The elaboration of orders and the introduction of minor orders represent a kind of specialization of function to meet the needs of the growing organism; but it was not until the fourth century that they were arranged in a kind of ladder of ascending importance which all must climb.[1] Cyprian was only a layman when he was made bishop of Carthage, and so in the fourth century was Ambrose when forced by the people to undertake the office of bishop of Milan. Such were, of course, exceptional cases and not to be encouraged, as Cyprian himself clearly recognizes, for in supporting the claims of Cornelius against Novatian he points out that the former had not been raised at one step to the episcopate but had risen through the various lower grades (*Epist.*, LV). The inscriptions contain a number of interesting records of clerical progression. That of Flavius Latinus, Bishop of Brixen, appears to belong to the third century:

FL. LATINO EPISCOPO
AN. III. M.VII PREASB.
AN. XV. EXORC. AN. XII.[2]

The father of Damasus, Bishop of Rome (366–84), had been *exceptor, lector, levita* (i.e., deacon), and *sacerdos*.[3]

THE ORGANIZATION OF THE GREAT CHURCH

Parallel to the development of organization in the different Churches went the development of the "Great Church" as Celsus called it. There had been a sense of unity from the first amongst the Jewish Christians, who regarded themselves as the New Israel; and this same sense was fostered among the Gentiles by St. Paul, as also, no doubt, by other Christian teachers. The actual term "Catholic", which in our day represents the unity and universality of the Church, is first found in Ignatius (*Smyrn.*, VIII) as applied to the Great Church to distinguish it from local Churches (but not yet as opposed to heretical and schismatic bodies). He looked upon the bishop as the centre of each particular Church, as Jesus was the centre of the Church universal.

We are apt to think of the bishop's jurisdiction in terms of territory, the diocese over which he rules; but it may, in primitive times, have been thought of rather in terms of persons, as in the Celtic Church in Ireland and Northern England. It was the primitive custom to have a bishop in every town and so long

---

[1] Abailard thought that such a ladder existed from the beginning, having been taken over from the Jews (*Epist. ad Hel.*, VII).

[2] Syxtus, II, p. 183. [3] *Bull. Arch. Crist.*, 1881, p. 48.

as the Christian body was small this was a very convenient custom; for the bishop could know all his flock and be known by them.[1] But as the Church grew, much of the work of the bishop had to be handed over to subordinates and this close intercourse was not always possible. The need for taking effective measures against heresy and faction also made the old simple type of bishop unequal to the position, as men in sufficient numbers could not be found. There was need for a higher rank, even among the bishops, to give definite leadership. This higher rank, which arose from the rest of the bishops, naturally tended to exalt the great patriarchal sees above the smaller ones and especial value was attached to sees founded by apostles. But as the Church grew up within the geographical boundaries of the Roman Empire it naturally tended to imitate its organization, and so Rome as the imperial city began to take a prominent place. In the West, indeed, it had no serious rival. Here it may be well to point out that though the Church's system was modelled on that of the Empire, taking up and preserving its various geographical divisions, in one most important respect it differed from it; for, in the words of J. R. Green: "its self-made constitution, its elected rulers, its deliberative assemblies, kept alive the free democratic traditions of a world strangled by Caesarism" (*Stray Studies*, II, p. 200).

The title of Patriarch, probably taken over from the Jews, was first applied to Alexander, Bishop of Caesarea in Palestine,[2] it did not come into general use until well beyond our period. That of pope seems to have begun with the bishops of Alexandria. Strangely enough, although the Roman clergy address Cyprian as pope, the title was not used of the bishop of Rome until the beginning of the fourth century,[3] and it was not until long after our period that they had any exclusive use of it. The term is often applied to Augustine, and as late as the end of the fifth century Sidonius so addresses the bishops of Rheims, Lyons, Arles, and other cities.

Although the various patriarchs stood out above the other bishops, in theory at least all bishops were equal, and anything in the nature of a primacy would have been repugnant to the ideas of the times. Tertullian is especially scornful of any bishop who should desire to be a "pontiff".[4] The usual practice seems to

[1] The *Apostolic Church Order* contemplates cases where the bishop would not have more than a dozen people over whom to rule: see *Texte und Unters.*, II, Pt. V, p. 7. This was, of course, in the East.

[2] See Germer-Durand, *Rev. Bibl.*, 1894, p. 255.

[3] It is used in an inscription of Marcellinus (d. 304). See De Rossi, *Inscr.*, I, p. cxv.

[4] *Pontifex scilicet maximus, quod est episcopus episcoporum, edicit* (*De Pudic.*, XXXI). So Gregory the Great later rejected the title *sacerdos universalis* as suggesting the pride which makes men forerunners of Anti-Christ.

have been for the bishop senior by consecration to act as metro-politan; this was especially the case in North Africa, except in Africa Proconsularis.

The West was more interested in organization and practice than in doctrines and theories; none the less, it was in the West that a theory of the episcopate was, in the middle of the third century, actually worked out. This, as we have seen, was the work of Cyprian, Bishop of Carthage. He regarded the episcopate as expressing the unity of the Church, and as the instrument of the Church's authority. He would, indeed, make the authority of the bishop and of the Church identical. Those who claim to have special powers must exercise them in subordination to the bishop. He held a kind of mystical idea of the episcopate which was really one, although embodied in the individual bishops (*De Unit.*, V, *Epist.*, LV, 24). All bishops are equal, as were the apostles, and any kind of primacy is ruled out. No bishop is to judge another or is himself liable to judgment. All alike must await the judgment of Christ from whom alone their office is derived. The unity of the Church and of the episcopate does not depend on the bishop of Rome or of any other see; but on the mutual recognition by all bishops of their independent responsi-bility.

The synodical system, like other ecclesiastical innovations, had its origin in the East, for Tertullian refers to such gatherings among "the Greeks" and expresses the wish that something similar could be organized in the West.[1] Such councils did not as yet form part of the regular machinery of the Church; to assemble them before the Empire began to look on the Church with favour would, indeed, have been difficult, if not actually dangerous. There were, however, meetings from time to time to discuss urgent questions, such as the date of Easter (Euseb., V, xxiii, 2; xxiv, 8). In the West, Cyprian, in this as in other matters a pioneer, seems to have been the first to make regular use of them. In Africa (except Africa Proconsularis), and in Spain, the synod was presided over by the senior bishop.[2] The bishops appear to have been the representatives of their dioceses and not mere delegates. This was something novel in the ancient world where the idea of representation was not highly developed. After the triumph of the Church a regular system of holding annual synods was instituted covering a definite area, corre-sponding to the civil province and presided over by the metro-politan. In addition, councils on a large scale became an important feature in the ecclesiastical organization; in fact there

---

[1] *De Jejun.*, XIII. He mentions councils in connexion with the refusal to recognize the canonicity of *The Shepherd* of Hermas (*De Pudic.*, X).
[2] Cyprian seems to have presided over councils *qua* bishop of Carthage.

was a glut of them in connexion with the Arian controversy.

The development of the Church's machinery involved the increase of restrictions. Some of these were really alien to the spirit of Christianity, and capable, as subsequent ages were to prove, of becoming a hampering burden on free spiritual growth. But heresy had to be met, and after Constantine's rise to power there was an insistence on uniformity of belief which tended to restrain the healthy progress of thought and to foster the narrowing idea that the Church was the only ark of salvation. Even for the higher ranks of the clergy there would be a loss of freedom, for when they first came into general use synods were consultative, not executive bodies, and attendance was voluntary. Synods were, as Benson was fond of pointing out, the only free, representative assemblies in the Empire. But when councils of the whole Church met under imperial protection all was changed and their findings had the force of law.

The tightening-up of organization led also to an additional emphasis on the distinction between cleric and layman, and to the development of a professional ministry. The clergy, in fact, came to be regarded as the *ordo*, corresponding to the senatorial order, as distinct from the *plebs* or people.[1] Later, the State would give them the privileges and immunities of the heathen priesthood as well as the endowments which exempted them from the necessity of pursuing other callings. It would also confer upon them legal jurisdiction.

The displacement of the pagan priesthood by the Christian ministry, however, not only gave the presbyter a new place in the social and political system; it also involved almost inevitably the transfer to him of heathen conceptions of his office and the use concerning it of similar terms. In the New Testament there is no trace of what may be called sacerdotalism, the theory that is, that importance attaches to persons who perform ritual acts on the ground that such acts depend for their efficacy on the skill, knowledge, or special relation of such person to the deity. The careful avoidance of sacrificial language in connexion with the Christian ministry can hardly be an accident: ἱερεύς, for example, is never used by a Christian writer with such a reference before the end of the second century.[2] The first known instance, as a matter of fact, occurs in a heathen author (Lucian, *De Mort. Peregr.*, XI). No "presbyter" would have desired to identify his office with the priesthoods of paganism or even with that of the Old Testament. When sacerdotal terms were adopted,

[1] By the end of the first century the distinction between the "people" and those who minister to them is clearly recognized (I *Clem.*, XL, 5).

[2] In spite of the absence of the term, it has been claimed that the Christian ministry was sacerdotal from the first: see B. J. Kidd, *Hist. of the Church*, I, p. 40, n. 1.

important though subtle distinctions were made so as to do away with any idea of "magic". The sacramental acts were not really those of the priest, but of the Lord whom he represented. "He who baptizes and consecrates", said St. Bernard centuries later, "is Christ Himself" (*Epist.*, CCCLIII). Such distinctions would be hard to grasp and still more to maintain by those who had been brought up in heathen surroundings.

Even before the recognition of Christianity by the State, there had been considerable developments through the analogy of the pagan priesthoods, especially those of Isis and Mithras.[1] "Before Rome became Christian it had become clerical", wrote H. A. L. Fisher (*Hist. of Europe*, I, p. 90), and with much truth. Priesthood in the early days had been the characteristic of the community, not of the individual minister, to whom were committed the exercise of priestly functions;[2] even the power of the keys belonged to the society, not to the ministry.[3] In the same way, medieval political thinkers held that the administrative authority of the magistrate was exercised on behalf of the community (*universitas* or *populus*), a specialization of function rendered necessary for the sake of good order.

Though such specialization of function was undoubtedly necessary in the case of the Church, its effects were in some ways to prove disastrous; for it led to a rigid division between the clergy and the laity which some regard as the fundamental apostasy. Creighton once quoted what he called a terrible saying of a very wise man: "There has been no *Church* since the end of the third century. There have been two bodies, one offering, the other accepting, Christian privileges" (*Life of Mandell Creighton*, II, p. 375). This danger seems at present to be facing the Church of England, where two distinct conceptions of religion, one held by the priesthood and the other by the laity, seem definitely to be emerging.

Sacerdotal claims for the Christian clergy seem, so far as evidence is available, to have had their origin in the West, in that part of the Church in which afterwards they were to blossom so luxuriously and to play so vital a part. They are first advanced in the writings of Tertullian, who claimed that the Christian ministry was a *sacerdotium* and applied the term *sacerdos* without qualification to the individual minister. At the same time he recognized the validity of lay baptism, using the somewhat hazardous argument that anyone can give what he has himself received (*De Bapt.*, XVII). In his Montanist period,

---

[1] See Dill, *Roman Society from Nero to Marcus Aurelius*, p. 580.
[2] No indelible *character* was apparently presupposed. "For Cyprian, to all intents and purposes the *sacerdotium* is annulled if the bishop or presbyter . . . is repudiated by the Church": see *Early Hist. of the Church and Ministry*, p. 232 f.   [3] So Westcott on John 20 : 22 f.

Tertullian asserted the rights of laymen when no clergy are available to act as priests, and even to offer the eucharist (*De Exhort. Cast.*, VII).[1] In this extension he is at variance with the practice of *Apost. Trad.*, XXVI, 12. It is Tertullian also, who first applies *ordo* to the clerical body[2] (*De Monog.*, XII). His ideas, however, can scarcely have originated with himself and must be presumed to be those current in North Africa. Similar ideas, it may be pointed out, are found in Hippolytus (e.g., *Refutatio*, pref.) at about the same time or a little later. Tertullian is at pains to draw a parallel between the hierarchy of the Old Testament with its High Priest, Priest and Levite and the ministry of the Christian Church (*De Bapt.*, XVII). Similar lan-gauge had been used in I *Clem.*, XL, 5, but with no suggestion that the grades of ministry of the two dispensations were in any way identical each to each. It is improbable that the Jews had any responsibility for introducing sacerdotal ideas into the Church, for by this time Judaism, after the Fall of Jerusalem, had itself ceased to be sacerdotal. None the less, the Old Testa-ment descriptions of the Temple worship must ever have been before the minds of its readers, and there was also the wonderful idealization contained in Ecclesiasticus 50 : 5–21.

Tertullian's claim that the layman might in an emergency act as a priest should remind us that in the primitive Church the laity were much less dependent on the ministry than in later times. A very high standard of spiritual competence and re-sponsibility was expected from all instructed Christians, who were considered capable of providing for their own spiritual nourishment. This has been brought out by Harnack in his treatise *Bible Reading in the Early Church*, and receives illustra-tion in the advice given by *Apost. Trad.*, XXXVI, 1, that when no public instruction is available lay people should read a "holy book" at home. (Incidentally this presupposes a high standard of literacy among Christians.) In regard to the whole matter of the relations of the clergy and laity it is easy to go astray, for "theologians and historians, themselves almost always of the clergy, have read into their picture of the primitive centuries the conditions of their own day, and have unduly minimized the position of the laity and their share in the active life

---

[1] Too much should not be read into this claim, which referred to an emergency only. Probably Tertullian would still have felt, as he did when he wrote *De Praes.*, XLI, that to deny any distinction between clergy and laity was a mark of heresy.

[2] *Ordo* is the equivalent of the Greek κλῆρος, the original word behind "clergy". Its meaning is "lot" and the beginnings can be found in Acts 1 : 17 where the "lot" fell on Matthias. Later, it came to mean the office itself; and, later still, those who held it. The term was not restricted to this technical use, for Eusebius can speak of κλῆρος τῶν μαρτύρων (V, i, 10).

of the Church and in the shaping of its destinies."[1]

When once the distinction between clergy and laity had been recognized, as it was everywhere by the middle of the second century or a little later, due respect and deference would be paid by the members of the one order to those of the other. In the worship of the Church this would of necessity be the case for those of the clergy who were actually taking the services; but beyond this it seems to have been the custom for members of the clergy who were present to be provided with seats, whereas the body of the congregation remained standing. Sohm had an interesting theory that it was in some such connexion that the distinction originally arose, suggesting that the Lord's Supper was exactly represented, with the celebrant taking the place of the Master and the presbyters sitting at the table to represent the disciples.[2] If this theory is correct, it would mean that the eucharist not only had a share in the elevation of the bishop above his fellow presbyters, but the elevation of the whole order above the laity.

So far as outward distinctions are concerned, such as the wearing of a special dress, our period knows of none. Probably this came about much later when after the barbarian conquest the clergy, as distinct from the laity, persisted in the use of Roman costume. In the matter of marriage, differences were beginning to grow up, even in our period. Hippolytus, for example, regards marriage after ordination as sinful, though a married man might be ordained (IX, 12). This was probably the Church's rule and it is expressly stated to be such in *Apostolical Canons*, XXV, and the *Apostolical Constitutions*, VI, 17, so far as the higher orders of the clergy are concerned, though the lower orders, who also ranked as clergy by later custom, from sub-deacons downwards, were permitted to marry even after having been appointed to their office. In their case there was no "ordination". By the *Canons of Hippolytus*, VIII, 50, a bachelor was not to be ordained unless he bears a good character with his neighbours.

Up to the end of the third century, most bishops and presbyters probably had a secular calling which provided them with an income, though they were entitled to receive an allowance out of the offerings of the faithful. In the days of Cyprian in North Africa they received a daily *sportula* as well as a monthly allowance. Such support was only right in view of the time which they might have to spend in the Church's interests. But these

---

[1] C. H. Turner, *Catholic and Apostolic*, p. 279. This reminder comes very aptly from an Anglo-Catholic layman who occupied a chair of Divinity at Oxford, but refused to take a D.D. because he was not in orders.
[2] *Wesen und Ursprung des Katholizismus*, p. 141.

interests might be seriously neglected by those who depended mainly upon trade for their living;[1] some, indeed, were not at all careful as to their employment, engaging in traffic in slaves and even in usury[2] (cf. Cyprian, *De Lapsis*, V).

The Church prided itself on the fact that it made no charge for the services of its ministers. Tatian jibes at the heathen philosophers who required payment for their instruction (*Ad Graec.*, XXV) and boasts that even poor Christians are instructed gratuitously (*op. cit.*, XXXII). This was always the custom of the Rabbis. A stipendiary ministry was, indeed, regarded as a mark of heresy. It was customary apparently among the Montanists (Euseb., V, xviii, 2) and the Monarchians (V, xxviii, 28).

Cupidity seems to have been one of the besetting dangers of the clergy and even in the New Testament there are constant warnings against the love of money by the Church's officials (e.g., I Tim. 3 : 3, 8; Titus I : 7; I Pet. 5 : 2). This seems very strange to us and makes one wonder what kind of opportunities could arise by which money could be made out of the clerical profession at this early date. But the warnings are constantly repeated in Christian writings, the most surprising of them all is that in *Didasc.*, II, 5: "Let not the bishop be given to base gain, especially as regards the heathen". This may, of course, refer to commercial transactions carried on apart from his ecclesiastical office.

THE MINISTRY OF WOMEN

The consideration of the question of the ministry of women is complicated by the difficulty, found also in the case of men, of distinguishing between an office and a function. It would be natural, if not inevitable, for those who possessed certain gifts to exercise them on behalf of the Church; but this would not mean inevitably that any definite status was granted. In all ages the Church has owed much to the voluntary labours of its female members. None the less, from the earliest times some kind of ministry of women seems to have been recognized. St. Paul, for example, calls Prisca his fellow labourer (Rom. 16 : 3) and refers to the activities of Phoebe (Rom. 16 : 1 f.); though there is no sound reason for giving her the title of "deaconess", as is done by the margin of the Revised Version.[3] In other passages also he

---

[1] Jerome, *Epist. ad Nepontian*, could write: *Negotiatorem clericum . . . quasi quandam pestem fuge.*

[2] The Council of Nicaea made deposition the penalty for clerics who engaged in usury (canon 17).

[3] Hort regarded Phoebe as a wealthy woman who was a patroness of the Church, and not the holder of any official position: see *Christian Ecclesia*, p. 207 f.

gladly acknowledged the help which women had rendered him (Rom. 16 : 12; Phil. 4 : 3). But none of these instances demands or even suggests the existence of any definite order in the latter sense of the word. Some kind of organized work by women for the necessitous, however, seems to be required by the command given to Hermas (*Vis.*, II, iv, 3) to write a small book and send it to Grapte [1] who would exhort the widows and orphans.

In the period with which we are concerned, an organized ministry of women seems to have been the mark of heretical or schismatic bodies. Tertullian condemns the heretics for allowing women to teach and occupy positions of prominence,—and comments on their "pertness" (*De Praes.*, XLI: *quam procaces*). Among the Gnostics women were very active, and some of their writings (*Pistis Sophia* and the *Second Book of Jeu*) actually set out a list of female apostles, headed by Mary Magdalene.[2] The Marcionites, also, allowed a prominent place to women.[3] It was, however, among the Montanists that they played the greatest part. The Spirit, it was held, made no distinctions of sex, and a woman might be His instrument just as readily as a man. So the Montanist prophetesses baptized and even celebrated the eucharist. That women should be thus prominent was in accord with the social traditions of Asia Minor, or at least the Western part of it; a further illustration of this may be found in the famous romance *Paul and Thecla*, where Thecla is represented as having been commissioned by the apostle to go forth and teach the word of God (§ 41: *Apoc. N.T.*, p. 281).

The incident referred to by Pliny in his correspondence with Trajan (*Epist.*, XCVI) belongs, like the instances cited above, to the East, and not the West; none the less, in the absence of other material it calls for notice. He speaks of having tortured two female slaves (*ancillae*) who were known among the Christians as *ministrae*. This last term is often rendered "deaconesses". This, it seems to me, is to read too much into the term. They may quite well have been used in some quite menial task. It has also been suggested that the Christians to whom Pliny refers were members of some heretical body, which might account for the prominence of women (granted that they were prominent) amonst them. It is worthy of remark that these various heretical sects were characterized by a tendency to take from women their true pre-eminence, for some of them forbade marriage, and all of them encouraged similar ascetic practices.

Among heretical sects prophesying was the principal activity

[1] The name is strange and no instance of its recurrence is found in the Christian inscriptions as it is missing from Diehl's Index.
[2] Schmidt, *Gnostische Schriften*, p. 452.
[3] See Epiphanius, *Haer.*, XLII, and Jerome, *Epist.*, CXXXI.

of women. This was a function which was recognized as legitimate by St. Paul (1 Cor. 11 : 5 f.) though he would not allow women to be heard in the congregation (1 Cor. 14 : 34 f.; cf. 1 Tim. 2 : 11 f.). But those who feel that they are possessed of divine inspiration are not easy to control, and female prophets were discouraged in the West. Even in his Montanist days, Tertullian retained his prejudice against any kind of woman worker who was inclined to exceed her office. But the prophetess, in any case, cannot be regarded as an "official" or the member of even a minor order.

It is sometimes stated that there were three orders of women in the Early Church: widows, deaconesses, and virgins; though there seems to be considerable difficulty in assigning to them their different functions. Such a statement, however, would not be true of the West during our period. In his essay on the subject in *Catholic and Apostolic*, p. 316 ff., C. H. Turner finds nothing that can in any real sense be described as an order before the fourth century. I think that he is probably mistaken in the case of "widows"; but as far as the other two orders are concerned I am in full agreement. Certainly deaconesses are entirely unknown. Even in the East, the term διακόνισσα is not found before canon 19 of Nicaea. Up to this date "deacon" (διάκονος) was used of either sex. The new term was also used of the wives of deacons (just as *episcopa* was used in the early Middle Ages of the wife of a bishop), which might cause confusion. In the East, the order seems definitely to have been established by the time of the *Didascalia*, possibly as early as the latter part of the second century, which gives to it a regular status and defines its duties as what we should call *zenana* work (the seclusion of the female sex in the East debarred women from the ministry of men), the visiting of the sick, and the care of women catechumens. *The Apostolic Constitutions* place deaconesses between deacons and sub-deacons, and the order became very prominent in the Byzantine Church.

As deaconesses became prominent in the Byzantine Church, so in the Western Church did virgins, after the institution of monasticism; but in our period there is no trace of anything approaching an order. The *Apostolic Tradition*, XII, lays it down that virginity is a matter for personal decision, and virgins are not appointed or ordained. There was great emphasis in the pre-Nicene Church on secrecy in regard to vows of virginity taken by either sex. Ignatius, in the East, advises men not to make the matter public (*Ad Polyc.*, V); and Tertullian, in the West, gave the same advice to women (*De Virg. Vel.*, II). Such secrecy precludes the thought of a definite order.

Last of all we come to widows, and here I think we can discern at least the beginnings of a definite order. Lightfoot suggested that widows were of two types, those who received alms, and those who, in addition, rendered service in return. The latter he regarded as an order (II, i, p. 322). C. H. Turner, however, rejects the distinction (*op. cit.*, p. 321) and considers that all widows were merely recipients of alms. Certainly the widows mentioned in the list of Cornelius of Rome together with "persons in distress"—they numbered fifteen hundred—were of this category. But, on the other hand, Tertullian seems to look upon them as in some sort an order (*De Praes.*, III; *De Pudic.*, XIII); and so, it seems to me, does *The Apostolic Tradition*. In the special section devoted to them (XI) it refuses ordination because they have no "ministry" (§ 4) and appoints prayer as their special function, which, it points out, is the function of all Christians (§ 5). But though they are not to be ordained, in contradistinction to virgins they are "instituted". In the East they bulked large. The *Apostolic Church Order* appoints three to each congregation; two for prayer and the third for sick nursing. Whilst, in the *Testament of our Lord*, I, 34, thirteen widows are spoken of who sat "in front", that is, among the clergy; thus balancing the bishop and twelve presbyters, of whom mention is also made.

CHAPTER VII

CHRISTIAN LIFE

What was it like to be a Christian under the Roman Empire in the first few centuries after Christ? It is difficult to say with any precision. We have, indeed, a few precious glimpses of the life which was lived and a number of expositions of what was fitting. We can also find useful and enlightening parallels from the Mission Field to-day, for development there was not altogether different from developments in Europe centuries ago.

In each locality, the first generation of Christians had come to Christ as a Saviour; but, with the growth of a second or third generation, this aspect of His work tended to become less prominent, and there was a tendency to look upon Him as a lawgiver who had disclosed a new way of living by means of which salvation might be obtained. Hermas, for example, speaks of God's law being preached (*Sim.*, VIII, iii, 2) and of Christians suffering for the law (*op. cit.*, 6), and even of "life" as the reward of those who keep the commandments of the Lord (*op. cit.*, vii, 6). The same tendency is also found in Justin (I *Apol.*, LXI). The prevalence of this idea, although it was not bound up with any observation of the minute regulations of Judaism, makes all the more important the task of studying the Christian way of life as understood in the West.

The author of the *Epistle to Diognetus* has pointed out that Christians are not to be distinguished from others by any special customs; they follow those of the place in which they live (V, 4), sharing all things as citizens, though suffering all things as strangers (V, 5). This continued to be true; Tertullian, for example, claimed that Christians did not neglect to observe public festivals, although they kept them in their own way (*Apol.*, XXXV). But Minucius Felix explains that Christian banquets were less luxurious than those of the heathen and free from all licence or excess (*Octavius*, XXXI). In the earlier days especially, however, there was much insistence on separation from the world. It was not long since the fourth gospel had been written and it taught that the world was lying under the power of the Evil One.

Such separation was necessary, even though it involved the Christians in suspicion and dislike. All life, whether that of the individual or the community, is conditioned by its environment; and a recollection of the state of the Roman Empire and its inhabitants, of their moral and social standards, will excuse the attitude of aloofness which the Christians adopted. Apart from such low standards, most aspects of life were entwined by pagan customs and observances. It was therefore impossible for Christians to accept public offices since these involved participation in pagan rites; for the same, as well as for other reasons, military service was difficult for the Christian.[1] Even the teaching profession had its difficulties, for the subjects taught were pagan, and pagan festivals had to be observed by instructors and pupils alike. The state of public festivals and the popular theatre is sufficiently well known to explain why Christians abstained from attending them. Art and literature, things innocent in themselves, might, as in the time of the Puritans, be an occasion of stumbling. The extent, however, to which use was made of even pagan art, in the catacombs, has only recently been realized, as the later part of this chapter will describe. As Christianity became more widespread and Christians less careful, the barrier between heathen and Christian became less formidable, and Christians permitted themselves to attend many public functions which an earlier generation would have regarded with horror; there were even Christians who undertook official duties in connexion with pagan festivals and some who, as tradesmen, were engaged in the manufacture of idols.[2] In point of fact great care had to be exercised by Christians in the matter of their avocations, and lists of forbidden trades were drawn up to guide them.[3]

The permeation of all activities and occupations by religious observances and religious sanctions, as with the Hindus, was a real danger and a continual temptation to the weaker brethren. The Christians met it by trying to live their lives in the realized presence of God. "At every step and advance, in all our going out and coming in, when we dress and put on our shoes, at the bath and at the table, when we light our lamps, or go to bed, or take a seat, in every action of our lives, we sign our forehead with the cross." So Tertullian describes the custom of Christians in North Africa at the end of the second century (*De Cor. Mil.*, IV).

Internally, Christian life was remarkable for the spirit of fellowship, for the care which Christians had for one another. The name "brethren", which had been given to them by their Lord (Matt. 12 : 48; 23 : 8), was typical of the relationship which they bore to each other. The name might indeed have been taken

---

[1] See for this Harnack, *Militia Christi*.   [2] Euseb., VIII, i, 2; ix, 7; xi, 2.
[3] See for example the list in *Apost. Trad.*, XVI, 9 f. Later lists based upon it made various alterations to adjust the prohibitions to different circumstances: see Gregory Dix's edition, p. 24 ff.

over from Judaism (Acts 2 : 29, 37), and be shared with the participants in the mysteries;[1] but membership of a mystery religion could not give that sense of comradeship which was the right and privilege of the Christian. For one thing, it was customary for the various mystery cults to welcome those who had already been initiated into other cults and so cut across the fellowship which the new aspirant may have had with his fellow members; the real fellowship of the devotee, however, was not with his fellow members but with the object of the cult itself. One feature of the mysteries must also have worked against the realization of true fellowship: the presence in them of different grades of knowledge and initiation (in Mithraism there were seven). In the Church, all men, when once they had been fully received, were on the same level of privilege and standing. Nor could such a one expect the same care which the Christians bestowed on any member who was sick, a care which aroused the admiration of the heathen (Tertullian, *Apol.*, XXXIX), nor that general kindliness which called forth the sarcasm of the satirist Lucian (*De Mort. Peregr.*, XI).

A description of Christian life when it was perhaps at its purest and highest has been preserved by Justin Martyr in the middle of the second century. The remarkable thing about it is the difference which belief in the true God has made, and the contrast with the old life of paganism and lax morality. "We who formerly delighted in fornication", he says, "now embrace purity alone; we who formerly used magic arts now dedicate ourselves to the good and unbegotten God; we who loved the path to wealth and possessions above all, now bring what we have into the common stock, and give to any in need; we who hated and destroyed one another and would not sit even at the same fire as those of another tribe on account of their different customs, now, since the coming of Christ, live familiarly with them, and pray for our enemies, and try to persuade those who hate us without a cause to live in accordance with the fair precepts of Christ so that they with us may become partakers of the joyful hope of obtaining from God, the ruler of all, the same reward" (I *Apol.*, XIV).

The means by which provision could be accumulated for the care of the poor and ailing was almsgiving, a practice which has ever taken a foremost place in the Christian scheme of living. It had even come to be regarded as a source of merit,[2] and, with

[1] The members of a religious corporation in the Serapeum at Memphis furnish an example: see Moulton and Milligan, *Vocabulary of the Greek Testament*, p. xvii.

[2] According to the present text of II *Clement*, XVI, 4, fasting is better than prayer, and almsgiving than either. There seems, however, to have been some disarrangement.

Origen in the East, as a help to the forgiveness of sins. Such charity was carefully organized, but room was allowed for the individual to exercise his own charity direct, not always with complete discretion. The danger of almsgiving by those who regard it as in some measure an act of merit is that they will care little about the objects upon whom their beneficence may fall. On the other hand, indiscriminate charity was actually commended by so great a teacher as Clement of Alexandria, who denied the right of the Christian to exercise judgment on others, a process which might well exclude some who were friends of God.[1] The later habit of beggars gathering outside places of worship, although a Jewish, and even a Roman custom (cf. Martial, I, 112), was, of course, impossible until Christianity became a recognized religion.

The duty and privilege of almsgiving were commonplaces to the Jewish Christian, for he had known them from childhood; more and more had almsgiving become prominent in Judaism, and in the New Testament there are several references to the high place which it occupied (cf. Luke 21 : 1; Acts 10 : 2). In the Christian Church as a whole it was taken up as part of the system of worship, and regular officials were appointed to attend to it.[2] There was a monthly collection for charity which was entirely voluntary (Tertullian, *Apol.*, XXXIX). The proceeds went to support various objects, in addition to making provision for the sick and needy. Such were the partial maintenance of the clergy, martyrs in prison during a persecution, and those sentenced to the mines. With the bishop's permission any special object might be brought to the notice of the faithful and their alms solicited (Tertullian, *De Jejun.*, XIII).

The efforts of the Christians, however, were not limited to the giving of alms; personal service was also rendered. This was something new in religion, and it made a deep impression on those outside, especially as it was by no means restricted to fellow Churchmen. It was noticeably evident during outbreaks of plague, and instances have been recorded both at Carthage (Pontius, *Vita Cypr.*, IX) and at Alexandria (Euseb., VII, xxii, 7 ff.; IX, viii, 14).

Fasting was a duty which is commonly associated with almsgiving. This, too, was a Jewish custom which our Lord assumed His followers would continue (Matt. 6 : 16). The early Christians had two fast days in the week, Wednesday and Friday, when they "kept station", as the term was. It was also customary to fast before baptism (Justin, I *Apol.*, LXI; Tertullian, *De*

---

[1] See G. Ulhorn, *Christian Charity in the Ancient Church*, p. 121 ff.
[2] The proceeds were entrusted to the custody of the president: see Justin, I *Apol.*, LXVII.

Bapt., XX). Of the later fasting periods of the West, Lent and the four ember seasons, there is only a trace. Ember days were first observed in the time of Leo I, and the forty days not until the seventh century, though from quite early times there was a preparatory fast before Easter extending to two days. The usage seems to have varied, and attempts to make it uniform were already being made in the days of Irenaeus (Euseb., V, xxiv, 12). So also the exact procedure in fasting had not been fixed. In Africa, some fasted until the ninth hour (3 P.M.), others until the evening.[1] In the Church of Rome the practice was not highly valued, if Hermas at all reflects the prevailing opinion, for he declares that God desired abstinence from evil rather than from food (*Sim.*, V, i, 4 f.).

Almsgiving and fasting were part of a normal Christian life in the Early Church, but there was little attempt to carry them to excess, or to give to ascetic practices in general the high place which later they were to occupy in the West. This restraint and moderation was quite in accord with the mind of Christ, who never countenanced sufferings inflicted merely for their own sake. "The hardships which He endured and enjoined upon others were the hardships that were incidental to His mission and His work" (Hastings Rashdall, *Conscience and Christ*, p. 157). Ascetic practices were, in the ante-Nicene age, a mark of heresy rather than Catholicism. This applies mainly to the attitude taken up towards the body and the exercise of its functions. Along with the inculcation of vegetarianism and the avoidance of wine, even in the eucharist, went, often enough, a denunciation of marriage. The apocryphal writings are full of such notions. In the *Assumption of the Virgin*, XI, St. John is preferred to the other apostles as the bearer of the palm before the bier because he alone was a virgin.[2] They also record attempts to forbid marriage and even the carrying out of the duties of married life by those already in that state. The Christian missionaries were referred to as the men who separate husband and wife,[3] and a blessing is pronounced upon those who "possess wives as though they had them not".[4]

Ideas of this character are definitely Oriental, for the East tends ever to identify holiness and asceticism, and are directly contrary to the Old Testament command to be fruitful and

[1] For fuller details see *Dict. of Christ. Antiquity*, I, p. 661 ff.
[2] *Apoc. N.T.*, p. 213: cf. *Acts of Paul*, VI and XII (pp. 273 and 275), and *Pistis Sophia* where St. John sits on the left hand of the Lord, the right being reserved for Mary Magdalene.
[3] *Acts of Philip.*, XLV (*Apoc. N.T.*, p. 443), and *Acts of Peter and Andrew*, VIII (*Apoc. N.T.*, p. 458).
[4] *Acts of Paul*, V, XI (p. 273 ff.): cf. *Acts of Peter*, XXXIV (p. 332 f.); *Acts of Thomas*, XII, LXXXVIII, and XCVI (pp. 369, 404, and 406).

multiply (Gen. I : 22, etc.). Hence the Rabbis regarded marriage as a far higher state than celibacy and one likely to lead to greater sanctity. With the Jews, as with the Christians, it was among heretics, such as the Essenes, that exaggerated asceticism most flourished. But such ideas had their origin in the gospel (Matt. 19 : 12) and could claim some support from St. Paul. They were by no means the monopoly of heresy. Later, they would achieve enormous proportions, mainly through the influence of Augustine, who regarded the begetting of children as a consequence of the Fall which had brought death into the world and so made necessary some means of continuing the race. Jerome also did much to make them popular in the West, and by his day the notion was already prevalent that celibacy was a more perfect way of life than that of the ordinary Christian.

In the pre-Nicene period there were many who practised complete continence, but were careful to refrain from boasting about it (Minucius Felix, *Octavius*, XXXI); such boasting was, in fact, looked upon as presumptuous and even dangerous (Ignatius, *Ad Polyc.*, V, 2). An exaggerated estimate of the sanctity of the unmarried state is found as early as Hermas (*Sim.*, IX ff.) and Justin (I *Apol.*, XV); whilst Tatian refers to pagan taunts on the matter (*Ad Graec.*, XXXII f.). For the notion that virginity is a superior state to married life we have to wait, as in other matters, until we come to the days of Cyprian (*De Habitu Virg.*, XXIII). On the other hand Clement of Alexandria was exceedingly anxious to show that Christians repudiated such notions, claiming that St. Peter had children, and even that the fellow worker of St. Paul (Phil. 4 : 3) was his wife.[1] In another passage he even professes to describe the parting between St. Peter and his wife and extols the perfection of their married life.[2] To later ideas, married apostles were a sore problem, and Jerome suggests that St. Peter's wife was already dead at the time of his call (*Adv. Jovin.*, I, 26). Gregory the Great, however, was not at all sensitive in the matter of clerical celibacy, as he makes a point of relating that his ancestor, Felix III, had been Bishop of Rome (*Dial.*, IV, 16).

Married chastity, however, continued to be valued, even in orthodox circles, as an inscription from Gaul testifies;[3] but it was

---

[1] Renan married St. Paul to Lydia!
[2] *Strom.*, III, vi, 52 f., and VII, xi, 63 f. According to *Clem. Recog.*, VII, xxv, she accompanied him on his missionary journeys: cf. 1 Cor. 9 : 5.
[3] See Le Blant, *Inscr. chrét. de la Gaule*, No. 391:

QVORVM VITA TALIS [FVIT VT LIN]
QVENS CONIVX MARITVM XX A[NNOS]
EXCEDENS IN CASTITATE PERPE[TVA]
PERDVRARET

discouraged by the greatest teachers of the West, especially when it took eccentric forms. Augustine, for example, reproved a certain Ecdicia who not only refused her husband his rights, but went about in widow's weeds (*Epist.*, CCLXII). Jerome also blamed Celantia for taking a vow of continence without the consent of her husband (*Epist.*, CXLVIII: it is not certain, however, that this letter is genuine).

Thus Christian life, in its queerly unsympathetic and oppressive environment, was being slowly hammered out. But there was failure and there was sin. How were these to be dealt with? In the teaching of the Lord, repentance and the desire for amendment brought forgiveness; but this was too simple, as Gwatkin has said, for men who lived under Caesar's government and measured God's mercy by Caesar's justice (*Early Church Hist.*, II, p. 83). A system of penance was therefore evolved. Some such system existed in the Jewish Church, which had means by which undesirable members might be excluded from the community (Luke 6 : 22; John 16 : 2). Since Jesus Himself left power with His apostles to remit or retain sins (John 20 : 23), it may be inferred that in the Christian Church duly qualified officials could declare their remission. But the standard fixed for the Christian was immeasurably high; the Church was to be a community of saints, and some even held that no sin after the reception of the truth could be forgiven (Heb. 10 : 26 ff.). A sinless life was possible (1 John 3 : 6; but cf. 2 : 1 f.). This seems to involve a conflict of opinion which may be explained by some distinction having been made between different classes of sins. Jesus had laid it down that certain sins were incapable of forgiveness, or so the early Christians believed (Matt. 12 : 31 f.); and major offences such as apostasy, idolatry, murder, adultery, and fornication may have been put in this class.

In *The Shepherd* of Hermas the subject of penance is very prominent and he allows that a single lapse can be condoned (*Mand.*, IV, i, 8), if followed by heartfelt penance, and the former status recovered (*Vis.*, III, xiii, 4). Here perhaps we can trace the beginnings of some definite system.[1] Such a development was natural for men confronted by the fear of the divine judgment, and it was not the Jews alone who had recognized this. Reitzenstein thinks that the habit of confession had been widespread in the primitive Graeco-Roman world, and having been lost for a time was recovered in the Hellenistic period.[2] It was common also in Egypt from the time of the Nineteenth Dynasty.

[1] For the history of the development of the penitential system in the early days, see A. d'Alès, *L'Édit de Calliste*. It is written from a Roman Catholic standpoint.
[2] *Die hell. Myst.*, p. 137, n. 1. See, further, R. Pettazzoni, "Confession of Sin and the Classics", in *Harvard Theol. Rev.*, 1937, XXX, p. 1 ff.

Ovid refers to confession of sins being made before the altar of Isis, but it is not certain that a priest was present (*Ex Pont.*, I, 51 ff.); whilst Plutarch also takes note of the practice (*De Superst.*, VII).

The confession of sins was at first made in public as a preparation for the approach to God. "In the congregation thou shalt confess thy transgressions and then thou shalt not go to thy prayer with an evil conscience" (*Didache*, IV, 14). But by the time of Tertullian many were finding the practice a heavy burden on their self-respect, and he asks them if it is better to confess openly, or to be damned? (*De Poen.*, X). Such confession was intended to humble the sinner, and at the same time to arouse the compassion of his fellow Christians (*op. cit.*, IX). Tertullian, with his legal outlook, was responsible for the further development of the system, for he introduced the idea of "penance", that is, the giving of satisfaction to an offended God, and with 1 John 5 : 16 in mind he made a distinction between mortal and venial sins. Excommunication was an anticipation of the Last Judgment (*Apol.*, XXXIX).

The development of the idea of penance may have been influenced by the Latin rendering. In the Greek μετάνοια means simply "change of mind"; the corresponding verb is actually used by the authorities when urging Polycarp to be reasonable (*Mart. Polycarp.*, IX, 2 : XI, 1), and the word itself, or its Latin equivalent, in Pliny's correspondence with Trajan when he points out that if opportunity for a change of mind is given men will conform to the recognized worship.[1] The real meaning was gradually lost in the Latin *poenitentia*,[2] although Lactantius tried to recover it by the rendering *resipiscentia* (*Div. Instit.*, VI, xxiv, 6).

The edict of Callistus marked a stage in the development of the penitential system, though it was probably not nearly so revolutionary as some Protestant writers seem to think.[3] It sought to regulate the position and gave increased powers to the bishop. It should be noted that it is concerned with sins of the flesh. The outbreak of persecution tended to greater strictness and raised many problems as to the terms upon which apostate Christians were to be restored, if restoration was possible in this life.[4] It was popular demand rather than official rigour which caused the tightening-up of the system, but the effect was still further to enhance the power of the clergy, and in particular of the bishop with whom in the last resort the right to grant

[1] *Epist.*, X, 96. The phrase *poenitentiae locus* which he uses is the equivalent of τόπος μετανοίας found in Wisdom 12 : 10; Heb. 12 : 7; I *Clem.*, VII, 5, etc.
[2] In the recent Westminster (Roman Catholic) version of the New Testament "repentance" is used and not "penance".
[3] cf. d'Alès, *L'Édit de Calliste*, p. ii.   [4] See above, pp. 153 ff.

absolution was held to lie. But even clerical absolution was not regarded as essential. The daily use of the Lord's Prayer was enough (Cyprian, *De Dom. Orat.*, XII), an idea which persisted as late as Augustine (*De Civ. Dei*, XXI, 27).

In some of the catacombs, seats have been found carved in the rock beside what may have been primitive altars.[1] These have been claimed as evidence for a system of confessional. There is little doubt that they were for the use of the bishop. There is no real trace in our period of anything like the vast penitential system which would later emerge, and in particular of the custom of confession to the ears of the priest alone.[2]

The status of penitents differed slightly in the East and the West, at least so far as their privileges of church attendance were concerned. In the West, they were allowed to remain during the celebration of the eucharist, but only in the porch.[3] In Syria, however, they were entirely excluded; whilst in Asia Minor, only those who had reached the third stage of penitence, the so-called consistents, were permitted to remain.[4]

SOCIAL CONDITIONS

In the first ages of the Church it was to the simpler relations of life alone that the teaching of the Gospel could be applied. It had its existence within the framework of the Empire, upon which it could exert no influence and whose institutions it was in general bound to accept. Later, when Christianity had become the dominant faith, opportunities would arise for extending its principles to the wider aspects of the life of the community. But even before this era great changes followed the acceptance of Christian teaching, for it was not those parts of man's life which we call spiritual which alone were transformed by the leaven of the Gospel. In particular, the conditions of family life were improved; slaves also were treated in a more humane manner, even if the institution of slavery was retained.

In Roman society, the status of women, as we have seen, was in a process of change, and fresh powers and wider liberties were being claimed by them, a transformation which was not without its dangers. Among the Jews, the position of women had not been high; a man could divorce his wife almost at will, whilst she had no rights against him. Polygamy was recognized, though by

---

[1] Marucchi, p. 404.
[2] R. P. P. Galtier, *L'Église et la rémission des péchés*, maintains that from early times a system of private penance existed alongside the public penance. This is most improbable: see, further, R. C. Mortimer, *The Origins of Private Penance in the Western Church*.
[3] Tertullian, *De Poen.*, VI; *De Pudic.*, I; Cyprian, *Epist.*, XXX; LXVII.
[4] See, further, Brightman in *Early Hist. of the Church and Ministry*, p. 367 f.

the Christian era it had become very rare. At the same time the Jews maintained a lofty standard of morality, and sexual relations outside the marriage bond were vehemently condemned. The Greeks, it may be remarked, saw nothing wrong in prostitution, so long as only foreign women were degraded in this way. With the Christians, the position of women was improved in every way. This affected their place in the life of the family in particular, and it was the duty of the mother (as well as the father) to see that the children were taught the Christian faith (Polycarp, *Phil.*, IV, 2; *Epist. Barn.*, XIX, 5). The relations of the father towards his children were also affected, and Roman sternness modified by the new law of love (Cyprian, *Test. adv. Jud.*, III). It need hardly be said that the practices of abortion and of exposing unwanted children were rigidly condemned.[1] One very difficult matter for Christian women was the "unequal yoke" of marriage with an unbeliever, and Justin has given examples of the straits to which wives might be reduced in these circumstances (II *Apol.*, II). The Council of Elvira forbade such unions (canon 15), but they were sufficiently common when the Council of Arles met in 314 (or 316) for this prohibition to be modified. The comparatively light punishment of temporary excommunication is provided—*aliquanto tempore a communione separentur* (canon 11).

As to slaves, there was a real improvement in their status and treatment, parallel to a similar development among the Romans themselves, through the growth of humanitarian ideas under Stoic influences, but no conception, as yet, that the whole institution was incompatible with Christian standards of life.

In pre-Christian times even the best of the pagans had regarded slaves as a kind of superior animal with none of the rights of man. Plato, although he advises considerate treatment, despised all slaves; and the high-minded Cato could go so far as to suggest that they should be worked to death so as to avoid the burden of keeping them when past fulfilling their duties.[2]

The New Testament is full of good advice on the question of the relations of masters and slaves (e.g., 1 Cor. 7 : 21; Eph. 6 : 5 ff.; Col. 3 : 22; 4 : 1; and the delightful epistle to Philemon: cf. also 1 Pet. 2 : 18). But in the prevailing state of society when slavery was a necessary institution there was no possibility of any abolition. Individual slaves might be emancipated, and those who remained as slaves receive consideration as fellow Christians. That this was not always easy we may judge from the fact that Ignatius had to tell Polycarp not to despise slaves; at the same time he must keep them in their place and not

---

[1] *Epist. Barn.*, XIX, 5; *Epist. ad Diog.*, V, 6; Justin, I *Apol.*, XXIX.
[2] So Plutarch informs us: *Cato*, XXI.

encourage them to expect emancipation at the expense of the congregation (*Ad Polyc.*, IV, 3). A clue to the difficulties which were bound to arise, difficulties already hinted at in the New Testament, may be found in the exhortations of Tertullian to both masters and slaves that they should exercise patience towards one another (*De Patient.*, XV).

But if there was no idea of abolishing the institution, or even of any large measure of redemption, the conditions of the slave were definitely improved. De Rossi has noted that there is no mention of "slave" in the catacombs.[1] A possible exception is an inscription in the cemetery of Commodilla which reads:

RECESSIT IN PACE IOANNIS
EVN[V]CVS CVBICVLARIVS [2]

On the other hand, there are inscriptions of freedmen expressing gratitude for their liberty. An example is to be found in the cemetery of Callistus:

MARCIE RVFINE DIGNE PATRONE
SECVNDVS LIBERTVS FECIT [3]

Furthermore the slave was not excluded from holy orders and might even become a bishop. Callistus had been a slave, and if Pius was the brother of Hermas, as the Muratorian Fragment states, he also was probably of servile origin.

This is the brighter side of the picture. But things were not always so favourable for the Christian slave and the Council of Elvira, *c.* 300, had to pass strict measures to protect them from the ill-treatment of their owners (canons 5 and 41). In later times, in spite of legislation,[4] the conditions of the slave were by no means satisfactory, as frequent protests show only too clearly.[5]

BURIAL CUSTOMS

From a consideration of the manner of life of the early Christians we turn now to their methods of disposing of the bodies of the dead, a matter to which great importance was attached. This we can see from the grief of the Christians at Lyons and Vienne when they were unable to recover the bodies of their martyred brethren (Euseb., V, i, 61). Our first really authentic information comes from the beginning of the second century and corresponds almost exactly with the sudden substi-

[1] *Bull. Arch. Crist.*, 1866, p. 124. The phrase "slave of Christ" or "slave of God" is, of course, quite common.
[2] Marucchi, p. 122. [3] De Rossi, *Roma Sotterran.*, I, Plate 20.
[4] See Theod. Code, IX, vi, 2 f.; VII, xiii, 8; IX, vii, 4; ix, 1; xii, 1.
[5] cf. Jerome, *Epist.*, LIV; Salvian, *De Gubern. Dei*, IV, 26.

tution in the Roman world of burial for cremation.[1] During the last century of the Republic and the first century of the Empire both methods of disposing of the dead had been practised, although cremation was probably the more common; then suddenly it was dropped, save in the case of the emperor where there was some connexion between cremation and apotheosis.[2] This very rapid change seems to have begun with the wealthy, which suggests that it was a matter of fashion rather than of principle and is no evidence of any alteration in the attitude to the hereafter. Although the Christians practised burial,[3] there can be no question of their having influenced others, nor is it likely that the mystery religions did so, nor the revival of Pythagoreanism.

By Roman Law, the dead had to be buried outside the walls of the city, and at first the Christians doubtless made use of the normal facilities. But soon there would be the desire—in this they followed the Jews[4] to possess their own burial grounds. And so land would be bought or provided by wealthy converts for the purpose. The Church itself owned and administered cemeteries and *Apost. Trad.*, XXXIV, lays it down that the charges were not to be extortionate, also that watchmen were to be provided by the bishop out of the proceeds of the collection.

Christians in Rome and in a few other places in the West, such as Naples and North Africa,[5] made use of catacombs or underground cemeteries for the disposal of their dead, as the Jews had done before them.[6] There was nothing secret about the matter. They must have been constructed with the permission of the owners of the surface land to which their boundaries had to conform and were registered with the authorities.[7] Burial places were sacrosanct and no attempt would be made to interfere with them except by evilly disposed persons. The idea that they were

---

[1] See A. D. Nock, "Cremation and Burial in the Roman Empire", in *Harvard Theol. Rev.*, XXV, 1932, p. 321 ff.

[2] The Christian emperors gave up the practice, though it may have been revived in the case of Julian: see Ammianus Marcellinus, XXV, v, 1; ix, 12; x, 5.

[3] The Christians had no dogmatic views on the subject; they looked upon burial as the older and better custom: so Minucius Felix, *Octavius*, XI, 4 f., XXXIV, 10.

[4] Six Jewish cemeteries have been discovered in Rome. Three on the Appian Way, and one each on the Via Labicana, Via Portuensis, and Via Nomentana. The latter was discovered in 1920: see R. Paribeni, *Notizie degli Scavi*, 1920, p. 143 ff.

[5] The latter are numerous and important: see Leynaud, *Les Catacombes africaines*. Together with sarcophagi they throw additional light on early Christian art.

[6] Jewish catacombs in Rome were at least a century earlier than Christian: see J. B. Frey, *Rendic. Pont. Accad.*, XII, p. 185 ff.

[7] After about A.D. 133 associations of poor persons (*collegia tenuiorum*) for the burial of their members were recognized. Whilst other associations required the permission of the senate or the emperor, they merely required a police permit.

largely used for worship must be abandoned in view of fuller knowledge, though during a persecution gatherings might well take place in them, just as in air-raids tube-stations became places of refuge. Organized worship in the catacombs belongs to the fourth and later centuries when the cult of the martyrs had developed.

A great deal of work has been carried out on the catacombs in recent years, both by way of excavation and of reconstruction. The monumental work of Paul Styger, *Die römischen Katakomben*, 1933, has done much to set the whole matter in its true proportions, even though it involves some revision of the views of previous scholars. He finds two distinct types of cemetery: an earlier, shaped like a grid with passages round the walls and cross gangways; this type was privately owned. About the middle of the third century another type emerges, with its main passage down the centre and passages branching from it; this type was in public ownership (*op. cit.*, p. 4).

It is in the dating of the cemeteries, however, that Styger's views are most revolutionary. He asserts that no inscription with a consular date or other reliable evidence has been discovered belonging to a period before the middle of the second century (*op. cit.*, p. 11), and he considers that the early dating of the so-called cemeteries of Domitilla and Priscilla is no longer possible in view of the dates stamped on the bricks with which they are constructed (*op. cit.*, p. 12 f.).

On one point Styger is very insistent: the presence of inscriptions or other matter gives no clue to the date of the cemetery in which they are found unless it can be proved that they are in their original positions. The history of the catacombs should be enough to warn scholars against the danger of being misled in this way; for not only were they repeatedly plundered, which necessarily involved immense disturbance in the position of their contents, but light shafts were driven down and extra passages provided to facilitate the movements of pilgrims during the ages when they were "show-places".[1] When the Goths were in possession of Rome some damage was done, such as plundering for marble, and probably also for relics. This would also destroy inscriptions.[2] The same thing occurred during the Lombard domination. Then the popes themselves deliberately removed all the relics upon which they could lay their hands; especially prominent was Paul I (757–67), and by the middle of the ninth century the process was practically complete. Thenceforth the

---

[1] Jerome tells us he used to visit the catacombs on Sundays with his schoolfellows (*Comm. on Ezek.*, xii, 50).

[2] cf. The inscription of Pope Vigilius (537–55) who tried to repair the damage: SED PERIIT TITVLVS CONFRACTO MARMORE SANCTVS.

catacombs were neglected and earth fell in, and with it no doubt remains from the pagan burial grounds which in many cases actually lay above the catacombs. It was not until the Renaissance that any interest was again taken in them.

Another interesting point raised by Styger is where heretics were buried. What, he asks, became of dead Gnostics, Donatists, Pelagians, and Arians? (*op. cit.*, p. 3). Most of these belong to a period later than that of our study, but there is more evidence of the existence of heretical cemeteries than Styger seems aware of. The Novatianists had their own burial ground,[1] and quite a large number of Gnostic remains have been discovered,[2] including a hypogeum in the Via Latina and another in the Via Manzoni which came to light in 1919; whilst the Valentinians had a small cemetery on the Via Latina discovered in 1903. There seems also to have been a Sabellian cemetery in the fourth century.[3] Otherwise they may have used the public cemeteries or even those of the Church, though this seems unlikely. Heretical cemeteries may have been seized in later times by the Catholics and all peculiar traces destroyed, though it is not necessary to suppose that there would normally be anything to distinguish the inscription on the tomb of a heretic from that of a Catholic.

One custom the Christians took over from both Jews and pagans, that of placing lamps in tombs.[4] Many of them are inscribed, again in imitation of earlier users, and sometimes with identical wording; Egyptian lamps, for example, of the Graeco-Roman period have been found with a frog (the symbol of the goddess Hekt) and the words "I am the resurrection".[5] In some Christian tombs in Palestine a favourite inscription was "The Lord (or Christ) is my light".[6]

CHRISTIAN ART

The fate of paintings in the ancient world is as tragic as it is notorious. When Pausanias visited Greece in the middle of the second century he found that they had nearly all perished; of the frescoes of Polygnotus which had once excited the admiration of antiquity nothing remained but "a little blue pigment on a ruined wall near Delphi".[7] All that we have is a list of names

[1] De Rossi, *Bull. Arch. Crist.*, 1863, p. 20.
[2] Marucchi, *Nuovo Bull.*, 1903, pp. 301–304; 1911, pp. 209–235.
[3] De Rossi, *Bull. Arch. Crist.*, 1866, p. 95; Marucchi, p. 673.
[4] There is a long article on the subject with numerous illustrations in the *Dict. of Christ. Antiq.* It is, of course, not quite up to date. Lamps were very common in Africa, especially in the catacombs: see Leynaud, *op. cit.*, pp. 200, 295, 325, etc. Many specimens are now in the museum at Carthage.
[5] Budge, *Egyptian Magic*, p. 63. These lamps are sometimes claimed as Christian.   [6] R. A. S. Macalister, *The Excavations of Gezer*, II, p. 228.
[7] J. G. Frazer, *Pausanias and other Sketches*, p. 92.

and of the subjects of their works. In the case of early Christian art the contrary is true; the paintings have largely been preserved, but the names of the artists are unknown. In the catacombs and elsewhere [1] enough has been preserved to throw light on the mental outlook of the early Church in Rome and Italy; though if we possessed examples of Christian art belonging to other phases of life our opinion might require modification.

In some quarters art was looked upon with suspicion by Christians; Tertullian, not unexpectedly, regarded it as positively sinful (*Adv. Hermog.*, I) and the powers of evil as the source of artistic inspiration (*De Spect.*, X). This was a continuance of the Jewish ban on art, a ban which had aroused the laments of the writer of IV Maccabees xvii, 7, since it prevented the sufferings of the martyrs from being so recorded. But the ban had not been entirely effective as the synagogue at Doura shows, as well as the paintings in Jewish catacombs. Among Christians, the general outlook was much broader, although the use of paintings in churches was forbidden by the Council of Elvira on the ground that they might attract worship (canon 36). This prohibition was entirely disregarded.

The catacombs reveal the employment of art in the service of religion,[2] and that of an excellent quality. The Christian spirit with its creative energy found an ally and means of expression in the popular art of Rome, which at the beginning of the Christian era gradually shook off its dependence on a purely classical tradition.[3] Early Roman art was that of a people or society dwelling in security, whose main interest was in the refinements of living; in this it resembled the graceful art of the Minoans, rather than the aggressive barbarism of the Assyrians. Later there would be a falling off and the craving after mere bulk, as seen in such vast structures as the Colosseum, the baths of Caracalla and of Diocletian (and in Christian times the great church of Constantine), show a barbarian spirit. Ostentation and magnificence are by no means identical, and it would be a poor taste which preferred the Pyramids to the Parthenon. The abandonment of the classical tradition, which may have been a sign of new life, laid the Romans open to influences from outside, and in the third century a flood of Orientalism came in through the Syrian emperors. This still further drove out classical realism

[1] The church at Doura built in A.D. 232 has extensive mural paintings which seem to have influenced religious art in the West (*Camb. Anct. Hist.*, XII, p. 496, n. 1). Among the subjects are the Sacrifice of Isaac; and, from the New Testament: the Good Shepherd, Jesus and St. Peter on the Lake, the healing of the Paralytic, and the three Marys going to the tomb.
[2] See especially Wilpert, *Pitt. delle cat. romane.* There are many first-rate reproductions in all the well-known collections, such as those of De Rossi, Marucchi, and Styger.
[3] *Camb. Anct. Hist.*, XII, p. 565.

and brought in a kind of Eastern expressionism.[1]

One very significant feature of the development of Christian art alongside and in conjunction with that of popular art in Rome was the manner in which 'Christians made use of elements borrowed from pagan sources, and quite possibly employed pagan workmen. As is well known, in some cases they retained on their tombs the old pagan dedication D M (*Dis manibus*)[2] and in the subjects represented on the walls of the catacombs pagan influence abounds; so much so that often enough there is nothing to distinguish Christian paintings from those which have survived from contemporary art.[3] Such subjects as winged *amoretti*,[4] heads with a fillet of vine-leaves, pictures of the four seasons, a subject frequently occurring in the East in the middle of the second century;[5] as well as landscapes, various animals and other natural objects. Nor were purely pagan subjects wanting, such as Cupid and Psyche. The figure of Orpheus is very common, as on a sarcophagus at Tipasa in North Africa, probably as a representation of Christ.[6] The Good Shepherd with the lamb, which appears on Egyptian tombs to represent Anubis,[7] was naturally capable of Christian application. More difficult to explain is a painting of Ulysses and the sirens in the cemetery of Callistus.[8]

Such pagan objects, however, are in the minority, and recourse has usually been had to the Old and New Testaments, or to the life and worship of the Church. There is naturally a good deal of repetition, as in the paintings of the Middle Ages; and, for the same reason, the growth of convention, and also the inability of a not very highly educated public to recognize more than a limited range of subjects.

Many of the subjects taken from the Old Testament[9] had already been used by the Jews, for, as we have seen, the ban on such representations was not strictly observed. Amongst those most frequently occurring are Noah and the Ark, Moses striking

[1] *op. cit.* (Plates), V, p. v.

[2] See the large number of examples in Diehl, III, p. 425 ff.

[3] Much fresh material has recently been brought to light in the cemetery of the Freedmen at Ostia by G. Calza.

[4] These may be distantly connected with the small birds with human heads used in Egyptian tombs to represent the soul.

[5] Vincent in *Rev. Bib.*, 1922, XXXI, p. 275.

[6] An Orpheus-like Christ appears on the famous Antioch chalice of uncertain date. A. B. Cook, *Zeus*, II, p. 1197 ff., would place it *c.* A.D. 100; others date it as late as the fifth century. A similar figure has been found in a fifth-century mosaic near the Damascus gate at Jerusalem: see S. A. Cook, *Schweich Lectures*, Plate XXXIX.

[7] Reitzenstein, *Die hell. Myst.*, pp. 36 and 107. Guthrie, *Orpheus and Greek Religion*, p. 264, thinks the figure was copied from Orpheus.

[8] Marucchi, p. 186.

[9] The North African Church seems to have been especially fond of subjects taken from the Old Testament, particularly on sarcophagi.

the Rock, the Sacrifice of Isaac, Daniel in the Lions' Den, and the Three Children in the Furnace. All of them, it will be observed, capable of topical application; the last two would be of especial value in days of persecution, whilst the ark suggested the Church, and Moses striking the Rock the waters of baptism. The Sacrifice of Isaac became a great feature in Rabbinic literature after the third century, and from that time onwards Christians may not have made so much use of it.[1] Another Old Testament prophecy appears in the catacomb paintings: Balaam is represented as standing before the Virgin and Child with the star shining above their heads (cf. Num. 24 : 17).[2] In a cemetery at Naples a representation of the expulsion of Adam and Eve from Paradise is also found.

Among subjects taken from the New Testament, that of the Baptism of Christ is very frequent; as are the Feeding of the Five Thousand, the Raising of Lazarus—a type, no doubt, of the Resurrection—the Annunciation, the visit of the Wise Men;[3] and, somewhat unexpectedly, the Woman at the Well of Sychar; this last, possibly, has eucharistic symbolism. Pictures of the crucifixion are not found in the West before the fifth century, although there are a few instances in the East.[4]

Towards the end of our period Christian sarcophagi begin to appear. Their subjects are much the same as those contained in wall paintings such as Jonah and the Whale, the Good Shepherd, as well as scenes from the life of the Lord and those of His followers. Two very beautiful examples, both from the Lateran Christian Museum, are reproduced in *Camb. Anct. Hist.*, Vol. V (Plates), p. 217. They are elaborately carved and full of figures. One represents the Good Shepherd, also a woman in prayer; the other, scenes from the life of the Lord and of St. Peter.

Of subjects in Christian art taken from the life of the Church and of the individual there are many examples, though in some cases identification has been a little hasty.[5] Such include Baptism, the Eucharist (a subject to which we shall return), the Judgment, and the Heavenly Feast. In both these later subjects the details seem to be borrowed from pagan models.

The use of symbols in religious art is a matter of course. In the

---

[1] I have noticed allusions in literature in Iren., IV, v, 4; Tertullian, *Adv. Jud.*, X; and Paulinus of Nola, *Epist.*, XXIX, 9.
[2] Others think that Isaiah, not Balaam, is represented: see Marucchi, p. 487.
[3] The number varies. Four are found in the cemetery of Domitilla (Marucchi, p. 171); two only in that of SS. Peter and Marcellinus, p. 328, besides the conventional three.
[4] Syxtus, II, ii, p. 107.
[5] Similar hasty identifications in other fields of archaeology are a warning in this matter. The British Museum seal, for example, on which a tree and two figures appear with a serpent, was long regarded as a Babylonian representation of the Fall, but is so no longer: see S. A. Cook, *Schweich Lectures*, p. 70.

Early Church it occurs not only in paintings, but also in numerous inscriptions, as well as on various articles of jewellery and such like. Most of these, unfortunately for our purpose, are of a date later than our period and can be used only by way of amplification. Here, again, we note the free use of pagan signs, or signs common to pagans and Christians. The cross itself is found on Cretan monuments and as the ANKH of the Egyptians. In the form of the *swastika* it occurs on tapestry from Akhmim, and frequently elsewhere. So, too, the anchor is a symbol of the sea-god as well as of hope. The well-known use of the fish to symbolize our Lord (its letters in Greek form the initials of the phrase "Jesus Christ, Son of God, Saviour") is interesting on account of its distribution, for, whilst it is very common in the Roman catacombs, for some reason or other it is scarcely found elsewhere until the fifth century; in Gaul, for example, no specimen is known before 474.[1] The lamb is used both for the Lord and the Christian soul. The peacock appears as a symbol of the Resurrection, either because of the yearly renewal of its feathers, or because its flesh was supposed to be incorruptible. One or two others may be mentioned, but no exhaustive survey is possible. The lighthouse represents the light of the Gospel, but also the end of the Christian voyage, since it is found with the palm and the crown.[2] The voyage itself, under a different figure, is represented by a horse (the spiritual course of 1 Cor. 9 : 24 and 2 Tim. 4 : 7); in one specimen from Sardinia it bears a sacred symbol on its flank.[3]

An exceptionally large number of symbols represent the eucharist, a testimony to the importance attached to it in the Early Church. Even if we reject some of the identifications as of doubtful validity, enough remain in number and variety to establish this beyond doubt. One common symbol is the five loaves and two fishes from the feeding of the five thousand. Other symbols are bread with a tripod, baskets of bread, grapes, manna, and even a pail of milk. In some cases what are regarded as actual celebrations are depicted; these may well represent such services, but they have a very close resemblance to heathen funeral feasts.[4]

The Christians, too, had their funeral feasts and anniversary commemorations. They were held in the cubicula in which the bodies had been deposited. The stone seats found in some cata-

---

[1] See Le Blant, *Nouveau Rec. des inscript. chrét.*, Nos. 136 and 334.
[2] See *Bull. Arch. Crist.*, 1868, p. 11.
[3] *op. cit.*, 1873, Plate XI.
[4] On representations of the eucharist see Syxtus, II, i, p. 168 ff., and II, ii, pp. 42 ff., 166 ff.; and especially an inscription from Modena on II, ii, p. 45; also *Dict. of Christ. Antiq.*, p. 625 ff. Many representations in the catacombs are rejected by Styger (e.g., pp. 107, 141, 203, 220, 340).

combs may have had a connexion with these rites.[1] Some of the rites were evidently of an undesirable character, for Monnica was reproved by Ambrose for practising them as she had been accustomed to do in North Africa.[2]

[1] As in S. Panfilo (Marucchi, p. 564) and the so-called Great Catacomb (p. 403 f.).
[2] See Augustine, *Conf.*, VI, ii.

CHAPTER VIII

CHRISTIAN WORSHIP

With Christianity a new type of religion spread over the West. And yet it was not entirely new, for it preserved many of the characteristics of its Jewish forerunner. What would impress the heathen, as Döllinger pointed out, would be that "a religion of prayer was superseding a religion of ceremonies and invocation of the gods; that it encouraged all, even the most uneducated, to pray" (*First Age of Christianity*, p. 344 f.). The habit of private prayer was certainly encouraged,[1] and about this a little may be said before going on to consider its corporate aspects. The custom was not, of course, the invention of the Church, for it is a habit instinctive in the human race when once the possibility of this great spiritual privilege has been realized. Knowing God and believing that He hears their petitions, men cannot but "lift up hands of prayer". Even the devotees of Serapis practised it,[2] as did the Jews. The Rabbis, indeed, traced the custom back to the fathers of the Hebrew race (*Berakoth*, 26 b), and it will be recalled that the disciples asked the Lord to teach them to pray because John the Baptist had so taught his disciples (Luke 9 : 1–4). With the Christians, prayer was to be offered three times daily, at the third, sixth, and ninth hours respectively.[3] In pious households there was also a reading of the Scriptures at the third hour, before the first meal was taken.

In modern times there are many devout souls who consider that private prayer and meditation are the only forms of intercession that are really worthy of the name. Such ideas, though uncommon in antiquity, were not unknown. Plotinus, for instance, regarded public worship as unbecoming in a philosopher; man's intercourse with the divine must be purely personal. Later Neoplatonists, however, took a different line, and in their desire to bolster up a dying paganism recognized the necessity of corporate acts of worship in order to appeal to the common folk.

From the earliest days corporate worship was a characteristic of the Christian Church. How could it have been otherwise in view of its Jewish antecedents? But even so there was a tendency

---

[1] See Cyprian, *De Dom. Orat.*, IV.

[2] Daily prayers (though possibly of a public nature) are mentioned in a papyrus of the first century A.D. published in the collection of the Berlin Museum, III, No. 846. There are also references to the practice in the Hermetic literature.

[3] Cyprian added prayers at morning and evening (*op. cit.*, XXXV).

on the part of some to absent themselves (cf. Heb. 10 : 25), and warnings against the danger of neglect and incitements to more frequent attendance are common in the Apostolic Fathers.[1] Tertullian, rather quaintly, urged the value of gathering together so that by sheer weight of numbers God might be compelled to grant the wishes of His worshippers, a violence which He approved (*Apol.*, XXXIX, 2).

It is impossible to exaggerate the importance attached to corporate prayer by the primitive community. They realized to the full Lietzmann's dictum that "The heart of the Christian life is to be found in the act of public worship" (*The Founding of the Church Universal*, p. 161). Moreover, such worship had immense value in fostering that sense of fellowship which was abundantly necessary if the Church was to survive. Fellowship gave to the individual, as to the Church as a whole, strength in face of temptation, and courage to meet persecution, stimulating zeal and promoting unity. As in the case of the associations, there was a large social element in Christian assemblies, especially in the first days when the agape was combined with the Lord's Supper.[2] Although scandals in connexion with this combination were already manifest in Corinth in St. Paul's day it does not seem to have been broken off until a century later. By this time the Church had grown to such an extent that it may not have been convenient; and possibly the entry of converts of a higher social class may have made it difficult to maintain its original intention.

The social side of worship would be no novelty to the Gentile convert; the other deeper, more spiritual side, he would need to learn, for in his own religions, apart from the mysteries, the idea of worship had been the correct performance by duly appointed officials of a stated ritual. This conception began in time to invade the Christian Church, giving it a kind of magic efficacy in the eyes of the ignorant and uninstructed; and with the tendency to emphasize ceremonial acts and to substitute ritual ordinances for spiritual worship. But worship was no haphazard affair, it must be duly ordered and controlled; so Clement reminds the Corinthians that the Lord had appointed fixed times and seasons and even a regular ministry and stated localities (I *Clem.*, XL). Later, undisciplined worship would be regarded as a peculiarity of heresy (Tertullian, *De Praes.*, XLI). A testimony to the value which early Christians set upon an exact performance of the services of the Church can be found in Lucian, who tells us that his hero Peregrinus gave up Christianity owing

---

[1] cf. Ignatius, *Eph.*, V, 3, XIII, 1; *Magn.*, IV, 1 (here there is a reference to "unlawful assemblies"); *Epist. Barn.*, IV, 10; II *Clem.*, XVII, 3.
[2] See Batiffol, *Étude d'hist. et de théol. positive*, p. 277 ff.

to a quarrel over a point of ritual (*De Morte Peregr.*, XIV).

One great advantage of a fixed ritual is that those who may not hold exactly the same views can join it; for ritual is often uniting when dogmas separate. In it, moreover, belief and emotion react upon one another, the very human desire for united action is met, as well as man's instinct to give corporate expression to his beliefs.

Daily worship was an ideal, but the principal day with Jewish Christians would continue, for a time, to be the Sabbath. From a very early period, however, the day of the Lord's resurrection began to be specially hallowed, and at length it entirely ousted the Sabbath, and Sunday became the day set aside for Christian worship.[1] The gradual influx of Gentiles would strengthen a tendency already at work. In the East, the Sabbath is still regarded as of peculiar sanctity, the Ethiopian Church places it on almost the same level as Sunday; but, in the West, it has little to distinguish it from other week-days.

No one who studies the early history of the Christian Church can fail to be impressed by the manner in which it spread without such advantages as might come from the possession of special edifices set apart for divine worship. The contrast between the past and the present is, in this respect, remarkable. At first, the Christians would not need any special buildings, since the temple at Jerusalem and the synagogues in that and other cities would still be frequented by them. But very soon other provision had to be made. Some Jewish Christians seem to have started their own synagogues, as Jewish custom indeed allowed. Even in the New Testament the word is used for a Christian assembly (Jas. 2 : 2) and in the sub-apostlic age Hermas uses it (*Mand.*, XI, 9), as well as Ignatius (*Ad Polyc.*, IV, 2),[2] whilst with Jewish Christians it long continued (Epiphanius, *Haer.*, XXX, 18).

When purely Christian places of assembly began to be required, use would at first be made of private houses belonging to the wealthier members of the community. Some of these might be exceedingly large, for Sallust speaks of Roman houses that were like cities (*Catilina*, XII). Worshippers going in and out of such houses would attract no comment, in view of the constant stream of clients and slaves. The owners might easily acquire, as hosts, the right to preside over the proceedings in their own houses; and it is even possible that separate "house-churches" might present difficult problems if they developed along different lines. But not all the "hosts" were people of wealth, for Celsus

[1] Ignatius, by implication, condemns those who still "sabbatize": *Magn.*, IX, I.
[2] So too in Christian interpolations in the *Testaments of the Twelve Patriarchs*, Test. Ben., XI. It is also found in the *Acts of Peter*, IX, and in Theophilus, *Ad Autol.*, II, 14.

could taunt the Christians with meeting in the shops of cobblers and other small tradesmen (III, 55). In Rome, the cemeteries and catacombs seem to have been used for worship, though probably only in times of persecution. Later, as Christians became more numerous and less liable to maltreatment, halls attached to the house of the bishop would be established. In Justin's day these were apparently not set apart for worship only (*Acta*, III), for, like the synagogues, they would probably be used for all kinds of purposes, such as centres for charitable and social efforts, for work and instruction, as well as the headquarters for evangelistic work.[1]

The New Testament already knew of "house-churches". We hear of two at Colossae (Col. 4 : 15 and Philem. 2); of that of Aquila and Priscilla at Ephesus (1 Cor. 16 : 19) and at Rome (Rom. 16 : 5). Tradition speaks of this house and that of Pudens being on the sites respectively of the present churches of St. Prisca and St. Pudenziana. But the New Testament seems also to contemplate special buildings or rooms set aside for worship. This seems a possible inference from St. Paul's protest in 1 Cor. 11 : 22: "Have ye not houses to eat and drink in? or despise ye the church of God?"[2] A little later the statement in I *Clem.*, XL, noticed above, that there were "fixed places" for worship, is evidence for Rome in the latter part of the first century. By the time of Tertullian, church buildings, in Africa at least, seem to have been in use (*De Spect.*, XXV, *De Idol.*, VII); some were quite elaborate structures with outbuildings (*De Pudic.*, IV). So, too, in the Decian persecution, penitents who had lapsed are said never to leave the threshold of the church (Cyprian, *Epist.*, LVII).

Some difficulty has been occasioned by the statement of Minucius Felix, who was a contemporary of Tertullian, that the Christians had no "temples" (*delubra*) (*Octavius*, XXXII). This does not, however, mean that they had no places for worship. A "temple" was a place where sacrifices were offered, and such were not a Christian custom. The same statement is made by Arnobius, *Adv. Gent.*, VI, 1, and by Lactantius, *De Mort. Persec.*, II, 2, more than a century later when Christian churches admittedly existed in large numbers.

In the reign of Severus Alexander (222–35) a dispute with a guild of tavern-keepers over the possession of a building was decided in favour of the Christians on the ground that it was better that God should be worshipped in it.[3] It was not, however, until the second half of the third century, when persecution

---

[1] cf. the description of the church at Cirta in *Gesta apud Zenoph.* (*P.L.*, VIII, col. 731), which was being used for storing materials for charitable distribution.
[2] But "church" may mean "congregation" as in 11 : 16 and 14 : 34.
[3] Lampridius, *Vit. Alex.*, XLIX.

was thought to have spent its force, that large buildings became at all usual.[1] Optatus of Milevis[2] speaks of more than forty basilicas in Rome alone at the beginning of the fourth century. When Christianity became a recognized religion the order was made in the so-called "edict of Milan", that buildings which had been seized should be restored to the Christian body (*corpori Christianorum*).[3]

During the greater part of our period the interior arrangements and decorations of Christian places of worship would be very simple and even meagre, especially in the eyes of converts from paganism. Tertullian himself contrasted their simplicity with the splendour of heathen temples (*Adv. Val.*, III); a contrast which would cease in the fourth century after the influx of pagan customs. One reason why Christians were denounced as atheists was that they had no images, altars, or even a priesthood. To this the apologist could reply: "He who cultivates innocence supplicates God; he who cultivates justice makes offerings to God; he who abstains from fraud propitiates God; he who snatches man from danger slays the most acceptable victim. These are our sacrifices, these are our rites of divine worship."[4]

It has been suggested that Christian churches, in their more developed form, were copied from the meeting-halls of the mystery religions. These required larger buildings than the ordinary temples, and so a form of the basilica was adopted, with nave and aisles, and an apse at the end. An example can be cited in the first-century basilica discovered in 1915 near the Porta Maggiore in Rome. This might well have been taken for a Christian church, did not the imagery on the walls reveal its different character.[5]

Church furniture would be very simple; an altar or holy table, a term which was preferred as late as Bede,[6] for the celebration of the eucharist, and a lectern or platform for the reading of the Scriptures, would be the most prominent features. In North Africa, altars were usually of wood, though stone was sometimes

[1] See Macarius Magnes, *Apocriticus*, IV, 21.

[2] II, 4. We need not infer that these were exceptionally large buildings, for basilicas might be attached to private houses: see R. Burn, *Rome and the Campagna*, p. 1.

[3] The wording suggests that Christians assembled in other places besides the churches, from which *ea loca . . . ad quae convenire consuerunt* are distinguished (Lactantius, *De Mort. Persec.*, XLVIII).

[4] Minucius Felix, *Octavius*, XXII.

[5] See G. McN. Rushforth in *The Legacy of Rome*, p. 407. A fuller account will be found in G. Leroux, *Les Origines de l'édifice hypostyle*, p. 318 ff. It was an underground building measuring twelve by six metres, and in excellent preservation. The atrium and the main hall were supported by six rectangular pillars. The stucco reliefs are in the style of the first century A.D.

[6] *Hist. Eccles.*, V, x: *habentes . . . tabulam altaris vice dedicatam.*

used.[1] There was little in the way of ritual. Even lights and incense were not found in this connexion as a rule. It is true that lights were often used, but for practical reasons, when meetings were held before daybreak. That there were attempts to extend the use may be judged from Tertullian's sarcastic remarks on those who encroach on the day with lamps or useless candles (*Apol.*, XXXV, XLVI). At a later date Lactantius adds his condemnation; to offer candles and tapers to the God of light seems to him a sign of madness (*Div. Instit.*, VI, 2). The ceremonial use of lights may have come in eventually in connexion with the festivals of martyrs, for their use in cemeteries during the daytime is forbidden by the Council of Elvira (canon 34). Incense was used because of its supposed sanitary properties and to cover bad smells, so Tertullian informs us (*De Cor. Mil.*, X). In another passage he condemns even this use as recalling the cult of the demons (*Ad Uxor.*, II). The ceremonial use of incense is later than Augustine (see *Enarr. in Ps. XLIX*, XXI).

Clement of Alexandria tells us that in the *Preaching of Peter* Christians were urged not to imitate either Greeks or Jews in their worship (*Strom.*, VI, v, 39). In point of fact, the worship of the Church was from the first closely modelled on that of the Synagogue.[2] Common to both were the reading of psalms and other Scriptures, the homily or sermon, the use of liturgical phrases, and even the separation of men and women. There was, of course, no set form incumbent on all Churches, but each community worked out its own forms, keeping to a broad general outline. For the West, we are particularly fortunate in having two reasonably detailed descriptions of worship; one from about the middle of the second century, the other from its close. The latter is in Tertullian, *Apol.*, XXXIX; the former in Justin Martyr, I *Apol.*, LXV–LXVII. Justin says that Sunday was the day for the chief worship and all were expected to attend it. It began with a reading from the memoirs of the apostles or the writings of the prophets, which went on as long as time allowed. Then came an exposition by the president, evidently of a practical nature, which exhorted the congregation to imitate the examples which had been put before them. After prayers, bread, wine, and water were brought in.[3] Then the president prayed and offered thanks, using his own words, and the people added Amen.[4] Then there was a distribution "of that for which thanks

---

[1] Gsell, *Les Monuments antiques*, II, p. 145.

[2] cf. Dix, *The Apostolic Tradition*, p. xl ff., and C. W. Dugmore, *The Influence of the Synagogue upon the Divine Office*.

[3] In the Sarum use water was added to the wine in the sacristy before low mass: see Pearson, *The Sarum Missal in English*, p. lix.

[4] In North Africa, the people said "Amen" on receiving the sacrament Tertullian, *De Spect.*, XXV.

had been given", absentees receiving their share by the hands of the deacons. Then followed a collection, the proceeds of which were handed to the president to be used for those in need, such as widows and orphans, the sick, prisoners and strangers. Two things stand out in this description; its very informal nature, and the large part taken by the president.

If the so-called *Egyptian Church Order* is really the *Apostolic Tradition* of Hippolytus we have additional information about the customs of the Roman Church at a slightly later time. It allows the use of a set prayer at the eucharist in case the celebrating bishop is unable to compose such a prayer for himself and provides a model (X, 3 ff.). No doubt many service books perished during the persecution of Diocletian, when there was a special effort to destroy Christian writings of every kind. Although many ancient liturgies and forms have survived, some even bearing the names of apostles, none of them is of ante-Nicene date. This is to be regretted, for worship and dogma are closely allied and an early liturgy would perhaps have thrown interesting light on the proportions of belief, even if it did nothing else to add to our knowledge.

In that part of the service which was devoted to praise there would be considerable scope for human invention, for, in addition to the psalms, hymns and other spiritual songs would find a place.[1] Pliny speaks of the Christians singing hymns to Christ as God,[2] and it may be that the custom of direct address to Jesus, found indeed in the New Testament (e.g., Acts 7 : 59), in this way became widespread. Paul of Samosata forbade it as a recent invention (see Euseb., VII, xxx, 10). At a date still later the Council of Laodicea (by canon 59) endeavoured to put an end to the singing of private compositions in church.

During worship different attitudes were apparently adopted by the congregation. For prayer, they stood (except certain penitents who remained on their knees, a posture which was really prostration), as the Jews had done before them. Some worshippers seem to have made a habit of sitting or squatting, possibly from laziness, for it called forth a strong rebuke from Tertullian (*De Orat.*, XII).[3] Sitting was usual when reading or instruction was going on, except that the congregation stood for the gospel. A distinction was made between the clergy and the

[1] Tertullian mentions that the praises of God were sung in Scriptural language or in Christian compositions (*Apol.*, XXXIX). Some other early references to Christians singing hymns are: Acts 16 : 25; *Mart. Ignat.*, VII; and Euseb., V, xxviii, 5.

[2] *Epist.*, XCVI. His actual words are *Carmen Christo quasi deo dicere*: which are interesting as containing a technical term, *carmen dicere*, though probably it is not used in this sense.

[3] They have their modern successors in those who loll forward instead of kneeling or remain on their knees when the epistle is read instead of sitting.

laity, seats being provided for the bishops and presbyters. Men and women sat or stood apart (*Apost. Trad.*, XVIII, 2; Cyprian, *De Dom. Orat.*, XXXI). In the East, at a later date, the practice of separating the sexes was carried so far that different entrances were used by them (*Apost. Const.*, II, 61).

Preaching was probably on very simple lines. As described by Justin (I *Apol.*, LXVII) it was of a practical nature and given by the president on the basis of the passage which had been previously read. It seems largely to have been the right of the bishop, especially in the North African Churches (cf. Cyprian, *Epist.*, LII, LVI, LXXX). In the New Testament, all who had spiritual gifts (if of the male sex) were allowed to deliver their message in church (1 Cor. 14 : 31 ff.). Later on, presbyters, if duly licensed by the bishop, were allowed to preach; a custom which developed but slowly in the West, where even in the days of Augustine it was unusual (Possidius, *Vit. Aug.*, V). A deacon preached but rarely. In Pionius's *Life of Polycarp* we are told that the saint, while yet a deacon, had a great reputation as a preacher. This statement is more likely to represent the possibilities and conditions of the time when the *Life* was written, in the late fourth century, than the custom of the second.

SACRAMENTS

So far, I have said nothing about the two rites which played so considerable a part in the life and worship of the Primitive Church, rites to which the name sacrament [1] was afterwards applied, baptism and the Lord's Supper. Both of them, it may be pointed out, were in the New Testament connected with the risen Saviour (cf. Rom. 6 : 4 and 1 Cor. 11 : 26). Sacraments were no mere symbols, but means of grace as well as acts of worship, and God's part was at least as important as man's.[2] This aspect continued to be emphasized, especially in the East, until at last it might almost have seemed that sacraments were the exclusive channels of divine help. This use of material means suited an age which demanded outward and visible signs in religion and found such everywhere available.[3] Some scholars

[1] The word itself, being Latin, was not in use until the second century. *Sacramentum* was the soldier's oath and as such especially applicable to baptism. The worshippers of Mithras employed it of the initiatory rites to one of its numerous grades. See, further, Bethune-Baker, *Early Hist. of Christian Doctrine*, p. 376.

[2] This was true even of the baptism of John, which in the synoptic gospels is "not only a symbol of purification on repentance, but is thought of as in some way guaranteeing salvation": Schweitzer, *Paul and His Interpreters*, p. 242. The same idea may also be found in the fragment of the *Gospel according to the Hebrews* quoted by Jerome, *Contra Pelag.*, III, 2 (*Apoc. N.T.*, p. 6).

[3] Harnack considers that the Marcionites were exceptional in having no sacramental theology: *Mission und Ausbreitung*, p. 250 (E.T., I, p. 289).

have regarded the extent to which the sacraments were emphasized, even in apostolic times, as evidence that Christianity was really a species of mystery religion. There is no justification for such a theory, although, from at least the latter part of the second century the Christians were at pains to secure the eucharist from the presence of outsiders, even the catechumens being excluded from its celebration. In the Early Church there was no disputing as to the meaning of the sacraments, as is demonstrated by the absence of any conciliary decisions about them. Christians recognized their practical worth and importance as means of grace and fellowship and, for the time, were content not to formulate any theory concerning them.

(a) *Baptism*

In the New Testament no attempt is made to explain the meaning of baptism. It was not even the means by which our Lord's first followers were admitted to discipleship, perhaps because some at least of them had been already baptized by John. Later it became the normal method of initiation. The rite was doubtless taken over from the Jews, and with it, in all probability, the use of anointing in connexion with the ceremony.[1] In the first ages of the Church baptism was administered without any apparent preparation, the simple confession of belief in Jesus being considered to fulfil all requirements (cf. Acts 8 : 35–38; 16 : 30–33). The need for preparation, however, soon became evident and a definite class of catechumens was recognized. The period of preparation was sometimes extended to as much as three years, and it included moral instruction and testing, as well as the teaching of doctrine.[2] To baptize without adequate preparation was one of the signs of heresy, according to Tertullian (*De Praes.*, XLI: cf. *De Bapt.*, XX).

For the administration of the rite in the West we are fortunate in having accounts from Justin, Tertullian, and *The Apostolic Tradition* of Hippolytus.[3] The candidates, after the appointed prayer and fasting, assembled in the church at night, usually on the eve of Easter. At cockcrow they proceeded to the baptistry or to some place where there was running water, where the actual ceremony was performed.[4] The water was blessed, the

---

[1] See F. Gavin, *The Jewish Antecedents of the Christian Sacraments*, p. 112.

[2] See *Apost. Trad.*, XVII, and canon 42 of the Council of Elvira. Justin, although he assumes that instruction will take place before baptism, does not necessarily imply anything elaborate or prolonged (I *Apol.*, LXI). But, as he was writing for the heathen, a simple statement was all that was required; even in his day there may have been a considerable period of preparation.

[3] For fuller details see F. E. Brightman in *Early Hist. of the Church and Ministry*, p. 342 ff.

[4] The baptism did not take place in church: cf. Justin, *op. cit.*, LXI; Tertullian, *De Cor. Mil.*, III; *De Bapt.*, IV.

candidates renounced the powers of evil (*De Spect.*, IV) and were, as a double precaution, then exorcised. Then followed the confession of faith and the actual baptism by threefold immersion.[1] The newly baptized then returned to the church to be confirmed by the imposition of the bishop's hands, and in both Rome and the East by unction. They had previously been anointed with the oil of thanksgiving and had partaken of a cup of milk and honey, a symbol of the food of the promised land into which they were now come. The administration was the right of the bishop, but he might delegate it to presbyters, or even to deacons (Tertullian, *De Bapt.*, XVII). Such was the rite in outline. Certain peculiar features may now be specified. In the Roman Church, oil was used in the exorcism of the candidate; in the African, only the imposition of hands. In the former, at this period, no baptismal formula was used; but, instead, immersion after each paragraph of the creed had been repeated. The unction in the confirmation was also confined to Rome among Western Churches.

Immersion was the usual custom for those in health, and, since this involved the removal of the clothes, men and women were baptized separately. The importance of immersion can be illustrated by the efforts supposed to have been made by St. Peter in baptizing Theon when on shipboard in the Adriatic. According to the *Acts of Peter*, V, they had to wait for a calm day and descend into the sea (*Apoc. N.T.*, p. 308). When possible, running water seems to have been used, though this was not essential, as Tertullian is careful to point out when referring to St. Peter's baptizing in the Tiber (*De Bapt.*, IV). The preference for running water would probably rule out the early existence of baptistries; certainly the claim that a tank found in the cemetery of Priscilla was used for baptism is most unlikely.[2]

Baptism into the name of the Trinity was usual, but at first the name of the Lord Jesus was enough. There seems to have been some confusion between the two usages, for in *Didache*, VII, 1, that into the Trinity is enjoined, but in IX, 5, there is reference to baptism "in the name of the Lord". When Thecla baptized herself by plunging into a tank after wrestling with animals in the arena she cried: "In the name of Jesus Christ do I baptize myself".[3]

Baptism was held to be necessary to salvation, though in the

---

[1] Threefold immersion is at least as old as the end of the second century: see Tertullian, *Adv. Prax.*, XXVI.

[2] See A. Profumo, *Un battistero cristiano*. In any case it is exceedingly improbable that baptism would have been administered among the tombs of the dead: cf. Styger, p. 143.

[3] *Acts of Paul and Thecla*, XXXIV (*Apoc. N.T.*, p. 279).

case of martyrs their own blood sufficed.[1] The extent to which this idea was carried can be seen from Hermas, *Sim.*, IX, xvi, where it is even considered necessary for the "spirits in prison" who were freed from Hades. As a rule our Lord's descent is enough,[2] but Hermas considers that instruction and the "seal" must be added. The use of the term "seal" was probably borrowed from the Jews, who used it of circumcision (cf. Rom. 4 : 11 f.; *Epist. Barn.*, IX, 6). It suggests ratification rather than origination. So common was the usage that Abercius, Bishop of Hieropolis, could speak of Christians as "the people with the bright seal".[3] The actual wording varies a little though "the seal of the Lord" or "of Christ" is perhaps the most frequent.[4] In at least one passage the phrase "the seal of the Word" occurs.[5]

Various beliefs about the efficacy of baptism were current, and the desire for its repetition (as in the case of the *taurobolium*) had to be severely condemned.[6] The rise of the penitential system was a consolation to those who believed that no post-baptismal sin could be forgiven. Thecla regarded it as a safeguard against temptation itself. "Only give me the seal of Christ," she cries to St. Paul, "and temptation shall not touch me."[7]

The question of heretical baptism which caused such fierce controversies in the third century has already been noticed in connexion with them; here it may be added that the Roman custom of "conditional" baptism dates only from the twelfth century, and was not much used before the sixteenth.

In view of the later practice of baptizing infants, something may conveniently be said of its first use in the West, where it seems to have been introduced earlier and practised more freely than in the East. The earliest definite notice is contained in a statement by Irenaeus that through Christ all are born again, including infants and children (II, xxii, 4). There can be little doubt that the reference is to baptism. By the time of Tertullian the custom was so common that he felt that he ought to protest against those who are innocent and untaught being

---

[1] Tertullian, *De Bapt.*, XVI (he refers to Luke 12 : 50); Cyprian, *Epist.*, LXXIII; Euseb., VI, iv, 3.

[2] See the various accounts of the harrowing of Hell in the *Acts of Pilate, etc.*

[3] See Lightfoot, II, i, p. 480.

[4] Hermas is fond of using the term absolutely: see *Sim.*, VIII, ii, vi; IX, xvi, xvii, xxxi; and so II *Clem.*, VII, "the seal of baptism". The "seal of the Lord" occurs in *Acts of Paul and Thecla*, XXV (*Apoc. N.T.*, p. 277), and *Acts of Peter*, V (*op. cit.*, p. 308). Basilides, the pupil of Origen, is described as receiving "the seal in the Lord" (Euseb., VI, v, 6).

[5] *Acts of Thomas*, XXVI (*op. cit.*, p. 375).

[6] cf. Tertullian, *De Bapt.*, XVIII.

[7] *Acts of Paul and Thecla*, XXV (*Apoc. N.T.*, p. 277): cf. *Acts of Thomas*, XLIX (*op. cit.*, p. 388).

baptized (*De Bapt.*, XVIII).[1] But his protest went unheeded and in the *Apostolic Tradition* of Hippolytus, XXI, 4, infants are included as fit subjects for baptism, their parents or other relations acting as sponsors.

(b) *The Eucharist*

To present-day Christians accustomed to the eucharist as a service held in church and often surrounded by an elaborate ritual, it is difficult to recollect that for the early Christians it was a real meal held in a private house. The ordinary supper at which the family gathered might by prayers and rites be transformed into a eucharist; this custom persisted even in Cyprian's day, though such celebrations did not rank with the official morning eucharist (*Epist.*, LXIII).

Baptism was the necessary preliminary to partaking of the eucharist, as the Lord's Supper (1 Cor. 11 : 7) came to be called.[2] In New Testament times the disciples seem to have met daily for worship and a common meal. The first description of the actual service speaks of a weekly assembly on Sunday (Justin, I *Apol.*, LXVI). More frequent celebrations would later become the rule. It is in North Africa that the process can most easily be traced (cf. Tertullian, *De Orat.*, XIV), culminating in a daily eucharist in the more important centres (Cyprian, *De Dom. Orat.*, XVIII).

But if the Lord's Supper was eventually transformed into the eucharist there does not seem at first to have been any exclusive link between it and the Upper Room. It has been suggested that "it had one of its roots in a customary 'breaking of bread' practised by Jesus and His disciples during His earthly life, and perpetuated in the Church after His death and resurrection".[3] Probably there was always an eschatological element in men's thoughts of the eucharist, for, if it looked back to previous custom, it also looked forward "to that heavenly banquet which was the august and mysterious symbol of the perfection of the age to come".[4] The only primitive liturgical commemoration of the Death was the *Pascha*, which was the Jewish Passover under a Christian form. This actually commemorated both the Passion and the Resurrection.[5] The date of the festival was, as we know, the subject of much disputing. In Asia, it coincided with the actual Passover; in other parts, it took place on the following Sunday, being preceded by a fast. No special notice was taken of "Good Friday", save that it also was observed

[1] Children, according to Cyprian, need baptism even if they have not themselves offended, for they partake of the original sin of Adam (*Epist.*, XIV).
[2] St. Luke refers to it as "the breaking of bread" (24 : 35; Acts 2 : 42, 46; 20 : 7). [3] *Doctrine in the Church of England*, p. 160, note.
[4] C. H. Dodd, *The Apostolic Preaching*, p. 233.
[5] See *J.T.S.*, XXV, 1924, p. 268.

with a fast in preparation for the *Pascha*.[1]

Some scholars consider that St. Paul was responsible for linking together the eucharist and the Last Supper (cf. 1 Cor. 11 : 24) and that the command to continue it as a memorial in the synoptic gospels is no part of the original record.[2] However Justin is quite clear that in his day what was done at Rome was such a memorial (I *Apol.*, LXVI), as is the *Apostolic Tradition* of Hippolytus (IV).

In the first days, the eucharist had been combined with a common meal, the agape or love-feast. The connexion was soon abolished,[3] and the agape continued as a mainly social event, although prayers were still part of the procedure.[4] When this divorce actually took place it is not possible to discover. As late as the beginning of the second century Ignatius regards the holding of the agape as equally with baptizing the chief work of the bishop, for it was his presence which apparently made the difference between an ordinary meal and a eucharist.[5] Gradually the social side of these assemblies came to outweigh the religious, until in the fourth century it was forbidden to hold them in churches.[6] Begun as a symbol of the brotherhood of all believers, they came to be an occasion for showing charity to the poorer members of the community.[7] As time went on, they probably took on a special character, and were held in connexion with definite occasions such as the "birthdays" of martyrs, the dedication festivals of churches, as well as events in the private lives of individuals, such as marriages and funerals. In the cemetery of Peter and Marcellinus in Rome there is a representation of a feast, probably of the early fourth century, in which those seated at a table are waited upon by two female servants named Agape and Irene. Marucchi (p. 326 f.) thinks that the heavenly banquet, with the "love" and "peace" which would attend it, is represented; but Styger (p. 203) considers that it is a funeral feast. In any case the use of the name Agape, though common among Christians, is remarkable.[8]

---

[1] G. Dix, *Apost. Trad. of St. Hippolytus*, p. 73 f.

[2] The Western text of Luke 22 : 19b–20 omits it, and the omission is accepted by Westcott and Hort.

[3] It seems to have been retained until the third century in Alexandria: see Clement of Alex., *Paed.*, II, i, 10 ff. The memorial and the agape are connected in the so-called *Epistle of the Apostles* (*Apoc. N.T.*, p. 490). This last would be evidence for Asia Minor, but not for the West. Dix knows of no evidence to show that the Roman Church ever gave official recognition to such feasts (*op. cit.*, p. 83 f.), though they are described in *Apost. Trad.*, XXVI.

[4] They are mentioned by Tertullian, *Apol.*, XXXIX.

[5] *Smyrn.*, VIII, 2. See Lightfoot's comments, II, i, p. 386 f. and ii, p. 313.

[6] By the Council of Laodicea (canon 28) and by the third Council of Carthage (canon 30).

[7] cf. *Apost. Trad.*, XXVII, and Augustine, *Contra Faustum*, XX, 20.

[8] See, for its occurrence in the inscriptions, Diehl, III, p. 6. There are several

The eucharist was normally celebrated by the bishop but, as in the case of baptism, he soon delegated his powers to others. In the celebration, he was assisted by the deacons who handed the elements to the worshippers,[1] who received them with crossed hands.[2] All those who were present communicated, even when there was a daily celebration, for, as Cyprian said, "we pray that our Bread, which is Christ, may be given to us daily" (*De Dom. Orat.*, XVIII). In the fourth century an exception would be made in the case of certain penitents, the *consistentes*, who, although allowed to be present, were forbidden to take part. When the bishop was celebrating, the presbyters there do not seem to have taken any part in the service. With the growth of the Christian community and the establishment of several churches in a city, opportunities of celebrating would be theirs. In Rome the bishop sent a fragment of the bread to each presbyter in the principal churches of the city, to be placed with the bread of his celebration, and so the link was kept up. It should be noted that two or more altars were not allowed in one church —such an idea provoked the scorn of Augustine—so that the presbyter had less opportunity of celebrating than under later conditions.

The use of wine was avoided by certain semi-heretical sects, such as the Ebionites and the followers of Tatian, who flourished mainly in the East. One such sect was known as the Hydroprastae from their use of water only. They existed as late as the fourth century.[3] One curious reason for the avoidance of wine is reported by Cyprian, who, when he ordered certain bishops to resume its use, was informed that the smell of it in early morning aroused the suspicions of the heathen and betrayed Christians (*Epist.*, LXIII). In some instances there seems to have been administration in one kind only,[4] and the rather late *Martyrdom of Matthew*, XXV (*Apoc. N.T.*, p. 461) refers to the use of the juice of the grape which was pressed into the cup.

The custom of consuming the elements in the houses of the

---

instances of sisters being named Agape and Irene: see *C.I.L.*, 1897, XIV, *Bull. Arch. Crist.*, 1882, p. 113 ff., and Silvagni, *Inscr. Christ. urbis Romae*, p. 350.

[1] According to Justin, I *Apol.*, LXV, they handed the bread as well as wine and water. Cyprian mentions the cup only (*De Lapsis*, XXV). Tertullian seems to infer that the president himself handed the elements to each worshipper (*De Cor. Mil.*, III).

[2] So in North Africa: *Passio S. Perpetuae*, IV: *junctis manibus*.

[3] Some Jewish authorities regard the grape as being the fruit of the "forbidden tree": *Apoc. Abraham*, XXIII; *Berakoth*, 40 a; *Apoc. Baruch*, IV, 8. The more usual identification is with the fig.

[4] cf. *Acts of John*, CIX f. (*Apoc. N.T.*, p. 268); *Acts of Thomas*, XXVII (p. 376), CXXXIII (p. 422); cf. CXXI (p. 418) where bread and water are mentioned, and CXX (p. 418), wine mingled with water. These instances probably come from unorthodox bodies and refer to the East; similar ideas may, however, have spread in the West.

worshippers seems to have been common. Justin, as we saw above, speaks of the deacons taking them to absent communicants, whilst Tertullian reveals what seems to later ideas an extraordinary state of affairs. Lay people, apparently, were in the habit of storing up the elements at home to eat at their leisure (*De Uxor.*, II); whilst some Christians refused to partake of the eucharist on vigils so as not to break their fast. He advises them to attend the service but to take back the consecrated elements for later consumption at home (*De Orat.*, XIX).[1] Cyprian reports an incident during persecution when a woman, who had lapsed, on opening the receptacle in which she kept the reserved sacrament was met by a burst of flame (*De Lapsis*, XXVI). Christians were not always as careful as they ought to have been in this matter, and the *Apost. Tradition* (XXXII, 2) warns them to see that no unbaptized person nor a mouse or other animal consumes the eucharist.

Into the theological and philosophical beliefs concerning the eucharist it is not possible to enter here; many excellent summaries are in existence.[2] It will suffice to point out that already in the middle of the second century there was a distinct recognition that after the consecration the bread and wine are no longer the same. Justin (I *Apol.*, LXVI) says "the food which was blessed by the prayer of the Word . . . is, we are taught, both the flesh and blood of that Jesus Who was made flesh". This clear statement in a writing intended for pagans is most striking. So, too, Irenaeus in his casual allusions to the eucharist,[3] takes the same point of view, and argues back from it to refute docetic and Gnostic theories as to matter and the Lord's body. Similar teaching is to be found in the great African fathers. Tertullian marks a distinct advance on Justin and Irenaeus, for, whilst they look to an invocation of the Logos (the invocation of the Holy Spirit is not found in liturgies until after our period) as making the body and blood, he concentrates upon the words of institution.[4] The bread, however, is only a figure (*figura*) of the body (*Adv. Marc.*, IV).[5] Elsewhere he says that the words of the

---

[1] In view of the later practice of "reservation" it is interesting to notice that he applies the term to the Lord's body (*reservato*).

[2] See, for example, Bethune-Baker, *Early Hist. of Christian Doctrine*, p. 397 ff.

[3] cf. Harvey, *Irenaeus*, I, p. clxxiii.

[4] The idea of attaching value to the "moment of consecration", however, is very much later. The ordinary worshipper was not made aware of it, in the West, until the eleventh century at the very earliest: see Edmund Bishop in the Appendix to R. H. Connolly, *Homilies of Narsai* (*Texts and Studies*, VIII, No. 1, p. 128).

[5] Dr. Swete has commented: "in his judgment, the Bread and Cup are figures, although not bare figures, since by Christ's ordinance they are authorized and effective representations of the realities which they symbolize" (in *J.T.S.*, III, p. 161).

Lord's Prayer, "give us this day our daily bread", included His body (*De Orat.*, VI). This recalls the opinion, still current at the end of the sixth century,[1] that the apostles consecrated the eucharist with the Lord's prayer only. There can be but little doubt that the accusation of cannibalism brought against the Christians was due to a misunderstanding of current theories of the eucharist.[2]

The idea that the eucharist is not only a memorial and a means of grace, but also the offering of a sacrifice, also goes back to quite early times in the West. It underlies the parallel drawn between the ministries of the two covenants (I *Clem.*, XLIV), and by the time of Irenaeus was well established. None the less, Justin clearly recognized that prayers and thanksgivings from faithful hearts are the only perfect sacrifice (*Dial.*, CXVII). Elsewhere he says that the offering of the bread and wine are a fulfilment of Mal. 1 : 10 ff. (*Dial.*, XLI). In Cyprian, the sacrificial aspect of the eucharist is well to the fore. The Christian priest stands in the place of Jesus Christ and makes the same offering (*Epist.*, LXIII). It is, however, pointed out that the sacrifice differs from those of both Jews and pagans, by being "spiritual" and not "material"; none the less, it is the body of Christ which is offered.[3]

How far Christian ideas about the eucharist were influenced by Jewish and pagan sacrificial meals it is impossible to say with any exactness. The Old Testament describes eating bread before Jehovah (Ezek. 44 : 3; cf. Exod. 24 : 11); whilst, as we have already seen, the structure and prayers of the liturgy have been considerably influenced by Jewish models. In the very full and detailed descriptions of the eucharist as celebrated in the West early in the third century, the large element of Jewish material is remarkable.[4] There are also close parallels with pagan ceremonies, with Mithraism in particular, as both Justin (I *Apol.*, LXVI) and Tertullian (*De Praes.*, XL) observed. They attribute the resemblances to the malice of the demons. The borrowing in this instance may be on the pagan side, for it is not always the Church which copies its rivals, as many scholars like to think. Often enough no direct borrowing on either side need be inferred, sacrificial meals are very ancient, and even the Hittite ritual at Boghaz-Keui contained something very like a consecration of bread and wine.[5] None the less, the Church was a frequent borrower, as is admitted by Canon Barry, the learned Roman

---

[1] See the letter of Gregory the Great to John of Syracuse.
[2] The critic in Macarius Magnes, *Apocriticus*, III, xv, condemns the Christian view as "beast-like and absurd".
[3] cf. Bethune-Baker, *op. cit.*, p. 406.
[4] See Dix, *Apost. Trad. of St. Hippolytus*, I, p. xl ff.
[5] See E. Burrows in *Zeitschrift der morgenländ. Gesellschaft*, 1922, p. 190.

Catholic historian, who recognizes that when the Romans became Christians, "they took over . . . the language, the ritual, the yearly observances, the festal adornments, and even the artistic symbols to which they had been brought up" (*The Papal Monarchy*, p. 11). Some even take this power of adaptation, a legacy, surely, from the old Roman spirit which was accustomed to retain old forms when the meaning had departed from them, and give them a new content, as a testimony to the vitality and excellence of Catholicism.[1]

We have seen already that the Christian churches, when freedom for development and expansion became possible, were very similar to the teaching halls of the heathen; from the heathen, too, they adopted the tradition of a splendid pageantry. Much was taken over with little alteration, save that the names were changed to give the appearance of orthodoxy; but, as S. A. Cook has said in another connexion, "the old canvas still shows through the coatings it has received" (*The Relig. of Anct. Palestine*, p. 114).

THE CULT OF THE SAINTS

One development which was doubtless suggested by the pre-Christian experience of converts from paganism was the cult of saints, and, in particular, of the Blessed Virgin Mary. This began in the East and then spread to the West. One quite early instance may be cited, from the *Acts of John* (probably belonging to the first half of the second century). The apostle is reported to have raised a man and his wife from the dead. In gratitude they obtain a picture of him, and, during his lifetime, place an altar with lamps before it. St. John protested that this was a heathenish custom, to which the reply was given: "My only God is He who raised me up from death with my wife: but if, next to that God, it be right that the men who have benefited us should be called gods—it is thou, father, whom I have had painted in that portrait, whom I crown and love and reverence as having become my good guide".[2] Such a feeling was natural in one who had been brought up to believe in demi-gods, and, in a later age, and again in the East, there could be rejoicing (in which Christians of the West no doubt had their share) that the glories of the pagan deities had been transferred to the saints.[3]

If the West did not originate such customs, it quickly followed the example of the East,[4] and in various parts of Italy and else-

[1] E. G. Gourmont, *La Culture des idées*, p. 137.
[2] *op. cit.*, XXVII (*Apoc. N.T.*, p. 233).
[3] cf. A. Maury, *La Magie et l'astrologie*, p. 151 ff.
[4] The cult of the saints is found even in Islam, for " they fill a void which monotheism has left between the humble peasant and the Lord of the World.

where the cult of the Blessed Virgin took over the sanctuaries and even the rites of various female deities, such as Ceres, Vesta, and Venus. Here some shrewd words by N. P. Williams may be quoted: "the more extravagant developments of devotion to the Mother of Christ represent not so much the impression made by the Mary of the New Testament upon the earliest disciples, as the unconscious transference to her person of ideas and sentiments connected with the pre-Christian 'Queen of Heaven' whose worship was denounced by Jeremiah in the Old Testament" (in *Northern Catholicism*, p. 224). The cult of St. Joseph also became very popular in the West, but was of much slower growth. It seems to have originated in Egypt.

The cult of the saints may have had its beginnings in the high regard which was paid to the martyrs, which certainly goes back to quite early times and may have owed something to the attitude of the Jews towards such heroes of the faith as the Maccabees.[1] In the West, no doubt, it followed on the pagan cult of the dead. To a Roman, the tomb was, as Dill has said: "a chapel or an altar as well as a last home. . . . The cult of the dead long survived in the cult of the martyrs and the pagan feasting at their tombs disturbed and perplexed Augustine, and Paulinus of Nola" (*Roman Society from Nero, etc.*, pp. 486 and 488). Anniversary feasts in honour of the martyrs are found in Asia Minor before the end of the second century, though in Rome not until a hundred years later. Perhaps the first sign of the beginning of a cult is connected with the death of Polycarp at Smyrna in 155, especially in *Mart. Polycarp.*, XVIII. By the time of Cyprian, memorials are a regular feature (*Epist.*, XXVIII, XXXIV).

In the Syrian calendars, the list of martyrs begins with Ignatius; those of North Africa, with the Scillitan Martyrs of 180; but the Roman *Depositio Martyrum*, which dates from 354, contains no names from the first two centuries except St. Peter and St. Paul. In the contemporary *Depositio Episcoporum*, the list of popes from 254 to 352, whilst containing a careful record of the day and month of their death, often omits the year. This record was in view of the annual memorial celebration. In this connexion it may be recalled that it was not a Christian custom to celebrate birthdays, either one's own or those of other people, and Origen has pointed out that in Holy Scripture it is only evil men, Pharaoh and Herod, whose birthdays are referred to.[2] The

They are interested in individuals, not in the universe, and they specialize in different ailments": *The Legacy of Egypt*, p. 390.

[1] In the parish of Milton Damarel in Devon a chapel was dedicated in 1315 to St. John the Baptist and the Seven Maccabees; see *Register of W. Stapeldon*, p. 123.

[2] See *Selecta in Genes* (*P.G.*, XII, col. 132); *Hom. in Lev.*, viii (*P.G.*, XII, col. 495), and *Comm. in Matt.*, xiv. (*P.G.*, XIII, col. 89).

birthday of the martyr was the day on which he sealed his faith by the offering of his blood and entered into a new life.[1]

Another practice which was probably inspired by pagan custom was that of invoking the saints for their aid. The earliest known example in the West is the appeal of Hippolytus (*In Dan.*, ii, 30): "Remember me I beseech you, in order that I also may obtain with you the same lot of steadfast witness". It will be noticed that the appeal is made, not to Christian martyrs, but to the Three Children (a favourite subject in the catacombs).[2] The practice was not unknown among orthodox Jews,[3] but it is to pagan sources that we shall most readily turn, and there we find that a whole host of various supernatural beings was available to those who called upon them. They presided over every kind of activity and had their shrines in many localities. It was not a long step to substitute for them, not the supreme object of Christian worship, but various lesser beings. In some cases magic came in with ignorant Christians, and even demons were invoked, either as an attempt to make the best of both worlds or simply through crass ignorance.[4] A study of the inscriptions suggests that there was a belief that any dead person could intercede for the living, and in the memorials of quite ordinary people in the catacombs one finds such phrases as PETE PRO NOBIS and PETAS PRO SORORE TVA,[5] in addition to requests to apostles and martyrs. An inscription from Narbonne may also be cited here:

LAGGE FILI

BENE QVIESCAS

MATER TVA ROGAT TE

VT ME AD TE RECIPIAS [6]

Cyprian, who considered that the saints have no power in things of this life, since they need to pray for their own avenging (Rev. 6 : 10), would limit their influence to the next world and the day of judgment (*De Lapsis*, XVIII).

The regard for the saints, which sometimes under pagan influences became excessive, may have owed something to the somewhat similar worshipping of angels which began even in the Apostolic Age (Col. 2 : 18). The strange idea that the dead become angels when they die was not unknown,[7] and speculations

---

[1] See, further, P. H. Delahaye, *Les Origines du culte des martyrs.*
[2] The cult of the Three Children was widely practised in North Africa: see *C.I.L.*, VIII, 13543. It will be recalled that Justin includes them in his list of Christians before Christ (I *Apol.*, XLVI).
[3] See my note on "Intercession of Saints in Jewish Literature" in *Jeremiah* (*Westminster Commentaries*), p. 129 f.
[4] cf. Le Blant, *Nouveau Recueil des inscript.*, p. xvi.
[5] Marucchi, pp. 165 and 557.   [6] Le Blant, *L'Épig. chrét. in Gaule*, p. 4.
[7] Hermas, *Vis.*, II, ii, 7; *Sim.*, IX, xxv, 2; *Mart. Polycarp.*, II, 3; *Acts of Paul and Thecla*, V (*Apoc. N.T.*, p. 273).

about angels and the angelic orders were very common in both Jewish and Christian writers.[1] In the *Ascension of Isaiah*, a Christian document in spite of its title, two great angels find a place in the seventh heaven—they are the Holy Spirit and Jesus Himself. Thus the category of "angel" was very inclusive. In a strange passage, already referred to, Justin Martyr states that Christians worship and adore not only God and His Son but the host of the other good angels who are made like Him (I *Apol.*, VI).

[1] "The air was full of angelology" wrote Lightfoot: II, i, p. 391.

EPILOGUE
THE CHURCH AND THE EMPIRE

THE CHURCH AND THE EMPIRE

In November 1872, Canon Lightfoot, as he then was, delivered a lecture in St. Paul's Cathedral on the position of the early Christians under the Roman Empire.[1] He began with the following passage: "Living, as we do, in an age when the rights of the individual are loudly proclaimed and scrupulously respected, it is difficult for us to conceive the tyranny which in ancient times the State exercised over the thoughts and the actions of the subjects". Later in his lecture he spoke of the "vast moral gulf" which in this regard separated modern from ancient society. That gulf, as we know only too well, no longer exists. The tyranny which the State can exercise over the subject is as familiar to us, by hearsay if not by actual experience, as it was to the men of the ancient world. We can therefore understand more fully than could our fathers the position of the first generations of Christians. The history of the relation of the Church and the Empire in their period is no longer a theme of merely academic interest. From the contemplation of their struggles and endurance we may gain fresh strength and inspiration for worthy living in our own day. Otherwise, to brood over their sufferings would be a morbid and futile exercise. All stories of persecutions and atrocities may, as Croce has said: "fill human memory with grief, horror, and indignation, but they do not merit the interest of the historian . . . except as they provide the incentives and the material for generous human activity " (*History as the Story of Liberty*, p. 162).

So far as Church and Empire had any contact, the relations between them at first were friendly. It is true that the founder of Christianity had been put to death by a Roman magistrate; but the responsibility could hardly be laid at the door of the government, for it was so obvious that the weakness of a subordinate official had led to what was in effect a judicial crime. The tragedy on Calvary furnished no clue to the considered attitude of the Roman State. As the missionaries of the Gospel went forth on their work of propaganda they were not unmindful of the protection which the officials of the Empire could afford. St. Paul, in particular, on more than one occasion was indebted to them, and in his writings he represents the government as playing a beneficent part. It is Rome which preserves

[1] Reprinted in *Historical Essays*, p. 26 ff.

civilization itself from unknown dangers (2 Thes. 2 : 5–7), and the powers that be are ordained of God to be His ministers for the preservation of order and justice (Rom. 13 : 1 ff.). A similar attitude is taken up by St. Peter (1 Pet. 2 : 13 f.). In the Revelation, it is true that Rome is represented as Babylon drunk with the blood of the saints (17 : 1–6), but this attack stands almost alone in early Christian literature.

The policy of the Roman government, as we have seen, towards the various religious faiths within the Empire was one of toleration, unless there was suspicion on political or moral grounds. How was it, then, that the Church came in for such harsh treatment?

At first, Christians would not be distinguished from Jews; and Christianity, from the point of view of the government, would rank as a Jewish sect. The outbreak under Nero must, however, have shown, once and for all, that Christians were not simply nonconforming Jews, but members of a new religion, and, as such, demanding separate notice and treatment. Gradually the Church was seen in its true light, as an alien body within the State; with its own laws and customs, living a life which had not been derived from it, and prepared, if need be, to defy its authority. This, whatever may have been the actual charges brought against Christians, was the underlying cause of persecution; they were different from other people and a disintegrating element in society.

The most serious offence of which the Christians were guilty was abstinence from participation in the official cultus. As the welfare of the Empire was thought to be bound up with the due performance of the prescribed rites, the gods might be justly offended by their aloof attitude. There was also difficulty over military service. The Christian had no necessary objection to military service as such, but he was not prepared to take the oath to the emperor, an act which seemed to involve treason to his divine Lord.[1]

In the latter half of the second century a wave of archaism seems to have spread over the East and Italy, which must have brought with it a fresh appreciation of the value of traditional ideas and practices. A general enthusiasm might easily lead to persecution, especially in the more remote regions where matters would be taken more seriously than among the sophisticated Italians. A century later came the determined effort of Decius to revive the ancient Roman spirit, and one consequence· was that the Church, which was obviously an obstruction to his plans, encountered the first organized persecution.

It has often been regarded as a paradox, and a most regret-

.   [1] See Harnack, *Militia Christi*.

table paradox, that the best emperors were the worst persecutors. J. S. Mill, for example, saw in the persecution of Marcus
Aurelius "one of the most tragical facts of all history". In his
case, however, it is easy to make too much of his inconsistency,
for it was by no means the only one in that tortured soul.[1] A
professed lover of peace and a believer in the brotherhood of
man, he could, with all the cruel disregard of an Assyrian
monarch, condemn whole peoples to destruction or deportation
if the needs of the State demanded it. It was, in any case, natural
that the best emperors should persecute, for they were more
careful for the good of the State, against which the Christians
were a standing menace. Persecutions can arise very readily in a
well-ordered community and justice itself may be invoked in
their support. It was in no barbarous land, but in Athens itself,
after a legal trial, that Socrates met his death.

The abstention of the Christians from the traditional rites
would, by itself, have constituted a reason for persecution. The
question must be faced as to whether there were not more positive reasons for regarding the Church as definitely aiming at the
subversion of the State. Modern emphasis on the moral teaching
of Jesus tends to obscure other aspects of Christianity; above
all, the proclamation of a new Kingdom upon earth. Many of
those who joined the Church may have been attracted by this
feature of the Gospel preaching, and it seems highly probable
that among them would be agitators, and advocates of the use
of force similar to the Jewish zealots. The anarchical and dis-
orderly elements in the primitive Church were probably much
more considerable than later ages recognized or cared to remember.[2] Possibly one reason why the term "Kingdom of God"
appears so seldom outside the synoptic gospels was the fear that
it might be misunderstood among Gentile readers; whilst the
notable emphasis on the sacred character of the civil order in
the New Testament, and in subsequent writings, may have been
an attempt to counteract such elements.[3] It is not suggested
that they formed any really appreciable portion of the new
society; Christians probably came chiefly from the small shopkeepers and artisans, a type usually averse to social unsettlement; and in the literature at least, if we except Ignatius, there
is nothing to suggest the material from which revolutionaries
are made. None the less, they were open to the suspicion of hold-

---

[1] Tertullian, it may be noted, claimed that Marcus favoured the Church
(*Apol.*, V), but he is clearly mistaken. The presumptuous "cocksureness" of
the Christians must have been very galling to a philosopher.
[2] See A. J. Carlyle, *Hist. of Medieval Political Theory in the West*, I, p. 89.
He cites Acts 17 : 7; 1 Thes. 2 : 12, 4 : 10 f., 5 : 14; 2 Thes. 3 : 6 ff.; 1 Cor.
6 : 12, 10 : 23 f.; and the later example of the Anabaptists (p. 96).
[3] Carlyle, *op. cit.*, p. 157 f.

ing dangerous views. Justin Martyr definitely complains that the Roman government, when it heard that Christians were seeking a Kingdom, rashly concluded that it was an earthly kingdom (I *Apol.*, XI). In the first centuries of our era it must have been difficult for the government to realize that men might be rebels in religion and yet remain perfectly constant in their allegiance to the State.

Prayers for the government had been a regular feature of Christian worship from the days of the New Testament onwards, as they were also a feature of Rabbinic teaching.[1] There are references to them in Clement of Rome (LXI. 1) and later in Tertullian (*Apol.*, XXXII, *De Resr. Carnis*, XXIV); in fact it may be said that they are common in all the apologists. How could Christians be disloyal, was their plea, when they make regular intercession for the welfare of the State? The fact that the emperor claimed some kind of divine status seems not to have been realized as an objection by either side to prayers being made for his welfare. In present-day Japan, with greater realism, prayers for the emperor are forbidden, since he is above the need of them, being himself divine.

Some perplexity must have been aroused in the minds of many officials, for they could hardly fail to recognize that the Christians were a very orderly section of the community. The situation provided opportunities for a species of blackmail by which the nervous Christian secured a precarious immunity and the official a welcome addition to his stipend.[2] The better type of Roman civil servant, however, must have been exceedingly perturbed at having from time to time to punish good citizens merely because they held eccentric views in religion. Others, no doubt, were glad of the chance of indulging a natural love of cruelty; such was the pro-consul Scapula so fiercely condemned by Tertullian.[3]

If the government had grounds for suspicion, so, too, had the common people. The Christians were so secret and mysterious that a general feeling of disquiet which could not fail to end in opposition prevailed widely. They might complain that their enemies could give no reason for the ill-feeling which they aroused (*Epist. ad Diognetum*, V, 17), nor why they should be regarded as the foes of the human race, and like the Jews before them, as atheists.[4] The charge of atheism may have been

[1] cf. *Aboth*, III, 2: "Pray for the welfare of the government since but for the fear thereof men would swallow each other alive".

[2] Tertullian speaks of blackmail by soldiers (*Apol.*, VII, 3).

[3] This is the first occasion, so far as I know, of the Christian turning on his oppressor. Later, there came an elaboration of the theme in Lactantius, *De Mort. Persec.*

[4] Tacitus, *Ann.*, XV, 44, and *Epist. ad. Diog.*, VI, 5. For the Jews, see Josephus, *Contra Apion.*, II, 6.

due in large measure to their worshipping a "nameless" god. This seemed to be resented by the mob at Lyons (Euseb., V, i, 52). Even the pleasures of life seemed to be avoided by them and its legitimate amusements condemned; they were not to be seen at public spectacles and processions, or even at private banquets.[1] What could be done with such people? Moreover, their own meetings were kept so secret. There must be something wrong about them. And so stories of fearful orgies which extended even to incest and cannibalism began to grow,[2] and with them the common accusation, dangerous in itself, of practising magic arts. By the beginning of the third century, such slanderous stories were accepted by the few, so Origen affirms (*Contra Cels.*, VI, xxvii, 40). It is true that Caecilius, the pagan advocate in the *Octavius* of Minucius Felix, repeats the common accusations against the Christians, but one can hardly imagine that he believed that his friends would have had anything to do with a society which allowed such things. They must be dismissed as mere rhetoric. But whilst the belief in these slanders persisted among the vulgar they would always suffice for an excuse for rioting, and outbreaks against Christians. At the same time, they gave the mob an opportunity for demonstrating its own zeal and loyalty. The common herd, Tertullian tells us, was ever ready to shout for the death of the Christians, or itself to use fire and stones in attacks upon them (*Apol.*, XXXV, 8; XXXVII, 2; XL, 2). Crowds, as a rule, are not so cruel or hardened to suffering as despots; but those who habitually attended the gladiatorial shows would not be unduly squeamish. But even they, as we shall see, were impressed by the constancy of the victims.

Behind many of the popular outbreaks lay personal motives. In the days of St. Paul the menace of Christianity to certain trades had been recognized (Acts 16 : 19; 19 : 23 ff.), and one may be sure that those who derived their living from soothsaying and the manufacture of idols would continue to be aware of the danger.[3] Well might Tertullian specify among the accusors of the brethren such people as panders, pimps, astrologers, and wizards (*Apol.*, XLIII). Economic causes thus provided motives for denunciation. Other causes of a more delicate nature were not wanting. The father of a family might punish his slaves or children for being Christians, and, if they proved obdurate, hand them over to the government.[4] The relations and friends of a convert might feel aggrieved and denounce him or her out of revenge. An instance of the latter type of accusation is recorded

[1] Minucius Felix, *Octavius*, XII. Tertullian, *De Spect.*, is a warning against their dangers.
[2] Suetonius condemned Christianity as *superstitio nova et malefica* (*Nero*, XVI). [3] cf. The fodder-sellers of Bithynia: Pliny, *Epist.*, X, 96.
[4] Domestic tribunals are referred to by Tertullian, *Apol.*, I.

under Antoninus Pius when a certain Ptolemaus was reported to the Prefect of Rome by the husband of one of his converts. There is also the puzzling case of Apollonius, who, perhaps for some petty grievance, was denounced by one of his own slaves.[1] The informer had his legs broken; but the charge was investigated, it is said, by the senate of which he was a member,[2] and Apollonius executed.

In periods of revolution or public danger, opportunities for paying off private scores may easily arise; under a totalitarian state such opportunities are ever present. It is not surprising therefore to find the malice of individuals instigating action when official complacence would gladly have remained dormant. The age was one, moreover, in which the informer flourished almost as freely as in some modern states.[3] Roman law allowed the successful *delator* to claim part of the property of the condemned. In fact, delation became a recognized profession, and in some cases a very lucrative one.

Such personal motives might be extended to include the exercise of influence by individuals upon the emperors. Valerian, for example, is said to have been worked upon by Macrianus, "the master and chief ruler of the Egyptian magi" (Euseb., VII, x, 4); whilst the persecution inaugurated by Diocletian is generally supposed to have been inspired by Galerius. From time to time, the Jews also may have roused up trouble for the Church or its members.

Last of all may be considered causes which were really accidental or fortuitous. Christians might suffer, like other people, at the whim of a tyrant. This was the case under Maxentius;[4] whilst, under Maximin the Thracian, they were persecuted because they had enjoyed some favour from his predecessor, Severus Alexander. There were, in addition, what may be called more general causes; sudden outbreaks of pestilence or famine; floods on the Tiber or low water on the Nile; for these and other like disasters the Christians might serve as scapegoats, might, indeed, be regarded as responsible owing to their neglect of the gods. Eusebius, whose treatment of the whole subject of persecutions can hardly be called "scientific", has the merit of viewing the last persecution from a lofty standpoint and seeing in it a punishment for the sins of the Church, such as pride, sloth,

---

[1] In certain cases of treason the evidence of the accused's own slaves was admitted: Cod. IX, viii, 4, 6, 7.

[2] The Greek and Armenian versions of his *Acta* were discovered towards the close of the nineteenth century: see F. C. Conybeare, *Early Monuments of Christianity*, pp. 35–48. The fact of his martyrdom is now generally accepted, but it is doubtful whether he was a senator, or, in any event, that he was tried by the senate.

[3] cf. Melito of Sardis (*c.* 175), quoted by Euseb., IV, xxvi, 5.

[4] Optatus of Milevis, I, 2 ff., 16 ff.

internal strife, and so forth (VIII, i, 7). Behind all persecution there might be one constant cause, and especially such persecutions as seem to arise haphazard—the demons whose allegiance had been renounced by the adherents of the new faith.[1] The sufferings of the present, bad as they might seem, were but a foretaste of what would occur when the devil himself was let loose upon the earth (Euseb., V, i, 5).

As to the exact charge upon which Christians were punished there is some difference of opinion as to the years before 250. Was it crime enough simply to be a Christian? Under Nero, it might be claimed that the offence for which the victims suffered was arson; but Pliny, under Trajan, after making careful inquiries, decided that the popular notion that the Christians committed all kinds of horrible deeds was unfounded. None the less, since they refused to abjure their religion when ordered to do so by the magistrate they must be punished.[2] Such defiance was in itself a crime, and a very serious one in Roman eyes. There was a great mass of anti-Christian sentiment in existence which would influence the authorities. This affected their estimate of the legal position, and political rather than juridical or religious considerations were paramount. The Christians, as such, did not fit in. If, however, they were willing to offer sacrifice, all would be well, and no questions would be asked about their private beliefs. That was the crux, for the Christians refused absolutely to perform an act which members of other faiths found harmless enough, because they regarded it as taking from the honour due to the One God whom they worshipped. Hence they suffered "for the name" (Hermas, *Vis.*, III, i, 9; ii, 1; cf. Justin, I *Apol.*, IV).

There seems, however, to have been no regular procedure against the Christians, and it is very significant that Pliny, as late as 112, professes to be ignorant on the point and has to consult Trajan in the matter. The whole subject is beset with difficulties and uncertainties, and no clear conclusion seems to be possible with our present knowledge. Professor Merrill, approaching the consideration of the persecutions from the standpoint of Roman Law, concludes that they have been greatly exaggerated, and points out (as others had done before him) that the term *collegium illicitum* which was applied to the Christian Church did not signify an illegal society, but merely one that was not recognized by law and had therefore no legal standing; it could not, for example, hold property. He dismisses the outbreak under

---

[1] Justin, I *Apol.*, V; II *Apol.*, XII; Minucius Felix, *Octavius*, XXVII, 8.
[2] It has been suggested that there was an attempt to suppress associations at this time: hence the order to dissolve the Christian Church. The evidence, however, is by no means conclusive.

Nero as a mere incident which in itself could not have rendered Christians, as such, definite lawbreakers. The proceedings under Domitian he refuses to regard as being in any way concerned with Christianity; they were, in his opinion, directed against a group of aristocrats who had adopted Jewish superstitions.[1]

After Trajan, however, the matter becomes clearer, and the definite question of conforming to the religion of the Empire is the real point at issue. However, in the last and most serious persecution, under Diocletian, the actual cult of the emperor played but a subordinate part.[2] The decree of Valerian seems to be the first enactment to make actual profession of Christianity a statutable offence.[3]

The extent of the persecutions is difficult to estimate, for, doubtless, many suffered of whom no record has been preserved. This would apply especially to soldiers dealt with under military discipline. No doubt there were many sporadic local outbursts. An example may be cited of an inscription on a milestone which refers to an otherwise unknown persecution of some magnitude which took place at Ancyra under Domitian or Trajan.[4] In this connexion the absence of reference by Christian writers to persecutions of which we have knowledge should be noted. The troubles in Bithynia in Pliny's day, for instance, were apparently unknown to Melito of Sardis.[5]

Both East and West, in varying degrees, and by no means at the same time, were subjected to persecutions. But the outbreak under Nero was probably confined to Rome, as Orosius in the fifth century is the first writer to record any extension to the provinces (*Hist. adv. Pagan*, VII, 7). None the less, it is possible that there were repercussions elsewhere, and also further outbreaks in Rome itself, when once the Christians had come to be regarded as criminals.[6] One inscription, which is an obvious forgery, has been found at Maravesar (Marquesia) in Lusitania. It thanks Nero for having rid the province of brigands and those who wished to propagate a new superstition.[7] If the Revelation belongs to the reign of Domitian, it testifies to a very sharp persecution having taken place in the neighbourhood of Smyrna.

[1] See his interesting volume, *Essays in Early Christian Hist.*
[2] So N. H. Baynes in *Camb. Anct. Hist.*, XII, p. 659.
[3] Ulpian is said to have codified the edicts against the Christians, *c.* 215 (Lactantius, *Div. Inst.*, V, 11).
[4] See Ramsay and Bell, *Thousand and One Churches*, p. 514.
[5] It has been suggested that these Christians were heretics, hence Melito's omission: see W. Bauer, *Beiträge zur Hist. Theol.*, 1934, X, p. 94 ff. The suggestion is interesting and ingenious, but in the absence of definite evidence remains a mere conjecture.
[6] Suetonius, *Nero*, XVI, may refer to a wider and longer activity. Gwatkin, *Early Church Hist.*, I, p. 75, was of the opinion that there were other persecutions and that the Revelation was a Christian counterblast.
[7] Leclercq, *L'Espagne chrét.*, p. 29.

But the date is uncertain, and may well belong to a slightly earlier period and refer to extensions of the persecution under Nero.[1] Until the beginning of systematic persecution in the middle of the third century the most widespread attacks seem to have occurred under Marcus Aurelius.

A study of the procedure against the Christians reveals a development in technique. Trajan, in 112, ordered that they were not to be sought out, even though worthy of punishment; an attitude which later provoked the scorn of Tertullian—they were to be treated as innocent until they were caught! Trajan had no sympathy for Christians, as such, but he was anxious that public order should be maintained and nothing done which was unworthy of the Empire. For this reason anonymous accusations were to be ignored. Pliny had much the same point of view, but that did not prevent his torturing certain "deaconesses" to obtain evidence. As a rule torture was applied to Christians to make them abandon their faith. This procedure seemed to Minucius Felix, as a lawyer, most inconsistent. The object of torture was to get at the truth; now it was being used to make men deny the truth (*Octavius*, XXVIII). Tertullian also made his protest. Christians were only too ready to acknowledge their faith, and so the crime of which they were accused; why torture them in the hope of compelling them to deny it? (*Apol.*, II).

Hadrian was a ruler of humane disposition (he abolished human sacrifices in pagan temples); and his rescript to Fundanus, if genuine, gave some measure of protection to Christians, for it laid down that mere clamour or malicious charges were to be disregarded. If, however, definite accusations are brought, the guilty must be punished. The principal object of the rescript may well have been to protect good pagans from needless annoyance and the possibility of blackmail by delators. Septimius Severus, whose son Caracalla had a Christian foster-mother (so Tertullian, *Adv. Scap.*, IV), took the line of trying to prevent fresh conversions rather than of punishing those already Christian. He adopted the same method towards Judaism, which seems to have been showing some activity at the beginning of the third century.

With Decius, came the first real attempt to abolish Christianity altogether. Hitherto the main object had been to restrain proselyting zeal or to compel outward conformity; now there was to be a root and branch destruction. In his desire to restore

---

[1] So Edmundson. He suggests that the seer may have seen volcanic eruptions, which were frequent about A.D. 70, "in the neighbouring island of Thera" (*The Church of Rome*, p. 178). But as Thera (Santorin) is about 80 miles from Patmos it is not likely that he could have seen more than a distant glow.

ancient ways and discipline, Decius ordered every citizen[1] to declare by an act of sacrifice his allegiance to the gods, and so obtain their much-needed aid. It is not quite certain that the measure was primarily directed against the Christians; but its effect was to reveal their numbers and persons. Sacrifice was to be offered on a fixed day, and local authorities were to see that it was duly performed; and, further to stimulate them, travelling commissioners would see that they did their duty. The penalty for non-compliance was death, but it does not seem always to have been enforced, though no doubt additional deaths followed severe torture. In some places the magistrates issued certificates or *libelli* to those who had not actually made the sacrifice.[2] This salved the consciences of weaker brethren, but by the rest they were regarded as being in exactly the same state as actual apostates. There were many victims in all parts of the Empire, and included among them were many of the leaders of the Church. Some of the bishops, including Cyprian of Carthage, deliberately avoided death, realizing that they could serve the Church and its Lord more usefully by their lives. This attitude, which was not always understood by the more fanatical, was certainly wise, for the organization of the Church undoubtedly suffered in many parts through the deaths of its leaders.

The methods of Decius and his advisers were strangely modern. Their chief object seems to have been to frighten the Christians into submission by a threat of force; in other words, what we now call a "war of nerves". Hence the avoidance of extremes, and even a disinclination to make martyrs.[3] C. H. Turner has suggested that even if the hiding-place of Cyprian himself had been known to the authorities "It is at least not impossible that . . . they would have preferred to leave the Carthaginian prelate under the odium that attached to a fugitive rather than to confer on him the dignity of a martyr" (*Studies in Early Church Hist.*, p. 109).

The defeat and death of Decius brought relief to the Church. But it was not of long duration, for his successor Gallus reissued the order to sacrifice and some of the clergy went into exile, including Cornelius of Rome, who died before he could return. Six years or so later Valerian put out two edicts or rescripts which laid down an elaborate scale of penalties for the profession of Christianity.[4] They may be summarized as follows: All persons

[1] This seems almost certain from the discovery of *libelli* given to pagans. There is one to a pagan priestess (Wilcken, *Chrestomathie*, No. 125), and a *libellus* in the Brugsch collection in the Berlin Museum is granted to certain Aurelii who claimed that they had always offered sacrifice to the gods.
[2] See J. R. Knipfing, "The Libelli of the Decian Persecution", in *Harvard Theol. Rev.*, 1923, XVI, p. 345 ff.   [3] cf. Cyprian, *Epist.*, LVI, 7.
[4] The original rescripts no longer exist, but their contents are known from the records of the trial of Cyprian and his letter, *Epist.*, LXXX.

are to conform to the ceremonies of the Roman people; those of rank who fail to do so will be degraded and their property confiscated; continued obduracy will render them liable to the death penalty, except in the case of women, who will be banished; public servants will be sent to the mines;[1] bishops and clergy will be executed, and all assemblies must be closed; the use of the catacombs and burial-grounds is forbidden. This last clause was immediately defied by Sixtus of Rome, who conveyed thither bodies believed to be those of St. Peter and St. Paul. The Church had been purified by its previous struggles under Decius and bore the attack with greater calm and courage. This time there was no need for the bishops to save their lives in order to rally their flocks, and Cyprian and Sixtus both made the supreme sacrifice for their faith in 258.

There followed more than forty years of peace, during which the Church even received some measure of recognition.[2] This period came to an end with the outbreak of the last and decisive contest in February 303. But the period of peace had not been without its martyrs; quite a number are recorded as having suffered, but for the most part they had come under military law, and were almost confined to the West, where Maximian bore rule. They included St. Sebastian, the commander of a cohort at Milan who died at Rome, and a certain Ferrutius who suffered at Mainz (c. 296). To this period is attributed the strange story of the Theban Legion already referred to in Part II, Chap. VI, all of whom are said to have been Christians and to have been massacred, together with their commanding officer. Non-military victims include St. Peregrinus, Bishop of Auxerre, and his deacon Jovinus. The authenticity of all these stories is doubtful; the legend of the Theban Legion, for example, is not found before the sixth century.

The persecution proper began on February 23, 303, with an attack on the great church at Nicomedia. This initial act foretold the policy to be pursued—the destruction of the buildings, which had by this time become numerous and even imposing. In addition, special efforts were to be made to destroy Christian writings. In other respects older methods would be followed. Property was to be confiscated, rank lost, and in some cases enslavement would be the punishment for obstinate clinging to the faith. Later, orders were given for the arrest of the clergy. Later still, the Christians were offered their freedom in return for sacrificing; and torture was employed as an added incentive

---

[1] Prayers for those working in the mines are often found in early liturgies. Tertullian scornfully remarks that it was only right that Christians should be sent to the mines, for it was out of the mines that the gods of the pagans had come (*Apol.*, XII). [2] See below, p. 396.

to accepting this piece of generosity. The policy seems to have been to avoid extreme measures against ordinary Christians and to concentrate on the leaders.

At the end of 303, Diocletian had a mental breakdown and Maximian, his colleague, was given a free hand. Being less wise and more violent than Diocletian, he issued a further edict in April 304 demanding sacrifice from all. The result was a new outbreak of fanaticism and a large crop of martyrs. In that part of the West which was under the direct rule of Constantius extremes were avoided. He seems, indeed, to have done little beyond pulling down a few churches. On the resignation of both Diocletian and Maximian in May 305, Constantius became Augustus and persecution was relaxed in most of the West. It continued, however, in Italy and Africa until the revolt of Maxentius in October 306, but even he seems to have sent two bishops of Rome into exile. After his defeat by Constantine a new era of toleration began. Meanwhile, in the East persecution had been raging bitterly under Galerius, the new Augustus, and his nephew, Maximin Daza. There, for six long years, the Church had to endure; but at last it conquered, and Galerius, dying of a terrible disease, issued an edict of toleration in April 311.

Toleration as the official policy of the government is usually dated from the meeting of Constantine and his ally, Licinius, at Milan in 313, when a document generally known as the Edict of Milan was drawn up. This title is probably incorrect; strictly speaking, there was no "Edict of Milan", for it "has gone the way of many another symbolic representation of historical truth".[1] The victors evidently drew up a series of regulations for issue to the various provincial governors, but no edict as such. The exact text has not survived, but most of the original Latin has been preserved by Lactantius (*De Mort. Persec.*, XLVIII, 2 ff.), and additional matter is to be found in Eusebius (X, v, 2 f.). Permission was given for Christians and all others to adopt that form of religion which best pleased them in order that "whatever gods might be" (*quidquid divinitatis in sede coelesti*) should extend their benevolent interest over the Empire.

The full end of persecution was not yet attained, for the unfortunate East was still in the power of Maximin Daza. He hit upon some novel methods, such as an order for the expulsion of all Christians by the municipal authorities; made an attempt (later to be taken up by Julian) to found a great pagan Church; to control education and produce propagandist literature. He had, however, but a short time for his experiments, as he was defeated by Licinius and died soon after 313. Licinius himself,

---

[1] N. H. Baynes in *Camb. Anct. Hist.*, XII, p. 686. See, further, his volume *Constantine the Great and the Christian Church*, p. 69 ff.

after his breach with Constantine, began to show favour to Mithras and in 323 another wave of persecution threatened the East. Then came his defeat at Hadrianople; and at last it could be seen, *pace* Julian, that Christianity was destined to become the religion of the Roman Empire, although its actual establishment would still be delayed for more than a generation.

Among the various methods adopted by the Roman government in its persecution of the Christians, two seem to call for special notice—burnings, and the destruction of cemeteries. Burnings began under Nero, when some of his victims had to serve as torches. The method was continued in the case of St. Polycarp, and by Decius, received classic prominence in the case of St. Lawrence and his grid-iron, and was much used by Diocletian. In the literature of the times there are also references to this form of punishment,[1] which in the later acts of the martyrs become very frequent.[2]

Attacks on cemeteries are unexpected in view of the Roman attitude to all places of burial. It is often stated that they regarded them as sacred. This is not quite accurate; they were really considered taboo owing to the presence of dead bodies, and were thus, in technical language, *loca religiosa* and not *loca sacra*.[3] The effect, however, was the same, and burial-grounds were respected and considered safe from violation. To desecrate a grave was a horrible thing.[4] None the less, such desecrations did take place, if not with the consent of the authorities, at least by the violence of the mob; and Tertullian can complain of the profanation of Christian burial-places and of the dead being torn from the quiet of the tomb and shamefully mangled (*Apol.*, XXXVII).

What, it may now be asked, were the effects upon the Church and individual Christians of all these attempts at suppression? The answer may be divided under two heads—direct and indirect.

Persecution was always a test of the faith and constancy of the disciple; on a large scale it was also a menace to the very existence of the Church itself in any particular area. In nerving itself to meet the challenge of this menace the Church found its soul and put the divine powers with which it was endowed to full proof. Whilst the struggle lasted its members would at least be sincere Christians, for others would be afraid openly to pro-

---

[1] cf. *Acts of Peter*, XXVIII (*Apoc. N.T.*, p. 328).
[2] They are fond of quoting Ps. 65 (66) : 12: *Transivimus per ignem et aquam et induxisti nos in refrigerium.* There is a probable reference to this psalm in an inscription from Aubagne, cited by Le Blant, *L'Épigr. chrét. en Gaule, etc.*, p. 11: O FORTVNATI QVI VIM [IGNI]S PASSI SVNT.
[3] See Warde Fowler, *Relig. Experience of the Roman People*, p. 37.
[4] Josephus, *Antiq.*, XVI, vii, 1 ff.

fess the faith. The body was thus kept pure and vigorous; whilst those who were called upon to suffer helped to strengthen the faith and endurance of the rest. The fact that other Christians and other Churches might be enduring the same trials at the same time forged a close link between them. One thing which had made the Decian persecution so dangerous to the Church was the great increase in merely nominal Christians which had taken place during the years of tranquillity which had preceded it. Those who recanted were divided into distinct classes. The *sacrificati* had sacrificed at the altar; the *thurificati* had merely cast incense into the flame; the *libellatici* had obtained certificates of conformity from the heathen magistrates. For those who had gold to offer, the means of escape were perhaps easy; it was not only in the Paris of François Villon that prisons were, what R. L. Stevenson has called, "leaky".

Indirect results were the controversies which arose over the status of those who had recanted and wished to be received back into the Church. Perhaps, also, the beginnings of Monasticism within the Church (it was, of course, a pre-Christian movement) may be traced to those who fled into solitary places in order to escape, and there found a peace and calm which they were by no means willing to abandon when the storm had passed over. The use of the Scriptures and men's views on their teaching must also have been considerably affected. There must, for example, have been a great stimulus of interest in apocalyptic writings, especially among Jewish Christians, after the outbreaks under Nero and Domitian; for in the Old Testament the endurance of persecution is followed by the vindication of the righteous. The policy of Diocletian of destroying sacred books must have compelled the Church, and individual Christians even more, to decide which books actually were sacred, and which capable of being handed over without real sin. No doubt many valuable writings disappeared at this time, and MSS. of the inspired writings themselves which might have thrown much light on the text. Official copies used in Church were much more likely to be seized than those in the possession of individuals, who would have better opportunities of hiding them; but the former would no doubt contain the better and more accurate text. In Africa, both rolls (*libri*) and codices are mentioned as having been destroyed.

THE TRIUMPH OF THE CHURCH

In spite of all the measures of the Roman government to suppress it, the Church triumphed at length and the Empire had to recognize it. The "ripple on the Galilean lake" had overflowed the Mediterranean. Such an end to the conflict would have seemed outrageous and impossible to Romans of the first century when Empire and Church were setting out side by side on their dual career. But the Church was full of vigorous and primitive life; the Empire, although a superficial examination could not detect it, was already beginning to suffer from the exhaustion of the Roman people.

For the Church, the Empire, in spite of its refusal to recognize the Christian religion and the sporadic outbursts of persecution, was doubtless a benefit. The late Professor Bury, indeed, considered that the existence of the Empire was a condition of the spread of Christianity, and that the hindrances thrown in the way "were more than compensated by the facilities of steady and safe intercourse and communication, which not only helped the new idea to travel, but enabled its preachers and adherents to organize their work and keep constant touch with one another" (*Life of St. Patrick*, p. 3).

To attempt to explain the triumph of Christianity in terms of opportunity and so forth, as Gibbon did in the fifteenth chapter of his great work, is entirely unsatisfactory, for it ignores the real issue and regards the Word, not as leaven, but as "the artificial result of the strange ferment of religious excitement, superstitions, philosophical mysticism, desperate aspirations which stirred among the peoples of the Levant". But this will not do, for, as Professor Powicke (from whom I have just quoted) goes on to say: "only those who accept the dogma of the divinity of Christ as the central fact in a long procession of divine revelation can escape bewilderment in the contemplation of the spread of Christianity".[1]

Christianity had its rivals. It appeared, indeed, in the midst of a series of religious movements which ultimately stretched from the seventh century B.C. to the seventh century A.D. The opening of this period had seen the beginnings of Judaism, following on the teaching of the great prophets, Jeremiah, Ezekiel, and the second Isaiah; Lao-tze and Confucius, in China; Gautama, in India; possibly Zoroaster, in Persia; and the birth of philosophy and the rise of mystic cults in the Greek world. At the close it would see the rise of Islam. The zenith of the whole awakening can be found in the centuries immediately following the birth of Christ. There then spread a new demand for higher ethical standards and a greater measure of ethical attainment. This demand Christianity alone could meet, for it promised salvation, not only for a world to come and in the life after death, but from the power of sin itself; no other religion dared to proclaim that "Sin must no longer have dominion over you" (Rom. 6 : 14).

[1] *The Christian Life in the Middle Ages*, p. 2 (reprinted from *The Legacy of the Middle Ages*, p. 24): cf. Lightfoot, *Hist. Essays*, p. 7 f.

The older cults, and especially those which, like Christianity itself, had come from the East, enjoyed for a season their measure of popularity; but, sooner or later, they had to succumb before the growing might and deeper purity of their younger rival. No impartial or complete estimate of their worth can be made at this distance of time; because a religion needs to be judged in action, as manifested in the lives of its adherents; and such a manifestation is no longer possible. The followers of Isis and the disciples of Mithras have alike disappeared from the face of the earth, and what we learn from literature and archaeology does not take us very far. But time has given its verdict: they perished; Christianity remains. And no one will question that it was a just verdict.

Various secondary causes may no doubt be brought in to account for the triumph of Christianity, but the primary cause was that it possessed a life which was lacking in all its rivals. It could bring new hope into the world and had the ability, which they had not, to meet the needs, moral, emotional, and intellectual, of mankind. Its morality was the fruit of a vision, and a new law, not of dead ordinances, but of a living Lord. It had a message, moreover, not only for the wealthy and the learned, but also for the poor and ignorant. Celsus, when he scoffs at Christianity for welcoming sinners and outcasts, unwittingly reveals the utter impotence of the accepted religions to bring about a moral reformation in their votaries; he could even argue that it was next to impossible for the character of one who was habituated to evil to be changed. But Christian love and Christian fellowship found the task by no means beyond its power; and this love, we may firmly believe, played as great a part as Christian courage and the logic of the apologists in the Church's triumph.

In some instances the reason for the acceptance of the Christian faith must be sought on the intellectual plane, though converts in this class were probably not numerous. For cultivated persons the Old Testament had an especial appeal, and for two reasons. The fulfilment of prophecy was very impressive; but even more so was the demonstration that Christianity was no new-fangled religion, but had, on the contrary, a long pedigree behind it. Both Justin and his disciple Tatian were affected by this argument.

The strength of the Christian faith was revealed, above all, in the fortitude of the martyrs. They might be dismissed by Marcus Aurelius as unlearned and ignorant men whose motives were beyond his comprehension;[1] but others were moved to adopt the

---

[1] *Meditations*, XI, 3; Pliny also put their conduct down to mere obstinacy: *Epist.*, X, 96.

faith which they adorned and even to imitate the same example. Tertullian, in a passage which seems to be based on his own experience, tells how curiosity is aroused as to the source of such endurance, then follows conviction (*Apol.*, L; *Ad Scap.*, V). Palm-wreathed and radiant, the martyrs faced death in the firm conviction that it was not merely a way of escape from suffering, but the gateway to life eternal. When sentence was passed upon them, they rejoiced, holding that man's condemnation was God's absolution. With some, the desire for martyrdom became a passion; especially in Africa, where Cyprian had to console those who feared that the cessation of persecution might rob them of so precious a crown. What really mattered, he pointed out, was the faith that made martyrdom possible, not the act which witnessed to it (*De Mart.*, XVII). Some actually provoked the authorities to put them to death; but such martyrs were often a source of embarrassment to the Church, and their fanaticism would sometimes break down, when faced by torture and death, to be followed by a shameful recantation. The truly Christian action of Cyprian himself in withdrawing in face of danger they could not understand.[1]

The title of martyr was not lightly given in the Early Church, and even then some kind of official confirmation was required before it could be attached even to those who had died for the faith.[2] At the same time, those who had witnessed a good confession, but had escaped with their lives, were sometimes allowed to assume the title; but this was liable to arouse criticism if not fully justified. Tertullian, for example, pours scorn on Praxeas who prided himself on his good confession (*martyrii*) which consisted in a short and uneventful imprisonment (*Adv. Prax.*, I).

It is worth while pointing out an aspect of martyrdom which is generally forgotten; it had a social as well as a religious significance, for the martyr died for the right of private judgment and the independence of the individual. In this, of course, he was but showing forth in more vivid terms the underlying faith of every genuine follower of His Lord.

Closely linked with the witness of the martyrs was that of the miracles which Christians were believed to have performed. When, in the fourth century, they were no longer held to occur, Hilary of Poitiers declared that it was because they were no longer necessary, since the occasion for martyrdom had also ceased.

---

[1] His flight was the more courageous in view of the *Quo vadis?* legend of St. Peter, whose supposed excuse for leaving Rome was the same as Cyprian's: see *Acts of Peter*, XXXV (*Apoc. N.T.*, p. 333).

[2] This seems to be the meaning of *sed necdum vindicati* in Optatus, I, 16.

In the New Testament, the power of working miracles is taken for granted; and those who had read the Old Testament must inevitably have expected such signs in connexion with the revelation which fulfilled it. In the pre-Nicene age, miracle was the natural language of revelation. Thus the evidential value of miracles was not so great as we are apt to suppose ; they were too common, could, indeed, be worked, so some Christians admitted, by the advocates of other faiths, though by the help of evil demons. No religious teacher, unless he were some strange philosophic novelty, would have had any chance of gaining a hearing in that superstitious age unless he could claim to work miracles.

Although the triumph of Christianity was not assured before Constantine took it under his protection, certain of his predecessors had in a measure prepared the way. The Syrian emperors, with their eclectic outlook, had not ignored the Gospel, and it has been claimed that Philip the Arabian was actually a convert (Euseb., VI, xxxiv). More significant of the growing prestige of the Church than such doubtful patronage was the act of Gallienus in restoring to the bishops, as the Church's representatives, cemeteries which had been seized during the persecution of the previous reign. He thus recognized their right to hold property. Gallienus, however, was no patron of the Gospel and hoped indeed that the work of the Neoplatonists and other philosophers would soon convince the Christians of their errors. A further recognition of the Church's right to hold property was the decision of Aurelian that the disputed temporalities of the see of Antioch should go to the claimant favoured by the Churches of Italy and Rome.

The motives which led Constantine to take the Christian Church under his protection have often been discussed and no agreed result has been reached.[1] Probably they were very complicated. He may have realized that although the Christians formed but a minority of the population, especially in the West, they were an organized and well-established body, as the failure of the persecuting efforts of Diocletian and Galerius had demonstrated. His statesmanlike mind may have foreseen that, sooner or later, the Church must triumph;[2] but reasons of policy perhaps prevented any complete identification with the Church during

---

[1] In his pamphlet *Der Glaube Konstantins der Grossen*, Lietzmann accepts the genuineness of Constantine's religious convictions.

[2] cf. G. La Piana, *Harvard Theol. Rev.*, 1927, p. 340: "To turn the enemy into an ally was the obvious device of political wisdom; and the attempt was made to bring about a gradual absorption of Christian universalism into the universalism of the state and to bind the church to the wheels of the government by bestowing privileges and protection upon the Christian religious organization".

the early years of his rule. As we look back, knowing the future course of events, we can see that his decision was a wise one, when judged by worldly standards, for the Church was alive and vigorous; the Empire already in decline. The one had its face turned to the past; the other was stretching out eager hands to possess the future.

If Christianity had to wait for more than half a century before Theodosius I would definitely establish it as the faith of the Roman people, Constantine at least began the process by which it was worked into the main pattern of the Empire's development. The opportunity thus presented to the Church was immense. The ancient world and its civilization was in process of disintegration; old boundaries, social and intellectual as well as geographical, were being obliterated; but soon it would be ripe for a fresh synthesis. The older religions had nothing to offer which could meet the situation; they were corrupt and inadequate and no sentimental feeling need be allowed, like a sunset glow, to linger over the passing of paganism. Its inadequacy had, indeed, long been apparent, for the decay of civic morality had robbed the Hellenic world of any stable tradition, whilst the failure of the worship of the Emperor to provide a religion which would bind the Empire together was completely obvious.

By the beginning of the fourth century the Church had all the characteristics of a universal religion, having long ago shed the national and racial limitations taken over from Judaism. Its doctrinal system had been sufficiently closely assimilated to current thought to meet the needs of the vulgar and to present to the learned a theology which would at least merit their respect. This adaptation to its intellectual environment might have been disastrous and dragged the Church down into the welter of syncretistic religions which surrounded it. The persistence of Jewish influences, especially as enshrined in the Scriptures, prevented this. Finally the Church had an adequate disciplinary system and set forth a high standard of morality such as was urgently needed if the moral fibre of the State was to be restored. The immediate effect of the alliance was an influx, not only of new ideas, but of new energy as well. Even older ideas which had been in circulation but had never been adopted found fresh recognition and reinforcement. The Church, it can be admitted, no longer lived in that tremendous wave of enthusiasm which flowed from Christ's open grave and the gift of Pentecost; that seems to have died down after the first generation (cf. Rev. 2 : 4; Heb. 2 : 1; 10 : 32 f.); but by solid organization and capable leadership—less romantic and ideal characteristics—it had been prepared to take its part.

For the Church, recognition was far from being an unmixed benefit. It had, indeed, shown itself capable of overcoming persecution, but success was to prove an even greater challenge. In the course of the long struggle many compromises had been made; it was through compromise that much of its progress had been possible, and the position of privilege and prestige which awaited the official faith exposed the Church to new dangers and made it more open to many that were old. So long as it was separated from the world, the Church was strong to influence the world; once they became allies, half the Church's power seemed to be gone. Even the cessation of persecution was not all gain, for it removed a very keen mode of testing the sincerity of converts. Popularity and imperial favour would act exactly in the reverse way and attract the insincere and the ambitious. But the effects of the final recognition must not be exaggerated; worldliness, for example, may have come in like a flood, but it was already more than a stream, as Cyprian's description of the Church of North Africa and the findings of the Council of Elvira abundantly testify. The process of "compromise", even of paganization, had begun long before; but now it received a fresh impetus which would prove irresistible. Christianity took the place of its defeated rival in the world of politics and the name of Christ was substituted for that of Jupiter. Henceforward, allegiance to Him and to Caesar would no longer be incompatible.

The Church, in its relief at the passing of danger and persecution, and in gratitude to Constantine, its deliverer, gave to that emperor almost complete liberty of action in settling its relations with the State. The Church, indeed, had no choice in the matter, for if Constantine took it into partnership, it was he alone who drew up the terms. It was no concordat, but a dictated peace.

One thing which Constantine postulated in his new instrument was unity and a fixed basis of belief. So synods and councils would be held to pass decrees which the State would enforce; and, since the acceptance of imperial protection involved submission to the imperial will, it came about that it was the emperor, and not the bishops, who summoned councils and who gave or withheld approval of their findings. Thus there was inaugurated that protracted series of conflicts over doctrines and definitions which, for the time, tended to sap the spiritual life of the Church and engendered fierce hatreds within its ranks. The West was, it is true, less subject to such disputes than the East; but it had to experience the gradual gathering of power into the hands of the Roman bishop, and the consequent growth of a secular spirit within the Church.

Constantine ruled the Church with an iron hand and his successors adopted the same policy. The nobler Churchmen attempted to resist, especially when there was interference in spiritual and doctrinal matters; Hosius of Cordova, for example, protested to Constantius, and even reminded him that it was for rulers to learn from bishops in such matters. A like independence was shown by Athanasius and Ambrose. But, for the most part, the headship of the emperor was taken almost as part of the natural order. He simply retained the position which, as Pontifex Maximus, he had occupied in the pagan system.[1] God alone was his superior.[2]

The Church, perhaps because of its obsession with the conflicts over creeds, showed no disposition to trample on the paganism which it had supplanted. In many households the men remained pagan when their women-folk accepted the new faith; this continued as late as the time of Jerome, for some of his most notable disciples had pagan husbands. Even when laws were promulgated against paganism—the Theodosian Code contained twenty-five of them—their enforcement was often in the hands of officials who secretly favoured the old ideas. Soon after the beginning of the fifth century, however, the task was taken over by the bishops. Even so, Claudian, as late as the reign of Honorius, could draw the emperor's attention to the ring of pagan temples which still encircled the imperial palace as if to protect it (*De Sex. Cons. Hon.*, XLIV).

The emperors had no wish to oppress their pagan subjects, but policy did not enable them to extend the same consideration to schismatics and heretics. Certain steps, however, were taken, such as the removal of the sanctuary of Aphrodite which stood over the supposed site of the Holy Sepulchre at Jerusalem. Heathen shrines also suffered immense damage in the process of adding to the glories of Constantinople. Among the objects taken thither was the famous tripod of Apollo from Delphi—it still survives although in a mutilated condition. The leaders of the Church, afraid of the influence of the traditional religion, would gladly have seen more drastic measures against pagan remains, and their efforts were encouraged by the populace, eager to obtain free building material. The emperors, however, continued to protect as many ancient memorials as possible;[3] a policy which later appealed to Prudentius, himself an ardent hater of paganism, but a lover of all that was magnificent and beautiful (*Contra Symm.*, I, 501).

[1] The Christian emperors still continued to bear the title until the accession of Gratian. It was Gratian who disendowed the sacred colleges.
[2] This is stated quite plainly by Optatus of Milevis *cum super imperatorem non sit nisi solus Deus* (*P.L.*, XI, col. 999).
[3] See Theod. Code, XVI, x, 15 ff.

REASONS FOR THE FALL OF THE EMPIRE

Gibbon, in a long note at the end of Chap. XXXVIII of his *Decline and Fall of the Roman Empire*, amongst other causes for that process instances "the introduction, or at least the abuse of Christianity" (IV, p. 162). Not many scholars of more recent times would be disposed to agree with him. On the contrary, it might well be argued that, had the Church retained more of its primitive zeal and purity, it might even at that late hour have succeeded in saving it; though probably when Christianity came to power the Empire was already too far advanced along the road of decay and dismemberment for any hope of arresting its progress. In this connexion it is interesting to note the conclusion of a modern historian of unusual insight. Professor Toynbee regards the whole imperial era as a species of "Indian summer", and concludes that the Empire was doomed before it was founded, since "its establishment was nothing but a rally which could only delay, but not permanently arrest, the already irretrievable ruin of a Hellenic Society which the Roman Empire temporarily embodied" (*A Study of Hist.*, IV, p. 61).

The prevailing school of history would doubtless attribute the fall of the Empire in the West to economic causes, though it is perhaps wiser to see in such the accompaniment and symptom of the loss of creative energy rather than its origin (so Toynbee, *op. cit.*, IV, p. 42). Certainly the economic conditions of the later Empire were unhealthy. Wealth had become concentrated in the hands of a few great families who took little interest in public affairs and devoted their energies to culture. The burden of maintaining public life fell more and more on the middle classes until they collapsed beneath it. The civil wars at the beginning of the fourth century and all the unsettlement which followed in their train were blows from which trade never fully recovered. The process, was, however, gradual, and not the result of sudden and violent calamities. Slowly, though unperceived, the resistless effect of social and economic laws was being exerted, whilst the ignorant zeal of statesmen and the selfishness of the wealthy only brought nearer the fate which the one tried to avert and the other regarded as outside their consideration.

An added cause was the penetration of the West by German tribes. This, too, was a gradual process. The barbarian peoples came in at first by infiltration, for the military power of Rome prevented anything like mass immigration until the final collapse. And, since the decay of a political organism is exactly similar to that of an animal, its earliest manifestations appeared at the extremities. The heart of the Empire was protected by the "linked concave of the Alps", but the frontiers beyond were already endangered. To defend them was the supreme task of coming generations. But the strain was too severe, though valiant efforts were made. Indeed it almost seemed in the end that the Empire existed for the sake of the armies which strove vainly to preserve it. Certainly to the rude soldiers who assumed the purple the civilian world was so much taxing material.

Too great an exaltation of the interests of the State at the expense of its subjects has also been put forward as a contributory cause[1]—a warning to totalitarians. The citizens on their part, even as early as the days of Tacitus,[2] were strangely indifferent to the State and its welfare. But so long as subjects obey orders and refrain from criticism, indifference is no unwelcome virtue under a totalitarian state. But this indifference, together with excessive oversight on the part of the government, prevented the Roman people from ever becoming politically mature. They never acquired what Gertrude Bell once called "the Anglo-Saxon acceptance of a common responsibility in the problems that beset the State" (*Amurath to Amurath*, p. 5).

But, behind all these minor causes, behind economic failure and a general sense of dissatisfaction, behind the decay of public spirit, there lay another which contained within it the explanation of the whole complicated process of decadence. The soil of humanity within the bounds of the Graeco-Roman world was exhausted, and must needs go through a time of fallow before the ploughshare, wielded by younger, more vigorous races, should prepare it for a new seed-time and a new harvest. The seed for this sowing would in no small measure be preserved by the Christian Church. This would be its highest secular service, if not to the Roman Empire, at least to the peoples of Europe. Looking back, we can discern that the really significant feature of the centuries which followed immediately upon the birth of Christ was not the decline and fall of the Roman Empire, but the expansion of the one Christian society which was, in its turn, to foster the growth of a new civilization. This, surely, is the only worthy point of view to adopt; for the historian, although he has to set out the story of the past, must ever keep his eyes on the future; not the things that are decaying and ready to pass away are his chief concern, but the fresh life that in every case is stirring among them. "Creativeness, and it alone, is the true and sole subject of history."[3]

[1] Rostovtzeff, *Soc. and Econ. Hist of the Roman Empire*, p. 330.
[2] *Hist.*, I, 1: *inscitia rei publicae ut alienae.*
[3] Croce, *History as the Story of Liberty*, p. 162.

INDEX

Abailard, 64, 168, 182, 288, 326
Abdon and Sennen, Martyrs, 120
Abercius, Bishop of Hieropolis, 120, 366
Acilius Glabrio, 100
Acolytes, 56, 111, 325
Actium, Battle of, 20
Adam and Eve, Book of, 56, 343
Adamantus, Manichee, 283
Adoptionism, 298
Aelia Capitolina (Jerusalem), 78
Aelius Aristides, 57
Aesculapius, 55
Africa, North, 143 ff.; Religion in, 58, 62, 147, 235, 278, 283; Christianity in, 147 ff., 160 ff., 170, 219, 257 ff., 288, 360 f., 398; Disappearance of, 142, 158
Africans in Rome, 102, 106 ff.
Africanus, Julius, 262
Agape, The, 357, 368
Agricola, 37, 65, 197 f.
Alba Longa, 19
Alban, St., 202
Albigenses, 283
Alcibiades, 60
Alcibiades of Apamaea, 120, 272
Aldhelm, St., 94, 167, 205
Alesia, 175, 179
Alexander, Bishop of Rome, 109 f.
Alexander of Abonuteichos, 280
Alexander the Great, 34, 51, 72
Alexandria, 143, 213 f., 225, 277; and Rome, 138, 221; Christianity in, 90, 122, 126, 264, 317 f.; Jews in, 73, 84; School of, 22, 120, 246 f., 257, 264 ff., 296
Allegory, Use of, 25, 81, 251, 257, 266
Almsgiving, 339 f., 362
Altars, 56, 62, 360 f., 369, 372
Ambrose, St., Bishop of Milan, 22, 122, 134, 194, 326, 355
Ambrosius, friend of Origen, 255, 265
Amiens, 183
Ammianus Marcellinus, 38, 40, 174, 180, 193
Ammonius Saccas, Neoplatonist, 68 f.
Ancyra, 386
Andernach, 189
Andrew, Acts of, 236 f.
Anencletus, Bishop of Rome, 104
Angels, 82, 182, 374 f.
Anglo-Saxons, 94, 199, 203 f., 401
Anicetus, Bishop of Rome, 105, 106 f., 279, 321

Anointing, 364 f.
Anterus, Bishop of Rome, 109
Antioch, 20, 22, 58, 96, 213, 257, 313 f.; Chalice of, 352
Antium (Anzio), 97, 136
Antoninus Pius, Emperor, 62, 252
Antony, Mark, 20, 38, 46
Apelles, Marcionite, 121, 281
Apocalypses, 239 ff.
Apocryphal Writings, 9, 230 ff., 276 f., 283, 285 f., 306 f., 341
Apollonius, Martyr, 257, 384
Apollos, 126
Apologists, 61, 246 f., 250 ff., 260 f., 265 f., 287, 382
Apostles, 85, 90, 122 f., 310 f., 313
Apostles, Acts of the, 74 f., 85, 89, 92, 99, 231
Apostles, Epistle of the, 96, 239, 273, 305 f., 368
Apostolical succession, 82, 284, 287, 319 f.
Apostolic Church Order, 85, 96, 249, 327, 336
Apostolic Constitutions, 85, 244, 248 f.
Apostolic Fathers, 22, 222 ff., 230
Appii Forum, 136 f.
Apuleius, 38, 52, 54, 57, 60, 119, 146 f., 230, 259
Aquileia, 19, 62, 130 f., 183
Aquinas, St. Thomas, 25
Arabs, Arabic, 72, 90, 144, 158
Architecture, 148 f., 174, 186, 204 f., 263, 360
Aricia, 136 f.
Aristides, Apologist, 252
Aristotle, 69, 292
Arles, 176, 178, 182 f., 187, 346; Council of, 114, 131 ff., 157, 185, 202, 323
Arnobius, 49, 218, 263
Arpi, 140
Art, 40, 62, 166, 197, 308, 338, 351; Christian, 56, 82, 350 ff.; Medieval, 33, 192, 232, 234, 352
Artemon, Monarchian, 297 ff.
Asceticism, 276, 334, 341 f.
Asia Minor, 22, 106 f., 113, 187, 213, 290, 297, 305, 321; Literature, 96, 236, 239, 271; Thought, 29, 271, 288; and the Western Text, 220
Associations, 46 f., 312 f., 357, 385
Asti, 133
Athanasius, St., 22, 190, 212, 318

403

411